Making Global Value Chains Work for Development

Making Global Value Chains Work for Development

Daria Taglioni
Deborah Winkler

1818 H Street NW, Washington, DC 20433
Telephone: 202-473-1000; Internet: www.worldbank.org

1 2 3 4 19 18 17 16

ISBN (paper): 978-1-4648-0157-0
ISBN (electronic): 978-1-4648-0162-4
DOI: 10.1596/978-1-4648-0157-0

Cover image: © Patrick Ibay. Used with permission. Further permission required for reuse.
Cover design: Bill Pragluski, Critical Stages LLC

Library of Congress Cataloging-in-Publication Data has been requested.

CONTENTS

Foreword		*xiii*
Preface		*xv*
Acknowledgments		*xvii*
About the Authors		*xix*
Abbreviations		*xxi*
Overview	**Making GVCs Work for Development**	**1**
	Introduction	1
	Part I: Why GVCs Require Fresh Thinking	1
	Part II: Quantifying a Country's Position in GVCs	2
	Part III: Strategic Questions and Policy Options	4
	Part IV: Country Engagement	7
	Note	7
	References	7
PART I	**Why GVCs Require Fresh Thinking**	**9**
Chapter 1	**Here's Why**	**11**
	Introduction	11
	Firm and Policy Perspective	13
	Evolution of GVC Trade	16
	Assessment of a Country's Potential in GVCs	20
	Policy Dimension: Entering GVCs, Expanding Participation, and Ensuring Sustainable Development	25
	Notes	30
	References	32
Chapter 2	**Consider Bulgaria**	**35**
	Introduction	35
	Bulgaria's Domestic Value Added in Exports	35
	Channels for Increasing Domestic Value Added in Exports	36
	Bulgaria's GVC Participation and Firm-Level Productivity	45
	What Must Be Done?	47
	Notes	50
	References	50
	Annex 2A	51

PART II Quantifying a Country's Position in GVCs 53

Chapter 3 What Do Imports and Exports Say about GVC Participation? 55
GVC Participation Using Gross Trade Data 55
Informed Classifications 58
GVC Participation Using Data on Trade in Value Added 62
Buying and Selling Sides 62
Notes 63
References 70

Chapter 4 Buyer-Related Measures 71
Introduction 71
Intermediates in Gross Imports 71
Imported Inputs Embodied in Gross Exports 71
Value Added in Gross Exports 73
Length of Sourcing Chains 80
Buyer Dimension: Summary 85
Notes 86
References 86

Chapter 5 Seller-Related Measures 87
Introduction 87
Intermediates in Output or Gross Exports 87
I2E Trade in Gross Exports 88
Domestic Value Added in Gross Exports of Third Countries 88
Who Are the Ultimate Consumers of a Country's Value Added? Value Added in Final Domestic Demand 91
Length of Selling Chains: Distance to Final Demand 94
Domestic Gap between Buying and Selling Chains 97
Seller Dimension: Summary 98
Notes 99
References 100

Chapter 6 Other Measures of GVC Participation: From Macro to Micro 101
Introduction 101
GVC Participation Index 101
Network Metrics and Visualizations 104
Role of Services in Value Added 108
Main Actors and Their Links in GVCs Using Firm-Level Measures 112
Notes 115
References 116

Chapter 7 Use of GVC Measures to Assess the Drivers and Impacts of GVC Participation 117
Introduction 117
What Are the Determinants of GVC Links? 117
Do GVC Links Matter for Economic Upgrading? 121
Quantifying the Labor Market Dimension of GVCs 125
Summary 130
Annex 7A. Regression Results 132
Annex 7B. Factors Mediating Productivity Spillovers from Foreign Direct Investment 137
Annex 7C. Factors Mediating Productivity Spillovers from GVC Integration in Bulgaria 139
Notes 143
References 143

PART III Strategic Questions and Policy Options 145

Chapter 8 Entering GVCs 147
Introduction 147
Attracting Foreign Investors and Facilitating Domestic Firms' Entry into GVCs: Strategic Questions 147
Policy Options 161
Notes 174
References 175

Chapter 9 Expanding and Strengthening GVC Participation 179
Introduction 179
Promoting Economic Upgrading and Densification in GVCs: Strategic Questions 179
Strengthening Absorptive Capacity: Which Domestic Firm Characteristics Help Internalize Spillovers? 185
Policy Options 186
Notes 193
References 194

Chapter 10 Turning GVC Participation into Sustainable Development 199
Introduction 199
Promoting Social Upgrading and Cohesion: Strategic Questions 199
Promoting Environmental Sustainability: What Benefits from Environmental Regulation? 205
Policy Options 205
Notes 211
References 211

PART IV Country Engagement 213

Chapter 11 Designing a Country Engagement Strategy Based on Sound Analytics 215
What Is the Goal of This Guide? 215
Who Is This Guide For? 217
Steps in Component 1 219
Annex 11A Interview Guide for Fieldwork 223
Annex 11B Checklist of Topics from Combined Desk Research and Fieldwork 228

Appendixes 231

Appendix A Dimensions of GVC Participation: A Tentative Checklist 233
Appendix B Broad Economic Categories Classification 237
Appendix C Customized versus Generic Intermediates 239
Appendix D Parts and Components 241
Appendix E Value Chain Categories 243
Appendix F Sector and Product Clusters 245
Appendix G Main Types of Data Used to Measure GVC Participation 251
Appendix H The World Bank Export of Value Added Database 255
Appendix I Survey Year and Number of Domestic and Foreign Manufacturing Firms, by Country 259

Notes 261
References 262

Boxes

1.1 Defining GVCs 12
1.2 The Disruptive Effects of Computer-Aided Technologies and Digital Innovation 19
1.3 What Is Special about Network Analysis? Finding Structure in Economic Problems 24
2.1 Methodology for the Identification of Key GVCs and Peer Countries 36
4.1 Choice of Comparator Countries 72
6.1 Why Firm-Level Analysis? 112
6.2 GVC Measures Based on World Bank Enterprise Surveys 114
7A.1 Data: GVC Indicators and Policy Variables 132
8.1 Network Analysis of a Product Value Chain Using I-O Tables 150
8.2 The Moroccan Aerospace Industry 154
8.3 Examples of Strategic Analysis and the Dynamics of Change Management: The Ventilation Industry and the Truck Cluster in Sweden 155
8.4 The Impact of Thailand's 2011 Flooding 157
8.5 Why the Form of Governance Matters 158
8.6 Four Strategies to Widen Power Asymmetries in GVCs 160
8.7 Lessons from Failed Industrial Policies 163
8.8 Chile: ProChile Internationalization Plan 165
8.9 Case Study: Regulatory Reform and Infrastructure Building in Greek Logistics 173
9.1 The Czech Republic's Supplier Development Program 188
9.2 Case Study: Renault-Dacia Regional Design and Development Activities in Romania 189
9.3 Own Design and Branding in Turkey 193
10.1 Succeeding in New Knowledge-Intensive Niche Sectors 206
10.2 Bangladesh's Minimum Wage in the Apparel Industry 206
11.1 World Bank Group Approach to Diagnostic Work and Formulation of Action Plans to Strengthen a Country's Position within Specific GVCs 216
G.1 Major Input-Output Databases 252
H.1 Value Added in Exports 258

Figures

O.1 Strategic Policy Framework 5
1.1 Supplier-Buyer Links between China and Japan in the Automotive Industry 14
1.2 Stylized Facts about GVCs: A Multipolar World with Diverging Performances 17
1.3 Services Trade 18
1.4 Services Forward Links, 2007 19
1.5 Two Perspectives When Measuring GVC Participation 20
1.6 Two Perspectives When Measuring GVC Seller and Buyer Functions 21
1.7 GVC-Driven Development 22
1.8 From Sector to Functional Upgrading 23
1.9 Achieving Functional, Product, and Inter-sector Upgrading in All of a Country's Agricultural, Manufacturing, and Services Production through Skills, Capital, and Process Upgrading 23
1.10 Network Representation of Value-Added Trade, 2011 25
1.11 GVC Transmission Channels 28
2.1 Growth of Domestic Value Added Embodied in Gross Exports, 1995–2011 36
2.2 Decomposition of Domestic Value Added Generated through Exports 37
2.3 Share of Firms Exporting Directly or Indirectly 37
2.4 Share of Total Inputs Sourced Locally 38
2.5 Share of Total Sales Exported Directly or Indirectly 38
2.6 Share of Firms Using Material Inputs/Supplies of Foreign Origin 38
2.7 Domestic and Foreign Value Added Embodied in Gross Exports: Bulgaria and Selected Countries, 1995 and 2008 39

2.8	Coefficients from Regression Results for Value-Added Components of Gross Exports, Overall Country Sample and Bulgaria	39
2.9	Coefficients from Regression Results for Value-Added Components of Gross Exports, by Sector, Overall Country Sample	40
2.10	Bulgaria's Buying and Selling Patterns, 1995 and 2009	41
2.11	Final Demand, by Destination, Bulgaria and Peer Countries, 1995 and 2008	42
2.12	Domestic Value Added in Third Countries' Gross Exports, Bulgaria and Peer Countries, 1995 and 2008	43
2.13	Import and Export Upstreamness and Gap, Bulgaria and Peer Countries, 2000 and 2012	44
2.14	Strategic Policy Framework Applied to Bulgaria	47
2.15	Doing Business Indicator: Overall and Protecting Investors, 2014	48
2.16	Logistics Performance Index: Overall and Customs Efficiency, 2014	49
2.17	Innovation Capacity and Skills, 2012	50
3.1	Malaysia's Top 50 Exports and Imports, 2012	58
3.2	Most Relevant Buyers of Computer Storage Devices	61
3.3	Most Relevant Suppliers for Computer Storage Devices	61
3.4	Buying and Selling Patterns: Japan, 1995 and 2011	64
3.5	Buying and Selling Patterns: China, 1995 and 2011	65
3.6	Buying and Selling Patterns: Poland, 1995 and 2011	66
3.7	Buying and Selling Patterns: Mexico, 1995 and 2011	67
3.8	Buying and Selling Patterns: Germany, 1995 and 2011	68
3.9	Buying and Selling Patterns: United States, 1995 and 2011	69
4.1	Intermediate Imports, 1996–2012	72
B4.1.1	Country Positioning in the Global Economic Space	73
4.2	Countries' Integration in GVCs: Share of Intermediate Imports in Gross Imports and Electrical and Electronics, 2009 and 2012	73
4.3	Intermediate Imports Embodied in Exports and Electrical and Optical Equipment, Selected Countries, 2009 and 2011	74
4.4	Re-imports and Re-exports in Supply Chain Trade	75
4.5	Decomposition of Gross Exports	76
4.6	Quantifying the Value Added of Gross Exports	76
4.7	Decomposition of Gross Exports, Selected Countries, 2011	77
4.8	Foreign Value Added in a Country's Gross Exports, 1995 and 2011	77
4.9	Comparison of Four Buyer-Related Measures of GVC Participation, Selected Countries, 2009	78
4.10	Value-Added Trade: US$10 Million in Mexican Car Exports to the United States	79
4.11	Foreign Value Added in Thailand's Transport Equipment Sector Exports, by Source Region, 1995–11	80
4.12	Foreign Value Added in Gross Exports and Electrical and Optical Equipment, by Source Region, Selected Countries, 2011	80
4.13	Foreign Value Added in Gross Exports and Electrical and Optical Equipment, Selected Countries, 2011	81
4.14	Foreign Value Added in Gross Exports in the U.S. Electrical and Optical Equipment Sector, by Source Industry, 2011	81
4.15	Foreign Value Added in Gross Exports, Electrical and Optical Equipment, by Source Sector, Selected Countries, 2011	82
4.16	Foreign Value Added in Gross Exports, Chemicals and Chemical Products, by Source Sector, Selected Countries, 2011	83
4.17	Length of Sourcing Chains, by Industry, 2008	84
5.1	Intermediate Exports, 1996–2012	88
5.2	Domestic Value Added Embodied in Third Countries' Exports, 1995 and 2011	89
5.3	Domestic Value Added Embodied in Third Countries' Exports, Excluding Mining and Quarrying and Coke, Refined Petroleum Products, and Nuclear Fuel, 2011	90

5.4 Domestic Value Added Embodied in Third Countries' Exports, Global Market Share, Selected Countries, 1995 and 2011 91
5.5 Domestic Value Added Embodied in Third Countries' Exports, Global Market Share, Chemicals and Chemical Products and Electrical and Optical Equipment, Selected Countries, 1995 and 2011 91
5.6 RCA in Chemicals and Chemical Products and Electrical and Optical Equipment, 1995 and 2011 92
5.7 Domestic Value Added in Gross Exports, by Destination Region, 1995 and 2011 92
5.8 Domestic Value Added in Gross Exports in Electrical and Optical Equipment, by Destination Region, 1995 and 2011 93
5.9 Domestic Value Added in Gross Exports in Chemicals and Chemical Products, by Destination Region, 1995 and 2011 93
5.10 The Ultimate Consumers of a Country's Export Value Added 94
5.11 Domestic Value Added Embodied in Foreign Final Demand, 2011 95
5.12 Foreign Value Added Embodied in Domestic Final Demand, 2011 95
5.13 Domestic Value Added in Foreign Final Demand, Top Five Partner Shares, Selected Exporters, 2011 96
5.14 Upstreamness of Industries in Malaysia 97
5.15 Upstreamness in Malaysia and Comparators, 2012 and Progression Since 2000 97
5.16 Import Upstreamness, Export Upstreamness, and Domestic Gap, Malaysia, 2000–13 98
6.1 GVC Participation Index, 2011 102
6.2 GVC Participation Index, Excluding Mining and Quarrying and Coke, Refined Petroleum Products, and Nuclear Fuel in the Numerator, 2011 102
6.3 GVC Participation Index, Malaysia and Peer Countries, Chemicals and Chemical Products, 2011 103
6.4 GVC Participation Index, Selected Countries, Electrical and Optical Equipment, 2011 103
6.5 Breakdown of Malaysia's GVC Participation Index, 2011 103
6.6 Evolution of the Network of Value-Added Trade, 1995 and 2011 104
6.7 Buyer and Seller Perspectives, 2011 105
6.8 World Gross Trade Network for Apparel, 2013 108
6.9 Bangladesh's Gross Trade Network: Main Buyers of Bangladeshi Apparel (Cotton) Consumption Products, 2013 109
6.10 Domestic Value Added of Services Sectors Embodied in Manufacturing Gross Exports, All Countries, 2009 110
6.11 Contribution of Services Sectors to Export Value Added of Goods Sectors in Morocco, 2007 111
6.12 Forward and Backward Links in Export Value Added, Trade and Transport Services, 2001 and 2007 111
6.13 Forward and Backward Links in Export Value Added, Other Private Services, 2001 and 2007 112
6.14 Input Sources of Multinationals in Agribusiness, 2012 113
6.15 Domestic Suppliers' Output Sold to Multinationals in Agribusiness, 2012 115
6.16 Sales Channels of Domestic Suppliers in Agribusiness, 2012 115
7.1 GVC Integration and Overall Logistics Performance Indicator, 2008 119
7.2 GVC Integration and Skill Levels, 2008 119
7.3 GVC Integration and Geographical Distance to the Closest Knowledge Center (Germany, Japan, and the United States), 2008 120
7.4 Labor Value Added in Chinese Machinery and Equipment Exports, 1995–2011 126
7.5 Labor Value Added in Indian Other Private Services Exports, 1995–2011 127
7.6 GVC Participation and the Labor Component of Domestic Value Added in Exports 128
7.7 Growth in the Labor Component of Domestic Value Added in Exports by Level of GVC Participation Growth and Foreign Value Added 128

7.8 Jobs in the Business Sector Sustained by Foreign Final Demand, 1995 and 2008 129
8.1 Malaysia: RCA, Gross Exports, and Domestic Value Added Embodied in the Country's Gross Exports, 2009 149
B8.1.1 Manufacturing Inter-Sector Links, NAICS 31–33, 2007 151
B8.1.2 Most Relevant Buyers of Computer Storage Devices 152
B8.1.3 Most Relevant Suppliers for Computer Storage Devices 152
B8.1.4 Computer Storage Devices Network for Malaysia 153
B8.1.5 Malaysia as an Importer of Downstream Products 153
B8.1.6 Malaysia as an Exporter of Downstream Products 153
B8.2.1 Upward Mobility: Approximate Employment in the Moroccan Aerospace Industry 154
8.2 Five GVC Governance Structures 159
8.3 Logistics Services in a Typical Supply Chain 166
8.4 Reducing Supply Chain Barriers: Impact on GDP and Trade Growth 167
8.5 Services Involved in the Internationalization of Production (at Sandvik Tooling) 172
9.1 Example of Possible Inter-Sector Upgrading in Nicaragua 181
9.2 Standards in Agrifood GVCs 190
9.3 Diffusion of Standards and Other Codes of Conduct in GVCs 191
9.4 Tasks Performed by Apparel Industries in Torreon, Mexico 191
10.1 Social Cohesion as an End of, and a Means for, Development 200
10.2 Social "Grading" of Jobs 201
10.3 Upgrading and Downgrading 202
10.4. Economic and Social Upgrading and Downgrading in Apparel, 1990s to 2000s 203
B10.2.1 Minimum Wage per Month for Selected Countries 206

Tables

O.1 Selected Policy Objectives and Performance Indicators by Focus Area 6
2A.1 Bulgaria's Position in the Global Network of Trade in Value Added, 2008 51
2A.2 Logistics Performance, Domestic Component, 2014 52
3.1 Malaysia's Top 50 Exports, 2012 56
3.2 Malaysia's Top 50 Imports, 2012 57
3.3 Turkey's Share of Exports and Value Added, 2003 and 2010 59
3.4 Auto Cluster 60
4.1 Indicators of Value Added Embodied in Gross Exports 79
4.2 Summary of the Main Buyer-Related Measures 85
5.1 Indicators of Value Added Embodied in Final Demand 96
5.2 Summary of the Main Seller-Related Measures 99
6.1 Network Measures 106
6.2 Network Measures, All Sectors, E&E, and Chemicals, 2009 107
6.3 Indicators of Services Value Added 110
7.1 Jobs Generated by Five Components of Foreign Trade, 2009 130
7.2 Manufacturing GVC Workers, 1995 and 2008 131
7A.1 GVC Integration as a Buyer and Domestic Value Added, National Characteristics, 1995–2011 133
7A.2 GVC Integration as a Buyer and Domestic Value Added, National Characteristics, Selected Years, 1995–2011 134
7A.3 GVC Integration as a Seller and Domestic Value Added and the Role of National Characteristics, 1995–2011 135
7A.4 GVC Integration as a Seller and Domestic Value Added, National Characteristics, Selected Years, 1995–2011 136
7C.1 Structural Integration in GVCs from a Buyer's Perspective and Its Impact on Productivity, the Role of Absorptive Capacity, Manufacturing Firms, OLS 139

7C.2	Structural Integration in GVCs from a Seller's Perspective and Its Impact on Productivity, the Role of Absorptive Capacity, Manufacturing Firms, OLS	139
7C.3	Structural Integration in GVCs and Its Impact on Productivity, the Role of Absorptive Capacity, Manufacturing Firms, OLS	140
7C.4	Structural Integration in GVCs from a Buyer's Perspective and Its Impact on Productivity, the Role of National Characteristics, Manufacturing Firms, OLS	141
7C.5	Structural Integration in GVCs from a Seller's Perspective and Its Impact on Productivity, the Role of National Characteristics, Manufacturing Firms, OLS	142
8.1	Addressing Obstacles at the Border: Policy Objectives and Performance Indicators	168
8.2	Increasing the Connectivity of Domestic Markets: Policy Objectives and Performance Indicators	169
8.3	Improving Cost Competitiveness While Avoiding the Trap of Low-Cost Tasks: Policy Objectives and Performance Indicators	170
8.4	Improving Drivers of Investment: Policy Objectives and Performance Indicators	171
8.5	Encouraging and Protecting Foreign Investment: Policy Objectives and Performance Indicators	172
8.6	Improving Domestic Services Infrastructure and Market Structure: Policy Objectives and Performance Indicators	173
9.1	Fostering Innovation and Building Capacity: Policy Objectives and Performance Indicators	189
9.2	Improving Standards: Policy Objectives and Performance Indicators	191
10.1	Promoting Social Upgrading: Policy Objectives and Performance Indicators	208
10.2	Engineering Equitable Distribution of Opportunities and Outcomes: Policy Objectives and Performance Indicators	210
11.1	Desk-Based Analysis	218
11.2	Stakeholders to Target during Fieldwork	220
A.1	A Multidimensional Checklist of a Country's Participation in GVCs	234
B.1	Broad Economic Categories Classification	237
C.1	Customized Intermediates in the Apparel and Footwear Sector	239
D.1	List of Manufacturing Parts and Components	241
E.1	Assignment of Products to Five Value Chain Categories in Five Main GVC Sectors	243
F.1	GVC Clusters	245
BG.1.1	International Input-Output Databases	252
H.1	Turkey's Exports, Gross and Value-Added Measures, by Sector, 2007	258
I.1	Survey Year and Number of Domestic and Foreign Manufacturing Firms, by Country	259
I.2	Survey Year and Number of Domestic and Foreign Manufacturing Firms, Selected Countries	261

FOREWORD

The global value chain (GVC) revolution has transformed trade, leading to changes in trade-growth-development links, trade-competitiveness links, and trade-governance options. In my view, twentieth century globalization is about made-here-sold-there goods crossing borders: the trade system helped nations sell things. But twenty-first century globalization is also about factories crossing borders, so intra-factory flows of goods, know-how, investment, training, ideas, and people are now international commerce. The trade system helps nations make things, not just sell things.

GVCs also denationalized comparative advantage, and that changed the options facing all nations. Instead of building the whole chain domestically to become competitive internationally (the twentieth century way), in the twenty-first century, low- and middle-income nations join GVCs to become competitive and then industrialize by densifying their participation. The flip side is that the competitiveness options of high-income nations have changed. Globally competitive firms knit together national comparative advantages to make components in the most cost-effective location. Firms and nations that eschew GVCs must struggle to compete. In short, GVCs killed import substitution for low- and middle-income countries and naively nationalistic industrial policies for high-income countries.

Making Global Value Chains Work for Development is very timely in that those facts are now coming into focus in the global discussion on development. Some low- and middle-income nations—for example, most East and Southeast Asian economies—have fully embraced the GVC revolution, but they are struggling with the challenge of making GVCs work better for their national development strategies. Other low- and middle-income nations—especially in Africa and South America—still view GVCs as some sort of trap, creating a new core-periphery pattern with "good" jobs in the North and "bad" jobs in the South. Yet even the most reluctant are coming around to the idea that the success of nations such as China in the GVC competition means that all other low- and middle-income nations have to face the sort of competition that comes when GVCs combine high-tech with low wages. In essence, GVCs killed import substitution as a viable industrialization strategy, so that pursuing strategies that nations such as the Republic of Korea and the United States pursued in the past became almost unthinkable. In that domain, the book is extremely welcome. The GVC revolution requires fresh thinking; twentieth century paradigms are insufficient or misleading when applied to twenty-first century challenges. This book is a solid step in that direction. Much research remains to be done, but the book will help governments—and policy scholars—understand the issues. The basic structure of the book is well thought through.

Part I introduces key concepts to provide an accessible and highly logical framework for thinking about GVCs and—importantly—for why GVCs require new thinking. That is a key element, because I find that many policy makers in low- and middle-income countries (and many academics in high-income countries) view GVCs as just a new buzzword for rationalizing old policy ideas. It is essential to get this message out, so that governments will stop using old analytics to think through new challenges. Firms in all nations are much further along in view of the changes, but they do not really have a way to conceptualize them simply. The first chapter will help on both scores.

Part II provides a review of the many concepts and measurement tools that have been discussed over the 20 years or so since GVCs really took off. In the past three or four years, the range of GVC measurements exploded with new data sets, including the Trade in Value Added data set of the Organisation for Economic Co-operation and Development and the World Input-Output Database. The critical concepts used in those data sets are a bit tricky, because they are so far from the standard, black box/production-function approach to trade. Again, this book provides a good, accessible introduction to the measures and how they compare.

Part III is less well developed simply because the research does not exist to support a diagnostic approach to policy. In the economic literature, a great deal of storytelling and macro data purport to show that nations participating in GVCs are seeing faster growth and expanding exports on the intensive and extensive margins, but we do not really know enough to guide policy makers' decisions on exactly what to do.

Overall, this book is an excellent product. It is too early to write a definitive work on GVCs and development. My guess is that at least a decade of research will be necessary to reach that point. But governments face challenges that must be met today. This book is an excellent contribution to making such decisions on a more solid, evidence-based foundation. I wholeheartedly commend it.

Richard Baldwin
Professor, International Economics, Graduate Institute, Geneva, Switzerland
Director, Centre for Economic Policy Research, London, England
Founder and Editor-in-Chief, VoxEU.org

PREFACE

From banana chips to computer chips, the way the global economy produces and exchanges goods has never been more dynamic or more interconnected. The fragmentation of production across global chains and the importance of foreign inputs in virtually all sectors affect everybody: participants, nonparticipants, and countries at all income and development levels. Increasingly complex global value chains (GVCs) are a dominant economic reality in the twenty-first century. They present critical new challenges to the ways of evaluating and improving a country's trade and competitiveness.

This book comes at the perfect moment for low- and middle-income countries seeking to join or upgrade in GVCs. Until now, the development community has had a very emulative, unidirectional discourse. A narrow focus on the success stories among GVCs has resulted in policy prescriptions that too often seek to make each country the next Singapore; that simply will not suffice. Over the past few years, as some of the initial success stories—such as Ireland or even my home country, Costa Rica—have come to face challenges in the sustainability of their position in GVCs, questions and concerns rightly have been raised.

In light of the new reality of GVCs, a thorough review of tools and policies is in order. The time has come to reevaluate conventional wisdom. How can the risk of investment attraction policies be more accurately assessed? What might their impact be on domestic investors? What are the inherent tensions between GVC attraction strategies—often based on low wages—and achieving higher labor productivity and better wages? For which type of countries are export-processing zones a viable tool of industrialization? Will firms in those zones actually generate more spillovers than those outside the zones?

This book presents a crucial starting point for applying fresh thinking to the GVC revolution and its implications for policy and development. It does so by providing three main contributions to the current debate on GVCs. First, it provides a framework for more easily conceptualizing GVCs and thus, for more structured discussions and debates on GVCs and their implications for development. Second, it serves as a repository of analytical tools—on which the World Bank Group will work to expand as new tools become available. Third, it is a collection of best-practice policies illustrated through case studies, which will also be expanded to include evidence-based data. All this is accomplished through an innovative mix of methodologies from the economic and business school literature, embracing top-down and bottom-up approaches.

I see this work as the spearhead of the World Bank Group's newly established Trade and Competitiveness Global Practice effort to lead the intellectual and policy agenda on GVCs. It is a promising first step for better understanding the role of GVCs in economic development in the twenty-first century—especially the impact of GVCs on increasing the prosperity of the bottom 40 percent of global citizens. I strongly believe that continuing to develop innovative tools is not only necessary but essential. Now is the time for questions, reflections, and nuances—and that is what this work brings.

Anabel González
Senior Director, Trade and Competitiveness Global Practice
World Bank Group

ACKNOWLEDGMENTS

Making Global Value Chains Work for Development was prepared by Daria Taglioni (Task Team Leader) and Deborah Winkler, under the guidance of Anabel González, Senior Director of the World Bank Group's Trade and Competitiveness Global Practice. The book is part of a broader, multiyear work program of the Trade and Competitiveness Global Practice, which is aimed at offering a comprehensive framework and analytical instruments that can be used to undertake a systematic assessment of a country's competitiveness and trade performance. The book draws on contributions, background notes, and discussions from a variety of experts. These include Olivier Cattaneo (policies for entering and strengthening participation in global value chains), Massimiliano Calì and Alen Mulabdic (labor content of exports), Claire Hollweg (measures of social upgrading and computations of some of the measures in part II), Asier Mariscal (skills and transmission of knowledge), Miles McKenna (environmental sustainability), Anasuya Raj (methodology for the selection of comparator countries), Gianluca Santoni (measures of network analysis), as well as Emiliano Duch, Thomas Farole, Sumit Manchanda, Syed Akhtar Mahmood (specific aspects of country engagement strategies), Laura Alfaro, Pol Antras, Paola Conconi, Ana Paula Cusolito, Thomas Farole, Ana Margarida Fernandez, Jan de Locker, Asier Mariscal, Timothy Sturgeon, Ezequiel Zylberberg, and the International Finance Corporation/International Labour Organization Better Work Programme (key issues to cover in firm interviews and surveys). The authors are grateful to Richard Baldwin for his invaluable expertise and consultation on the overall narrative of the book, and to Gary Gereffi on specific concepts.

Special thanks go to our peer reviewers, Paulo Correa (Lead Economist, Trade and Competitiveness Global Practice), Emiliano Duch (Lead Finance and Private Sector Development Specialist, Trade and Competitiveness Global Practice), Frederico Gil Sander (Senior Country Economist, Macroeconomics and Fiscal Management Global Practice), and Loraine Ronchi (Lead Economist and Global Agribusiness Lead, Trade and Competitiveness Global Practice), as well as peer reviewers from the World Trade Organization and the Organisation for Economic Co-operation and Development (OECD) (Development Centre; Statistics Directorate; Directorate of Science, Technology, and Industry; and Trade and Agriculture Directorate), and the OECD Initiative for Policy Dialogue on Global Value Chains, Production Transformation, and Development, which has been provided without explicitly identifying the names of the authors.

The authors would also like to thank other experts and consultants who contributed valuable discussions, comments, and other inputs, including Guillermo Arenas, Jean François Arvis, Bertram Boie, Christina Busch, Ana Paula Cusolito, Roberto Echandi, Thomas Farole, Michael Ferrantino, Mona Haddad, Eric van der Marel, William Milberg, Jose Daniel Reyes, Frank Sader, and Sebastian Saez, as well as participants in the CompNet Research Network of the Eurosystem, OECD.

During the development and piloting of parts of the book in different countries and regions across the world, including Bulgaria, Cambodia, China,

Malaysia, Morocco, Poland, South Africa, Turkey, and Vietnam, the authors benefited from the support, comments, and suggestions of colleagues at the World Bank Group, including Enrique Aldaz-Carroll, Fabio Artuso, Jean-Pierre Chauffour, Julian Latimer Clarke, Doerte Doemeland, Thomas Farole, Frederico Gil Sanders, Mariem Malouche, Sandeep Mahajan, Kamer Karakurum Ozdemir, Catriona Mary Purfield, Richard Record, Jose Guillherme Reis, Martin Reiser, Emilia Skrok, and Chunlin Zhang.

Thanks also go to Premachandra Athukorala, Xiao Jiang, Sebastien Miroudot, Timothy Sturgeon, and Marcel Timmer, as well as the Asian Development Bank; the Center on Globalization, Governance, & Competitiveness; Japan Automobile Manufacturers' Association; Kommerskollegium; OECD; Proceedings of the National Academy of Sciences of the United States of America; and the World Economic Forum for permission to use their material.

The authors are grateful to Communications Development Incorporated, led by Bruce Ross-Larson, and Sandra Gain for editing the book; Paola Scalabrin, Susan Graham, and Denise Bergeron from the World Bank's publishing and knowledge unit for overseeing the publication and dissemination process; Patrick Ibay for providing the overall layout and graphical design of the figures and the graphical concept of the cover. Amir Alexander Fouad and Patrick Ibay provided support during the book's preparation and Patrick also coordinated the publication process.

This project was supported in part by the governments of Finland, Norway, Sweden, and the United Kingdom through the Multi-Donor Trust Fund for Trade and Development.

ABOUT THE AUTHORS

Daria Taglioni

Daria Taglioni is a lead economist and the Global Solutions Lead on Global Value Chains in the Trade and Competitiveness Global Practice of the World Bank Group. Ms. Taglioni's published work in economic policy analysis covers topics in international trade and finance, including countries' competitiveness in the global economy and the relationship between financial markets and performance. Ms. Taglioni is the author of the book *Valuing Services in Trade: A Toolkit for Competitiveness Diagnostics* (with Sebastian Saez, Erik van der Marel, Claire Hollweg, and Veronika Zavacka). Her articles have appeared in peer-reviewed journals, including the *Journal of International Economics*, *Economic Policy*, *Journal of Banking and Financial Economics*, *Journal of Economic Integration*, *World Economy*, *Emerging Markets Review*, *European Economy*, *OECD Journal*, and *Journal of Financial Transformations*, as well as in edited volumes by the World Bank Group, Centre for Economic Policy Research, European Central Bank, and Organisation for Economic Co-operation and Development (OECD). Before joining the World Bank Group, Ms. Taglioni worked at the European Central Bank and the OECD. She holds a PhD in international economics from the Graduate Institute Geneva.

Deborah Winkler

Deborah Winkler is a senior consultant in the World Bank Group's Trade and Competitiveness Global Practice. Deborah has worked on issues of global value chains, export competitiveness, foreign direct investment, trade in services, and the welfare effects of international trade and offshoring. She is the author of *Outsourcing Economics: Global Value Chains in Capitalist Development* (with William Milberg) and *Services Offshoring and Its Impact on the Labor Market*. Ms. Winkler is the editor of *Making Foreign Direct Investment Work for Sub-Saharan Africa: Local Spillovers and Competitiveness in Global Value Chains* (with Thomas Farole). Her recent articles have appeared in *World Development*, *Journal of Economic Geography*, and *World Economy*, as well as edited volumes by the World Bank Group, Centre for Economic Policy Research, International Labour Office and World Trade Organization, and Oxford Handbook Series. She received her PhD in economics from Hohenheim University in Germany.

ABBREVIATIONS

ASEAN	Association of Southeast Asian Nations
BEA	Bureau of Economic Analysis (United States)
BEC	Broad Economic Categories
BONwin	inflows of value added
BONwout	outflows of value added
BPO	business process outsourcing
CCw	clustering index
CI	CzechInvest
cm	centimeter
CRI	competitiveness reinforcement initiative
E&E	electrical and electronics
E&O	electrical and optical
EPZ	export processing zone
EU	European Union
EXIOPOL	Environmental Accounting Framework Using Externality Data and Input–Output Tools for Policy Analysis
FAO	Food and Agriculture Organization (of the UN)
FDI	foreign direct investment
g	gram
GDP	gross domestic product
GTAP	Global Trade Analysis Project
GVC	global value chain
HS	Harmonized System
HSE	health, safety, and environmental
I2E	import to export
ICIO	inter-country input-output
ICT	information and communications technology
IDE	Institute of Developing Economies
IFC	International Finance Corporation
IKTIB	Istanbul Textile and Apparel Exporter Association

ILO	International Labour Organization
I-O	input-output
IPR	intellectual property rights
ISIC	International Standard Industrial Classification
IT	information technology
JETRO	Japan External Trade Organization
JV	joint venture
KPI	key performance indicator
LACEX	Labor Content of Exports
LMIC	low- and middle-income country
LP	logistics performance
LPI	Logistics Performance Index
m	meter
M&A	merger and acquisition
M&E	monitoring and evaluation
MC-GVC	Measuring Competitiveness in Global Value Chains
MF	mediating factor
MNC	multinational corporation
MNE	multinational enterprise
MRIO	multi-regional input-output tables
NACE	General Industrial Classification of Economic Activities within the European Communities
NAFTA	North American Free Trade Agreement
NAICS	North American Industry Classification System
nec	not elsewhere classified
NEM	nonequity mode of investment
nesoi	not elsewhere specified or included
OECD	Organisation for Economic Co-operation and Development
OEM	original equipment manufacturer
R&D	research and development
RCA	revealed comparative advantage
RMG	ready-made garment
RTR	Renault Technologie Roumanie
SEZ	special economic zone
SITC	Standard International Trade Classification
SMEs	small and medium enterprises
TiVA	Trade in Value Added
UN	United Nations
UNCTAD	United Nations Conference on Trade and Development
WDI	World Development Indicators
WIOD	World Input-Output Database
WTO	World Trade Organization

Overview

MAKING GVCS WORK FOR DEVELOPMENT

Introduction

Making Global Value Chains Work for Development provides a framework, analytical tools, and policy options. The book shows why global value chains (GVCs) require fresh thinking. It presents a methodology for quantifying the extent of a country's participation in GVCs, based on available data. It also proposes a strategic framework to guide policy makers in identifying the key objectives of GVC participation and development and in selecting suitable economic strategies to achieve them.

Part I: Why GVCs Require Fresh Thinking

Part I begins by asserting that the economic implications of GVCs must be rethought for the twenty-first century. GVCs entail four key features that set them apart from traditional production and trade. These are customization of production, sequential production decisions going from the buyer to the suppliers, high contracting costs, and global matching not only of goods and services, but also production teams and ideas (Antràs 2015).

Goods and services produced in GVCs are frequently customized to the needs of their intended buyers. Customization, in turn, entails sequential production and sales decisions that go from the final buyer backward to the producers of upstream inputs. Global production of customized goods and services also entails intensive contracting between parties, often subject to distinct legal systems. Because of the fragmented contracting environment, a significant share of GVC trade is intra-firm.[1] GVCs also lead to matching production teams globally, with unprecedented skill and knowledge transfer, but also with important distributional consequences, as world income shifts toward countries involved in GVCs and a "superstar effect" is generated in many countries, with the risk of growing inequalities domestically.

Internationally fragmented production is not new. For decades, low- and middle-income countries (LMICs) have imported parts from countries with more advanced technology. But generally these imports were only for the assembly of locally sold goods. Because the goods produced were not part of a global network, flows of know-how and the rate of technology transfer were less intense. And because there were fewer opportunities to buy and sell on global markets, the push to improve productivity was also less strong.

The new characteristic of GVCs from a development perspective is that factories in LMICs have become full-fledged participants in international production networks, and this fact can present important development prospects.

- LMICs no longer are just importing parts for assembly for local sales; they are absorbing valuable foreign technology and know-how and importing inputs that they process and export in the form of goods, parts, components, and services used in some of the most sophisticated products today. Baldwin and Lopez-Gonzalez (2013) call this process import to export, or I2E.
- LMICs no longer have to master the entire production process of a good. They can specialize in only a segment of the international production process while reaching sufficient production scale

to meet their bottom line, thanks to the access to global markets.

- As firms from different countries no longer just trade goods and services, but work together in vertically integrated systems of production, sharing blueprints, technicians, managerial practices, and productivity-enhancing tools and techniques, GVCs provide access to "accelerated learning" and transfer of tacit knowledge, at a rate unthinkable in a traditional trade setting.
- With GVCs, the range of actors in international trade and production has expanded. South-South trade flows and investment are rapidly gaining importance. Outward foreign direct investment (FDI) by the BRICS (Brazil, the Russian Federation, India, China, and South Africa) rose from US$7 billion in 2000 to US$145 billion in 2012 and US$200 billion in 2013, that is, almost one-third of global FDI (Gómez-Mera and others 2015). It is not just manufacturing. In countries such as India, the Philippines, and Vietnam, to name just a few, dynamic knowledge intensive software and business services have emerged and are showing strong growth. And it is not just the story of large multinationals anymore. The fragmentation of production together with advances in information and communications technology are creating new entrepreneurial possibilities for small and medium enterprises to access markets abroad, giving rise to a new category of so-called micro-multinationals, which are small firms that develop global activities from their inception (Mettler and Williams 2011).
- Participation is not a given but raises new challenges. Competition is fierce and LMICs face a set of challenges to enter international production, upgrade to higher value-added products, tasks, and sectors, and ensure social upgrading and cohesion from participation.
- Countries are also faced with new policy tradeoffs. High growth and development potential are associated with exposure to the increasing complexity and uncertainty that is associated with organizing production across several locations.

Opening borders and attracting offshore factories is important, and those steps help jump-start entry into GVCs. But retaining GVCs, maximizing their benefit to the domestic economy, and ensuring their sustainability require well-designed and well-targeted policies. From a policy perspective, the critical issue is how GVCs integrate into the economy as a whole. If GVCs remain de-linked from the local context, lead firms will keep driving most decisions and governments may have limited influence and ability to leverage these decisions for domestic economic development. The policy challenge therefore extends to creating and strengthening links with domestic firms and ensuring that the host country benefits from technology transfers, knowledge spillovers, and increased value addition in the country. It is equally important to ensure that GVC participation benefits domestic society through more and better paid jobs, better living conditions, and social cohesion. In a nutshell, the key question is, how can LMICs make GVCs work for development?

To exemplify how this book can help policy makers find answers to that challenge, part I ends with a case study of Bulgaria. The study shows how analysts can make use of the quantitative tools described in part II of the book, as well as the strategic policy framework developed in part III, to identify a country's position in GVCs, its scope for upgrading, and policies that can help achieve that goal. Finally, part IV closes the book, offering guidelines on how to design and implement a national strategy to achieve GVC-led development. The guidelines are based on experience on the ground by World Bank Group teams.

Part II: Quantifying a Country's Position in GVCs

Integrating a country's domestic suppliers into GVCs increases the possibility for GVC spillovers through exporting to a buyer abroad or supplying to a multinational in the country. But countries should also consider from a buyer's perspective the opportunities that GVC participation can provide. Firms can join existing global and regional value chains through importing parts and components that are used in production at home without the need to build a complete array of value chains at home. In the past, for a country to become an apparel exporter, for example, it would need design capabilities and textile mills; to export in the automotive sector, it would need to produce engines and all the subcomponents, and be able to produce on the scale necessary to compete with foreign producers. Under the new trade dynamics, a country can specialize in certain activities (for example, sewing, specific components, or subassemblies) and import the balance of manufacturing needs. Although such a situation does not guarantee significant value capture and upgrading from inception, it does provide a vital first step toward producing world-class, high-quality goods and services. Nowhere is that more evident than in China, and more widely across East Asia, where GVCs are at the heart of the open-economy growth model that has been responsible for the growth and poverty reduction success story of the region in recent decades.

Quantitative measures of GVC participation and guidelines for analysis make it possible to deliver informed policy suggestions. Correct identification of constraints and remedial actions, and assessment of the efficacy of new policy measures cut across the gamut of the statistical information system, including macro and, crucially, micro (firm-level) data. The organizing framework and indicators in part II make it possible to answer questions related to a country's GVC participation and the economic and social gains from such participation. The key takeaway from part II is that a sound analysis of countries' participation in GVCs requires assessing performance across a wide range of indicators and concepts. No single measure or concept can be used to determine success or failure in GVC integration. The development of value-added trade data represents a fundamental step forward in understanding GVC trade.

Nevertheless, currently, measures of GVC participation and domestic value added in trade are not widely available. Existing GVC databases are presented at a fairly aggregated level of goods and services, and do not always cover LMICs. No single database in isolation provides a complete picture of GVC participation and how much value added in trade is being generated domestically. By shifting emphasis from the broad country level to an increased focus on firms and narrowly defined sectors, part II suggests moving further in the direction of better measures of GVC participation and domestic value added embodied in trade.

Questions that can be addressed with the tools described in part II include the following:

- How extensive is a country's or sector's GVC participation? What is a country's, sector's, or product's degree of centrality and structural integration in GVCs?
- Which are the source countries of foreign value added that are used as an input in the exports by the country of interest?
- Which countries are the final consumers of domestic value added embodied in the exports by the country of interest?
- What is a country's performance and what are its main functions in GVCs (buyer or seller; predominantly headquarters, factory, or assembly location)?
- Are domestically owned firms well integrated in GVCs?
- Through which channels and in which sectors do domestic value-added products and services contribute most to the country's gross exports?
- Does the position (upstream/downstream) of the country's and sector's participation in GVCs matter for domestic value added and growth of domestic value added?
- What is the impact of GVC participation on task trade (goods and services) and the factors of production (such as workers, ideas, and investments)?
- Is GVC participation creating positive effects and spillovers to the domestic economy?

Part II assesses a country's GVC participation through three types of measures:

1. GVC participation measures, by country and sector (including trade in value added)
2. Network analysis of international trade
3. Firm-level measures of direct links in GVCs

GVC participation measures differentiate between buyer- and seller-related measures and combine those measures to assess countries' overall GVC participation. Growing GVC participation on the buying side indicates that a country's exports increasingly rely on intermediate imports. Growing GVC participation on the selling side indicates a country's growth in domestic value added caused by own or third-country exports. So various measures drawing on trade in value-added data estimate the source of value (domestic or foreign, by country and industry) that is added in goods and services produced for export or final demand. Emphasis is placed on how value addition from gross exports has changed over time and how it is linked to the country's participation in GVCs. Meanwhile, the narrow view of whether a country captures a growing share of the value of exports is dismissed, as it misses the key benefit of growth of domestic value added (in levels) originating from GVCs: positive changes in foreign sourcing are associated with positive changes in the per capita domestic value added in exports, which suggests that greater use of foreign inputs is complementary to growing per capita domestic value added in exports.

Network metrics typically focus on a country's gross trade, trade in value added, trade in parts and components, or other groupings of trade flows that proxy for GVC trade. The metrics can be computed for overall trade, individual sectors, or individual products in three ways. First, there are several indicators that examine a country's centrality and structural integration in GVCs. Second, the network trade index is an improved measure of assessing a country's trade openness overall (Santoni and Taglioni 2015), its openness in a sector, or its trade of an individual product relative to peers. The index accounts not only for direct trade relationships with partner countries, but also for the interactions of the countries with their partners, in an iterative process that covers the entire network. Third, bilateral network relations can be visualized as a world map of proxies for vertical trade networks. In this context, concepts such as minimal spanning trees visually identify the trade partners with the strongest or most relevant links, according to a chosen parameter. Overall, network analysis helps to capture heterogeneity between the individual nodes in the networks (for example, countries or combinations of countries and sectors, or countries and products) and in the links between the nodes, to understand the complex, multidimensional phenomena that characterize GVCs.

Firm-level measures focusing on direct links in GVCs add more granularity to the analysis. They can be aggregated up to the sector and country levels, but—where data are sufficiently available—they can also be used to look at the dispersion around the average for any given measure of interest. Firm-level survey data directly capture the main actors in a value chain—buyers and suppliers—and allow comparisons of GVC links across industries or between types of actors (for example, foreign-owned versus domestically owned firms, or firms of different sizes) in a country or a single industry across countries. The links between buyers and suppliers include multinational corporations and domestic suppliers in a country, domestic final producers and suppliers abroad, and domestic suppliers and buyers abroad.

Part III: Strategic Questions and Policy Options

GVC participation does not automatically generate development. Part III shows that development requires getting more value added from a country's productive factors (economic upgrading and densification), improving the quality and quantity of those factors (especially labor skills and technological capabilities), redressing market failures, and engineering equitable distribution of opportunities and outcomes—which all add up to social cohesion. All this must occur while reinforcing living standards, including employment, wages, working conditions, economic rights, gender equality, economic security, and protection of the environment—altogether known as social upgrading. The internationalization of production processes helps with very few of those development challenges, but it provides the policy space to address them.

The book offers policy makers analytical tools and policy options to formulate a country's GVC participation strategy—how the country can enter a GVC and then leverage its position to expand GVC participation by shifting and improving resources in a way that advances development goals. Formulating a country's GVC participation strategy includes determining whether a GVC delivers labor market–enhancing outcomes for workers at home. Thinking at the country level brings to the fore constraints such as the supply of various types of labor, skills, and absorptive capacity. GVCs can create new opportunities on the labor demand side, but supply and demand cannot meet if the supply is missing. That fact emphasizes the importance of embedding national GVC policies in a broader portfolio of policies aimed at upgrading skills, improving physical and regulatory infrastructure, and enhancing social cohesion.

The strategic policy framework in part III focuses on strategies to help LMICs maximize their gains from participation in GVCs. To develop an effective and sustainable strategy of GVC participation, governments must identify key binding constraints and design the necessary policy and regulatory interventions—as well as infrastructure and capacity building—which allow them to achieve distinct objectives and address specific challenges (figure O.1):

1. Entering GVCs: attracting foreign investors and facilitating domestic firms' entry into GVCs

Figure 0.1. Strategic Policy Framework

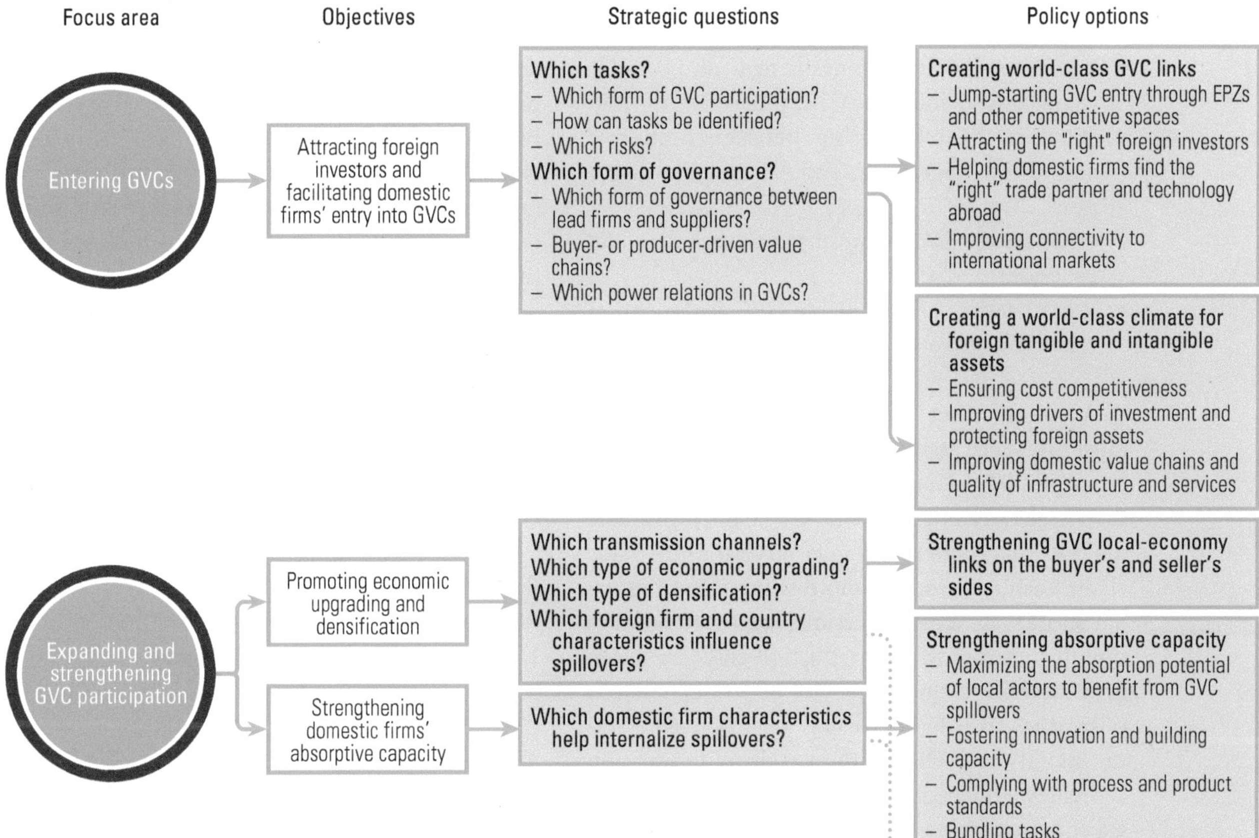

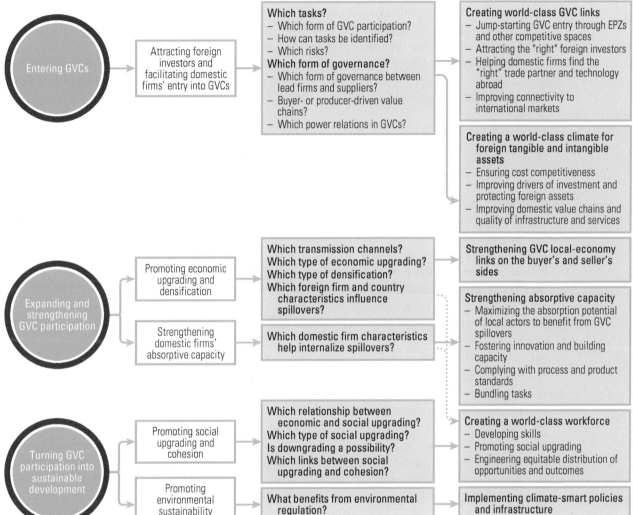

Note: EPZs = export processing zones; GVCs = global value chains.

2. Expanding and strengthening GVC participation: promoting economic upgrading and densification, and strengthening domestic firms' absorptive capacity
3. Turning GVC participation into sustainable development: ensuring skill upgrading, social upgrading, and equitable distribution of opportunities and outcomes while promoting environmental sustainability.

The goal is to enable policy makers to make informed choices. All in all, GVCs offer a role to play for economies at different levels of development at any point in time. Economies that have in place a supporting environment and well-functioning institutions can, in addition, move along the value chain, strengthen participation, and achieve higher added value in a sustainable way. Therefore, the book raises strategic questions in each of the three focus areas, offers a range of possible answers, and points to critical issues that must be considered.

- Which form of GVC participation can a country pursue?
- How can GVC tasks be identified?
- What are the possible risks of GVC participation?
- Which forms of governance exist between lead firms and suppliers?
- Which power relations characterize specific GVCs?

- What are the GVC transmission channels?
- Which type of economic upgrading, densification, and social upgrading can countries pursue?
- Which foreign firm, domestic firm, and country characteristics influence GVC spillovers?
- What is the relationship between economic and social upgrading, and is downgrading a possibility?
- What are the links between social upgrading and cohesion?
- What benefits to sustainable GVC participation can originate from environmental regulation?

A country that seeks to participate in GVCs must ask which tasks it should focus on and which types of GVC governance are possible. A country that is already integrated in GVCs must evaluate the risks that could threaten its survival in the value chain, such as becoming more vulnerable to external shocks. By locating various stages of production in countries where production costs are lower, firms decrease the marginal cost of production, but raise other costs by increasing the complexity and uncertainty associated with organizing production across several locations. Changes in this "trade-off" affect outsourcing and offshoring decisions, and can be heavily influenced by national policy choices. In recent years, some evidence has started to emerge on "back-shoring" activities because of rising costs, intellectual property rights concerns, digitalization of the economy, and changing perceptions about the stability and reliability of GVCs.

Countries also need to be aware of the power relations in GVCs between the lead firm and other firms, and the scope for diversifying specific supply chain risk. Because a large part of GVC integration happens through FDI, countries must examine whether FDI leads to positive spillovers for local actors (especially domestic firms and workers), and they must know about possible factors at the foreign investor, domestic firm, and national and institutional levels that could—positively or negatively—mediate such benefits. Countries also have to decide which type of economic upgrading (product, functional, or inter-sector), densification, and social upgrading (employment, wages, or labor standards) they want to pursue, and assess the relevance of implementing climate-smart policies and infrastructure in their GVC integration strategies.

Finally, policy options are proposed for each of the three focus areas:

1. Which policies support GVC entry?
2. How can policies influence the expansion and strengthening of GVC participation?
3. Which policies help turn GVC participation into sustainable development?

To guide policy makers in prioritizing policies, part III lists performance indicators that can be used to identify the most important challenges that a country must address. Table O.1 presents selected performance indicators, of those described in part III, for illustration.

Table O.1 Selected Policy Objectives and Performance Indicators by Focus Area

Focus area	Policy options	Selected performance indicators
Entering GVCs	Improving connectivity to international markets	LPI (international)—overall and components; efficiency of customs (WDI)
	Ensuring cost competitiveness	Unit labor costs
	Improving drivers of investment	Ease of doing business index—overall (WDI)
	Protecting assets	Ease of doing business index—protecting investors (WDI)
	Improving domestic value chains and quality of infrastructure and services	LPI (domestic)—quality of infrastructure, quality and competence of services (WDI)
Expanding and strengthening GVC participation	Fostering innovation and building capacity	R&D intensity
	Complying with process and product standards	Diffusion of voluntary standards and ISO certification ownership (WDI, national statistics); surveys/field assessments in country
Turning GVC participation into sustainable development	Developing skills	Education statistics
	Promoting social upgrading	Wage statistics; employment statistics; labor standards
	Engineering equitable distribution of opportunities and outcomes	Indicators on access to information; antidiscrimination laws and rights; social insurance and assistance

Note: GVCs = global value chains; ISO = International Organization for Standardization; LPI = Logistics Performance Index; R&D = research and development; WDI = World Development Indicators.

Governments that seek to join GVCs have to create (1) world-class GVC links and (2) a world-class climate for foreign tangible and intangible assets. The first item requires attracting the right foreign investors and improving connectivity to international markets; the second requires assets protection and high-quality infrastructure and services. The ease of doing business indicator, for example, can provide an overview of how attractive a country is to foreign investors, especially in its protection of assets. The logistics performance index can help countries assess how well they fare on connectivity to international markets and border efficiency. The logistics performance index can also help in examining the quality of a country's infrastructure and services.

To expand and strengthen a country's GVC participation, policy makers must focus on strengthening existing GVC–local economy links, as well as the absorptive capacity of local actors, to help them maximize the benefits from GVC spillovers. Absorptive capacity includes innovation capacity, which, for example, could be measured by research and development intensity.

Turning GVC participation into sustainable development also means creating a world-class workforce with policies that promote skill development, social upgrading, and equitable distribution of opportunities and outcomes, and implementing climate-smart policies and infrastructure. Performance indicators include, but are not limited to, education, wage, and employment statistics, as well as indicators on labor standards, access to information, antidiscrimination laws and rights, and social insurance and assistance.

Part IV: Country Engagement

To complement the content of parts I to III, part IV offers guidelines to engage with country stakeholders for implementing a national strategy to achieve GVC-led development. The odds of success in GVCs are affected by policy and its implementation in a wide range of influencing areas. Part IV is intended to bring attention to the synergies between the various areas of policy and help support countries' efforts to identify the necessary reforms to trigger a virtuous cycle of "reform-GVC entry and upgrading-development."

The following are important recommendations and lessons learned for interventions at the country level that the World Bank Group experience of working with countries across the globe suggests:

- The creation of synergies on the ground requires multiple interventions (advisory, analytics, financing, advocacy) and long-lasting engagement.
- Policy advice supporting GVC-based growth models requires sound analytics, evidence, and data. It also requires 360-degree assessment of the competitiveness of a country's economy, in its entirety, and drilling down to specific sectors, GVCs, tasks, and activities, to identify, prepare, and inform all interventions.
- Interventions need to build on analytical foundations and follow well-targeted and action-bound action plans, but they do not need to follow a standard sequence or timeline abstracting from country-specific and context-specific conditions. Coordination, information sharing, and leveraging synergies between different interventions are important. Coordination demands are high within government agencies, GVC stakeholders, and donor partners.
- A participative approach, with alignment on and ownership of the agenda by all stakeholders, is critical. Effective stakeholder engagement mechanisms are a central anchor for continued, long-lasting results (but are often the least funded).
- Network effects and positive spillovers from GVC participation across sectors, based on integrated solution packages, are achievable over time. Dynamic learning, replication, and scale-up can be fostered through global and cross-country platforms.
- A shared vision and a common understanding of the project goals and objectives between implementing teams, local and international stakeholders, and other development partners are important for success.

The rest of part IV shares World Bank Group experience in leveraging the combination of quantitative, desk-based analysis, fieldwork, and in-country capacity building to produce sound, country-specific diagnostics.

Note

1. About 50 percent of total U.S. exports, for example, are intra-firm, according to Antràs (2015).

References

Antràs, Pol. 2015. *Global Production: Firms, Contracts, and Trade Structure.* Princeton, NJ: Princeton University Press.

Baldwin, Richard, and Javier Lopez-Gonzalez. 2013. "Supply-Chain Trade: A Portrait of Global Patterns and Several Testable Hypotheses." NBER Working Paper 18957, National Bureau of Economic Research, Cambridge, MA.

Gómez-Mera, Laura, Thomas Kenyon, Yotam Margalit, Josó Guilherme Reis, and Gonzalo Varela. 2015. *New Voices in Investment: A Survey of Investors from Emerging Countries.* Washington, DC: World Bank.

Mettler, Ann, and Anthony Williams. 2011. *The Rise of the Micro-Multinational: How Freelancers and Technology-Savvy Start-Ups Are Driving Growth, Jobs and Innovation.* Policy Brief, Lisbon Council, Brussels, Belgium.

Santoni, Gianluca, and Daria Taglioni. 2015. "Networks and Structural Integration in Global Value Chains." In *The Age of Global Value Chains,* edited by João Amador and Filippo di Mauro. Washington, DC: Center for Economic and Policy Research.

PART I

WHY GVCs REQUIRE FRESH THINKING

Part I begins by asserting that global value chains (GVCs) must be rethought for the twenty-first century. Chapter 1—"Here's Why"—shows that the new GVC-enabled flow of know-how from high-income countries to low- and middle-income countries is a key factor in determining the role of GVCs in industrialization and development. From a policy perspective, the critical issue is how GVCs integrate into the economy as a whole and how to maximize the benefits from technology transfers, knowledge spillovers, and increased value addition. But it is equally important to ensure that participation in GVCs benefits domestic society through more and better-paid jobs, better living conditions, and social cohesion.

To exemplify how this book can help policy makers find answers to that challenge, chapter 2—"Consider Bulgaria"—provides a case study of Bulgaria. The study shows how analysts can make use of the quantitative tools described in part II of this book, as well as the strategic policy framework developed in part III to identify a country's position in GVCs, its scope for upgrading, and policies that can help achieve that goal.

Chapter 1

HERE'S WHY

Introduction

Global value chains (GVCs) can be thought of as factories that cross international borders (box 1.1).[1] Producing high-quality goods and services in GVCs involves more than simply trading goods and services internationally; it also entails the cross-border movement of know-how, investments, and human capital. When Toyota makes car parts in Thailand, it does not rely on local know-how. Instead, it imports Toyota technology, management, logistics, and any other bits of know-how not available in Thailand, because Thai-made parts have to fit seamlessly with parts made in Japan and elsewhere. GVCs, in effect, "unbundle" factories by offshoring firm-specific know-how along the stages of production, and those international flows of know-how are a key reason why GVCs offer unprecedented development opportunities to participating countries.

Internationally fragmented production is not new. For decades, low- and middle-income countries (LMICs) have imported parts from countries with more advanced technology, although generally only for the assembly of locally sold goods. Because the goods produced were not part of a global network, flows of know-how were less intense. The new characteristic of GVCs from a development perspective is that factories in LMICs have become full-fledged participants in international production networks. They are no longer just importing parts for assembly for local sales. They are exporting goods, parts, components, and services customized to the needs of the intended buyers and used in some of the most sophisticated products on the planet.

Given the need for customization and integration of production facilities internationally, large multinational corporations (MNCs) seek to improve local innovation, knowledge-based capital, and competencies. The Samsung Group—which employs 369,000 people in 510 offices worldwide—worries about shortages of technical and engineering skills in Africa and how those shortages affect its efforts to embed its African workforce in Samsung's global production networks. In 2011, to address such shortages, Samsung launched Samsung Electronics Engineering Academies in Kenya, Nigeria, and South Africa. Outstanding performers are sent to annual Learnership Programs in Seoul as part of Samsung's program for young leaders. The initiative serves the company's broader goal to develop 10,000 electronics engineers across the continent by 2015.[2] Other corporations are investing in building the skill base in LMICs, too.[3] Lucent Technologies supports education and learning programs in 16 countries throughout Africa, Asia, Europe, and Latin America; Nike and the United Kingdom's Department for International Development run a program to support access to economic assets for adolescent girls; Microsoft provides support to incorporate information technology (IT) into the daily lives of young people in the Philippines, Poland, the Russian Federation, and South Africa; Cisco provides funds, expertise, and equipment to create national networks of IT training centers in India, Mexico, South Africa, and the West Bank and Gaza, in addition to the work of the Cisco Networking Academy, which has 10,000 academies in 165 countries; finally, Nokia enhances life skills and leadership skills of young people in several countries, including Brazil, China, and Mexico.

The new GVC-enabled flow of know-how from high-income countries to LMICs is a key factor in determining the role of GVCs in industrial

Box 1.1. Defining GVCs

From a business organization perspective, *value chains* describe the sequence of productive (value-added) activities that capital and labor (or firms and workers) perform to bring a good or service from its conception to end use and beyond.[a] "Value chain analysis" is intended as the science of identifying bottlenecks and opportunities between different stages of production and tasks. Value chains are said to be "global" when they include steps, processes, and actors from at least two countries;[b] they can be regional if the scope of production takes place within the same geographic region. From an economic perspective, the phenomenon of *global value chains* (GVCs) identifies a production structure in which tasks and business functions are distributed among several companies, globally, or regionally.[c] The key features of GVCs are therefore the international dimension of the production process and the "contractualization" of buyer and seller relationships, often across international borders.

GVCs, in effect, integrate the know-how of lead firms and suppliers of key components along all the stages of production and in multiple companies and offshore locations. Typically coordinated by lead firms, GVCs involve international trade flows within their networks of foreign affiliates (foreign direct investment), contractual partners (non-equity modes of investment), and arm's-length external suppliers.[d] Well-functioning *supply chains*—which define the physical movement of goods all along the value chain, including domestic and international segments—are a key concern in GVCs. This is the case because good *logistics*, which defines the art of managing the supply chain and includes good connectivity, streamlined procedures for imports and exports, and low cost of logistics services, is an important determinant of countries' ability to join and strengthen participation in GVCs and a key factor in determining the costs of sourcing from and supplying to global markets. Getting to the border is one of the most pervasive constraints for exports of firms in low- and middle-income countries (LMICs), while the costs of logistics services can be disproportionately high for smaller and younger firms or for more remote locations. Improving logistics is also where LMICs have the most potential to reduce trade costs, according to recent surveys. Finally, well-functioning trade facilitation measures enable GVC trade by reducing the time, cost, and uncertainty involved in importing and exporting.

But most production processes do not happen in a sequence of dependent activities. Instead, they take place in more complex networks of production, in which participating firms are specialists in one activity and external international sourcing arrangements imbue inter-firm trade with characteristics similar to intra-group trade: better control from the center, higher levels of bilateral information flow, tolerance of asset specificity, and harmonization and immediate integration of business processes that increase the potential for foreign activities to integrate seamlessly with activities performed at home. Large brand-carrying multinational enterprises (MNEs), such as IBM, Siemens, and Toyota, nowadays rely on a complex web of suppliers, vendors, and service providers of all kinds and in multiple locations. At the same time, a set of highly influential global buyers gained scale and influence in the 1990s, including retailers such as Walmart and Tesco and branded merchandisers such as Nike, Zara, and Uniqlo.[e] Building on successful experiments in the 1970s and 1980s by a handful of pioneering retailers, such as J. C. Penney and Sears, global buyers nowadays place huge orders with suppliers around the world without establishing any factories or farms of their own.[f] Unlike traditional MNEs, where equity ties link headquarters with foreign affiliates, global buyers link to their suppliers through non-equity external sourcing ties. Often, intermediaries (for example, trading companies such as Hong Kong SAR, China's Li & Fung) are used to link buyers to producers in multiple countries.

To highlight the complexity of the interactions among global producers, recent literature makes reference to the concept of global production "networks" rather than "chains."[g] Accordingly, in the more realistic metaphor of networks, links can be seen as connecting nodes, some more central and some more peripheral. Given the predominance of the term GVCs in the literature, this report uses it to refer generically to chains, networks, or both. When more specific references are needed, they will be explicitly mentioned in the text.

Capital and labor are not the only factors of production. "Ideas" can be singled out as a third factor of production, although they could also be understood as high-skilled labor input. In a global context, the value-added activity performed in one country crosses international borders in goods or services tasks. Different tasks of the value chain contain a different amount of such factors of production. For example, specialized workers tend to be necessary in higher value-added tasks of the GVC. In the automotive, electronics, and electrical appliance industries, ideas are more strongly embedded in the early preproduction stages, such as research and development and design, or in postproduction (logistics, marketing, and branding), thus requiring such specialized workers in those tasks. In other industries, notably the craft-based ones (such as furniture making), innovation development is maximized when ideas (product design) and manufacturing operations are joint,[h] because innovation in those sectors often stems from a bottom-up approach.[i]

a. Porter (1985); Sturgeon (2001).
b. Gereffi and others (2001); Gereffi, Humphrey, and Sturgeon (2005).
c. Grossman and Rossi-Hansberg (2012).
d. UNCTAD (2013).
e. Feenstra and Hamilton (2006).
f. Gereffi (1999); Ponte and Gibbon (2005).
g. Henderson and others (2002).
h. Buciuni, Coro, and Micelli (2013); Pisano and Shih (2009).
i. Breznitz and Murphree (2011).

development. LMICs can now industrialize by joining GVCs without the need to build their own value chain from scratch, as Japan and the Republic of Korea had to do in the twentieth century.[4] That enables LMICs to focus on specific tasks in the value chain rather than producing the entire product, thereby lowering the threshold and costs for industrial development. LMICs can benefit from foreign-originated intellectual property; trademarks; operational, managerial, and business practices; marketing expertise; and organizational models.

The result is that a new policy framework has emerged in which imports matter as much as, if not more than, exports and in which the flows of goods, services, people, ideas, and capital are interdependent and must be assessed jointly (box 1.1). Countries that understand the opportunities that GVCs offer and adopt the appropriate policies to mitigate the risks associated with them have the opportunity—through GVCs—to boost employment and productivity in all their agriculture, manufacturing, and services production. Job creation and labor productivity growth are sometimes viewed as competing goals, as higher labor productivity enables firms to produce a larger amount of value added without necessarily increasing the number of workers at the same rate (static productivity effects).

Research shows that GVC integration leads to higher net jobs but lower job intensity[5] and has strong potential for productivity gains via several transmission channels (dynamic productivity effects), as discussed later in this chapter, which go in hand with increased labor demand caused by more vertical specialization and higher output in GVCs.

Firm and Policy Perspective

Connecting Factories and Protecting Assets When Doing Business Abroad: The Firm Perspective

The international location of new production facilities is ultimately in the hands of GVC lead firms. Conceptually, the new possibilities created by globalization and the information and communications technology revolution create two distinct sets of necessities for firms, which countries must address: (1) connecting factories and (2) protecting assets. Because cross-border factories must work as a unit, lead firms in GVCs care about efficiently connecting local factories with the relevant international production network and protecting proprietary assets.

The predictability, reliability, and time sensitivity of trade flows are important factors behind firms' decision about a location, according to major trade and competitiveness indexes and case studies.[6] In many cases, countries cannot participate in certain parts of GVCs because of requirements for timely production and delivery. In effect, time is money in GVCs. A day of delay in exporting has a tariff equivalent of 1 percent or more for time-sensitive products.[7] Slow, unpredictable land transport keeps most of Sub-Saharan Africa out of the electronics value chain.[8] Lead firms and intermediate producers in GVCs need reliable, predictable, and timely access to inputs and final products to satisfy demand on time. Hence, good infrastructure and efficient borders are critical, as they relate to the predictability, reliability, and time sensitivity of trade flows.

Strong, well-enforced property rights are the other element essential to attracting and keeping foreign investors.[9] Firms export valuable, firm-specific technology and know-how, only part of which can be protected through patents, trademarks, and other forms of intellectual property regulations (IPRs). The know-how embodied in business and organizational models, operational and managerial practices, production processes, and export processes cannot be patented or trademarked; and even when intellectual property can be patented or trademarked, IPR treaties and domestic regulations aimed at promoting fair competition only imperfectly protect such know-how. Because GVCs necessarily involve contracting relationships between agents located in countries with heterogeneous legal systems and contracting institutions, "contracts are often neither explicit nor implicit; they simply remain incomplete."[10] The way in which different national systems deal with contractual frictions and incomplete contracts and the way host countries enforce contracts between private parties are additional elements driving firms' choice of location, and those elements also factor into firms' boundaries in global sourcing.[11]

The connectivity of factories and the nature of contracting across countries are therefore key determinants—along with capital intensity—of a firm's decision to make or buy and whether to do so domestically or internationally. Figure 1.1 illustrates

Figure 1.1. Supplier-Buyer Links between China and Japan in the Automotive Industry

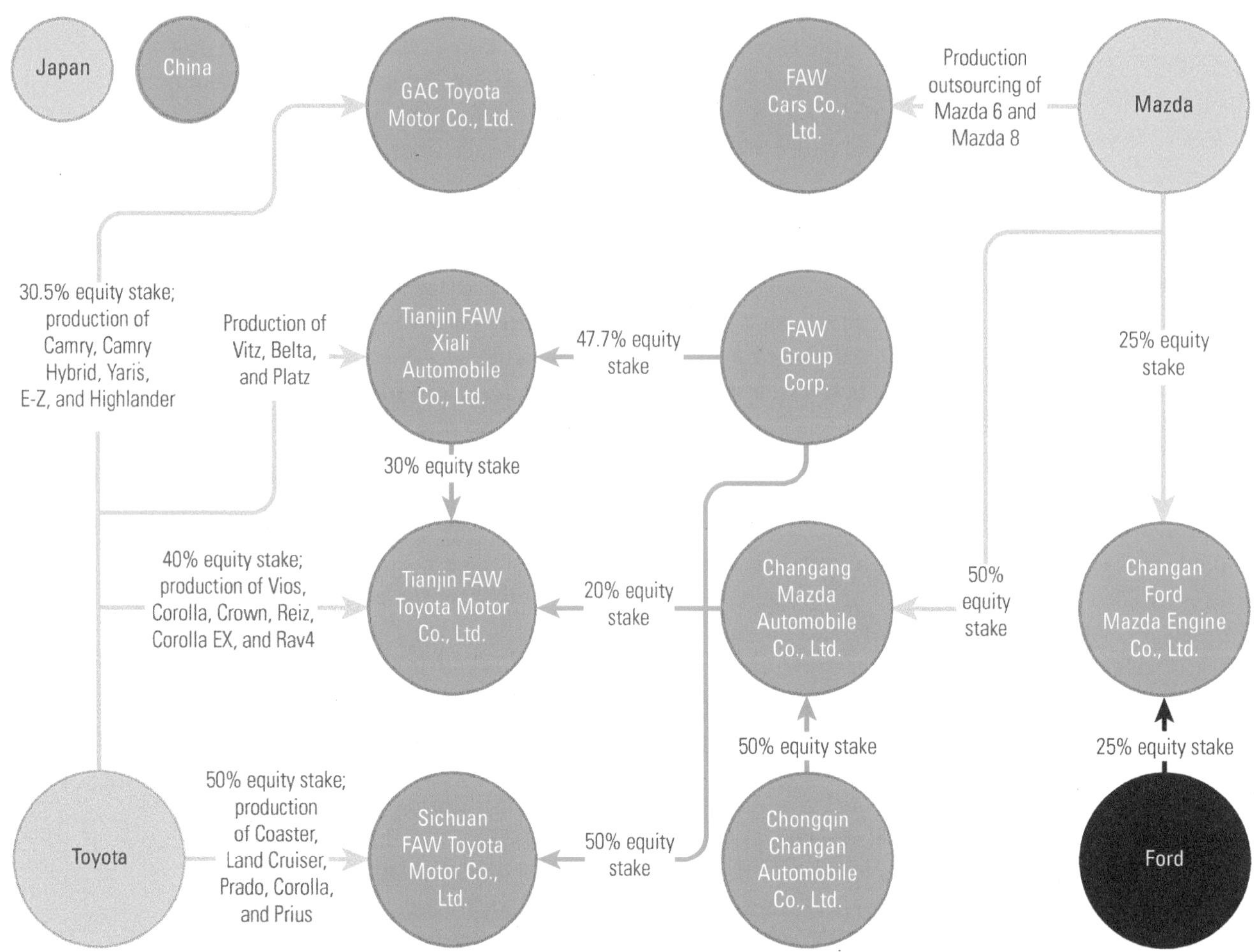

Source: Japanese Automobile Manufacturers Association 2013, 55, adapted as of March 2013.
Note: Japanese companies are yellow, Chinese counterparts are green. The arrows indicate ownership or other forms of control. The Japan Automobile Manufacturers Association states: "In principle, the tie-ups shown above cover only technical cooperation related to motor vehicle production and exclude sales tie-ups."

these concepts using actual ownership relationships between some of the key suppliers and buyers in the Sino-Japanese auto industry. Those relationships move from Japan to China—that is, from the higher-income to the lower-income country and from the technological hub to the production site. The good connectivity between China and Japan and the proximity of the two countries satisfy the first concern of lead firms: connecting factories. Meanwhile, the correspondence between the type of control and the strategic importance of assets in the Sino-Japanese automotive sector accurately illustrates the second key concern of global investors: protecting assets.

Control of the subsidiary takes place in a variety of ways. The most strategic assets are tied to the lead firm through forms of direct capital control over the supplier (such as majority equity stakes). Assets of lower importance (such as older technologies) are instead just handed over through licensing agreements or other non-equity investments. Technical cooperation and arm's-length trade signal looser forms of collaboration. With the dramatic growth of outsourcing practices, competition between companies has shifted from horizontal (with firms competing in the same sector for the same customer base) to vertical (with firms in the same value chain competing to perform specific and specialized tasks). Lead firms compete with first-tier and lower-tier suppliers.[12]

The links between Mazda, the fifth largest Japanese car manufacturer in production volume, and China's FAW Car Group (FAW) illustrate the complexity of vertical competition (figure 1.1). Whereas Mazda outsources the production of the Mazda 6 and the Mazda 8 to FAW, the latter also competes with the former. FAW produces other models, under different brands, using technology from Mazda's competitors, including Daihatsu, Toyota, and Volkswagen. Mazda also has its own line of luxury cars that directly compete with models from the lead firms.[13]

Creating Links to the Local Economy: The Policy Maker Perspective

In the same way that import substitution industrialization gave way to export-oriented industrialization, the latter is now being replaced by efforts to identify an entry point into vertically specialized industries and upgrade within GVCs. Attracting offshore factories and ensuring domestic firm participation in international GVCs has become a major priority for many policy makers in LMICs.

From a policy perspective, however, the critical issue is how GVCs integrate into the economy as a whole. Attracting and keeping offshore factories is not enough. Opening borders and attracting investment are important and help jump-start entry in GVCs. But to retain GVCs, maximize their benefit to the domestic economy, and ensure their sustainability, countries must integrate the domestic productive sector. The policy challenge extends, therefore, to creating and strengthening links with domestic firms and ensuring that the host country benefits from technology transfers, knowledge spillovers, and increased value addition in the country. If GVCs remain de-linked from the local context, lead firms drive many decisions, and governments may have limited influence and ability to leverage such decisions for domestic economic development. It is equally important to ensure that GVC participation benefits domestic society through more and better-paid jobs, better living conditions, and social cohesion.

The right strategies can help LMICs increase and strengthen their participation in GVCs and foster development. Those strategies will be discussed at length in part III. Nevertheless, a point to remember is that to create an effective and sustainable strategy of GVC participation, governments must focus on identifying key binding constraints and designing the necessary policy and regulatory interventions—as well as infrastructure and capacity building—with a "whole of value chain approach." Such an approach is needed to achieve development objectives through GVC participation and address specific challenges in entering GVCs, expanding and strengthening participation, and ensuring sustainability and inclusive growth. Trade and investment policies need to be connected with a wide-ranging domestic reform agenda aimed at helping countries enhance firms' productivity by building internal capacities and providing access to capital and connectivity, and ensuring a responsive and effective governance structure for identifying opportunities and addressing challenges from GVC participation.

GVCs require targeted policies and analysis across a wide range of areas, which may not always be easy for a country's policy makers to formulate and connect to each other and to GVCs. Governments may not necessarily be aware of the effects of domestic policies on integration and upgrading in GVCs. The odds of success in GVCs are affected by policy and its implementation in areas as different as trade (tariff and nontariff barriers), domestic services regulations, investment regulations and incentives, compliance with process and product standards, innovation, industry, entrepreneurship, labor markets, education, and infrastructure and connectivity. Countries may not appreciate fully the importance of the synergies between the core areas of trade and investment regulation and well-tailored complementary measures. Countries also may not be able to identify the appropriate investment in education and vocational training, infrastructure, and connectivity; the best setting for labor market policies; which international standards to adopt; how to design and develop adequate supplier programs; effective cluster development programs and competitive spaces (special economic zones, growth poles, growth corridors, and so forth); or services regulations conducive to business efficiency. Finally, countries may not be able to identify and implement sustainable and effective financing and incentive schemes.

Even when governments are aware of these issues, putting in place regulations that do not unnecessarily restrict effectiveness in GVC participation may be difficult. In most countries, many agencies have a role in setting and enforcing regulation that may affect value chains and the efficiency of their supply chain.[14] Those agencies also often legislate and implement regulation in an uncoordinated manner because regulators set policies with domestic regulatory objectives in mind. As a consequence, international coordination is not necessarily able to foster GVCs' production and trade along the corresponding supply chain. International coordination conflicts with domestic regulatory objectives may explain why existing trade agreements, investment agreements, and similar forms of international cooperation are rarely designed to foster GVC participation (Hoekman 2014).

Given this background, the policy maker's priority should be to identify and lift binding constraints, unlock productivity growth, and improve the overall competitiveness of the country. Many governments are willing to invest significant time and effort to adopt policy that influences the cost of production and trade within a GVC. The appropriate analysis and policy strategies can help trigger a virtuous cycle of "reform—GVC entry and upgrading—development," whereby the private sector is encouraged to keep investing retained earnings in the continued improvement of existing activities, new activities, and comparative advantage tasks in countries' agriculture, manufacturing, and services sectors, thereby generating a process of inclusive growth for the host country.

Evolution of GVC Trade

Once concentrated among a few large economies, global flows of goods, services, and capital now reach an ever larger number of economies worldwide. Global gross exports of goods increased tenfold over 1980–2013, and that of services, 9.8-fold. Foreign direct investment (FDI) net inflows were 34 times higher in 2013 than in 1980. By 2013, as many as 3,000 bilateral investment treaties had been signed to create the framework of deep agreements necessary to connect factories and protect the assets of foreign firms, and the sales of foreign-owned firms amounted to US$26 trillion.[15]

All these flows have grown over time, creating increasingly dense and complex networks. The value of most bilateral goods flows between major world regions (Asia, Eastern Europe, Latin America, the United States, and Western Europe) is now greater than the gross domestic product (GDP) of the participants. In 1980, by contrast, the only flows of goods exceeding the value of GDP were those connecting the United States with Western Europe and Western Europe with the Middle East, North Africa, and Sub-Saharan Africa. The globe has grown into a multipolar world economy with diverging performances (figure 1.2). The triad formed by China, the European Union, and the United States accounts for 53.6 percent of world goods and services exports and 53.9 percent of world goods and services imports. India's trade, by comparison, is very small, accounting only for one-fifth of China's goods and services exports.

GVC participation and trade costs remain heterogeneous. Although East Asia, Central and Eastern Europe, Mexico, and parts of the Middle East, such as Morocco and Turkey, are increasingly integrated in GVCs, other parts of the world remain marginal. That is also the case for most of Africa, Mercosur (the trade bloc comprising Argentina, Brazil, Paraguay, Uruguay and Venezuela as full members, and Bolivia, Chile, Colombia, Ecuador, and Peru and Suriname as associate countries), and South Asia. Another key difference between the group of countries and regions that is more integrated into GVCs and the group with low integration is that whereas the latter remain resource-based economies, the former have shifted their specialization to manufacturing.

An initial trigger has been the integration of China, India, and Russia, which added new massive product and labor markets that had been marginal to the multilateral trading system before 1989. The integration of these countries into the world economy nearly doubled the scope of play for globalization.[16] Faced with slow growth at home, large enterprises from high-income countries set up operations in the newly opened markets, especially in China. Although relocation was partly to carve out brand recognition and a market share in rapidly expanding consumer markets, the firms also saw an opportunity, through GVCs, to cut costs on goods produced for export to international and home markets. Moreover, under pressure from financial markets, large American and European enterprises embarked on a "second unbundling" of corporate functions during the 1990s.[17] In an effort to focus on "core competencies," nearly every business function that was considered "noncore" became subject to possible external sourcing from more specialized, more competitive, and often less unionized suppliers.[18]

According to Hoekman (2014), the heterogeneity in GVC participation is largely caused by persistent heterogeneity in trade costs. In addition to trade costs, which are determined by a country's connectivity among domestic markets and with international markets, a country's drivers of investment—including its skills and technological capacity and the protection of foreign assets—further determine its extent of GVC participation. Improvements in industrial capabilities in many LMICs have created many more opportunities for their firms in the past 20 years. What previously had to be done within the boundaries of multinational enterprises (MNEs) can now be externally sourced from newly competent suppliers and service providers with offices and factories around the world.[19] While the twin trends of external and international sourcing meant that

Figure 1.2. Stylized Facts about GVCs: A Multipolar World with Diverging Performances

Triad: China, European Union, and the United States

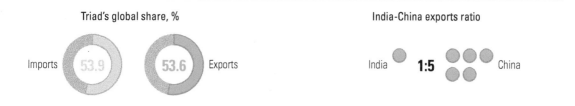

Heterogeneous trade costs

Heterogeneous GVC participation

Resource based	Shifted to manufacturing
Africa, South Asia, and MERCOSUR	East Asia, Central and Eastern Europe, Mexico, and Turkey

Role of FDI

GVC trade

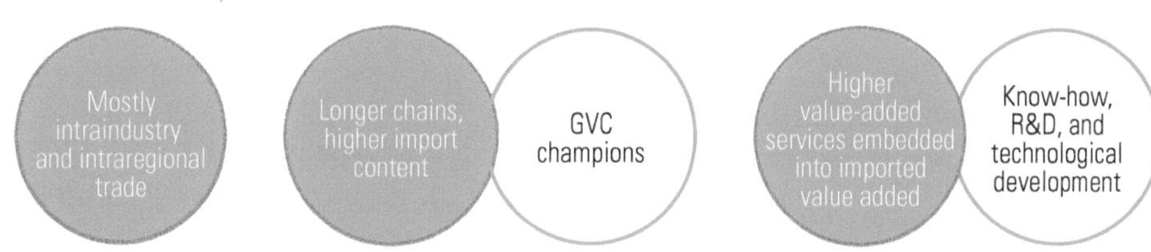

Sources: Adapted from UN Comtrade Database; UNCTAD 2013; Manyka and others 2014; Hoekman 2014.
Note: FDI = foreign direct investment; GVC = global value chain; Mercosur = Southern Common Market (Bolivia, Chile, Colombia, Ecuador, and Peru); R&D = research and development.

existing suppliers received vast quantities of new work and were pressured to follow their customers to offshore locations,[20] at the same time and for the same reasons, the most efficient suppliers that were based in LMICs grew rapidly from being small companies to becoming MNEs in their own right.[21]

Although production systems today are very complex, with multi-layered international sourcing networks and fast-evolving, technology-enabled business models that constantly change the geography of GVC trade, the bulk of it is intra-industry and intraregional. Many goods require shorter supply lines, which has allowed countries near large consumer markets to attract export processing activity. Eastern Europe, in particular, joined traditional "export processing" locations such as Mexico and North Africa.

Yet, the fragmentation of production implies that in most manufacturing processes value chains have become longer. A mechanical consequence is that most countries have increased their dependence on foreign inputs, measured by the share of foreign value added as a percentage of their gross exports, as they increasingly rely on imported inputs that are processed and subsequently exported. But that is not important. What matters is that those additional imports are helping countries to grow faster the domestic value added that is exported, and that the imports enrich the skill set available in the country. And indeed, not only GVC champions, such as China; Poland; Taiwan, China; Turkey; and Vietnam, to name a few, but also late adopters of GVCs, such as Bulgaria and Cambodia, have seen their domestic value added embodied in gross exports increase significantly and at par with increasing foreign sourcing.

Manufacturing functions were among the first to be externally sourced, but services soon followed. By the 2000s, the computerization of work and the emergence of low-cost international communications enabled a surprisingly wide range of service tasks to be standardized, fragmented, codified, modularized, and more readily sourced externally and cheaply transferred across long distances. Even aspects of research and development (R&D) are now sourced from foreign suppliers. As in goods production, the application of IT to the provision of services has allowed some degree of so-called mass customization, which is the association of customization to increasing process automation and high-volume production.[22] Services trade and the role of services in boosting the economy as a whole have increased: more than 60 percent of the current stock of global FDI is in services. The composition of services has also changed, with modern services, such as business services, gaining in relative importance at the expense of traditional services, such as travel.[23] FDI is also a main engine of growth for services trade. Mode 3 (delivery through foreign affiliates) covers about 50 percent of overall services trade (figure 1.3).

The explosion of services trade is a result of falling trade and investment barriers as well as new digital technology, which have reduced the costs of delivering services across borders and transformed many goods into services (box 1.2). The deregulation in air and road transport, abolition of antitrust exemptions for maritime liner transport, privatization of ports and port services, and divestiture and breakup of telecom monopolies are, according to Hoekman (2014), the main examples of regulatory measures reducing the cost of delivering services across borders.[24] In addition, services have increased in importance as a determinant of competitiveness. Countries with a higher content of services in the downstream economy are also those producing more complex goods (figure 1.4).

Figure 1.3. Services Trade

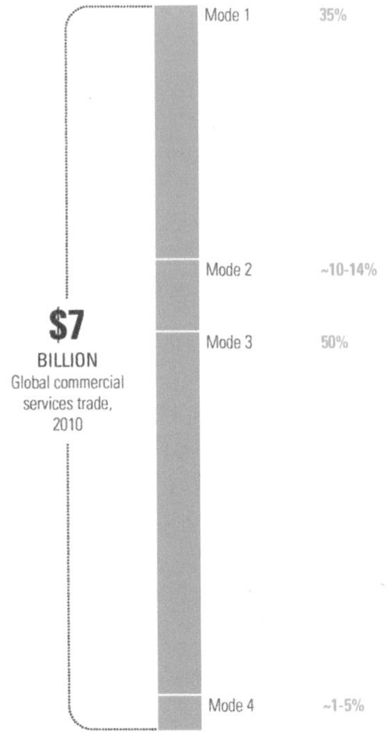

Source: Adapted from Saez and others 2015.
Note: Values are U.S. dollars. Mode 1 = cross-border trade; mode 2 = consumption abroad; mode 3 = commercial presence; mode 4 = presence of natural persons.

The agriculture sector has also evolved. It now represents just 2 percent of global trade (down from 9 percent in the 1960s) and—just as with services—the composition of trade in agriculture has changed from the dominance of traditional commodities to increasing trade in higher-value processed products. The shift is also tightly linked to GVCs. In addition to the barriers to connecting to the agrifood GVC in the first place,[25] the efficiency and functioning of the agrifood value chain depends on the availability and quality of a variety of embedded services, including quality control, logistics, storage facilities, packaging, insurance, and distribution.

For example, avocados are portrayed in a case study by the U.S. Agency for International Development for Chile.[26] The fruit can be sold locally or internationally—at very different stages of processing. At the most basic "ingredient" level, the fruit is grown with little control over its quality, harvested, and sold to intermediaries at low profit margins. The same producers of avocados can instead achieve better bargaining power and profit margins by entering or setting up more complex and sophisticated value chains, and by focusing on producing higher-quality primary products (production tasks) that can be sold in faraway and demanding markets. They can do so by embedding the range of services just mentioned (quality control and so on) and by adding to the production technology that enhances the quality of the fruit and better controls the ripening of the fruit to ensure that it happens at the point of destination—whether that be next door or on the other side of the globe.

To achieve the standards demanded in global markets, the producers of the primary good (the fruit) need a quality management system that grants higher quality standards by controlling harvest and postharvest procedures. By doing so, the producer improves the tasks of comparative advantage (agricultural production) with the assistance of more technology and services.

In conclusion, what matters is the value addition generated domestically and the longer-term

Box 1.2. The Disruptive Effects of Computer-Aided Technologies and Digital Innovation

Value chains are rapidly changing under the pressure of digital innovation. Cloud computing, the "Internet of Things" and "Big Data" are transforming business models, power relations, and sources of value added in entire industries as diverse as the health industry, distribution services, and the automotive sector. The ubiquity of e-mails, sensors, electronic data collection, social networks, tools for virtual collaboration (Dropbox or Google Docs), online labor marketplaces, platforms such as eBay and Alibaba, and other cost-convenient sites for sales and professional collaborations by small and medium enterprises are all productivity-enhancing instruments—albeit some possibly disruptive—grounded in digital technology.

As companies develop more sophisticated ways to leverage digital technology, they are also shifting many processes that used to be labor intensive to computer-aided machinery. The digitization of manufacturing may soon allow customized production at no incremental cost and in smaller quantities (which means lower overall costs) than with assembly lines. The result is not only that the advantages of standardized mass production may be fading away, but also the distinction between preproduction, production, and postproduction may become less and less relevant. Analogously, the distinction between goods and services production may become more and more a statistical artifact.

Model-based definition, additive manufacturing (such as 3D printing), and copy-exact techniques are only three of the cutting-edge technologies transforming value chains and processes. Such computer-based technologies can be disruptive—particularly for companies and countries specializing in standardized production and assembly activities and not investing in human capital and technological empowerment—because they have the potential to change the conventional upgrading patterns. The technologies do so by transforming goods into online transfers of data, which allow production at the consumer's location. For instance, 3D printing is a process by which individual machines build products by depositing layer upon layer of material. Model-based definition instead uses a fully annotated 3D digital model as a master and provides a seamless flow of digital thread through the product life cycle. Copy-exact techniques allow for duplicating entire production processes in remote locations and on larger or smaller scales. The technique was used, for example, by Intel to match its manufacturing site to its development site at all levels, from equipment to process, and data collected at several levels were compared with data from research and development (R&D) sites to get an exact match.

Although these methods are still used mainly for R&D, prototypes, and the construction of very complex components, there are increasing examples of the methods being used for manufacturing consumer products, from toys to bicycles and even housing.

Sources: WEF 2012; World Bank 2016.

development prospects that inflows of world-class technology and a richer and more sophisticated skill set allow. The value added embodied in a country's exports can be generated directly by exporters or indirectly by the rest of a country's productive system—in other words, by producers in upstream sectors that supply inputs to the export sector. Particularly important is whether that value addition—which should be measured in absolute levels and not as a share of exports—increases over time. The combination of traditional drivers of internationalization (arm's-length trade and intra-firm trade related to FDI) combined with extensive and complex models of external international sourcing leads to cross-country, inter-firm relationships increasingly similar to intra-group characteristics. Patterns of cross-border investment and trade based on product cycles—where producers in less developed countries receive older, outmoded products from more advanced economies[27]—are rapidly giving way to more unified global production systems and markets, with different countries specializing in specific aspects, or stages, of the development and production of leading-edge goods and services.

Figure 1.4. Services Forward Links, 2007

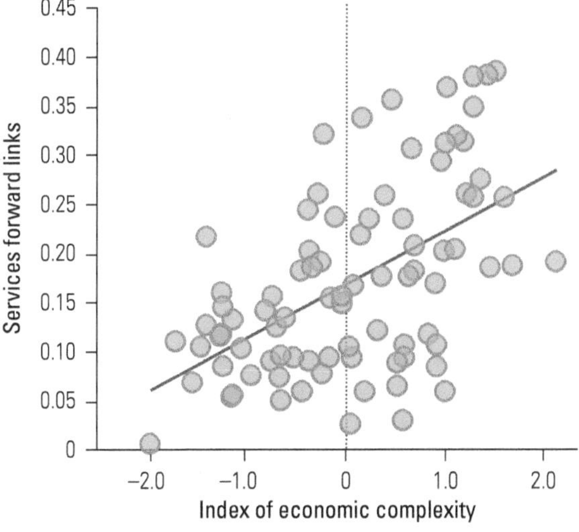

Source: Saez and others 2015.

GVCs offer countries that embrace them the chance to grow faster, import skills and technology, and boost employment and productivity in all the country's agriculture, manufacturing, and services activities.

Assessment of a Country's Potential in GVCs

To guide policy makers in achieving development through GVC integration requires investigating the key concepts and metrics of a country's GVC participation. Understanding how countries fare in such key concepts and metrics allows a better identification and analysis of specific value chains, activities, and business segments, which are the object of case studies, such as those based on Michael Porter's five forces.[28]

Assessments of country GVC participation focus on three concepts:

1. Function in GVCs: the buyer's and seller's perspectives
2. Specialization and domestic value-added contribution: specialization in low or high value-added activities, and patterns of upgrading and development through GVCs
3. Position in GVC network and type of GVC node: hub, incoming spoke, or outgoing spoke; clustering properties; and centrality in the global network

The multidimensional nature of GVCs can be captured by looking at the relationships between goods, services, workers, ideas, and investments (box 1.1)—going beyond value added to look at the actors in GVCs and assess the effects of GVCs on jobs and wages.

Function in GVCs: Buyer's and Seller's Perspectives

Classic trade involves goods made 100 percent in one country and sold in another. Measures of GVC trade quantify deviations from that classic trade concept—essentially, how much of a country's exports consist of value that was added in another country. The basic concept is "importing to export," or I2E, as Baldwin and Lopez-Gonzalez (2013) call it. As figure 1.5 illustrates, one country (Japan in this example) exports parts that are incorporated in the exports of another country (China here). That single flow of intermediate goods is the basis of two key measures of GVC integration:

- On the sales side, it indicates that Japanese exporters are selling to a GVC.
- On the sourcing side, it indicates that China is buying from a GVC.

The term GVC trade typically refers to I2E manufactured goods and related services, but more generally it also includes imported raw materials used in exports.[29] The relevance of I2E on the seller's and buyer's sides is illustrated in detail in part II.

To put the I2E concept in an operational context, the book introduces a distinction between the seller's and buyer's sides of GVC participation. In many cases, countries are GVC buyers and GVC sellers, but that distinction reflects the difference in economic mechanisms and determinants that lead to a country's successful performance in absorbing valuable foreign value added compared with growing domestic value embodied in GVC trade flows. We consider three types of buyer roles in GVCs: input purchases (1) for production of final exports, (2) for production of intermediate inputs in the value chain, and (3) for assembly. There are also three main seller functions: supply of (1) turnkey components, (2) primary inputs, and (3) other inputs (figure 1.6).

The types of flows (goods, services, people, ideas, and capital) predominantly associated with the buyer's or seller's role are more easily discussed by first focusing on the buyer's or seller's functions separately and then considering them jointly. That evaluation

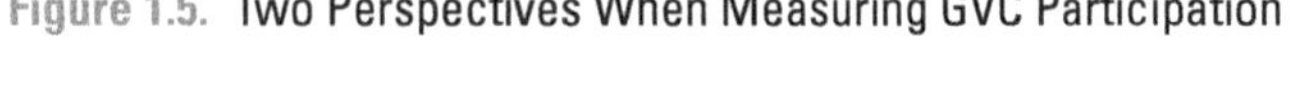
Figure 1.5. Two Perspectives When Measuring GVC Participation

Source: Adapted from Baldwin and Lopez-Gonzalez 2013.

Figure 1.6. Two Perspectives When Measuring GVC Seller and Buyer Functions

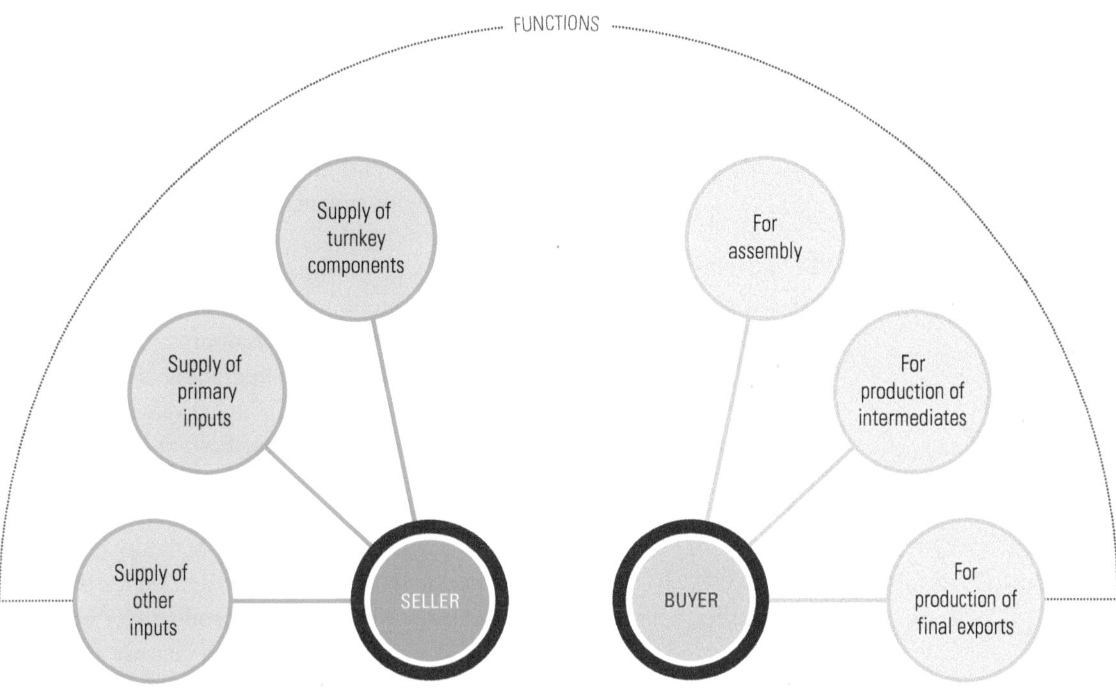

is more easily actionable from the policy angle. If, for example, the domestic value chain is found to be short, or little transformation is taking place domestically, the supply-side bottlenecks and opportunities for expansion on the buying side could be more readily identified than those on the selling side.

Specialization and Value Addition

Ultimately, what matters is the value addition generated in the country and whether it increases over time, which is not a new question for economics. Value addition is a function of productivity, but it is associated with the breadth, variety, and sophistication of tasks and activities in which a country specializes.

The range of activities in a value chain is very broad. The activities range from manufacturing inputs, outputs, and assembly operations to inbound and outbound logistics, marketing, sales, and a range of other service activities. And there are activities as diverse as the production of other inputs, machinery, and equipment, as well as R&D, technological development, and functions aimed at organizing the firm's infrastructure, human resource management, and procurement. Broadly, the value-added content of such activities and tasks tends to grow as the technological and know-how requirements needed to perform the task increase.

In many value chains, the highest value added lies with intangible activities, which are intensive in human capital and technology.[30] In some industries, such as electronics and apparel, the latter tend to be located either at the beginning of the value chain (preproduction activities, such as basic and applied R&D and design) or at the end (postproduction activities driven by marketing knowledge, such as marketing, commercialization, advertising, brand management, specialized logistics, and after-sale customer services). In other industries, such as furniture, the intangible, high value-added activities (such as design) are likely to take place jointly with production.[31] Finally, in sectors such as chemicals, high value-added activities tend to be concentrated upstream.

The value added in different industries can be in different segments of the value chain, but invariably, higher-income countries have a stronger specialization in higher value-added activities within value chains. This fact reflects the greater use of technology and service inputs—whether in agriculture, manufacturing, or services, and whether in preproduction, production, or postproduction. Greater use of technology and service inputs is, in turn, the outcome

Figure 1.7. GVC-Driven Development

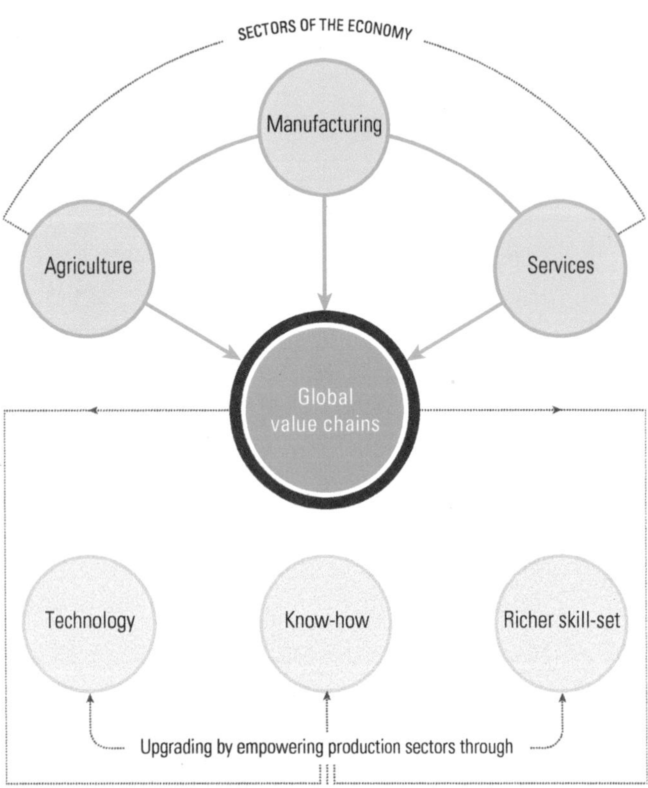

of more complex knowledge- and capital-intensive activities (figure 1.7).

The ability of a small country such as Denmark to establish and maintain its position among the top eight world exporters of food products exemplifies the relationship. Denmark achieved that position by massively applying information and communications technologies and support services (R&D, logistics, commercialization, advertising, and after-sale services) to the production and processing of food. Moreover, and linked to the first item, Denmark has made continuing efforts to upgrade products, processes, and functions, by introducing capital-intensive inputs, thereby increasing value addition.

Digitization also makes every step of the production process more productive and, in some cases, changes the nature of production. Digitization transforms some goods into services (e-books, digital news, and entertainment), and 3D printing transforms goods into online transfers of data that locate the production process next to the consumer (box 1.2). Cloud computing, the "Internet of Things," and "Big Data" are transforming business models, power relations, and sources of value added in entire industries as diverse as the health industry, distribution services, and the automotive sector. The ubiquity of e-mails, sensors, electronic data collection, social networks, tools for virtual collaboration (Dropbox or Google Docs), online labor marketplaces, eBay, and similar platforms as cost-convenient sites for sales by small and medium enterprises (SMEs) are all productivity-enhancing instruments grounded in digital technology.

In a world dominated by complex and fragmented production processes, economic development can occur through economic upgrading and densification. Economic upgrading is largely about gaining competitiveness in higher value-added products, tasks, and sectors. Densification involves engaging more local actors (firms and workers) in the GVC network. In some cases, this could mean that performing lower value-added activities on a larger scale can generate large value addition for the country. Raising domestic labor productivity and skills contributes to the overall goal to increase a country's value added as a result of GVC participation.

The proponents of the "new paradigm" emphasize the role of functional upgrading (figure 1.8), moving to higher value-added tasks. But other forms of economic upgrading are equally relevant. Upgrading does not necessarily mean transitioning from an agricultural to a services economy, as traditional development views suggest (development in broad sectors, or the "old paradigm," as dubbed by the GVC literature). It can instead mean increasingly embracing higher value-added production with the contribution of better skills and know-how, capital and technology, and processes (figure 1.9). In that sense, economic upgrading in GVCs via skills, capital, and process upgrading overcomes the old paradigm and extends the new paradigm focused solely on functional upgrading (figure 1.8); it allows achieving higher value-added production in the form of product, functional, and inter-sector upgrading. Denmark's strength in global food production and Chile's production of high-quality avocados for export provide a clear case for improvement. Improvement can occur by identifying (1) the tasks or activities of initial comparative advantage within sectors, and then (2) policies to empower such activities of comparative advantage, and (3) policies to empower the underlying existing skills with technology and better human capital inputs. Following these steps may help countries to produce better quality products, establish more efficient processes, and

Figure 1.8. From Sector to Functional Upgrading

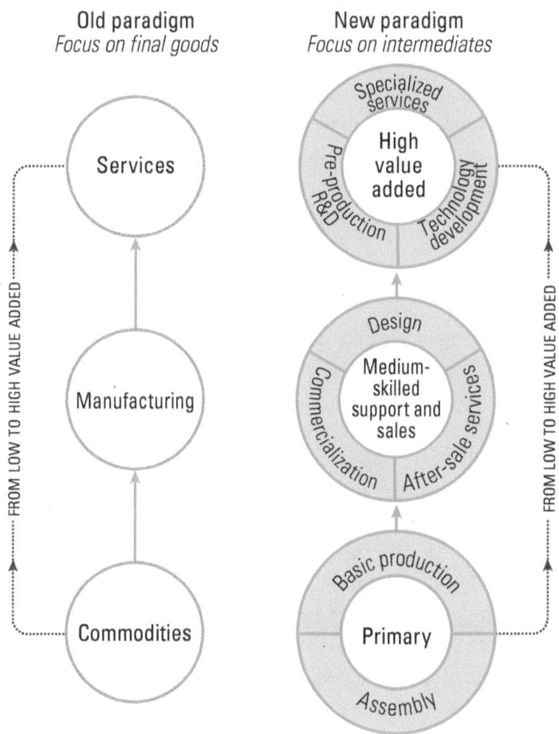

Source: Adapted from Cattaneo and Mirodout 2013.
Note: R&D = research and development.

Figure 1.9. Achieving Functional, Product, and Inter-sector Upgrading in All of a Country's Agricultural, Manufacturing, and Services Production through Skills, Capital, and Process Upgrading

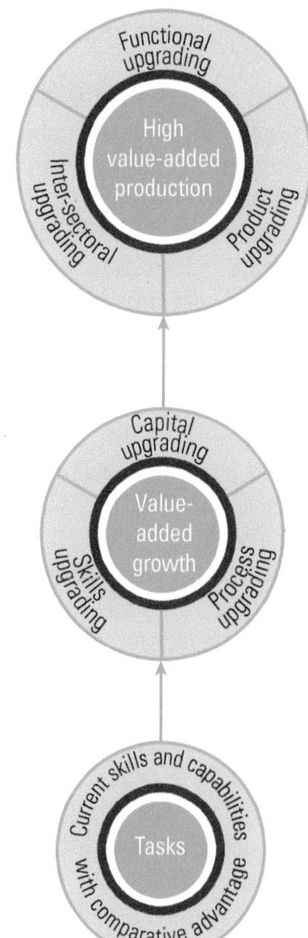

jump to higher value-added functions or develop specialization in more profitable industries (figure 1.9). Part III outlines strategies that countries pursue to do so.

Position in GVC Networks and Type of GVC Node

In the complex, multidimensional space of GVCs, how do countries fare overall? Network analysis and metrics shed some light on this topic by capturing the complexity and heterogeneity of actors and trade links (box 1.3). Large and dense networks may be assessed more easily by creating a network topology, consisting of a set of centrality measures that capture different aspects of the network. Stylized representations of the network make it easier to visualize some dominant aspects of the network and the actors.

The following are relevant measures:

1. *Strength:* average flow for country *c*
2. *Closeness:* mean distance from country *c* to all other countries
3. *Centrality:* the location of country *c* relative to the overall structure of the network through measures of "structural integration" in the network—for example, as measured by the Bonancich power index (Bonancich 1987)
4. *Clustering:* the transitivity of the network—how much the neighbors of country *c* are connected to each other
5. *Visualization through a minimal spanning tree:* a process that illustrates the network reporting the strongest flow for each node (box 1.3). The most connected countries—the central nodes, as they are the main trade partner for several countries—are the "roots" of the tree, distinguished from the peripheral countries, the "leaves." The size of the node reflects a country's strength or centrality in the network (figure 1.10).

Network indexes and tree representations are useful in many ways. They can be constructed to account for the heterogeneity of trade links and, accordingly, to visualize trade flows relevant to GVCs, such as

Box 1.3. What Is Special about Network Analysis? Finding Structure in Economic Problems

Network analysis and metrics are primarily about finding structure in the data describing the link between the nodes (agents, countries, and firms). This approach differs from traditional econometrics in many ways.

The first difference is that network analysis accounts for heterogeneity in the links between individual observations. That is not the case for traditional econometrics, which assumes one of two corner cases, both assuming uniform links: a fully connected network or random connections. The difference is key, as it has conceptual and computational implications. It also clearly underscores that the usefulness of network analysis goes beyond visualizations of phenomena. In trade, for example, measures of eigenvector centrality are to be preferred to openness measures, as the former account not only for direct links, but also for indirect links.[a] And the links suggest new insights, for example, that a relatively central position in a production network (a new input is used by already central technologies) makes an input's wide diffusion across the network more likely.[b]

The second difference lies in the assessment of the structure of the network. Network analysis allows for several metrics to synthesize a node's complex and multidimensional set of characteristics in one indicator, such as centrality metrics, with the nodes retaining their full set of characteristics (or complexity). Standard econometrics would proceed otherwise to explore the structure of the network. It would, for instance, regress the values of the adjacency matrix against independent variables, working de facto with averages. And the structure of the network matters. It determines the nature and size of impacts. For example, in GVCs, input-output links can generate a cascade effect induced by the propagation of micro-shocks through the production network.[c] In traditional statistical concepts, the law of large numbers would suggest that micro-shocks cancel out, as the distribution of a large universe of firms would tend to have a normal distribution. But the "granular" hypothesis of Gabaix shows that with asymmetric distributions of firms, firm-level shocks do not necessarily cancel out.[d] Instead, the shocks affect aggregate fluctuations through general equilibrium channels. The size of the impact depends on the network structure, that is, the properties of the matrix corresponding to the underlying production relations, which can play a key role in determining the depth and frequency of large economic shocks, such as downturns.[e]

A third difference is that in econometrics, indicators need to be related to independent variables. The network toolbox is more eclectic and flexible, and it allows the analysis to accommodate nonlinearity and topology, and, generally speaking, the full set of relationships between variables, including those traditionally covered by econometrics. Gravity modeling, the workhorse of empirical international and spatial economics, for example, can also be addressed through network analysis. The resulting concept of connectivity is associated with economic benefits for the more connected nodes on transport networks.

A previous generation of dimensionality reduction tools—principal component analysis, multidimensional scaling, and clustering—also looked for structure in the data, but network analysis allows more visual identification of the relevant dimensions. For example, a network representation of a proximity matrix will be more visual than the traditional dendrogram of a clustering analysis. However, some more recent tools from complexity and computer science can be superior—strictly speaking—to a network toolbox for certain applications and retain some of its advantages in representing the same data. Two examples include Kohonen's[f] self-organizing map and nonlinear (exponential) component analysis.

a. Santoni and Taglioni (2015).
b. See the results from the input diffusion model by Carvalho and Voigtländer (2015).
c. Acemoglu and others (2012); Acemoglu, Akcigit, and Kerr (2015); Acemoglu, Ozdaglar, and Tahbaz-Salehi (2015a, 2015b); Carvalho (2014).
d. Gabaix (2011).
e. Acemoglu and others (2015).
f. Kohonen (1982).

value-added trade. They can also illustrate other types of flows (for example, parts, components, services, or FDI) or flows in individual sectors or of specific products. Network indexes allow observers to identify the position of individual countries in GVC networks, their centrality, and the nature of the trade flows.

Moreover, network measures, such as centrality and clustering, reveal the indirect links between countries.[32] For example, trade in intermediates for many Central American countries is connected to the United States through Panama, the region's main logistics hub. Looking at various network measures in combination allows analysts to detect that aspect of Panama's participation in trade and GVC networks.

Multidimensional Nature of GVCs

A multifaceted, multidirectional approach examines the nexus of goods, services, investments, workers, and ideas in GVCs (box 1.1). Specifically, the framework covers tasks to produce goods and services and factors of production—that is, capital flows, including FDI, as well as workers, ideas, information, and intellectual property (patents, trademarks, and copyrights). Connecting tasks with factors of production has become increasingly important because the quality and availability of production factors in a country affect downstream activities in the GVC.

Looking at the relationships between some of those components is not new. Economists have

Figure 1.10. Network Representation of Value-Added Trade, 2011

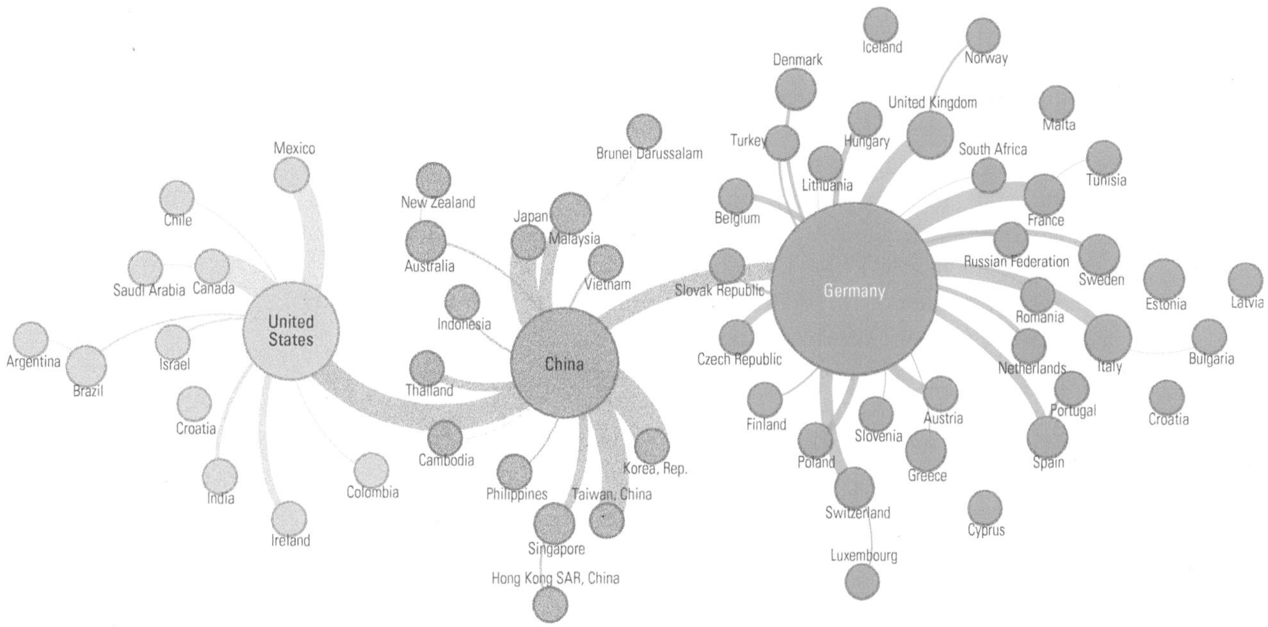

Source: Santoni and Taglioni 2015.
Note: In 2011, China, Germany, and the United States formed the three main roots of the value-added trade network. That is, those three countries were the most relevant sources and destinations for the value added embodied in other countries' exports, especially neighboring economies.

examined the relationship between trade and investment for quite some time. The economics profession has traditionally tended to view trade and investment as separate phenomena; the standard question was whether they were complements or substitutes.[33] The emphasis now is to look at them jointly. Similarly, economists and policy makers should analyze the tasks and production factors of a GVC jointly.

To capture this concept of "jointness," table A.1 in appendix A describes examples of patterns expected in goods and services tasks as well as in the factors of production, including workers, ideas, and investments, depending on their role in GVCs. This additional information is rarely available in the form of hard data and must be gathered primarily through surveys or field assessments.

Policy Dimension: Entering GVCs, Expanding Participation, and Ensuring Sustainable Development

GVCs represent a new path for development. They can help LMICs accelerate industrialization and the "servicifying" of the economy. For policy makers, the focus is on shifting and improving access to resources while also advancing development goals—and on whether GVC participation delivers labor market–enhancing outcomes for workers at home as well as social upgrading and cohesion.

GVCs can lead to development. But at the country level, such constraints as inadequate skills, labor, and absorptive capacity remain.[34] GVCs can create new opportunities on the labor demand side, but supply and demand cannot meet if the supply is missing. That potential gap illustrates the importance of embedding national GVC policies in a broader portfolio of policies aimed at upgrading skills, improving physical and regulatory infrastructure, and enhancing social cohesion.[35]

To address all these policy dimensions of GVC-led development, part III proposes a framework that identifies three focus areas: (1) entering GVCs; (2) expanding and strengthening participation in GVCs, through upgrading to higher value-added activities and densifying economic participation; and (3) turning GVC participation into sustainable development. The text links these focus areas with specific objectives, strategic questions, and ensuing policy options (figure O.1 in the Overview).

Joining GVCs: Policy Options to Facilitate GVC Entry

Integrating domestic firms (suppliers and final producers) into GVCs can help LMICs accelerate their industrialization. Facilitating GVC entry requires creating world-class GVC links and a world-class climate for foreign tangible and intangible assets. However, GVC participation is a necessary but not sufficient condition for development. Although GVCs open doors, they are not magical. Most of the hard work still has to be done at home, with domestic pro-investment, pro-skills, pro-jobs, and pro-growth reforms. Creating demand for high-productivity workers must be matched with a supply of capable workers who have the relevant skills. In other words, when thinking about the first step in facilitating GVC entry, policy makers must have a clear road map of how entry will lead to strengthened and broader participation and economic and social upgrading. Policy makers must keep a keen eye on the workforce's competencies and how they match up with foreign investment.

Creating World-Class GVC Links

Countries can join GVCs by facilitating the entry of domestic firms or by attracting foreign investors. The FDI option includes more direct access to foreign know-how and technology. Costa Rica and Thailand have managed to attract FDI and turn it into sustainable GVC participation in very different ways. In all cases, however, ensuring a set of conditions that includes excellent infrastructure, streamlined export procedures, and a tariff-friendly environment is necessary.

For LMICs that face significant infrastructure and regulatory gaps, establishing a broadly competitive national environment for offshore FDI is difficult. As a result, many of those countries seek to establish "competitive spaces"—enclave locations such as special economic zones (SEZs) and export processing zones (EPZs), where the rules of business are different from those that prevail in the national territory and the costs of factors of production are lower. The zones usually are rapidly built sites equipped with excellent infrastructure; streamlined customs, regulatory, and administrative procedures; and favorable tax conditions (such as tariff drawbacks on imports of intermediates). Competitive spaces have played a central role in the development of GVCs in many sectors in "Factory Asia" and "Factory North America." And in many lower-income countries, exports come overwhelmingly from such spaces. For SEZs, EPZs, and other competitive spaces to contribute to sustained economic development, however, they have to be linked to the rest of the economy. The problem is that, by their nature, they resist such links for several reasons. Most studies of the backward links of firms in EPZs find the links to be minimal, with domestic trade remaining very low and technology spillovers rare.[36]

Ultimately, however, a sustainable and inclusive policy of GVC participation and upgrading requires establishing a broadly competitive national environment for offshore FDI and domestic firms. Overall investment attraction policies matter greatly. In designing investment promotion measures, various factors are important for policy makers to consider, particularly measures that explicitly target foreign investors. However, policy makers should ensure that the measures do not discriminate against domestic investors. Policy makers also must identify and attract "the right" foreign investors. That endeavor includes assessing the nature of investment and the motivations of potential foreign investment (efficiency-seeking, resource-seeking, or a market-seeking export platform), as well as its technology contribution and the technology gap with domestic firms. Investment promotion should not only focus on lead firms in GVCs, but also target turnkey global suppliers, and possibly, important lower-tier suppliers.[37]

Moreover, countries can facilitate the participation of domestic firms through arm's-length trade by helping them find the right trade partners and technology abroad. That help can include setting up firm directories, offering practical advice, and promoting exports and imports more generally. Government assistance can also include e-tools to help domestic companies commercialize their intellectual property, identify and take advantage of freely available technologies, or assist them to establish licensing agreements.

GVC entry also requires the improvement of a country's connectivity with international markets. Bad connectivity means high costs, low speed, and high uncertainty. Thus, successful participation in GVCs requires policy makers not just to ensure efficient cross-border connections, but also to increase the connectivity of domestic markets and enhance the resilience and efficiency of the domestic segment of the supply chain.

Creating a World-Class Climate for Firms' Assets

Low wages may be a way for countries to enter GVCs, and low-wage industrial jobs can be a big productivity step-up from subsistence agriculture, underemployment, and low-skill service jobs. However, the goal should be higher labor productivity, so the country can remain cost-competitive despite rising wages and living standards. Although static labor productivity effects may be negative for employment creation (if the same amount of value added is created with fewer workers), GVC integration has strong potential for dynamic productivity gains via several transmission channels, as will be discussed in the next section.

What matters are unit labor costs, not wages. Chinese labor, for example, remains cost-effective despite rising wages, because labor productivity is also rising. Moreover, lower unit labor costs alone are not sufficient; the capacity to meet production requirements also must be taken into consideration.[38] Put simply, lower labor costs will not attract GVC-linked foreign investors without the right infrastructure and capacity building. Labor policies aimed at attracting foreign investment should therefore be matched by other initiatives, including packages of infrastructure and public-private vocational training.

Removing restrictions and barriers to foreign investment and increasing the protection of foreign assets are keys to attracting foreign investors. Those efforts imply policies such as (1) allowing more foreign equity into domestic companies,[39] (2) facilitating the movement and employment of key personnel, (3) relaxing domestic content rules when their role and purpose are not clearly defined, (4) relaxing rules on foreign exchange and repatriation of benefits, and (5) strengthening investor protection and the right to challenge domestic regulations and decisions.

The sophistication and competitiveness of domestic firms are essential conditions in the host economy. Countries that are home to large and competitive firms have an advantage in attracting foreign investors and fostering the participation of domestic firms through arm's-length trade, because the domestic firms can act as turnkey suppliers. Some domestic firms also have the potential to become lead firms. Countries with predominantly SMEs find entering GVCs more difficult unless the SMEs are part of a well-established and integrated industrial cluster, such as the Italian industrial districts.[40]

The benefits of efficient transportation and logistics at the border could be undermined by inefficient domestic links (such as the unreliability or high cost of domestic transportation or the lack of cold chains for fresh products), as well as regulatory bottlenecks. Foreign investors evaluate the ease of access to efficient services and infrastructure in the host country, including access to cheap and reliable energy, finance and trade support, telecommunications (for e-commerce or electronic transfers), and transport. For example, Indonesia reduced vessel dwell time by reforming storage fees, which improved the country's Logistics Performance Index score.

Meanwhile, a light-handed industrial policy can foster entry into GVCs by overcoming market failures or capturing coordination externalities. An analogy is urban policy. If individual initiatives are completely uncoordinated, the result can be over-congested cities that fail in their basic goal of improving the lives of residents. At the other extreme, government control of every investment decision can stifle growth and innovation and fail to improve lives. A key difference between GVC-led development and classical models of development—through structural transformation from agriculture to manufacturing to services—is that government coordination in GVC-led models must take place at the micro level. Countries do not have to pick a sector as the "winner"; they must assess the existing skills and capabilities in the country, domestic and international demand conditions, and competition from other countries. Based on such information, the government may then set in place the appropriate incentive framework on the supply and demand sides. In this way, governments can help plan and encourage entry into the appropriate tasks and, consequently, densification of the GVC participation that has already begun, while also fostering domestic demand for goods and services produced domestically—all on a market-driven basis.

Completing the Firms' Ecosystem: Policy Options to Expand Development beyond the Initial GVC Enclave

Strengthening GVC–Local Economy Links

After a country enters GVCs, the next set of policy considerations must ensure that the GVCs are as integrated as possible into the domestic economy. The logic of this effort is that strong links with the domestic economy should result in greater diffusion of knowledge, technology, and know-how from foreign investors. The problem is that foreign investors do not actively pursue—and sometimes resist—such integration, for reasons that range from economic constraints, to technological and quality gaps with domestic suppliers, to shortages of specialized workers and skills.

For policy makers, the goal is to turn economic upgrading and densification through GVC participation into sustainable development. Part of that effort should include understanding how the potential for FDI spillovers differs across firms, sectors, and tasks—and designing investment attraction policies that do not discriminate against domestic players.[41]

It is also important to ask what economic upgrading through GVCs means for average living standards—such as employment, wages, work conditions, and economic security—and for wider social upgrading, distributional concerns, and nonmaterial factors such as democracy, labor rights, human rights, gender equality, environment, cultural issues, respect for minority rights, and more.

The main transmission channels for economic and social upgrading include the following:

- *Forward links:* sales of GVC-linked intermediates to the local economy, spurring production and/or productivity in various downstream sectors
- *Backward links:* GVC-linked purchases of local inputs, spurring production and/or productivity in various upstream sectors
- *Technology spillovers:* improved productivity of local firms in the same or related downstream or upstream sectors as a result of GVC production
- *Skills upgrading:* similar to technology spillovers, but transferred through the training of and demand for skilled labor
- *Minimum scale:* for example, GVC participation may stimulate investments in infrastructure that would otherwise not be profitable and that may spur local production in other sectors

These transmission channels enable GVCs to support development and industrialization efforts in four ways (figure 1.11).[42]

First, GVCs—through backward value chain links—generate a demand effect and an assistance effect in the host country:

- *Demand effect.* Lead firms tend to require more or better inputs from local suppliers.
- *Assistance effect.* Lead firms can assist local suppliers through knowledge and technology sharing, advance payments, and other types of assistance.

In addition, the forward and backward links generate technology spillovers, improving the productivity of local firms through two mechanisms:

- *Diffusion effect.* The assistance effect leads to diffusion of knowledge and technology in the suppliers' industry.
- *Availability and quality effects.* GVC participation increases the availability and quality of inputs in the buyer's industry.

Second, GVC participation can translate into pro-competitive, market-restructuring effects that

Figure 1.11. GVC Transmission Channels

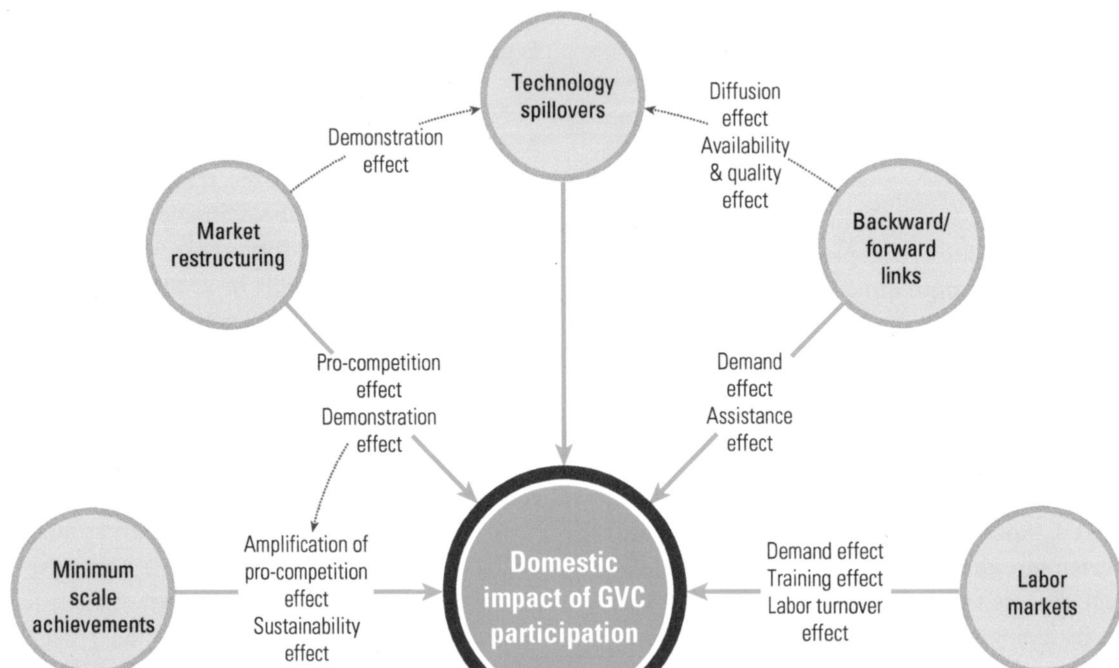

are not limited to GVC participants but extend to nonparticipants:

- *Pro-competition effect.* GVC participation increases competition for the limited resources in the country (between foreign investors and local firms, but also between participants and nonparticipants in GVCs), increasing overall average productivity in the medium run.[43]
- *Demonstration effect.* Knowledge and technology spillovers arise from direct imitation or reverse engineering by local firms (GVC and non-GVC participants) of GVC products, business models, marketing strategies, production processes, and export processes.

Third, minimum scale achievements have a twofold impact:

- *Amplification effect.* Minimum scale achievements amplify pro-competition effects. The achievements stimulate investment in infrastructure and backbone services, which would not be realized without the scale of activity generated by GVCs. Once the infrastructure is in place, it is likely to spur local production in other sectors and the non-GVC economy.
- *Sustainability effect.* Minimum scale achievements also strengthen the ability of the country to sustain GVC participation over time. The GVC literature is rife with examples of the key role of improvements in backbone infrastructure and services, such as logistics, to improve timeliness and reliability in transporting goods, parts, and components, and therefore enable countries to integrate vertically into GVCs.[44]

Fourth, GVCs benefit labor markets through the following mechanisms:

- *Demand effect.* GVC participation is characterized by higher demand for skilled labor from MNCs or other GVC participants. Multinationals may temporarily bid away human capital by paying higher wages or offering enhanced employment benefits. The effect tends to dim, however, as soon as the productivity of domestic firms is raised or the market adjusts to the tighter labor supply.
- *Training effect.* Local firms participating in GVCs are more likely to receive training (say, from MNCs or their international buyers).
- *Labor turnover effect.* Knowledge embodied in the workforce of participating firms (such as MNCs or their local suppliers) moves to other local firms.

Strengthening Absorptive Capacity

The degree to which local firms and workers benefit from knowledge and technology spillovers ultimately depends on the absorptive capacity of domestic actors. This is the most important area of GVC spillover policy, particularly in helping local firms and workers access opportunities. Building the absorptive capacity of local firms requires general and industry-specific investments to upgrade technical capacity and, most important, to achieve quality and efficiency standards for production and export.

Industry-specific and general policies—for education, standard-setting, and innovation—and complementary policies—such as development of adequate supplier programs or effective clusters—are critical for sustaining long-term spillovers. Bolstering productivity and production and innovation capacities, including human capital and other resources, can be achieved through coordinated efforts over a range of initiatives. The initiatives may include developing public-private partnerships aimed at research and development collaboration, increasing the supply of sufficiently qualified researchers in local universities, and aligning higher education curricula and training specializations with local economic activities. Policy makers should also help domestic firms comply with process and product standards. Such public, private, or voluntary standards must be respected throughout the entire value chain, because every stage of production can affect the quality of the final product or service, which could affect the lead firm's reputation. Over the long term, a country cannot be competitive in GVCs by offering a single task (for example, assembly); it must offer a bundle of tasks. Diversifying into service tasks and promoting service exports offer a largely untapped income potential for many LMICs.[45]

Creating a World-Class Workforce

Developing skills is a key element of competitiveness, and it affects the ability to participate in GVCs and achieve economic and social upgrading within GVCs. Economic upgrading requires the availability of new skills and knowledge by increasing the skill content of a country's activities (and thus its workforce) or developing competencies in niche market segments.[46] Economic upgrading and social upgrading are thus linked to and dependent on each other. Indeed, lead firms have strong incentives to train their workforces to comply with the firms' standards. Beyond private initiatives, there is a strong case for public investment in skills development to meet the needs of international trade and participation in GVCs.[47]

Economic upgrading may drive social upgrading, but that is not automatic. Complementary policy could promote social upgrading and maximize the sustainable development impact of GVC activities. Social policies are needed to create an equitable distribution of opportunities and outcomes. Without social cohesion and policies ensuring that all segments of society benefit from GVC participation, development would be unsustainable. Social upgrading can derive from labor regulation and monitoring, such as occupational safety, health, and environmental standards in GVC production sites. Well-functioning labor markets are also important, because integrating into GVCs requires reallocating resources.

For social upgrading to translate into social cohesion through better living standards, countries must ensure equal opportunities to strengthen social cohesion by (1) creating a sense of belonging and active participation, (2) promoting trust, (3) offering upward social mobility, and (4) fighting inequality and exclusion. Equal access to jobs (including for women and minorities) is the most important opportunity in GVCs. Access to widely advertised information about job vacancies and practical advice on how to get those jobs (through job search assistance) is a precondition for equality of access to jobs. In addition, workers need to be informed about their rights. Despite their important roles in the labor market, farmers, the self-employed, and informal workers in particular often are unaware of their rights in relation to landowners, traders, or employers. Cooperatives, associations, and trade unions can be effective channels of information.

But those information channels require that freedom of association and collective bargaining rights already exist in the country. Such provisions encourage proactive social dialogue that can address tensions before they lead to conflict. And facilitating access to jobs for excluded or disadvantaged groups helps economies tap a largely idle segment of the workforce with productive potential, and increases social cohesion. Antidiscrimination laws and mandatory or voluntary affirmative action programs—such as proactive measures for hiring women, minorities, or other groups—are important measures for achieving greater equality of opportunity.[48]

Implementing Climate-Smart Policies and Infrastructure

Firms today are more vulnerable than ever to shifts in the economy and exogenous disruptions, such as climate change. Climatic disruption can impair firms' ability to access inputs and deliver final products, making countries' preparedness an increasingly critical factor in firms' location decisions. Climate change is a multi-sector, uncertain phenomenon, which makes evaluating economic impacts and designing robust and appropriately prioritized adaptation strategies difficult for countries.

The global trade landscape is trending toward more climate-friendly international standards and mandatory sustainability reporting regimes, including on issues of (1) wildlife trafficking, (2) illegal logging, (3) sustainable management of ocean and coastal resources, (4) energy efficiency, (5) infrastructure for electric vehicles, (6) responsible mining practices, (7) chemical health and safety cooperation, (8) trade in environmental goods, and (9) aviation emissions.

But for countries to comply with such standards, long-term strategic policy responses will be necessary. This will require the mainstreaming of a triple bottom-line approach to planning, one that accounts for financial, social, and environmental policy implications. Increasing the scale of global production requires carefully planned investments in infrastructure. With an effective strategic vision, countries can strengthen the ability of their firms to sustain GVC participation over time.

Notes

1. The phenomenon has been called "vertical specialization" by Balassa (1967) and Findlay (1978), "slicing up of the value chain" by Krugman (1995), and many other names by other economists, including "international fragmentation of production" (Arndt and Kierzkowski 2001), "transnational production" (Feenstra 1998), and "global production networks" (Ernst and Kim 2002; Henderson and others 2002). Vertical specialization identifies a production structure in which tasks and business functions are spread over several companies that are globally or regionally dispersed. Tasks, rather than sectors, define the specialization of countries in the value chains, as indicated by Grossman and Rossi-Hansberg (2008).
2. ACET (2014).
3. Dunbar (2013).
4. Baldwin (2012).
5. Cali and Hollweg (2015).
6. WEF (2013).
7. Hummels and others (2007).
8. Christ and Ferrantino (2011).

9. Feenstra and others (2013).
10. Rodrik (2000, 179).
11. Antràs and Yeaple (2014). Antràs and Chor (2013) lists a range of reasons for incomplete contracting in international settings, including the limited amount of repeated interactions; lack of collective punishment mechanisms associated with international transactions; and natural difficulties in contract disputes involving international transactions, such as determining which country's laws are applicable to the specific contract. Finally, even when the relevance of the law to the contract in question is clear, local courts may be reluctant to enforce a contract involving residents of foreign countries.
12. The extent of vertical competition varies, depending on the power relations within the specific value chain (see, for example, Milberg 2004). Interestingly, horizontal and vertical competition are driven by similar forces: the interplay between traditional cost advantages, institutional factors, and proximity to the final consumer, which together determine which tasks are more profitable in given locations (Cattaneo and others 2013).
13. Daihatsu licenses the Terios SUV technology (an older technology that has been phased out in the Japanese domestic market) to FAW (Paultan.org). The latter engages in the manufacture and sale of passenger cars and related accessories. FAW offers its products under three brand names: Benteng, Mazda6/Atenza, and Hongqi. Some of the Benteng cars are produced using old models of the Mazda sedan, and others using the second-generation Volkswagen Jetta. The company also produces the Mazda6/Atenza for the Chinese and Japanese markets. The production and commercialization of this model is outsourced by Mazda Japan, a competitor of Daihatsu. The advantage for Mazda is that it can focus on models that are more strategic from a corporate point of view, such as Premacy and Familia. Finally, FAW has its own brand: the Hongqi luxury car (FAW corporate website: http://www.faw.com/). Hongqi cars have been manufactured since 1958; the original models were reserved for the high-ranking party elite of the communist party. They remained in production until 1981 (*The Economist*, "The Home Team," November 13, 2008, www.economist.com/node/12544893). The current Hongqi fleet includes the H7, which is an executive car based on the Toyota Crown platform. This intricate system of collaboration and business relationships is an excellent example of the degree of vertical competition in the automotive sector.
14. For the distinction between value chains and supply chains, refer to box 1.1.
15. UNCTAD (2013).
16. Freeman (2006).
17. Baldwin (2011).
18. See Sturgeon (2002) for a detailed case study on the trend toward external sourcing in the electronics industry.
19. Sturgeon and Lester (2004).
20. Humphrey (2003).
21. Kawakami (2011).
22. Pine (1999).
23. Saez and others (2015).
24. Hoekman (2014).
25. WTO-OECD (2013).
26. Sagrario, Pierrestegui, and Mas (2009).
27. Vernon (1966, 1979).
28. Porter (2008).
29. Importing to export on the sales and sourcing sides is related to the bilateral concepts of backward and forward vertical specialization introduced by Lopez-Gonzalez and Holmes (2011), in which "backward" refers to sourcing and "forward" to sales. That usage contradicts the standard usage of backward and forward links from economic geography, in which "backward links" refer to sales and "forward links" refer to sourcing (Ottaviano and Puga 2003).
30. Gereffi and Frederick (2010).
31. Buciuni, Coro, and Micelli (2013).
32. Santoni and Taglioni (2015).
33. Brainard (1993); Helpman (1984); Horstmann and Markusen (1992).
34. Kummritz, Taglioni, and Winkler (2016).
35. Kummritz, Taglioni, and Winkler (2016).
36. Milberg and Winkler (2013).
37. Farole and Winkler (2014b).
38. Cattaneo and others (2013).
39. China has been effective in attracting FDI, even with restrictions on joint ventures. However, that success is largely a result of China-specific conditions: a large domestic market and a large pool of low-cost but well-trained workers. Countries that do not have specific factors to attract investors or to use as leverage will have less space for maneuvering when dictating joint venture conditions with foreign investors.
40. Becattini (1990); Porter (1990).
41. Understanding the spillover potential of different FDI at the micro level is likely to become an important policy priority in the coming years. This is not the case only for small and lower-income countries that rely increasingly on FDI and have a limited pool of resources to devote to attracting foreign investors, but also for large countries. Another important priority in designing FDI-related policy should be ensuring that the incentives used to attract foreign investors do not create a bias against local integration. Moreover, policy makers must leverage investment incentives to promote spillovers actively, including local supplier development, provision of technical assistance, and training of workers, joint research, and more. The spotlight should be on value addition rather than in-country ownership. Instead of establishing rigid local content requirements, the focus should be on collaborative development of flexible localization plans, in which investors come up with their own proposals on how they will deliver spillovers to the local economy. Incentivizing foreign investors to collaborate with local universities, research institutes, and training institutes is also important (Farole and Winkler 2014a).
42. The discussion on mechanisms triggered by GVC participation evolves partially from the taxonomy introduced by Farole, Staritz, and Winkler (2014).
43. In the short run, average productivity may decrease and local firms may lose market shares because of intensified competition.
44. WEF (2013).

45. Cattaneo and others (2013).
46. Humphrey and Schmitz (2002).
47. Cattaneo and others (2013).
48. OECD (2011); World Bank (2013).

References

Acemoglu, Daron, Ufuk Akcigit, and William Kerr. 2015. "Networks and the Macroeconomy: An Empirical Exploration." *NBER Macroeconomics Annual 2015*, volume 30. National Bureau of Economic Research, Cambridge, MA.

Acemoglu, Daron, Vasco M. Carvalho, Asuman Ozdaglar, and Alirez Tahbaz-Salehi. 2012. "The Network Origins of Aggregate Fluctuations." *Econometrica* 80 (5): 1977–2016.

Acemoglu, Daron, Asuman Ozdaglar, and Alireza Tahbaz-Salehi. 2015a. "Microeconomic Origins of Macroeconomic Tail Risks." NBER Working Paper 20865, National Bureau of Economic Research, Cambridge, MA.

———. 2015b. "Networks, Shocks, and Systemic Risk." NBER Working Paper 20931, National Bureau of Economic Research, Cambridge, MA.

ACET (African Center for Economic Transformation). 2014. *2014 African Transformation Report: Growth with Depth.* Accra, Ghana: ACET.

Antràs, Pol, and Davin Chor. 2013. "Organizing the Global Value Chain." *Econometrica* 81 6: 2127–204.

Antràs, Pol, and Stephen R. Yeaple. 2014. "Multinational Firms and the Structure of International Trade." *Handbook of International Economics*, 4: 55–130.

Arndt, Sven W., and Henryk Kierzkowski. 2001. *Fragmentation: New Production and Trade Patterns in the World Economy.* Oxford: Oxford University Press.

Balassa, B. 1967. *Trade Liberalization among Industrial Countries.* New York: McGraw-Hill.

Baldwin, Richard. 2011. "Trade and Industrialisation after Globalisation's Second Unbundling: How Building and Joining a Supply Chain Are Different and Why It Matters." NBER Working Paper 17716, National Bureau of Economic Research, Cambridge, MA.

———. 2012. "Global Supply Chains: Why They Emerged, Why They Matter, and Where They Are Going." Discussion Paper 9103, Centre for Economic Policy Research, London.

Baldwin, Richard, and Javier Lopez-Gonzalez. 2013. "Supply-Chain Trade: A Portrait of Global Patterns and Several Testable Hypotheses." NBER Working Paper 18957, National Bureau of Economic Research, Cambridge, MA.

Becattini, Giacomo. 1990. "The Marshallian Industrial Districts as a Socio-Economic Notion." In *Industrial Districts and Interfirm Co-Operation in Italy*, edited by Frank Pyke, Giacomo Becattini, and Werner Sengenberger. Geneva: International Institute for Labor Studies.

Bonancich, Phillip. 1987. "Power and Centrality: A Family of Measures." *American Journal of Sociology* 92 (5): 1170–82.

Brainard, S. Lael. 1993a. "An Empirical Assessment of the Factor Proportions Explanation of Multinational Sales." NBER Working Paper 4583, National Bureau of Economic Research, Cambridge, MA.

Breznitz, Dan, and Michael Murphree. 2011. *Run of the Red Queen. Government, Innovation, Globalization, and Economic Growth in China.* New Haven, CT: Yale University Press.

Buciuni, Giulio, Giancarlo Coro, and Stefano Micelli. 2013. "Rethinking the Role of Manufacturing in Global Value Chains: An International Comparative Study in the Furniture Industry." *Industrial and Corporate Change* (4): 1–30.

Cali, M., and C. Hollweg. 2015. "The Labor Content of Exports in South Africa: A Preliminary Exploration." World Bank, Washington, DC.

Carvalho, Vasco M. 2014. "From Micro to Macro via Production Networks." *Journal of Economic Perspectives* 28 (4): 23–48.

Carvalho, Vasco M., and Nico Voigtländer. 2015. "Input Diffusion and the Evolution of Production Networks." Economics Working Papers 1418, Department of Economics and Business, Universitat Pompeu Fabra, Barcelona, Spain.

Cattaneo, Olivier, Gary Gereffi, Sébastien Miroudot, and Daria Taglioni. 2013. "Joining, Upgrading and Being Competitive in Global Value Chains: A Strategic Framework." Vol. 1. Policy Research Working Paper 6406, World Bank, Washington, DC.

Cattaneo, O., and S. Miroudot. 2013. "From Global Value Chains to Global Development Chains: An Analysis of Recent Changes in Trade Patterns and Development Paradigms." In *21st Century Trade Policy: Back to the Past?* Volume in Honor of Professor Patrick Messerlin, edited by E. Zedillo and B. Hoekman. New Haven, CT: Yale University Press.

Christ, Nannette, and Michael J. Ferrantino. 2011. "Land Transport for Exports: The Effects of Cost, Time, and Uncertainty in Sub-Saharan Africa." *World Development* 39 (10): 1749–59.

Dunbar, Muriel. 2013. "Engaging the Private Sector in Skills Development." Health and Education Advice and Resource Team, Oxford, United Kingdom.

Ernst, Dieter, and Linsu Kim. 2002. "Global Production Networks, Knowledge Diffusion, and Local Capability Formation." *Research Policy* 31: 1417–29.

Farole, T., C. Staritz, and D. Winkler. 2014. "Conceptual Framework." In *Making Foreign Direct Investment Work for Sub-Saharan Africa: Local Spillovers and Competitiveness in Global Value Chains*, edited by T. Farole and D. Winkler, 23–55. Washington, DC: World Bank.

Farole, Thomas and Deborah Winkler. 2014a. "Policy Implications." In *Making Foreign Direct Investment Work for Sub-Saharan Africa: Local Spillovers and Competitiveness in Global Value Chains*, edited by Thomas Farole and Deborah Winkler, 263–79. Washington, DC: World Bank.

———. 2014b. "The Role of Mediating Factors for FDI Spillovers in Developing Countries: Evidence from a

Global Dataset." In *Making Foreign Direct Investment Work for Sub-Saharan Africa: Local Spillovers and Competitiveness in Global Value Chains*, edited by T. Farole and D. Winkler, 59–86. Washington, DC: World Bank.

Feenstra, Robert C. 1998. "Integration of Trade and Disintegration of Production in the Global Economy." *Journal of Economic Perspectives* 12 (4): 31–50.

Feenstra, Robert, and Gary Hamilton. 2006. *Emergent Economies, Divergent Paths: Economic Organization and International Trade in South Korea and Taiwan, China.* Cambridge, UK: Cambridge University Press.

Feenstra, Robert C., Chang Hong, Hong Ma, and Barbara J. Spencer. 2013. "Contractual versus Non-Contractual Trade: The Role of Institutions in China." *Journal of Economic Behavior & Organization* 94 (C): 281–94.

Findlay, Ronald. 1978. "An 'Austrian' Model of International Trade and Interest Rate Equalization." *Journal of Political Economy* 86: 989–1008.

Freeman, Richard 2006. "The Great Doubling: America in the New Global Economy." Usery Lecture, April 8, Georgia State University. http://emlab.berkeley.edu/users/webfac/eichengreen/e183_sp07/great_doub.pd.

Gabaix, Xavier. 2011. "The Granular Origins of Aggregate Fluctuations." *Econometrica* 79 (3): 733–72.

Gereffi, Gary. 1999. "International Trade and Industrial Upgrading in the Apparel Commodity Chain." *Journal of International Economics* 48: 37–70.

Gereffi, Gary, and Stacey Frederick. 2010. "The Global Apparel Value Chain, Trade, and the Crisis: Challenges and Opportunities for Developing Countries." In *Global Value Chains in a Postcrisis World*, edited by O. Cattaneo, G. Gereffi, and C. Staritz, 157–208. Washington, DC: World Bank.

Gereffi, Gary, John Humphrey, Raphael Kaplinsky, and Timothy J. Sturgeon. 2001. "Introduction: Globalisation, Value Chains and Development." *IDS Bulletin* 32 (3): 1–8.

Gereffi, Gary, John Humphrey, and Timothy J. Sturgeon. 2005. "The Governance of Global Value Chains." *Review of International Political Economy* 12 (1): 78–104.

Grossman, Gene M., and Esteban Rossi-Hansberg. 2008. "Trading Tasks: A Simple Theory of Offshoring." *American Economic Review* 98 (5): 1978–97.

———. 2012. "Task Trade between Similar Countries." *Econometrica* 80 (2): 593–629.

Helpman, Elhanan. 1984. "A Simple Theory of International Trade with Multinational Corporations." *Journal of Political Economy* 92 (3): 451–71.

Henderson, Jeffrey, Peter Dicken, Martin Hess, Neil Coe, and Henry Wai-Chung Yeung. 2002. "Global Production Networks and the Analysis of Economic Development." *Review of International Political Economy* 9 (3): 436–64.

Hoekman, Bernard. 2014. "Supply Chains, Mega-Regionals and Multilateralism: A Road Map for the WTO." Research Paper RSCAS 2014/27, Robert Schuman Centre for Advanced Studies, Centre for Economic Policy Research, London.

Horstmann, Ignatius J., and James R. Markusen. 1992. "Endogenous Market Structures in International Trade (Natura Facit Sal-tum)." *Journal of International Economics* 32 (1–2): 109–29.

Hummels, David, Peter Minor, Matthew Reisman, and Erin Endean. 2007. "Calculating Tariff Equivalents for Time in Trade." Technical Report submitted to the U.S. Agency for International Development, Nathan Associates, Arlington, VA.

Humphrey, John. 2003. "Globalization and Supply Chain Networks: The Auto Industry in Brazil and India." *Global Networks* 3 (2): 121–41.

Humphrey, J., and H. Schmitz. 2002. "How Does Insertion in Global Value Chains Affect Upgrading in Industrial Clusters?" *Regional Studies* 36 (9): 1017–27.

Japan Automobile Manufacturers Association, Inc. 2013. *The Motor Industry of Japan 2013.* Tokyo, Japan: Japan Automobile Manufacturers Association, Inc.

Kawakami, Momoko. 2011. "Inter-firm Dynamics of Notebook PC Value Chains and the Rise of Taiwanese Original Design Manufacturing Firms." In *The Dynamics of Local Learning in Global Value Chains; Experiences from East Asia*, edited by Momoko Kawakami and Timothy Sturgeon, chapter 1. Basingstoke, UK: Palgrave Macmillan.

Kohonen, Teuvo 1982. "Self-Organized Formation of Topologically Correct Feature Maps". *Biological Cybernetics* 43 (1): 59–69.

Krugman, Paul. 1995. "Growing World Trade: Causes and Consequences." *Brookings Papers on Economic Activity* 26 (1): 327–77.

Kummritz, Victor, Daria Taglioni, and Deborah Winkler. 2016. "Economic Upgrading through Global Value Chain Participation: Which Policies Increase the Value Added Gains?" World Bank, Washington, DC.

Lopez-Gonzalez, Javier, and Peter Holmes. 2011. "The Nature and Evolution of Vertical Specialisation: What Is the Role of Preferential Trade Agreements?" Trade Working Paper No. 2011/41, Swiss National Centre of Competence in Research, Bern, Switzerland.

Manyka, James, Jacques Bughin, Susan Lund, Olivia Nottebohm, David Poulter, Sebastian Jauch, and Sree Ramaswamy. 2014. "Global Flows in a Digital Age: How Trade, Finance, People, and Data Connect the World Economy." McKinsey Global Institute Report, McKinsey & Company, Washington, DC.

Milberg, William. 2004. "The Changing Structure of Trade Linked to Global Production Systems: What Are the Policy Implications?" *International Labour Review* 143 (1–2): 45–90.

Milberg, William, and Deborah Winkler. 2013. *Outsourcing Economics: Global Value Chains in Capitalist Development.* New York: Cambridge University Press.

OECD (Organisation for Economic Co-operation and Development). 2011. "Perspectives on Global Development 2012: Social Cohesion in a Shifting World." OECD, Paris.

Ottaviano, Gianmarco I. P., and Diego Puga. 2003. "Agglomeration in the Global Economy: A Survey of the 'New Economic Geography.'" *World Economy* 21 (6): 707–31.

Pine, B. Joseph, II. 1999. *Mass Customization: The New Frontier in Business Competition.* Cambridge, MA: Harvard Business School Press.

Pisano, Gary P., and Willy C. Shih. 2009. "Restoring American Competitiveness." *Harvard Business Review* 87 (7–8).

Ponte, Stefano, and Peter Gibbon. 2005. "Quality Standards, Conventions and the Governance of Global Value Chains." *Economy and Society* 34 (1): 1–31.

Porter, Michael E. 1985. *Competitive Advantage: Creating and Sustaining Superior Performance.* New York: Free Press.

———. 1990. "The Competitive Advantage of Nations." *Harvard Business Review* 78 (2): 73–93.

———. 2008. "The Five Competitive Forces That Shape Strategy." *Harvard Business Review* 86 (1): 78–93.

Rodrik, Dani. 2000. "How Far Will Economic Integration Go?" *Journal of Economic Perspectives* 14 (1): 177–86.

Saez, Sebastian, Daria Taglioni, Erik van der Marel, Claire H. Hollweg, and Veronika Zavacka. 2015. *Valuing Services in Trade: A Toolkit for Competitiveness Diagnostics.* Washington, DC: World Bank.

Sagrario, Ins, Mara Pierrestegui, and Gabriel Mas. 2009. "Combining Strategic Analysis and Change Management: A Tool for Improving the Competitiveness of Firms." Micro Report No. 154, U.S. Agency for International Development, Washington, DC.

Santoni, Gianluca, and Daria Taglioni. 2015. "Networks and Structural Integration in Global Value Chains." In *The Age of Global Value Chains,* edited by Joao Amador and Filippo di Mauro. Washington, DC: Center for Economic Policy Research.

Sturgeon, Timothy J. 2001. "How Do We Define Value Chains and Production Networks?" *IDS Bulletin* 32 (3): 9–18.

———. 2002. "Modular Production Networks: A New American Model of Industrial Organization." *Industrial and Corporate Change* 11 (3): 451–96.

Sturgeon, Timothy, and Richard K. Lester. 2004. "The New Global Supply-Base: New Challenges for Global Suppliers in East Asia." In *Global Production Networking and Technological Change in East Asia,* edited by Shahid Yusuf, M. Anjum Altaf, and Kaoru Nabeshima. Washington, DC: World Bank.

UNCTAD (United Nations Conference on Trade and Development). 2013. "World Investment Report 2013—Global Value Chains: Investment and Trade for Development." UNCTAD, Geneva.

Vernon, Raymond. 1966. "International Investment and International Trade in the Product Cycle." *Quarterly Journal of Economics* 80 (2): 190–207.

———. 1979. "The Product Cycle Hypothesis in a New International Environment." *Oxford Bulletin of Economics and Statistics* 41 (4): 255–67.

WEF (World Economic Forum). 2012. "The Future of Manufacturing." Global Agenda Council on the Future of Manufacturing, WEF, Cologny, Switzerland.

———. 2013. "Enabling Trade: Valuing Growth Opportunities." WEF, Geneva.

World Bank. 2013. *World Development Report: Jobs.* Washington, DC: World Bank.

———. 2016. *World Development Report 2016: Digital Dividends.* Washington, DC: World Bank.

WTO-OECD (World Trade Organization and Organisation for Economic Co-operation and Development). 2013. *Aid for Trade and Value Chain in Agrifood.* Geneva: WTO.

Chapter 2

CONSIDER BULGARIA

Introduction

This chapter examines the case of Bulgaria, which we use to illustrate how the tools described in this book exemplify a country's integration and economic upgrading in global value chains (GVCs). The chapter shows how analysts can make use of the quantitative tools described in part II of the book—as well as the strategic policy framework developed in part III—to identify a country's position in GVCs, its scope for economic upgrading, and policy suggestions to achieve that goal. In particular, the chapter explores how value addition from gross exports has changed over time in Bulgaria and how it is linked to the country's participation in GVCs. For easy navigation, the measures and concepts in this chapter reference the relevant chapters or charts in the book.[1]

Identifying the effect of GVC integration on country performance is exacerbated by the fact that the exogeneity of GVC participation is often difficult to establish. If GVC integration is endogenous to changes in the overall economic environment or to developments in politically influential parts of the economy, the causality between GVC participation and country performance could run in both directions. This makes Bulgaria a good candidate to evaluate, as it became a member of the European Union (EU) in 2007. The close supervision of reform progress by the European Commission represents a rare example of a mostly exogenous policy reform, including the country's openness to flows of capital, labor, trade, and ideas. This suggests that the opening of sectors in Bulgaria was an exogenous development rather than a response to domestic lobbying or other unobservable factors.

Bulgaria's Domestic Value Added in Exports

In a world of GVCs, what matters is the growth of a country's domestic value added embodied in gross exports, because a significant share of gross exports may consist of foreign value added (via imported inputs). Domestic value added consists of value added that is created in an industry (direct domestic value added), value added that is created in other sectors supplying the industry (indirect domestic value added), and re-imported intermediates (see chapter 4). Bulgaria's growth of domestic value added embodied in gross exports shows moderate overall performance compared with its peer countries. Bulgaria's compound annual growth rate between 1995 and 2008 reached 10.7 percent and, thus, was higher than the rate in established GVC countries such as Germany (6.9 percent), the United States (5.7 percent), and Japan (3.3 percent). However, Bulgaria trailed China (17.5 percent) and the regional peers, in particular, Romania (14.8 percent), Poland (13.8 percent), and the EU-10[2] (13.1 percent). Among the comparator countries, only Turkey (10.4 percent) and Portugal (6.7 percent) performed worse than Bulgaria (figure 2.1).

Bulgaria's growth in domestic value added embodied in gross exports varies significantly across sectors (for the methodology to identify key GVCs in a country, see box 2.1 and chapter 3). Agriculture, textiles, leather and footwear, and basic metals and fabricated metal products performed well compared with the EU-10 average over 1995–2008, but the performance of other product groups was lackluster. Growth in agriculture was 9 percent, placing

Figure 2.1. Growth of Domestic Value Added Embodied in Gross Exports, 1995–2011

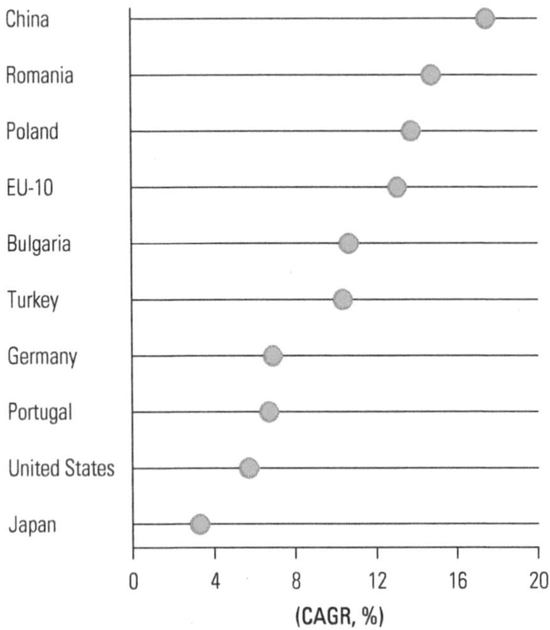

Source: Adapted from the Organisation for Economic Co-operation and Development–World Trade Organization Trade in Value Added database.
Note: See chapter 4 for more information on the decomposition. CAGR = compound annual growth rate; EU = European Union.

the country third after Romania (13 percent) and Portugal (10 percent) and above the EU-10 average (8.3 percent). Bulgaria's growth also exceeded that of the EU-10 in textiles, leather and footwear, and basic metals but fell significantly short of the EU-10 average in machinery, transport equipment, electrical and optical equipment, and in particular food and beverages. Overall, Bulgaria's growth seems to have been largely driven by the traditional sectors and has lagged in the medium- and high-tech sectors, showing a structure similar to that of Portugal.

Channels for Increasing Domestic Value Added in Exports

Between 1995 and 2008, the main source of growth in domestic value added embodied in exports was the increase in direct value added generated by exporters, which was 62.1 percent of the total (figure 2.2). The value-added growth contribution generated through backward links—that is, by the domestic supply sectors—was 37.8 percent. Growth of reimported intermediates was negligible. The growth of the direct value added by Bulgarian exporters is likely to be associated with improvements in productivity and export competitiveness via participation in GVCs. Chapter 1 discusses the transmission channels for economic and social upgrading in GVCs (see figure 1.11 in chapter 1).

International GVC Links

Macro Perspective: Bulgaria's Structural Integration in GVCs

Network analysis and metrics help capture the complexity and heterogeneity of actors and trade links in GVCs (see chapter 6). Bulgaria exhibits a low to

Box 2.1. Methodology for the Identification of Key GVCs and Peer Countries

The desk-based selection of potentially important sectors for global value chains (GVCs) is based on three quantitative analyses—based on the concept of a sector's revealed comparative advantage, assessment of total forward and backward GVC participation measures, and the composition of the top 50 to 100 export and import products (which usually account for roughly 50 to 70 percent of countries' total exports and imports). The last are identified at the most disaggregated statistical level available and categorized by final use (capital, consumption, and intermediate goods) and by chain category (final products, main inputs/parts, standard inputs, raw materials, and machinery and equipment [see also chapter 3]). Crossing gross trade data with informed classifications (see chapter 3) provides additional insights.

The analysis for Bulgaria focuses on eight specific GVCs, which play a significant role (actual or potential) in the country. The GVCs include (1) agriculture; (2) food and beverages; (3) textiles, leather, and footwear; (4) chemicals and nonmetallic mineral products; (5) basic metals and fabricated metal products; (6) machinery and equipment not elsewhere classified; (7) electrical and optical equipment; and (8) transport equipment. Although Bulgaria's involvement in the automotive GVC is still small, the country intends to expand its GVC participation in that area. This enables us to contrast Bulgaria with other countries—in particular, Romania—that successfully integrated into the transport equipment value chain.

Peer countries include Bulgaria's regional neighbors, which are Poland, Portugal, Romania, and Turkey, and the European Union-10 average (whenever possible), as well as key GVC benchmark countries, which are China, Germany, Japan, and the United States (for the methodology for selecting the peer countries, see box 4.1 in chapter 4).

medium level of structural integration in GVCs, which is slightly worse on the selling side. Table 2A.1 in annex 2A shows buyer-related and seller-related measures of structural integration in GVCs, as measured by the Bonacich power index (Bonacich 1987). They are denoted with the terms BONwin and BONwout, respectively. Bulgaria's overall extent of structural integration in GVCs as a buyer (BONwin) lies in the medium spectrum and is weakest in transport equipment. The country's overall structural integration in GVCs as a seller (BONwout) lies in the low to medium range across the country sample, and is lowest in agriculture, food and beverages, electrical and optical equipment, and transport equipment. The countries with the highest levels of structural integration in GVCs are China, Germany, and the United States.

Minimal spanning trees help in visualizing the complexity and heterogeneity of actors and trade links in GVCs (for the concept of network visualizations, see chapter 6). Figure 1.10 in chapter 1 illustrates a minimal spanning tree based on trade in value-added data (as computed by Santoni and Taglioni 2015). The main root of the tree is Germany, making it the most relevant source of the "imported" value added in other countries' exports, including Bulgaria, but also in peers such as Poland, Portugal, and Turkey, as well as China. Bulgaria's structural integration in GVCs is less peripheral compared with Portugal, Romania, and Turkey. From the regional perspective, value-added trade flows between Germany and Poland are the most relevant.

Micro Perspective: Firms' Integration in GVCs

A country's integration in GVCs is the outcome of firms' GVC links. Domestic firms can become sellers in GVCs by supplying to multinational firms in the country or by exporting inputs or final products to international buyers. Domestic firms can also act as buyers by sourcing intermediates from abroad (for a description of GVC measures based on World Bank Enterprise Surveys, see box 6.2 in chapter 6).

Bulgaria's domestic firms are less well integrated in GVCs on the selling side than are local subsidiaries of multinationals. Whereas 66 percent of the foreign firms sampled in Bulgaria export at least 1 percent, the share drops to 18 percent for domestic firms (figure 2.3). The share of domestic firms that export is higher in Poland (23.1 percent) and Romania (21.1 percent), and almost twice as high in Turkey (35.9 percent). In Bulgaria, domestically owned manufacturing firms tend to source only 65.3 percent of their inputs locally, which is lower than for most comparator countries. Foreign manufacturing firms in Bulgaria source about 52.6 percent of their inputs locally, which suggests that backward links of foreign direct investment (FDI) are in the medium range (figure 2.4). Shifting the focus to Bulgarian exporters' GVC links, the picture looks slightly better. Domestic exporters in Bulgaria export the second highest share of their sales (8.9 percent), but they still have a long way to go to reach the share of sales exported by Turkey (16.7 percent) (figure 2.5).

On the buying side, Bulgaria's domestic firms are much better integrated into GVCs compared with firms in the peer countries. GVC integration on the

Figure 2.2. Decomposition of Domestic Value Added Generated through Exports

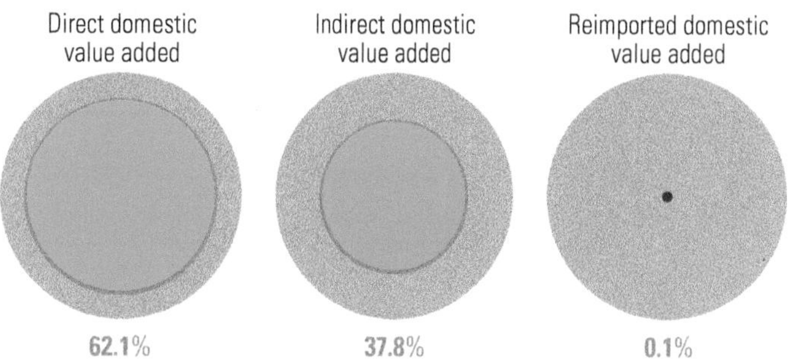

Source: Adapted from the Organisation for Economic Co-operation and Development–World Trade Organization Trade in Value Added database.
Note: See chapter 4 for more information on the decomposition.

Figure 2.3. Share of Firms Exporting Directly or Indirectly

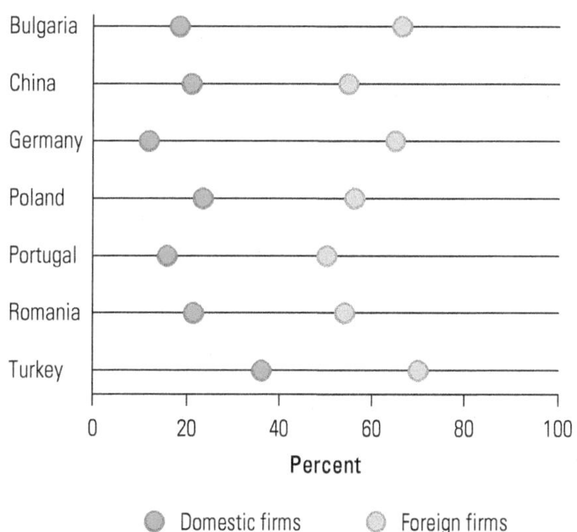

Source: Adapted from Enterprise Surveys (World Bank).
Note: The relevant data for each country are as follows: Bulgaria (2013), China (2012), Germany (2005), Poland (2013), Portugal (2005), Romania (2013), and Turkey (2008).

Figure 2.4. Share of Total Inputs Sourced Locally

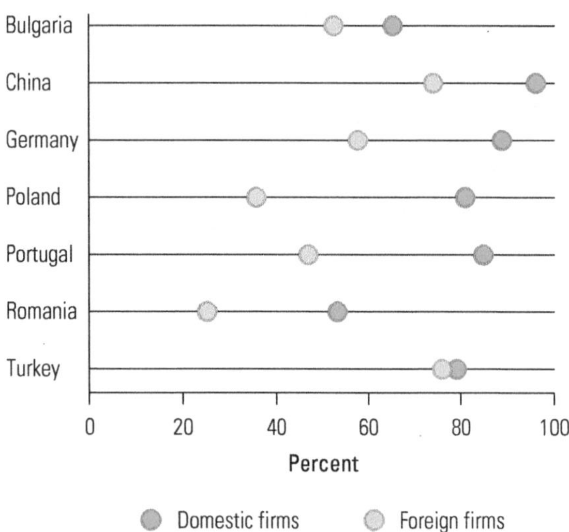

Source: Adapted from Enterprise Surveys (World Bank).
Note: The relevant data for each country are as follows: Bulgaria (2013), China (2012), Germany (2005), Poland (2013), Portugal (2005), Romania (2013), and Turkey (2008). The data include manufacturing firms only. See box 6.2 in chapter 6 for the definition of this measure.

Figure 2.5. Share of Total Sales Exported Directly or Indirectly

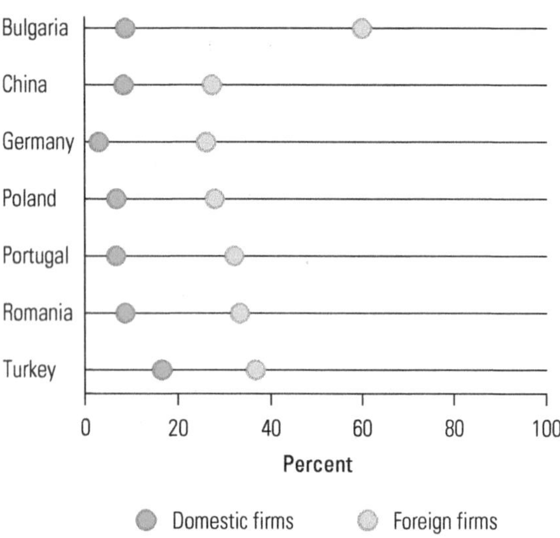

Source: Adapted from Enterprise Surveys (World Bank).
Note: The relevant data for each country are as follows: Bulgaria (2013), China (2012), Germany (2005), Poland (2013), Portugal (2005), Romania (2013), and Turkey (2008). See box 6.2 in chapter 6 for the definition of this measure.

buying side provides information on the sources of technology transfer and the types of GVCs a country is likely to join. In Bulgaria, more than 60 percent of domestically owned manufacturing firms source inputs of foreign origin, which is the second highest share in the sample after Romania. In China, by contrast, only 12.9 percent of domestic manufacturing firms import intermediates (figure 2.6). The extent of GVC links on the buying side is also greater for domestic manufacturing firms in Bulgaria, reaching 34.7 percent, which is the second highest share after Romania (46.6 percent) (100 percent minus the share of total inputs sourced locally, as shown in figure 2.4).

Domestic versus Foreign Content of Gross Exports

Some countries, interest groups within countries, and even international organizations (see, for example, UNCTAD 2013) still view GVCs as a trap that creates a new core-periphery pattern with "good" jobs in the North and "bad" jobs in the South. The key piece of evidence that GVC skeptics present to support their view is that the share of domestic value added embodied in exports as a percentage of gross exports tends to shrink for emerging countries. Indeed, the share of domestic value added embodied in exports as a percentage of gross exports has fallen in Bulgaria and all its peer countries. Bulgaria's share declined from 62.7 percent in 1995 to 60 percent in 2008, which is less than the share in any of the peer countries (figure 2.7).

Evidence of decreasing domestic value added in total exports is a reflection of the increased sophistication and length of value chains. All countries

Figure 2.6. Share of Firms Using Material Inputs/Supplies of Foreign Origin

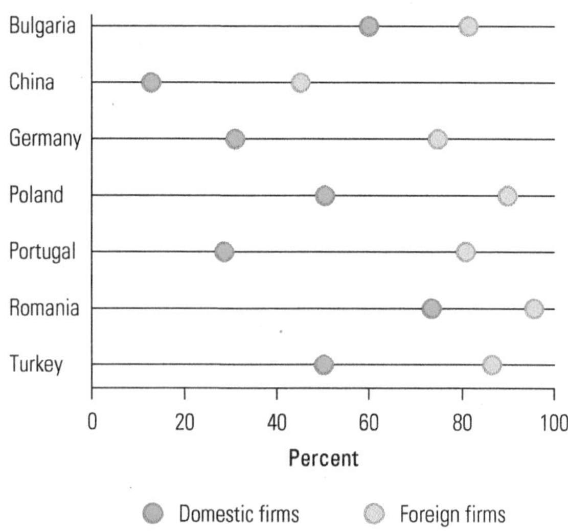

Source: Adapted from Enterprise Surveys (World Bank).
Note: The relevant data for each country are as follows: Bulgaria (2013), China (2012), Germany (2005), Poland (2013), Portugal (2005), Romania (2013), and Turkey (2008). The data include manufacturing firms only. See box 6.2 in chapter 6 for the definition of this measure.

Figure 2.7. Domestic and Foreign Value Added Embodied in Gross Exports: Bulgaria and Selected Countries, Total, 1995 and 2008

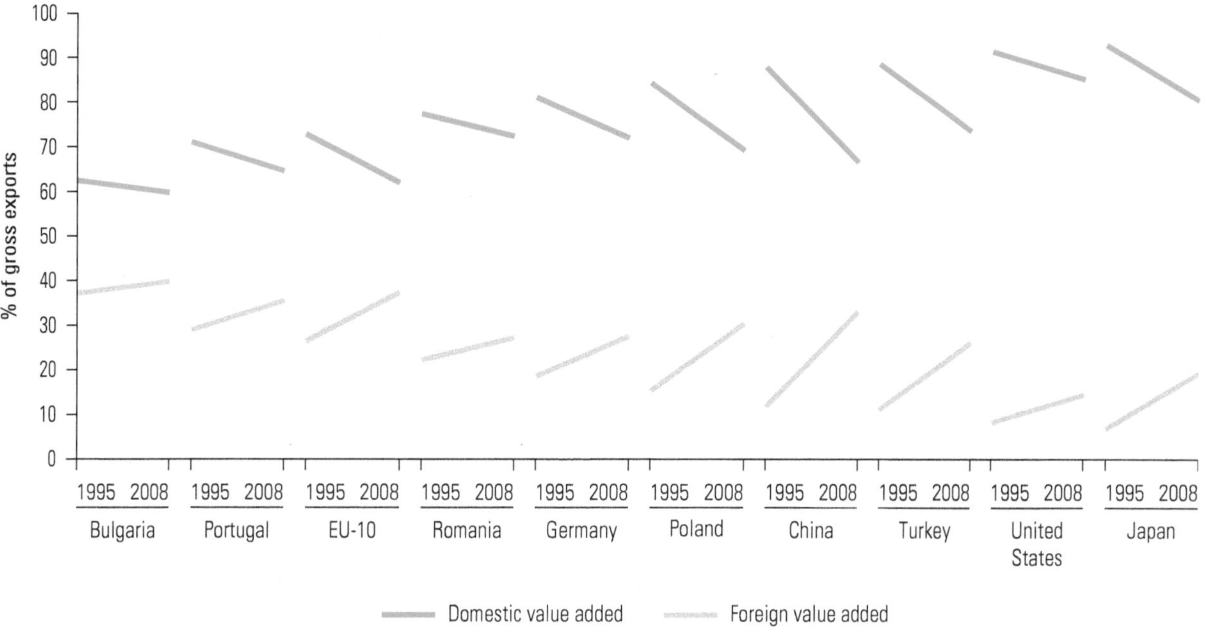

Source: Adapted from the Organisation for Economic Co-operation and Development–World Trade Organization Trade in Value Added database.

increasingly rely on foreign value added (imported inputs) in GVCs. One way to demonstrate this increase is by measuring the correlation between the growth rate of gross exports and developments in the direct (intrasector) domestic value added embodied in gross exports, the indirect (upstream) domestic value added embodied in gross exports, and the foreign value added embodied in gross exports (for definitions of these measures, see chapter 4; for the econometric model, see chapter 7).

The econometric results indicate that domestic value added gains substantially from increases in gross exports. More specifically, all the value-added components of gross exports are positively correlated with growth of gross exports. In Bulgaria, growth of the direct domestic value added embodied in gross exports shows the highest correlation with growth of gross exports (figure 2.8). In the overall sample of countries, growth of gross exports shows the highest correlation with growth of the indirect (upstream) domestic value added embodied in gross exports. For the overall sample and for Bulgaria, growth of foreign value added embodied in gross exports shows the weakest correlation with growth of gross exports.

The results by sector indicate that the growth of indirect (upstream) domestic value added embodied

Figure 2.8. Coefficients from Regression Results for Value-Added Components of Gross Exports, Overall Country Sample and Bulgaria

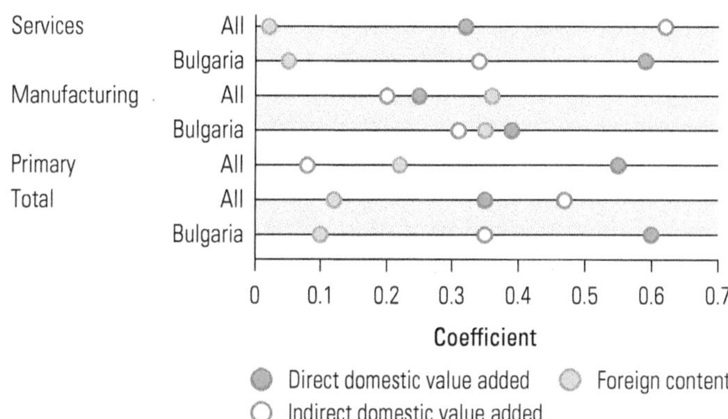

Source: Adapted from the Organisation for Economic Co-operation and Development–World Trade Organization Trade in Value Added database.
Note: Computations are based on econometric results (not reported).

in gross exports increases most in the services sector, in particular for the overall sample of countries (figure 2.8). Figure 2.9 reports the coefficients for individual industries in the overall country sample (the number of observations was too low to estimate the model for Bulgaria alone). The main observation is that overall gains in the domestic content of gross exports are always greater than those in

Figure 2.9. Coefficients from Regression Results for Value-Added Components of Gross Exports, by Sector, Overall Country Sample

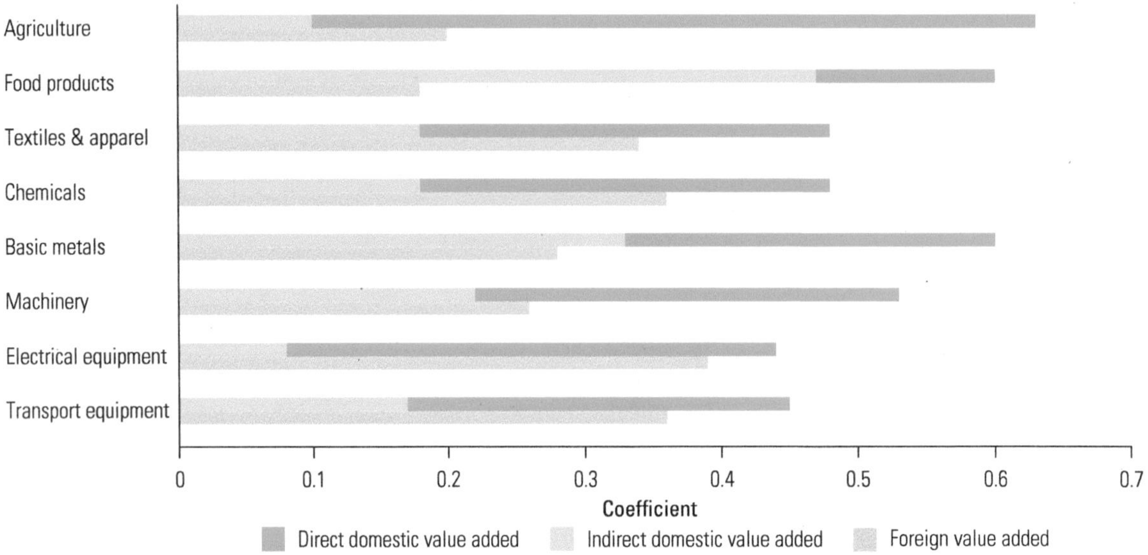

Agriculture
Food products
Textiles & apparel
Chemicals
Basic metals
Machinery
Electrical equipment
Transport equipment

0 0.1 0.2 0.3 0.4 0.5 0.6 0.7
Coefficient

Direct domestic value added Indirect domestic value added Foreign value added

Source: Adapted from the Organisation for Economic Co-operation and Development–World Trade Organization Trade in Value Added database.
Note: Computations are based on econometric results (not reported).

foreign content. At the same time, the results for specific industries point to substantial heterogeneity in composition.

Imports-to-Exports Patterns

The basic concept of GVC trade is "importing to export," or I2E, as Baldwin and Lopez-Gonzalez (2013) call it. Essentially, the measure of GVC trade captures how much of a country's exports consist of value that was added in another country. The measure includes the sourcing side in GVCs (that is, how much a country is buying) and the selling side in GVCs (how much a country is selling) (for more details, see chapter 3). Bulgaria buys its I2E mainly from Germany, Italy, the Russian Federation, and Turkey (figure 2.10). Between 1995 and 2009, Bulgaria's reliance on sourcing I2E from Russia dropped sharply and, to a lesser extent, also from Germany, whereas the I2E sourcing share from Romania and Turkey showed a relatively strong expansion over the period. On the selling side, Bulgaria sold its I2E products mainly to Belgium, Germany, Italy, Romania, and Turkey. The country's reliance on those I2E destinations—especially Belgium and Germany—increased between 1995 and 2009, with the exception of Italy. Other EU countries, such as France, the Netherlands, and the United Kingdom, also lost in relative market share as destinations of I2E products over the period.

Final Demand for Value Added in Gross Exports

Despite Bulgaria's EU integration, the final demand for Bulgarian value added embodied in gross exports (for the measure, see chapter 5) from the EU-27 has increased only slightly and remains significantly lower than the EU average. Between 1995 and 2008, Bulgaria's share increased from 52.5 to 54.7 percent (figure 2.11). Bulgaria's share in 2008 was thus substantially less than the EU-10 average of 69.1 percent and the shares for other EU peers, such as Poland (71.3 percent) and Romania (64.7 percent). For Bulgaria, final demand from the EU-27 market grew only in transport equipment and, to a lesser extent, food and beverages and machinery and equipment. The final demand for Bulgarian value added embodied in its gross exports from other countries increased from 27.8 to 32.5 percent over the same period, whereas final demand from East Asia declined from 10.9 to 5.3 percent.

International GVC Links and Growth in Bulgaria's Domestic Value Added That Is Exported

Does the intensity and nature of GVC links matter for growth in domestic value added that is exported? This study explores this question through econometric and statistical analysis from several angles. First, the analysis explores whether the degree of structural integration in global value-added trade matters.

Figure 2.10. Bulgaria's Buying and Selling Patterns, 1995 and 2009

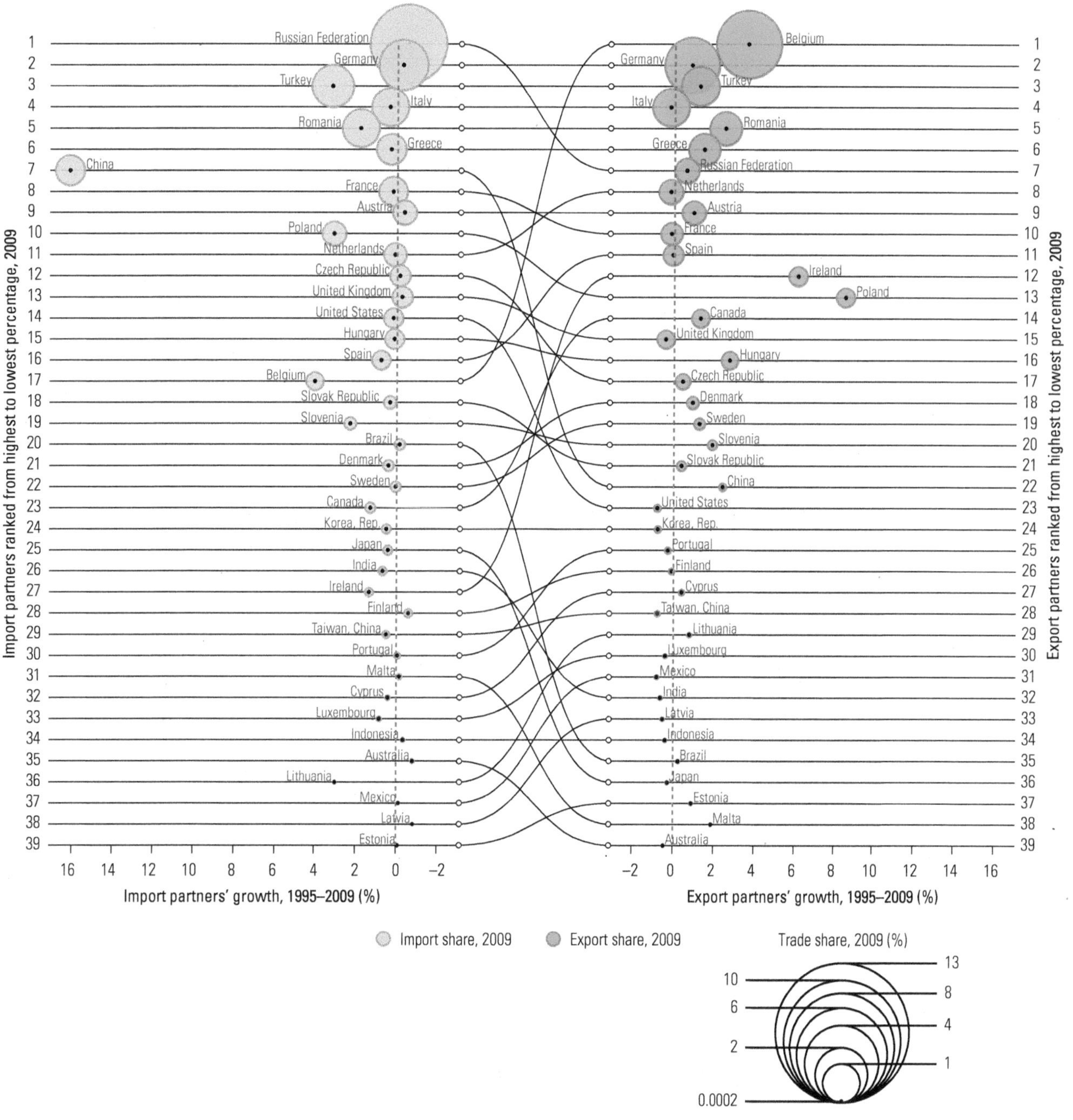

Source: Adapted from Baldwin and Lopez-Gonzalez 2013.

Second, the analysis asks whether the greater integration of Bulgaria in GVCs as a buyer (relative to the weaker integration as a seller) negatively affects Bulgaria's domestic value-added growth from gross exports. Third, the analysis looks more closely at the relation between the growth of foreign value added embodied in gross exports and the growth of the domestic value-added component. The underlying econometric and statistical frameworks can be found in chapter 7.

Bulgaria's increasing GVC integration is correlated with value-added gains. We find a positive correlation between growth of GVC participation and growth of domestic value added embodied in

Figure 2.11. Final Demand, by Destination, Bulgaria and Peer Countries, Total, 1995 and 2008

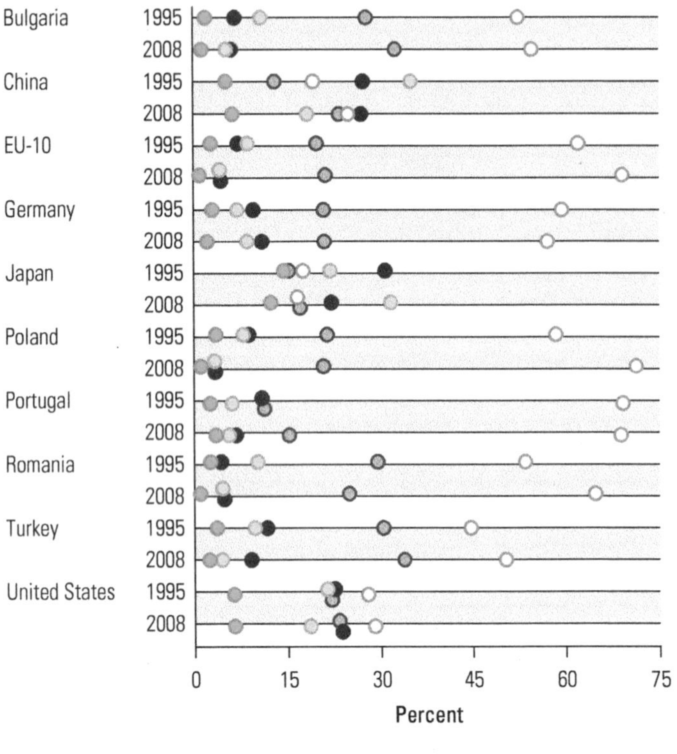

Source: Adapted from the Organisation for Economic Co-operation and Development–World Trade Organization Trade in Value Added database.
Note: Destinations are only available at the aggregated level. ASEAN = Association of Southeast Asian Nations; EU = European Union; NAFTA = North American Free Trade Agreement.

gross exports. Although that correlation suffers from problems of endogeneity, the correlation is higher in Bulgaria compared with the full country sample in the Trade in Value Added database developed by the Organisation for Economic Co-operation and Development and the World Trade Organization (for more information on this database refer to Appendix G). The value-added premium for Bulgaria's integration in GVCs is even higher on the selling side than on the buying side. The highest positive correlation stems from the manufacturing sector, whereas it is weakest for the services sector. A breakdown by sectors indicates that the correlation is highest for textiles and apparel and metals, sectors in which the premium for Bulgaria over the full country sample is also highest. These results may be associated with Bulgaria's comparative advantage in those sectors.

Interestingly, the unbalanced extent of integration in GVCs on the buying side (higher) versus the selling side (lower) does not seem to harm Bulgaria, but rather tends to be associated with a gain in domestic value-added exports. The correlation is highest for the primary sectors, followed by manufacturing and services. The premium, which is highest in textiles and apparel, agriculture, and machinery, may be driven by the beneficial effects of importing foreign know-how and technology.

Finally, higher growth of foreign value added in gross exports is associated with higher growth of domestic value added embodied in gross exports. In other words, higher rates of imported inputs enable Bulgaria and all the other countries in the sample to increase their production, productivity, and value-added content in exports. The elasticity is slightly lower for Bulgaria compared with the overall sample. The results make a clear case for integrating in GVCs and encouraging imports by demonstrating that more imports are linked to more value addition from exports.

Scope for Further Value-Added Growth

Low Domestic Value Added in Third Countries' Exports

There remains large scope for further value-added growth. Bulgaria's sales of inputs to third countries—which are used in those countries' exports—tend to be of low value added (for the measure, see chapter 5). Although all countries in the sample increased their domestic value added in third-country exports as a percentage of gross exports, Bulgaria's expansion is among the lowest (figure 2.12). Its share is among the lowest in the sample for chemical and nonmetallic mineral products, metals, and machinery and equipment; however, the country managed a strong increase in its share for electrical and optical equipment.

Large Distance to Final Demand and Lower Opportunities for Increasing Domestic Value Added along the Chain

A final useful metric is to combine import and export "upstreamness"—the distance of a country's import and export baskets to the final consumer—to compute the gap between the buying and selling chains, which is defined as the difference between import and export upstreamness (for more on upstreamness and the domestic gap between the buying and selling chains, see chapter 5). A positive gap indicates that exports are relatively more downstream compared with the import mix, or that exports are closer to

Figure 2.12. Domestic Value Added in Third Countries' Gross Exports, Bulgaria and Peer Countries, Total, 1995 and 2008

Source: Adapted from the Organisation for Economic Co-operation and Development–World Trade Organization Trade in Value Added database.

final demand than are imports. Conversely, a negative gap indicates that a country's export profile is more upstream than its import profile. Alternatively, a negative gap may indicate that the country has a sophisticated consumer market and therefore is an intensive importer of finished consumer goods, such as the United States.

Bulgaria's exports and imports are in a relatively upstream position, far from the final consumer, and have moved up further over time. Bulgaria's import upstreamness in 2012 was the third largest after China and Japan, whereas its export upstreamness was the largest of the sample. As for most countries, both measures increased over 2000–12, reflecting that GVCs have become longer with the increased fragmentation of production. Only Germany and Poland managed to move their exports closer to the final consumer (figure 2.13).

Bulgaria's gap is relatively short, which implies that the average number of production steps and, thus, opportunities to increase domestic value added along the chain are fewer than elsewhere. This situation will not change unless the country manages to enter tasks that are not carried out domestically. Bulgaria showed the second smallest gap after the United States, which resulted from similarly high import and export upstreamness. The gap is slightly positive, which suggests that exports are relatively closer to final demand than are imports. A larger gap implies a larger average number of production steps performed in the country. Bulgaria's small gap could be an indicator of lower opportunities to expand domestic value added along the chain.

In Bulgaria, textiles and transport equipment and, to a lesser extent, food and beverages and machinery and electronics are closest to final demand. Although food and beverages moved slightly upstream, machinery and electronics moved even closer to final demand, as did chemicals and transport equipment. By contrast, metals and agriculture—the two sectors that are the most upstream—moved further from final demand.

Does the position in the value chain (upstreamness) and the length of the domestic segment of GVCs matter for the growth rate of domestic value added that is exported? This question can be addressed econometrically by examining the growth rate of the upstreamness and the domestic length of sourcing chains—that is, the distance between a sector of interest and the first supplier in the value chain (for an econometric model, see chapter 6).

Going upstream has no impact on the growth of domestic value added embodied in manufacturing exports for the overall sample of countries. The correlation between growth of upstreamness and growth in the domestic value-added content of exports is statistically insignificant in manufacturing, although a statistically significant correlation exists

Figure 2.13. Import and Export Upstreamness and Gap, Bulgaria and Peer Countries, 2000 and 2012

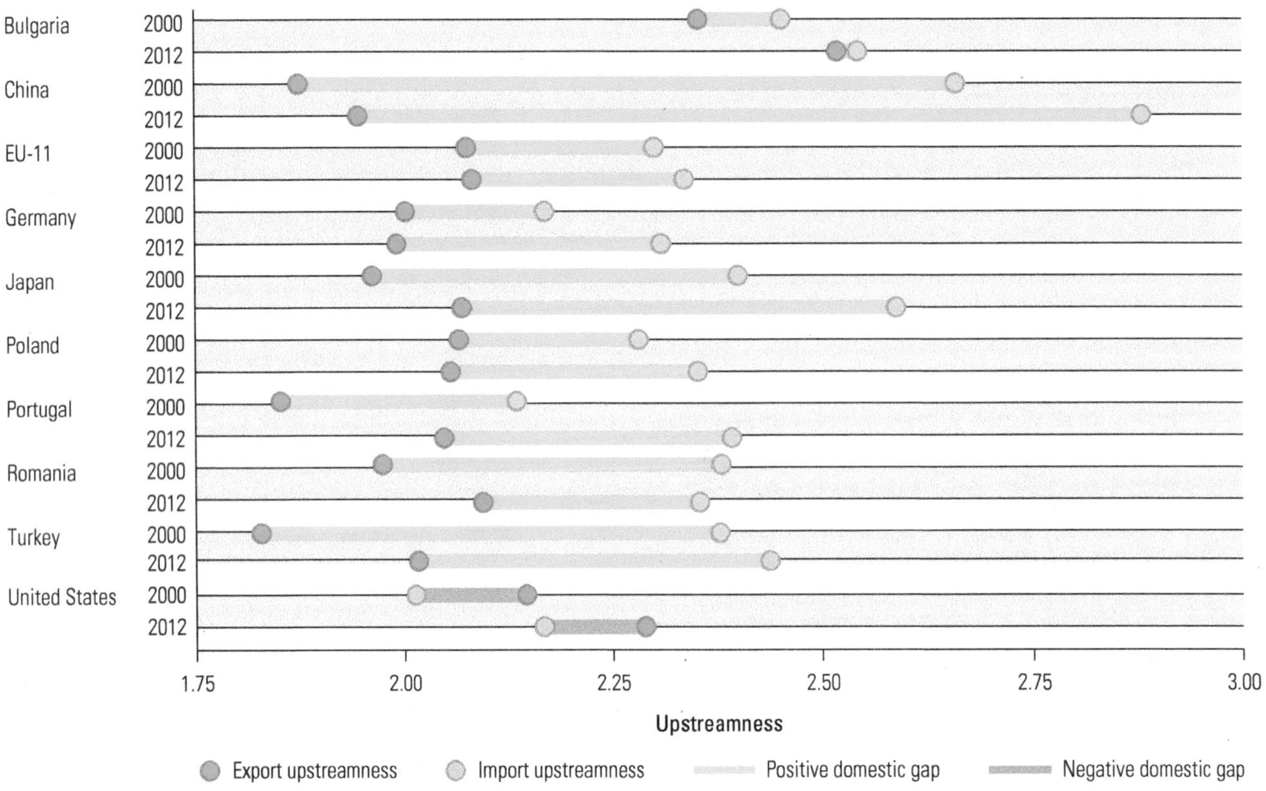

Upstreamness

Export upstreamness · Import upstreamness · Positive domestic gap · Negative domestic gap

Sources: Adapted from Chor 2014; United Nations Comtrade database.

for agriculture and services. By contrast, for Bulgaria, the relationship is mostly statistically significant, even in manufacturing industries. A breakdown by industry suggests that Bulgaria's moving upstream in the value chain is associated with greater growth of domestic value added that is exported in agriculture, food and beverages, and textiles.

By contrast, in chemicals, metals, and electronics, moving downstream creates a positive association. The results for the full country sample indicate instead that the relationship is statistically insignificant for all the individual manufacturing sectors. In agriculture, however, we find that moving downstream is associated with growth in the domestic value added embodied in gross exports, a result that is at odds with the case of Bulgaria, where moving upstream generates greater value addition. Finally, in the results for the full country sample, upstreamness in the services sector is associated with growth of the value added embodied in exports. The results for the services sector may be driven by the fact that research and development (R&D) and design activities are located at the beginning of many value chains. Interestingly, however, the correlation coefficient for the services sector in Bulgaria is again at odds with the results for the overall country sample—that is, significantly negative. In other words, being closer to final demand in the services sector in Bulgaria pays off.

Finally, expanding the length of domestic sourcing chains is associated with greater domestic value-added content in Bulgarian gross exports of food and beverages, textiles and apparel, metals, and transport. By contrast, the association is negative for services, agriculture, and chemicals, which suggests that in these sectors, specialization in core activities and higher import intensity may be associated with better quality, higher value-added output.

Summary

The analysis so far suggests that a key priority for Bulgaria, after having successfully integrated into regional and GVCs, is to target economic upgrading and densification. The econometric results suggest a positive correlation between Bulgaria's integration in GVCs and its ability to boost the domestic value-added content of exports. However, the indicators for Bulgaria's position in GVCs point to a still low to medium level of integration and positioning in the low value-added segment. The results suggest ample scope for upgrading.

Bulgaria's GVC Participation and Firm-Level Productivity

What is the potential of GVCs to enhance the productivity of firms located in Bulgaria (domestic and foreign)? This question may be addressed by modifying the analysis by Farole and Winkler (2014) and applying it to Bulgaria. The model assesses how a firm's absorptive capacity and a country's institutional variables influence firm productivity from structural integration in GVCs in manufacturing industries (see annex 7B in chapter 7; for a literature review of the mediating factors, see chapter 9). The data consist of a cross-section of domestic manufacturing firms in low- and middle-income countries (LMICs) from the World Bank's Enterprise Surveys. Because the effect of GVC participation is the topic of interest, we merged the data set with two sector measures of structural integration in GVCs: BONwin (buyer's perspective) and BONwout (seller's perspective), as computed by Santoni and Taglioni (2015). The data include measures for more than 14,000 manufacturing firms in 22 LMICs (see table I.2 in appendix I).

A sector's structural integration in GVCs—as buyer and seller—has a positive impact on firm productivity. The estimations for the full country sample clearly confirm that GVC participation increases the productivity of firms in a country—be they domestic or foreign firms (see tables 7C.1 to 7C.3 in annex 7C in chapter 7). The various transmission channels through which GVC participation can increase productivity at home are depicted in figure 1.11 in chapter 1. The positive impact in the full sample is stronger for the seller-side measure than for the buyer-side measure. In other words, GVC integration as a buyer (via importing intermediates) in the short term leads to higher productivity gains than does GVC participation as a seller (via exporting).

The following subsections discuss the role of absorptive capacity and national characteristics for the GVC integration-productivity nexus.

Absorptive Capacity

Several characteristics at the firm level—in particular, a firm's lower technology gap—can increase the productivity spillovers from a sector's structural integration in GVCs (see annex 7B and tables 7C.1 to 7C.3 in annex 7C in chapter 7 for definitions of the variables and the regression results). A lower technology gap of a firm (relative to the median productivity level of foreign firms in the same sector) positively mediates productivity gains from GVC participation on the buying and selling sides in the full country sample, and the positive effect is even larger for Bulgaria. In other words, firms that lag further behind foreign firms in their median productivity also benefit less from GVC integration.

Exporters and foreign firms in Bulgaria gain less from structural integration in GVCs than do the same types of firms in the overall sample of 22 countries. Other factors that positively mediate the impact of structural integration in GVCs from a buyer's and seller's perspective are the firm's technology level, size, export share, and FDI status; these findings hold for the average firm in the full country sample. In Bulgaria, the positive effects from export share and FDI status are smaller. These results may be related to infrastructural challenges or barriers at the border, which do not support a firm's openness to trade and FDI as much in Bulgaria as in other countries.

Although the firm's location in an agglomeration reduces the productivity gains from the sector's structural integration in GVCs as a buyer and as a seller in the full country sample, the effect in Bulgaria is more positive for buyers and more negative for sellers. In other words, agglomerations entail positive urbanization economies, large consumer markets, deep labor pools, links to international markets, and clusters of diverse suppliers and institutions—when firms rely on imported inputs in GVCs, lowering production costs and increasing firm productivity. These benefits outweigh the potential negative congestion costs that occur because of increased demand for resources in agglomerations (such as power outages and waiting times). By contrast, firms that are selling in GVCs may face higher negative congestion costs, which seem to be higher than the potential benefits of agglomeration.

Why are productivity spillovers for sellers in Bulgarian agglomerations lower in the short run? One reason could lie in the short-term nature of the regressions: buyers in Bulgaria may benefit more quickly from GVC integration (for example, through the availability of high-tech inputs)—especially when located in agglomerations—whereas the productivity gains for sellers may take more time to materialize. In the short run, sellers in Bulgaria may face negative competition and rivalry effects—which could be even greater in agglomerations—which hamper productivity. The weaker GVC links for sellers in GVCs might magnify those potential mechanisms. In the long run, it could be that multiple positive effects offset the negative competition and rivalry effects for sellers.

National Characteristics and Institutions

The productivity spillovers from structural integration in GVCs are lower in more open trade regimes and more developed countries in the full country sample (see annex 7B and tables 7C.4, and 7C.5 in annex 7C in chapter 7 for definitions of the variables and the regression results). A country's share of exports (as a percentage of gross domestic product [GDP]), less trade protectionism, and a higher GDP reduce the positive productivity spillovers on firms from GVC participation, as a buyer and as a seller. GVC participants in an outward oriented trade setting may focus more strongly on international distribution and marketing, whereas in an inward oriented policy regime, they might bring newer technologies to the host countries (Crespo and Fontoura 2007). Local firms in an open trade regime may also be more exposed to competitive pressures through international trade competition, which could lead to negative spillovers in the short term.

The more advanced a country is in income level, the lower are the productivity spillovers from GVC participation. If income is accepted as a broad measure of national competition (and other institutional factors), the findings suggest that more developed countries with higher levels of competition benefit less from GVC integration. In such contexts, firms may have lower incentives to improve (Barrios and Strobl 2002).

Productivity spillovers from structural integration in GVCs are lower in countries with higher education, whereas they are higher in countries with high innovation capacity, according to the full country sample. Government spending on education (as a percentage of GDP) and the share of people who have completed secondary and tertiary education reduce the positive productivity spillovers on firms from GVC participation, as a buyer and as a seller. By contrast, higher R&D intensity shows a positive and significant impact on productivity spillovers for both types of GVC integration. Meyer and Sinani (2009), for instance, include three measures of a country's availability of human capital and show evidence that the share of workers with tertiary education, the R&D intensity in the private sector, and the number of patents (per billion U.S. dollars) granted to host country residents significantly affect spillovers in GVCs. This relationship takes a U-shaped form, that is, the extent of spillovers increases only below or above certain threshold levels of human capital (Meyer and Sinani 2009). It is possible that the countries in the sample (which covers only LMICs) are in the medium level of the U-curve for skills and the low level of the U-curve for R&D intensity.

National and institutional characteristics in Bulgaria positively mediate the productivity spillovers from structural integration in GVCs as a buyer—that is, on the sourcing side. The results show a positive association between integration in GVCs and measures of financial freedom (such as banking efficiency and independence from government control and interference in the financial sector). The same holds true for more government spending on education (as a percentage of GDP), higher share of people who have completed secondary and tertiary education, higher R&D intensity, higher share of exports (as a percentage of GDP), less trade protectionism, and higher per capita income, which all show a positive and significant mediating relationship with firm productivity in Bulgaria. Although many of these characteristics reduce productivity spillovers in the full country sample, in Bulgaria they can help increase the productivity gains from GVC integration as a buyer.

By contrast, many national and institutional characteristics in Bulgaria are negatively associated with the productivity spillovers from structural integration in GVCs as a seller. Less restricted labor or financial markets, more government spending on education, higher share of people who have completed secondary and tertiary education, higher share of R&D intensity, more freedom to invest, higher share of exports in GDP, less trade protectionism, and higher GDP have a negative and statistically significant correlation with firm-level productivity in Bulgaria. Compared with the full country sample, the negative mediating effects of national characteristics are weaker for Bulgaria from a buyer's perspective but stronger from a seller's perspective. This was also the case for firm location in agglomerations.

What explains the negative mediating relationship with GVC participation as a seller but the positive mediating relationship with GVC integration as a buyer in Bulgaria? Buyers in Bulgaria might benefit more quickly from GVC integration (for example, through the availability of high-tech inputs), which is further supported by a business-friendly environment—in particular, trade openness, skilled workforce, and R&D intensity. Sellers, by contrast, may face negative competition and rivalry effects in the short run, and a business-friendly environment may lead only to greater competition and, thus, more negative effects. The weaker GVC links for sellers in GVCs might magnify the effect. In the long run, however, multiple positive effects can be expected to offset the negative competition and rivalry effects for sellers.

What Must Be Done?

Applying the strategic policy framework to Bulgaria reveals two priority areas for policy intervention, as discussed in World Bank (2015): (1) facilitating domestic firms' entry into GVCs and (2) strengthening Bulgaria's GVC integration—particularly on the selling side—by fostering better links with domestic producers and enhancing absorptive capacities. The GVC analysis described in this chapter, combined with selected performance indicators of Bulgaria's regulatory and institutional framework related to GVCs (see table O.1 in the Overview), reveals that to integrate further into GVCs, Bulgaria must improve (1) connectivity to international markets as well as to the domestic segment of the supply chain and (2) the quality of infrastructure. The country also must focus on strengthening its links, maximizing the absorption potential of local actors to benefit from GVC spillovers and fostering its innovation capacity to expand and strengthen its GVC participation (figure 2.14).

Figure 2.14. Strategic Policy Framework Applied to Bulgaria

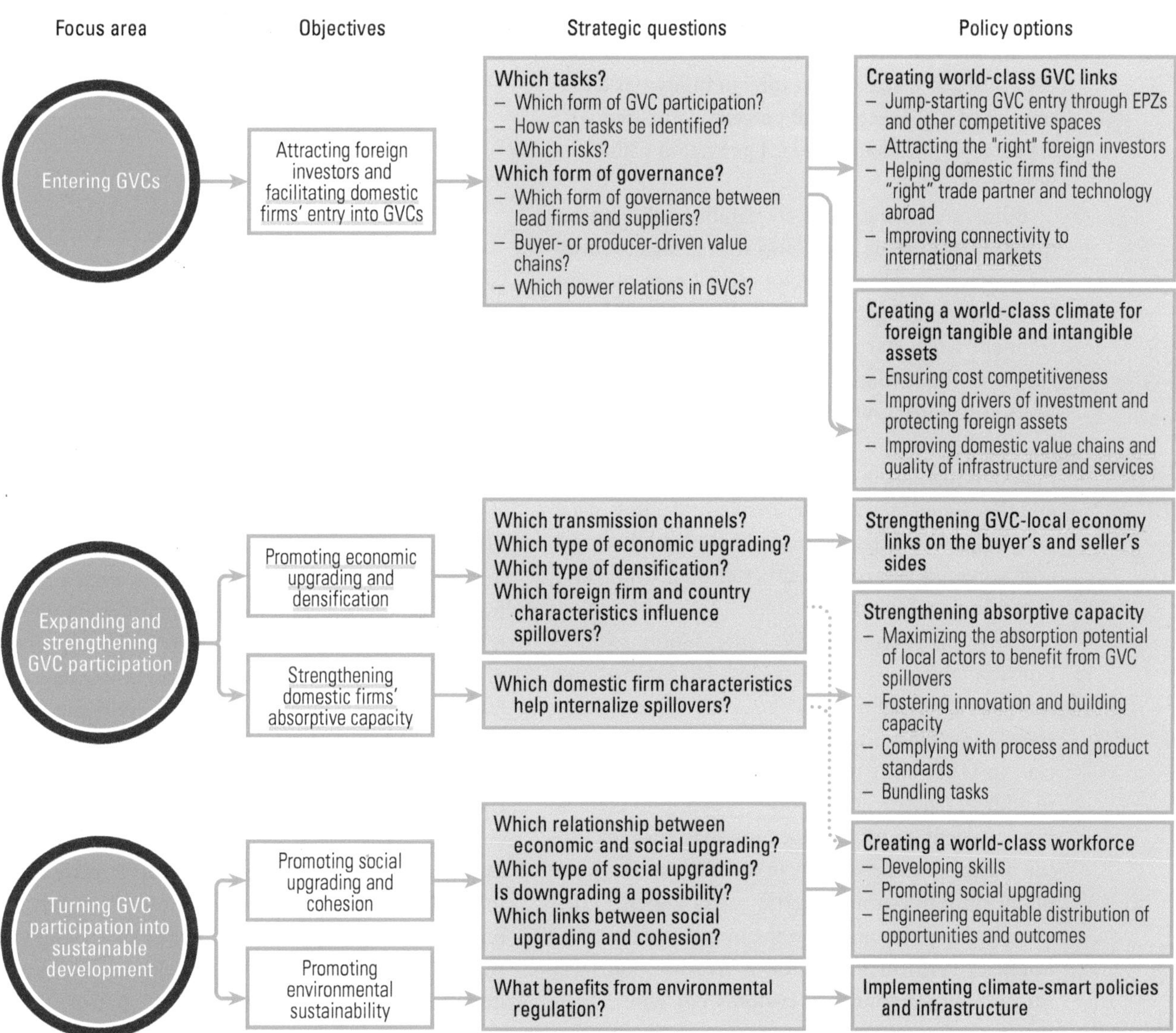

Note: The orange lines highlight priority areas for policy intervention in Bulgaria. EPZs = export processing zones; GVCs = global value chains.

Facilitate Domestic Firms' Entry into GVCs

Macro- and micro-level indicators reveal that there is scope for Bulgarian firms to enter GVCs, especially on the selling side. The analysis points out that Bulgaria exhibits a low to medium level of structural integration in GVCs—in particular in agriculture, food and beverages, electrical and optical equipment, and transport equipment, the last being slightly worse on the selling side. At the micro level, Bulgaria's domestic firms are less well integrated in GVCs on the selling side. More scope exists for domestic firms to become exporters. In the following, we analyze some policy options that can help achieve this goal.

Countries can join GVCs either by facilitating domestic firms' entry or by attracting foreign investors. Bulgaria's relatively favorable business environment, in conjunction with the country's accession to the EU in 2007, led to large inflows of FDI, especially during the years around EU membership. Between 2005 and 2009, average net foreign inflows as a percentage of GDP reached 20 percent, compared with 6.4 percent in Romania and 4.4 percent in China and Poland.

Bulgaria's business climate exhibits solid performance relative to its peers, also with regard to investor protection. The country's overall ease of doing business, which captures a country's regulatory environment when starting and operating a local firm, ranges in the medium spectrum compared with its peers and global GVC players (figure 2.15). Business is more difficult to do in China, Romania, and Turkey than in Bulgaria, but much easier in Germany, Japan, and the United States. In the area of protecting investors, Bulgaria is at the same level as Poland, Portugal, and Romania, but is ranked better than China and, surprisingly, Germany.

However, successful GVC integration requires Bulgaria to improve its connectivity to international markets. Poor connectivity means high costs, low speed, and high uncertainty. Successful participation in GVCs thus requires policy makers not just to address barriers at the border, but also to increase the connectivity of domestic markets and enhance the resilience and efficiency of the domestic segment of the supply chain. Bulgaria ranks lowest (47th) among its peer countries in the overall international Logistics Performance Index, a measure that takes into account a country's customs efficiency, quality of trade and transport infrastructure, ease of arranging shipments, quality of logistics services, ability to track and trace consignments, and delivery times (figure 2.16). Bulgaria also lags behind its peers in customs efficiency (64th), whereas its peers and global GVC players, including China, perform much better in both regards.

Figure 2.15. Doing Business Indicator: Overall and Protecting Investors, 2014

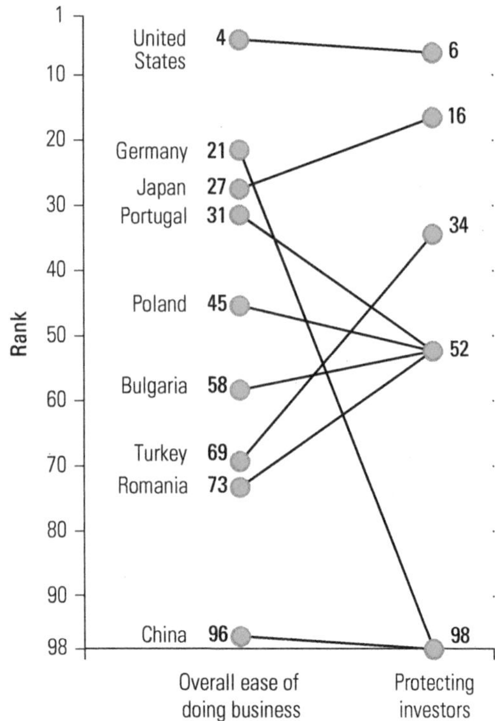

Source: Adapted from World Bank Logistics Performance Index and Doing Business data.

Although Bulgaria's quality of services performs relatively well in most aspects, the quality of its infrastructure lags behind that of most of its peers. According to the domestic Logistics Performance Index,[3] Bulgaria is trailing its peers in the quality of trade and transport-related infrastructure, especially ports and airports. The country also lacks quality in roads (ranking as the second worst performer after Poland) and rail (alongside Poland, Turkey, and the United States) (see table 2A.2 in annex 2A). Bulgaria's competence and quality of trade and logistics-related services, by contrast, are relatively high in most aspects (especially freight forwarders, warehousing and distribution services, customs agencies and brokers, and road-haulers and consignees/shippers). By contrast, health/sanitary and phytosanitary and quality/standards inspection agencies perform relatively poorly.

Figure 2.16. Logistics Performance Index: Overall and Customs Efficiency, 2014

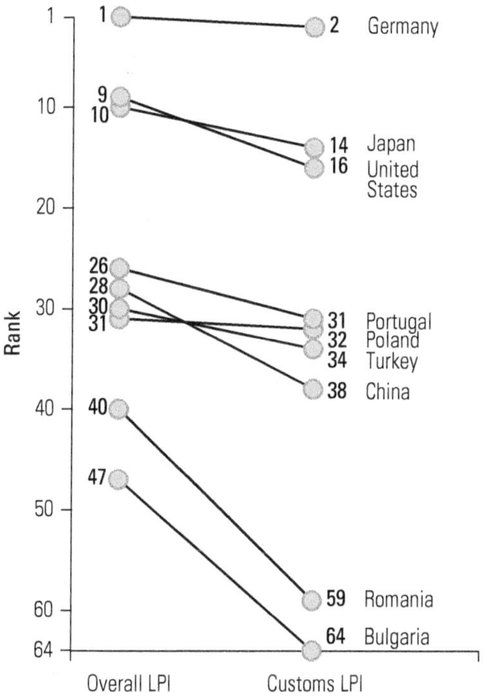

Source: Adapted from World Bank Logistics Performance Index and Doing Business data.

Strengthen GVC–Local Economy Links on the Selling Side

Firm-level analysis indicates there is scope to strengthen GVC-local economy links, especially on the selling side. Although the share of FDI inflows as a percentage of GDP is very high in Bulgaria, the challenge lies in linking FDI with the local economy. The analysis reveals that the share of local inputs sourced by multinational manufacturing firms in Bulgaria lies only in the middle spectrum; and although Bulgarian exporters' GVC links are stronger, scope for growth remains.

Weaker links on the selling side in Bulgaria may have magnified the negative mediating effect on productivity spillovers for sellers in GVCs—in particular, in the short run. Strong links with the domestic economy should offer greater benefits of GVC participation at home via several transmission channels (figure 1.11 in chapter 1). Linkage development can focus on the breadth of links (variety of local inputs) and their depth (degree of local value added), so making that distinction is key (Morris, Kaplinsky, and Kaplan 2011). Policies promoting links between GVCs and the local economy target foreign investors primarily, but those policies can also include other international buyers outside the country. Several policy options are available (see chapter 9).

Strengthen Bulgaria's Absorptive Capacity

GVCs can lead to benefits, but at the country level constraints remain, such as inadequate capacity to absorb such potential gains. Attracting foreign investors and other international buyers and linking them to the domestic economy should create optimal conditions for local firms and workers to benefit from spillovers of knowledge and technology. The degree to which they ultimately benefit, however, depends crucially on the absorptive capacity of domestic actors. That is the area of spillover policy in which government has the most important role to play, in particular by the absorptive capacity of firms and workers and helping local firms and workers access opportunities.

The analysis indicates that innovation capacity—at the firm and country levels—matters for positive productivity spillovers from GVC integration. The econometric analysis shows that a higher level of technology positively mediates spillovers in GVCs. In particular, a smaller technology gap relative to foreign firms is beneficial for productivity spillovers in GVCs, and that effect is even stronger for Bulgaria compared with the average firm in the full country sample. Similarly, higher R&D intensity at the country level increases the productivity gains from GVC integration in the full country sample. In this area, the gains are even higher in Bulgaria for buyers in GVCs, but lower for sellers.

Although the share of skilled workers in Bulgaria is high, the country's innovation capacity has room to expand further. More than one-quarter of Bulgaria's workforce has tertiary education, putting the country at a level similar to Germany and Poland. The proportion of educated workers in Portugal, Romania, and Turkey is less than 20 percent (figure 2.17). Public and private expenditures for basic research, applied research, and experimental development, however, are the second lowest after Romania (0.64 percent of GDP)—at only one-quarter the levels of Germany, Japan, and the United States and only one-third the level of China (figure 2.17). Reduction of the skills gap will require the active engagement of universities and research institutes.

Building absorptive capacity goes beyond increasing R&D intensity. Measures to build the absorp-

Figure 2.17. Innovation Capacity and Skills, 2012

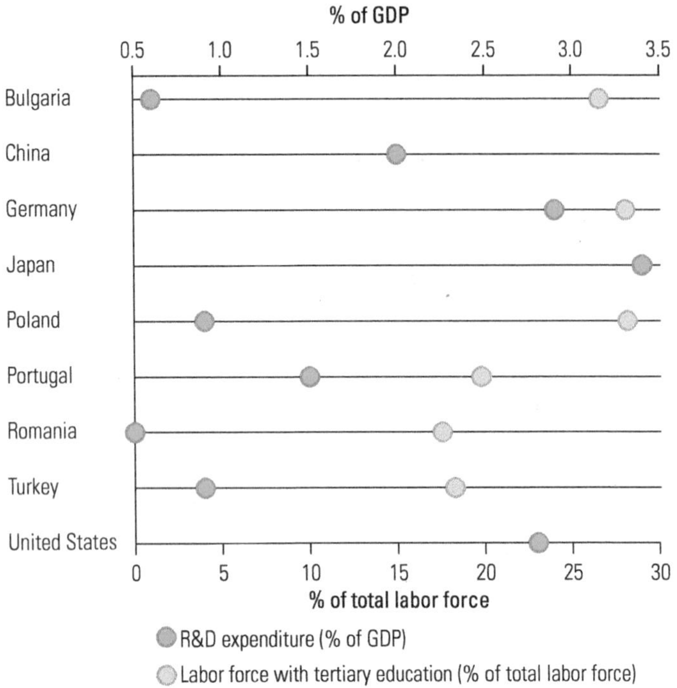

Source: Adapted from World Bank 2012.
Note: No labor force data are available for China, Japan, or the United States.

tive capacity of local firms require general and industry-specific investments to upgrade technical capacity and, most important, achieve quality standards. Because licensing of technology from foreign investors and other international buyers is a significant source of technical spillovers, governments should provide incentives for that licensing.

Notes

1. A significant part of this chapter is based on a technical background paper written by the authors for World Bank (2015). It shows how to analyze a country's participation in GVCs, using Bulgaria as an example. The chapter uses only publicly available data.

2. EU-10 comprises Bulgaria, the Czech Republic, Estonia, Hungary, Lithuania, Latvia, Poland, Romania, Slovak Republic, and Slovenia.

3. http://data.worldbank.org/data-catalog/logistics-performance-index.

References

Baldwin, Richard, and Javier Lopez-Gonzalez. 2013. "Supply-Chain Trade: A Portrait of Global Patterns and Several Testable Hypotheses." NBER Working Paper 18957, National Bureau of Economic Research, Cambridge, MA.

Barrios, Salvador, and Eric Strobl. 2002. "Foreign Direct Investment and Productivity Spillovers: Evidence from the Spanish Experience." *Review of World Economics* 138 (3): 459–81.

Bonacich, Phillip. 1987. "Power and Centrality: A Family of Measures." *American Journal of Sociology* 92 (5): 1170–82.

Chor, Davine. 2014. "Where Are Countries Positioned along Global Production Lines?" *Macroeconomic Review*: 94–99. Monetary Authority of Singapore.

Crespo, N., and M. P. Fontoura. 2007. "Determinant Factors of FDI Spillovers—What Do We Really Know?" *World Development* 35 (3): 410–25.

Farole, Thomas, and Deborah Winkler. 2014. "The Role of Mediating Factors for FDI Spillovers in Developing Countries: Evidence from a Global Dataset." In *Making Foreign Direct Investment Work for Sub-Saharan Africa: Local Spillovers and Competitiveness in Global Value Chains*, edited by Thomas Farole and Deborah Winkler, 59–86. Washington, DC: World Bank.

Meyer, Klaus E., and Evis Sinani. 2009. "When and Where Does Foreign Direct Investment Generate Positive Spillovers? A Meta-Analysis." *Journal of International Business Studies* 40 (7): 1075–94.

Morris, M., R. Kaplinsky, and D. Kaplan. 2011. "Commodities and Linkages: Meeting the Policy Challenge." MMCP Discussion Paper 14, Making the Most of Commodities Programme, The Open University, U.K.

Santoni, Gianluca, and Daria Taglioni. 2015. "Networks and Structural Integration in Global Value Chains." In *The Age of Global Value Chains*, edited by Joao Amador and Filippo di Mauro. Washington, DC: Center for Economic and Policy Research and VOXEU.

UNCTAD (United Nations Conference on Trade and Development). 2013. "World Investment Report 2013—Global Value Chains: Investment and Trade for Development." UNCTAD, Geneva.

World Bank. 2012. *World Development Indicators.* Washington, DC: World Bank.

———. 2015. *Productivity Growth in Bulgaria: Trends and Options.* Washington, DC: World Bank.

Annex 2A

Table 2A.1 Bulgaria's Position in the Global Network of Trade in Value Added, 2008

Sector	Total			Agriculture			Food and Beverages			Textiles, apparel, and footwear			Chemicals and non-metal minerals			Basic metals and fabricated metals			Machinery and equipment, nec			Electrical and optical equipment			Transport equipment		
Country	CCw	BONwin	BONwout	CCw	BONwin	BONwout	CCw	BONwin	BONwout	CCw	BONwin	BONwout	CCw	BONwin	BONwout	CCw	BONwin	BONwout	CCw	BONwin	BONwout	CCw	BONwin	BONwout	CCw	BONwin	BONwout
Argentina	0.63	0.12	0.13	0.52	0.14	0.13	0.58	0.14	0.14	0.52	0.13	0.13	0.54	0.12	0.12	0.51	0.11	0.12	0.48	0.10	0.11	0.47	0.10	0.11	0.51	0.13	0.12
Australia	0.68	0.13	0.14	0.54	0.14	0.14	0.59	0.14	0.14	0.50	0.11	0.14	0.58	0.12	0.14	0.60	0.15	0.14	0.56	0.13	0.14	0.52	0.11	0.14	0.53	0.12	0.14
Austria	0.68	0.14	0.14	0.50	0.12	0.14	0.59	0.15	0.14	0.55	0.14	0.14	0.60	0.14	0.14	0.60	0.15	0.14	0.59	0.16	0.14	0.57	0.14	0.14	0.58	0.16	0.14
Belgium	0.70	0.15	0.14	0.55	0.15	0.14	0.61	0.16	0.14	0.57	0.15	0.14	0.64	0.16	0.14	0.61	0.16	0.14	0.59	0.15	0.14	0.56	0.14	0.14	0.58	0.16	0.14
Brazil	0.67	0.13	0.14	0.56	0.15	0.15	0.61	0.14	0.15	0.53	0.12	0.14	0.59	0.13	0.14	0.58	0.14	0.14	0.55	0.13	0.14	0.53	0.12	0.13	0.55	0.14	0.14
Brunei Darussalam	0.54	0.09	0.10	0.36	0.07	0.09	0.36	0.05	0.09	0.42	0.11	0.09	0.37	0.04	0.10	0.35	0.02	0.10	0.43	0.00	0.09	0.34	0.04	0.10	0.34	0.02	0.09
Bulgaria	0.60	0.12	0.11	0.47	0.14	0.10	0.50	0.11	0.10	0.47	0.12	0.11	0.53	0.12	0.11	0.52	0.13	0.11	0.50	0.12	0.11	0.48	0.11	0.10	0.45	0.10	0.10
Cambodia	0.50	0.10	0.08	0.37	0.12	0.05	0.39	0.10	0.06	0.43	0.12	0.08	0.37	0.07	0.07	0.36	0.07	0.06	0.34	0.08	0.06	0.35	0.08	0.06	0.33	0.06	0.06
Canada	0.69	0.14	0.14	0.57	0.16	0.14	0.59	0.14	0.14	0.53	0.13	0.14	0.61	0.14	0.14	0.60	0.15	0.14	0.58	0.14	0.14	0.56	0.14	0.14	0.58	0.16	0.14
Chile	0.64	0.12	0.13	0.52	0.15	0.12	0.56	0.14	0.12	0.46	0.10	0.12	0.54	0.12	0.13	0.51	0.10	0.14	0.50	0.10	0.13	0.39	0.03	0.13	0.48	0.10	0.13
China	0.75	0.16	0.15	0.56	0.14	0.16	0.64	0.16	0.16	0.65	0.19	0.17	0.66	0.16	0.16	0.65	0.17	0.16	0.66	0.18	0.16	0.66	0.18	0.16	0.62	0.17	0.16
Czech Republic	0.67	0.14	0.13	0.49	0.13	0.12	0.54	0.13	0.13	0.53	0.14	0.13	0.57	0.14	0.13	0.58	0.14	0.13	0.58	0.15	0.13	0.57	0.15	0.13	0.57	0.15	0.13
Denmark	0.68	0.14	0.13	0.54	0.14	0.14	0.60	0.16	0.14	0.53	0.13	0.13	0.59	0.14	0.14	0.56	0.13	0.13	0.58	0.15	0.13	0.55	0.14	0.13	0.53	0.13	0.13
Estonia	0.59	0.11	0.11	0.44	0.12	0.09	0.49	0.12	0.10	0.45	0.12	0.09	0.50	0.11	0.10	0.49	0.11	0.10	0.46	0.10	0.10	0.48	0.11	0.10	0.44	0.10	0.10
Finland	0.67	0.14	0.13	0.46	0.10	0.13	0.54	0.12	0.13	0.50	0.12	0.13	0.58	0.13	0.13	0.58	0.14	0.13	0.58	0.15	0.13	0.57	0.15	0.13	0.54	0.13	0.13
France	0.73	0.15	0.15	0.61	0.18	0.16	0.65	0.17	0.16	0.60	0.16	0.16	0.65	0.16	0.15	0.63	0.16	0.15	0.64	0.17	0.16	0.61	0.16	0.15	0.63	0.18	0.16
Germany	0.76	0.16	0.16	0.60	0.16	0.17	0.67	0.17	0.17	0.62	0.16	0.17	0.68	0.17	0.16	0.67	0.18	0.17	0.68	0.19	0.17	0.64	0.17	0.17	0.66	0.19	0.17
Greece	0.65	0.13	0.13	0.50	0.13	0.12	0.54	0.13	0.13	0.50	0.12	0.13	0.55	0.12	0.13	0.55	0.13	0.12	0.49	0.10	0.12	0.50	0.11	0.12	0.45	0.08	0.12
Hong Kong SAR, China	0.67	0.13	0.13	0.42	0.07	0.13	0.47	0.08	0.13	0.42	0.06	0.14	0.56	0.12	0.13	0.50	0.09	0.13	0.52	0.11	0.13	0.54	0.12	0.14	0.49	0.10	0.13
Hungary	0.66	0.14	0.13	0.51	0.15	0.12	0.55	0.13	0.12	0.50	0.13	0.12	0.56	0.13	0.12	0.56	0.14	0.12	0.55	0.14	0.13	0.56	0.16	0.12	0.56	0.16	0.13
Iceland	0.55	0.10	0.10	0.38	0.10	0.07	0.44	0.10	0.08	0.37	0.08	0.08	0.46	0.10	0.09	0.42	0.08	0.09	0.40	0.08	0.09	0.45	0.11	0.09	0.38	0.07	0.09
India	0.69	0.14	0.14	0.53	0.13	0.15	0.59	0.14	0.14	0.59	0.16	0.15	0.61	0.14	0.14	0.59	0.14	0.14	0.57	0.14	0.14	0.56	0.13	0.14	0.55	0.14	0.14
Indonesia	0.66	0.13	0.13	0.50	0.12	0.14	0.59	0.14	0.14	0.56	0.15	0.14	0.58	0.13	0.13	0.55	0.12	0.13	0.55	0.14	0.13	0.54	0.13	0.13	0.51	0.12	0.13
Ireland	0.68	0.14	0.13	0.51	0.13	0.13	0.60	0.16	0.13	0.50	0.11	0.13	0.61	0.15	0.14	0.53	0.11	0.13	0.54	0.13	0.13	0.57	0.15	0.13	0.50	0.11	0.13
Israel	0.65	0.13	0.12	0.51	0.15	0.12	0.51	0.11	0.12	0.50	0.13	0.12	0.57	0.14	0.12	0.53	0.12	0.12	0.52	0.12	0.12	0.54	0.14	0.12	0.51	0.12	0.12
Italy	0.72	0.15	0.15	0.57	0.15	0.16	0.63	0.16	0.15	0.62	0.17	0.16	0.64	0.16	0.15	0.63	0.16	0.15	0.64	0.17	0.16	0.60	0.15	0.15	0.61	0.16	0.16
Japan	0.73	0.15	0.15	0.51	0.11	0.16	0.57	0.12	0.15	0.57	0.14	0.16	0.64	0.15	0.15	0.63	0.16	0.16	0.64	0.16	0.16	0.63	0.16	0.16	0.63	0.17	0.16
Korea, Rep.	0.71	0.15	0.14	0.48	0.10	0.14	0.57	0.13	0.14	0.58	0.15	0.15	0.63	0.15	0.14	0.61	0.15	0.14	0.61	0.15	0.15	0.62	0.17	0.15	0.60	0.17	0.15
Latvia	0.58	0.11	0.11	0.44	0.12	0.10	0.49	0.11	0.10	0.45	0.11	0.10	0.48	0.09	0.11	0.48	0.11	0.10	0.44	0.09	0.10	0.44	0.09	0.10	0.43	0.09	0.10
Lithuania	0.59	0.11	0.11	0.47	0.13	0.10	0.51	0.12	0.11	0.47	0.12	0.11	0.53	0.12	0.11	0.48	0.11	0.10	0.45	0.10	0.10	0.46	0.10	0.10	0.45	0.10	0.10
Luxembourg	0.64	0.13	0.12	0.46	0.11	0.11	0.52	0.12	0.12	0.50	0.13	0.12	0.54	0.12	0.12	0.55	0.14	0.12	0.51	0.12	0.12	0.49	0.11	0.12	0.44	0.08	0.12
Malaysia	0.69	0.14	0.14	0.57	0.17	0.14	0.59	0.14	0.14	0.54	0.14	0.13	0.60	0.15	0.13	0.56	0.13	0.13	0.59	0.16	0.13	0.60	0.16	0.14	0.52	0.12	0.14
Malta	0.54	0.10	0.09	0.36	0.09	0.07	0.41	0.09	0.08	0.34	0.07	0.08	0.43	0.09	0.08	0.36	0.06	0.08	0.37	0.07	0.08	0.46	0.11	0.09	0.38	0.08	0.08
Mexico	0.67	0.14	0.13	0.51	0.13	0.13	0.55	0.13	0.13	0.52	0.14	0.13	0.57	0.13	0.13	0.57	0.14	0.13	0.55	0.13	0.13	0.58	0.16	0.13	0.57	0.16	0.13
Netherlands	0.71	0.15	0.14	0.60	0.18	0.15	0.65	0.18	0.15	0.56	0.14	0.15	0.64	0.16	0.15	0.61	0.15	0.14	0.61	0.16	0.15	0.58	0.15	0.15	0.58	0.15	0.15
New Zealand	0.60	0.12	0.11	0.49	0.14	0.11	0.54	0.14	0.12	0.48	0.12	0.11	0.50	0.11	0.11	0.50	0.11	0.11	0.46	0.10	0.11	0.46	0.10	0.11	0.45	0.10	0.11
Norway	0.68	0.13	0.14	0.54	0.14	0.14	0.59	0.14	0.14	0.48	0.09	0.14	0.59	0.13	0.15	0.59	0.14	0.14	0.58	0.14	0.14	0.54	0.12	0.14	0.53	0.13	0.14
Philippines	0.63	0.13	0.12	0.43	0.10	0.11	0.46	0.09	0.11	0.49	0.13	0.11	0.48	0.09	0.11	0.47	0.09	0.11	0.48	0.10	0.12	0.56	0.15	0.13	0.49	0.11	0.12
Poland	0.68	0.14	0.13	0.52	0.14	0.13	0.58	0.15	0.13	0.55	0.15	0.13	0.59	0.14	0.13	0.60	0.15	0.14	0.58	0.15	0.14	0.57	0.14	0.13	0.59	0.16	0.14
Portugal	0.64	0.13	0.12	0.47	0.12	0.12	0.54	0.13	0.12	0.54	0.15	0.13	0.56	0.13	0.12	0.54	0.13	0.12	0.52	0.12	0.12	0.53	0.13	0.12	0.53	0.14	0.12
Romania	0.63	0.12	0.12	0.48	0.13	0.11	0.49	0.10	0.12	0.52	0.14	0.12	0.54	0.13	0.12	0.55	0.14	0.12	0.53	0.13	0.12	0.51	0.12	0.12	0.52	0.13	0.12
Russian Federation	0.71	0.14	0.16	0.59	0.15	0.17	0.59	0.12	0.16	0.53	0.11	0.16	0.64	0.14	0.17	0.64	0.15	0.17	0.61	0.14	0.16	0.55	0.12	0.15	0.57	0.14	0.16
Saudi Arabia	0.66	0.12	0.14	0.49	0.10	0.15	0.56	0.12	0.14	0.50	0.10	0.15	0.61	0.13	0.15	0.56	0.12	0.15	0.48	0.08	0.14	0.49	0.09	0.14	0.47	0.08	0.14
Singapore	0.71	0.15	0.14	0.47	0.10	0.14	0.58	0.14	0.14	0.51	0.12	0.14	0.63	0.16	0.14	0.57	0.14	0.13	0.59	0.16	0.14	0.60	0.16	0.14	0.56	0.14	0.14
Slovak Republic	0.64	0.13	0.12	0.47	0.13	0.11	0.52	0.13	0.11	0.50	0.14	0.11	0.55	0.13	0.12	0.55	0.14	0.12	0.54	0.14	0.12	0.54	0.14	0.12	0.55	0.15	0.12
Slovenia	0.61	0.12	0.11	0.43	0.11	0.10	0.48	0.11	0.10	0.48	0.13	0.10	0.53	0.13	0.11	0.53	0.13	0.11	0.52	0.13	0.11	0.50	0.12	0.11	0.50	0.13	0.11
South Africa	0.63	0.13	0.12	0.50	0.15	0.11	0.52	0.13	0.11	0.46	0.11	0.11	0.54	0.12	0.12	0.56	0.14	0.13	0.53	0.00	0.12	0.48	0.10	0.12	0.53	0.14	0.12
Spain	0.70	0.14	0.14	0.56	0.16	0.14	0.61	0.15	0.14	0.58	0.15	0.15	0.63	0.15	0.14	0.60	0.15	0.14	0.59	0.15	0.14	0.58	0.14	0.14	0.60	0.16	0.15
Sweden	0.70	0.14	0.14	0.51	0.12	0.14	0.59	0.14	0.14	0.53	0.13	0.14	0.61	0.15	0.14	0.60	0.15	0.14	0.61	0.16	0.15	0.58	0.15	0.14	0.59	0.16	0.14
Switzerland	0.69	0.14	0.14	0.50	0.12	0.14	0.59	0.15	0.14	0.54	0.14	0.14	0.62	0.15	0.14	0.59	0.14	0.14	0.60	0.16	0.15	0.59	0.15	0.14	0.55	0.13	0.14
Taiwan, China	0.69	0.14	0.14	0.49	0.12	0.13	0.52	0.11	0.13	0.55	0.15	0.14	0.61	0.15	0.13	0.59	0.15	0.14	0.59	0.15	0.14	0.61	0.16	0.15	0.55	0.13	0.14
Thailand	0.68	0.14	0.13	0.51	0.13	0.13	0.59	0.15	0.14	0.57	0.16	0.13	0.58	0.13	0.13	0.55	0.13	0.13	0.55	0.13	0.13	0.59	0.16	0.14	0.54	0.13	0.13
Turkey	0.67	0.13	0.13	0.51	0.13	0.13	0.56	0.13	0.13	0.58	0.16	0.14	0.58	0.14	0.13	0.60	0.15	0.13	0.56	0.14	0.13	0.53	0.13	0.13	0.56	0.15	0.13
United Kingdom	0.72	0.15	0.15	0.55	0.13	0.16	0.63	0.15	0.16	0.59	0.15	0.16	0.65	0.16	0.15	0.63	0.15	0.16	0.62	0.16	0.16	0.61	0.15	0.15	0.62	0.17	0.16
United States	0.75	0.15	0.16	0.64	0.18	0.18	0.67	0.17	0.17	0.61	0.15	0.17	0.68	0.16	0.17	0.64	0.15	0.17	0.66	0.17	0.17	0.63	0.16	0.17	0.65	0.18	0.17
Vietnam	0.63	0.13	0.12	0.53	0.17	0.11	0.56	0.15	0.12	0.54	0.16	0.12	0.51	0.11	0.11	0.50	0.11	0.11	0.48	0.11	0.11	0.50	0.12	0.11	0.46	0.10	0.11

Source: Calculations using data from Santoni and Taglioni 2015.

Note: The cells are colored according to the strength of the metrics—a green cell indicates a strong measure, an orange cell indicates a weak measure, and a white cell indicates an average measure. BONwin = eigenvector centrality based on inflows of value added; BONwout = eigenvector centrality based on outflows of value added; CCw = clustering index; nec = not elsewhere classified.

Table 2A.2 Logistics Performance, Domestic Component, 2014

Quality of infrastructure: Evaluate the quality of trade- and transport-related infrastructure in your country of work (% of respondents answering low/very low)

	Bulgaria	China	Germany	Japan	Poland	Portugal	Romania	Turkey	United States
Ports	66.7	5.4	0.0	50.0	0.0	33.3	0.0	12.5	11.1
Airports	33.3	0.0	0.0	0.0	0.0	0.0	0.0	16.1	5.6
Roads	44.4	0.0	0.0	0.0	50.0	0.0	33.3	12.5	16.7
Rail	55.6	5.3	0.0	0.0	50.0	33.3	0.0	61.3	50.0
Warehousing/transloading facilities	22.2	0.0	0.0	0.0	0.0	0.0	0.0	3.1	5.6
Telecommunications and IT	0.0	5.3	0.0	0.0	0.0	0.0	0.0	6.3	0.0

Competence and quality of services: Evaluate the competence and quality of service delivered by the following in your country of work (% of respondents answering high/very high)

	Bulgaria	China	Germany	Japan	Poland	Portugal	Romania	Turkey	United States
Road	66.7	28.2	90.0	50.0	50.0	100.0	33.3	80.7	50.0
Rail	44.4	15.8	68.4	50.0	0.0	0.0	0.0	20.0	33.3
Air transport	55.6	43.6	94.4	50.0	0.0	66.7	33.3	70.0	66.7
Maritime transport	44.4	50.0	84.2	50.0	50.0	33.3	100.0	83.3	55.6
Warehousing/transloading and distribution	77.8	38.5	90.0	50.0	50.0	66.7	66.7	77.4	50.0
Freight forwarders	88.9	44.7	85.0	50.0	100.0	66.7	66.7	80.7	66.7
Customs agencies	77.8	33.3	85.0	50.0	100.0	33.3	33.3	54.8	33.3
Quality/standards inspection agencies	33.3	18.4	85.0	50.0	50.0	33.3	33.3	46.7	29.4
Health/SPS agencies	22.2	23.7	76.5	50.0	0.0	33.3	33.3	33.3	22.2
Customs brokers	77.8	29.0	80.0	50.0	100.0	33.3	66.7	54.8	55.6
Trade and transport associations	44.4	34.2	77.8	50.0	50.0	0.0	66.7	67.7	50.0
Consignees or shippers	66.7	35.9	84.2	50.0	0.0	0.0	66.7	61.3	23.5

Source: Calculations using 2014 World Bank Logistics Performance Index data.
Note: The cells are colored according to the performance of the indicator—a green cell indicates strong performance an orange cell indicates weak performance, and a white cell indicates average peformance. IT = information technology; SPS = sanitary and phytosanitary.

PART II

QUANTIFYING A COUNTRY'S POSITION IN GVCS

To guide policy makers in achieving development through integration in global value chains (GVCs), the key concepts and metrics of the country's GVC participation must be investigated. Understanding how countries fare in such key concepts and metrics allows a better identification of specific value chains, activities, and business segments, which are the object of the case studies in this part.

The assessment of a country's GVC participation focuses on three concepts:

- *Role in GVCs:* the buyer's perspective versus the seller's perspective
- *Specialization and domestic value-added contribution:* specialization in low or high value added, preproduction, assembly, postproduction, or support activities
- *Position in GVC network and type of GVC node:* incoming spoke, hub, or outgoing spoke, clustering properties, or centrality in the global network

Chapter 3—"What Do Imports and Exports Say about GVC Participation?"—discusses how gross import and export flows can be used to gather some initial insights into a country's participation in GVCs. The chapter also delves into how much of the gross flows represent value addition in the country of interest and how to quantify the domestic value added embodied in a country's exports.

Chapter 4—"Buyer-Related Measures"—covers more indirect measures, such as the share of intermediates in gross imports based on combining gross trade data with informed classifications, and more direct quantifications of a country's position in GVCs, such as the foreign value added embodied in the country's gross exports or the length of sourcing chains. Adding information on factors of production (labor and wages, ideas, and investment) enables further characterization of the buyer function in GVCs for a country.

Similarly, in chapter 5—"Seller-Related Measures"—the measures can be more indirect, such as the share of intermediates in output or gross exports, or more direct, including the domestic value added embodied in gross exports of third countries and the length of selling chains. Like the analysis of the buyer dimension, information on factors of production further helps characterize a country's participation as a seller in GVCs.

Chapter 6—"Other Measures of GVC Participation: From Macro to Micro"—complements the buyer- and seller-related measures with additional measures of GVC participation at the macro and micro levels. The chapter includes the GVC participation index, network metrics and their visualizations, the role of services in value added, and firm-level links in GVCs.

Chapter 7—"Use of GVC Measures to Assess the Drivers and Impacts of GVC Participation"—presents selected topics for a research agenda on ways to test for the drivers and impacts of GVC participation using statistical methods or econometrics or by quantifying direct relationships in international input-output tables.

The multidimensional nature of GVCs can be captured by examining the relationships between goods, services, workers, ideas, and investments, going beyond value added to identify the actors in GVCs and how to assess the impacts of GVCs on jobs and wages.

This part uses country-specific examples to illustrate the concepts and suggested analysis.

Chapter 3

WHAT DO IMPORTS AND EXPORTS SAY ABOUT GVC PARTICIPATION?

GVC Participation Using Gross Trade Data

Gross export data indicate what products a country exports, whereas gross import data indicate what it imports. These data do not provide any indication of the domestic or foreign source of the inputs or the value addition generated in the country. To gather information on the latter requires more sophisticated data (discussed herein). Even so, a first assessment of a country's global value chain (GVC) participation can be based on gross exports and imports data.

The first consideration when investigating a country's potential in GVCs is what the country exports and imports. Looking at the top 50 to 100 export and import products of a country, classified at the most disaggregated level (at least Harmonized System [HS] 6-digit or Standard International Trade Classification 5-digit products) is a good starting point. For most countries, the top 50 exports and imports are likely to cover at least 50 percent of the total trade value in each direction, and the top 100 cover at least 75 percent.

A country's distribution of exports tends to follow a lognormal, power, or Zipf's law distribution. Zipf's law, originally applied to language, states that given some universe of items, the frequency of any item is inversely proportional to its rank in the frequency table. That is, a few items account for the bulk of the given universe; the contribution of most items is marginal. Exports and imports loosely follow such asymmetric distribution laws. Therefore, the marginal additional information that can be gathered from import and export products beyond the top 50 to 100 is generally small.

The usefulness of eyeballing the top imported and exported products as a starting point in GVC analysis can be seen in the example in table 3.1, which reports Malaysia's 50 top exports, and table 3.2, which reports the country's 50 top imports. The most important export product, other monolithic integrated circuits (HS code 854230), accounts for 10.5 percent of overall exports. The importance of individual items rapidly decreases. Two items, liquefied natural gas and petroleum and oils (not crude), cover more than 6 percent of exports each, and 11 additional products cover a share of 1 to 5 percent of total exports each. All other items, individually, represent less than 1 percent of total exports. Imports follow a similar distribution.

Refinements of such a first-cut analysis increase the relevance of GVC analysis. Four types of refinements should be considered:

- *Consider raw commodities separately from other products.* Although raw commodities are important import and export items for most countries worldwide, their relevance in a GVC analysis is limited. Therefore, the various analyses suggested in this chapter and elsewhere in part II of the book should be run in two ways—including raw commodities and excluding them—and the results compared.
- *Compare product-level imports with export values, volumes, and prices of the top traded products.* If exports and imports follow a similar distribution and the values or volumes traded have a similar growth or level, this may suggest that relatively little transformation may be taking place

Table 3.1. Malaysia's Top 50 Exports, 2012

Rank	HS-6 Code	Description	Value (US$)	Share (%)
1	854230	Monolithic integrated circuits	23,846,665	10.5
2	271111	Liquefied natural gas	17,974,365	7.9
3	271000	Petroleum oils/oils from bituminous minerals (not crude)	15,419,273	6.8
4	151190	Palm oil or fractions simply refined	10,935,036	4.8
5	270900	Petroleum oils/oils from bituminous minerals (crude)	10,440,086	4.6
6	847170	Storage units	5,881,013	2.6
7	847330	Parts & accessories of the machines of heading No. 84.71	5,331,637	2.3
8	151110	Crude oil	4,504,723	2.0
9	852812	Color television receiver	3,214,780	1.4
10	401519	Other gloves	3,072,135	1.4
11	854140	Photosensitive/photovoltaic/LED semiconductor devices	2,491,291	1.1
12	400122	Technically specified natural rubber (TSNR)	2,382,671	1.0
13	151620	Vegetable fats & oils & their fractions	2,348,416	1.0
14	854290	Parts of electronic integrated circuits, etc.	2,248,361	1.0
15	847180	Other units of automatic data processing machines	2,057,050	0.9
16	853710	Electrical control & distribution boards, <1kV	1,981,275	0.9
17	711319	Jewelry & parts of precious metal except silver	1,876,044	0.8
18	854129	Transistors, other than photosensitive transistors	1,743,263	0.8
19	400599	Compounded unvulcanized rubber in primary forms, nes	1,666,362	0.7
20	853400	Printed circuits	1,417,904	0.6
21	853690	Electrical switch, protector, connector for <1kV, nes	1,361,028	0.6
22	903090	Parts & accessories, electrical measuring instruments	1,352,642	0.6
23	441213	Plywood, outer ply of tropical wood	1,305,017	0.6
24	852520	Transmission apparatus incorporating reception apparatus	1,262,680	0.6
25	999999	Commodities, nes	1,241,447	0.5
26	852990	Parts of radio/TV transmit/receive equipment, nes	1,126,296	0.5
27	854190	Parts of semiconductor devices & similar devices	1,049,935	0.5
28	851780	Electronic apparatus for telephone line	926,542	0.4
29	271129	Petroleum gases & gaseous hydrocarbons, nes, liquefied	925,991	0.4
30	844359	Other printing machinery	910,630	0.4
31	841510	Window or wall types, self-contained	900,525	0.4
32	382319	Other industrial monocarboxylic fatty acids	840,678	0.4
33	940360	Other wooden furniture	793,101	0.3
34	800110	Tin, not alloyed	780,070	0.3
35	854110	Diodes, other than photosensitive or light emitting diodes	778,835	0.3
36	903040	Gain/distortion & crosstalk meters, etc.	772,792	0.3
37	852320	Magnetic discs	764,608	0.3
38	382490	Chemical prep. allied in	712,140	0.3
39	852540	Still image video cameras & other video camera recorders	691,899	0.3
40	850910	Vacuum cleaners	654,134	0.3
41	847990	Parts of machines & mechanical appliances, nes	599,320	0.3
42	851790	Parts of telephone line/telegraph equipment, nes	596,025	0.3
43	390110	Polyethylene having a specific gravity of less than 0.94	587,103	0.3
44	392690	Plastic articles, nes	585,215	0.3
45	940350	Wooden furniture of a kind used in the bedroom	583,510	0.3
46	382370	Industrial fatty alcohols	581,726	0.3
47	880330	Other parts of airplanes or helicopters	572,487	0.3
48	903082	Instruments for measuring or checking semiconductors	569,050	0.3
49	151329	Palm kernel or babassu oil & fractions thereof	564,780	0.2
50	844390	Parts of printing machinery & ancillary equipment	559,765	0.2

Source: Adapted from the United Nations Comtrade database.

Note: Products from the electrical and electronics sector are color-coded in green, whereas those from the oil, gas, and petrochemical sector are color-coded in yellow, and products from all other sectors in gray. HS = Harmonized System; kV = kilovolts; LED = light-emitting diode; nes = not elsewhere specified.

Table 3.2. Malaysia's Top 50 Imports, 2012

Rank	HS-6 Code	Description	Value (US$)	Share (%)
1	271000	Petroleum oils/oils from bituminous minerals (not crude)	15,596,099	7.9
2	854230	Monolithic integrated circuits	15,193,085	7.7
3	854290	Parts of electronic integrated circuits, etc.	10,704,458	5.4
4	270900	Petroleum oils/oils from bituminous minerals (crude)	8,963,271	4.6
5	847330	Parts & accessories of the machines of heading No. 84.71	3,672,195	1.9
6	880240	Airplanes & other aircraft, of an unladen weight <15,000kg	3,246,371	1.7
7	852520	Transmission apparatus incorporating reception apparatus	2,168,024	1.1
8	270119	Other coal, whether or not pulverized, but not agglomerated	2,103,913	1.1
9	852990	Parts of radio/TV transmit/receive equipment, nes	2,061,850	1.0
10	853400	Printed circuits	1,961,253	1.0
11	870323	Automobiles, spark ignition of 1500-3000cc	1,880,437	1.0
12	740311	Refined copper: Cathodes & sections of cathodes	1,674,219	0.9
13	710813	Non-monetary: Other semi-manufactured forms	1,534,985	0.8
14	853120	Indicator panels incorporating LCD or LED	1,438,878	0.7
15	854190	Parts of semiconductor devices & similar devices	1,267,170	0.6
16	847130	Portable digital automatic data processing machines, >10kg	1,156,743	0.6
17	400110	Natural rubber latex, whether or not pre-vulcanized	1,134,514	0.6
18	710812	Non-monetary: Other unwrought forms	1,116,523	0.6
19	711590	Articles of, or clad with, precious metal, nes	1,041,547	0.5
20	999999	Commodities nes	1,017,398	0.5
21	847170	Storage units	1,010,919	0.5
22	170111	Cane sugar w/o flavoring or coloring matter	973,042	0.5
23	847989	Other machines & mechanical appliances	940,269	0.5
24	853690	Electrical switch, protector, connector for <1kV, nes	921,485	0.5
25	151190	Palm oil or fractions simply refined	908,447	0.5
26	400122	Technically specified natural rubber (TSNR)	898,192	0.5
27	180100	Cocoa beans, whole or broken, raw or roasted	877,533	0.4
28	151110	Crude oil	796,517	0.4
29	870421	Diesel powered trucks, >5tonnes	782,424	0.4
30	300490	Medicaments nes, in dosage	775,336	0.4
31	880330	Other parts of airplanes or helicopters	717,258	0.4
32	392690	Plastic articles, nes	707,399	0.4
33	847990	Parts of machines & mechanical appliances, nes	703,534	0.4
34	851780	Electronic apparatus for telephone line	689,394	0.4
35	853710	Electrical control & distribution boards, <1kV	657,043	0.3
36	870829	Other parts & accessories of bodies (including cabs)	653,313	0.3
37	901380	Other devices, appliances, & instruments	624,489	0.3
38	310420	Potassium chloride	624,451	0.3
39	903090	Parts & accessories, electrical measuring instruments	616,256	0.3
40	230400	Soybean oil: Oil-cake & other solid residues	611,933	0.3
41	760110	Aluminum, not alloyed	609,133	0.3
42	100630	Semi-milled or wholly milled rice	599,986	0.3
43	210690	Food preparations, nes	596,375	0.3
44	730511	Pipeline submerged arc welded steel, diameter >406mm	587,927	0.3
45	870322	Automobiles, spark ignition of 1000-1500cc	572,274	0.3
46	850440	Static converters	561,011	0.3
47	520100	Cotton, not carded or combed	546,293	0.3
48	844390	Parts of printing machinery & ancillary equipment	542,525	0.3
49	100590	Maize except seed corn	535,904	0.3
50	854129	Transistors, other than photosensitive transistors	481,679	0.2

Source: Adapted from the United Nations Comtrade database.

Note: Products from the electrical and electronics sector are color-coded in green, whereas those from the oil, gas, and petrochemical sector are color-coded in yellow, and products from all other sectors in gray. cc = cubic centimeters; HS = Harmonized System; kV = kilovolts; LCD = liquid crystal display; LED = light-emitting diode; mm = millimeters; nes = not elsewhere specified; w/o = without.

domestically, with the domestic segment of the country's major GVCs being relatively short.

- *Use informed classifications to extract as much information as possible from gross trade data.* Regrouping data in meaningful clusters or categorized by informed classifications is also very helpful.
- *Document trade flows at the subnational level.* Acknowledging the fact that subnational differences may exist, data that take into account the subnational perspective should be used when available.

Informed Classifications

Informed classifications are useful for identifying features and investigating specific aspects of GVC trade, including parts and components, technical functions, and so forth. Multiple classifications exist, with concordance tables that allow matching them with standard trade data, and researchers are constantly developing new ones. Some examples of useful classifications that are widely available include the following:

- The United Nations (UN 2002) Broad Economic Categories focus on the final use and distinguish between consumer goods, capital goods, and intermediates.[1]
- Athukorala (2010) identifies parts and components at a very detailed level of aggregation for East Asia.
- Sturgeon and Memedovic (2011) show how to identify final goods and intermediate goods—the latter further categorized in standard or customized intermediates—in specific GVCs (electronics, vehicles and parts, and textiles/apparel/footwear, and more recently raw and processed food and chemicals and related products).
- Taymaz, Voylvoda, and Yilmaz (2011), based on engineering considerations—and in a paper applied to Turkey—similarly assign products and activities to five value chain categories (final products, main inputs/parts, standard inputs, raw material, and machinery and equipment). The system focuses on five typical GVCs: televisions, motor vehicles, food, machinery, and textiles and apparel, the last distinguishing cotton, wool, synthetic, and other.

A discussion of these classification systems can be found in appendixes B to E. The following examples illustrate how the classifications can enrich the analysis of a country's imports and exports. We use the case of Malaysia for the illustrations.

Illustration #1: Final Use

To start, the analysis focuses on the most basic classification, the UN Broad Economic Categories. The majority of Malaysia's top 50 exports and imports, measured at the HS 6-digit level, are intermediate products from two sectors: oil, gas, and petrochemicals (color-coded in yellow in the figures) and electrical and electronics industry (in green) (tables 3.1 and 3.2).

Comparison of the top imports and exports of a country provides further preliminary insights on their participation in GVCs. Figure 3.1 provides such

Figure 3.1. Malaysia's Top 50 Exports and Imports, 2012

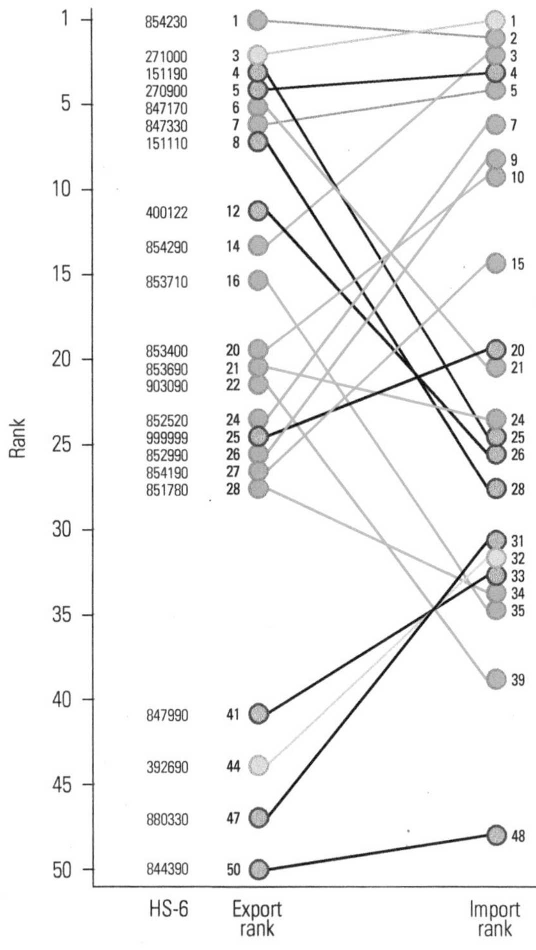

Products from the electrical and electronics sector
Products from the oil, gas, and petrochemical sector
Products from all other sectors

Source: Adapted from the United Nations Comtrade database.
Note: HS = Harmonized System.

a comparison for Malaysia. The figure shows that not only are they intermediate goods, parts, and components that feed into the production of other products, but the majority of the top products also appear as top imports and top exports. This fact raises the question of how much value added is provided within segments of GVCs located in the country. This type of preliminary test therefore flags whether participation in GVCs remains marginal, with little domestic transformation.

Illustration #2: Value Chain Category

The second example uses the classification of Taymaz, Voylvoda, and Yilmaz (2011) to categorize firm-level export and production data (measured as firm value added) for the motor vehicles, textiles and apparel, and agrifood sectors in Turkey (table 3.3).[2] This classification assigns exports to one of five value chain categories, namely: final products, main inputs/parts, standard inputs, raw materials, and machinery and equipment. Although this information is only available for five industries—motor vehicles, televisions, food, machinery, and textiles and apparel—it is nevertheless useful, as these five industries represent important GVCs in many countries. The key stylized facts that emerge from the analysis of production and exports in Turkey are the following:

- For motor vehicles in 2010, more than 70 percent of the sector's exports were final products. The second most important production stage in the Turkish automotive value chain, by export value, is standard input production. Exports of standard inputs accounted for nearly 25 percent of total exports. Although the share of main parts and components exports increased from 2003 to 2010, those exports remained marginal (less than 3 percent in 2010).
- Similar to motor vehicles, Turkish textile exporters tend to concentrate in the final stage of textile production. About 70 percent of the export value and more than 50 percent of value addition is generated by final goods exports.
- The agrifood sector stands apart from the previous two. Although the majority of production is in final goods, the majority of export growth has been concentrated in fairly unsophisticated products, such as grains, nuts, and lentils, a fact that is reflected in the high export share of raw materials.
- Overall, the numbers in the table reveal that Turkish participation in the agrifood value chain

Table 3.3. Turkey's Share of Exports and Value Added, 2003 and 2010
(% of total)

	Final	Main inputs	Standard inputs	Raw materials	Machinery and equipment	Total
			Motor vehicles			
Export share, 2003	73.5	0.4	24.8	0.2	1.1	100
Value-added share, 2003	48.0	2.7	46.9	0.2	2.1	100
Export share, 2010	72.3	2.4	23.9	0.3	1.1	100
Value-added share, 2009	38.4	1.1	53.3	0.7	6.5	100
			Textiles and apparel			
Export share, 2003	78.8	11.9	7.3	1.7	0.3	100
Value-added share, 2003	55.5	19.1	13.5	9.2	2.7	100
Export share, 2010	70.0	15.0	8.6	5.7	0.7	100
Value-added share, 2009	56.0	17.0	13.2	11.8	2.0	100
			Agrifood			
Export share, 2003	34.3	19.2	n.a.	44.6	1.8	100
Value-added share, 2003	48.9	18.5	n.a.	17.4	15.2	100
Export share, 2010	37.4	17.9	n.a.	42.0	2.7	100
Value-added share, 2009	56.0	16.8	n.a.	13.3	13.9	100

Source: World Bank 2014.
Note: n.a. = not available.

is less advanced than in the other two sectors. The low specialization in machinery and equipment is also a symptom that Turkish GVC participation tends to concentrate in low value-added segments of GVCs.

Illustration #3: Customized Trade and the World Bank MC-GVC Database and Country Dashboards

Distinguishing customized from standard intermediates can be used to assess participation and links at the industry and product levels. The World Bank Group for example has constructed a database for measuring competitiveness in GVCs, the Measuring Competitiveness across Global Value Chains (MC-GVC) database, which allows tracking of six categories of goods trade in three archetypal GVC industries: electronics, apparel and footwear, and autos and motorcycles. For each of these industries, the database identifies whether goods are for intermediate or final use and, for intermediates, if they are classified by Sturgeon and Memedovic (2011) as customized or standard parts and components. A global view of international trade through these lenses suggests that:

- High-income countries specialize in final assembly—but assembly is also an important activity in upper-middle-income countries (such as Argentina, Hungary, Mexico, South Africa, and Turkey), as well as in some poorer countries (such as Cambodia and India).
- The supply chain for customized parts and components extends widely into the middle-income level, but not to low-income countries. A drill-down shows that ignition wiring sets for autos, for example, are widely exported from middle-income countries.
- Japan keeps more of its customized parts and components at home than North America or Western Europe does (unlike in electronics, where the supply chain is more widely distributed).

Table 3.4. Auto Cluster

Nomenclature of Economic Activity	
Revision 2 code	**Revision 2 description**
1392	Manufacture of made-up textile articles, except apparel
2219	Manufacture of other rubber products
2222	Manufacture of plastic packing goods
2229	Manufacture of other plastic products
2433	Cold forming or folding
2511	Manufacture of metal structures and parts of structures
2550	Forging, pressing, stamping and roll-forming of metal; powder metallurgy
2572	Manufacture of locks and hinges
2573	Manufacture of tools
2593	Manufacture of wire products, chain, and springs
2732	Manufacture of other electronic and electric wires and cables
2740	Manufacture of electric lighting equipment
2790	Manufacture of other electrical equipment
2822	Manufacture of lifting and handling equipment
2841	Manufacture of metal forming machinery
2849	Manufacture of other machine tools
2892	Manufacture of machinery for mining, quarrying, and construction
2899	Manufacture of other special-purpose machinery, nec
2910	Manufacture of motor vehicles
2920	Manufacture of bodies (coachwork) for motor vehicles; manufacture of trailers and semi-trailers
2931	Manufacture of electrical and electronic equipment for motor vehicles
2932	Manufacture of other parts and accessories for motor vehicles
3299	Other manufacturing, nec

Source: World Bank 2013.
Note: NACE = Nomenclature of Economic Activities; nec = not elsewhere classified.

Information at the country level can be used to leverage firm-level hypotheses on participation rates and trends, export and import links, specific products of interest, two-way trade in differentiated products, and competition in destination markets. An example is the production of color television receivers. Analysis of gross trade flows at the product level matched with information on customized trade shows that Tunisian color televisions have an increasing market share in France, but there is ruthless competition at the global level, as the same market segment is populated by important global actors, such as LG from the Republic of Korea.

Illustration #4: Product Clusters

Another useful method to enrich the data is to combine production or export data that belong to different sectors but to the same GVC (or cluster of products). An example of a cluster for the auto sector is illustrated in table 3.4, which reports the clustering of sectors by economic activity carried out by a regional development agency in Romania, the Romania-West Development Agency (following the Nomenclature of Economic Activities, revision 2). The table shows that the auto GVC includes not only vehicles and their parts and components, but also molding and other metallurgy activity, production of specialized textiles, rubber products, packaging goods, plastics, and a variety of additional products from the electric and electronics industry, machinery, and equipment. Appendix F provides examples of clusters for agrifood, construction, energy, health, information and communications technology, textiles, and tourism. Although such cluster classifications tend to be similar across countries, some differences at the very granular level can be expected. Different market segments and business models affect the way activities are clustered together.

Input-output (I-O) tables are a useful first step in identifying clusters of activities across sectors. Figure 3.2 shows the main sectors buying computer storage devices (North American Industry Classification System [NAICS] product 334112), and figure 3.3 identifies the main inputs of this product, based on U.S. I-O tables. The green nodes in figure 3.2 are downstream industries that use NAICS 334112 as inputs in production and for which computer storage devices (red) represent at least 1 percent of the total input requirements for their production (nodes and links are built using network analysis metrics, illustrated in chapter 6; for more details, see box 8.1 in chapter 8). The buyer industries are as follows:

- Sector 334510: electromedical and electrotherapeutic apparatus
- Sector 334111: electronic computer manufacturing with small business administration standards, which includes manufacturing and/or assembling electronic computers, such as mainframes, personal computers, workstations, laptops, and computer servers
- Sector 33411A: other computer manufacturing
- Sector 334511: search, detection, navigation, guidance, aeronautical, and nautical system and instrument manufacturing
- Sector 33451A: other measuring and controlling device manufacturing.

What sectors are the most important suppliers for this sector? The green nodes in figure 3.3 show the following suppliers of inputs to 334112:

- Sector 334610: software reproduction
- Sector 33411A: other computer manufacturing
- Sector 334418: printed circuit assembly
- Sector 335999: all other miscellaneous electrical equipment and component manufacturing
- Sector 33441A: other electronic component manufacturing
- Sector 332800: metal treating

Figure 3.2. Most Relevant Buyers of Computer Storage Devices

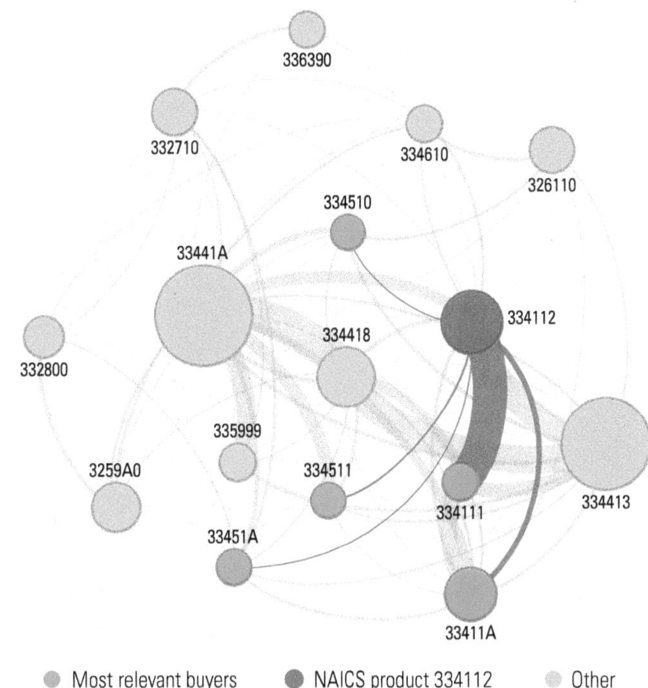

Source: Santoni and Taglioni forthcoming. Adapted from Benchmark Input-Output Data, Bureau of Economic Analysis, U.S. Department of Commerce.
Note: Red lines designate flows of computer storage devices (red circle) to main buying sectors (green circles). NAICS = North American Industry Classification System.

Figure 3.3. Most Relevant Suppliers for Computer Storage Devices

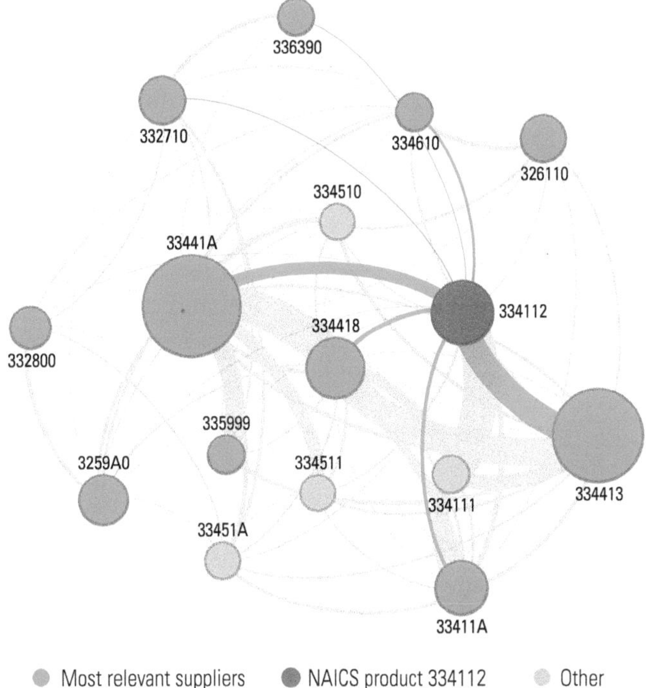

Source: Santoni and Taglioni forthcoming. Adapted from Benchmark Input-Output Data, Bureau of Economic Analysis, U.S. Department of Commerce.
Note: Green lines designate main input flows from supplying sectors (green circles) to the computer storage sector (red circle). NAICS = North American Industry Classification System.

- Sector 3259A0: other chemical product and preparation manufacturing
- Sector 326110: plastics packaging materials and unlaminated film and sheet manufacturing
- Sector 334413: semiconductor and related device manufacturing
- Sector 332710: machine shops
- Sector 336390: other motor vehicle parts manufacturing.

The upstream products that computer storage devices use as inputs are more numerous than the downstream products. Such mappings enable the definition of clusters of activities or products for further analysis.

Clustering can also include information on the geographic location of activities in countries. Examples include the U.S. Cluster Mapping project and the European Union Cluster Portal.[3] Acknowledging that clusters and their impacts can vary across regions in a country, the projects also take into account the subnational perspective.[4]

GVC Participation Using Data on Trade in Value Added

The previous section discussed how to use gross import and export flows, as well as production data, to gather some initial insights into a country's participation in GVCs. Gross trade flows can be decomposed in various ways. The most obvious distinction is between domestic and foreign value added (see chapter 4 for more details). As stated in the introduction, because in GVCs countries import inputs to export them after processing, what matters is the value addition generated in the country. This section delves into how much of the gross flows represent value addition in the country of interest (chapter 2 illustrates the relevance of this exercise in the example of Bulgaria).

Addressing this question requires moving beyond traditional trade data. New databases have greatly facilitated this task—particularly the World Input-Output Database (WIOD), created by a consortium of 11 institutions; the Organisation for Economic Co-operation and Development–World Trade Organization's Trade in Value Added database;[5] the United Nations Conference on Trade and Development–EORA GVC database; and the World Bank Export of Value Added database, which is based on the Global Trade Analysis Project database (appendixes G and H). Drawing on these databases, this part of the book introduces GVC participation measures. Most of the measures illustrated in chapters 4 to 7 require the use of these databases. Furthermore, some of the measures can only be computed with some of the databases mentioned; when that is the case, it is explicitly mentioned in the text.

To facilitate the illustration of some of the underlying economic concepts, key measures of GVC participation that draw on these databases are discussed by differentiating between buyer-related (chapter 4) and seller-related (chapter 5) measures and combining the measures to assess the overall GVC participation of countries (chapter 6). These databases can also be used for network analysis—for example, to construct measures of centrality and structural integration in GVCs (chapter 6). Finally, the data can be used in econometric and statistical methods (chapter 7) that go beyond the illustration of countries' participation in GVCs. These proposed methods allow for testing the economic relevance of specific measures and examining the drivers and effects of GVC participation.

The quantifications in this part of the book can be analyzed at the aggregate and sector levels. The level of detail depends on data availability. Some of the most sophisticated measures are available at fairly aggregate sector levels, whereas most of the less sophisticated measures are available for narrowly defined industries. Because aggregate trends may hide important developments in underlying industries, it is suggested to use a range of tools of different sophistication levels, which combined reveal a general overview of how countries fare in GVCs and provide the ability to zoom into specific issues.

Buying and Selling Sides

A key role of GVCs in industrial and economic development is boosting the competitiveness of the exports of low- and middle-income countries by facilitating the combination of foreign technology with the countries' labor, capital, and technology. Imports are important for competitiveness. A country's ability to participate in GVCs depends as much on its capacity to import world-class inputs efficiently as the country's capacity to export. A country cannot become a major exporter in GVCs without first becoming a successful importer of intermediate imports, because imported intermediate inputs contain foreign technology.

This section suggests ways to identify the extent to which countries source—domestically or internationally—the intermediates they use in exporting, which will provide a first indication of their participation in GVCs. The section then shows ways to quantify the domestic value added embodied in countries' exports.

Import to export (I2E) patterns are a useful starting point. Figures 3.4 through 3.9 illustrate I2E on the sales and buying sides for six important actors in GVCs: Japan, China, Poland, Germany, Mexico, and the United States, respectively. The sales and buying patterns for I2E for each country are normalized by the country's exports (on the sales side) or imports (on the buying side). The result shows where the country sources the intermediates it uses to export, as well as where it sells the intermediates used in its partners' exports.

In the figures, each graph has two matched sides. The left side shows the country's I2E buying pattern—that is, the share of its exports made up of imported intermediates from the partners in the list. The right side shows the country's bilateral exports of I2E trade as a share of its total exports. For each partner, the shares are shown for 2011 (size of circle), while the position on the x-axis illustrates the evolution of buying and selling patterns (growth between 1995 and 2011 in percent), respectively. Countries are ranked in decreasing order for 2011; tiny partners have been removed to improve readability.

The distinction between the buying and selling sides of I2E is clear in Japan's I2E with China (figure 3.4). China is a very important destination for Japanese parts and components that are embodied in other countries' exports. In 2011, more than 10 percent of Japan's exports consisted of intermediate goods sold to China and subsequently embodied in Chinese exports—shown on Japan's sales side of I2E (right side). In figure 3.5, which shows China's I2E, the exact same flow of GVC intermediates is shown as China's I2E on the buying side as almost 5 percent (it is normalized by China's imports instead of Japan's exports).

Japan and China have noticeably different participation in GVCs. According to the I2E measure, Japan imports I2E goods from few countries, mostly China, the United States, Saudi Arabia, and Australia (in decreasing order of importance) (figure 3.4, left side); but a large fraction of Japan's exports are of parts embodied in other countries' exports (right side). China sources its I2E inputs from many more countries, mainly from Japan; United States; Korea; Taiwan, China; and Germany (figure 3.5, left side), but sells a much lower share of I2E goods to a wide variety of countries (right side), indicating China's specialization in final goods exports.

Compared with China, the selling patterns are different for Poland (figure 3.6). Poland's participation is on par on the buying side (left side). It buys from a variety of countries, mainly Germany, Russia, and China (in decreasing order) and other European partners, but sells a higher I2E share primarily to Germany and other European markets. This finding underscores the importance of the regional dimension, particularly for the European GVCs. Mexico's dependence on inputs from the United States emerges clearly (figure 3.7): almost 12 percent of Mexico's I2E originates from the United States. The other important suppliers (in decreasing order) are China, Japan, Germany, Canada, and Korea.

Germany's I2E (figure 3.8) and that of the United States (figure 3.9) are more similar to that of Japan. In both cases, the countries sell domestic parts and components that are then embodied in many other countries' exports. The most important buyers for the United States are (in decreasing order) China, Canada, and Mexico (figure 3.9, right side). German intermediates, by contrast, feed into Chinese and most of its regional partners' exports (figure 3.8, right side). On the buying side, the United States seems to rely very little on foreign countries. I2E inputs are mainly sourced from Canada, China, and Mexico (in decreasing order) (figure 3.9, left side). Germany's most important sources of I2E (in decreasing order) are the United States, France, United Kingdom, Russian Federation, and Italy (figure 3.8, left side).

Notes

1. Note that the OECD STAN Bilateral Trade Database by industry and end-use category (BTDxE), which is based on the Broad Economic Categories, distinguishes the following end-use categories: intermediate goods, household consumption, capital goods, and mixed end-use (personal computers, passenger cars, personal phones, precious goods, packed medicines, and miscellaneous).
2. World Bank (2014).
3. For the U.S. Cluster Mapping project, see http://www.clustermapping.us; for the EU Cluster Portal, see http://ec.europa.eu/growth/smes/cluster/index_en.htm.
4. The U.S. Cluster Mapping project has the information broken down to the county level; the EU Cluster Portal shows the data at the Nomenclature of Territorial Units for Statistics (NUTS-2) level.
5. Access the World Bank's Trade in Value Added database at http://data.worldbank.org/data-catalog/export-value-added.

Figure 3.4. Buying and Selling Patterns: Japan, 1995 and 2011

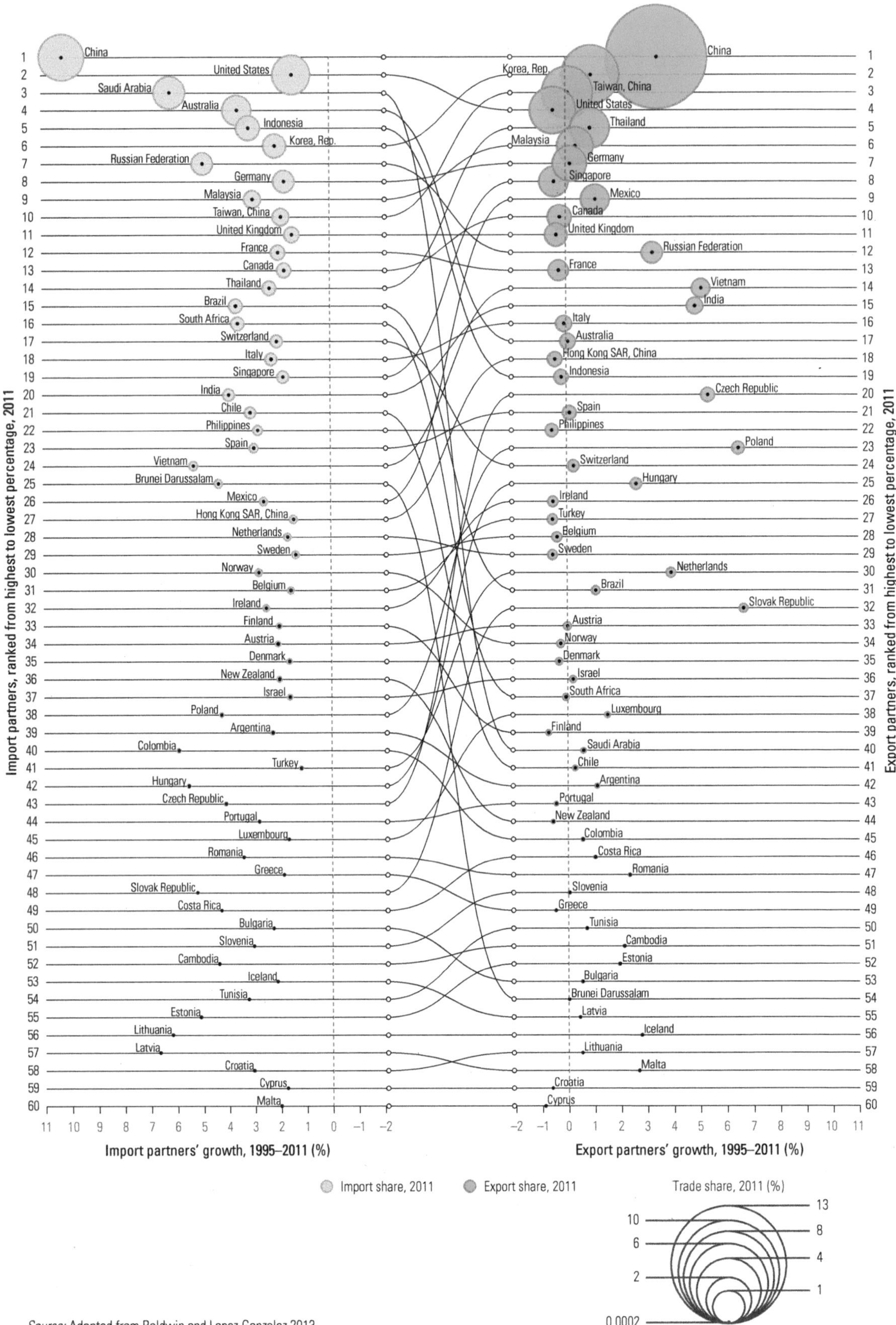

Source: Adapted from Baldwin and Lopez-Gonzalez 2013.

Figure 3.5. Buying and Selling Patterns: China, 1995 and 2011

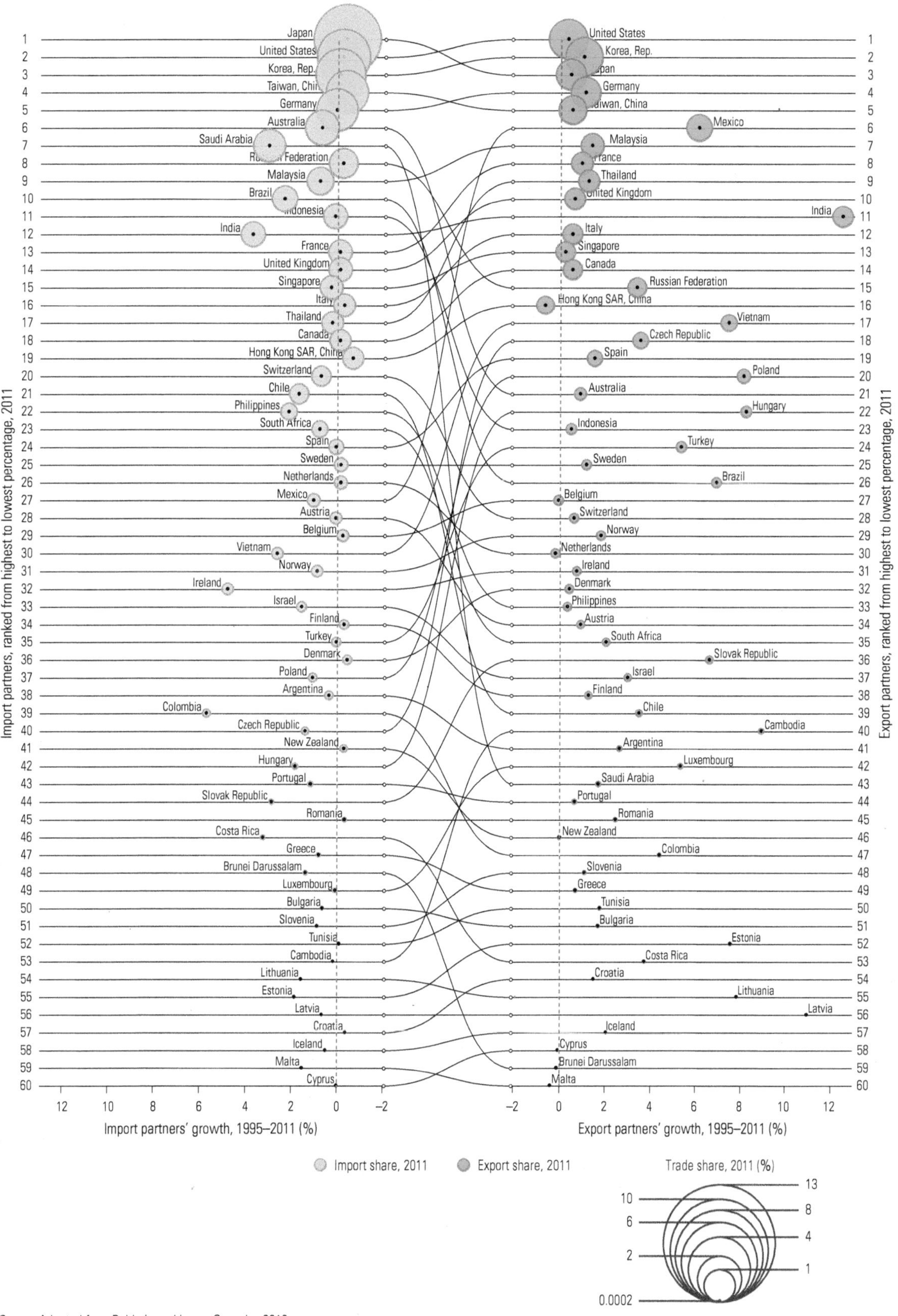

Source: Adapted from Baldwin and Lopez-Gonzalez 2013.

Figure 3.6. Buying and Selling Patterns: Poland, 1995 and 2011

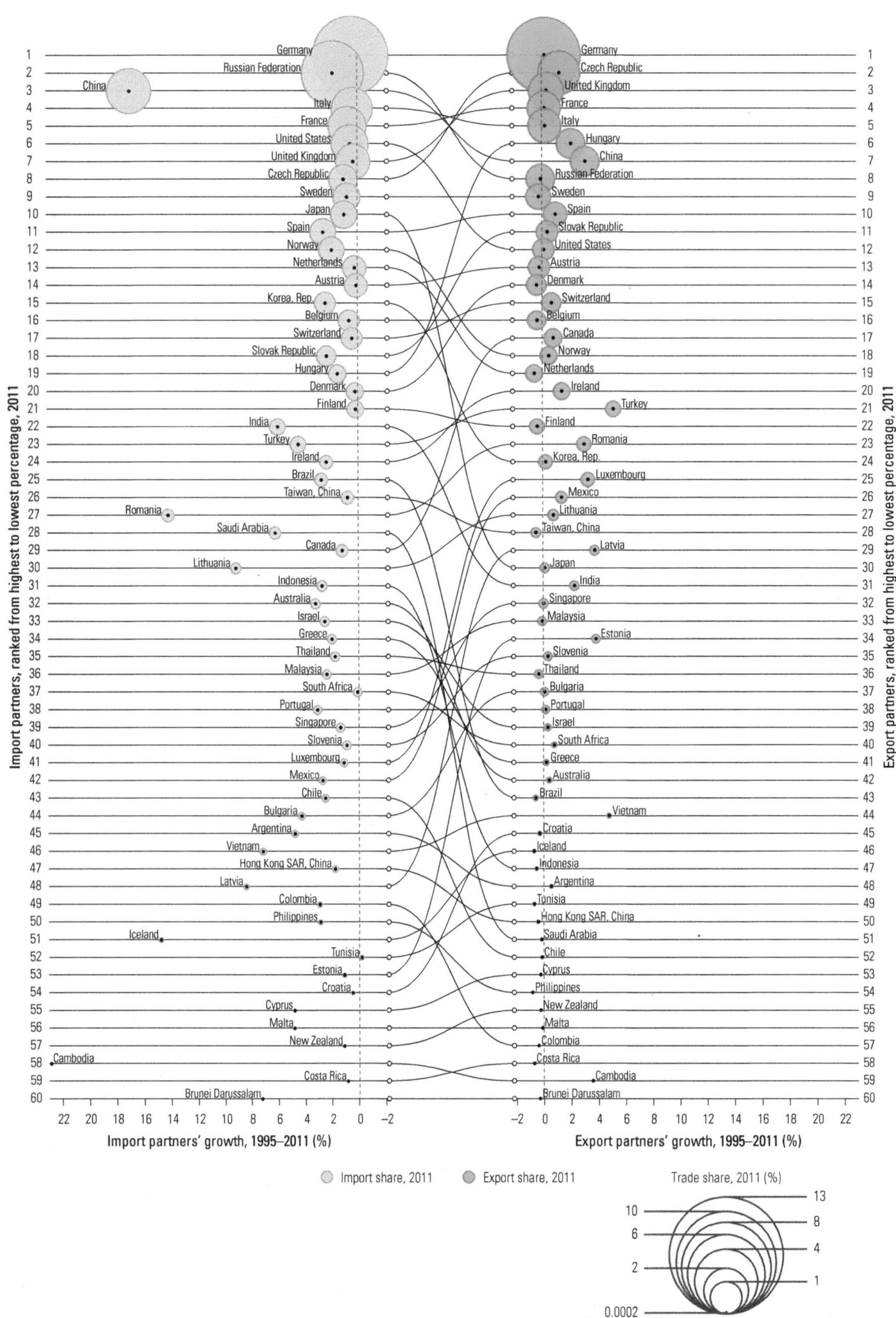

Source: Adapted from Baldwin and Lopez-Gonzalez 2013.

Figure 3.7. Buying and Selling Patterns: Mexico, 1995 and 2011

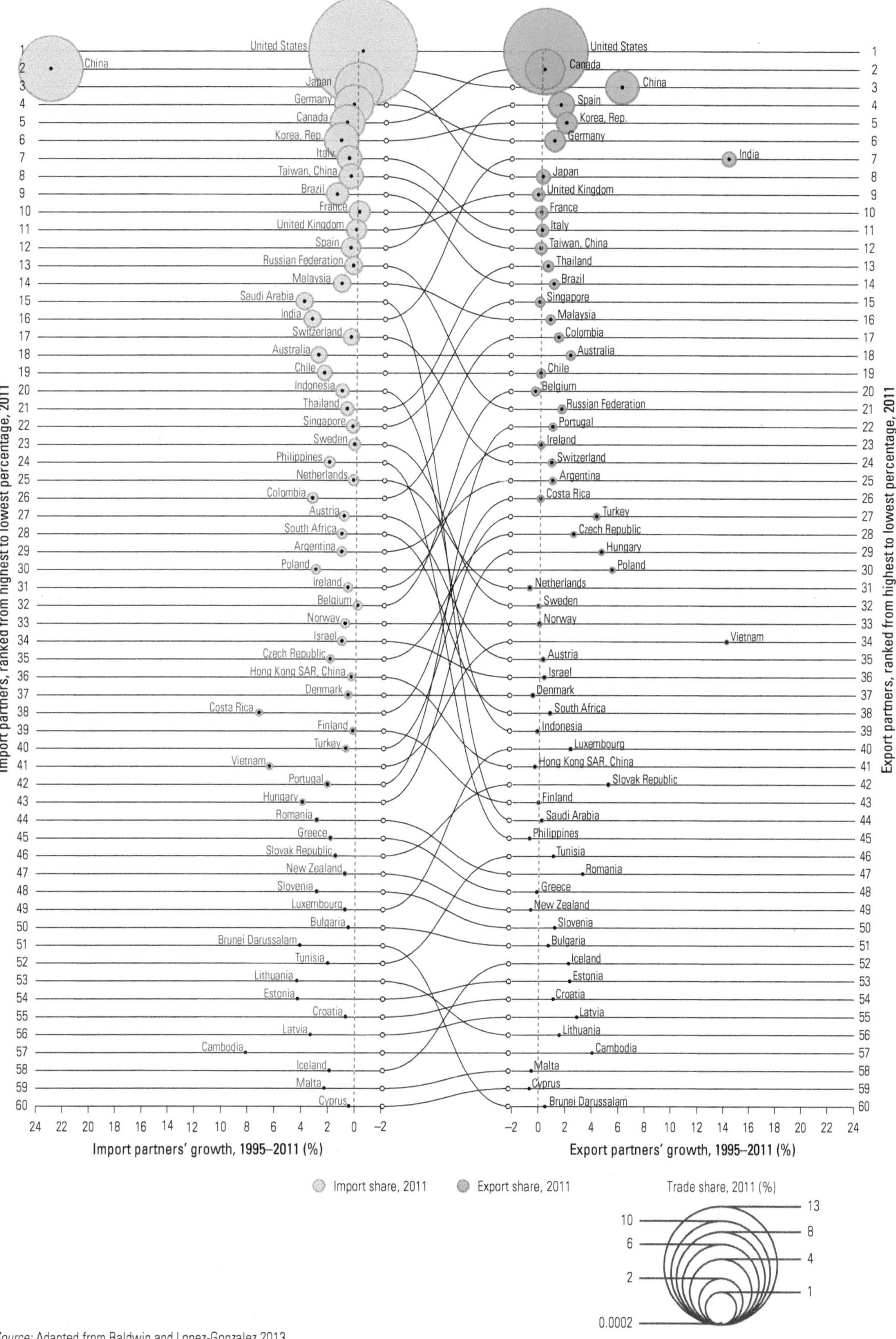

Source: Adapted from Baldwin and Lopez-Gonzalez 2013.

Figure 3.8. Buying and Selling Patterns: Germany, 1995 and 2011

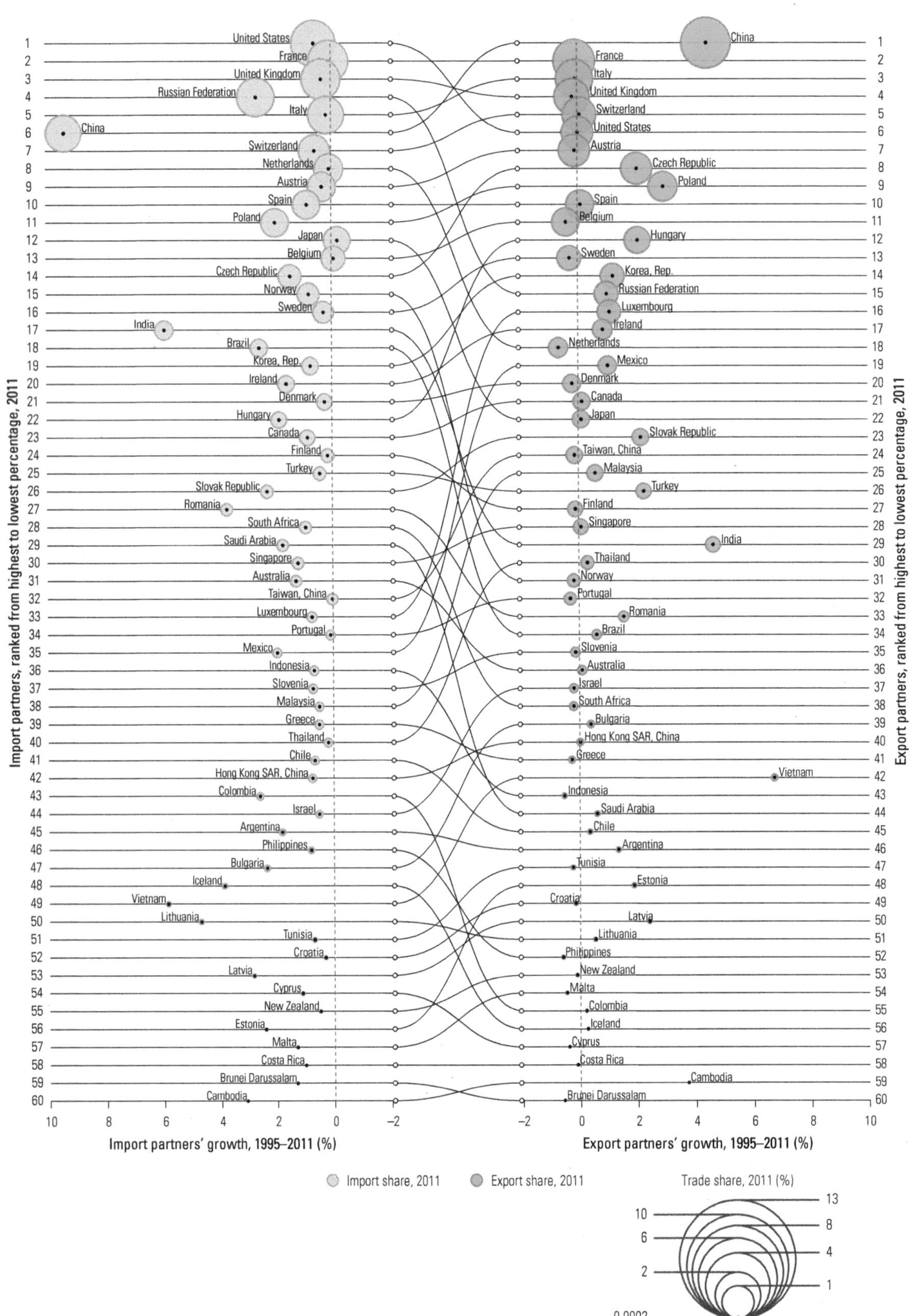

Source: Adapted from Baldwin and Lopez-Gonzalez 2013.

Figure 3.9. Buying and Selling Patterns: United States, 1995 and 2011

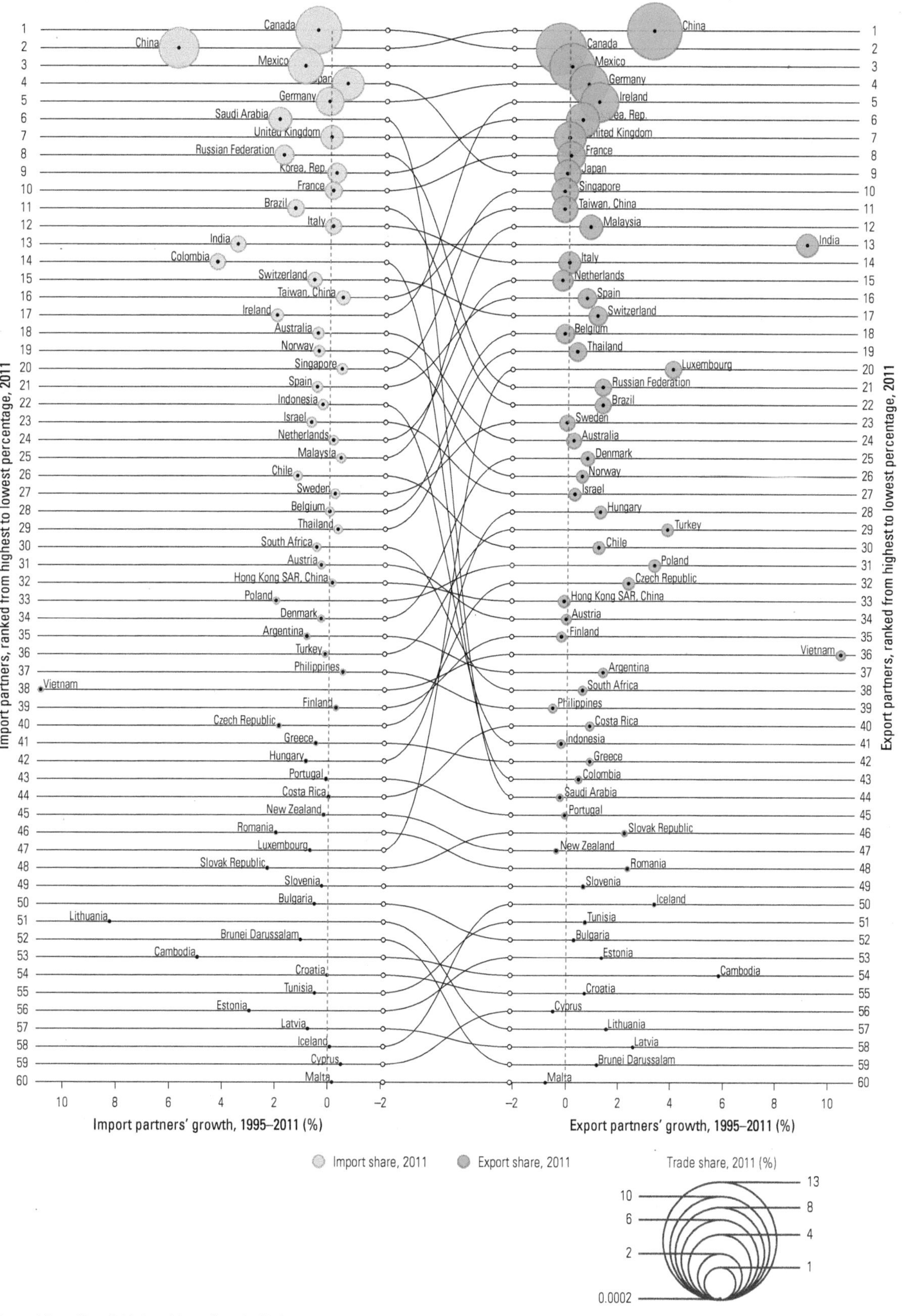

Source: Adapted from Baldwin and Lopez-Gonzalez 2013.

References

Athukorala, Premachandra. 2010. "Production Networks and Trade Patterns in East Asia: Regionalization or Globalization?" Working Paper Series on Regional Economic Integration 56, Asian Development Bank, Manila.

Baldwin, Richard, and Javier Lopez-Gonzalez. 2013. "Supply-Chain Trade: A Portrait of Global Patterns and Several Testable Hypotheses." NBER Working Paper 18957, National Bureau of Economic Research, Cambridge, MA.

Santoni, Gianluca, and Daria Taglioni. Forthcoming. *Network Analysis Using U.S. Benchmark Input-Output Data.* Washington, DC: The World Bank.

Sturgeon, Timothy J., and Olga Memedovic. 2011. "Mapping Global Value Chains: Intermediate Goods Trade and Structural Change in the World Economy." Working Paper 10/2010, United Nations Industrial Development Organization, Vienna.

Taymaz, Erol, Ebru Voylvoda, and Kamil Yilmaz. 2011. "Uluslararasi Üretim Zincirlerinde Dönüşüm ve Türkiye'nin Konumu." TUSIAD-Koc Universitesi Ekonomik Arastirma Forumu Calisma Raporlari Serisi. "The Transformation of International Production Linkages and Turkey." TUSIAD-Koc University, Economic Research Forum Research Reports. http://eaf.ku.edu.tr/sites/eaf.ku.edu.tr/files/eaf_rp_1101.pdf.

UN (United Nations). 2002. "Classification by Broad Economic Categories." United Nations, Department of Economic and Social Affairs, Statistical Papers Series M No. 53, Rev. 4.

World Bank. 2013. "Romania Western Region Competitiveness Enhancement and Smart Specialization Final Report." Paper presented at the World Bank and the Agency for Regional Development–Region West, Romania closing-project conference, "Advisory Services on Competitiveness Enhancement and Smart Specialization Policies in the West Region," Timişoara, Romania.

———. 2014. "Turkey: Trading up to High Income: Country Economic Memorandum." Report 82307, World Bank, Washington, DC.

Chapter 4

BUYER-RELATED MEASURES

Introduction

The global value chain (GVC) participation measures in this chapter focus on the sourcing side in GVCs. The key questions are, where are a country's exports made, and where is their value created? This is the buyer's perspective, as shown on the left side in figures 3.4 to 3.9 in chapter 3.

Intermediates in Gross Imports

The first indicator is the share of intermediates by Broad Economic Categories (BEC) in gross imports, as shown for high-income countries (HICs) and low- and middle-income countries (LMICs) between 1996 and 2012 (figure 4.1).[1] Two patterns stand out. First, the share of intermediates in gross imports rose most in HICs, which reflects the global fragmentation of production and the offshoring of tasks from HICs to LMICs. Second, the share is substantially higher for LMICs, reaching 71 percent in 2012 against 61 percent in HICs. That phenomenon probably occurs because LMICs specialize in processing intermediates for subsequent export (which could be shown by further separating processed from primary intermediates), whereas final goods had a larger share of the imports of HICs.

In this chapter, the measure is illustrated for Malaysia and selected peer countries, including Chile, China, Mexico, the Philippines, Poland, the Republic of Korea, Singapore, South Africa, Thailand, and Vietnam (box 4.1). The countries are all middle to high performers in GVCs.

High shares of intermediate imports in total imports are common for these countries, reflecting the importance of primary commodities in the import basket of dynamic and rapidly industrializing economies (figure 4.2). The far lower shares of intermediates of imports in electrical and electronic equipment support this finding. The difference also suggests that sector analysis of this indicator is very important. The indicator can be computed using the concepts and classifications discussed in chapter 3 (BEC, value chain category, customized trade, and other classifications).

The measure does not reveal whether the inputs are used domestically or exported. The following measures address this topic, focusing on imported inputs or foreign value added embodied in gross exports.

Imported Inputs Embodied in Gross Exports

I2E in Intermediate or Total Imports

The indicator importing to exports (I2E) in intermediates measures the buyer's intermediate imports embodied in its gross exports as a percentage of the buyer's total intermediate imports.[2] A very similar measure was presented in chapter 3. The only difference in this chapter, compared with chapter 3, is that the denominator here includes intermediate rather than total imports, resulting in smaller shares. Figure 4.3 reports the measure for the selected group of countries, as well as for Germany, Japan, and the United States.

Figure 4.1. Intermediate Imports, 1996–2012

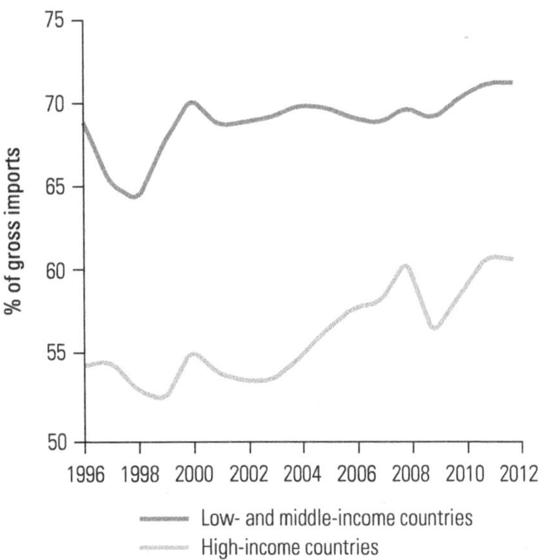

Source: Adapted from the United Nations Comtrade database.
Note: Calculations are based on the Broad Economic Categories classification (appendix B).

Survey data confirm that, in the aggregate, a large share of the imports of goods and services is used as inputs for exports. According to a recent business survey of 250 lead firms and suppliers in the agrifood sector, more than 80 percent of businesses in GVCs perceive imports of goods and services as being important or critical for their exports.[3] This finding challenges the mercantilist approach to trade and trade negotiations, in which the focus is on market access and the reciprocity of concessions. The new trade paradigm, by contrast, would reward opening import access as a key ingredient of strategies that reinforce a country's competitiveness.

I2E by Source Country

Imported intermediate inputs contain foreign technology. A key role of GVCs in industrial development is to boost the competitiveness of the exports of LMICs by facilitating the combination of foreign technology with their labor, capital, and technology. A very useful indicator of GVC participation, then, is the origin of the imported inputs embodied in a country's gross exports, as was illustrated in the left-hand side of figures 3.4 to 3.9 in chapter 3.

Distinguishing between Domestic and Foreign Value Added in Imports

Although imported inputs embodied in gross exports is a very useful indicator for a country's participation in GVCs, it does not distinguish between the foreign and domestic contents of the value of the imported inputs. Imported inputs may contain domestic value added that is exported to a foreign location, processed, and re-imported. An example is U.S. inputs imported by Canada and used to produce Canadian exports.[4] The imported inputs from the United States may already contain Canadian value added from upstream processes in which the United States has imported inputs from Canada. Those products are called "re-imports" from a Canadian perspective and "re-exports" from a U.S. perspective (figure 4.4).

BOX 4.1. Choice of Comparator Countries

International comparisons set countries' competitiveness in context; therefore, several examples in this part of the book discuss results for a subset of countries. The challenge is to select comparable countries. The following methodology was adopted.

Malaysia was selected as an example. Malaysia was an early adopter of global value chains, but is a middle performer, with areas of excellence and areas in which it needs to catch up (see World Bank 2014). To put the country's performance in context, the most appropriate peer countries were identified (listed in the main text).

Selection of the peer countries was based on a data-driven method, informed by the judgments of country experts. The method identifies countries similar in size or economic development, competitors with export baskets of similar composition, or neighboring countries. The World Bank Group has constructed a world database of peer countries to inform export competitiveness analyses. The matching of countries with their peers is available at https://mec.worldbank.org/buildercompare#comparator countries. Benchmark countries for each of the 121 countries in the data set are determined based on the following five indicators: population, human capital, physical capital, gross domestic product per capita, and export basket composition. Countries are ranked by similarity in decreasing order, enabling the analyst to select the most similar ones as benchmark countries. Figure B4.1.1 shows the global network of countries.

(Box continues next page)

BOX 4.1. (continued)

Figure B4.1.1. Country Positioning in the Global Economic Space

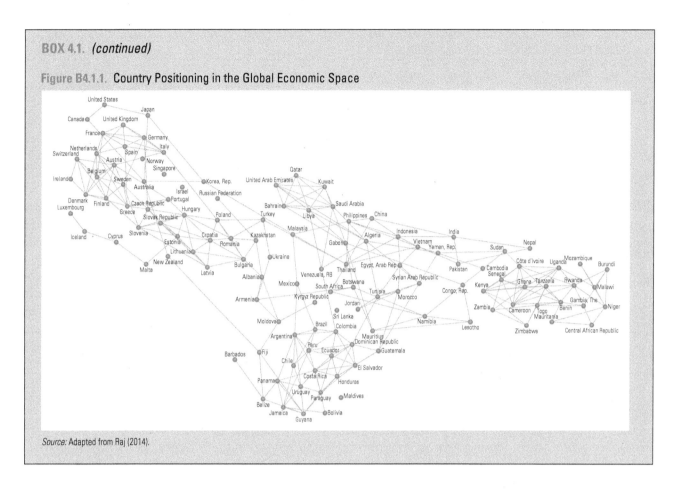

Source: Adapted from Raj (2014).

Re-importing and re-exporting can be quite important for some industries and countries.

Value Added in Gross Exports

Value-added trade statistics can be used to single out the domestic or foreign value added embodied in exports. The advantage of these data is that they help determine where things are actually made. For example, the data can be very important for quantifying the impact of GVC participation on jobs. Because about three-quarters of domestic value added comes from labor, value-added trade statistics roughly show where the export-linked jobs are located, by country and sector.

Gross exports are decomposed in various ways, the most obvious being between domestic and foreign value added (see the bars in figure 4.5). A first set of indicators looks at the value added embodied in gross exports. The first-pass indicator simply distinguishes between domestic and foreign value added, usually expressed as a share of gross exports. The second pass digs deeper into where the domestic value added is actually created. This indicator breaks

Figure 4.2. Countries' Integration in GVCs: Share of Intermediate Imports in Gross Imports and Electrical and Electronics, 2009 and 2012

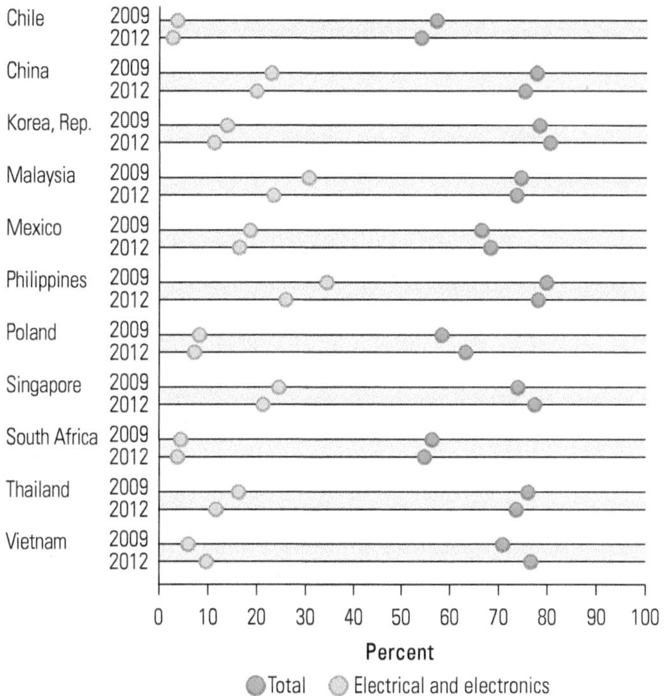

Source: Adapted from the United Nations Comtrade database.

Figure 4.3. Intermediate Imports Embodied in Exports and Electrical and Optical Equipment, Selected Countries, 2009 and 2011

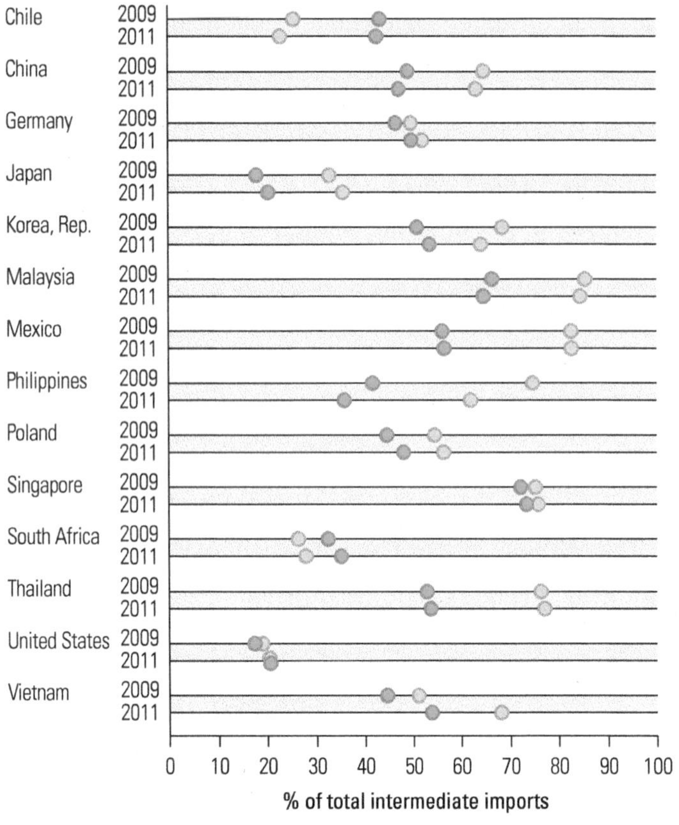

Source: Adapted from the Organisation for Economic Co-operation and Development–World Trade Organization Trade in Value Added database.

out the total domestic value added into (1) domestic value added in the particular sector (autos, in the example), (2) domestic value added in upstream sectors supplying the sector with parts, and (3) domestic value added in intermediates first shipped abroad for further processing and then re-imported.

Combining information from input-output tables with information from trade flows makes such computations possible. Four data sets for trade in value added are discussed in chapter 3 and appendixes G and H. The data sets make it possible to assess the domestic or foreign value-added content of countries' gross exports.

Model-based computations enable quantifying the value added of a given export (good or service). If information is available on the geographic origin of the inputs, the value added specific to inputs produced domestically can be quantified, following an iterative process (figure 4.6). The schematic in figure 4.6 distinguishes between domestic value added (green) and foreign value added (yellow), and clarifies differences between the following key concepts:

- *Gross exports.* The total value of exports as shown in traditional trade and balance-of-payments statistics (for goods and services) captures the value added embodied in the production of the good or service exported, as well as all domestically sourced and imported inputs embodied in the good or service.
- *Direct domestic value added embodied in exports.* Gross exports minus domestically sourced (EXGR_IDC), re-imported (EXGR_RIM), and foreign inputs (EXGR_FVA) capture the true sector-specific domestic value added of exports (EXGR_DDC). This information is important in an environment in which global production is fragmented across countries. For example, a business process outsourcing (BPO) service in India contains telecommunications services from local providers and foreign owners of satellites. The measure EXGR_DDC nets out domestic and foreign inputs and captures the true value added generated in India's BPO sector.
- *Total domestic value added of exports.* For the total, the direct domestic value added of exports is added to the value added of the inputs sourced domestically (indirect domestic content of gross exports [EXGR_IDC]) and the value added of re-imported inputs (EXGR_RIM). In the BPO example, the measure captures the value added of the BPO service plus the value of the domestic satellites used as input in the underlying telecommunications service, but the measure does not include the value of the foreign-owned satellite input. The measure captures the full domestic value added of an exported service or good. Quantitatively, however, in most countries re-imported inputs tend to be very small, so the sum of the direct and indirect value added contribution is highly correlated with the total domestic value added embodied in exports.

To exemplify the relevance of these concepts, gross exports (of goods and services) are decomposed in the four measures, for the same countries (figure 4.7). The share of foreign value added is lowest in commodity exporters and HICs. The lower the ratio is, the higher is the domestic value-added content in gross exports, and thus the lower is the importance of I2E. Commodity goods often are exported in their

Figure 4.4. Re-imports and Re-exports in Supply Chain Trade

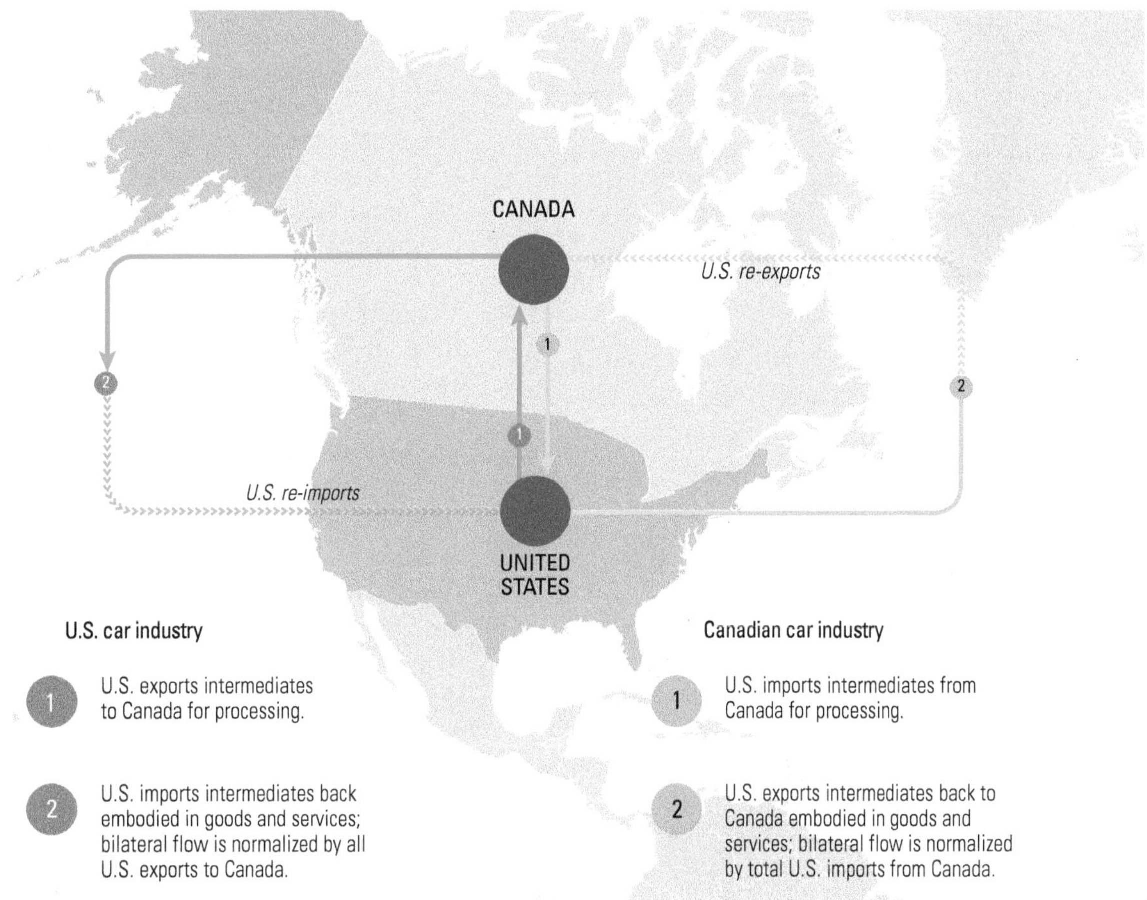

Source: Adapted from Baldwin and Lopez-Gonzalez 2013, figure 5.
Note: U.S. re-exports are Canadian re-imports but with different normalizations.

raw form or embody only low additional value from other sectors or from abroad, which explains the high share of direct domestic value added. By contrast, HICs tend to have a more diversified domestic supply base that requires them to rely less on foreign imports. China's gross exports rely more on indirect value added (37 percent) in supplying sectors.

By contrast, most other emerging countries and Germany, Japan, and the United States (44, 48, and 52 percent, respectively) strongly depend on direct domestic value added. That countries relatively marginal to GVCs (such as Chile and South Africa) and countries at their core (Germany, Japan, and the United States) post a low I2E ratio suggests that the measure—in isolation—is not indicative of failure or success. Its relevance needs to be assessed in combination with the wider range of measures presented in this book.

Reflecting the fact that the domestic value added in re-imported intermediates is generally very low for most countries, in the sample in figure 4.7, that amount adds up to 1 percent of total gross exports only for China and Germany.

Foreign Value Added in Gross Exports

Subtracting the total domestic value-added of exports measure as a percentage of gross exports from 1 yields the foreign value added embodied in gross exports as a percentage of gross exports. This figure captures the country's GVC position as a user of foreign value added in its exports. For the world as a whole, only 20 percent of gross exports constitutes value that was added in a foreign country.[5]

By plotting the foreign value added in a country's gross exports as a percentage of gross exports, three patterns stand out (figure 4.8):

- Almost all countries saw their numbers increase between 1995 and 2011. The expansion was

Figure 4.5. Decomposition of Gross Exports

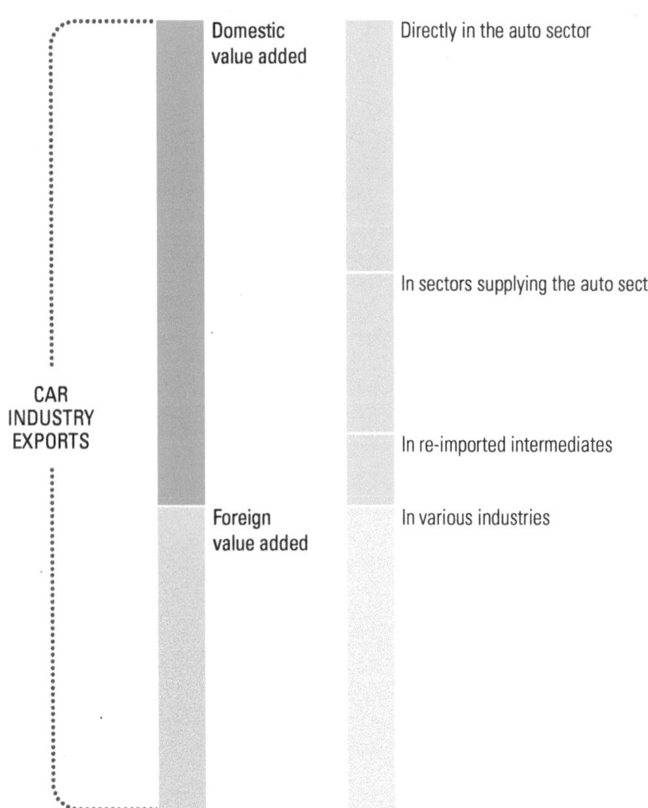

Source: Adapted from Baldwin and Lopez-Gonzalez 2013.

particularly strong in emerging countries, such as Cambodia, Hungary, Korea, Poland, and Turkey.

- The share is lower for large countries—especially the manufacturing giants—but Germany and even China are almost twice as integrated internationally as the United States.
- The share rises to very high levels in the smallest countries, such as Ireland, Luxembourg, and Singapore.

The difference between gross exports and value-added exports can be extremely stark for some products. China's exports of iPhones, for example, include less than 10 percent of Chinese value added, whereas Norway's exports of oil contain almost 100 percent of Norwegian value added. At the national level, however, the difference is moderate for most countries, with some standouts: Korea has a remarkably high foreign content for a country of its size and level of industrialization. Australia is a standout for its low number, but that surely reflects its reliance on primary product exports, which are naturally high in local content.

How do the four key measures compare for individual countries? Figure 4.9 shows the share of imported intermediate inputs in total imports,

Figure 4.6. Quantifying the Value Added of Gross Exports

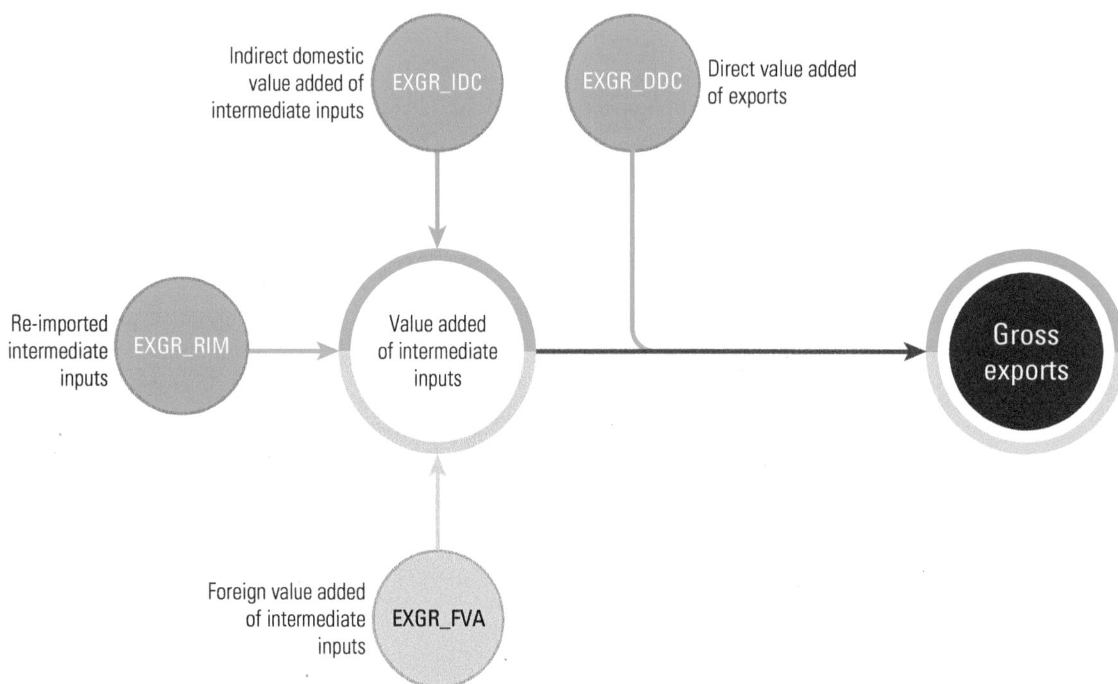

Note: Foreign value added is highlighted in yellow and domestic value added is highlighted in green.

Figure 4.7. Decomposition of Gross Exports, Selected Countries, 2011

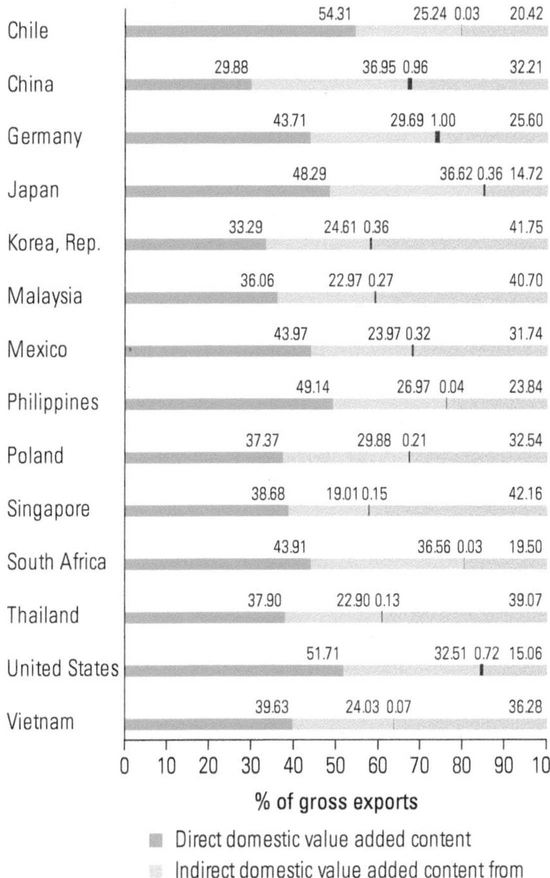

Source: Adapted from the Organisation for Economic Co-operation and Development–World Trade Organization Trade in Value Added database.

Figure 4.8. Foreign Value Added in a Country's Gross Exports, 1995 and 2011

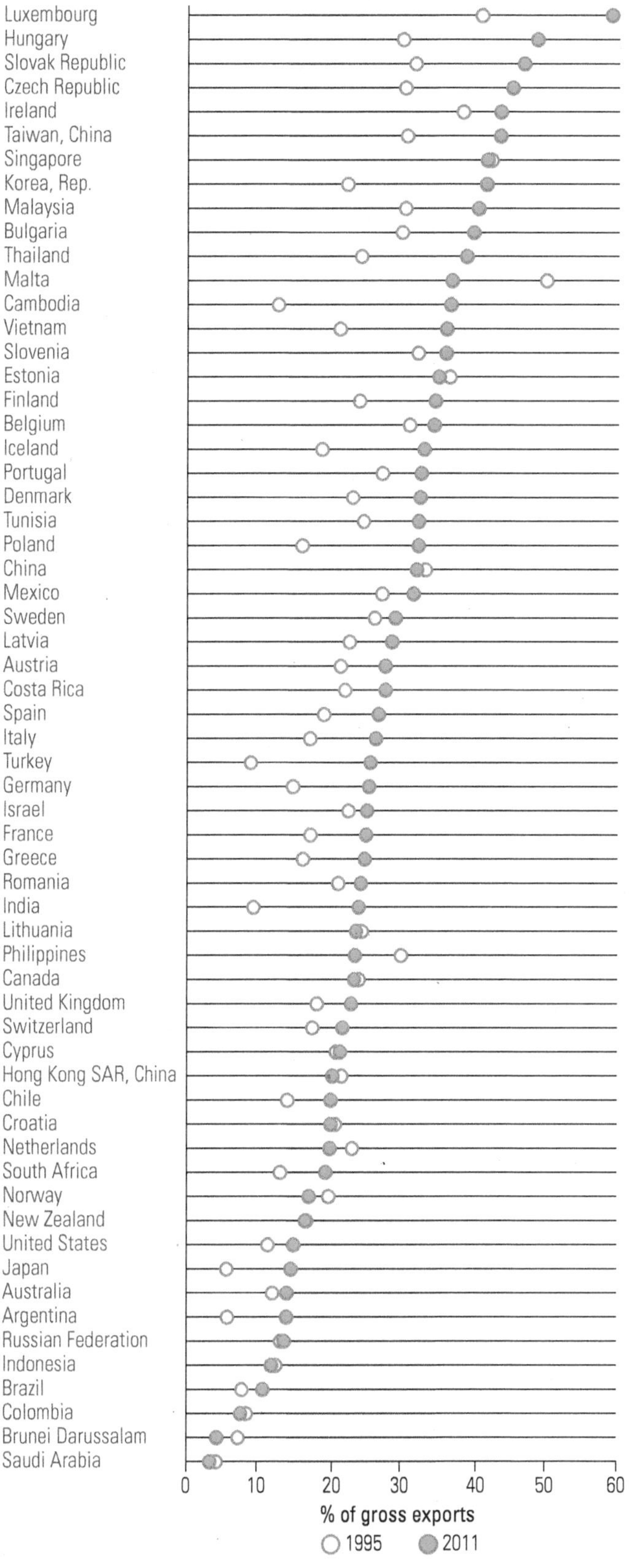

Source: Adapted from the Organisation for Economic Co-operation and Development–World Trade Organization Trade in Value Added database.

the share of I2E in total imports, the foreign value-added content in gross exports as a percentage of gross exports, and the domestic value added in gross exports as a percentage of gross exports for 2009.

Full Decomposition of Value Added by Sector and Source Country

The decomposition of gross exports illustrated in figures 4.5 and 4.6—and applied to specific countries in figures 4.7 to 4.9—can be used further to identify the source of value added by sector and country. The decomposition addresses where and in which industries the value added that makes up a country's gross exports is produced. Figure 4.10 breaks down US$10 million of Mexican auto exports. The first column shows that US$10 million in car exports

Figure 4.9. Comparison of Four Buyer-Related Measures of GVC Participation, Selected Countries, 2009

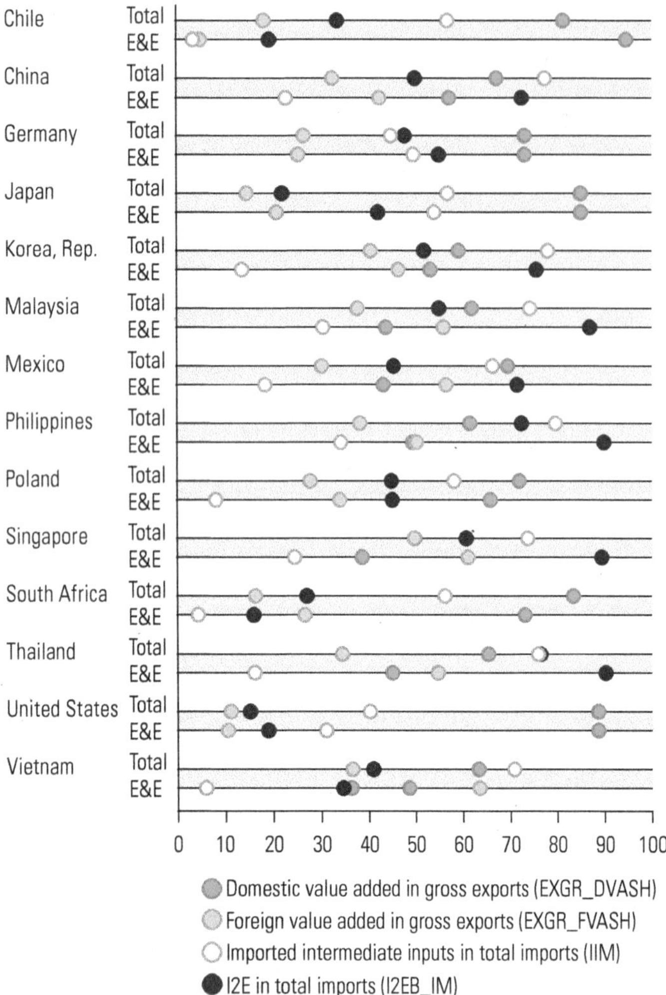

Source: Adapted from the Organisation for Economic Co-operation and Development–World Trade Organization Trade in Value Added database.
Note: E&E = electrical and electronic equipment; GVC = global value chain; I2E = importing to export.

from Mexico to the United States, in this example, contains intermediates of iron and steel sourced abroad worth US$3 million, intermediates of rubber and plastics sourced in Mexico worth US$2.5 million, and US$4.5 million of Mexican value added in the car industry. The US$4.5 million consists of payments to productive factors in Mexico (wages, interest, dividends, and so on) and the Mexican firm's profit margin on the export sale.

The iron and steel inputs embodied in the Mexican cars exported to the United States come from the iron and steel sectors in Australia, Mexico, and the United States (US$1 million each). The imported iron and steel has Mexican value added because the U.S. iron and steel industry uses Mexican inputs in its exports to Mexico (US$1 million of Mexican value added). The value added in the rubber and plastic intermediates comes from Mexico and the United States, because the Mexican rubber and plastics sector imports some inputs from the United States. The only figure that requires no further calculation is the Mexican value added in the car sector.

Although the measures that have been discussed so far can be computed using any of the databases illustrated in chapter 3, the Organisation for Economic Co-operation and Development–World Trade Organization Trade in Value Added (TiVA) database and WIOD are the only two international data sets that provide decompositions that drill down to the individual "country of origin by sector" level. With the full value-added breakdown of a country's gross exports to the world or to specific destinations, the information can be arranged in two basic ways: by source country or by source industry. The necessary indicators in the TiVA database are listed in table 4.1; the left column shows the TiVA indicator names; the right column provides their definitions. Similar measures are available in WIOD.

Value Added in Gross Exports by Source Country

The breakdown of foreign value added into source countries or industries is useful from a buyer's perspective because it identifies which foreign sources add the most value to its exports. Figure 4.11 shows the shares of foreign value added in gross exports as a percentage of gross exports for Thailand's transport equipment sector by source region. The share of total foreign value added in gross exports (sum across all source regions) rose from 48 percent in 1995 to 55 percent in 2011. Among the source countries, East Asian economies (China; Hong Kong SAR, China; Japan; Korea; and Taiwan, China) contributed approximately 23 percent to Thailand's gross exports of transport equipment. East Asia's contribution remained constant over the period, whereas other source regions expanded their shares, in particular, other regions, the Association of Southeast Asian Nations without Thailand, and South and Central America.

For the subsample of countries discussed earlier, the source of value added is shown for total exports and electrical and optical (E&O) equipment (figure 4.12). Germany (from European Union–28, EU-28), Mexico (from North American Free Trade Agreement, NAFTA), Malaysia (from East Asia), Poland (also from EU-28), Thailand (from East Asia), and Vietnam (also from East Asia) source the highest shares of foreign value added from a single

Figure 4.10. Value-Added Trade: US$10 Million in Mexican Car Exports to the United States

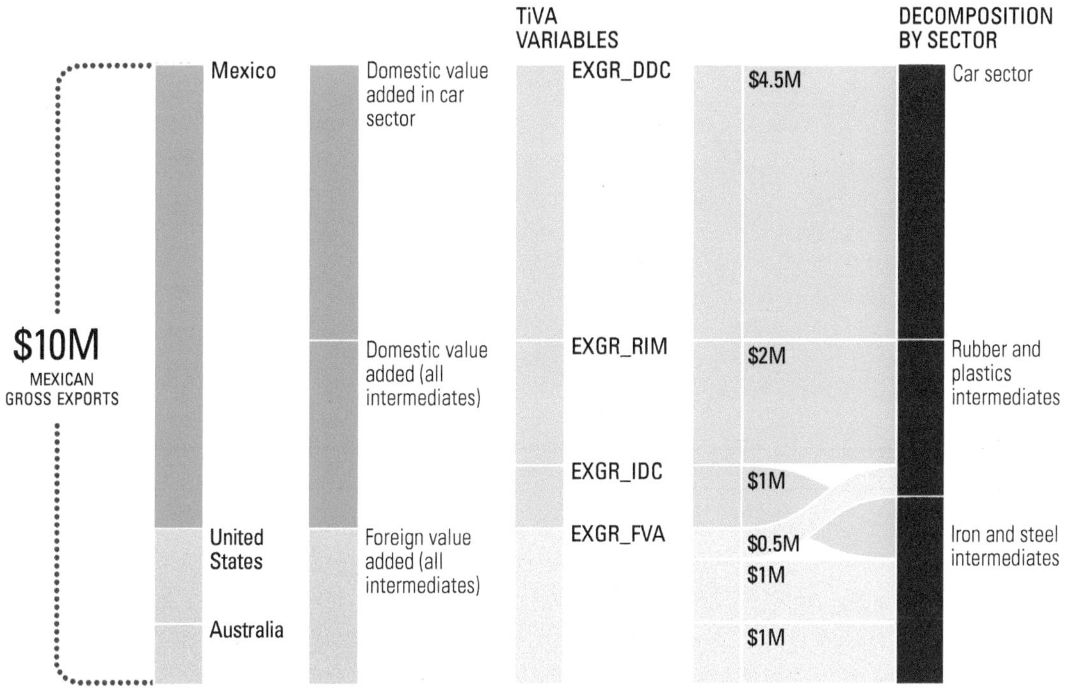

Source: Baldwin and Lopez-Gonzalez 2013.
Note: TiVA = Trade in Value Added.

Table 4.1. Indicators of Value Added Embodied in Gross Exports

Indicator	Definition
EXGR	Gross exports, by sector (US$ millions)
EXGR_DVA	Total domestic value added embodied in gross exports, by sector (US$ millions)
EXGR_DVASH	EXGR_DVA in EXGR, by sector (%)
EXGR_DDC	Direct (intrasector) domestic value added embodied in gross exports, by sector (US$ millions)
EXGR_IDC	Indirect (upstream) domestic value added embodied in gross exports, by sector (US$ millions)
EXGR_RIM	Re-imported domestic value added embodied in gross exports, by sector (US$ millions)
EXGR_FVA	Foreign value added embodied in gross exports, by sector and source country (US$ millions)
EXGR_FVASH	EXGR_FVA in EXGR, by sector and source country (%)

Source: Adapted from the Organisation for Economic Co-operation and Development–World Trade Organization Trade in Value Added database.

region—in the range of 12 to 17 percent. In the E&O industry, reliance on a single source region is higher. More than 35 percent of Vietnam's gross exports contain value added originating from East Asian locations, whereas the share ranges from 12 to 29 percent in China, Malaysia, the Philippines, Singapore, and Thailand. The regional dimension of GVCs, in the aggregate and in the E&O sector, emerges clearly.

Advanced countries (Germany, Japan, and the United States) post lower shares of foreign value added from any source region (figure 4.13). U.S. gross exports show the lowest foreign value-added content, a little over 15 percent (15 percent in E&O). Japan's foreign value-added share in gross exports is also low, making up less than 15 percent (17 percent in E&O). Germany's share of foreign value added is higher, representing about 26 percent of gross exports (25 percent in E&O), mainly sourced from the EU-28.

Value Added in Gross Exports by Source Industry

Similarly, foreign value added can be disaggregated by source industries. For the U.S. E&O equipment sector in 2011, the total share of foreign value added embodied in exports as a percentage of gross exports was 14.8 percent (figure 4.14). As might be expected, intra-industry foreign value added contributed one of the largest shares (2.8 percent), followed by foreign value added from mining and quarrying (1.9 percent) and real estate, renting, and business activities (1.5 percent). Wholesale and retail trade; hotels

Figure 4.11. Foreign Value Added in Thailand's Transport Equipment Sector Exports, by Source Region, 1995–11

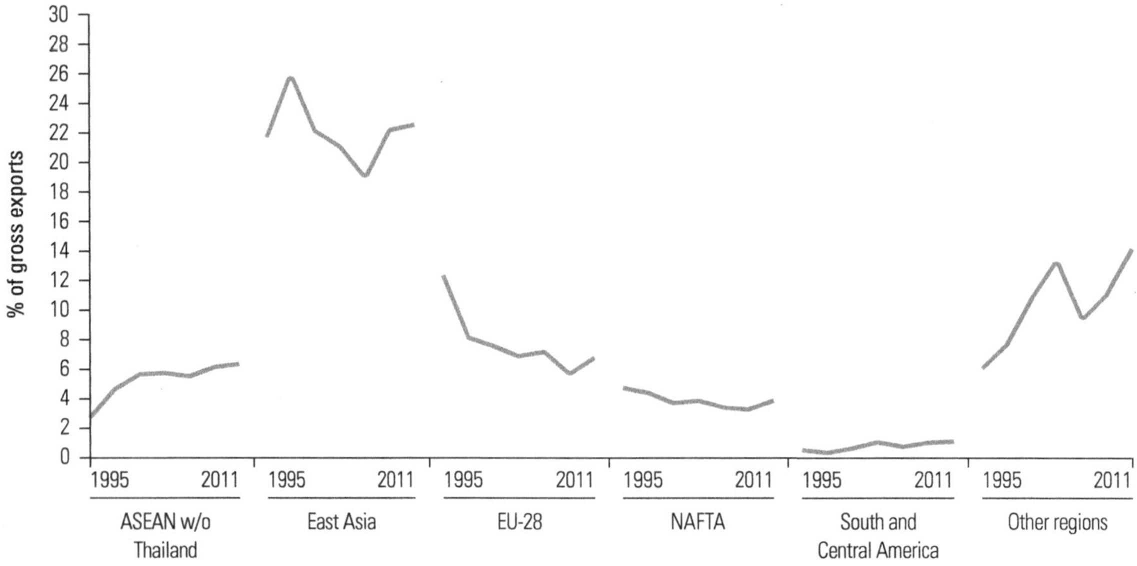

Source: Adapted from the Organisation for Economic Co-operation and Development–World Trade Organization Trade in Value Added database.
Note: ASEAN = Association of Southeast Asian Nations; EU = European Union; NAFTA = North American Free Trade Agreement.

Figure 4.12. Foreign Value Added in Gross Exports, Total and Electrical and Optical Equipment, by Source Region, Selected Countries, 2011

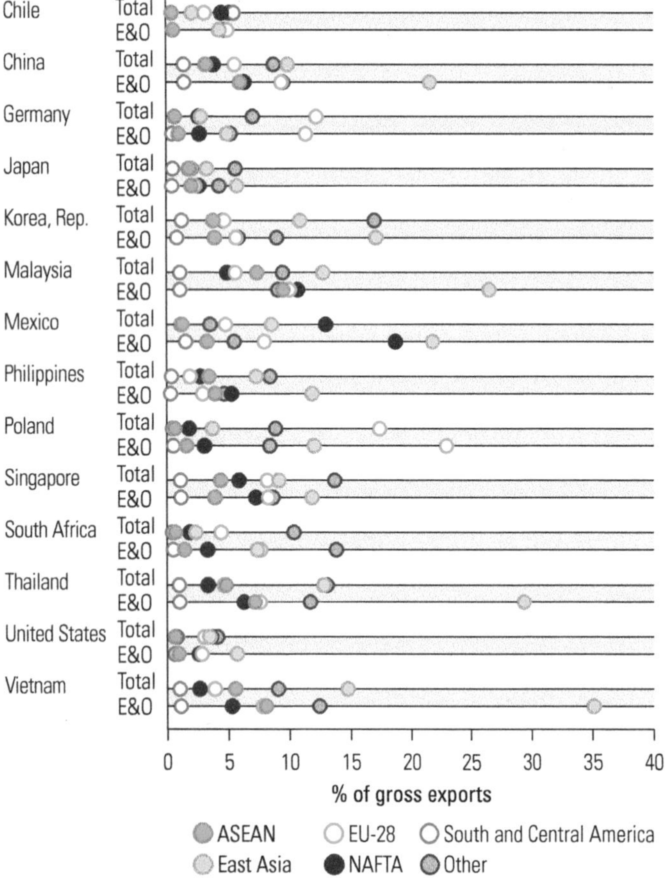

Source: Adapted from the Organisation for Economic Co-operation and Development–World Trade Organization Trade in Value Added database.
Note: ASEAN = Association of Southeast Asian Nations; E&O = electrical and optical; EU = European Union; NAFTA = North American Free Trade Agreement.

and restaurants (2.8 percent) was the largest contributor of foreign value added share in gross exports, pointing to the importance of services in GVCs.

Here we shift the focus to cross-country comparisons, to investigate the share of foreign value added embodied in gross exports as a percentage of gross exports, by source sectors, in the E&O equipment and chemicals industries. Figures 4.15 and 4.16 confirm the importance of business services and wholesale and retail trade, in particular for middle-income countries and HICs. The most important source sectors are highlighted in yellow. Most foreign inputs are sourced from the same industry in the E&O equipment sector (panel j in figure 4.15). For chemicals, the main foreign source industry is upstream mining and quarrying (panel c in figure 4.16).

Length of Sourcing Chains

The I2E concept focuses on bilateral relations—essentially, who a country is involved with in GVCs. Although it is informative for some issues, I2E misses the "chain" aspect of GVCs. The Japanese components used in Chinese exports, for example, are likely to contain imported components from, say, Korea or the United States.

One measure that reflects such multi-country considerations is the length of value chain sourcing. The measure developed by Fally (2011) and applied to the TiVA data by DeBacker and Miroudot (2013) captures this attribute by looking at a recursive measure of I2E on the sourcing side. To illustrate the concept, it is useful to consider a simple value chain, in which the automotive industry in Germany requires 40 cents of auto parts from Poland for each dollar's worth of automotives produced (the other 60 cents being value added by the German-based automotive industry). Assuming the Polish parts are 100 percent Polish value added, the length of the sourcing chain is 1.4; that is, the German stage always counts as 1 stage and the 40 percent value added in Poland counts as 0.4 stage. The term "sourcing chain" can be somewhat misleading, in that it also takes into account the direct domestic value added contribution of the sector of interest, and does not only consider the upstream sectors from which inputs are sourced.

The concept is recursive in more complex examples. For instance, if the 40 percent Polish value added included parts made in France, the sourcing chain would be longer. If the French parts were 100 percent made in France and made up 30 percent of the value of the Polish parts exports to Germany, the Polish parts chain would be 1.3 (1 for Poland and 0.3 for France). Thus, the German auto industry's chain length would be $1 + 0.4(1.3) = 1.52$.[6] The TiVA data provide a handy means for comparing the average number of production stages in a given industry and country.

Figure 4.13. Foreign Value Added in Gross Exports, Total and Electrical and Optical Equipment, Selected Countries, 2011

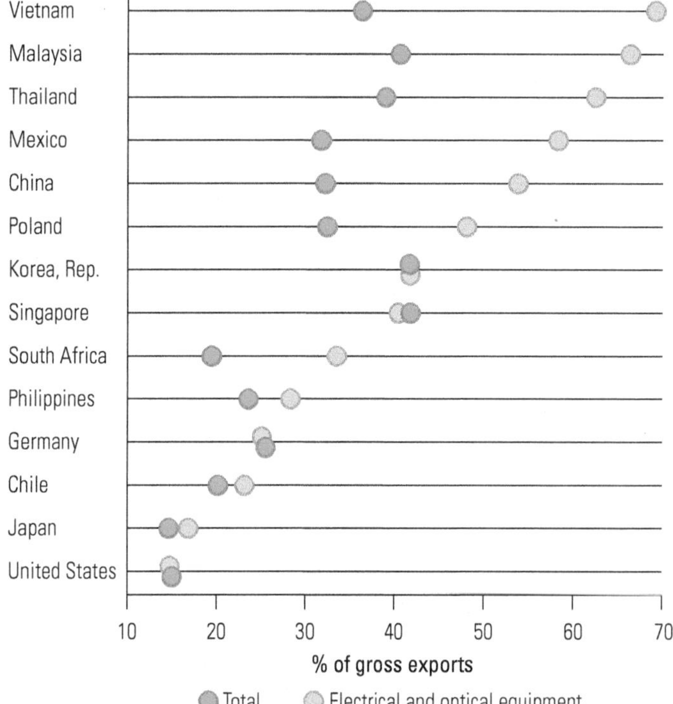

Source: Adapted from the Organisation for Economic Co-operation and Development–World Trade Organization Trade in Value Added database.

Figure 4.14. Foreign Value Added in Gross Exports in the U.S. Electrical and Optical Equipment Sector, by Source Industry, 2011

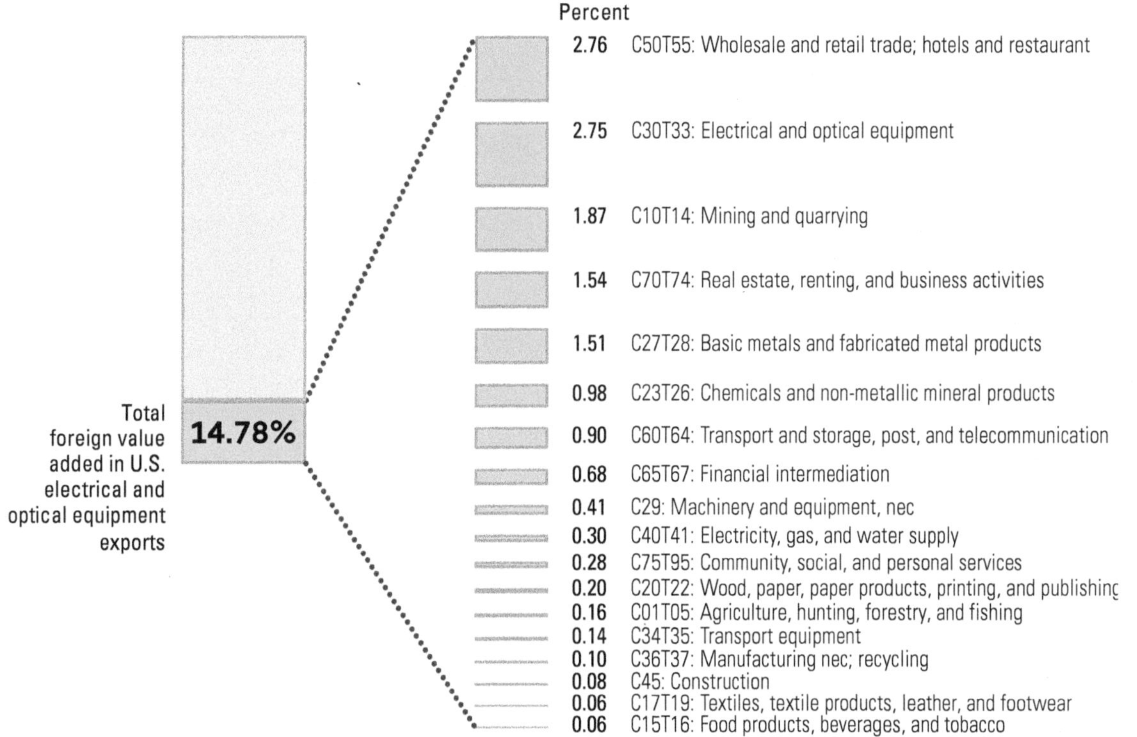

Source: Adapted from the Organisation for Economic Co-operation and Development–World Trade Organization Trade in Value Added database.
Note: nec =not elsewhere classified.

Figure 4.15. Foreign Value Added in Gross Exports, Electrical and Optical Equipment, by Source Sector, Selected Countries, 2011

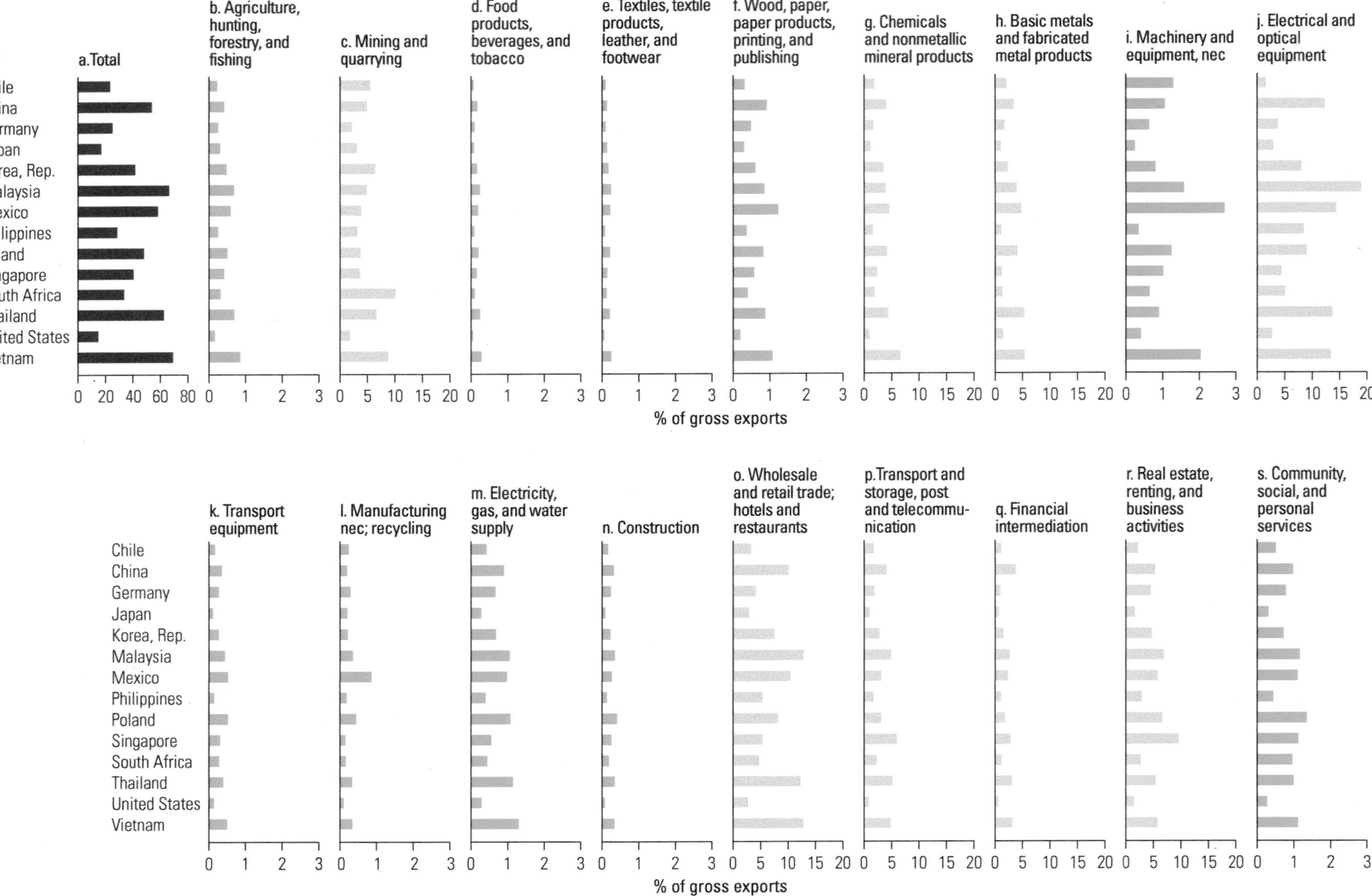

Source: Adapted from the Organisation for Economic Co-operation and Development–World Trade Organization Trade in Value Added database.
Note: The most important source sectors are in yellow and use a scale ranging from 0 to 20. Less relevant source sectors are in green and use a scale ranging from 0 to 3. nec = not elsewhere classified.

Figure 4.16. Foreign Value Added in Gross Exports, Chemicals and Chemical Products, by Source Sector, Selected Countries, 2011

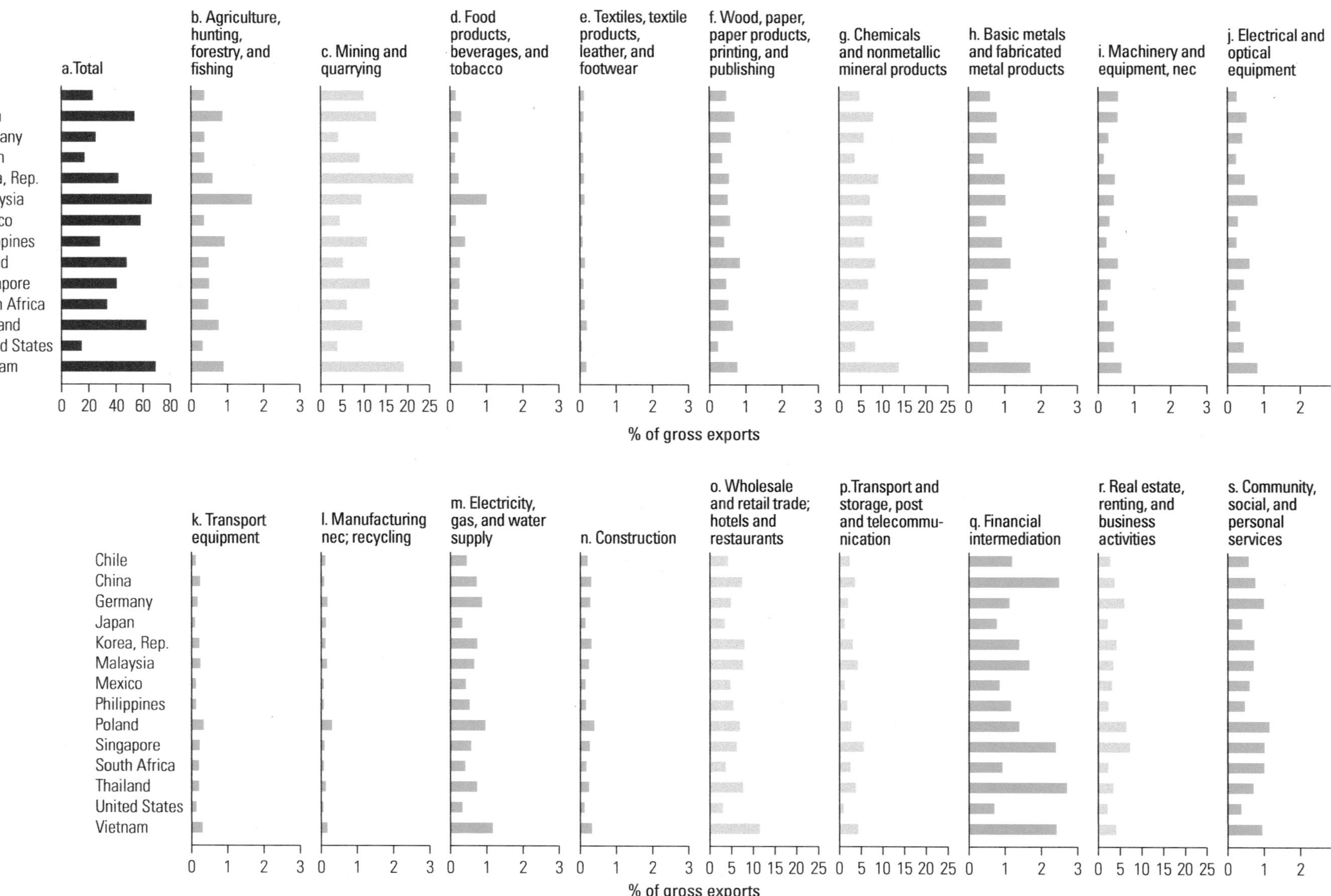

Source: Adapted from the Organisation for Economic Co-operation and Development–World Trade Organization Trade in Value Added database.

Note: The most important source sectors are in yellow and use a scale ranging from 0 to 25. Less relevant source sectors are in green and use a scale ranging from 0 to 3. The minimum value of the index is 1 when no intermediate inputs are used to produce a final good or service. nec = not elsewhere classified.

Figure 4.17. Length of Sourcing Chains, by Industry, 2008

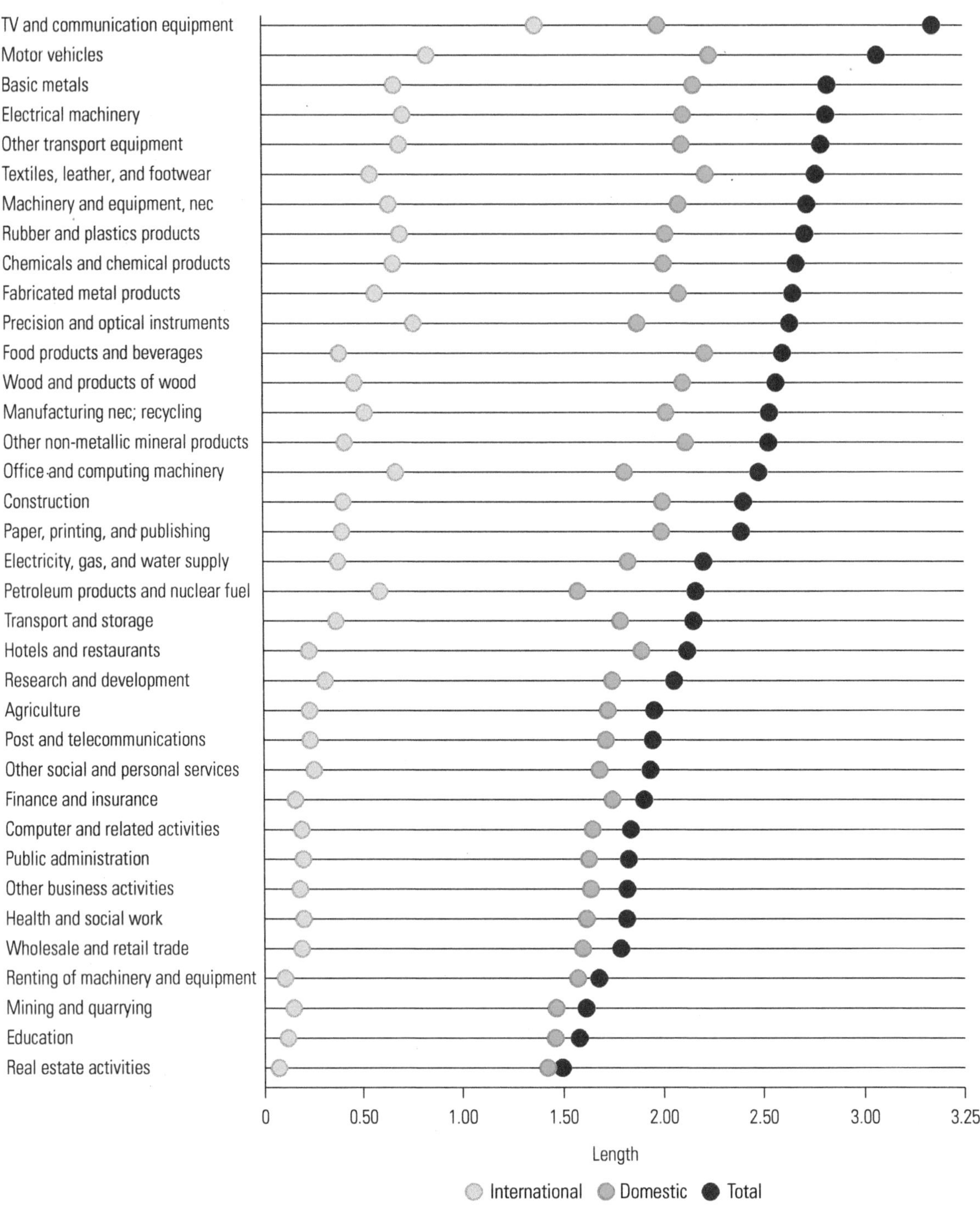

Source: Adapted from OECD Global Value Chains Indicators, May 2013.
Note: The minimum value of the index is 1 when no intermediate inputs are used to produce a final good or service. nec = not elsewhere classified.

Figure 4.17 shows the length of sourcing chains averaged across all countries in the TiVA data set, differentiating between the domestic and international production stages. The six industries with the longest chains are television and communication equipment; motor vehicles; basic metals; electrical machinery; other transport equipment; and textiles, leather, and footwear. Services, on average, have shorter value chains, with notable exceptions, such as transport and storage.

The measure can be useful in several ways. For instance, an increase in GVC length over time suggests that the value chain has become more complex, with stages done in more countries. The measure also can show the relative complexity of the GVCs of which a country is part—associating long GVCs with complex ones.

Buyer Dimension: Summary

Table 4.2 summarizes the main measures of the buyer dimension. More indirect measures—such as the share of intermediates in gross imports based on informed classifications—are easily available, whereas more direct quantifications of a country's performance in GVCs—such as the full decomposition of a country's gross exports—are available for only a limited set of countries. The table indicates whether the measures are available for goods tasks, services tasks, or both, as well as the level of analysis (country, sector, or firm). For easy reference, the table refers to the respective sections of the book, in which the measures are introduced. For more information on the underlying data, see appendixes G and H.

The measures presented so far cover only trade in tasks (goods and services). Chapter 1 shows that GVCs are a multidimensional phenomenon that also involves the flow of factors of production. From a buyer's perspective, several measures can be analyzed to complement the task-based assessment. Although a wider set of examples can be found in table A.1 in appendix A, the following are some of the key indicators:

- *Wages.* High wages are likely to be associated with buyers that are also final producers, close to final demand, and able to generate high value added. Low wages are likely to be associated with buyers that are mainly assemblers or are involved in activities with little transformation.

Table 4.2. Summary of the Main Buyer-Related Measures

Measure	Task	Level of analysis	Data sources	Where to find in book?
Share of intermediates in gross imports	Goods	Country, sector	Gross import data (UN Comtrade, BACI, WITS), categorized using informed classifications (BEC, parts and components, technical classifications)	Chapter 4, p. 71
Share of intermediates in gross imports, range of imports, bundle of imported products, and countries	Goods	Country, sector, firm	Gross import data (customs firm-level), categorized using informed classifications (BEC, parts and components, technical classifications)	Chapter 4, p. 71
Imported inputs embodied in exports, as percentage of gross imports	Goods and/or services	Country, sector	International I-O data (WIOD, World Bank Export Value Added database)	Chapter 4, p. 71
Imported inputs embodied in exports, as percentage of gross imports and by source country	Goods and/or services	Country, sector, source country	International I-O data (WIOD)	Chapter 4, p. 72
Share of foreign value added in gross exports	Goods and/or services	Country, sector	International I-O data (WIOD, TiVA, World Bank Export Value Added database)	Chapter 4, p. 75
Share of foreign value added in gross exports by source country	Goods and/or services	Country, sector, source country	International I-O data (WIOD, TiVA)	Chapter 4, p. 78
Share of domestic value added in gross exports	Goods and/or services	Country, sector	International I-O data (WIOD, TiVA, World Bank Export Value Added database)	Chapter 4, p. 74
Multinational's share of inputs from domestic suppliers in total inputs	Goods and/or services	Country, sector, firm	Enterprise surveys or other firm-level surveys	Chapter 6, p. 113
Domestic producer's share of imported inputs in total imported inputs	Goods and/or services	Country, sector, firm	Enterprise surveys or other firm-level surveys	Chapter 6, p. 115
Length of sourcing chains	Total	Country, sector	International I-O data (WIOD, TiVA); U.S. I-O table and gross trade data (Comtrade, BACI, WITS)	Chapter 4, p. 80

Note: BACI = International Trade database by CEPII; BEC = Broad Economic Categories; I-O = input-output; TiVA = Trade in Value Added; WIOD = World Input-Output Database; WITS = World Integrated Trade Solution.

- *Ideas.* Buyers that aim to create value addition from GVC participation are likely to be active buyers of international patents and foreign technology licenses. The existence or absence of a sound framework for intellectual property is likely to be associated with buyers specializing in higher value-added tasks—unless GVCs happen predominantly or exclusively within the boundaries of multinational corporations.
- *Investments.* Buyers are likely to observe foreign direct investment (FDI) inflows and high FDI stocks in sectors and products of GVC specialization, sometimes also associated with FDI in downstream or upstream sectors. If a country is a strong buyer overall, support for upstream services is also likely to be of interest to foreign investors, including banks and companies in distribution, transport, telecommunications, and so on.

Notes

1. The share of imported intermediates in gross imports, IIM, is defined as $IIM_{cs} = \frac{IMINP_{cs}}{IMGR_{cs}}$ where IMINP denotes intermediate imports and IMGR gross imports. The measure is easily available; intermediates can, for instance, be detected using the BEC classification in appendix B. It enables analysis of the extent to which a buyer imports intermediate inputs. Categorizations of the numerator informed by technical considerations, such as those discussed previously and reported in appendixes C to E, are also possible. Intermediates include energy imports.
2. I2EB_IMINP: $I2EB\_IMINP_{cs} = \frac{I2EB_{cs}}{IMINP_{cs}}$ where I2EB denotes the buyer's intermediate imports embodied in its gross exports and IMINP the buyer's total intermediate imports in a sector.
3. OECD-WTO 2013.
4. Baldwin and Lopez-Gonzalez 2013.
5. Baldwin and Lopez-Gonzalez 2013.
6. Technically, the upstream-length index—which Fally (2011) denotes as "N" because it can be interpreted as the number of upstream stages—is defined as $N_{cs} = 1 + \sum_{br} \mu_{br} N_{br}$. Here, N_{cs} is the GVC weighted number of stages for country "*c*" in sector "*s*." It is 1 (for the processing done in country *c*) plus a weighted sum of the length of the GVC for inputs that country *c*'s sector *s* uses. The weights are the value shares of inputs from partner nation *b*'s sector *r* (that total is defined for each nation, but the national subscript is omitted to reduce clutter in the formula). The formula focuses on international stages, but the same formula can be applied to parts sourced domestically by sector *s*, which allows the analysis to quantify the length of the domestic chain too.

References

Baldwin, Richard, and Javier Lopez-Gonzalez. 2013. "Supply-Chain Trade: A Portrait of Global Patterns and Several Testable Hypotheses." NBER Working Paper 18957, National Bureau of Economic Research, Cambridge, MA.

DeBacker, Koen, and Sébastien Miroudot. 2013. "Mapping Global Value Chains." OECD Trade Policy Papers No. 159, Organisation for Economic Co-operation and Development Publishing, Paris.

Fally, Thibault. 2011. "On the Fragmentation of Production in the U.S." University of Colorado, Boulder. http://sciie.ucsc.edu/14AIEC/Fragmentation_Fally.pdf.

OECD and WTO (Organisation for Economic Co-operation and Development and World Trade Organization). 2013. Aid for Trade at a Glance 2013: Linking to Value Chains. Paris: Organisation for Economic Co-operation and Development.

Raj, Anasuja. 2014. "Peer Countries." World Bank, Washington, DC.

World Bank. 2014. "Boosting Trade Competitiveness." *Malaysia Economic Monitor,* June 2014, Washington, DC.

Chapter 5

SELLER-RELATED MEASURES

Introduction

The global value chain (GVC) participation indicators discussed in chapter 4 focus on the sourcing side in GVCs. The touchstone question was: where are a country's exports made, and where is the value created? Key questions for the selling dimension are: who are the ultimate customers for a country's value added, and to what countries is the country exporting its value added? Australia, for example, exports iron ore to China, but part of that product ends up in the United States and Germany rather than China. That is the seller's perspective, as shown on the right-hand side in figures 3.4 to 3.9 in chapter 3.

Intermediates in Output or Gross Exports

A first basic measure of the seller's involvement in the production of inputs, as opposed to final goods, is the share of intermediates in gross output.[1] This measure is akin to the share of intermediates in gross imports presented in chapter 4, but focuses on domestic production rather than trade. The measure quantifies participation in GVCs, measured by the importance of intermediates in a country's overall production.[2] Interesting variations of this measure can be constructed by focusing on different types of intermediate inputs, using one or more of the informed classifications illustrated in chapter 3 and reported in appendixes B to E or by identifying production by clusters, as discussed in chapter 3 and appendix F.[3] However, the measure suffers from two main limitations. First, it is useful if it is quantified at a very disaggregated level. Therefore, to be useful, the measure requires survey, industry, or firm data sufficiently disaggregated to disentangle production according to one of the classifications. Second, the measure does not indicate whether intermediate output is used domestically or exported.

The share of intermediates in gross exports takes the exporting perspective into account. Again, the intermediates can be identified according to one of the informed classifications discussed in chapter 3 and appendixes B–F. In some countries, such as Malaysia, intermediates dominate the export basket (see figure 3.1 in chapter 3). This measure quantifies GVC participation, measured by the importance of intermediates in the export basket of a country or, put differently, whether the country supplies products used as intermediates for further processing in other countries. Over time, the measure for specific countries and sectors—and relative to peers—can provide a first-pass indication of whether a country has become a more important supplier in GVCs. The same limitations plague this measure as for the share of intermediates in gross imports, which is discussed in chapter 4. The measures do not reveal the use of the inputs in the export destination—whether they are used domestically or processed and exported to third countries. The measure that addresses this caveat focuses on the role of foreign inputs or value added for third countries' exports.

Before turning to that topic, however, there are two stylized facts about intermediate exports worldwide that are worth highlighting. First, the share of intermediates in gross exports has increased over the past one and a half decades (figure 5.1), which reflects greater global fragmentation of production, but may also be the result of rising commodity prices, especially in the 2000s. Second, the share is slightly higher for low- and middle-income countries, which

Figure 5.1. Intermediate Exports, 1996–2012

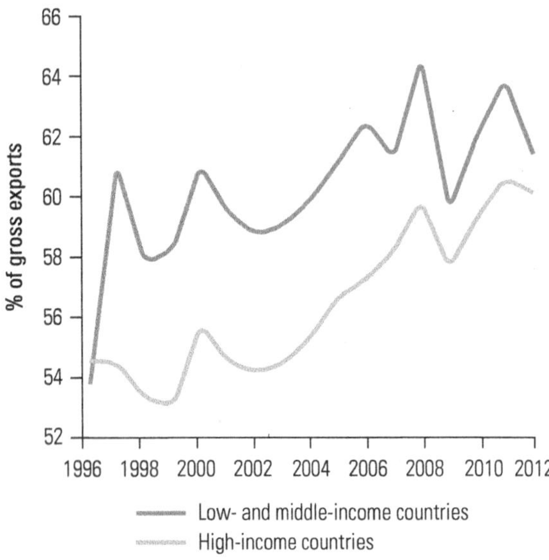

Source: Adapted from the United Nations Comtrade database.
Note: Calculations are based on the Broad Economic Categories classification (see appendix B).

suggests that high-income countries export more final goods, although the difference has become narrower since the late 1990s.

I2E Trade in Gross Exports

The indicator importing to exports (I2E) in gross exports measures intermediates sold by a country to a buyer for use in the buyer's exports (I2E from the buyer's perspective) as a percentage of the seller's gross exports.[4] The measure can be computed for the economy as a whole and for individual sectors.

Figures 3.4 to 3.9 in chapter 3 show the measure (the selling side) for Japan, China, Poland, Mexico, Germany, and the United States, respectively. The figures show, for example, that in 2011 over 10 percent of Japan's gross exports consisted of intermediate goods sold to China and subsequently embodied in Chinese exports (figure 3.4, right side). Similarly, almost 6 percent of Poland's gross exports contained I2E goods sold to Germany and embodied in German exports (figure 3.8, right side).

Domestic Value Added in Gross Exports of Third Countries

This indicator is very similar to the previous one, as it indicates the contribution of domestically produced intermediates to exports in third countries. The only difference is that this indicator accounts only for the seller's intermediates that are domestically produced, whereas in the previous case the intermediates could also contain some foreign value added. The portion of a country's exports used as imported inputs in the buyers' exports is formalized as DVA3EX.[5] DVA3EX can be related to the total gross exports in a country to obtain DVA3EX_EX.

From 1995 to 2011, almost all countries increased their GVC participation; the few exceptions were Cambodia, Croatia, and Luxembourg (figure 5.2). The increase was partly the mechanical effect of longer value chains and increasing specialization in GVCs worldwide. Nevertheless, cross-country differences exist. The leading countries are all natural resource exporters, including Brunei Darussalam, Norway, the Russian Federation, and Saudi Arabia, whose gross exports consisted of 38 to 43 percent domestic value added embodied in third countries' exports. Japan and the United States—two large, non-natural resource–intensive countries—did not come very far (at approximately 33 and 25 percent, respectively). On the other side of the spectrum are countries with very low export shares of domestic value added embodied in third countries' exports, ranging from only 12 percent in Cambodia and Luxembourg, to 14 to 16 percent in China, Croatia, Ireland, Mexico, Thailand, Turkey, and Vietnam.

The aggregate measure tends to give a somewhat biased picture, because natural resource–intensive countries, especially oil and gas exporters, unsurprisingly show the largest shares. It therefore makes sense to show this indicator excluding mining and quarrying and coke, refined petroleum products, and nuclear fuel in the numerator (figure 5.3). The indicator for total gross exports remains in the denominator. The picture is somewhat different from the previous figure, with natural resource–intensive exporters ranked behind Japan and closer to non-natural resource–intensive countries. Despite the correction, Brunei Darussalam, Chile, Norway, Russia, and Saudi Arabia still exhibit one of the largest shares: 29 to 30 percent of their total gross exports is made up of domestic value added subsequently embodied in third countries' exports. Among high-income countries, Austria; Iceland; Japan; the Republic of Korea; the Netherlands; Switzerland; Taiwan, China; and the United States show relatively large shares of 24 to 32 percent.

Another useful way to look at the data is through changes in global market share. To the extent that such

Figure 5.2. Domestic Value Added Embodied in Third Countries' Exports, 1995 and 2011

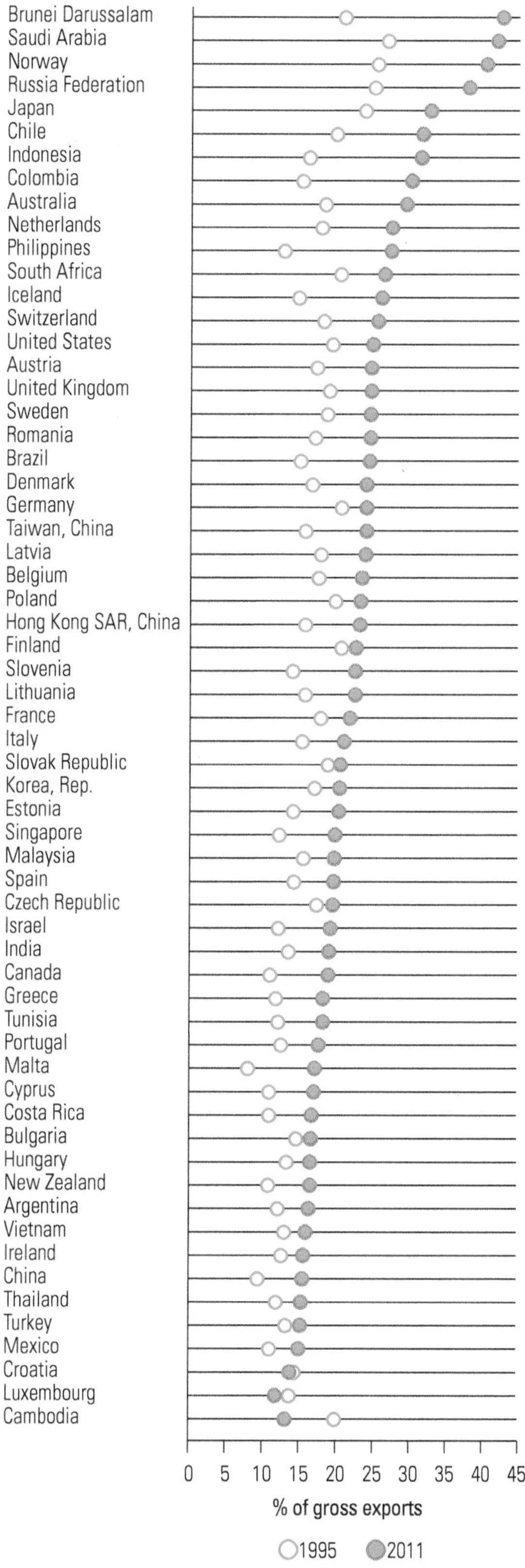

Source: Adapted from the Organisation for Economic Co-operation and Development–World Trade Organization Trade in Value Added database.

changes can be considered an indicator of competitiveness,[6] measuring a country's global market share changes in domestic value added embodied in third countries' exports can be considered a measure of increasing comparative advantage in GVCs. Figure 5.4 illustrates this measure for the selection of emerging countries used in the previous examples: Chile, China, Korea, Malaysia, Mexico, the Philippines, Poland, Singapore, South Africa, Thailand, and Vietnam. All market shares are expressed in percent of global value added embodied in third countries' exports. All countries in the sample—except South Africa—saw their market share increase. The most spectacular increase was for China, which jumped from 1.3 percent to 6.6 percent in global value-added market share.

Similar indicators can be constructed at the sector level. Figure 5.5 shows examples of the chemicals and chemical products and the electrical and optical (E&O) equipment sectors. In chemicals and chemical products (highlighted in green), global market shares are broadly unchanged over the period—except for China, which had a market share of less than 1 percent in 1995 and almost 5 percent in 2011; Japan, whose value-added market share diminished from 7.3 to 4.3 percent; and Germany, whose value-added market share shrunk by almost 40 percent during this period. In E&O (highlighted in yellow), the increase was spectacular for the Asian countries (except Japan and Singapore), including China, Korea, Malaysia, and Vietnam, which managed to gain a small but valuable market share (0.35 percent), given that it was starting from close to nothing.

Figure 5.6 illustrates another indicator of competitiveness and specialization patterns—the revealed comparative advantage (RCA) indicator for the E&O and chemical sectors. The figure shows the way in which countries' comparative positions changed between 1995 and 2011. Instead of using gross exports, the measure is constructed using domestic value added embodied in gross exports. This method is a more accurate representation of comparative advantage, because it nets out foreign value added imported into the country (see chapter 4). As in traditional RCA measures, a country is said to have a comparative advantage in the sector if the RCA measure is greater than 1 (to the right of the RCA line). All Asian countries in the sample—Vietnam aside—reveal a comparative advantage in E&O goods. Chile, Poland, South Africa, the United States, and Vietnam, by contrast, post a relatively weak specialization in E&O. From a dynamic point of view, the Philippines shows

Figure 5.3. **Domestic Value Added Embodied in Third Countries' Exports Excluding Mining and Quarrying and Coke, Refined Petroleum Products, and Nuclear Fuel, 2011**

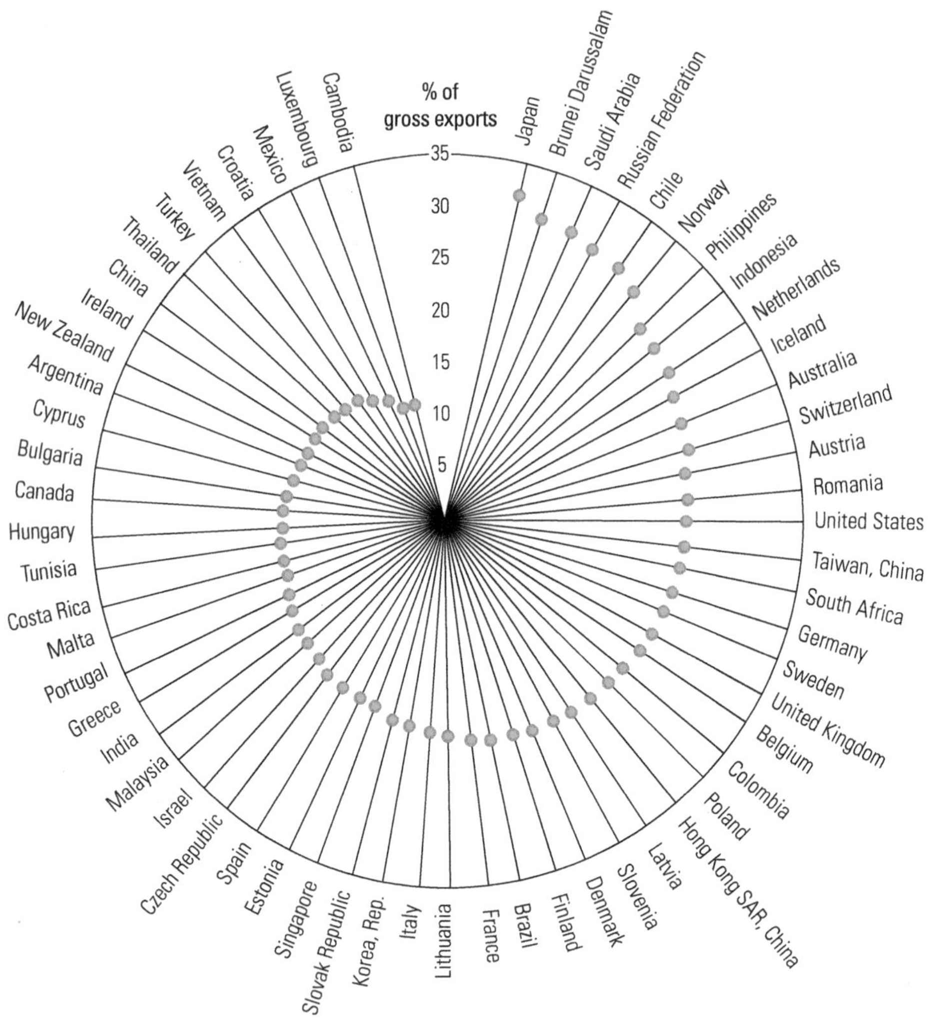

Source: Adapted from the Organisation for Economic Co-operation and Development–World Trade Organization Trade in Value Added database.
Note: Gross exports include the country's total exports.

a sizable reorientation toward E&O, with an RCA that went from 2 in 1995 to almost 3 in 2011. In chemicals, only five countries report an RCA greater than 1: Germany, Korea, Singapore, Thailand, and the United States. These results mesh with results found throughout the indicators—that Southeast Asia as a region is important for value-added trade in E&O goods, as opposed to chemicals, for which value added is concentrated in other world regions.

From a seller's perspective, identifying which foreign sources most demand its exported value added is useful. Domestic value added can be separated by destination countries. Figures 5.7 to 5.9 focus on the geographic side and show, for the countries in the preceding sample, the shares of domestic value added in gross exports in total, as well as in E&O and chemicals by destination region. The European Union (EU), East Asia, and North American Free Trade Agreement (NAFTA) countries differ in importance for those sectors.

In the aggregate, as well as for E&O, the most important trend has been the shift of Asian countries from NAFTA countries toward intraregional demand. For example, in 2011, Thailand's overall exports in value-added terms went mostly to destinations in East Asia (32 percent), other destinations (28.4 percent), and ASEAN countries (16.8 percent), and only marginally to the EU and NAFTA (10.5 and 10.4 percent, respectively). The Asian comparator countries display similar patterns.

Figure 5.4. Domestic Value Added Embodied in Third Countries' Exports, Global Market Share, Selected Countries, 1995 and 2011

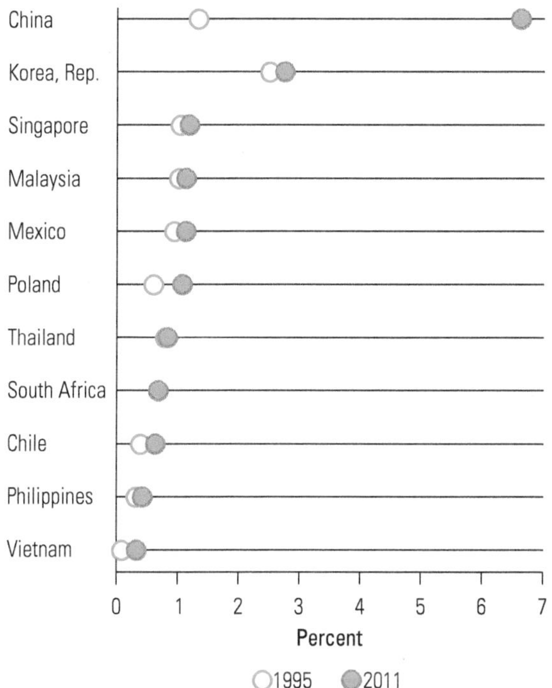

Source: Adapted from the Organisation for Economic Co-operation and Development–World Trade Organization Trade in Value Added database.

Figure 5.5. Domestic Value Added Embodied in Third Countries' Exports, Global Market Share, Chemicals and Chemical Products and Electrical and Optical Equipment, Selected Countries, 1995 and 2011

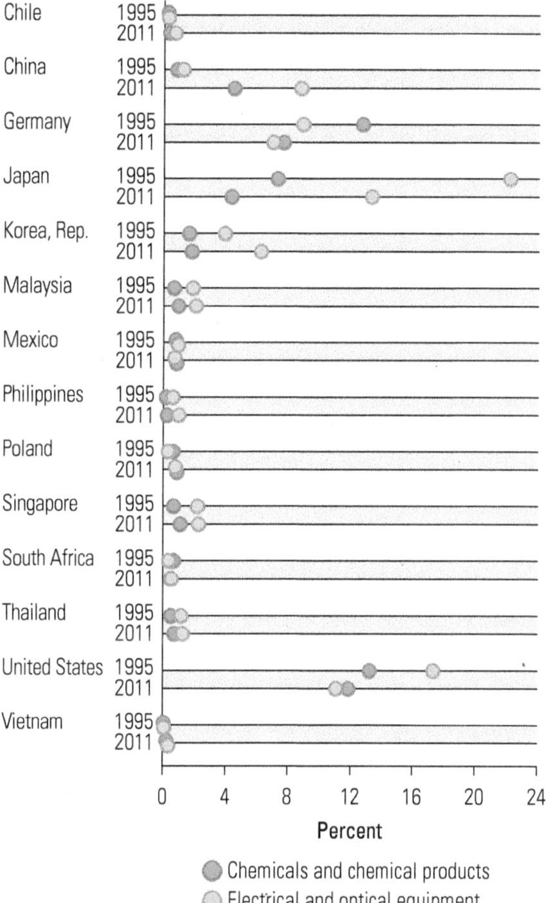

Source: Adapted from the Organisation for Economic Co-operation and Development–World Trade Organization Trade in Value Added database.

Mexico's total domestic value added in gross exports in 2011 went, in large part, to NAFTA and Poland's mostly to the EU. Finally, Germany's value added was exported to the EU first (52 percent), then to other destinations (22 percent), and only marginally to countries in East Asia and NAFTA (11.7 and 10.4 percent, respectively). U.S. exports of domestic value added were more spread out: EU (24 percent), NAFTA (23 percent), other destinations (23 percent), East Asia (19 percent), and South and Central America and ASEAN (6 and 5 percent, respectively).

Who Are the Ultimate Consumers of a Country's Value Added? Value Added in Final Domestic Demand

The previous discussion focused on direct links between a country and the buyers of its exports. The Trade in Value Added (TiVA) and World Input-Output databases can also provide an understanding of the final consumers of a country's value-added activities. The TiVA database contains a set of readily available indicators that focus on the share of value added in final demand by country of origin. The concepts can be understood by revisiting the simplified Mexican car industry example, which assumes that car production uses only two types of intermediate inputs: (1) iron and steel, and (2) rubber and plastics.

Figure 5.10, panel a, shows the observed trade flow between three countries (Australia, Mexico, and the United States). Australia and the United States export iron and steel to Mexico, and the United States also exports rubber and plastics to Mexico. Mexico exports final cars to the United States. The implicit trade flows—which keep track of the ultimate consumers of value added—are shown in figure 5.10, panel b. Australia's iron and steel sector is really exporting to U.S. consumers, not Mexican ones, and the United States is "exporting" iron and steel to itself.

Figure 5.6. RCA in Chemicals and Chemical Products and Electrical and Optical Equipment, 1995 and 2011

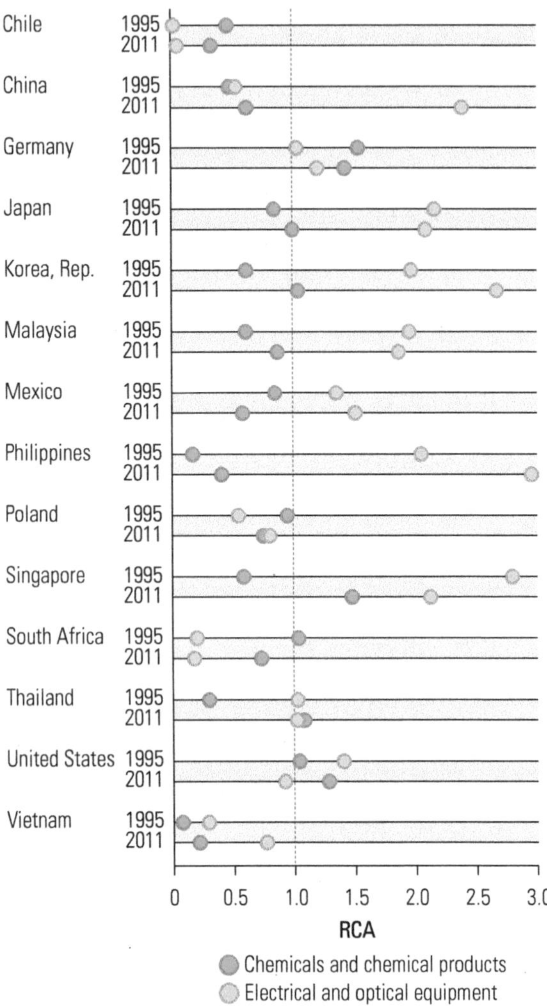

Source: Adapted from the Organisation for Economic Co-operation and Development–World Trade Organization Trade in Value Added database.
Note: RCA line = 1. RCA = revealed comparative advantage.

Figure 5.7. Domestic Value Added in Gross Exports, by Destination Region, 1995 and 2011

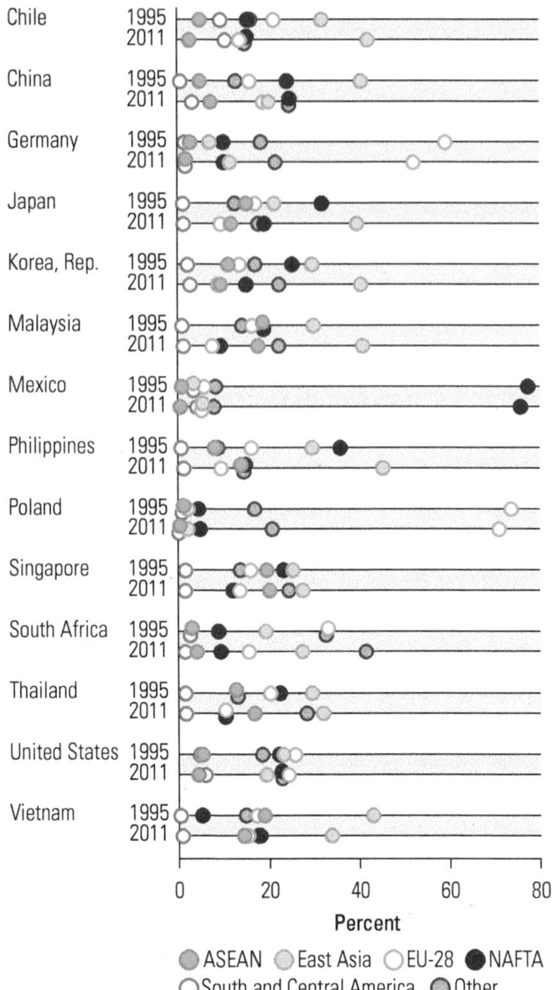

Source: Adapted from the Organisation for Economic Co-operation and Development–World Trade Organization Trade in Value Added database.
Note: ASEAN = Association of Southeast Asian Nations; EU = European Union; NAFTA = North American Free Trade Agreement.

This sort of information is useful in several ways. For example, Australian steel exports are affected by any U.S. trade barriers against Mexican autos. Thus, U.S.–Australian trade relations are not solely dependent on their bilateral trade. Moreover, the information may be helpful in understanding how changes in demand patterns—say, caused by an economic crisis or a simple recession—can affect a country's exports.

The domestic value added embodied in foreign final demand—FDDVA in the TiVA data set—shows how sectors export value through direct final exports and indirect exports of intermediates by way of other countries to foreign final consumers (households, charities, government, and investment). The measure illustrates the full upstream impact of final demand in foreign markets on domestic output.

The FDDVA measure looks at the sales side of this "final consumer" measure. A corresponding measure on the buying side also exists—the foreign value added embodied in domestic final demand (FDFVA)—which looks at where the value is added in a particular country's final demand. This measure can be interpreted as "imports in value added."[7]

The value added in final demand is a function of trade openness and GVC integration. As expected, the domestic value added embodied in foreign final demand as a share of a country's gross domestic product (GDP), FDDVA_GDP, is largest in small, open economies, such as Brunei Darussalam, Luxembourg, and Singapore. The indicator is also large in countries whose inputs are exported to other countries, including countries in Eastern

Figure 5.8. Domestic Value Added in Gross Exports in Electrical and Optical Equipment, by Destination Region, 1995 and 2011

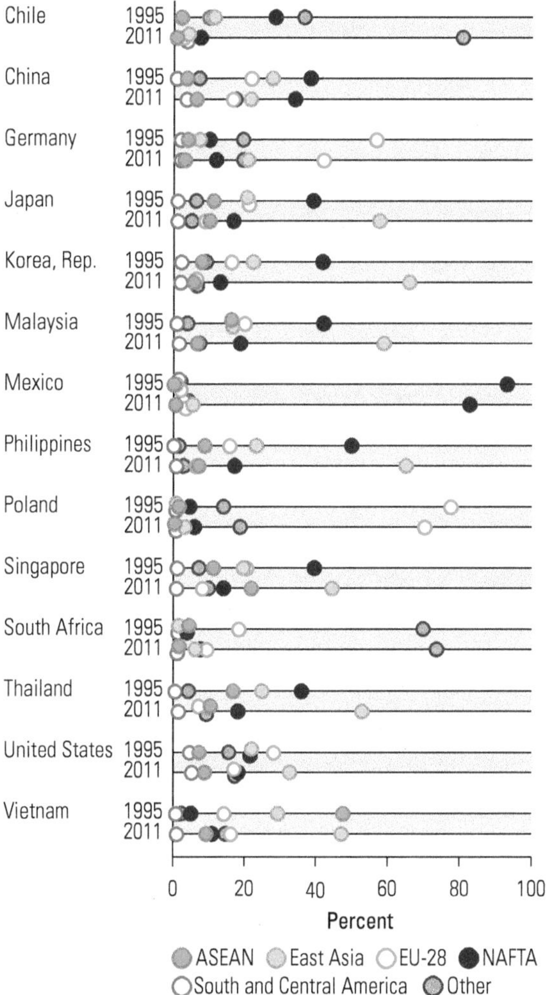

Source: Adapted from the Organisation for Economic Co-operation and Development–World Trade Organization Trade in Value Added database.
Note: ASEAN = Association of Southeast Asian Nations; EU = European Union; NAFTA = North American Free Trade Agreement.

Figure 5.9. Domestic Value Added in Gross Exports in Chemicals and Chemical Products, by Destination Region, 1995 and 2011

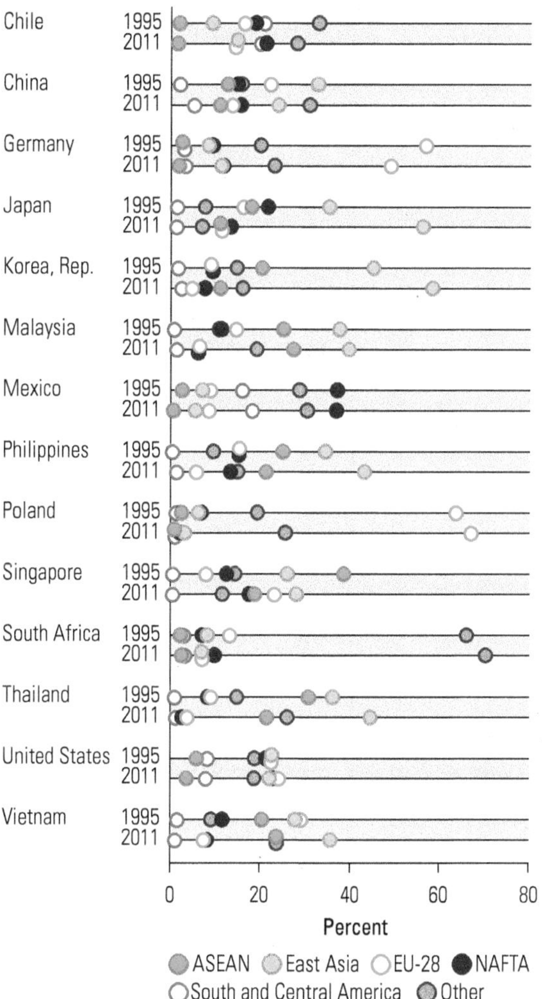

Source: Adapted from the Organisation for Economic Co-operation and Development–World Trade Organization Trade in Value Added database.
Note: ASEAN = Association of Southeast Asian Nations; EU = European Union; NAFTA = North American Free Trade Agreement.

Europe and Southeast Asia. The indicator is small in large countries, such as Japan and the United States (figure 5.11).

Foreign value added embodied in domestic final demand as a share of GDP, FDFVA_GDP, is highest in countries well integrated in GVCs and dependent on imported inputs from other countries, especially in Eastern Europe and Southeast Asia (figure 5.12).

The indicator also allows for identification of the ultimate buyer of a country's value added, which figure 5.13 shows for the set of selected countries used in the previous examples. The main final buyers of the value added of all countries in the data set are China and the United States. The exception is Poland, whose value added is ultimately consumed in Germany, the United Kingdom, France, Italy, and the United States, in that order. The markets of China, Germany, Japan, Mexico, the Philippines, Singapore, and Vietnam rely most on the United States for final demand of its value-added exports, with Mexico a clear outlier (64 percent). China is the most important final consumer for some countries' value added, including Chile, Korea, Malaysia, South Africa, and Thailand, while Japan also matters strongly as final consumer for all countries in the sample except Germany and Poland.

This trend is different from that observed when considering gross exports, in which the importance of the United States for many of the countries in the sample was less pronounced for overall exports.

Figure 5.10. The Ultimate Consumers of a Country's Export Value Added

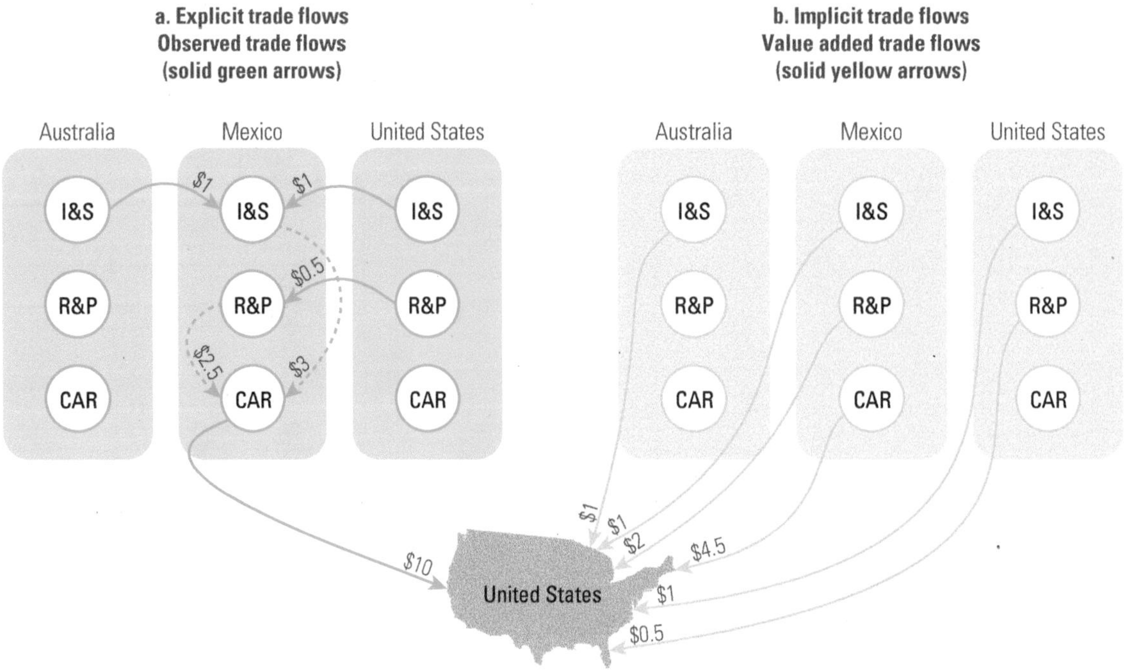

Source: Adapted from Baldwin and Lopez-Gonzalez 2013, 10.
Note: The car exports from Mexico to the United States (worth US$10 million) contain intermediates of iron and steel worth US$3 million and intermediates of rubber and plastics worth US$2.5 million (dashed green arrows). For more detail, see figure 4.10 (chapter 4). I&S = iron and steel; R&P = rubber and plastics.

Using the example of Malaysia, China is responsible for 16 percent of Malaysia's domestic value added embodied in foreign final demand. Japan and the United States (12 percent each) are also important final consumers of Malaysia's domestic value added embodied in foreign final demand. Using gross exports, the United States accounts, instead, for 9 percent of total Malaysian exports, only the fourth largest export partner behind Singapore (14 percent), China (13 percent), and Japan (12 percent).

Table 5.1 summarizes the indicators of value added embodied in final demand available in the TiVA database.

Length of Selling Chains: Distance to Final Demand

GVC length on the buying side of importing to export measures the number of upstream stages for a specific sector in a specific country. Another useful measure looks at a similar concept on the sales side. That measure gauges the "upstreamness" of a country's exports—roughly, the number of downstream stages between the country's producers and final consumers. Antràs and others (2012) call it the "distance to final demand."

For example, countries specialized in very upstream activities produce raw materials—say, iron ore—or the intangibles at the start of the production process—say, research and design. Countries that specialize in, for example, final assembly or customer services will be very close to final demand. Countries in activities at the center of the value chain focus on the standardized, labor-intensive manufacturing jobs. However, these assumptions do not hold for every type of production and GVC. They are true for some sectors and value chains (such as electronics, particularly in East Asia), but not for others (such as high-end furniture manufacturing, where acquisition of raw materials and design usually take place at the same stage of production).[8]

Keeping in mind the caveats, the analysis that follows asks how to assign a specific country to a category of upstreamness. The analysis draws on the work of Chor (2014), and applies it to measure where a country (Malaysia in our example) is positioned along the global production line. The analysis assesses whether Malaysia's exports tend to be in relatively upstream industries, near the start of the production process and far from final demand, or in downstream industries, closer to the final consumer. Chor (2014) calculates a measure of the production

Figure 5.11. Domestic Value Added Embodied in Foreign Final Demand, 2011

Brunei Darussalam
Luxembourg
Singapore
Ireland
Malaysia
Saudi Arabia
Vietnam
Hungary
Estonia
Iceland
Malta
Slovak Republic
Thailand
Czech Republic
Bulgaria
Taiwan, China
Slovenia
Hong Kong SAR, China
Switzerland
Norway
Cambodia
Cyprus
Latvia
Lithuania
Austria
Korea, Rep.
Belgium
Tunisia
Sweden
Denmark
Chile
Germany
Poland
Costa Rica
Netherlands
Russian Federation
Croatia
Finland
Israel
New Zealand
Romania
Portugal
South Africa
United Kingdom
Philippines
Spain
Canada
Indonesia
Italy
Mexico
France
Argentina
Australia
Greece
India
Turkey
Colombia
China
Japan
Brazil
United States

0 15 30 45 60 75
% of GDP

Source: Adapted from the Organisation for Economic Co-operation and Development–World Trade Organization Trade in Value Added database.

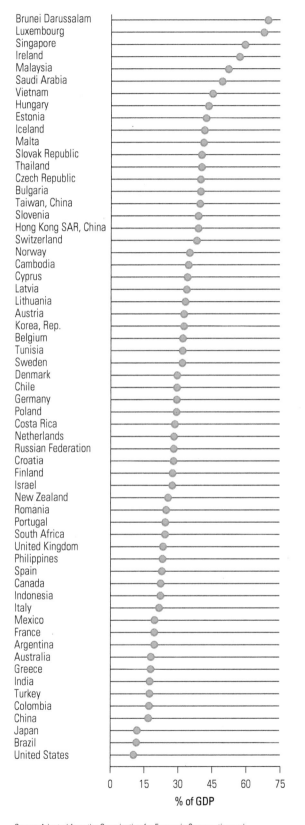

Figure 5.12. Foreign Value Added Embodied in Domestic Final Demand, 2011

Source: Adapted from the Organisation for Economic Co-operation and Development–World Trade Organization Trade in Value Added database.

Figure 5.13. Domestic Value Added in Foreign Final Demand, Top Five Partner Shares, Selected Exporters, 2011

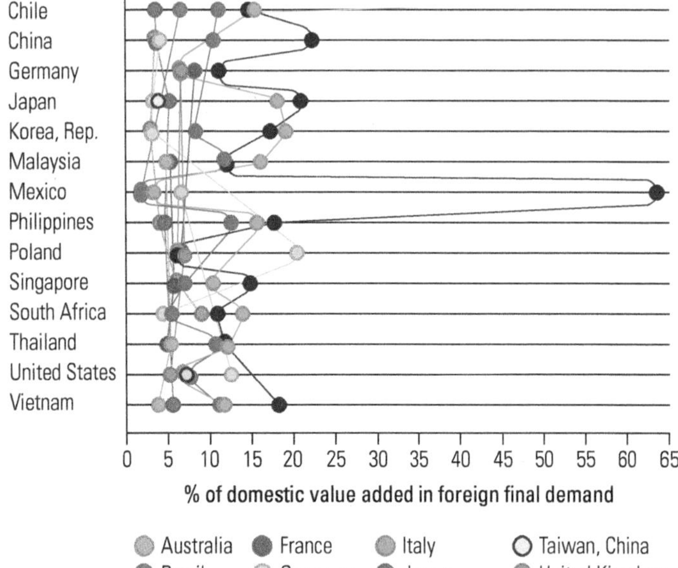

Source: Adapted from the Organisation for Economic Co-operation and Development–World Trade Organization Trade in Value Added database

line position, or upstreamness, for 426 industries (279 of which are manufacturing) using 2002 data from U.S. input-output (I-O) tables. The measure is based on I-O relationships, or how much sector u purchases from each sector s as inputs.[9]

The average position of Malaysia's exports from final demand can then be calculated as the average upstreamness measure for each industry, weighted by the importance of that industry in Malaysia's export basket. Figure 5.14 provides that calculation for each year from 2000 to 2013 for total exports, as well as electrical and electronic (E&E) equipment (combined and separately), petrochemicals, and manufacturing exports.

The petrochemical industry remains the furthest from final demand, significantly more so than total exports or E&E. The electrical industry is the closest, followed by manufacturing and electronics. E&E and manufacturing exports have moved upstream since 2000—or further away from final demand—unlike petrochemicals, which has moved downstream (despite remaining an upstream industry in general).

Compared with its peers, Malaysia has one of the highest upstreamness measures, behind only Australia, Chile, Indonesia, and South Africa (figure 5.15). This finding is no surprise, given that the most upstream industries tend to be related to the extraction and processing of raw materials and resources, and those comparator countries are all natural resource exporters. The results show that in the GVCs in which Malaysia participates, the country maintains a position relatively further from final consumption.

Among Malaysia's peers, only two countries have managed to move downstream (New Zealand and Vietnam), and two other countries (the Philippines and Poland) have moved marginally downstream. The largest upstream movers are Australia; Chile; Hong Kong SAR, China; Indonesia; Malaysia; and South Africa. Most countries have increased their upstreamness because the overall lengths of the value chains have increased with the fragmentation of production, and the countries herein are no exception. Moreover, the offshoring-outsourcing process that lengthens GVCs primarily tends to affect the early stages of production, so that the countries that are most upstream are likely to be relatively more affected. That fact notwithstanding, a new wave of service offshoring and outsourcing has been taking place in recent years, which may affect such conclusions in the future.

Table 5.1 Indicators of Value Added Embodied in Final Demand

Indicator	Definition
FDDVA	Domestic value added embodied in foreign final demand, by importing country and exporting sector (US$)
FDDVASH	FDDVA, by importing country and exporting sector (% of total FDDVA)
FDDVA_GDP	FDDVA, by importing country and exporting sector (% of GDP)
FDFVA	Foreign value added embodied in domestic final demand, by origin country and origin sector (US$)
FDFVASH	FDFVA, by origin country and origin sector (% of total FDFVA)
FDFVA_GDP	FDFVA, by origin country and origin sector (% of GDP)
TSVAFD	Bilateral trade balances in value added, by partner country, FDDVA minus FDFVA (US$)
TSVAFD_GDP	Bilateral trade balances in value added, by partner country (% of GDP)
TSVAFD_TSGR	Difference in trade surpluses, value added in final demand minus gross trade

Source: Adapted from the Organisation for Economic Co-operation and Development–World Trade Organization Trade in Value Added database.
Note: These indicators are in the Trade in Value Added database, which covers 61 economies. GDP = gross domestic product.

Domestic Gap between Buying and Selling Chains

A final useful metric is to combine import and export upstreamness to compute the domestic gap between the buying and selling chains of individual sectors (for the concept of upstreamness or distance to final demand, see the previous section). We calculate the export and import upstreamness for each year from 2000 to 2013 for total trade as well as trade in the E&E and petrochemical industries of Malaysia. Figure 5.16 plots the export or import upstreamness on the left axis, and their difference (import upstreamness minus export upstreamness) on the right axis, which is an indicator of the domestic gap between the buying and selling chains. A positive gap indicates that exports are relatively more downstream compared with the import mix, or that exports are closer to final demand than are imports. This is the case in economies in which the manufacturing sector has been a key source of export-led growth, such as China, Japan, and Thailand. Conversely, a negative gap indicates that a country's export profile is more upstream than its import profile. This is the case in economies whose exports are concentrated in agricultural products and primary commodities, such as Australia and New Zealand. Another scenario is that the negative gap indicates that the country is a large importer of finished consumer goods, rather than being a reflection of the composition of its exports; the United States is one example.

The domestic gap between the buying and selling chains in Malaysia has been changing since 2000. Whereas it was positive before 2010, it has become negative since then. The shift is being driven by exports that have become more upstream or further from final demand; import upstreamness has not changed significantly over the past decade. Malaysia is apparently becoming less plugged into global production lines as an importer of upstream intermediate inputs that are subsequently processed and assembled.

Neither E&E nor petrochemicals seems to be behind the change. Although the domestic gap of the E&E industry has become smaller since 2008, it remains positive but low—as the preceding analysis of limited GVC participation in E&E shows—which points to the weak selling side. The domestic gap of the petrochemicals industry has been mainly negative since 2002, which indicates that Malaysia imports more complex (downstream) petrochemicals for domestic use than the less complex (upstream) petrochemicals that the country sells in GVCs.

Figure 5.14. Upstreamness of Industries in Malaysia

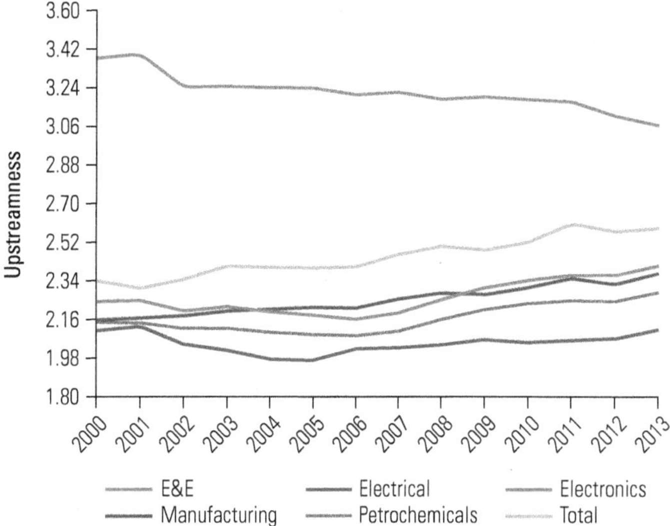

Sources: Adapted from Chor 2014; United Nations Comtrade.
Note: E&E = electrical and electronic.

Figure 5.15. Upstreamness in Malaysia and Comparators, 2012 and Progression Since 2000

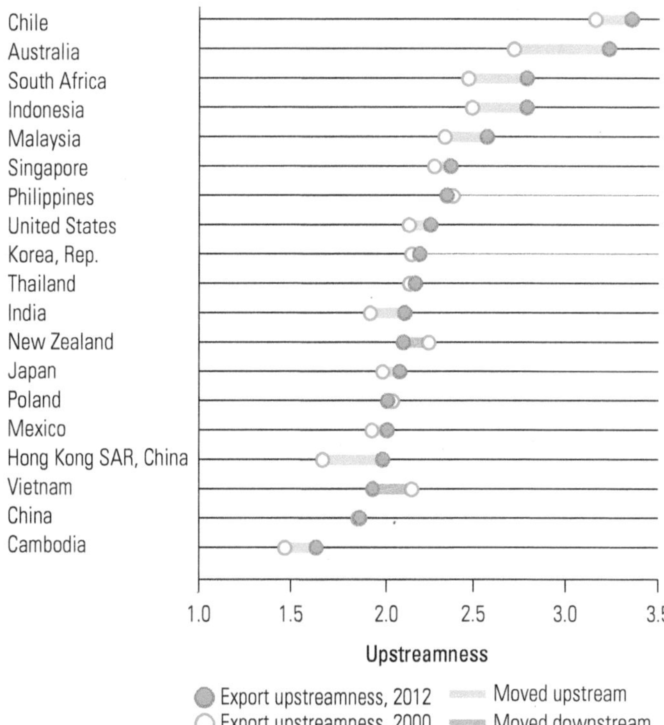

Sources: Adapted from Chor 2014; United Nations Comtrade.

Figure 5.16. Import Upstreamness, Export Upstreamness, and Domestic Gap, Malaysia, 2000–13

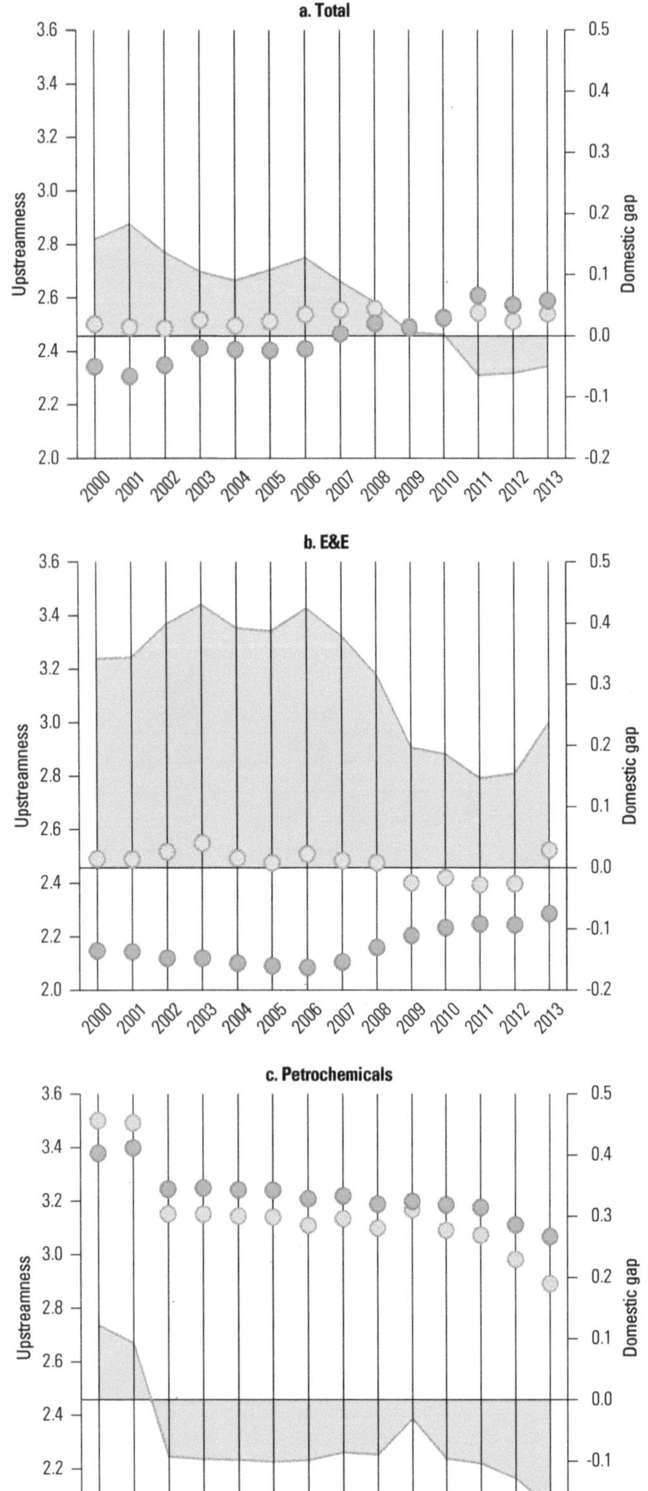

Sources: Based on the methodology in Chor 2014 and data from United Nations Comtrade.
Note: E&E = electrical and electronic equipment.

Seller Dimension: Summary

Table 5.2 summarizes the main measures of the seller dimension. The table indicates whether the measures are available for goods tasks, services tasks, or both, as well as the level of analysis (country, sector, or firm). For easy reference, the table refers to the respective sections in the book where the measures are introduced. For more information on the underlying data sets, see appendixes G and H.

GVCs are a multidimensional phenomenon that involves the flow of factors of production, as shown in chapter 1. From the seller's perspective, several measures can be analyzed to complement the task-based assessment that has been discussed. Although a wider set of examples can be found in table A.1 in appendix A, the following are some of the main indicators to consider:

- *Wages.* Low or high wages (relative to GVC partner countries) are a priori indeterminate. High wages are likely to be associated with sellers who are also owners of GVC assets, technology, and know-how.
- *Ideas.* Countries specializing in high value-added tasks are likely to export a lot of royalties and fee services. The existence or absence of a sound framework for intellectual property is likely to be associated with sellers specializing in higher value-added tasks, unless GVCs are predominantly or exclusively within the boundaries of multinational corporations.
- *Investment.* Outward direct investment is more prevalent for sellers than for buyers, predominantly in sectors of high GVC intensity, aiming at fostering large-scale production abroad. Foreign direct investment tends to be preferred to non-equity modes in transactions that embody more sophisticated technology and know-how.

Table 5.2 Summary of the Main Seller-Related Measures

Measure	Task	Level of analysis	Data sources	Where to find in book?
Share of intermediates in total output	Goods and/or services	Country, sector, firm	Production data (national statistics, UN-Stat manufacturing data set, firm-level data)	Chapter 5, p. 87
Share of intermediates in total exports	Goods	Country, sector	Gross export data (Comtrade, BACI, WITS), categorized using informed classifications (broad economic category, parts and components, technical classifications)	Chapter 5, p. 87
Share of intermediates in total exports, range of exports, bundle of exported products, and countries	Goods	Country, sector, firm	Gross export data (customs firm-level), categorized using informed classifications (broad economic category, parts and components, technical classifications)	Chapter 5, p. 87
I2E trade (% of gross exports)	Goods and/or services	Country, sector	International I-O data (WIOD, TiVA, World Bank Export of Value Added database)	Chapter 5, p. 88
Domestic value added (% of gross value of output)	Goods and/or services	Country, sector	International I-O data (WIOD, World Bank Export of Value Added database)	Chapter 6, p. 110
Domestic value added in gross exports of third countries	Goods and/or services	Country, sector	International I-O data (WIOD, TiVA, World Bank Export of Value Added database)	Chapter 5, p. 88
Domestic value added in gross exports (direct and forward or backward links)	Goods and/or services	Country, sector	World Bank Export of Value Added database	Chapter 6, p. 110
Domestic value added embodied in foreign final demand (% of GDP)	Goods and/or services	Country, sector	International I-O data (WIOD, TiVA)	Chapter 5, p. 92
Foreign value added embodied in domestic final demand (% of GDP)	Goods and/or services	Country, sector	International I-O data (WIOD, TiVA)	Chapter 5, p. 92
Domestic supplier's share of output to multinationals in total output	Goods and/or services	Country, sector, firm	Enterprise surveys or other firm-level surveys	Chapter 6, p. 113
Domestic supplier's share of exports in output	Goods and/or services	Country, sector, firm	Enterprise surveys or other firm-level surveys	Chapter 6, p. 113
Length of selling chains	Total	Country, sector	International I-O data (WIOD, TiVA) or national I-O data (for example, U.S I-O tables), and trade data	Chapter 5, p. 94
Domestic gap between buying and selling chains	Goods and/or services	Country, sector, firm	International I-O data (WIOD, TiVA) or national I-O data (for example, U.S I-O tables), and trade data	Chapter 5, p. 97

Note: BACI = international trade database by CEPII; GDP = gross domestic product; I2E = importing to export; I-O = input-output; TiVA = Trade in Value Added database; WIOD = World Input-Output Database; WITS = World Integrated Trade Solution.

Notes

1. $IIO_{CS} = \frac{OUTINP_{cs}}{OUTGR_{cs}}$ where OUTINP denotes intermediate output and OUTGR denotes gross output in country *c* and sector *s*.

2. $IIE_{CS} = \frac{EXINP_{cs}}{EXGR_{cs}}$ where EXINP denotes intermediate exports and EXGR denotes gross exports in country *c* and sector *s*. Note that intermediates include energy exports.

3. For example, following the Broad Economic Categories (BEC) classification (appendix B), or by looking at technical or customized classifications (appendixes C and E), at parts and components (appendix D), or at specific clusters of activity (appendix F).

4. $I2ES\_EX_{CS} = \frac{I2ES_{cs}}{EXGR_{cs}}$ where I2ES denotes intermediates sold by a country that are embodied in gross exports of third countries and EXGR denotes the seller's gross exports in a sector.

5. $DVA3EX\_EX_{CS} = \frac{DVA3EX_{cs}}{EXGR_{cs}}$ where DVA3EX denotes domestic value added embodied in third countries' exports and EXGR denotes the seller's gross exports in a sector.

6. Gaulier and others (2013).
7. OECD (2013).
8. Taglioni and Winkler (2014) discuss this issue.
9. Formally, the measure of upstreamness of industry s is computed as

$$U_{IS} = 1 * \frac{F_s}{Y_s} + 2 * \frac{\sum_u^N = 1 d_{su} F_u}{Y_s} + 3 * \frac{\sum_u^N \sum_{v=1}^N d_{sv} d_{vu} F_u}{Y_s} + \cdots$$

where Y_s is the total output of the industry, F_s is the value of that output that goes to final uses (final consumption or investment), and d_{su} is the value of inputs from industry s that are required by industry u to produce \$1 of the latter's output. With this definition, an industry that has its entire output channeled to final uses, namely with $F_s = Y_s$, will have $U_s = 1$.

References

Antràs, Pol, Davin Chor, Thibault Fally, and Russell Hillberry. 2012. "Measuring the Upstreamness of Production and Trade Flows." *American Economic Review Papers and Proceedings* 102 (3): 412–16. DOI:10.1257/aer.102.3.412

Baldwin, Richard, and Javier Lopez-Gonzalez. 2013. "Supply-Chain Trade: A Portrait of Global Patterns and Several Testable Hypotheses." NBER Working Paper 18957, National Bureau of Economic Research, Cambridge, MA.

Chor, Davine. 2014. "Where Are Countries Positioned along Global Production Lines?" *Monetary Authority of Singapore Macroeconomic Review*, April: 94–99.

Gaulier, Guillaume, Gianluca Santoni, Daria Taglioni, and Soledad Zignago. 2013. "In the Wake of the Global Crisis: Evidence from a New Quarterly Database of Export Competitiveness, Volume 1." Policy Research Working Paper 6733, World Bank, Washington, DC.

OECD (Organisation for Economic Co-operation and Development). 2013. *Science, Technology, and Industry Scoreboard 2013: Innovation for Growth.* Paris: OECD.

Taglioni, Daria, and Deborah Winkler. 2014. "Making Global Value Chains Work for Development." Economic Premise No. 144, Poverty Reduction and Economic Management Network, World Bank, Washington, DC.

Chapter 6

OTHER MEASURES OF GVC PARTICIPATION: FROM MACRO TO MICRO

Introduction

This chapter goes beyond the buying and selling sides in global value chains (GVCs) and complements the measures illustrated in chapters 4 and 5 with additional useful measures of participation. First, the chapter illustrates how the buyer and seller dimensions can be combined to quantify an overall indicator (the GVC participation index). Second, the chapter focuses on network metrics. It shows how a country's position overall, in a sector, in a specific GVC, and with respect to individual products can be measured and visualized using network metrics. Third, the chapter pays special attention to the role of services in value added. Fourth, the chapter introduces measures of direct links in GVCs using firm-level data—the micro perspective.

GVC Participation Index

Combining two measures that were previously introduced on the buying and sales sides provides a single measure of a country's involvement in vertically fragmented production, as a user of foreign value added for its own exports and as a supplier of domestic value added embodied in intermediate goods or services used in other countries' exports. This measure is captured by the GVC participation index.[1]

Conceptually, the index can be broadly considered a GVC-specific measure of trade openness. The higher is the foreign value added embodied in gross exports (see chapter 4) and the higher is the value of domestic inputs exported to third countries and used in their exports (see chapter 5), the higher is the participation of a given country in the value chain. The index is measured as the percentage of the country's gross exports.

Figure 6.1 shows the GVC participation index for 61 economies worldwide (highlighted in blue).[2] The results suggest that geographic size—particularly relative to regional peers—seems to matter. Smaller economies—such as Luxembourg; Singapore; Slovak Republic; and Taiwan, China—have participation rates of 60 to 70 percent. The participation of larger countries is lower. The participation of middle-size countries—such as Brazil, Mexico, and Turkey—is 35 to 50 percent. The index for China (48 percent) is relatively low, comparable to those of Germany and Japan. China's participation index reflects very low Chinese value added in third countries' exports, as well as medium foreign value added in China's gross exports, as commonly perceived. In addition to country size, the distance to consumer markets is another determinant of the participation in GVCs, giving New Zealand, for example, one of the lowest indexes (less than 33 percent).

Figure 6.1 provides a clear indication of whether countries tend to be specialized in buying activities (foreign value added embodied in gross exports, or backward links, highlighted in green) or selling activities (domestic value added embodied in gross exports of third countries, or forward links, highlighted in yellow). The buying side plays a larger role in most countries, except for resource-intensive countries, especially Brunei Darussalam, Colombia, Norway, the Russian Federation, and Saudi Arabia. Figure 6.2 shows the GVC participation measure, excluding mining and quarrying, and coke, refined petroleum products, and nuclear fuel in the numerator. To assess the impact of mining and quarrying

Figure 6.1. GVC Participation Index, 2011

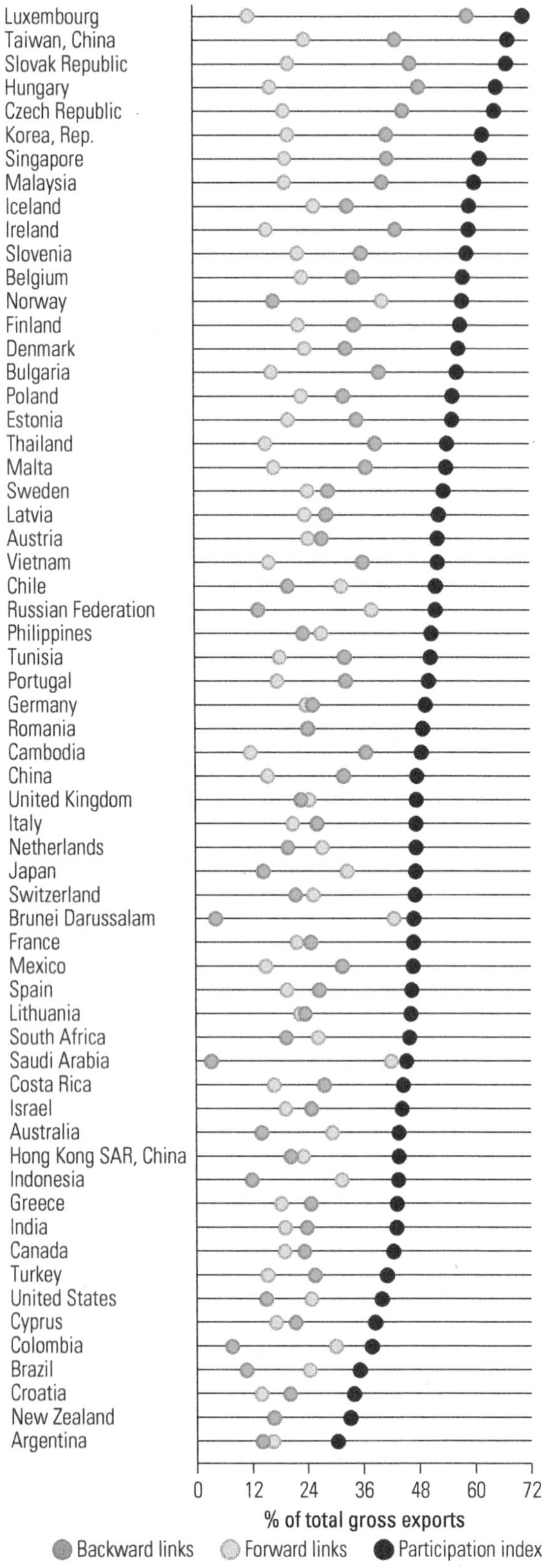

Source: Adapted from the Organisation for Economic Co-operation and Development–World Trade Organization Trade in Value Added database.

Figure 6.2. GVC Participation Index Excluding Mining and Quarrying and Coke, Refined Petroleum Products, and Nuclear Fuel in the Numerator, 2011

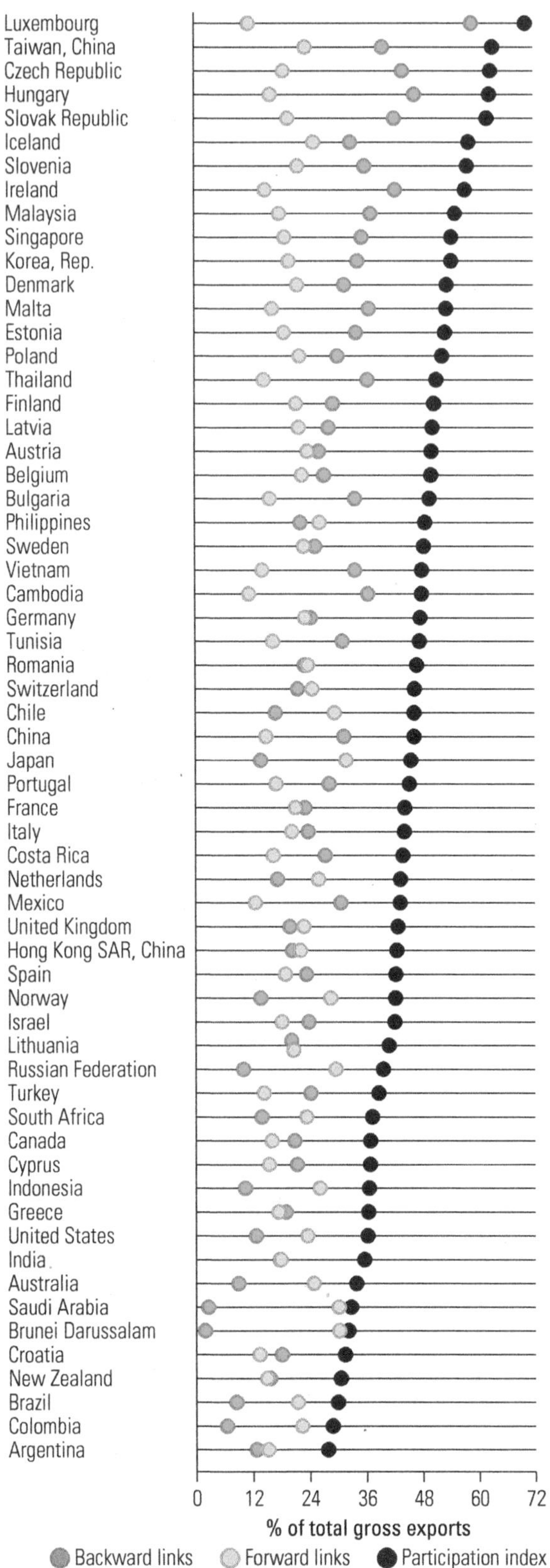

Source: Adapted from the Organisation for Economic Co-operation and Development–World Trade Organization Trade in Value Added database.

Figure 6.3. **GVC Participation Index, Malaysia and Peer Countries, Chemicals and Chemical Products, 2011**

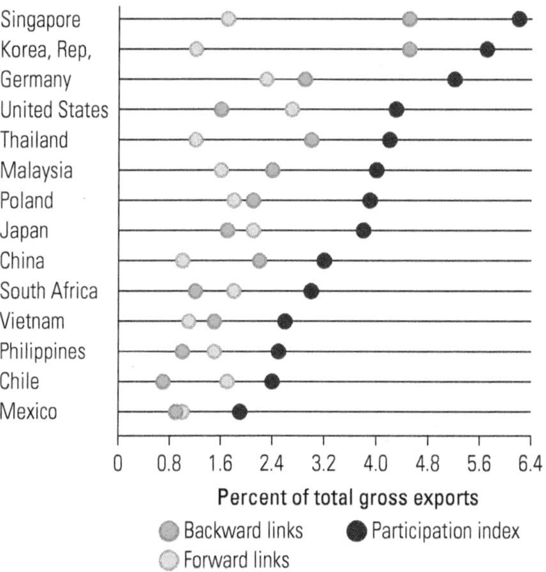

Source: Adapted from the Organisation for Economic Co-operation and Development–World Trade Organization Trade in Value Added database.

Figure 6.4. **GVC Participation Index, Selected Countries, Electrical and Optical Equipment, 2011**

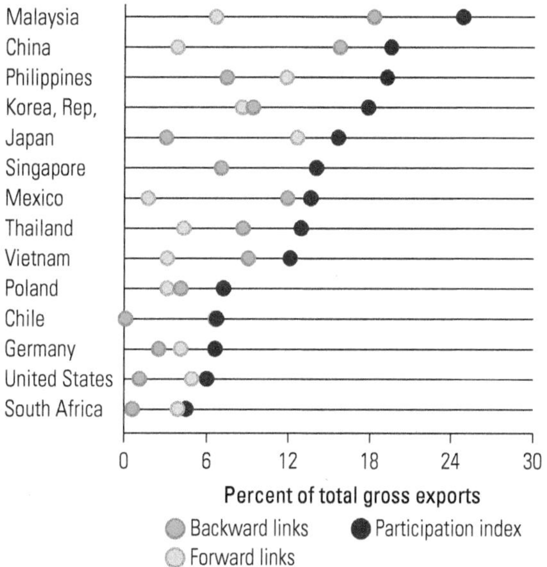

Source: Adapted from the Organisation for Economic Co-operation and Development–World Trade Organization Trade in Value Added database.

and petroleum and coke on the overall measure, we keep total gross exports in the denominator. Natural resource–intensive exporters are ranked at the lower end of the spectrum.

To illustrate how these concepts apply to specific countries, figures 6.3 to 6.5 focus on the GVC participation index for Malaysia and peer countries in the chemicals and chemical products sector (figure 6.3) and electrical and optical (E&O) equipment sector (figure 6.4). The sector participation index is computed using total exports as the denominator. Malaysia's GVC participation in the chemicals and chemical products sector is higher than the level in most of its peer countries, at 4 percent, and in the E&O sector Malaysia's GVC participation is the highest compared with its peers, at 25 percent. Moreover, chemicals reflect the general findings that the participation in GVCs is stronger on the buying side and weaker on the selling side. For E&O, Malaysia's performance on the buying side is considered stronger than on the selling side, following the patterns of China, Mexico, Thailand, and Vietnam. Together, the two sectors contribute more than one-half of Malaysia's overall participation in GVCs (figure 6.5). The contribution of E&O to overall participation is 41 percent (participation index of 25 percent relative to an overall participation index of 60 percent in 2011), whereas the chemicals sector contributes 15 percent (participation index of 4 percent relative to 60 percent).

Figure 6.5. **Breakdown of Malaysia's GVC Participation Index, 2011**

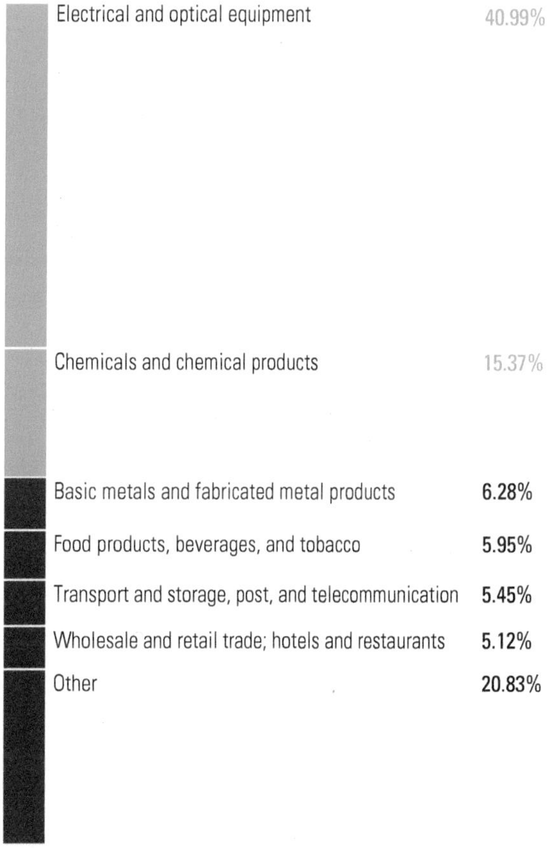

Electrical and optical equipment	40.99%
Chemicals and chemical products	15.37%
Basic metals and fabricated metal products	6.28%
Food products, beverages, and tobacco	5.95%
Transport and storage, post, and telecommunication	5.45%
Wholesale and retail trade; hotels and restaurants	5.12%
Other	20.83%

Source: Adapted from the Organisation for Economic Co-operation and Development–World Trade Organization Trade in Value Added database.

Network Metrics and Visualizations

Metrics and representations of trade networks can help identify the important suppliers and sellers of a country's value added (see box 1.3 in chapter 1). Plotting the network of value-added trade on a network space shows that China has moved to the center of the global trade network in the past 17 years, attracting most Asian countries with its gravitational pull (figure 6.6). The visualization is based on the undirected trade network (that is, without differentiating imports from exports) between 1995 (figure 6.6,

Figure 6.6. Evolution of the Network of Value-Added Trade, 1995 and 2011

a. In 1995, Germany and the United States were at the core of the network

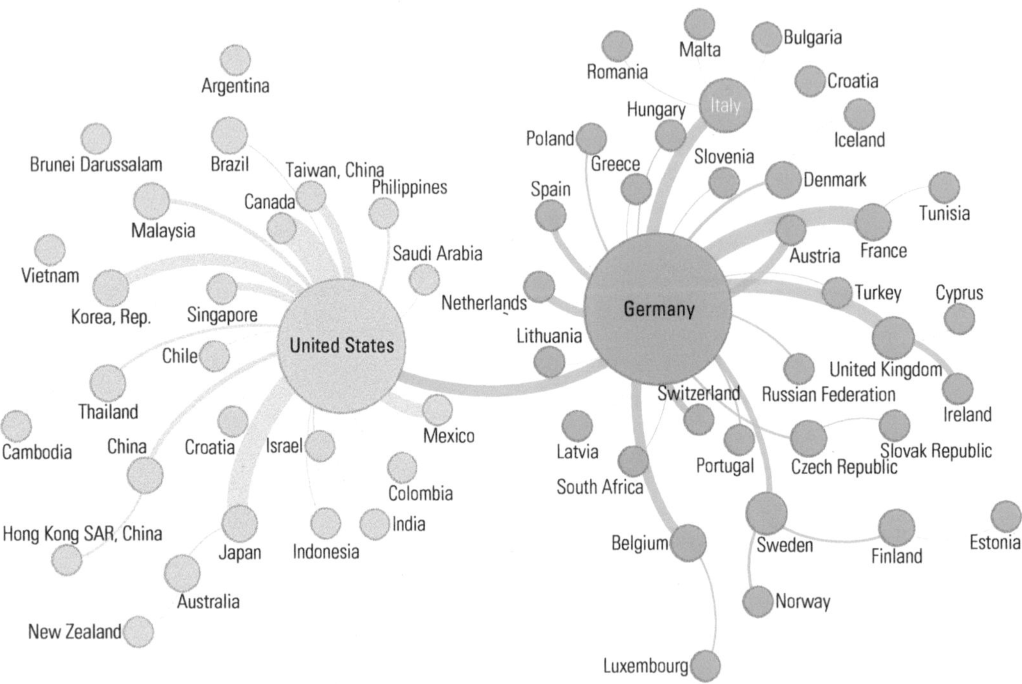

b. In 2011, Germany, China, and the United States were at the core of the network

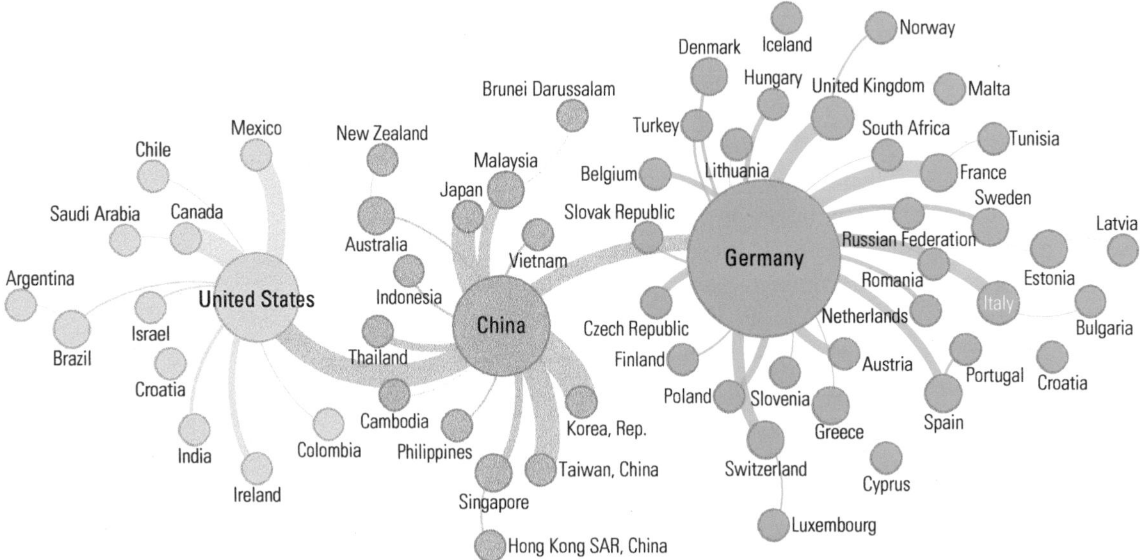

Source: Santoni and Taglioni 2015.

panel a) and 2011 (figure 6.6, panel b), and constructed using the measure of domestic value added embodied in gross exports.

In figure 6.6, the graphs visualize a minimal spanning tree—a reduced network that reports for each country only the strongest relation in value-added flows, considering imports and exports of value added. The most connected countries represent the roots of the tree (links are in darker colors and bigger), whereas links to peripheral countries (leaves) are in milder colors and smaller. The size of the nodes reflects a country's centrality.

China's move to the core, bringing it from the periphery to one of the three central nodes of the global trade and production networks, primarily results from the buying side (figure 6.7, panel b). On

Figure 6.7. Buyer and Seller Perspectives, 2011

a. Seller perspective, largest suppliers:[a] Most countries buy value added from the United States and Germany

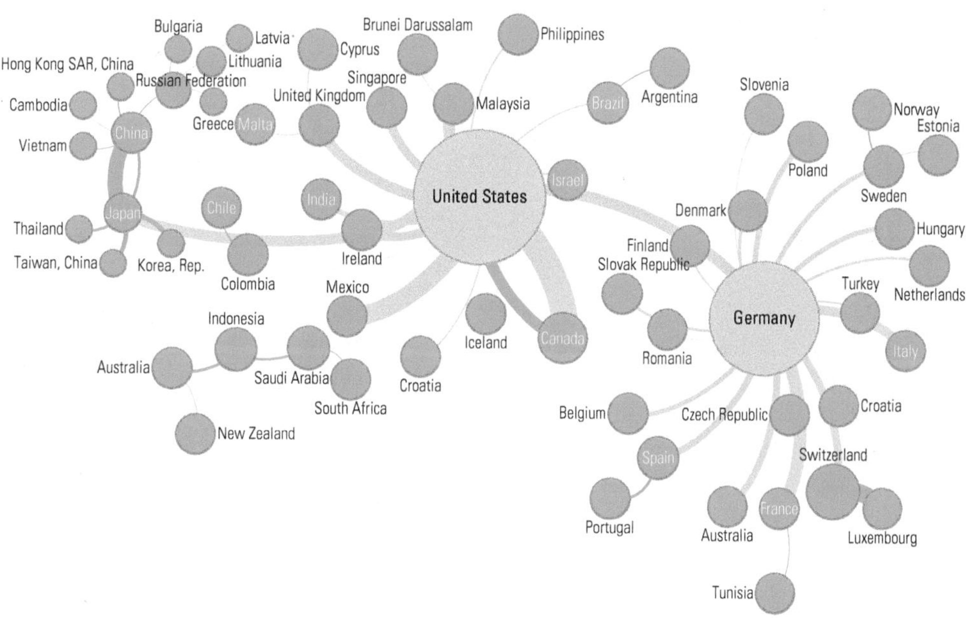

b. Buyer perspective, largest buyers:[a] Most countries sell value added to Germany and China

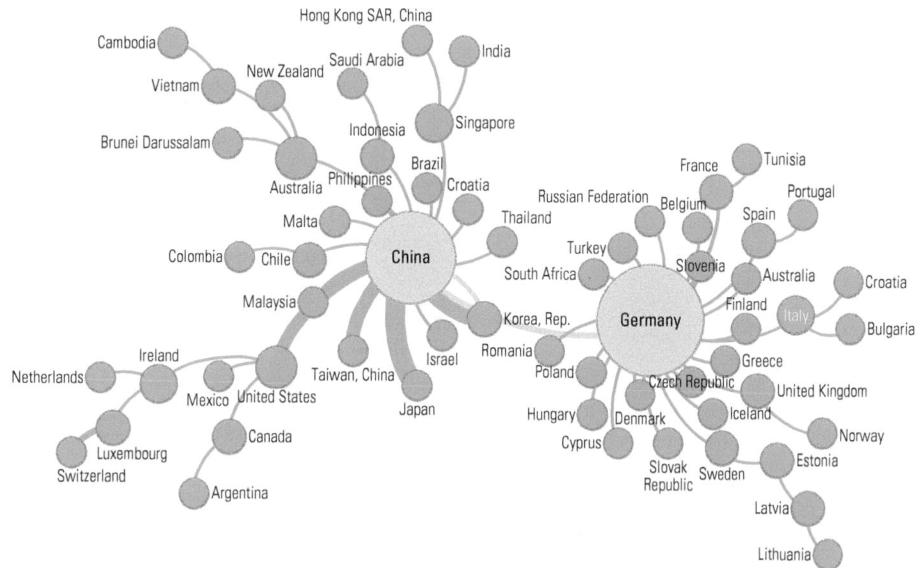

Source: Santoni and Taglioni 2015.
a. Reduced networks.

the selling side, Germany and the United States have remained the main suppliers of value added (figure 6.7, panel a). Thus, most Asian countries are in the supply system of the United States and in the buying system of China. For example, in 2011, Malaysia sourced more than 11.7 percent of overall imported value added from the United States, whereas China absorbed more than 29.8 percent of the value added Malaysia exported.

Network analysis allows much more than visualizations of dominant patterns. It can quantify full patterns of made-here-sold-there trade, as well as its evolution, using network metrics such as the eigenvector centrality (BONwin for inflows of value added, BONwout for outflows) and the clustering index (CCw)—see table 6.1.[3]

To illustrate how network metrics apply to trade in value added, table 6.2 reports the indexes for the two main concepts that underpin the preceding figures—eigenvector centrality and clustering—which are also constructed using domestic value added in gross exports. These measures are reported for total trade as well as for electrical and electronic and chemicals. The measure of eigenvector centrality—or structural integration—is a measure of the centrality of country *c* relative to the overall structure of the network. It is the most representative measure of the network and captures the strength of the links and their closeness or proximity. The eigenvector centrality can be computed from the buyer's (BONwin) or seller's (BONwout) perspective. The CCw is a measure of the transitivity of the network, measuring how much the neighbors of country *c* are connected to each other. It captures whether country *c* is strong because it trades a lot with other countries that are also strong.

For total trade, many of the countries central to the network from the buyer's perspective are also central from the seller's perspective—not only many high-income countries (HICs) in Europe and North America but also China. Still, China and Germany are more important from the buyer's perspective—demanding value added—whereas the United States is more important from the seller's perspective—supplying value added.

Again, Malaysia is used to illustrate the results in more detail. Of 56 economies, Malaysia ranks 13th from the buyer's perspective and 22nd from the seller's perspective, indicating that it is well integrated into GVCs from the buyer's and seller's perspectives but is stronger on the buyer's side. Malaysia is well clustered in the network (ranking 18th), suggesting that it trades with other countries that have strong links. Unsurprisingly, China, Germany, Japan, and the United States are the strongest economies.

Bangladesh's ready-made garments (RMG) industry is used to illustrate the use of network

Table 6.1 Network Measures

Measure	Description
In-strength and out-strength	Sum of values of inflows or outflows. The use of normalized link weights implies that the values for in-strength and out-strength report the market share of country *c*. The values show that usual market shares are a particular case of network centrality measures, when considering only first-order connectedness.
Eigenvector centrality (BONwin, BONwout)	Expresses the idea that the influence of a node is proportional to the influence of its neighbors: the node's eigenvector centrality is largely determined by the eigenvector centrality of its neighbors (multiplied by a constant).
Closeness	A measure of how close (topological distance) a node is to all other nodes. In general terms, the concept of distance in network analysis is related to the number of steps needed for some node to "reach" another network node. In the case of weighted networks, not the number of steps but the value of the links (the inverse of link value) is considered; the strongest flows result from shorter distance.
Clustering (CCw)	Expresses network transitivity, that is, how much the neighbors of country *c* are connected to each other.
Hubs and authorities	A drawback of eigenvector centrality with disconnected networks (with more than one strongly connected component) is that all nodes report a zero centrality. Hubs and authorities—also eigenvector-based centralities—represent a way to circumvent this problem. That is not the case with the network built from TiVA; only a strongly connected component results. So the out-eigenvector centrality is basically equal to the hub (99.9 percent correlation), whereas the in-eigenvector is equal to the authorities. The out-eigenvector then identifies hubs: nodes that point (sell) to highly connected nodes; in-eigenvector identifies authorities: nodes that are pointed to (buy from) highly connected nodes.

Note: TiVA = Trade in Value Added.

Table 6.2. Network Measures, All Sectors, E&E, and Chemicals, 2009

Country	Total			E&E			Chemicals		
	Cluster	BONwin	BONwout	Cluster	BONwin	BONwout	Cluster	BONwin	BONwout
Argentina	0.621	0.117	0.127	0.461	0.097	0.116	0.562	0.117	0.126
Australia	0.668	0.132	0.140	0.517	0.112	0.139	0.608	0.125	0.146
Austria	0.677	0.139	0.138	0.559	0.141	0.139	0.618	0.141	0.137
Belgium	0.698	0.147	0.143	0.561	0.136	0.145	0.664	0.160	0.148
Brazil	0.660	0.127	0.140	0.523	0.119	0.135	0.610	0.128	0.144
Brunei Darussalam	0.528	0.093	0.100	0.338	0.040	0.091	0.381	0.044	0.099
Bulgaria	0.597	0.118	0.113	0.473	0.106	0.108	0.538	0.123	0.106
Cambodia	0.505	0.099	0.084	0.360	0.083	0.064	0.388	0.071	0.072
Canada	0.677	0.139	0.139	0.552	0.137	0.138	0.630	0.143	0.142
Chile	0.631	0.122	0.129	0.386	0.034	0.128	0.569	0.119	0.128
China	0.748	0.163	0.157	0.660	0.187	0.168	0.693	0.166	0.159
Czech Republic	0.666	0.139	0.132	0.565	0.153	0.132	0.599	0.137	0.129
Denmark	0.678	0.141	0.136	0.549	0.137	0.135	0.615	0.137	0.138
Estonia	0.578	0.112	0.108	0.472	0.111	0.102	0.502	0.104	0.103
Finland	0.661	0.134	0.133	0.562	0.152	0.131	0.594	0.130	0.132
France	0.725	0.152	0.154	0.606	0.155	0.158	0.683	0.162	0.157
Germany	0.755	0.162	0.162	0.639	0.168	0.170	0.714	0.174	0.167
Greece	0.640	0.126	0.129	0.486	0.106	0.123	0.574	0.123	0.126
Hong Kong SAR, China	0.668	0.132	0.139	0.537	0.124	0.140	0.593	0.123	0.136
Hungary	0.653	0.136	0.127	0.557	0.155	0.127	0.587	0.136	0.123
Iceland	0.542	0.103	0.098	0.448	0.109	0.091	0.482	0.109	0.085
India	0.692	0.143	0.143	0.569	0.142	0.144	0.631	0.138	0.147
Indonesia	0.652	0.128	0.135	0.539	0.132	0.133	0.600	0.128	0.137
Ireland	0.680	0.142	0.137	0.567	0.150	0.137	0.642	0.151	0.143
Israel	0.644	0.131	0.127	0.535	0.136	0.127	0.589	0.134	0.125
Italy	0.715	0.148	0.152	0.595	0.150	0.155	0.669	0.158	0.153
Japan	0.718	0.146	0.156	0.625	0.162	0.165	0.667	0.149	0.158
Korea, Rep.	0.712	0.151	0.147	0.622	0.170	0.155	0.657	0.155	0.146
Latvia	0.571	0.107	0.109	0.431	0.089	0.102	0.488	0.092	0.107
Lithuania	0.580	0.112	0.109	0.448	0.098	0.100	0.533	0.118	0.108
Luxembourg	0.636	0.132	0.122	0.476	0.102	0.118	0.557	0.123	0.117
Malaysia	0.686	0.144	0.139	0.591	0.158	0.145	0.634	0.149	0.138
Malta	0.546	0.104	0.099	0.456	0.109	0.096	0.463	0.092	0.089
Mexico	0.660	0.138	0.130	0.572	0.160	0.131	0.586	0.127	0.131
Netherlands	0.709	0.151	0.146	0.581	0.147	0.149	0.675	0.165	0.150
New Zealand	0.593	0.115	0.114	0.446	0.098	0.106	0.517	0.106	0.109
Norway	0.672	0.134	0.141	0.531	0.121	0.138	0.612	0.127	0.147
Philippines	0.629	0.126	0.123	0.558	0.152	0.130	0.488	0.086	0.114
Poland	0.676	0.140	0.137	0.561	0.144	0.137	0.617	0.142	0.134
Portugal	0.638	0.128	0.126	0.518	0.131	0.121	0.577	0.129	0.123
Romania	0.626	0.124	0.124	0.510	0.125	0.123	0.560	0.126	0.116
Russian Federation	0.695	0.134	0.155	0.543	0.116	0.153	0.660	0.138	0.167
Saudi Arabia	0.648	0.118	0.143	0.470	0.080	0.140	0.627	0.131	0.154
Singapore	0.706	0.150	0.143	0.599	0.163	0.146	0.664	0.161	0.144
Slovak Republic	0.635	0.132	0.121	0.536	0.145	0.121	0.563	0.130	0.115
Slovenia	0.605	0.122	0.114	0.498	0.120	0.110	0.544	0.124	0.108
South Africa	0.626	0.124	0.124	0.472	0.100	0.121	0.554	0.115	0.122
Spain	0.698	0.144	0.145	0.572	0.141	0.147	0.652	0.152	0.147
Sweden	0.690	0.143	0.142	0.576	0.147	0.144	0.636	0.146	0.142
Switzerland	0.689	0.142	0.143	0.584	0.153	0.145	0.650	0.153	0.145
Taiwan, China	0.687	0.141	0.142	0.607	0.164	0.151	0.634	0.148	0.138
Thailand	0.673	0.139	0.136	0.584	0.161	0.139	0.604	0.133	0.134
Turkey	0.663	0.135	0.134	0.532	0.129	0.131	0.605	0.137	0.132
United Kingdom	0.717	0.148	0.153	0.603	0.154	0.157	0.674	0.157	0.158
United States	0.746	0.153	0.166	0.634	0.161	0.173	0.706	0.162	0.173
Vietnam	0.627	0.129	0.119	0.488	0.116	0.115	0.531	0.106	0.117

Source: Based on data from Santoni and Taglioni 2015.

Note: The colors of the cells are according to the strength of the metrics: a green cell indicates a strong measure, a yellow cell indicates a weak measure, and a white cell indicates an average measure. BONwin = eigenvector centrality based on inflows of value added; BONwout = eigenvector centrality based on outflows of value added; CCw = clustering index; E&E = electrical and electronic.

Figure 6.8. World Gross Trade Network for Apparel, 2013

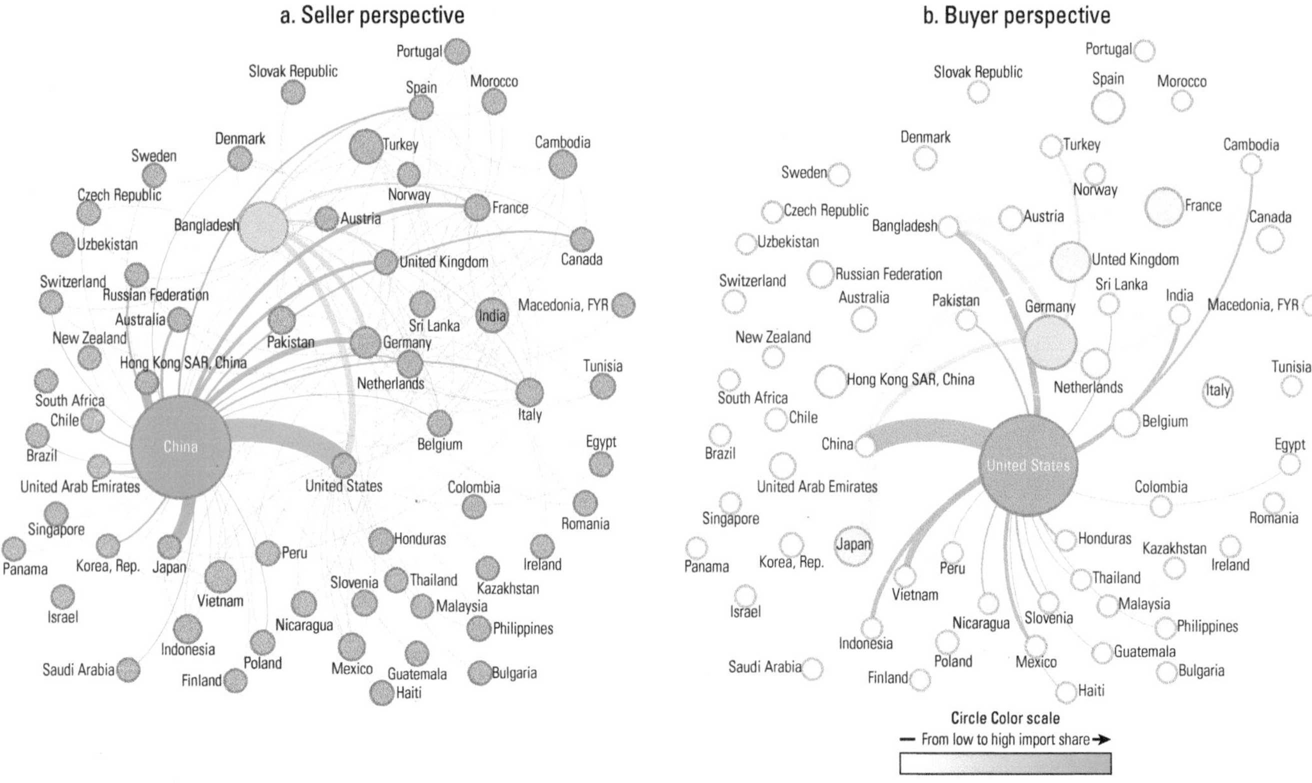

Source: BACI data from CEPII data.

Note: Both panels show apparel consumption product flows across economies; links are proportional to world market share. In the exporter graph (panel a), Bangladesh and China are highlighted as the two main exporters by using different colors: yellow for Bangladesh and green for China; the rest of the countries are gray; the node size is proportional to the export market share of each economy. For the buyer graph (panel b), a gradient color scheme is used to distinguish the largest importers (green) from the small importers (white); the node size is proportional to the import market share of each economy. The position of the circles in each graph reflects the number of links and relative weight (optimized using a force-directed algorithm, Gephi software). To improve readability, only trade flows (links) accounting for at least 0.001 percent of world trade are shown. The 62 economies in the network cover 91 percent of world trade in the selected apparel products. BACI = international trade database by CEPII.

visualization for GVC analysis. The Bangladeshi RMG industry is the second largest in the world in exports, after China (see figure 6.8, panel a). The total value of Bangladesh's RMG exports reached US$24.1 billion in 2013. The RMG industry accounts for more than 80 percent of Bangladesh's total exports and is the country's largest source of foreign currency. Around 60 percent of RMG exports go to the European Union, and an additional 19.6 percent go to the United States (figure 6.9).

Role of Services in Value Added

The focus of the measures in chapter 4 is on quantifying domestic and foreign value added in gross exports. A special case that deserves attention is the role of services value added in gross exports (see table 6.3, as explained later in this section). That concept is particularly important in the context of the internationalization of production.[4] A positive correlation, for example, exists between the specialization of a country in services in 1985 and its per capita gross domestic product in 2010; a positive correlation also exists between the overall economic complexity of an economy and the importance of the domestic services sector as a contributor of value added for downstream exports (figure 1.4 in chapter 1).[5]

Recent data on trade in value added suggest that services represent about 30 percent of the value added in manufacturing exports. Figure 6.10 illustrates the services share of value added embodied in gross exports as a percentage of gross exports in five manufacturing sectors by type of service input.

Measures quantifying the services dimension in GVCs are available in the Organisation for Economic Co-operation and Development—World Trade Organization Trade in Value Added database and the World Bank's Export of Value Added database. The

Figure 6.9. Bangladesh's Gross Trade Network: Main Buyers of Bangladeshi Apparel (Cotton) Consumption Products, 2013

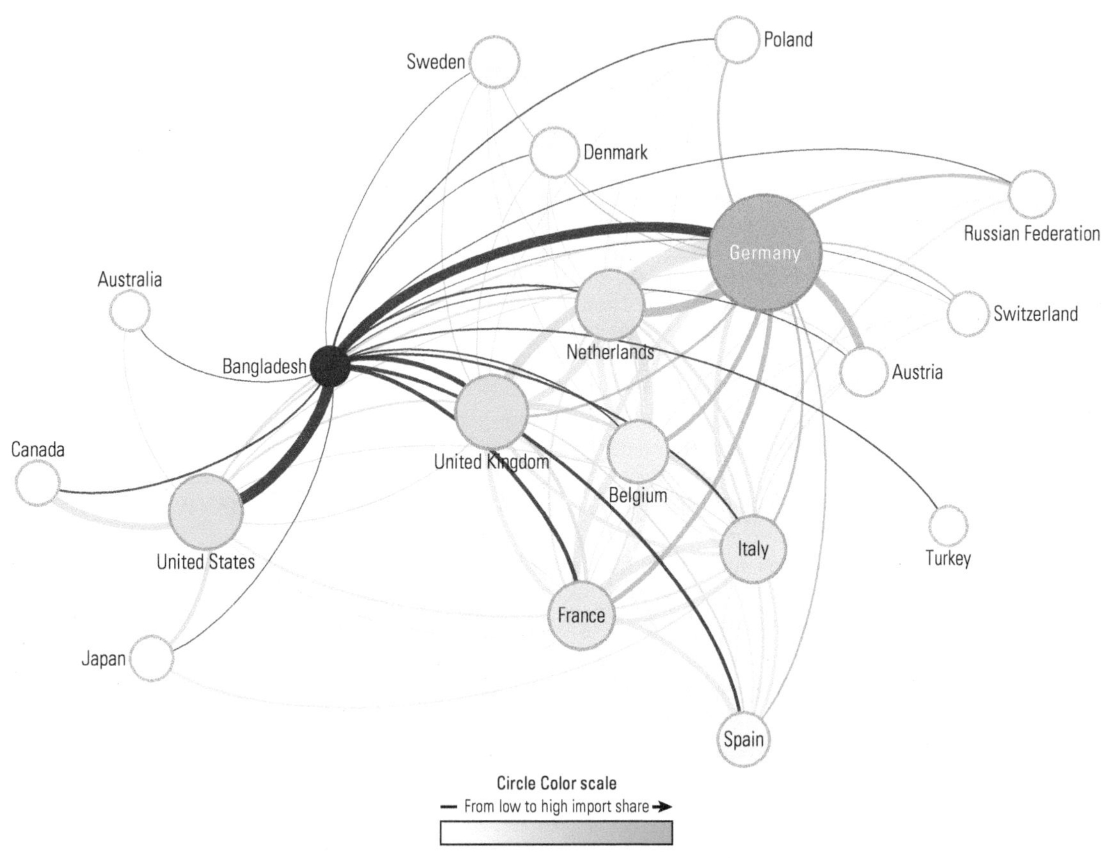

Source: BACI data from CEPII data.
Note: The graph shows Bangladesh's export relations for the selected apparel goods. The position of each circle in the graph reflects the number of links and relative weight (optimized using a force-directed algorithm, Gephi software). To improve readability, only trade flows (links) accounting for at least 1 percent of each country's exports are shown. BACI = international trade database by CEPII.

latter is based on data from the Global Trade Analysis Project database and work by Francois, Manchin, and Tomberger (2013), who constructed two matrices that allow identifying the value-added contribution of specific sectors to other sectors that either sell the final good to the domestic market (domestic value-added Sector_GMatrix) or export it (export value-added Sector_HMatrix) (see table 6.3). Rows indicate the supply sectors, and columns represent the demand sectors—that is, sectors that use a specific input. Forward links, VXsharefwd, designate the total share of a specific input being used across all sectors and are calculated as the sum over a row. Analogously, backward links, VXsharebwd, denote the share of different inputs used in a specific sector and are calculated as the sum over a column. The most recent matrix is available for 2011 (for more information on the database, see table 6.3 and appendix H).

Focusing on forward links in Morocco, figure 6.11 suggests that services represent a large share in most goods export sectors—in particular, in manufacturing exports. The share of total services (highlighted in dark gray) exceeds 30 percent in the metals (37 percent), paper and publishing (34.3 percent), and minerals and manufactures not elsewhere classified (both 30 percent) export industries. Services also contribute an important share to Morocco's most important manufacturing export sectors: chemicals (21.7 percent), machinery and equipment (23.7 percent), and transport equipment (13.6 percent). Among these export sectors, trade and transport services (highlighted in white) play the largest role, followed by other private services (highlighted in light gray).

Forward links of services are stronger than backward links in most countries, including Morocco. The following analysis focuses on a cross-country comparison of forward and backward links in export

Table 6.3 Indicators of Services Value Added

TiVA database, covering 61 economies

Indicator	Description
EXGR_SERV_DVASH	Domestic value added of the services sectors (ISIC Rev. 3 45-95), by sector (% of total gross exports).
EXGR_SERV_FVASH	Foreign value added of the services sectors (ISIC Rev. 3 45-95), by sector (% of total gross exports).
Other indicators	See table 4.1 (in chapter 4) and table 5.1 (in chapter 5) for other indicators that can be computed focusing on services value added only.

World Bank Export of Value Added database, based on GTAP database (105 countries worldwide)

Indicator	Description
Sector_GMatrix	This matrix contains the total domestic value added, based on links. Depending on whether rows or columns are considered, the sum corresponds to forward (row) or backward (column) links. Thus, reading a row for a given sector (sectors are presented on the y-axis) provides information about the value of the sector's inputs into each sector (on the x-axis). The matrix corresponds to matrix G, as described in the explanatory note in appendix H and in Francois, Manchin, and Tomberger (2013).
Sector_HMatrix	This matrix contains the total export value added, based on links. Depending on whether rows or columns are considered, the sum corresponds to forward (row) or backward (column) links. Thus, reading a row for a given sector (sectors are presented on the y-axis) provides information about the value of the sector's inputs into each sector (on the x-axis). The matrix corresponds to matrix H, as described in the explanatory note in appendix H and in Francois, Manchin, and Tomberger (2013).
DomVAshare	This vector denotes the domestic share of value added of gross value of output per sector. The diagonal matrix, B, as described in the explanatory note and Francois, Manchin, and Tomberger (2013), contains the shares on its diagonal.
GXshare	Denotes the share of each sector in total exports per country, based on the gross value of exports. See table 3 in Francois, Manchin, and Tomberger (2013).
DXshare	Denotes the share of each sector's exports of total exports per country, based on direct value added, ignoring links. See table 4 in Francois, Manchin, and Tomberger (2013).
VXsharefwd	Denotes the total value added in exports, based on forward links per sector and country. This vector corresponds to the row-sums of matrix H in the explanatory note in appendix H. See table 5 in Francois, Manchin, and Tomberger (2013).
VXsharebwd	Denotes the total value added in exports, based on backward links. It is obtained by taking the column-sums of matrix H. See table 6 in Francois, Manchin, and Tomberger (2013).

Sources: Export of Value Added database, Francois, Manchin, and Tomberger 2013; Organisation for Economic Co-operation and Development–World Trade Organization TiVA database; GTAP database.
Note: GTAP = Global Trade Analysis Project; ISIC = International Standard Industrial Classification; TiVA = Trade in Value Added.

Figure 6.10. Domestic Value Added of Services Sectors Embodied in Manufacturing Gross Exports, All Countries, 2009

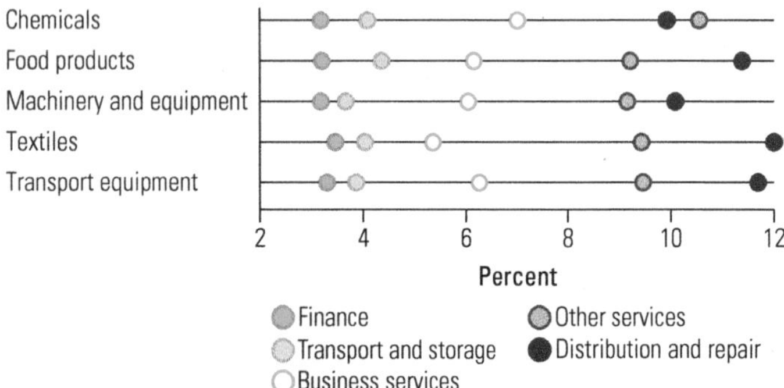

Source: Adapted from the Organisation for Economic Co-operation and Development–World Trade Organization database.
Note: The share of distribution does not include distribution services for final goods.

value added for trade and transport, as well as other private services, in 2007 (figures 6.12 and 6.13). The fact that most countries, including Morocco, are located below the 45-degree line indicates that forward links are stronger than backward links—that is, services contribute to export value added more strongly than they make use of export value-added contributions from other sectors, especially other private services.

Morocco's forward links of trade and transportation services were lower in 2007 compared with 2001, but higher than in most countries worldwide—that is, trade and transportation services were less important for export sectors (forward links) in 2007 than in 2001. Forward links of trade and transportation services declined from 26 to 22 percent of export value added, while backward links fell from 21 to 17 percent. Compared with its peers, Morocco shows lower forward and backward links of trade and transport services than the Arab Republic of Egypt, Tunisia, and Turkey; nevertheless, Morocco's links remain higher than those of most countries worldwide.

Strong forward (and also, to a lesser extent, backward) links characterize other private services in

HICs, but not in Morocco. The cross-country comparison reveals that other private services contribute more strongly to exports in HICs, whereas backward links play an important but less relevant role. Other private services in Morocco showed some progress between 2001 and 2007, increasing backward links from 6.0 to 8.8 percent and forward links from 7.9 to 9.8 percent; but other countries, such as Egypt and Romania, still show stronger links.

All this evidence emphasizes that a country's competitiveness, even in manufacturing, seems to be related to an efficient domestic services sector or to the degree of the country's openness to importing such services. In GVCs, the services sector is particularly important. Managing the complexity of the chain and preserving the production standards throughout the chain require strong coordination that relies on efficient services (such as business, technical, financial, transportation, and distribution services) and the movement of key personnel across borders (such as engineers, auditors, lawyers, and managers).

Part 2 of Saez and others (2015) discusses in detail the full range of measures for assessing the importance of services as a source of competitiveness in the economy.[6]

Figure 6.11. Contribution of Services Sectors to Export Value Added of Goods Sectors in Morocco, 2007

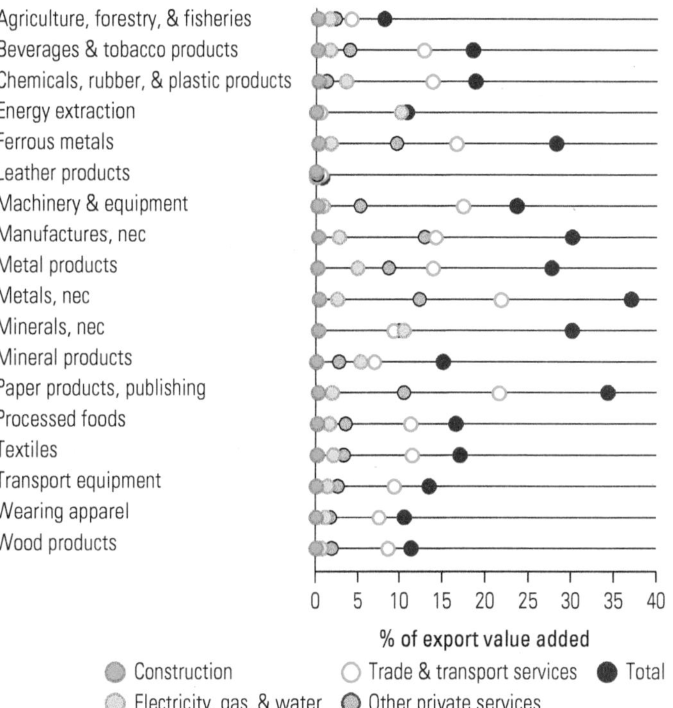

Sources: Adapted from Francois, Manchin, and Tomberger 2013; World Bank Export Value-Added database (World Bank); Global Trade Analysis Project (Purdue University).
Note: nec = not elsewhere classified.

Figure 6.12. Forward and Backward Links in Export Value Added, Trade and Transport Services, 2001 and 2007

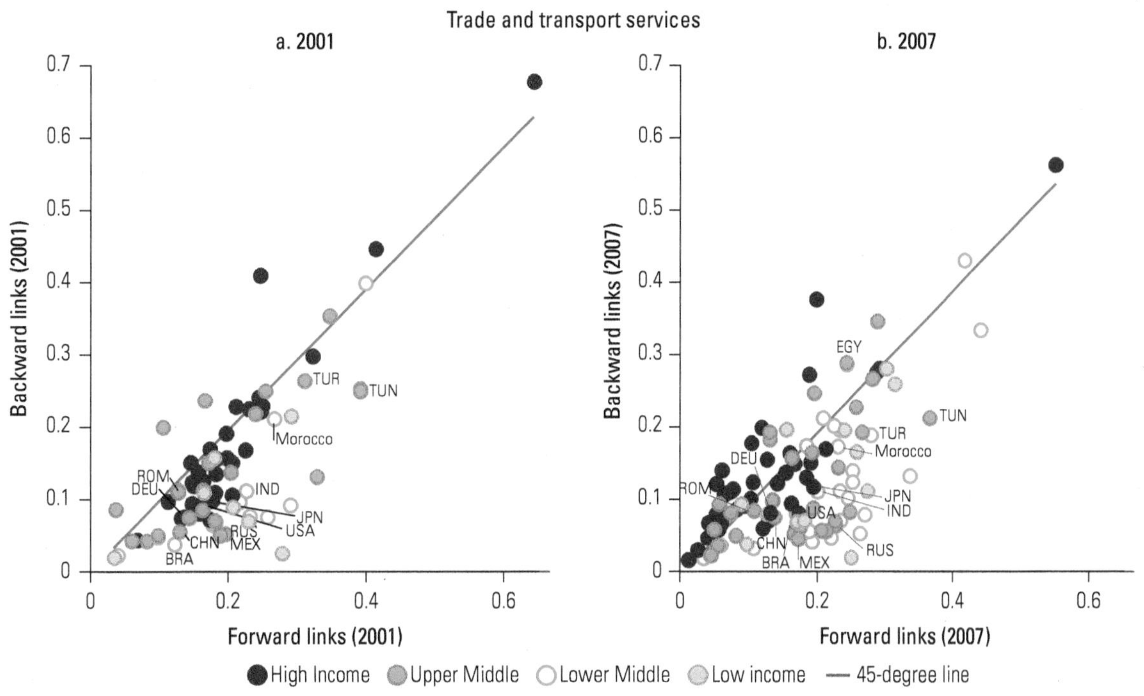

Sources: Adapted from Francois, Manchin, and Tomberger 2013; Export Value-Added database (World Bank); Global Trade Analysis Project (Purdue University).

Figure 6.13. Forward and Backward Links in Export Value Added, Other Private Services, 2001 and 2007

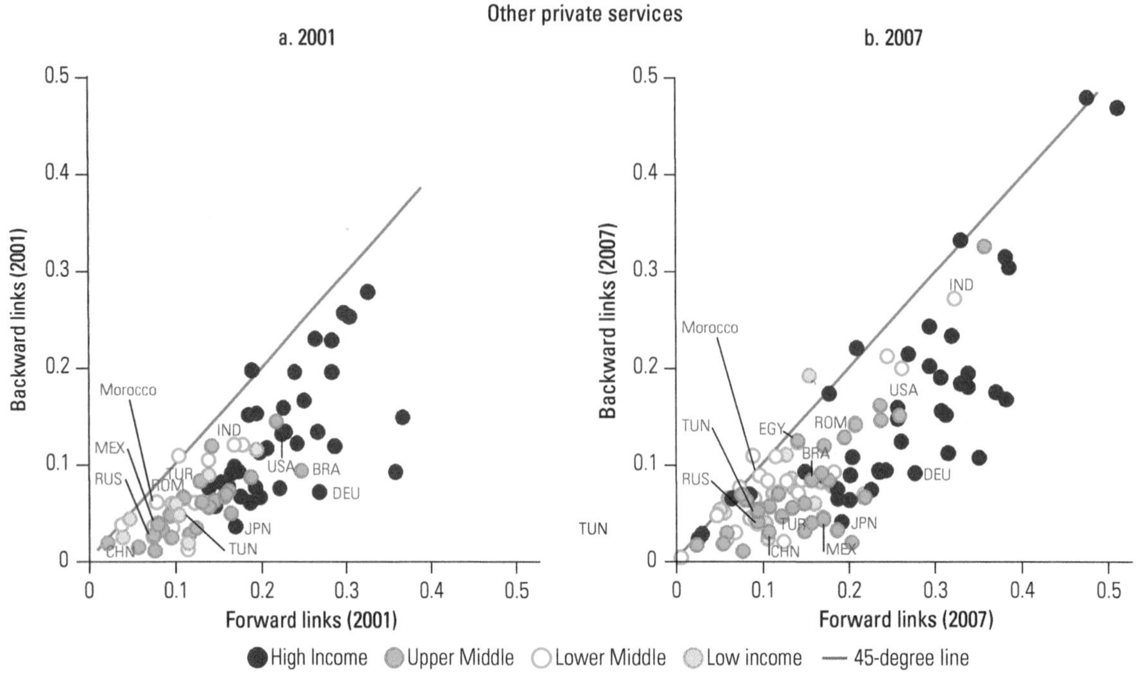

Sources: Adapted from Francois, Manchin, and Tomberger 2013; Export Value-Added database (World Bank); Global Trade Analysis Project (Purdue University).

Main Actors and Their Links in GVCs Using Firm-Level Measures

Firm-level data have the advantage of capturing directly the main actors in a value chain—final producers and their suppliers (other advantages are discussed in box 6.1). Depending on data availability, the extent of GVC links can be compared across industries in a country (if data are available for only one country) or in a single industry across countries (if data are available for several countries). Such comparisons allow countries to assess their level of integration in GVCs in a specific industry and identify possible areas for policy changes.

This section distinguishes between four types of firms that characteristically take part in GVCs:

Box 6.1. Why Firm-Level Analysis?

Aside from the fact that firms are heterogeneous in characteristics and performance, production models are seeing major changes worldwide, which deeply affect economies' transmission mechanisms—domestic and international.

But macro aggregations miss the critical features and effects of firm heterogeneity on the wider economy, because the aggregations are not adaptable to changes and innovations in the business landscape—either within countries or internationally. For policy initiatives to deliver the expected results in jobs, domestic growth, and exports requires identifying the typologies of actors in global value chains (GVCs) by answering a raft of questions. Are the companies that participate in GVCs domestic or foreign owned? Are they large multiproduct firms or small and medium enterprises? What is their function in the production process? Do they mainly sell inputs to domestic multinationals, or do they export? Do they rely on imported inputs? If so, from which source? Do they conduct research and development? Are they paying higher wages than non-GVC companies? Are they more intensive in technology and services?

These are just a few sample questions (for a more extensive list of questions, see annex 11A in chapter 11). Going deeper into firm-level dynamics can help policy makers and others not only improve their aggregate assessments of competitiveness and GVC participation, but also identify the drivers and the reaction of the real economy to policy interventions (an issue beyond the scope of this book).

In short, rounding out more aggregate assessments with firm-level data can improve policies to raise a country's competitiveness and secure the benefits of being in GVCs.

1. Multinationals relying on inputs from domestic suppliers
2. Domestic suppliers to multinationals in the country
3. Domestic suppliers that export
4. Domestic producers relying on imported inputs

Another type of firm is the hybrid case of non-equity modes of investment, whereby a multinational has a contractual relationship with a domestic firm in the host country and maintains some degree of control over the operation and conduct of business but has no ownership stake. This type of firm includes contract manufacturers that produce fully assembled goods for large retailers, as well as contract farming, business process outsourcing, franchising, contract management, strategic alliances, and joint ventures.[7] Such contractual relationships can fall into all four categories, which are discussed in the following subsections.

Figure 6.14. Input Sources of Multinationals in Agribusiness, 2012

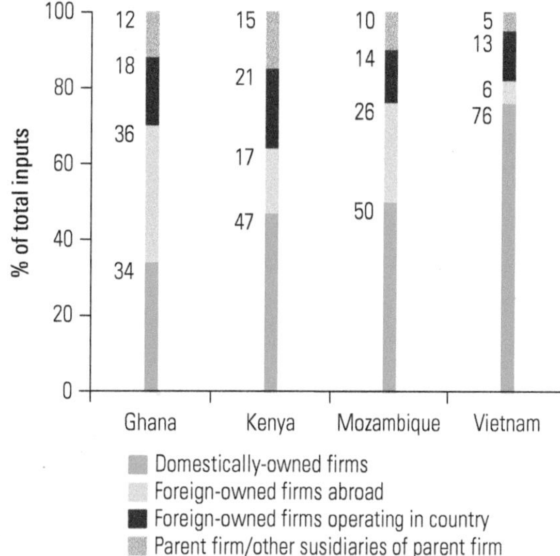

Source: Adapted from a survey by the World Bank International Trade Department (simple averages).

Multinationals' Share of Inputs from Domestic Suppliers

Most countries devote great attention and resources to attracting foreign direct investment (FDI). They hope not only to generate such benefits as jobs, foreign exchange, and tax revenues but also, perhaps more important, to realize dynamic benefits to the domestic economy through "spillovers." That term generally refers to productivity improvements resulting from knowledge diffusion from multinational affiliates to domestic firms. Although evidence on intra-industry spillovers is mixed, some studies have shifted the focus to vertical spillovers in upstream and downstream sectors.[8] Studies support the idea of positive backward spillovers from multinationals to local suppliers; the evidence on forward spillovers is more mixed.[9]

More links between multinationals for domestic inputs thus promise higher FDI spillover potential for the local economy, captured by its domestic sourcing intensity—the percentage of domestic inputs in a multinational's total intermediate inputs.[10]

The results of a World Bank International Trade Department survey of 30 multinationals in agribusiness in Ghana, Kenya, Mozambique, and Vietnam are only indicative, but they seem to suggest that input links between multinationals in agribusiness and suppliers are much higher in Vietnam (76 percent) than in African countries (50 percent or less), leading to higher FDI spillover potential in Vietnam (figure 6.14). Box 6.2 describes how this measure (and others) can be obtained from World Bank Enterprise Surveys.

Domestic Suppliers' Share of Output to Multinationals

The next measure is closely related to the previous one, as it also measures the percentage of a supplier's domestic output sold to a multinational.[11]

According to a survey by the World Bank International Trade Department of 88 supplier firms in agribusiness, the output share of suppliers to multinationals ranges from 21.5 percent in Ghana to 51.8 percent in Mozambique (figure 6.15). The percentage increased in all countries except Ghana after the domestic supplier started doing business with the multinational.

Domestic Suppliers' Share of Exports

The next measure for detecting a country's exposure to GVCs is the percentage of sales being exported.[12]

Depending on data availability, a supplier's exports can be further decomposed into direct exports, indirect exports, and sales to firms that use inputs for export products. The same survey of 88 suppliers in agribusiness shows that exports in the

Box 6.2. GVC Measures Based on World Bank Enterprise Surveys

Many of the indicators described herein can be obtained from the World Bank Enterprise Surveys. One major advantage of these surveys is that their questions are the same across all countries. Moreover, the data represent a random sample of firms using three levels of stratification: sector, firm size, and region.

(1) *A multinational's share of inputs from domestic suppliers can be calculated from the answers to two questions:*

- Question: What percentage of this firm is owned by each of the following?
- Answer: ___% foreign private individuals, companies, or organizations.
- ▸ Generally, foreign ownership of at least 10 percent qualifies a firm to be considered a multinational.

Based on foreign firms only, the multinational's share of domestic inputs can be obtained.

- Question: As a proportion of all material inputs or supplies purchased [that year], what percentage of this establishment's material inputs or supplies were of domestic origin?
- Answer: ___% material inputs or supplies of domestic origin.

(2) *A domestic supplier's share of exports can be calculated from the answers to three questions:*

- Question: What percentage of this firm is owned by each of the following?
- Answer: ___% domestic private individuals, companies, or organizations.
- ▸ Domestic ownership of at least 90 percent qualifies a firm to be considered domestic.

Domestic suppliers can be singled out based on the following question:

- Question: In the past fiscal year, this establishment's production falls into which category?
- Possible answers include (1) only goods for sale to final consumers, (2) semi-finished goods used as inputs by other firms, (3) mostly finished goods but also some semi-finished goods, and (4) mostly semi-finished goods but also some finished goods.
- ▸ Typical supplier firms should mainly focus on the production of intermediate goods, so categories 2 and 4 are the most appropriate to take into account. This question is not covered in all Enterprise Surveys, so the measure in some cases reflects a domestic firm's (rather than a supplier's) share of exports.

Based on this subsample, the share of exports in output can be calculated from the answer to one question:

- Question: In the past fiscal year, what percentage of this establishment's sales fell in each of the following categories?
- Possible answers include (1) national sales, (2) indirect exports (sold domestically to a third party that exports products), and (3) direct exports.
- ▸ A supplier's export share can be computed based on answer 3 only or on the sum of answers 2 and 3.

(3) *Finally, a domestic producer's share of imported inputs can be derived from the answers to three questions.*

- Question: What percentage of this firm is owned by each of the following?
- Answer: ___% domestic private individuals, companies, or organizations.
- ▸ Domestic ownership of at least 90 percent qualifies a firm to be considered domestic.

Domestic producers can be singled out based on the following question:

- Question: In the past fiscal year, this establishment's production falls into which category?
- Possible answers include (1) only goods for sale to final consumers, (2) semi-finished goods used as inputs by other firms, (3) mostly finished goods but also some semi-finished goods, and (4) mostly semi-finished goods but also some finished goods.
- ▸ Typical producer firms should focus mainly on the production of final goods, so categories 1 and 3 are the most appropriate to take into account. This question is not covered in all Enterprise Surveys, so the measure in some cases reflects a domestic firm's (rather than a producer's) share of imported inputs.

Based on domestic producers only, the firm's share of imported inputs can be obtained.

- Question: As a proportion of all material inputs or supplies purchased that year, what percentage of this establishment's material inputs or supplies were of foreign origin?
- Answer: ___% material inputs or supplies of foreign origin.

Source: Based on World Bank Enterprise Surveys.

broader sense made up 15 percent of total sales in Mozambique and 36 percent in Vietnam (figure 6.16). The survey results also reveal different underlying export structures: whereas the types of export channels in Kenya and Vietnam are very similar (dominated by direct exports), Ghanaian suppliers rely more on indirect exports or sell to firms that use their inputs for export products (box 6.2 describes how this measure can be obtained from World Bank Enterprise Surveys).

Figure 6.15. Domestic Suppliers' Output Sold to Multinationals in Agribusiness, 2012

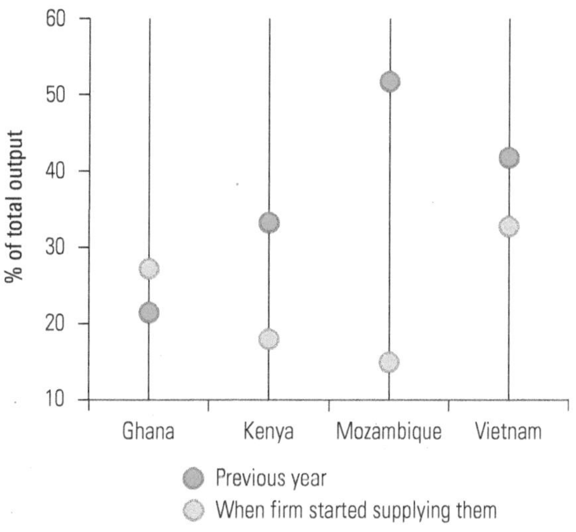

Source: Adapted from a survey by the World Bank International Trade Department (simple averages).

Figure 6.16. Sales Channels of Domestic Suppliers in Agribusiness, 2012

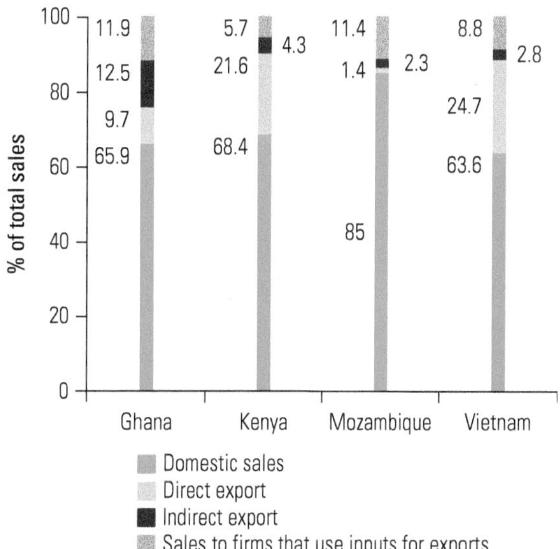

Source: Adapted from a survey by the World Bank International Trade Department (simple averages).

Domestic Producers' Share of Imported Inputs

The focus should be not only on domestic suppliers but also on domestic producers of final goods that can be part of GVCs if they rely on imported inputs. A domestic producer's percentage of imported inputs in total intermediate inputs is a widely accepted measure of offshoring.[13]

Notes

1. Developed by Koopman and others (2011), the index can be formalized as

$$GVC\_PART_{cs} = \frac{(EXGR\_FVA_{cs} + DVA3EX_{cs})}{EXGR_{cs}} = EXGR\_FVASH_{cs} + DVA3EX\_EX_{cs}$$

where EXGR_FVA is the foreign value added embodied in gross exports in sector *s* and country *c*, as defined in chapter 4, and refers to the sourcing side in GVCs. DVA3EX is the domestic value added of sector *s* and country *c* embodied in gross exports of third countries, which was defined in chapter 5 and relates to the selling side in GVCs. Both are measured as a percentage of gross exports, EXGR.

2. OECD (2012).

3. Those concepts, which underpin the graphical representations of figures 6.6 and 6.7, are described in chapter 1. They differ from econometric assessments in ways described in box 1.3 in chapter 1.

4. The concept can be formalized as

$SERV\_VAGR_{cs} = \frac{EXGR\_SVAC_{cs}}{EXGR_{cs}}$ where the EXGR_SVAC includes total domestic value added of the services sector embodied in gross exports and EXGR is gross exports.

The total decomposition of domestic value added of the services sector is formalized as $EXGR\_SVAC_{cs}=EXGR\_DDC\_SV_{cs}+EXGR\_IDC\_SV_{cs}+ EXGR\_RIM\_SV_{cs}$, where EXGR_DDC_SV is the direct domestic services value added, EXGR_IDC_SV the indirect domestic services value added, and EXGR_RIM_SV re-imported domestic services value added.

5. Saez and others (2015, 48).

6. Saez and others (2015).

7. UNCTAD (2011).

8. Javorcik (2004); Blalock and Gertler (2008).

9. See, for instance, the meta-analysis by Havranek and Irsova (2011).

10. The measure can be formalized as

$MULT\_DOM_{csi} = \frac{INP\_DOM_{csi}}{INP\_TOTAL_{csi}}$ where *INP_DOM* refers to the value of inputs that multinational *i* in sector *s* and country *c* purchases from domestic suppliers, and *INP_TOTAL* refers to the total value of inputs bought.

11. The measure is defined as

$SUP\_MULT_{csi} = \frac{OUTP\_MULT_{csi}}{OUTP\_TOTAL_{csi}}$ where OUTP_MULT refers to the value of output that supplier *i* in sector *s*, country *c*, sells to multinationals, and OUTP_TOTAL refers to the total value of output produced.

12. The measure is defined as

$SUP\_EX_{csi} = \frac{EX_{csi}}{OUTP\_TOTAL_{csi}}$ where EX denotes a supplier *i*'s exports and OUTP_TOTAL its total output in country *c* and sector *s*.

13. The measure can be formalized as $PROD\_IM_{csi} = \frac{INP\_IM_{csi}}{INP\_TOTAL_{csi}}$ where INP_IM denotes a domestic producer *i*'s value of imported inputs in sector *s* and country *c*, and INP_TOTAL represents the value of total inputs.

References

Blalock, G., and P. Gertler. 2008. "Welfare Gains from Foreign Direct Investment through Technology Transfer to Local Suppliers." *Journal of International Economics* 74 (2): 402–21.

Francois, J., M. Manchin, and P. Tomberger. 2013. "Services Links and the Value Added Content of Trade." Policy Research Working Paper 6432, World Bank, Washington, DC.

Havranek, Tomas, and Zuzana Irsova. 2011. "Estimating Vertical Spillovers from FDI: Why Results Vary and What the True Effect Is." *Journal of International Economics* 85 (2): 234–44.

Javorcik, Beata Smarzynska. 2004. "Does Foreign Direct Investment Increase the Productivity of Domestic Firms? In Search of Spillovers through Backward Linkages." *American Economic Review* 94 (3): 605–27.

Koopman, Robert, William Powers, Zhi Wang, and Shang-Jin Wei. 2011. "Giving Credit Where Credit Is Due: Tracing Value Added in Global Production Chains." NBER Working Paper 16426, National Bureau of Economic Research, Cambridge, MA.

OECD (Organisation for Economic Co-operation and Development). 2012. "Managing Aid to Achieve Trade and Development Results: An Analysis of Trade-related Targets." COM/DCD/TAD(2012)12/FINAL, OECD, Paris.

Saez, Sebastian, Daria Taglioni, Erik van der Marel, Claire H. Hollweg, and Veronika Zavacka. 2015. *Valuing Services in Trade: A Toolkit for Competitiveness Diagnostics*, Volume 1. Washington, DC: World Bank.

Santoni, Gianluca, and Daria Taglioni. 2015. "Networks and Structural Integration in Global Value Chains." In João Amador and Filippo di Mauro (eds) *The Age of Global Value Chains: Maps and Policy Issues*, London: CEPR.

UNCTAD (United Nations Conference on Trade and Development). 2011. WIR11. *World Investment Report 2011: Non-Equity Modes of International Production and Development.* New York and Geneva: United Nations.

Chapter 7

USE OF GVC MEASURES TO ASSESS THE DRIVERS AND IMPACTS OF GVC PARTICIPATION

Introduction

What are the determinants of global value chain (GVC) links? Do GVC links matter for economic upgrading? And what is the link between GVC participation and labor market outcomes? Although the GVC participation measures defined in the previous chapters are not suited to answer these questions, they can be used in combination with each other or with other measures to shed further light on two key questions policy makers need to ask: which policies help a country enter GVCs, and, more important, does GVC participation lead to development?

Although providing answers to these questions would go beyond the scope of this book, this chapter presents a research agenda and examples of possible estimation strategies for ways to test for the drivers and impacts of GVC participation using statistical methods or econometrics or quantifying direct relationships in international input-output tables.

What Are the Determinants of GVC Links?

The first section of this chapter focuses on the determinants of GVC links. The first step decomposes gross export growth into its components. If gross export growth is accepted as a measure of GVC links on the selling side, the decomposition allows for detecting how much of the value added is generated at home and abroad.

The second step adopts two measures of GVC links—GVC integration at the country or sector level and a GVC participation dummy at the firm level. The text focuses on different determinants of GVC links at the country, sector, and firm levels.

Decomposition of Gross Export Growth

What are the growth contributions of the different components of gross exports—as introduced in chapter 4—for export growth? We can decompose the growth rate of gross exports (EXGR) into the direct (intra-sector) domestic value added embodied in gross exports (EXGR_DDC), indirect (upstream) domestic value added embodied in gross exports (EXGR_IDC), and foreign value added embodied in gross exports (EXGR_FVA) (all in natural logarithms):

$$D.\ln EXGR_{cst} = \alpha + \beta D.\ln EXGR\_DDC_{cst} + \gamma D.\ln EXGR\_IDC_{cst} + \delta D.\ln EXGR\_FVA_{cst} + D_{cs} + D_t + \varepsilon_{cst}$$

D. denotes first differences, while subscripts c, s, and t designate country, sector, and time, respectively. All regressions control for country-sector and year fixed effects, denoted by D_{cs} and D_t, respectively.

This statistical relationship does not include re-imported domestic value added, EXGR_RIM, because in many cases that value is 0, and taking natural logarithms would yield many missing observations. Although all components are expected to show positive coefficient signs, comparing differences across countries or sectors within a country is nevertheless interesting.

This assessment can be based on data from the Trade in Value Added (TiVA) data set of the Organisation for Economic Co-operation and Development (OECD) and World Trade Organization (WTO), which covers 61 OECD and non-OECD countries and 34 sectors (two primary sectors, 17 manufacturing sectors, 10 commercial services sectors, and five other services sectors), for 1995, 2000, 2005, and 2008 to 2011. Because all the measures are reported in nominal values, applying appropriate deflators (preferably at the country or sector level) is important.

Correlations of GVC Integration with Country-Level Characteristics

What are the key country characteristics associated with GVC integration? Looking at the determinants of GVC participation requires developing a sound theoretical model. However, initial insights can be gathered by assessing the statistical correlation between measures of GVC integration with selected indicators at the country level. This analysis uses the measure of structural integration in GVCs—BONwin (buyer's perspective) and BONwout (seller's perspective), as computed by Santoni and Taglioni (2015) and introduced in chapter 6. Here we focus on the following three country characteristics, which, according to the economic literature, are important determinants of GVC participation: (1) logistics performance, (2) share of people with a tertiary education in the workforce, and (3) geographical distance to the closest global knowledge center.

Good logistics performance is important because key components of GVC production are time sensitive, and reliable connectivity allows firms to connect factories across borders more efficiently. A skilled workforce is recognized as an important determinant of countries' success in GVCs because it allows producing at the high standards of productivity, efficiency, sophistication, and timeliness required to serve global markets. Countries closer to the hubs in GVCs and to the global centers of knowledge are favored by easier access to tacit knowledge. Unlike knowledge embodied in technology, tacit knowledge requires frequent and continued face-to-face interaction between the staff and managers of lead firms or turnkey suppliers and those of other firms in the GVC, and the importance of tacit knowledge increases for more complex tasks. The analysis uses the overall Logistics Performance Index (LPI) to quantify logistics performance; the share of workers with tertiary education to quantify the skill level; and the geographical distance from Germany, Japan, and the United States as a proxy for distance from knowledge centers. Those three countries are identified as global knowledge centers through the network analysis illustrated in chapter 6 (eigenvector centrality of outflows of value added).

GVC Integration and Logistics Performance

Analysis of high- and middle-income countries based on information available in the OECD-WTO TiVA database in 2008 confirms that higher GVC integration, as a buyer and seller, hinges on better overall logistics performance (figure 7.1). The LPI takes into account a country's customs efficiency, quality of trade and transport infrastructure, ease of arranging shipments, quality of logistics services, ability to track and trace consignments, and delivery times. For high-income countries (HICs), the positive correlation is even stronger than for middle-income countries (not shown here), which suggests that the importance of efficient logistics may rise with more complex tasks.

GVC Integration and Skill Levels

Analysis of high- and middle-income countries with information available in the OECD-WTO TiVA database for 2008 suggests that a higher share of workers with tertiary education is positively correlated with GVC participation, from the buyer's and seller's perspectives (figure 7.2). The positive correlation seems to be stronger for GVC integration as a seller, which implies that becoming an exporter in GVCs depends more crucially on skills than importing GVC inputs.

GVC Integration and Geographical Distance to Knowledge Centers

Shorter geographical distance to major knowledge centers is positively correlated with higher GVC integration. Figure 7.3 plots the correlation between GVC integration and geographical distance to the closest (in kilometers) of three knowledge centers for a range of high- and middle-income countries with information available in the OECD-WTO TiVA database in 2008. The analysis takes into account the following knowledge centers: Germany, Japan, and the United States. Figure 7.3, panel a, suggests that longer distance to the closest knowledge center is negatively correlated with GVC integration as a buyer. This finding might support the view that countries that are geographically closer to technology centers are able to import more knowledge-intensive inputs, which increases their GVC integration as a buyer directly and perhaps also indirectly (in the sense that greater access to technology enables them to participate in more GVCs, which requires them to import more GVC inputs). Geographical distance to major knowledge centers is also negatively correlated

Figure 7.1. GVC Integration and Overall Logistics Performance Indicator, 2008

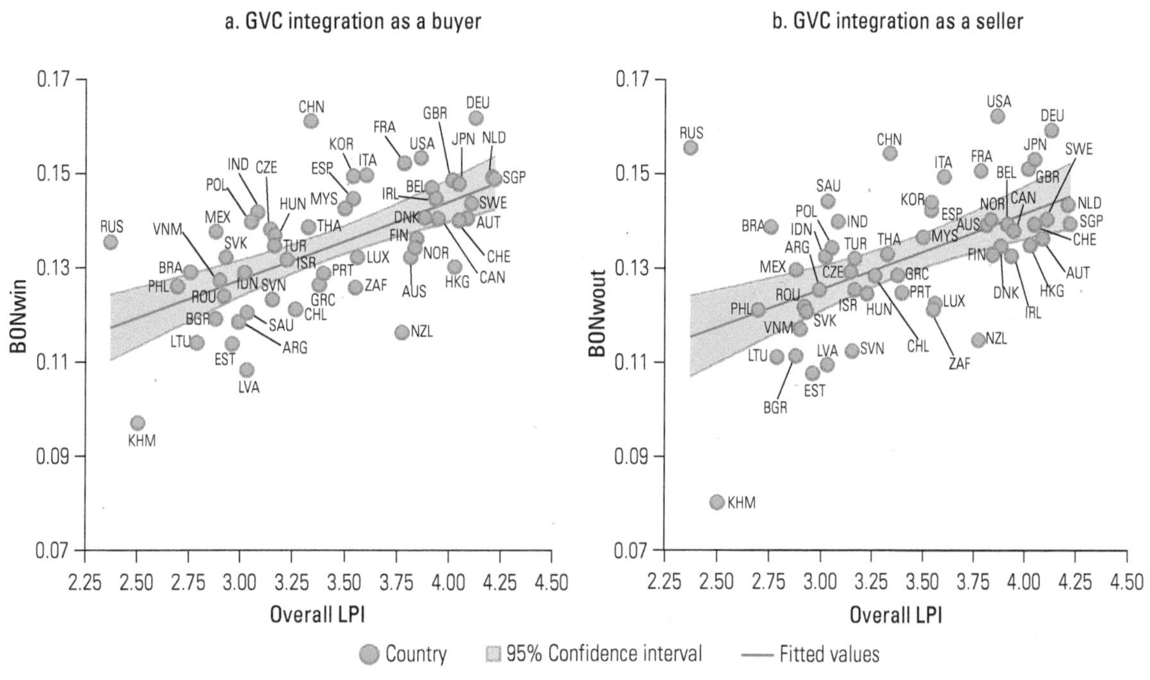

Sources: Adapted from Santoni and Taglioni 2015; Organisation for Economic Co-operation and Development–World Trade Organization Trade in Value Added database; World Bank World Development Indicators 2007.

Note: BONwin = buyer-related measure of structural integration in GVCs; BONwout = seller-related measure of structural integration in GVCs; GVC = global value chain; LPI = Logistics Performance Index.

Figure 7.2. GVC Integration and Skill Levels, 2008

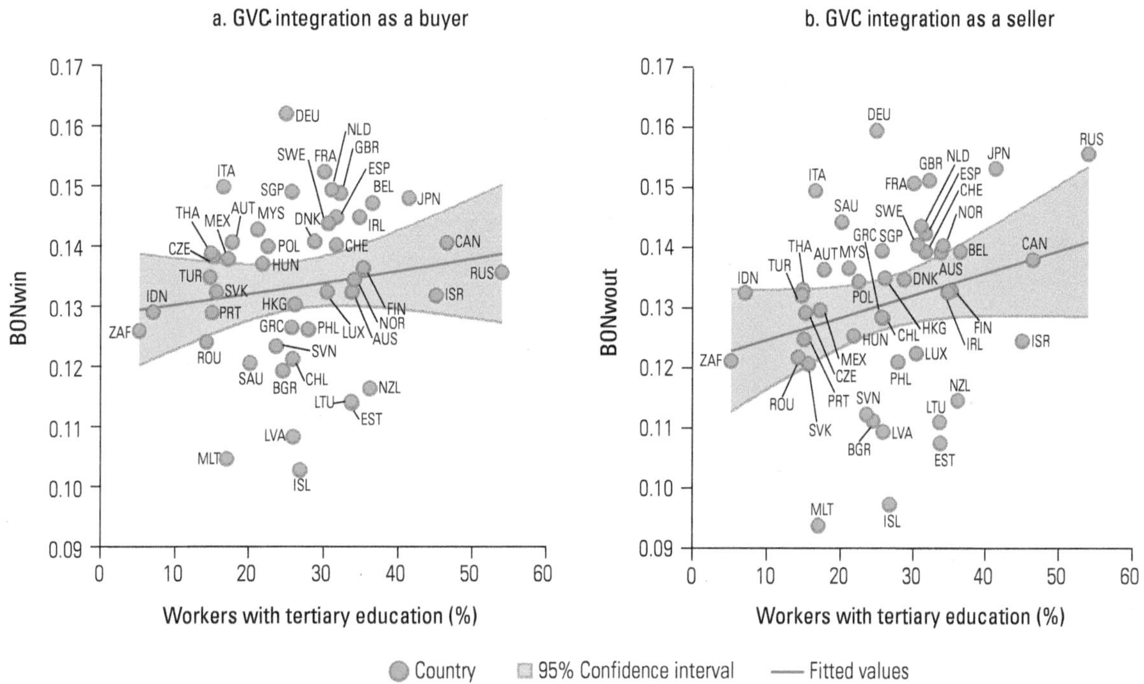

Sources: Adapted from Santoni and Taglioni 2015; Organisation for Economic Co-operation and Development–World Trade Organization Trade in Value Added database; World Bank World Development Indicators 2007.

Note: Education data are not available for many countries. BONwin = buyer-related measure of structural integration in GVCs; BONwout = seller-related measure of structural integration in GVCs; GVC = global value chain.

Figure 7.3. GVC Integration and Geographical Distance to the Closest Knowledge Center (Germany, Japan, and the United States), 2008

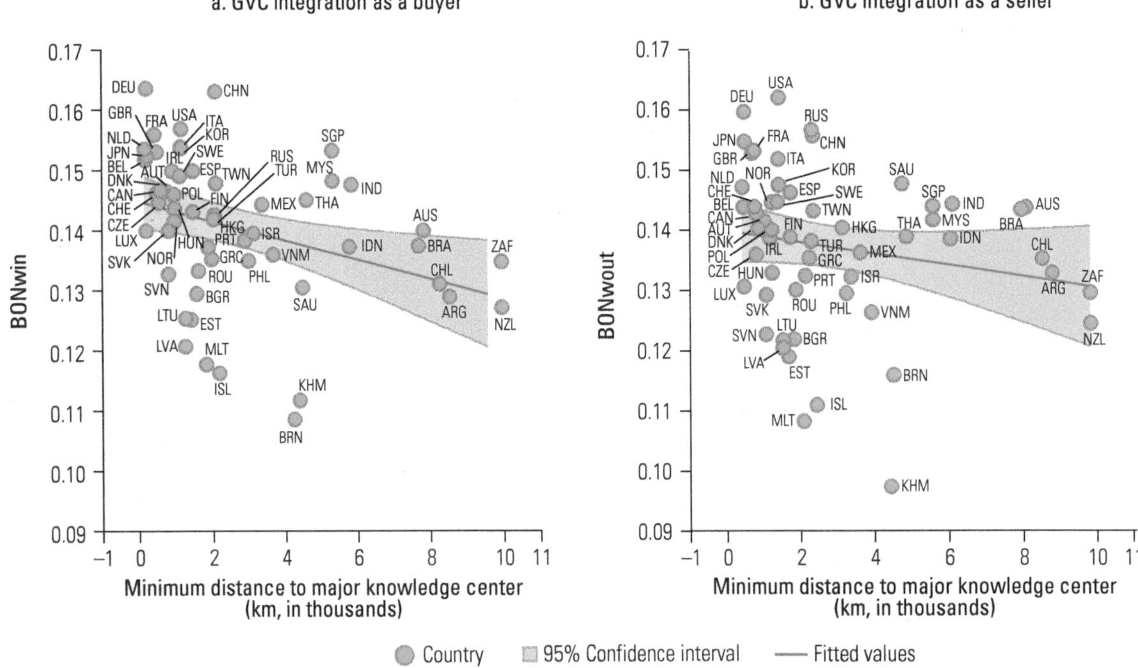

Sources: Adapted from Santoni and Taglioni 2015; Organisation for Economic Co-operation and Development–World Trade Organization Trade in Value Added database; CEPII 2012.

Note: BONwin = buyer-related measure of structural integration in GVCs; BONwout = seller-related measure of structural integration in GVCs; GVC = global value chain; km = kilometers..

with GVC integration as a seller, but the correlation seems to be weaker (figure 7.3, panel b). We find that resource-rich countries are located more remotely from knowledge centers.

Determinants of Firm-Level GVC Entry

This subsection amends the Roberts and Tybout (1997) theoretical model on the determinants of exporting. A firm *i*'s propensity to participate in a GVC at time *t* depends on the firm's expected profits, π, which, in turn, are influenced by expected revenues, *R*, and costs, *c*, plus sunk GVC entry costs, *S*:

$$\Pr(gvc_{it} = 1) = \Pr(R_{it} > c_{it} + S(1 - gvc_{it-1}),$$

where gvc denotes a GVC dummy at the firm level. The term $S(1 - gvc_{it-1})$ is 0 if the firm participated in GVCs in period $t - 1$, and 1 otherwise. In other words, the firm participates in GVCs if expected profits $\pi > 0$.

The firm's expected profits π are affected by firm-level characteristics and the policy environment, which can generate or lower revenues *R* or costs *c*. The equation then translates into the following:

$$\Pr(gvc_{ict} = 1) = \Pr(\pi_{ict} = \beta firm_{ict} + \gamma policy_{cst} + S(1 - gvc_{it-1}) > 0),$$

where subscript *c* denotes country, *s* is sector, firm is firm-level determinants of GVC participation, and policy is policy determinants.

The analysis focuses on the following estimation equation:

$$gvc_{ict} = \alpha_0 + \beta firm_{ict} + \gamma policy_{cst} + D_i + D_{cs} + D_t + \varepsilon_{ict}$$

where α_0 denotes the constant; D_i, firm fixed effects; D_{cs}, country-sector fixed effects; D_t, year fixed effects; and ε_{ict}, the idiosyncratic error term.

Following the literature on the firm-level determinants of exporting, the model includes firm size, firm age, foreign ownership status, as well as measures of workers' skills and productivity as determinants of GVC participation. This leads to the following version of the preceding equation:

$$gvc_{ict} = \alpha_0 + \beta_1 \ln emp_{ict} + \beta_2 \ln age_{ict} + \beta_3 fdi_{ict} + \beta_4 \ln wage_{ict} + \beta_5 \ln tfp_{ict} + \gamma policy_{cst} + D_i + D_{cs} + D_t + \varepsilon_{ict}$$

where emp denotes the total number of employees (in logarithms); age denotes the years of operation (in logarithms); fdi is a dummy that equals 1 if the foreign private ownership ≥ 10 percent, and 0 otherwise; wage is the average real wage per worker (in logarithms) as a proxy for worker skills; and tfp is total factor productivity (in logarithms).

Next, the focus is on the policy determinants of GVC entry, as discussed in part III of this book, including the following policy determinants at the country-sector level (depending on data availability, the determinants can also be measured at the country-region or country level only):

$$\begin{aligned} gvc_{ict} = {} & \alpha_0 + \beta_1 \ln emp_{ict} + \beta_2 \ln age_{ict} \\ & + \beta_3 fdi_{ict} + \beta_4 \ln wage_{ict} + \beta_5 \ln tfp_{ict} \\ & + \gamma_1 epz_{cst} + \gamma_2 open_{cst} + \gamma_3 \, connect_{cst} \\ & + \gamma_4 competitive_{cst} + \gamma_5 invest_{cst} \\ & + \gamma_6 domest_{cst} + D_i + D_{cs} + D_t + \varepsilon_{ict} \end{aligned}$$

where epz is a dummy that equals 1 if the country has an export-processing zone in a sector, and 0 if not; open denotes measures of openness to international trade and foreign direct investment (FDI); connect denotes measures of connectivity to international markets (for example, logistics performance, customs, and infrastructure); competitive covers measures of competitiveness in unit labor costs and labor productivity; invest captures drivers of investment (for example, intellectual property protection, level of competition, administrative burden, and corruption); and domest denotes measures of the quality of domestic value chains and the services infrastructure (for example, competence and quality of services). Depending on the type of variables chosen, it might be necessary to use logarithms.

The equation can be estimated using the probit/logit type of regression model where the dependent variable is a binary variable taking the value 1 or 0.

Determinants of Sector GVC Participation

If firm-level data—in particular, information on GVC participation—are not available, an alternative could be to estimate the impact of the policy determinants just discussed on sector GVC participation in a country, gvcpart, where GVC participation is not a dummy variable, but enters the equation in the form of values (in logarithms). The estimation equation then looks as follows:

$$\begin{aligned} \ln gvcpart_{ict} = {} & \alpha_0 + \gamma_1 epz_{cst} + \gamma_2 open_{cst} \\ & + \gamma_3 connect_{cst} + \gamma_4 competitive_{cst} + \gamma_5 invest_{cst} \\ & + \gamma_6 domest_{cst} + D_{cs} + D_t + \varepsilon_{cst} \end{aligned}$$

Do GVC Links Matter for Economic Upgrading?

The second part of this chapter focuses on the role of GVC links for economic upgrading. Three main measures of economic upgrading are adopted: (1) growth of domestic value added embodied in gross exports at the sector level in the first section, (2) level of domestic value added at the sector level in the second section, and (3) firm-level labor productivity in the third section. Different measures of GVC links are also explored, including GVC measures of structural integration as buyers and sellers in networks, foreign value added embodied in gross exports, domestic value added embodied in exports of third countries, GVC participation index, position in GVCs (upstreamness), domestic length of sourcing chains, and share of foreign output in a sector.

Growth of GVC Links and Domestic Value Added in Exports

Do the intensity and nature of GVC links matter for growth in domestic value added that is exported? This question can be explored through econometric analysis from several angles. First, the most obvious question to explore is whether the degree of structural integration in global value-added trade matters. Second, econometric analysis can be used to investigate how greater integration of a country in GVCs as a buyer—as opposed to weaker integration as a seller (that is, more unbalanced GVC integration)—affects domestic value-added growth from gross exports. Third, the analysis can examine more closely the relation between the growth of foreign value added embodied in gross exports and the domestic value-added component. Fourth, it can look at the role of a country's position in the value chain (upstreamness or distance to final demand). Finally, econometrics can be used to investigate the role of the domestic length of the sourcing chains.

Growth of GVC Participation and Domestic Value Added Embodied in Exports

What is the relationship between the growth rate of GVC participation and a country's growth of domestic value added embodied in exports? To address this question, we can correlate BONwin and BONwout growth measures of "eigenvector centrality" or structural integration in GVCs (as introduced in chapter

6) with the growth of domestic value added embodied in exports, EXGR_DVA:

$$D.lnEXGR\_DVA_{cst} = \alpha + \beta D.lnBON_{cst} + \gamma D.lnBON_{cst} * Dummy_{country\ of\ interest} + D_{cs} + D_t + \varepsilon_{cst}$$

The two measures of structural integration in GVCs, BONwin and BONwout, are suggested as measures of eigenvector centrality. These measures are preferred over other measures of trade openness or GVC participation, as the former account not only for direct links, but also for indirect links. For example, in accounting for the trade links between, say, Argentina and Mexico, BONwin and BONwout also take into consideration the full network of trade, including for example the trade links between China and the Republic of Korea. Alternative measures of GVC participation, such as the GVC participation index, can also be used.

The domestic value added embodied in exports is measured in logarithms. Because EXGR_DVA is reported in nominal values, appropriate deflators (preferably at the country-sector level) must be used.

To detect the correlation specific to the country of interest, the interaction term $\gamma lnBON_{cst}$* $Dummy_{country\ of\ interest}$—the dummy for the country of interest—is added, where the dummy takes the value 1 if that country is the one under analysis, and 0 otherwise. We also control for country-sector fixed effects, D_{cs}, and fixed year effects, D_t.

The signs of the coefficients of the correlations provide a first indication of whether a growing integration in GVCs may have the potential to increase the growth of domestic value added embodied in gross exports. Although the analysis does not allow for establishing causality, growing GVC integration can lead to higher output, productivity, and value added at home via several transmission channels (see figure 1.11 in chapter 1). The correlation can also be run at the sector level to detect differences across GVCs.

Growth of Balanced GVC Participation and Domestic Value Added Embodied in Gross Exports

To detect whether balanced GVC integration—as a buyer and as a seller—matters for economic upgrading, correlations can be run between the growth rate of balanced integration in GVCs (BONbal) and the growth rate of domestic value added embodied in gross exports (EXGR_DVA) (in logarithms):

$$D.lnEXGR\_DVA_{cst} = \alpha + \beta D.lnBONbal_{cst} + \gamma D.lnBONbal_{cst} * Dummy_{country\ of\ interest} + D_{cs} + D_t + \varepsilon_{cst}$$

The analysis can use an inverse measure of balanced GVC integration, defined as ln(BONwin–BONwout). Because EXGR_DVA is reported in nominal values, the use of appropriate deflators (preferably at the country-sector level) is important.

A larger difference designates less balanced GVC participation because GVC integration as a buyer is larger than as a seller. If the sign of the coefficient is positive, the results could point to the beneficial effects of importing foreign know-how and technology. Alternatively, the analysis can use a measure of balanced GVC participation in levels (rather than growth rates). Alternative measures of balanced GVC participation—for example, based on the forward and backward components of the GVC participation index—can also be used.

Growth of Foreign and Domestic Value Added Embodied in Gross Exports

A more direct way to look at the role of foreign inputs is to run correlations between the growth rate of EXGR_FVA and the growth rate of EXGR_DVA (in logarithms):

$$D.lnEXGR\_DVA_{cst} = \alpha + \beta D.lnEXGR\_FVA_{cst} + \gamma D.lnEXGR\_FVA_{cst} * Dummy_{country\ of\ interest} + D_{cs} + D_t + \varepsilon_{cst}$$

Because EXGR_DVA and EXGR_FVA are reported in nominal values, the use of appropriate deflators (preferably at the country-sector level) is important.

Although a positive sign on the coefficient would be expected, because importing enables exporting for most countries, the size of the coefficient by sector could indicate which sectors benefit more strongly from foreign know-how or technology.

Growth of Upstreamness and Domestic Value Added Embodied in Gross Exports

Does the position of a firm in the value chain (upstreamness or distance to final demand) matter for the domestic value added that is exported? The following computation illustrates correlations between the growth rate of upstreamness (UPSTREAM) and the growth rate of domestic value added embodied in gross exports (EXGR_DVA) (in logarithms):

$$D.\ln EXGR\_DVA_{cst} = \alpha + \beta D.\ln UPSTREAM_{cst} + \gamma D.\ln UPSTREAM_{cst}{}^{*}Dummy_{\text{country of interest}} + D_{cs} + D_t + \varepsilon_{cst}$$

Alternatively, the level rather than the growth of upstreamness can be included as the right-hand variable. Because EXGR_DVA is reported in nominal values, the use of appropriate deflators (preferably at the country-sector level) is important.

It is important to bear in mind that the results are clearly sector specific and depend on the current position of the country in a specific value chain, as well as the value-added contribution of the tasks upstream and downstream of the current ones. More upstreamness in the electronics sector, for example, can be beneficial if the country is specialized in assembly or production activities; higher value-added activities, such as research and development and design, are located at the beginning of the value chain. A move toward downstream postproduction activities (marketing, logistics, after-sales, and so forth) can also be beneficial.

Growth of Domestic Length of Sourcing Chains and Domestic Value Added Embodied in Gross Exports

The relationship between the growth rate of the domestic length of sourcing chains (LENGTH) and the growth rate of EXGR_DVA (in logarithms) is illustrated as follows:

$$D.\ln EXGR\_DVA_{cst} = \alpha + \beta D.\ln LENGTH_{cst} + \gamma D.\ln LENGTH_{cst}{}^{*}Dummy_{\text{country of interest}} + D_{cs} + D_t + \varepsilon_{cst}$$

Because EXGR_DVA is reported in nominal values, the use of appropriate deflators (preferably at the country-sector level) is important. Again, levels can be used instead of growth rates for the length variable.

GVC Links and Domestic Value Added[1]

This step focuses on the effect of GVC integration—as a buyer and a seller—on domestic value added, also taking into account the mediating role of national policy. Domestic value added is generated by combining labor with capital stock, and is dependent on a country's technology shifter. The technology shifter is assumed to be a function of international trade and innovation, which is consistent with the trade literature.

We estimate a standard fixed effects model for sector s in country c at time t of the following form:

$$\ln DVA_{cst} = \alpha + \beta \ln GVC_{cst} + \gamma \ln trade + \delta_1 \ln capital_{cst} + \delta_2 \ln emp_{cst} + D_{cs} + D_{st} + D_{ct} + \varepsilon_{cst}$$

where DVA denotes domestic value added, capital is capital stock, and emp is the number of employees. GVC captures our measures of GVC integration, which enter the function as part of the technology shifter. The first GVC indicator is the amount of EXGR_FVA; the second indicator is the amount of domestic value added re-exported by third countries (DVA3EX). EXGR_FVA quantifies a country's backward links into GVCs, or GVC integration as a buyer, while DVA3EX quantifies a country's forward links into GVCs, or GVC integration as a seller (see chapters 4 and 5 for more details).

In addition to GVC integration, we also include a measure of final goods trade (trade), to separate the potential positive GVC effect from the simple positive effect of trade openness. For this, we calculate the amount of foreign value added processed or consumed domestically. This covers imports of final goods and intermediate goods assembled and consumed domestically. Because the latter part might overlap with GVC trade, we might have a downward bias in our estimates. However, not controlling for openness would prevent us from separating the effects of GVC trade and final goods trade.

All variables are measured in logarithms at the sector level in a country. We also include country-sector fixed effects (D_{cs}), country-time fixed effects (D_{ct}), and sector-time fixed effects (D_{st}). The last are included to capture innovation that is part of the technology shifter.

As we are interested in the contribution of country-specific policy variables to economic upgrading through GVCs, we include an interaction term between a set of national characteristics and our GVC indicators:

$$\ln DVA_{cst} = \alpha + \beta_1 \ln GVC_{cst} + \beta_2 \ln GVC_{cst}{}^{*}policy_c + \gamma \ln trade + \delta_1 \ln capital_{cst} + \delta_2 \ln emp_{cst} + D_{cs} + D_{st} + D_{ct} + \varepsilon_{cst}$$

The sign of the coefficient β_2 indicates whether a certain policy helps increase ($\beta_2 > 0$) or reduce ($\beta_2 < 0$) the impact of GVC integration on domestic value added.

As measures for the policy variables (policy) we employ variables capturing a country's infrastructure, foreign presence, legal institutions, and innovation capabilities. Hence, we include variables that analyze a country's ability to join GVCs (infrastructure, foreign presence, legal system, and institutions) and its ability to upgrade (innovation). Because of the sometimes incomplete data, we use the average over the period.

The regression results for a set of 40 countries and 35 industries for 1995–2011 are shown in annex 7A. Many other aspects of a country's institutional characteristics (including education, trade openness, financial regulation, labor market regulation, business environment, competition, development, and so on) can also be assessed.

If we are interested in a country's performance in a specific role, we can add two more interaction terms to the equation:

$$\begin{aligned} \ln DVA_{cst} &= \alpha + \beta_1 \ln GVC_{cst} + \beta_2 \ln GVC_{cst} {*} policy_c \\ &+ \beta_3 \ln GVC_{cst} {*}\ Dummy_{\text{country of interest}} \\ &+ \beta_4 \ln GVC_{cst} {*} policy {*}\ Dummy_{\text{country of interest}} \\ &+ \gamma \ln trade + \delta_1 \ln capital_{cst} + \delta_2 \ln emp_{cst} \\ &+ Dummy_{\text{country of interest}} + D_{cs} + D_{st} + D_{ct} + \varepsilon_{cst} \end{aligned}$$

where the sign of the coefficient β_3 indicates whether the impact of GVC integration is higher or lower in the country of interest than for the rest of the country sample (β_1). The sign of the coefficient β_4 reveals whether the mediating effect of policy in the country of interest is more positive or negative than for the rest of the country sample (β_2).

GVC Participation and Firm-Level Productivity: Mediating Factors

Within-Industry Impact of FDI

Data constraints make it difficult to perform direct testing of the channels for FDI spillovers to the wider host economy. Farole and Winkler (2014) have developed an econometric analysis to assess how foreign investor characteristics, domestic firms' absorptive capacity, and a country's institutional variables influence intra-industry productivity spillovers to domestic firms from FDI (annex 7B). The method focuses on the within-industry impact of foreign output share on domestic firm productivity and the role of mediating factors. Specifically, Farole and Winkler ask, what is the potential of global production networks to enhance the productivity of domestic firms?

Foreign investor characteristics are likely to capture the effect of the effectiveness of intra-industry demand and assistance, technology spillovers that result from the willingness of foreign investors to provide technology and know-how, and the effect of increased competition with local firms for limited resources in the country (for a discussion of how foreign firm characteristics can influence spillovers, see chapter 9).

Measures of absorptive capacity, by contrast, allow for testing the preparedness of domestic firms to absorb new technology and know-how, using various channels. Measures of domestic institutional preparedness and other national characteristics indicate the ability of the domestic economy to facilitate technology spillovers, enhance the productivity of domestic firms, and generate positive effects on wages and skilled labor (for a discussion of how absorptive capacity and national institutions can influence spillovers, see chapter 9).

The econometric estimation uses a cross-section of more than 25,000 domestic manufacturing firms in 76 low- and middle-income countries (LMICs) from the World Bank's Enterprise Surveys (table I.1 in appendix I). The measure of intra-industry FDI spillovers in the strict sense captures only horizontal spillovers, but because sectors are defined at a broad level, FDI spillovers are likely to capture some vertical spillovers. For example, the rubric "auto and auto components" includes manufacturers of final automotive products and suppliers of automotive components, so FDI in this sector could affect domestic final producers of cars as well as domestic suppliers of auto components. Similar situations are likely in such sectors as food, electronics, and chemicals and pharmaceuticals.

Integrating a country's domestic firms into GVCs not only increases the possibility for productivity gains through supplying to a multinational firm in the country, but also through exporting to a buyer abroad. In addition, countries should not neglect the opportunities for productivity gains that GVC participation can provide from importing inputs that contain knowledge and technology. Alternatively, the model could also include firm-level measures of GVC integration as right-hand side variables, such as the share of exports in a firm's total output or the share of imported inputs in total inputs.

Within-Industry Impact of Structural Integration in GVCs

Similarly, the analysis can be used to examine the effect of GVC participation of an industry on a firm's productivity by merging the Farole and Winkler

(2014) data set with two sector measures of structural integration in GVCs: BONwin (buyer's perspective) and BONwout (seller's perspective), as described in chapter 6 and computed by Santoni and Taglioni (2015). Because the measures of structural integration are based on the OECD-WTO TiVA database, fewer observations are available, leading to a total of more than 14,000 manufacturing firms in 22 LMICs (table I.2 in appendix I). Alternative measures of GVC participation, such as the GVC participation index available in the TiVA database, might also be used.

The baseline equation follows the estimation equation in the previous section (annex 7B):

$$\begin{aligned}\text{lnlp}_{irst} = {} & \alpha + \beta\text{BON}_{cst} + \gamma(\text{BON}_{cst}{*}\text{MF}) \\ & + \delta(\text{BON}_{cst}{*}\text{MF}{*}\text{Dummy}_{\text{country of interest}}) \\ & + \zeta\text{lncapint}_{irst} \\ & + \text{Dummy}_{\text{country of interest}} + D_r + D_s + D_t + \varepsilon_{irst}\end{aligned}$$

lnlp_{irst} denotes the log labor productivity for domestic firm i in region r, country c, sector s at time t; lncapint_{irst} denotes capital intensity in natural logarithms. The key variable of interest is the interaction effect between the measure of structural integration in GVCs (BON) in country c and sector s at time t and the "mediating factors" (MF) that are specific to the country of interest (see annex 7B for the list of mediating factors and their definitions). This term is indicated in the equation as $\delta(\text{BON}_{cst}{*}\text{MF}{*}\text{Dummy}_{\text{country of interest}})$.

The total impact of GVC integration—taking into account the mediating role of absorptive capacity and host country characteristics—on firms located in the country can be obtained as follows:

$$\beta + \gamma\text{MF} + \delta(\text{MF}{*}\text{Dummy}_{\text{country of interest}})$$

A topic of interest is how the impact of mediating factors in the country of interest differs from the impact of the whole sample of countries in the data set—that is, the effects have to be interpreted relative to the full sample. Annex 7C shows an application of this model to Bulgaria. The results are described in chapter 2.

Quantifying the Labor Market Dimension of GVCs

The last part of this chapter addresses which GVC-oriented industries have a higher demand for labor, such that integrating into GVCs in those sectors has a greater potential to create jobs and increase household income. Using the newly developed LACEX database (table BG.1.1 in box G.1 in appendix G), economists at the World Bank found that in South Africa, GVC integration has led to higher net jobs but lower job intensity (Calì and Hollweg 2015; Hollweg 2015). Using a social matrix accounting approach, it appears that jobs per exports (in U.S. dollars) decline in GVC integration. Jobs growth comes through indirect links, and mainly services inputs (with implications for skill bias).

This section provides an overview of measures that can be used to identify the impact on labor and wages. The measures are categorized in two groups: indirect measures of social upgrading, and direct measures of social upgrading.

Indirect Measures of Social Upgrading

This subsection presents indirect measurements of the link between GVC participation and labor market outcomes. The specific sectors that are relevant for participation in GVCs can be analyzed using the following methods.

Descriptive Statistics

Descriptive statistics may be used to assess which sectors are associated with better labor market outcomes. The researcher would examine countries' sector averages of the number of employees, wages and salaries, wage rate (wages and salaries divided by the number of employees), or labor share (wages and salaries as a percentage of value added). Such statistics, for example, can be obtained from the United Nations Industrial Development Organization's Industrial Statistics database.

Analysis of Employment-Generating Industries and Their Level of GVC Integration

Analysis of employment-generating industries and their level of GVC integration may be carried out by running cross-country "controlled correlations" at the sector level, whereby the labor market indicators discussed in the previous section are regressed on indicators of GVC involvement while controlling for other factors, such as region and gross domestic product. The analyst can also run pooled regressions controlling for industry fixed effects to see which industries have more labor-market-enhancing outcomes conditional on GVC involvement. The sector-level GVC indicators may include the following:

- Network measure of structural integration in GVCs, to assess if centrality, clustering, closeness, or strength in a network has an effect on labor market indicators
- Domestic value added in gross exports, to consider whether value-added generation in exports can be associated with positive labor market outcomes
- GVC participation index or its individual components, to see whether countries that participate more as buyers and sellers generally have better labor market results
- Length of the sourcing chain—either domestic and international segments taken individually or both combined—to see how a greater number of production stages is related to labor market outcomes
- Upstreamness or distance to final demand, to see whether a country's position in the value chain matters for labor market results.

Direct Measures of Social Upgrading

This subsection presents more direct measurements of the link between GVC participation and labor market outcomes by drawing on various indicators already developed in the literature. The indicators can be applied across countries and industries if the data are available.

Labor Content of Gross Exports

The first direct measure of social upgrading is the labor content of gross exports. The newly developed World Bank data set on LACEX can be used to explore the social upgrading linked to GVC participation.[2] The data set is computed on the basis of the social accounting matrix data available in the Global Trade Analysis Project for intermittent years between 1995 and 2011. The matrix includes data for more than 100 countries and 24 or 57 sectors (see appendix G).

Two cases illustrate successful GVC insertion in the past two decades: (1) Chinese machinery and equipment and (2) Indian private services. The former contains non-transport machinery, including the electronics sector; the latter contains mainly information technology (IT)–enabled services, including back office and IT services exports.

China's labor value added in the machinery and equipment sector has expanded dramatically over time, particularly its backward link component (figure 7.4, panel a). This finding is confirmed by the ratio of backward to direct labor value added in exports, which has increased rapidly since 1997

Figure 7.4. Labor Value Added in Chinese Machinery and Equipment Exports, 1995–2011

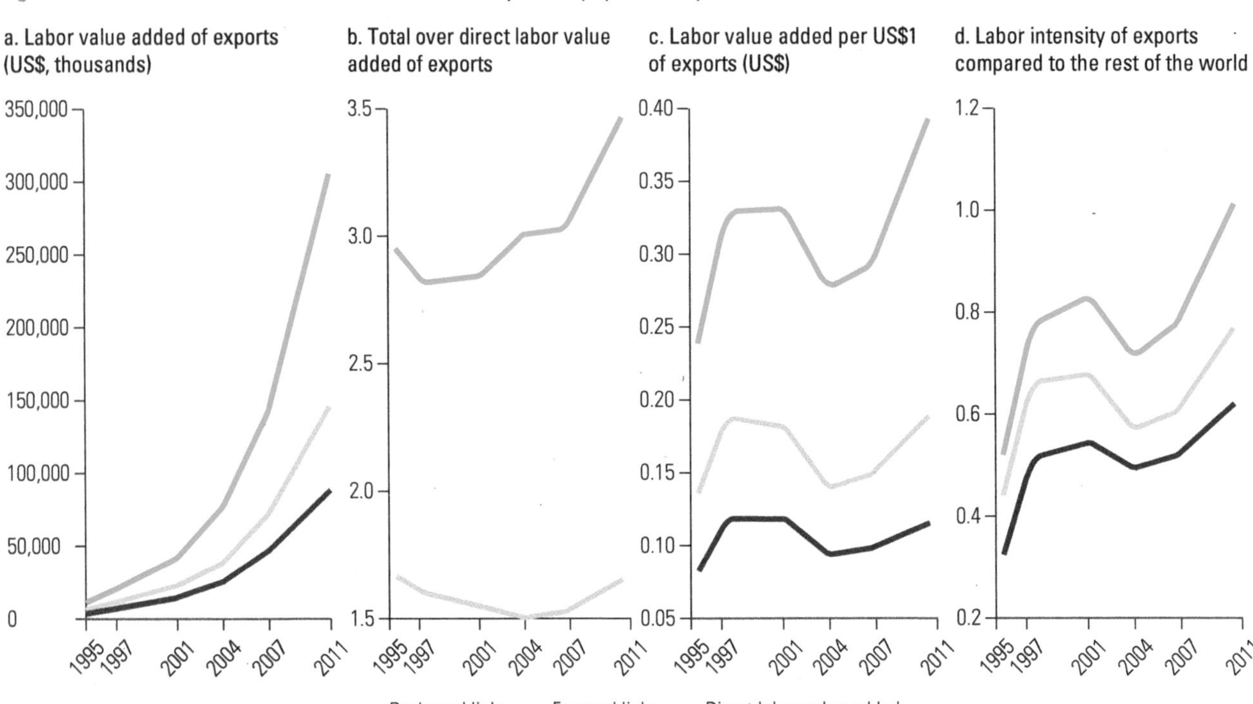

Source: Adapted from Cali and others forthcoming.

Figure 7.5. Labor Value Added in Indian Other Private Services Exports, 1995–2011

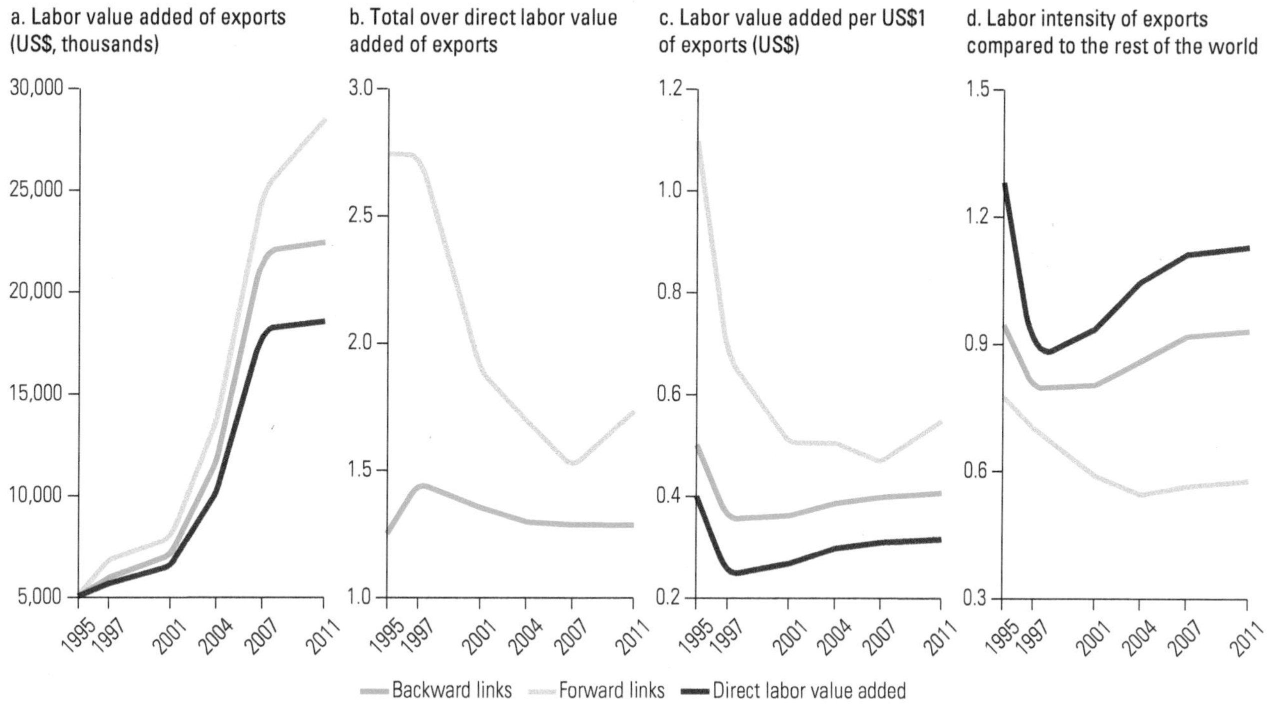

Source: Adapted from Calì and others forthcoming.

(figure 7.4, panel b)—unlike the forward links-direct ratio, which has remained constant. This suggests that China has increased its domestic production in the sectors providing inputs for final exports of machinery. The increase has also translated into an increase in the share of domestic labor value added in exports. The total labor content of machinery exports in backward links increased from US$0.23 per US$1 of exports in 1995 to almost US$0.4 in 2011 (figure 7.4, panel c). In other words, each $100 of machinery exports generated $40 of wages in the economy (in green), only $11 of which is a result of the direct labor in final production (in black). The increase has been much milder for direct and forward links. The increase in the labor intensity of China's machinery exports also has been more marked relative to the rest of the world (figure 7.4, panel d).

For India's other private services exports, the direct labor value added and total labor value added on the basis of forward links are more relevant than the value added generated through backward links (figure 7.5, panel a). Over time, the direct labor content of exports has grown more rapidly than the labor content of forward links (figure 7.5, panel b), but neither has grown relative to the value of exports. The labor content for each $100 of exports has declined for each of the three measures of labor value added since 1995 (figure 7.5, panel c). In particular, the total labor content of exports on the basis of forward links almost halved, from US$1.1 per US$1 of exports in 1995 to US$0.6 in 2011. But the direct and total labor content of exports on the basis of backward links have increased since 1997, also relative to the rest of the world (figure 7.5, panel d).

Labor Component of Domestic Value Added in Exports

A second direct measure of social upgrading, which was developed by the United Nations Conference on Trade and Development (UNCTAD 2013), is the labor cost component of domestic value added in exports, which acts as a proxy for the employment-generating potential of exports. Using the United Nations Conference on Trade and Development (UNCTAD) EORA GVC database for 187 countries, countries are ranked according to their 2010 GVC participation rates in decreasing order (figure 7.6). The labor component of domestic value added in exports increases with higher GVC participation: it reaches 43 percent of value added in exports for countries with the highest GVC participation rate (first quartile), compared with 28 percent for

Figure 7.6. GVC Participation and the Labor Component of Domestic Value Added in Exports

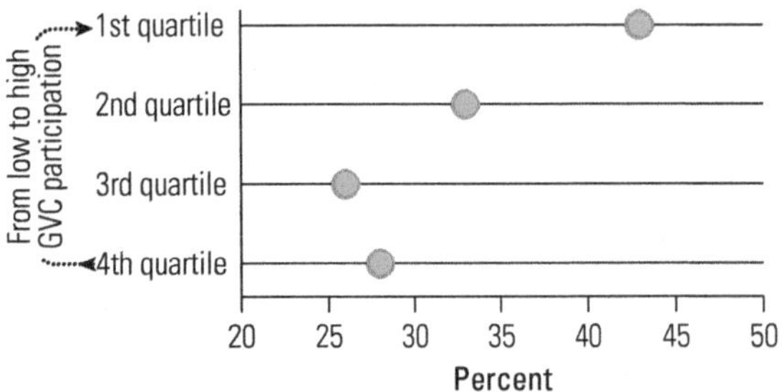

Sources: UNCTAD 2013; UNCTAD-EORA GVC database.
Note: The data are for 187 countries ranked according to the 2010 GVC participation rate in decreasing order and grouped in quartiles. Median values of the quartiles are reported. GVC = global value chain; UNCTAD = United Nations Conference on Trade and Development.

countries with the lowest GVC participation rate (fourth quartile).

In addition, countries with faster growth in GVC participation have faster growth in the labor component of domestic value added in exports (figure 7.7). From 2000 to 2010, the countries that experienced fast growth in GVC participation saw the labor component of exports rise faster (14 percent) than did countries with slow growth (9 percent). The relationship holds even when country participation in GVCs depends on higher foreign value added share, which reduces the share of domestic value added of exports.

Figure 7.7. Growth in the Labor Component of Domestic Value Added in Exports by Level of GVC Participation Growth and Foreign Value Added

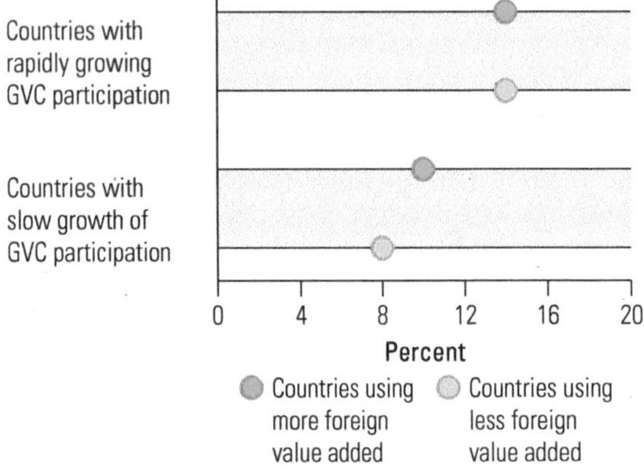

Sources: UNCTAD 2013; UNCTAD-EORA GVC database.
Note: The data are for 187 countries. "Countries with rapidly growing GVC participation" refers to the 50 percent of countries with the highest 2000–10 GVC participation growth rate. "Countries using more foreign value added" refers to the 50 percent of countries with the highest foreign value-added share in exports in 2010. GVC = global value chain; UNCTAD = United Nations Conference on Trade and Development.

Jobs Sustained by Foreign Final Demand

The third indicator, jobs sustained by foreign final demand, is being developed by OECD-WTO as part of the TiVA database for 40 countries.[3] The indicator calculates the number of jobs in the total economy sustained by foreign final demand, which captures the full upstream impact of final demand in foreign markets on domestic employment. Rather than consider the domestic value added in total exports (as was the basis of the previous indicator), which could be used as intermediates in third countries and be exported as final goods, the indicator considers the domestic value added in foreign final demand.

Between 1995 and 2008, a higher share of employment consisted of jobs sustained by foreign final demand (figure 7.8), yet that percentage varies according to countries' size and specialization. For example, based on preliminary estimates, the share for Germany almost doubled between 1995 and 2008, with about 10 million jobs sustained by foreign final demand. For China, the number increased by about two-thirds, from 89 million to 146 million. These figures are averages for the whole economy, including services sectors with lower exposure to international trade, but they can also be disaggregated by industry. For example, about one-third of U.S. jobs in electronics and almost two-fifths of Japanese jobs are derived from foreign final demand.

Jobs Generated by Foreign Trade in GVCs

The fourth indicator is the number of jobs generated by a country's trade in GVCs—jobs generated domestically and abroad—using the World Input-Output Database (WIOD) for 39 countries over the period 1995–2009. The sources of employment creation from international trade can be decomposed into five components: (1) exports, (2) imports, (3) import content of exports, (4) export content of imports, and (5) intermediates contained in imports.[4] The first two components are labor demand from final goods trade; the last three are from trade in intermediates, or the result of a country's GVC participation.

A country's participation in GVCs can lead to domestic or foreign labor demand. Because of the import content of exports, a country's exports generate jobs and incomes in foreign countries. Likewise, a country's imports from foreign countries might contain its own exports to those foreign countries as intermediate inputs. Because of the export content of imports, a country's imports generate jobs domestically. Given third-party intermediates contained in imports, trade between two countries will, in turn, create jobs in the third country. Therefore, the total domestic labor demand can be viewed for each country as the sum of labor demand by domestic exports and domestic content of imports. The sum of the remaining components yields the total foreign labor demand resulting from each country's trade position.

The jobs generated by each component can be computed for various industries. The sector-level information has been aggregated to a single employment figure for each country (table 7.1).[5] Large HICs tend to be the most responsible for GVC-based labor demand, with China, France, Germany, the Netherlands, and the United States having the greatest labor demand resulting from GVC participation. In 2009, most of the countries in the sample demanded more foreign labor than domestic labor through exports, with the exceptions including China, India, and Indonesia.

Jobs in GVC Manufacturing

The fifth indicator is for selected countries between 1995 and 2008, using the WIOD. The jobs in the GVC manufacturing indicator presents a broader picture of the structure of employment in GVCs within a country. It is the most direct measure in the literature of the domestic employment impacts of manufacturing GVC participation (table 7.2).[6] The indicator measures—directly and indirectly—the number of GVC jobs involved in the production of final manufacturing goods (also known as manufactures), as well as their sector of employment in a country.

Apart from China and Turkey, the share of manufacturing GVC jobs in overall employment declined, driven by manufacturing GVC job losses in agriculture and manufacturing. Only about one-half of the workers in manufacturing GVCs are employed in manufacturing; the other half are employed in nonmanufacturing industries that deliver intermediates.

At the same time, employment in manufacturing GVCs increased in the services sector. For some European countries, such as Germany, Italy, and Spain, GVC job increases in services were higher than job losses in manufacturing and agriculture, but that trend was not apparent in other countries.

Changes in the skill structure of GVC manufacturing workers and their average wages have been analyzed—between 1995 and 2008—and include low-, medium-, and high-skilled workers, proxied by educational attainment.[7] HICs in the European Union experienced a strong shift toward specialization in GVC activities performed by high-skilled workers. Relative to the overall labor force, the share of high-skilled workers in total GVC employment increased much faster than the share of medium-skilled workers.

Figure 7.8. Jobs in the Business Sector Sustained by Foreign Final Demand, 1995 and 2008

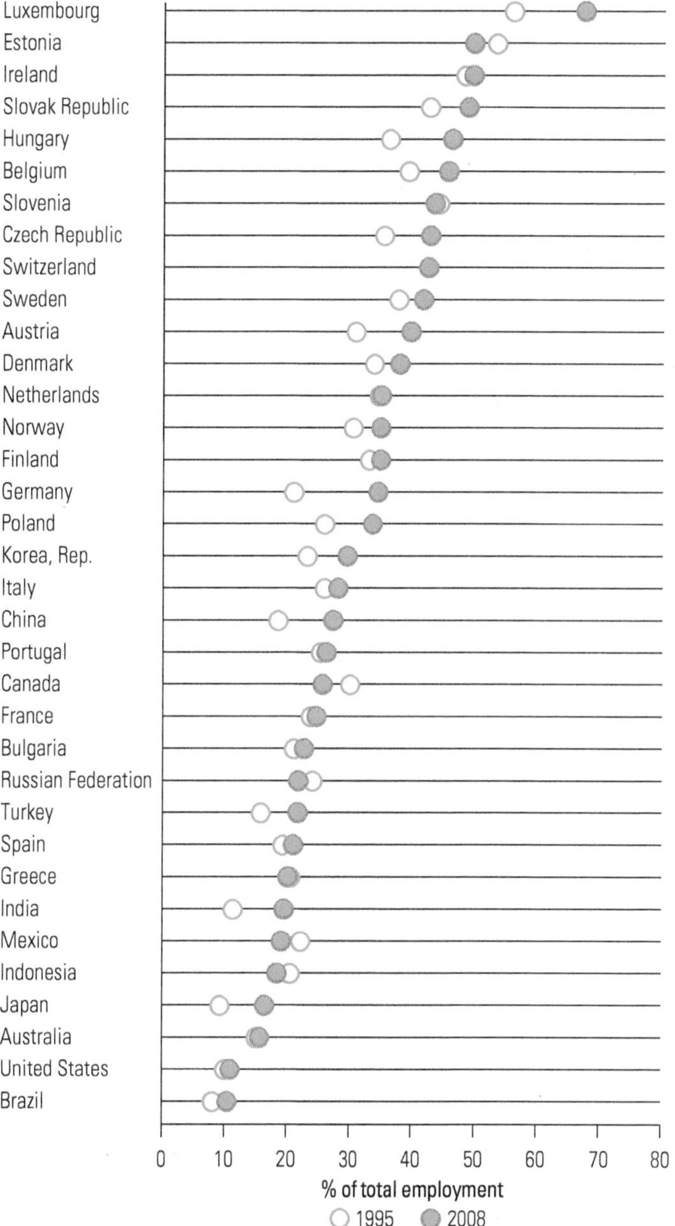

Source: OECD 2013, figure 7.8.1.
Note: The business sector is defined according to International Standard Industrial Classification Rev. 3, Divisions 10 to 74, that is, total economy excluding agriculture, forestry, and fishing (Divisions 01-05), public administration (75), education (80), health (85), and other community, social, and personal services (90–95).

Table 7.1. **Jobs Generated by Five Components of Foreign Trade, 2009**
(thousands)

Country	Domestic: Exports	Domestic: Export content of imports	Foreign labor: Imports	Foreign labor: Import content of exports	Foreign labor: Third-party imports in imports	Differences (domestic minus foreign labor)
China	140,249.1	3,270.9	17,462.8	4,221.9	2,238.0	119,597.4
India	34,914.8	89.6	8,064.4	1,291.5	496.6	25,151.9
Indonesia	10,236.6	24.0	3,891.8	448.4	289.0	5,631.4
Brazil	7,143.3	21.9	3,210.6	168.8	486.7	3,299.0
Bulgaria	882.3	1.4	465.3	97.9	98.2	222.4
Romania	1,597.0	6.0	1,097.3	186.6	293.7	25.4
Latvia	162.2	0.7	161.0	23.1	51.4	−72.5
Estonia	160.1	0.3	155.0	50.5	39.2	−84.3
Malta	45.1	0.0	119.0	33.9	23.8	−131.5
Cyprus	34.8	0.0	143.4	14.1	35.4	−158.1
Lithuania	250.5	1.0	383.8	102.7	68.5	−303.5
Slovenia	223.8	0.4	345.2	113.5	106.5	−340.9
Mexico	6,054.1	46.7	4,317.6	1,590.4	848.1	−655.2
Portugal	797.8	4.2	1,122.8	218.7	353.3	−892.8
Slovakia	738.4	4.9	977.2	458.0	264.7	−956.6
Poland	3,592.6	26.9	3,149.1	911.0	747.0	−1,187.6
Hungary	1,129.2	5.8	1,349.1	713.2	417.8	−1,345.1
Finland	433.5	2.0	1,644.0	449.7	323.2	−1,981.4
Czech Republic	1,674.7	15.9	2,176.4	993.2	544.1	−2,023.2
Turkey	2,056.6	6.2	3,146.6	456.5	506.2	−2,046.5
Greece	204.9	0.8	1,807.2	83.4	386.6	−2,071.5
Denmark	529.4	3.4	1,974.9	463.1	542.5	−2,447.7
Taiwan, China	3,119.7	23.2	3,807.2	1,681.9	517.2	−2,863.4
Russian Federation	6,532.3	47.3	8,398.5	225.3	897.5	−2,941.7
Ireland	578.8	2.4	2,278.2	897.9	440.0	−3,034.9
Sweden	828.5	6.7	2,520.9	697.5	694.6	−3,077.8
Austria	942.3	8.9	2,575.1	734.4	739.2	−3,097.4
Belgium	1,325.9	17.3	4,281.9	1,793.5	1,326.9	−6,059.2
Australia	1,081.5	5.4	7,268.1	470.9	563.1	−7,215.2
Spain	2,300.8	30.6	7,774.1	1,050.5	1,385.3	−7,878.4
Italy	3,427.0	45.6	9,109.3	1,437.0	1,891.9	−8,965.6
Canada	2,718.2	34.0	10,140.8	1,489.8	1,421.4	−10,299.8
Korea, Rep.	3,812.6	35.9	11,020.0	2,521.8	841.1	−10,534.4
France	3,114.5	70.5	11,471.2	1,898.5	2,674.1	−12,858.8
Netherlands	2,397.5	31.2	10,891.6	3,845.3	1,189.4	−13,497.7
England	3,897.1	80.0	15,583.6	1,746.0	2,499.5	−15,852.0
Japan	3,871.4	65.6	20,451.8	1,483.2	1,495.4	−19,493.2
Germany	8,473.3	366.8	22,449.3	5,591.3	4,619.4	−23,819.8
United States	6,851.7	510.9	61,198.0	3,101.0	6,484.2	−63,420.6
Total	268,383.9	4,915.2	268,383.9	43,755.9	38,840.7	−77,681.4

Sources: Jiang and Milberg 2013, 5, based on data from the World Input-Output Database.

Summary

This chapter focused on two basic questions in analyzing the relationship between GVC links and the domestic economy: what are the determinants of GVC integration, and what are its impacts? The quality of the assessment depends on the methodology that is applied, which, in turn, depends heavily on data availability. A fully developed regression model using firm- or sector-level data, for example, is preferable to bivariate correlations using country-level data, because the regression model allows the analysis to establish causality and dig into the drivers and impacts of GVC links at the micro level. For many LMICs, however, firm-level data are not available. Acknowledging this challenge, this chapter proposed several methodologies and data sources that can be used and combined, depending on the specific country context and data availability.

Regarding the determinants, the chapter began with the decomposition of gross export growth, which serves as a first assessment of where the growth of the value added embodied in gross exports is generated in terms of the country of origin (that is,

Table 7.2 Manufacturing GVC Workers, 1995 and 2008

	Manufacturing GVC workers (% of all workers in the economy)		Manufacturing GVC workers in 2008 (thousands) employed in				Change in manufacturing GVC workers between 1995 and 2008 (thousands) employed in			
Country	1995	2008	Agr.	Mfg.	Serv.	All sectors	Agr.	Mfg.	Serv.	All sectors
United States	16	11.1	1,143	8,837	6,892	16,872	–331	–3,144	–1,138	–4,612
Japan	22.6	19.4	1,298	6,491	4,417	12,207	–794	–2,225	148	–2,871
Germany	26.8	26.4	400	5,481	4,766	10,647	–161	–666	1,388	561
France	22	18.7	303	2,195	2,355	4,853	–96	–423	368	–151
United Kingdom	20.1	12.6	115	1,946	1,931	3,992	–128	–1,148	–347	–1,624
Italy	29.1	25.5	333	3,553	2,559	6,444	–192	–234	517	91
Spain	23.2	17.5	271	1,827	1,494	3,592	–97	185	353	440
Canada	20.8	16	157	1,138	1,482	2,777	–102	–136	193	–45
Australia	18.2	14.5	165	641	855	1,661	–48	3	196	150
Korea, Rep.	29.7	22.8	655	2,646	2,077	5,378	–468	–735	524	–679
Netherlands	22.8	19	89	643	929	1,661	–42	–87	158	29
China	31.7	33.3	121,342	87,568	49,468	258,378	9,963	20,508	11,965	42,436
Russia	24.7	21.9	4,259	6,749	6,228	17,237	–1,403	–2,120	2,198	–1,325
Brazil	29.6	28.7	8,347	9,490	9,823	27,660	–705	2,450	4,118	5,863
India	27.9	27.3	57,926	41,933	26,483	126,343	2,118	10,896	7,025	20,039
Mexico	30.3	24.4	2,817	6,128	3,205	12,150	–400	1,403	1,121	2,124
Turkey	27.1	30.4	1,778	3,115	1,554	6,446	–341	620	584	863
Indonesia	32.1	25.6	13,921	7,427	5,725	27,073	–1,899	–425	1,380	–944

Sources: Timmer and others 2014, appendix table 5; based on data from the World Input-Output Database.
Note: GVC = global value chain.

foreign versus domestic) and sector (within a sector or in upstream sectors). The section then looked in more detail at the determinants of GVC integration at the country, sector, and firm levels. At the country level, logistics performance, skill levels, and access to knowledge (measured as geographical distance to knowledge centers) were shown to be important factors for a country's extent of GVC links. Sector-level determinants can include the existence of an export processing zone, openness to international trade and FDI, connectivity to international markets, competitiveness in unit labor costs and labor productivity, drivers of investment, and the quality of domestic value chains and the services infrastructure. Firm-level determinants include size, age, foreign ownership status, workers' skills, and productivity.

As for the impacts of GVC integration, the chapter differentiated between economic and social upgrading. Economic upgrading is captured by measuring the growth of domestic value added embodied in gross exports, the level of domestic value added or productivity (for example, labor productivity or total factor productivity), which serve as dependent variables in the analyses presented. Although the first is only available at the sector level, the second and third can also be studied using firm-level data. Using regression analysis, measures of economic upgrading were then related to various measures of GVC integration at the sector level, including measures of structural integration in GVCs, foreign value added embodied in gross exports, domestic value added embodied in exports of third countries, upstreamness, length of sourcing chains, and the share of foreign output in total output. If firm-level data are available, the analysis could also include firm-level measures of GVC integration as right-hand-side variables, such as the share of exports in a firm's total output or the share of imported inputs in total inputs.

In addition to economic upgrading, the chapter also looked at the impact of GVC integration on social upgrading. Again, the analysis can assess the impact of the GVC-related measures listed previously on employment, wages and salaries, or the labor share, using regression analysis. The next step was to present a more direct way to measure the link between GVC participation and labor market outcomes, by drawing on various indicators already developed in the literature, which are based on international input-output data.

Finally, other impacts that were not explicitly covered in this chapter but warrant further investigation include the impact of GVCs on the macro economy, as well as the links with working conditions, education and skills, other aspects of the society (for instance, poverty), and the environment.

Annex 7A. Regression Results

Focusing on global value chain (GVC) integration as a buyer, table 7A.1 shows the results for the full sample of 40 countries in the World Input-Output Database (WIOD) covering the period 1995–2011. For a description of the data, see box 7A.1. Column 1 in table 7A.1 shows the results based on the estimation equation. The production factors labor and capital significantly increase domestic value added. The same applies to the trade-related variables foreign value added for domestic processing (trade) and, most important, our GVC measure of foreign value added embodied in exports (EXGR_FVA). A 10 percent increase in GVC integration as a buyer is expected to increase domestic value added by 0.7 percent. In other words, GVC integration as a buyer helps increase a country's domestic value added and thus fosters economic upgrading.

Next, we assess the role of national characteristics. We first focus on a country's infrastructure (table 7A.1, columns 2 to 8). Surprisingly, better logistics performance negatively mediates the impact of GVC integration as a buyer on value added (column 2). With the use of the OECD data set instead, which includes more emerging and low- and middle-income countries (but cannot control for capital stock and employment), the interaction term is positive and significant (table 7A.2). This result may be indicative of a lower policy threshold effect in emerging countries; that is, better infrastructure matters more.

Higher general infrastructure investment (table 7A.1, column 3), by contrast, shows the expected positive mediating effect. Better rail coverage and more investment in rails (columns 4 and 5) also positively mediate the effect. A higher value of air cargo (column 6) has no effect, while more investment in airports (column 7) shows a negative mediating effect. The latter effect is surprising, but could indicate that better airports may act as a driver to source more inputs internationally (or to offshore more inputs), which could reduce domestic value added if foreign production factors substitute for domestic ones. A higher value of air cargo positively mediates the impact of GVC integration as a buyer using the OECD data set (table 7A.2), which again may indicate a lower policy threshold effect. Finally, more investment in roads shows a positive effect (table 7A.1, column 8).

Second, we look at the role of foreign direct investment (FDI), which shows the expected positive

Box 7A.1. Data: GVC Indicators and Policy Variables

GVC Indicators

To calculate the global value chain (GVC) indicators, we rely on two databases that provide inter-country input-output (ICIO) tables, which allows us to track value-added flows across countries and industries. The first database is the World Input-Output Database (WIOD). It covers 40 countries, 35 industries, and the years 1995–2011. A major advantage of WIOD is that it also provides data on price levels, employment, and capital stocks at the industry level. This allows us to include the controls we need and to deflate the level variables (using 1995 as the base year).

The second database is the Organisation for Economic Co-operation and Development (OECD) ICIO database, which covers 61 countries, 34 industries, and the years 1995, 2000, 2005, and 2008–11. The advantage here is the extended country coverage, especially of low- and middle-income countries. However, since no additional variables are provided, we have to rely on our trade measure and fixed effects to get clean estimates. Therefore, the WIOD estimates represent our benchmark.

Policy Variables

We use seven proxies to measure a country's infrastructure: the infrastructure Logistics Performance Index (quality of trade- and transport-related infrastructure) and total infrastructure investment (percentage of gross domestic product [GDP]) capture the general quality of infrastructure. Kilometers of rail lines (per person) and investment in rail infrastructure (percentage of GDP), as well as the value of air cargo (percentage of GDP), investment in airport infrastructure (percentage of GDP), and investment in road infrastructure (percentage of GDP) capture specific aspects of a country's infrastructure.

The investment data are taken from the OECD transport database, but are only available for 35 countries in the sample. Therefore, we only include them in the WIOD regressions. The remaining variables are taken from the World Development Indicators (WDI) and are available for all countries except Taiwan, China..

To proxy for foreign presence and innovative capabilities, we use WDI data on foreign direct investment inflows (percentage of GDP), research and development (R&D) intensity, and patent applications (per person). In addition, we use OECD data on business sector R&D spending (percentage of GDP) for the WIOD sample. Finally, we rely on rule-of-law data from the World Governance Indicators to measure legal institutions.

Table 7A.1. GVC Integration as a Buyer and Domestic Value Added, National Characteristics, 1995–2011

Variable	(1)	(2)	(3)	(4)	(5)	(6)	(7)	(8)	(9)	(10)	(11)	(12)	(13)
EXGR_FVA	0.0713***	0.443***	0.0182	−0.0033	0.0196	0.0742***	0.178***	0.0409	0.0582***	0.0624***	0.121***	0.111***	0.0884***
	(0.0178)	(0.0886)	(0.0363)	(0.0150)	(0.0373)	(0.0186)	(0.0339)	(0.0364)	(0.0199)	(0.0170)	(0.0268)	(0.0312)	(0.0202)
Employment	0.346***	0.339***	0.362***	0.289***	0.337***	0.342***	0.332***	0.360***	0.338***	0.342***	0.347***	0.357***	0.341***
	(0.0585)	(0.0560)	(0.0622)	(0.0570)	(0.0684)	(0.0579)	(0.0680)	(0.0615)	(0.0582)	(0.0580)	(0.0584)	(0.0898)	(0.0574)
Capital stock	0.287***	0.290***	0.302***	0.292***	0.310***	0.302***	0.322***	0.307***	0.301***	0.287***	0.283***	0.312***	0.298***
	(0.0393)	(0.0376)	(0.0474)	(0.0386)	(0.0481)	(0.0389)	(0.0496)	(0.0473)	(0.0384)	(0.0390)	(0.0387)	(0.0570)	(0.0384)
Trade	0.164***	0.173***	0.168***	0.173***	0.178***	0.175***	0.177***	0.168***	0.173***	0.162***	0.166***	0.159***	0.179***
	(0.0221)	(0.0214)	(0.0221)	(0.0234)	(0.0261)	(0.0225)	(0.0246)	(0.0221)	(0.0226)	(0.0218)	(0.0219)	(0.0294)	(0.0224)
EXGR_FVA*infrastructure LPI		−0.116***											
		(0.0261)											
EXGR_FVA*infrastructure investment			0.0984**										
			(0.0403)										
EXGR_FVA*Rail line coverage				0.0003***									
				(4.36e–05)									
EXGR_FVA*rail investment					42.81***								
					(15.88)								
EXGR_FVA*air cargo						520,633							
						(538,886)							
EXGR_FVA*airport investment							−189.6***						
							(68.40)						
EXGR_FVA*road investment								12.32*					
								(6.815)					
EXGR_FVA*FDI inflows									0.0038***				
									(0.0014)				
EXGR_FVA*contract enforcement										0.0216			
										(0.0178)			
EXGR_FVA*total R&D intensity											−0.0436***		
											(0.0165)		
EXGR_FVA*business R&D intensity												−4.52e+06***	
												(1.75e+06)	
EXGR_FVA*patent applications													−7.99e-05***
													(2.10e-05)
Constant	3.554***	1.700***	−3.013***	2.516***	−4.138***	3.615***	−4.261***	5.535***	0.171	0.234	1.415***	−0.557	3.947***
	(0.462)	(0.473)	(0.691)	(0.523)	(0.739)	(0.470)	(0.789)	(0.407)	(0.511)	(0.525)	(0.527)	(0.816)	(0.473)
Observations	11,253	10,953	9,794	10,410	9,518	10,953	8,958	9,794	10,953	11,253	11,253	8,649	10,953
R–squared	0.869	0.876	0.872	0.880	0.874	0.874	0.874	0.872	0.875	0.869	0.870	0.853	0.875

Source: Data are from the World Input-Output Database.
Note: The dependent variable is domestic value added. EXGR_FVA is lagged. Robust standard errors are clustered at the industry-country level. All level variables are in natural logarithms. Country-year, industry-year, and industry-country fixed effects are included. EXGR_FVA = foreign value added embodied in exports; FDI = foreign direct investment; GVC = global value chain; LPI = Logistics Performance Index; R&D = research and development.
*** $p < 0.01$, ** $p < 0.05$, * $p < 0.1$.

Table 7A.2. GVC Integration as a Buyer and Domestic Value Added, National Characteristics, Selected Years, 1995–2011

Variable	(1)	(2)	(3)	(4)	(5)	(6)	(7)	(8)
EXGR_FVA	0.0874***	−0.0136	0.0586***	0.0751***	0.0701***	0.0709***	0.0404*	0.0888***
	(0.0128)	(0.0582)	(0.0181)	(0.0136)	(0.0141)	(0.0146)	(0.0206)	(0.0143)
Trade	0.286***	0.287***	0.297***	0.284***	0.284***	0.283***	0.273***	0.271***
	(0.0201)	(0.0212)	(0.0254)	(0.0202)	(0.0203)	(0.0202)	(0.0242)	(0.0221)
EXGR_FVA*infrastructure LPI		0.0333*						
		(0.0178)						
EXGR_FVA*rail line coverage			5.14e-05					
			(4.39e-05)					
EXGR_FVA*air cargo				2.08e+06***				
				(563,500)				
EXGR_FVA*FDI inflows					0.0026***			
					(0.000761)			
EXGR_FVA*contract enforcement						0.0309**		
						(0.0124)		
EXGR_FVA*total R&D intensity							0.0369***	
							(0.0126)	
EXGR_FVA*patent applications								1.03e-05
								(2.13e-05)
Constant	5.339***	5.476***	5.552***	5.444***	5.419***	5.462***	5.584***	5.912***
	(0.168)	(0.164)	(0.187)	(0.152)	(0.138)	(0.149)	(0.170)	(0.165)
Observations	8,488	8,235	7,408	8,348	8,348	8,488	8,098	8,096
R-squared	0.852	0.857	0.869	0.855	0.855	0.853	0.848	0.855

Source: Data are from the Organisation for Economic Co-operation and Development database.

Note: The dependent variable is domestic value added. EXGR_FVA is lagged. Robust standard errors are clustered at the industry-country level. All level variables are in natural logarithms. Country-year, industry-year, and industry-country fixed effects are included. EXGR_FVA = foreign value added embodied in exports; FDI = foreign direct investment; GVC = global value chain; LPI = Logistics Performance Index; R&D = research and development.

*** $p < 0.01$, ** $p < 0.05$, * $p < 0.1$.

sign (column 9). More foreign presence increases the gains from importing foreign value added for domestic value added, possibly because of more efficient distribution channels and/or investment put in place by foreign firms. Better contract enforcement has no mediating effect (column 10), while the mediating impact is positive in the OECD country sample. This could again suggest that in emerging countries better contract enforcement matters more.

Third, we assess the role of a country's innovation capacity. Surprisingly, the interaction terms with all three measures of innovation are negative and significant (table 7A.1, columns 11 to 13). One reason could be that GVC integration has a smaller positive impact on domestic value added in more innovative countries, possibly because domestic production factors contribute relatively more to value added. This explanation seems to be supported by the findings using the OECD country sample that includes more emerging countries (table 7A.2), where a higher research and development intensity positively mediates the relationship. More patents also show a positive coefficient sign, but are not statistically significant.

We now focus on GVC integration from a seller's perspective, using the amount of domestic value added re-exported by third countries (DVA3EX) as our GVC indicator. Table 7A.3 focuses on the effects using the full WIOD country sample. GVC integration as a seller substantially increases domestic value added (column 1). The elasticity is higher than those of all other control variables, while it was smaller when using the amount of foreign value added in exports (see table 7A.1), indicating that being a seller in GVCs contributes more strongly to boost economic upgrading than being a buyer only.

In the next step, we assess whether certain country characteristics influence the results. First, we look at the moderating role of infrastructure (columns 2 to 8). Surprisingly, only airport-related indicators matter. A higher value of air cargo shows a positive impact (column 6), while more investment in airports negatively mediates the effect (column 7). The latter effect is surprising, but confirms the findings from GVC integration on the buying side (see table 7A.1). These results could indicate that better airports may act as a driver to source more inputs internationally (or to offshore more inputs) to be used in a country's export products, which could reduce domestic value added if foreign production factors substitute for domestic ones. A higher value of the Logistics Performance Index and rail line coverage positively mediates the impact of GVC integration as

Table 7A.3. GVC Integration as a Seller and Domestic Value Added and the Role of National Characteristics, 1995–2011

Variable	(1)	(2)	(3)	(4)	(5)	(6)	(7)	(8)	(9)	(10)	(11)	(12)	(13)
DVA3EX	0.289***	0.286***	0.298***	0.248***	0.274***	0.286***	0.258***	0.296***	0.284***	0.293***	0.287***	0.275***	0.285***
	(0.0516)	(0.0510)	(0.0557)	(0.0533)	(0.0590)	(0.0512)	(0.0585)	(0.0542)	(0.0512)	(0.0521)	(0.0509)	(0.0746)	(0.0508)
Employment	0.243***	0.257***	0.249***	0.242***	0.251***	0.259***	0.261***	0.252***	0.260***	0.240***	0.242***	0.235***	0.256***
	(0.0378)	(0.0376)	(0.0451)	(0.0396)	(0.0460)	(0.0371)	(0.0456)	(0.0447)	(0.0369)	(0.0381)	(0.0377)	(0.0513)	(0.0374)
Capital stock	0.145***	0.159***	0.151***	0.151***	0.155***	0.158***	0.148***	0.151***	0.159***	0.144***	0.141***	0.135***	0.161***
	(0.0210)	(0.0211)	(0.0208)	(0.0223)	(0.0230)	(0.0212)	(0.0220)	(0.0207)	(0.0213)	(0.0207)	(0.0200)	(0.0249)	(0.0210)
Trade	0.193***	0.328	0.143	0.239***	0.206**	0.186***	0.402***	0.168*	0.161***	0.215***	0.163***	0.287***	0.199***
	(0.0424)	(0.202)	(0.0907)	(0.0690)	(0.0801)	(0.0429)	(0.0606)	(0.0988)	(0.0458)	(0.0525)	(0.0627)	(0.0688)	(0.0456)
DVA3EX*infrastructure LPI		−0.0466											
		(0.0595)											
DVA3EX*infrastructure investment			0.0866										
			(0.0677)										
DVA3EX*rail line coverage				−1.9e–05									
				(0.0002)									
DVA3EX*rail investment					13.23								
					(30.03)								
DVA3EX*air cargo						2.0e+06**							
						(789,801)							
DVA3EX*airport investment							−341.7**						
							(153.6)						
DVA3EX*road investment								10.76					
								(12.17)					
DVA3EX*FDI inflows									0.0055***				
									(0.00191)				
DVA3EX*contract enforcement										−0.0318			
										(0.0364)			
DVA3EX*total R&D intensity											0.0360		
											(0.0391)		
DVA3EX*business R&D intensity												−1.1e+06	
												(6.3e+06)	
DVA3EX*patent applications													−6.2e–05
													(5.0e–05)
Constant	3.554***	−2.701***	1.801***	5.862***	4.166***	3.836***	3.323***	8.067***	0.305	1.358***	2.601***	−0.852	−0.771
	(0.462)	(0.653)	(0.575)	(0.559)	(0.508)	(0.550)	(0.505)	(0.622)	(0.482)	(0.499)	(0.479)	(0.744)	(0.521)
Observations	11,253	11,012	9,845	10,460	9,568	11,012	9,008	9,845	11,012	11,312	11,312	8,680	11,012
R–squared	0.869	0.885	0.885	0.890	0.887	0.885	0.891	0.885	0.886	0.881	0.881	0.872	0.885

Source: Data are from the World Input-Output Database.
Note: The dependent variable is domestic value added. DVA3EX is lagged. Robust standard errors are clustered at the industry-country level. All level variables are in natural logarithms. Country-year, industry-year, and industry-country fixed effects are included. DVA3EX = domestic value added re-exported by third countries; FDI = foreign direct investment; GVC = global value chain; LPI = Logistics Performance Index; R&D = research and development.
*** $p < 0.01$, ** $p < 0.05$, * $p < 0.1$.

Table 7A.4. GVC Integration as a Seller and Domestic Value Added, National Characteristics, Selected Years, 1995–2011

Variable	(1)	(2)	(3)	(4)	(5)	(6)	(7)	(8)
DVA3EX	0.512***	0.270**	0.452***	0.511***	0.504***	0.478***	0.536***	0.564***
	(0.0245)	(0.109)	(0.0371)	(0.0263)	(0.0264)	(0.0288)	(0.0287)	(0.0216)
Trade	0.225***	0.223***	0.232***	0.225***	0.225***	0.225***	0.206***	0.205***
	(0.0142)	(0.0139)	(0.0165)	(0.0143)	(0.0143)	(0.0137)	(0.0130)	(0.0119)
DVA3EX*infrastructure LPI		0.0850***						
		(0.0314)						
DVA3EX*rail line coverage			0.0003***					
			(5.11e-05)					
DVA3EX*air cargo				700,776				
				(451,674)				
DVA3EX*FDI inflows					0.0017***			
					(0.0005)			
DVA3EX*contract enforcement						0.0564**		
						(0.0229)		
DVA3EX*total R&D intensity							0.0171	
							(0.0178)	
DVA3EX*patent applications								–4.94e-05
								(5.45e-05)
Constant	3.517***	3.610***	3.047***	3.628***	3.774***	3.565***	3.458***	3.600***
	(0.132)	(0.128)	(0.134)	(0.142)	(0.136)	(0.144)	(0.172)	(0.167)
Observations	8,502	8,240	7,409	8,362	8,362	8,502	8,103	8,101
R–squared	0.929	0.935	0.945	0.930	0.930	0.930	0.934	0.937

Source: Data are from the Organisation for Economic Co-operation and Development database.
Note: The dependent variable is domestic value added. DVA3EX is lagged. Robust standard errors are clustered at the industry-country level. All level variables are in natural logarithms. Country-year, industry-year, and industry-country fixed effects are included. DVA3EX = domestic value added re-exported by third countries; FDI = foreign direct investment; GVC = global value chain; LPI = Logistics Performance Index; R&D = research and development.
*** $p < 0.01$, ** $p < 0.05$, * $p < 0.1$.

a seller using the OECD sample of 61 industrialized and emerging countries (table 7A.4), which again may indicate a lower policy threshold effect.

Second, we find that FDI inflows clearly show a positive mediating impact on the relationship between GVC integration as a seller and domestic value added (table 7A.3, column 9). This result confirms the positive results for GVC integration on the buying side (see table 7A.1). The effect can also be confirmed using the OECD data set (table 7A.4), underlying the positive effect of FDI in GVCs on economic upgrading in industrialized and emerging countries.

Contract enforcement, by contrast, does not matter in the WIOD country sample (table 7A.3, column 10), although contract enforcement has a significant positive impact using the OECD country sample (table 7A.4). These results suggests that contract enforcement appears to be more important in emerging countries, supporting the findings for GVC integration as a buyer. Innovation does not matter in either data set (table 7A.3, columns 11 to 13).

The results suggest that GVC integration as a seller leads to higher domestic value-added gains than GVC integration as a buyer. However, national characteristics seem to matter less for the effect on economic upgrading in GVCs for sellers than for buyers, in particular in high-income countries. This finding could indicate that for more advanced economies, firm-level characteristics or absorptive capacities, such as productivity and skill intensity, are more important for becoming a seller in GVCs (which would confirm studies on the determinants of exporting that emphasize the role of productivity). When more emerging countries are included in the data set, the results suggest that national policies matter more strongly for economic upgrading from both buying and selling in GVCs. Policies also seem to have a generally positive impact in the enlarged country sample, suggesting a lower policy threshold effect.

Annex 7B. Factors Mediating Productivity Spillovers from Foreign Direct Investment

The baseline equation, estimated by ordinary least squares, takes the following form:

$$\begin{aligned}\text{lnlp}_{irst} = \alpha &+ \beta\text{FDI}_{cst} + \gamma(\text{FDI}_{cst}{*}\text{MF}) \\ &+ \delta(\text{FDI}_{cst}{*}\text{MF}{*}\text{Dummy}_{\text{country of interest}}) \\ &+ \text{lncapint}_{irst} + \text{Dummy}_{\text{country of interest}} + D_r \\ &+ D_s + D_t + \varepsilon_{irst}\end{aligned}$$

lnlp_{irst} denotes the log labor productivity for domestic firm i in region r, sector s, at time t. Foreign direct investment (FDI) is defined as the share of foreign output as a percentage of total output at the sector level in a country.

The key variable of interest is the interaction effect between the FDI variable in country c and sector s at time t and the "mediating factors" (MF), which are specific to the country of interest. That term is indicated in the equation as $\delta(\text{FDI}_{cst}{*}\text{MF}{*}\text{Dummy}_{\text{country of interest}})$. To avoid spurious results for the correlation of interest, the equation controls for a constant α, the FDI spillovers measure in country c and sector s at time t, its interaction with MF across all countries, the level in logs of capital intensity of domestic firm i—lncapint_{irst}—a dummy that takes the value 1 if the host country is the country of interest and 0 otherwise; as well as sector, region, and time fixed effects. Standard errors are robust to heteroskedasticity and clustered at the country-sector level.

The mediating factors tested are as follows:

1. *Measures of spillover potential by the foreign firm:*

   a. **own** = a sector's average percentage of foreign ownership in a country.

   b. **market** = a sector's average percentage of FDI sales to the domestic market in a country. This measure serves as a proxy for a sector's average FDI motive in a country, whereby a higher share is associated with market-oriented FDI.

   c. **inp** = a sector's average percentage of domestic input purchases of FDI firms in a country. This measure captures a sector's average sourcing strategy of foreign firms in a country, whereby a higher share is associated with more local sourcing.

   d. **tech** = iso + tech_for + website + email with $0 \leq \text{tech} \leq 4$, where iso = 1 if the firm owns internationally recognized quality certification and 0 otherwise; tech_for = 1 if the firm uses technology licensed from foreign firms and 0 otherwise; website = 1 if the firm uses its own website to communicate with clients or suppliers and 0 otherwise; and email = 1 if the firm uses email to communicate with clients or suppliers and 0 otherwise. The technology indicator serves as a proxy for a sector's average FDI technology intensity in a country.

2. *Measures of absorptive capacity in the host economy:*

   a. **gap** = domestic firm's labor productivity (LP) relative to median LP of multinational firms in the sector in natural logarithms; a higher number indicates a lower gap.

   b. **tech** = domestic firm's technology indicator as defined in the previous section, where tech $\in \{0, 1, 2, 3, 4\}$. The technology indicator serves as a proxy for research and development intensity, which is unavailable.

   c. **skills** = domestic firm's share of high-skilled labor in the firm's total labor force.

   d. **size** = domestic firm's total number of permanent and temporary employees, in natural logarithms.

   e. **aggl** = region's total number of manufacturing and services firms as a percentage of the country's total number of manufacturing and services firms. This measure is a proxy for urbanization economies (locational advantages) and covers domestic and foreign firms.

   f. **exp** = domestic firm's share of direct or indirect exports in firm sales.

3. *Measures of national characteristics and institutions:*

   a) **labor** = measure of labor freedom, in natural logarithms, from the Heritage Foundation; it captures labor market institutions. The variable ranges from 0 to 100 (highest labor freedom) and includes various aspects of the legal and regulatory framework of a country's labor market, such as minimum wages; laws inhibiting layoffs; severance requirements; and measurable regulatory burdens on hiring, hours, and so forth. The measure is mainly based on data from the World Bank's Doing Business annual studies.

   b) **finance** = measure of financial freedom, in natural logarithms, from the Heritage Foundation. The variable measures banking efficiency, as well as independence from government control and interference in the financial sector, with scores ranging from 0 to 100 (highest financial freedom). This measure relies on various underlying data sources, including (in order of priority) the Economist Intelligence Unit, International Monetary Fund, Organisation for Economic Co-operation and Development, and official government publications of each country.

c. **educ1** = government spending on education, as a percentage of gross domestic product (GDP), from the World Development Indicators (WDI) database.
d. **educ2** = people who have completed secondary and tertiary education, as a percentage of population ages 15 years and older, from Barro and Lee (2010).
e. **rd** = country's expenditures on research and development, as a percentage of GDP, from the WDI database.
f. **investment** = measure of investment freedom, in natural logarithms, from the Heritage Foundation; it serves as a proxy for investment promotion. The score ranges from 0 to 100 (highest investment freedom) and measures the ability of individuals and firms to move their resources in and out of specific activities internally and across the country's borders. This variable is mainly based on official government publications of each country on capital flows and foreign investment.
g. **trade1** = country's share of exports of goods and services as a percentage of GDP, from the WDI database.
h. **trade2** = measure of trade freedom, in logarithms, from the Heritage Foundation; a composite measure of the trade-weighted average applied tariff rate and nontariff barriers, with scores ranging from 0 to 100 (highest trade freedom), reflecting the absence of trade protectionism. The measure is based on various underlying sources, including data from the World Bank, World Trade Organization, and Economist Intelligence Unit.
i. **business** = measure of business freedom, in natural logarithms, from the Heritage Foundation; it is an outcome-based indicator of a country's institutional development. It is a measure that reflects the ability to start, operate, and close a business, with scores ranging from 0 to 100 (highest business freedom). The measure mainly relies on the World Bank's Doing Business annual studies.
j. **hhi** = measure of sector concentration, to capture competition in a domestic firm's sector. The hhi of sector concentration is defined as the sum of squares of a firm's output share by sector. If only one firm operates in a sector, the hhi would be 1. A lower hhi reflects higher sector diversity. This measure includes domestic and foreign firms.
k. **income** = a country's per capita GDP (US$ at 2000 prices), in natural logarithms, from the WDI database. It captures national competition, but also other aspects of the national and institutional environments.

Annex 7C. Factors Mediating Productivity Spillovers from GVC Integration in Bulgaria

Table 7C.1. Structural Integration in GVCs from a Buyer's Perspective and Its Impact on Productivity, the Role of Absorptive Capacity, Manufacturing Firms, OLS

Variable	(1) gap_{irst}	(2) $tech_{irst}$	(3) $skills_{irst}$	(4) $size_{irst}$	(5) $aggl_{rct}$	(6) exp_{irst}	(7) fdi_{irst}
$BONwin_{cst}$	2.3316	−2.6228**	0.7005	−4.2015***	0.8967	−1.3804	−0.5884
	(0.434)	(0.026)	(0.600)	(0.001)	(0.697)	(0.252)	(0.637)
$BONwin_{cst}$*MF	6.3302***	1.7829***	0.2092	1.0560***	−0.0492	3.3622***	3.8519***
	(0.000)	(0.000)	(0.637)	(0.000)	(0.993)	(0.000)	(0.000)
$BONwin_{cst}$*MF*$bulgaria_c$	1.7456**	0.4047	−0.4018	0.2034	17.8798	−1.8881**	−3.6582**
	(0.014)	(0.373)	(0.892)	(0.395)	(0.112)	(0.031)	(0.021)
$lncapint_{irst}$	0.0484***	0.2433***	0.2631***	0.2570***	0.2647***	0.2631***	0.2501***
	(0.000)	(0.000)	(0.000)	(0.000)	(0.000)	(0.000)	(0.000)
$bulgaria_c$	−1.1657***	−1.5192***	−1.1953***	−1.4954***	−1.5890***	−0.9818***	−1.1845***
	(0.000)	(0.000)	(0.001)	(0.001)	(0.000)	(0.001)	(0.001)
constant	7.8520***	6.2189***	4.3364***	5.8411***	5.8362***	4.6493***	4.6640***
	(0.000)	(0.000)	(0.000)	(0.000)	(0.000)	(0.000)	(0.000)
Observations	8,178	8,734	8,619	8,734	8,734	8,672	8,415
R-squared	0.91	0.50	0.47	0.49	0.47	0.48	0.49

Sources: Based on Farole and Winkler 2014, Santoni and Taglioni 2015.

Note: The dependent variable is log labor productivity ($lnlp_{irst}$). All regressions include sector, subnational region, and year fixed effects. Standard errors are clustered at the country-sector level. GVC = global value chain; OLS = ordinary least squares.

*p < 0.1, **p < 0.05, ***p < 0.01.

Summary

- Structural integration in global value chains (GVCs) has a positive effect from a buyer's perspective if all the mediating factors are taken into account (see table 7C.3, first column).
- A lower technology gap positively mediates productivity gains from GVC participation on the buying side in the full country sample, and the positive effect is even larger for Bulgaria (table 7C.1, column 1).
- Other factors that positively mediate the impact of structural integration in GVCs from a buyer's perspective are a firm's technology level (tech), size (size), export share (exp), and foreign direct investment (FDI) (fdi) status. However, that only holds for the full country sample. In Bulgaria, the positive effects from export share and FDI status are smaller (table 7C.1, columns 6 and 7).
- Although agglomeration (aggl) has a negative influence in the overall sample, the effect is positive for Bulgaria (table 7C.1, column 5; and table 7C.3, column 1).

Table 7C.2. Structural Integration in GVCs from a Seller's Perspective and Its Impact on Productivity, the Role of Absorptive Capacity, Manufacturing Firms, OLS

Variable	(1) gap_{irst}	(2) $tech_{irst}$	(3) $skills_{irst}$	(4) $size_{irst}$	(5) $aggl_{rct}$	(6) exp_{irst}	(7) fdi_{irst}
$BONwout_{cst}$	21.5631***	2.8876	7.0853*	0.3527	12.1879*	3.0935	6.0138*
	(0.003)	(0.392)	(0.058)	(0.922)	(0.076)	(0.336)	(0.076)
$BONwout_{cst}$*MF	6.4980***	1.8536***	0.2234	1.1055***	−16.0688	3.6661***	4.2005***
	(0.000)	(0.000)	(0.618)	(0.000)	(0.250)	(0.000)	(0.000)
$BONwout_{cst}$*MF*$bulgaria_c$	2.6355***	0.6088	−1.5955	0.2116	−352.6137***	−2.2371**	−4.0507**
	(0.000)	(0.246)	(0.603)	(0.472)	(0.001)	(0.017)	(0.020)
$lncapint_{irst}$	0.0401***	0.2420***	0.2628***	0.2563***	0.2642***	0.2626***	0.2491***
	(0.000)	(0.000)	(0.000)	(0.000)	(0.000)	(0.000)	(0.000)
$bulgaria_c$	−0.4180	−1.3305***	−0.8988**	−1.3411***	1.0230	−0.8387***	−0.9766**
	(0.200)	(0.000)	(0.016)	(0.004)	(0.164)	(0.008)	(0.013)
constant	5.1944***	5.4665***	3.4426***	5.2289***	4.4005***	3.9991***	3.7278***
	(0.000)	(0.000)	(0.000)	(0.000)	(0.000)	(0.000)	(0.000)
Observations	8,178	8,734	8,619	8,734	8,734	8,672	8,415
R–squared	0.92	0.50	0.48	0.49	0.48	0.48	0.49

Sources: Based on Farole and Winkler 2014; Santoni and Taglioni 2015.

Note: The dependent variable is log labor productivity ($lnlp_{irst}$). All regressions include sector, subnational region, and year fixed effects. Standard errors are clustered at the country-sector level. GVC = global value chain; OLS = ordinary least squares.

*p < 0.1, **p < 0.05, ***p < 0.01.

Summary

- Structural integration in GVCs has a positive effect from a seller's perspective if all mediating factors are taken into account (see table 7C.3, column 2). The positive impact is stronger for the seller-side measure compared with the buyer-side measure.
- A lower technology gap (gap) positively mediates productivity gains from GVC participation on the selling side in the full country sample, and the positive effect is even larger for Bulgaria (table 7C.2, column 1).
- As was the case for the buyer-related GVC measure, other factors that positively mediate the impact of structural integration in GVCs from a seller's perspective are a firm's technology level (tech), size (size), export share (exp), and FDI (fdi) status. However, that only holds for the full country sample. In Bulgaria, the positive effects from export share and FDI status are smaller (table 7C.2, columns 6 and 7).
- Interestingly, the mediating impact of agglomeration (aggl) turns negative from a seller's perspective, whereas the effect is positive from a buyer's perspective (table 7C.2, column 5; and table 7C.3, column 2). The interpretation could be that agglomerations entail positive urbanization economies when firms rely on external inputs in GVCs, which lowers production costs and increases firm productivity, and those benefits outweigh potential negative congestion costs. Firms that are selling within GVCs, by contrast, may face higher negative congestion costs (for example, related to transportation), which seem to be higher than the potential benefits in agglomerations.

Table 7C.3. Structural Integration in GVCs and Its Impact on Productivity, the Role of Absorptive Capacity, Manufacturing Firms, OLS

Variable	(1) $BONwin_{cst}$	(2) $BONwout_{cst}$
BON_{cst}	9.2658*	32.3833**
	(0.068)	(0.012)
BON_{cst}*gap_{irst}	6.2972***	6.4560***
	(0.000)	(0.000)
BON_{cst}*gap_{irst}*$bulgaria_c$	2.0540***	2.8115***
	(0.000)	(0.000)
BON_{cst}*$tech_{irst}$	0.2685***	0.2791***
	(0.004)	(0.004)
BON_{cst}*$tech_{irst}$*$bulgaria_c$	−0.2954	−0.0963
	(0.161)	(0.698)
BON_{cst}*$skills_{irst}$	0.0810	0.0767
	(0.514)	(0.568)
BON_{cst}*$skills_{irst}$*$bulgaria_c$	−1.2359	−0.9956
	(0.314)	(0.327)
BON_{cst}*$size_{irst}$	0.1264***	0.1131**
	(0.008)	(0.018)
BON_{cst}*$size_{irst}$*$bulgaria_c$	0.1545	−0.0556
	(0.474)	(0.712)
BON_{cst}*$aggl_{rct}$	−30.9621***	−37.9136
	(0.009)	(0.115)
BON_{cst}*$aggl_{rct}$*$bulgaria_c$	75.6443***	−943.2283***
	(0.001)	(0.002)
BON_{cst}*exp_{irst}	−0.0089	−0.0331
	(0.976)	(0.920)
BON_{cst}*exp_{irst}*$bulgaria_c$	−0.7764	−0.8087
	(0.571)	(0.556)
BON_{cst}*fdi_{irst}	0.3081	0.3633*
	(0.125)	(0.053)
BON_{cst}*fdi_{irst}*$bulgaria_c$	−0.5836	−0.5684
	(0.119)	(0.201)
$lncapint_{irst}$	0.0435***	0.0375***
	(0.000)	(0.000)
$bulgaria_c$	−1.2247***	5.6863***
	(0.002)	(0.000)
constant	6.9362***	3.6770**
	(0.000)	(0.030)
Observations	7,751	7,751
R-squared	0.92	0.92

Sources: Based on Farole and Winkler 2014; Santoni and Taglioni 2015.
Note: The dependent variable is log labor productivity ($lnlp_{irst}$). All regressions include sector, subnational region, and year fixed effects. Standard errors are clustered at the country-sector level. GVC = global value chain; OLS = ordinary least squares.
*p < 0.1, **p < 0.05, ***p < 0.01.

Table 7C.4 Structural Integration in GVCs from a Buyer's Perspective and Its Impact on Productivity, the Role of National Characteristics, Manufacturing Firms, OLS

Variable	(1) $labor_{ct}$	(2) $finance_{ct}$	(3) $educ1_{ct}$	(4) $educ2_{ct}$	(5) rd_{ct}	(6) $investm_{ct}$	(7) $trade1_{ct}$	(8) $trade2_{ct}$	(9) $business_{ct}$	(10) hhi_{sct}	(11) $income_{ct}$
$BONwin_{cst}$	18.4738	15.1480	15.4471*	5.8874	−9.0676**	−18.5153	5.4447*	46.2275***	50.0742	0.9948	14.6179
	(0.519)	(0.291)	(0.063)	(0.114)	(0.045)	(0.153)	(0.070)	(0.007)	(0.114)	(0.456)	(0.130)
$BONwin_{cst}$*MF	−4.2677	−3.7896	−83.5696*	−18.3914	1545.9797**	5.0911	−11.7106*	−10.9109***	−11.9946	−0.9732	−1.7905
	(0.537)	(0.309)	(0.058)	(0.100)	(0.029)	(0.148)	(0.052)	(0.007)	(0.118)	(0.470)	(0.134)
$BONwin_{cst}$*MF*$bulgaria_c$	1.8937*	2.2559**	72.6620*	30.3471***	1948.5219**	1.4553	18.7248**	3.2866***	2.3850***	0.0000	1.0696**
	(0.074)	(0.031)	(0.071)	(0.004)	(0.039)	(0.183)	(0.025)	(0.000)	(0.010)	(.)	(0.033)
$lncapint_{irst}$	0.2711***	0.2708***	0.2816***	0.2707***	0.2594***	0.2712***	0.2712***	0.2699***	0.2709***	0.2722***	0.2708***
	(0.000)	(0.000)	(0.000)	(0.000)	(0.000)	(0.000)	(0.000)	(0.000)	(0.000)	(0.000)	(0.000)
$bulgaria_c$	−2.1101***	−2.0583***	−2.8288***	−2.6351***	−2.0001***	−2.1376***	−3.3296***	−2.8066***	−2.2941***		−2.3292***
	(0.000)	(0.000)	(0.000)	(0.000)	(0.001)	(0.000)	(0.000)	(0.000)	(0.000)		(0.000)
constant	5.9350***	5.8794***	7.5136***	5.5893***	6.8063***	6.1145***	6.4155***	5.9171***	6.1632***	4.2449***	5.8306***
	(0.000)	(0.000)	(0.000)	(0.000)	(0.000)	(0.000)	(0.000)	(0.000)	(0.000)	(0.000)	(0.000)
Observations	8,515	8,515	6,579	8,515	6,673	8,515	8,515	8,515	8,515	8,263	8,515
R-squared	0.48	0.48	0.47	0.48	0.44	0.48	0.48	0.48	0.48	0.48	0.48

Sources: Based on Farole and Winkler 2014; Santoni and Taglioni 2015.
Note: The dependent variable is log labor productivity ($lnlp_{irst}$). All regressions include sector, subnational region, and year fixed effects. Standard errors are clustered at the country-sector level. GVC = global value chain; OLS = ordinary least squares.
*p < 0.1, **p < 0.05, ***p < 0.01.

Summary

- National and institutional characteristics in Bulgaria positively mediate the effect of structural integration in GVCs on firm productivity across the board when examining the buying side (table 7C.4).
- Higher financial freedom (finance), government spending on education (educ1), share of people with completed secondary and tertiary education (educ2), share of research and development (R&D) expenditures in gross domestic product (GDP) (rd), share of exports (trade1), absence of trade protectionism (trade2), and GDP (income) all show positive and significant mediating effects in Bulgaria.
- By contrast, some of those national characteristics have a negative effect in the full country sample—for example, government spending on education (educ1), share of exports (trade1), and the absence of trade protectionism (trade2). Therefore, for those variables, the net effect is less negative or even positive for Bulgaria.

Table 7C.5. Structural Integration in GVCs from a Seller's Perspective and Its Impact on Productivity, the Role of National Characteristics, Manufacturing Firms, OLS

Variable	(1) $labor_{ct}$	(2) $finance_{ct}$	(3) $educ1_{ct}$	(4) $educ2_{ct}$	(5) rd_{ct}	(6) $investm_{ct}$	(7) $trade1_{ct}$	(8) $trade2_{ct}$	(9) $business_{ct}$	(10) hhi_{sct}	(11) $income_{ct}$
$BONwout_{cst}$	−18.9168	80.4004	45.1467**	31.4952***	17.1380	−45.0303	11.8399*	188.8899***	271.4564**	6.8400*	99.3937***
	(0.803)	(0.177)	(0.030)	(0.006)	(0.201)	(0.500)	(0.092)	(0.000)	(0.022)	(0.056)	(0.008)
$BONwout_{cst}$*MF	6.3794	−19.2451	−256.3010**	−89.1525**	3533.6598*	13.3403	−14.8726	−43.2515***	−64.0242**	−0.7015	−11.2453**
	(0.736)	(0.203)	(0.032)	(0.016)	(0.077)	(0.443)	(0.339)	(0.000)	(0.024)	(0.616)	(0.011)
$BONwout_{cst}$*MF*$bulgaria_{c}$	−29.8746***	−34.3717***	−1.87e+03***	−426.7757***	−2.31e+04***	−32.1103***	−276.8090***	−38.9288***	−31.0791***	0.0000	−19.4073***
	(0.001)	(0.000)	(0.000)	(0.000)	(0.009)	(0.001)	(0.001)	(0.000)	(0.000)	(.)	(0.000)
$Incapint_{irst}$	0.2705***	0.2704***	0.2814***	0.2704***	0.2592***	0.2705***	0.2707***	0.2693***	0.2703***	0.2719***	0.2703***
	(0.000)	(0.000)	(0.000)	(0.000)	(0.000)	(0.000)	(0.000)	(0.000)	(0.000)	(0.000)	(0.000)
$bulgaria_{c}$	12.2958***	14.2412***	20.6887***	14.5512***	11.0190**	11.7757***	11.0847***	16.9562***	12.9836***		13.6429***
	(0.002)	(0.000)	(0.000)	(0.000)	(0.012)	(0.004)	(0.008)	(0.000)	(0.001)		(0.000)
constant	8,515	8,515	6,579	8,515	6,673	5.8825***	5.8061***	5.1181***	6.4553***	3.4222***	4.3802***
	0.48	0.48	0.47	0.48	0.44	(0.000)	(0.000)	(0.000)	(0.000)	(0.000)	(0.000)
Observations	8,515	8,515	6,579	8,515	6,673	8,515	8,515	8,515	8,515	8,263	8,515
R-squared	0.48	0.48	0.47	0.48	0.44	0.48	0.48	0.48	0.48	0.48	0.48

Sources: Based on Farole and Winkler 2014; Santoni and Taglioni 2015.
Note: The dependent variable is log labor productivity ($lnlp_{irst}$). All regressions include sector, subnational region, and year fixed effects. Standard errors are clustered at the country-sector level. GVC = global value chain; OLS = ordinary least squares.
$*p < 0.1$, $**p < 0.05$, $***p < 0.01$.

Summary

- National and institutional characteristics in Bulgaria negatively mediate the effect of structural integration in GVCs on firm productivity across the board when examining the selling side (table 7C.5).
- Less restricted labor (labor) or financial markets (finance), more government spending on education (educ1), a higher share of people with completed secondary and tertiary education (educ2), a higher share of R&D expenditures in GDP (rd), more freedom to invest (invest), a higher share of exports in GDP (trade1), more absence of trade protectionism (trade2), and higher GDP (income) all show a negative and significant mediating impact on productivity in Bulgaria.
- The full country sample also shows the negative effect of government spending on education (educ1), the share of people with secondary and tertiary education (educ2), the share of exports in GDP (trade1), the absence of trade protectionism (trade2), and per capita GDP (income). Therefore, the negative influence is even more pronounced for Bulgaria in those areas.
- The only variable in the overall sample with a positive impact is a country's R&D intensity.

Notes

1. This section draws on Kummritz, Taglioni, and Winkler (forthcoming), which is part of ongoing work at the World Bank that aims to develop a taxonomy of GVC participation and economic upgrading for a set of countries.
2. Calì and others (2016).
3. The World Bank's Trade in Value Added database can be accessed at http://data.worldbank.org/data-catalog/export-value-added.
4. Jiang and Milberg (2013).
5. Jiang and Milberg (2013).
6. Timmer and others (2014).
7. Timmer and others (2014).

References

Barro, Robert J., and Jong-Wha Lee. 2010. "A New Data Set of Educational Attainment in the World, 1950–2010." NBER Working Paper No. 15902, National Bureau of Economic Research, Cambridge, MA.

Calì, M., and C. Hollweg. 2015. "The Labor Content of Exports in South Africa: A Preliminary Exploration." World Bank, Washington, DC.

Calì, M., J. Francois, C. Hollweg, M. Manchin, D.A. Oberdabernig, H. Rojas-Romagosa, S. Rubinova, and P. Tomberger. 2016. "The Labor Content of Exports Database." Policy Research Working Paper No. 7615, World Bank, Washington, DC.

Farole, Thomas, and Deborah Winkler. 2014. "The Role of Mediating Factors for FDI Spillovers in Developing Countries: Evidence from a Global Dataset." In *Making Foreign Direct Investment Work for Sub-Saharan Africa: Local Spillovers and Competitiveness in Global Value Chains*, edited by Thomas Farole and Deborah Winkler, 59–86. Washington, DC: World Bank.

Hollweg, C. 2015. "The Labor Content of Exports in Belize: A Preliminary Exploration." World Bank, Washington, DC.

Jiang, Xiao, and William Milberg. 2013. "Capturing the Jobs from Globalization: Trade and Employment in Global Value Chains." Working Paper 30, Capturing the Gains: Economic and Social Upgrading in Global Production Networks, University of Manchester, Manchester, U.K.

Kummritz, Victor, Daria Taglioni, and Deborah Winkler. Forthcoming. "Economic Upgrading through Global Value Chain Participation: Which Policies Increase the Value Added Gains?" World Bank, Washington, DC.

OECD (Organisation for Economic Co-operation and Development). 2013. *Science, Technology and Industry Scoreboard 2013, Innovation for Growth.* Paris: OECD.

Roberts, M. J., and J. R. Tybout. 1997. "The Decision to Export in Colombia: An Empirical Model of Entry with Sunk Costs." *American Economic Review* 87 (4): 545–64.

Santoni, Gianluca, and Daria Taglioni. 2015. "Networks and Structural Integration in GVCs." In *The Age of Global Value Chains*, edited by João Amador and Filippo di Mauro. Washington, DC: Center for Economic and Policy Research.

Timmer, Marcel P., Abdul Azeez Erumban, Bart Los, Robert Stehrer, and Gaaitzen J. de Vries. 2013. "Slicing Up Global Value Chains." *Journal of Economic Perspectives* 28(2).

UNCTAD (United Nations Conference on Trade and Development). 2013. "World Investment Report 2013—Global Value Chains: Investment and Trade for Development." UNCTAD, Geneva.

PART III

STRATEGIC QUESTIONS AND POLICY OPTIONS

By integrating their domestic firms (suppliers and final producers) into global value chains (GVCs), low- and middle-income countries can help their economies industrialize, become services oriented faster, and move closer to their development goals. Part II suggests how to measure various aspects of GVC participation and, thus, how to identify key policy needs. This part of the book builds on those findings, suggesting "strategic questions" and approaches to addressing them—"policy options." Including real-world examples, the text proposes a diagnostics exercise to identify three focus areas.

Chapter 8—"Entering GVCs"—discusses ways for countries to enter global production networks. Those avenues include ways to attract foreign investors, as well as strategies to enhance the participation of domestic firms in GVCs. Suggestions for entering GVCs encompass measures to ensure that the country can offer world-class links to the global economy and create a friendly business climate for foreign tangible and intangible assets.

Chapter 9—"Expanding and Strengthening GVC Participation"—discusses ways for countries to lever their position in GVCs to achieve higher value addition through economic upgrading and densification. The concept of economic upgrading is largely about gaining competitiveness in higher-value-added products, tasks, and sectors. Densification involves engaging more local actors (firms and workers) in the GVC network. Strengthening GVC–local economy links, absorptive capacity, and skills contributes to the overall goal to increase a country's value added that results from GVC participation.

Chapter 10 tackles the challenge of "Turning GVC Participation into Sustainable Development." The chapter focuses on social and environmental sustainability of GVCs. Labor market–enhancing outcomes for workers at home and more equitable distribution of opportunities and outcomes create social support for a reform agenda aimed at strengthening a country's GVC participation. Climate-smart policy prescriptions and infrastructure can mitigate the challenges for firms from climatic disruptions, ensuring the long-term predictability, reliability, and time-sensitive delivery of goods necessary to participate in GVCs.

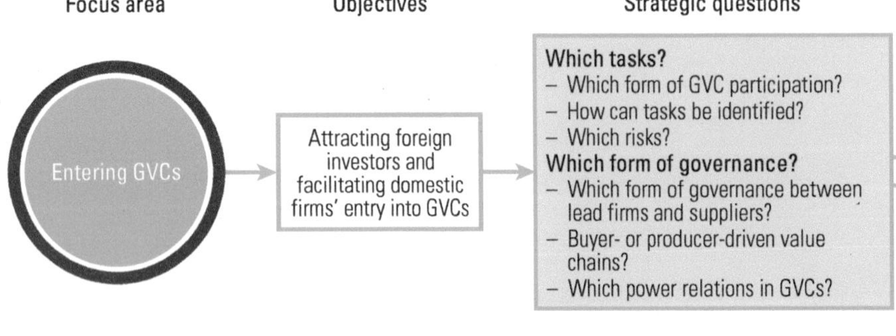
Focus area
Objectives
Strategic questions
Policy options
Entering GVCs
Attracting foreign investors and facilitating domestic firms' entry into GVCs
Which tasks?
– Which form of GVC participation?
– How can tasks be identified?
– Which risks?
Which form of governance?
– Which form of governance between lead firms and suppliers?
– Buyer- or producer-driven value chains?
– Which power relations in GVCs?
Creating world-class GVC links
– Jump-starting GVC entry through EPZs and other competitive spaces
– Attracting the "right" foreign investors
– Helping domestic firms find the "right" trade partner and technology abroad
– Improving connectivity to international markets
Creating a world-class climate for foreign tangible and intangible assets
– Ensuring cost competitiveness
– Improving drivers of investment and protecting foreign assets
– Improving domestic value chains and quality of infrastructure and services

Chapter 8

ENTERING GVCs

Introduction

This chapter focuses on the strategic questions, possible answers, and critical issues that policy makers must consider when seeking to enter global value chains (GVCs). A country that seeks to participate in GVCs must ask which tasks it should focus on and which types of GVC governance are possible. The chapter suggests that governments that seek to join GVCs have to create (1) world-class GVC links and (2) a world-class climate for foreign tangible and intangible assets. The first item requires attracting the right foreign investors and improving connectivity to international markets; the second requires high-quality infrastructure and services. Countries also need to be aware of the different power relations in GVCs between the lead firm and other firms, and the scope for diversifying specific supply chain risk.

Attracting Foreign Investors and Facilitating Domestic Firms' Entry into GVCs: Strategic Questions

Entering a GVC requires answering two strategic questions: (1) What tasks are performed in a GVC? (2) What form of governance does the GVC follow? The first is a more country-level question; the second emphasizes that entry into GVCs is ultimately a firm's decision.

Which Tasks?

The first strategic question has three sub-questions: (1) Which form of GVC participation? (2) How can tasks be identified? (3) Which risks? Before country analysts consider these questions, they should be aware of the pitfalls of basing their strategies on sector-based conceptual frameworks. Chapter 1 shows that reasoning along broad sector lines assumes that countries sell final goods to each other and that, as countries grow richer, they transition from specializing in the primary sector to manufacturing and ultimately to services.

In contrast to this sector-based vision, a "new paradigm" centered on tasks has recently gained popularity. Its premise is that in the world of GVCs—dominated by complex and fragmented production processes—development is best achieved by specializing in the tasks and activities of comparative advantage among the broad range available. After all, a firm's location decisions are task specific. Yet that approach, too, is partial, as it captures only functional upgrading efforts and strategies. Product and inter-sector upgrading—defined in chapter 9—are also necessary and can be achieved through the upgrading of skills, capital, and processes (see figure 1.9 in chapter 1). That higher-income countries have a stronger specialization in high-value-added manufacturing and services than lower-income countries indeed reflects the former's greater use of skills and know-how, capital and technology, and improved processes in its production, whether in agriculture, industry, or services—hence the term task-based development strategies. Therefore, this part discusses all three major forms of upgrading in GVCs—product, functional, and inter-sector—and three ways to achieve them—skills, capital, and process upgrading.

Which Form of GVC Participation?

Before identifying and focusing on the tasks and risks in GVCs, countries need to be aware of the two sets of approaches for entering GVCs: (1) attracting foreign investors and (2) facilitating domestic firms' access to GVCs ("internationalizing" those firms).

Regarding the first approach, why do countries go to great lengths to attract foreign direct investment (FDI)? One simple answer is that many countries have built up too little domestic capital to stimulate growth. FDI thus represents an important source of private capital. And given the relatively long-term outlook of direct (versus portfolio) investors, FDI generally is less risky than other financial flows, because it tends to be less vulnerable to rapid outflows caused by exogenous shocks. Moreover, pervasive information asymmetries—with powerful lead firms able to maintain and increase markups and with competitive suppliers subject to pressure from buyers on supply price, delivery time, quality, and payment schedule at the bottom—may lead to a suboptimal level of cross-border investment, justifying public intervention.[1]

But the more important answer is that FDI has the potential to deliver far greater "dynamic" benefits to host economies through the spillovers they deliver (mainly through technological and other advantages that stimulate higher productivity). Spillovers, in this context, generally refer to the diffusion of knowledge—unintentional or intentional, if sharing that knowledge is not compensated in some way—from multinational affiliates to local firms. Thus, spillovers encompass technology and all forms of codified and tacit knowledge related to production, including management and organizational practices. It also includes the benefits that can accrue to local participants when they link into the global networks of multinational investors.[2]

Not all FDI is the same, however; its development impact varies depending on the extent of foreign ownership. Fully foreign-owned FDI, for example, may induce the lead firm to transfer more knowledge—through technology, say—to the host country.[3] Partly foreign-owned FDI could also be beneficial for local firms; the lead firm's interests are less well protected, which makes technology leakages more likely. Larger domestic participation might also increase the chances of relying on domestic suppliers.[4]

Regarding the second approach—internationalizing domestic firms—one important spillover from foreign investors is the potential they create to help internationalize domestic firms, particularly their suppliers. They do this in two main ways: indirectly, by requiring domestic firms to meet international standards (as in quality and timely delivery) and by contributing to building the scale and productivity of their domestic suppliers; and directly, by providing access to their international marketing, supply, and distribution networks.[5]

Still, linking to foreign-owned subsidiaries of foreign firms is not the only way for domestic firms to join GVCs. They can consider other approaches that involve arm's-length trade:

- Exporting inputs to international buyers
- Becoming domestic final producers that import intermediates

Another approach to consider is the hybrid case of contract manufacturers that produce fully assembled goods for large retailers (such as Walmart or Gap) or lead firms that focus on design, development, and marketing and that outsource the actual production of their products, such as Nike, Calvin Klein, or Fisher-Price.[6] Contract manufacturers therefore fall into the latter two categories. They are part of non-equity modes of investment (NEMs), which also include business arrangements such as contract farming, business process outsourcing, franchising, contract management, strategic alliances, and joint ventures. In those cases, a multinational has a contractual relationship with a domestic firm in the host country and maintains some degree of control over the operation and conduct of business (more so than in the case of arm's-length trade), but has no ownership stake.[7] GVC participation through arm's-length trade and NEMs can also lead to spillovers.

This chapter clarifies that the form of GVC participation matters for development. The chapter also discusses how the form of governance in GVCs is not a prerogative of public policy, but endogenous to lead firms, although countries may adopt complementary policies to meet lead firms' needs to lever GVC opportunities.

How Can Tasks Be Identified?

It is often difficult for policy makers and analysts to identify the tasks in which a country has a comparative advantage, partly because full production- and trade-related statistics are rarely available at the task level in low- and middle-income countries (LMICs). Combining different approaches—complementary but different in data requirements—allows investigators to identify broad sectors, value chains, and specific activities, thereby enabling the country to determine its GVC entry strategy.

One strategy encourages entry into tasks—in sectors or value chains—in which the country already has expertise. The strategy internationalizes the existing production of goods or services, or that of new tasks—in a more aggregated sector or in a value chain in which the country already specializes. For example, Kenya—already an important producer of fruits and vegetables—later joined the horticulture GVC within the same industry.

Tasks can be identified in three steps. Step 1 identifies the broad export sectors in which a country has a revealed comparative advantage (RCA), which can be based on value-added export data. Step 2 analyzes the upstream and downstream output of a GVC product. Step 3 identifies differences in economic characteristics of tasks within those export sectors and value chains, such as tasks that may create the largest domestic value added or have important potential for diversification.

(Another strategy identifies a country's potential for entry into tasks in sectors in which the country is not yet active. In that case, countries can focus on the third step—identifying the optimal export sectors and value chains—and devote less attention to the starting sector or product specialization. Concepts of economic proximity between products may help identify the difficulties inherent in "jumping" to new sectors and activities.)

Step 1. Identify Sectors with the Highest RCA, Based on Value-Added Export Data

Identification of the export sectors in which a country has an RCA should be based on value-added rather than gross export data. Malaysia,[8] for example, has an RCA greater than one in four of nine manufacturing sectors—electrical and optical equipment (the most important GVC sector); machinery and equipment (not elsewhere classified); chemicals and non-metallic mineral products; and wood, paper, paper products, printing, and publishing—on both measures (figure 8.1). But for electrical and optical equipment, the value added–based RCA is about 15 percent lower—a key distinction.

Step 2. Analyze Upstream and Downstream Output of a GVC Product[9]

Network analysis applied to input-output (I-O) tables can help in assessing the features of the value

Figure 8.1. Malaysia: RCA, Gross Exports, and Domestic Value Added Embodied in the Country's Gross Exports, 2009

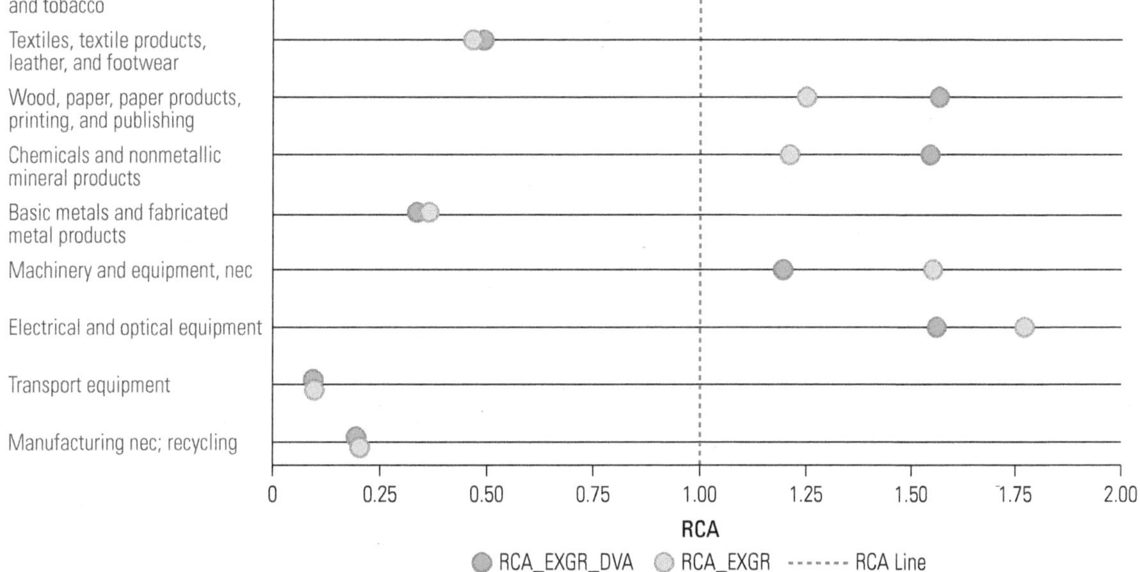

Source: Adapted from the Organisation for Economic Co-operation and Development–World Trade Organization Trade in Value Added database.
Note: RCA = revealed comparative advantage; RCA_EXGR = revealed comparative advantage based on gross exports; RCA_EXGR_DVA = revealed comparative advantage based on domestic value added in gross exports; nec = not elsewhere classified.

chains in which a country specializes. Using the U.S. I-O tables has the advantage of documenting I-O relationships at the finest level of disaggregation. But using those tables for assessing tasks in third countries has one important caveat: the analysis may be biased because of differences in technology across countries. Still, the richness from the very detailed documentation of the production structure in the U.S. I-O tables and the absence of comparable data for almost all countries worldwide justify their use.

The method of analysis has the following steps:

1. Identify the positioning of the export product of interest in the wider network of inter-sector production links.
2. Identify sectors that are the main buyers of the product and sectors that are the main suppliers and their relative economic contribution (measured in value added or exports).
3. Assess the relative position of countries of interest as suppliers of the product, as well as in the production of upstream and downstream products, and the relative value added or export contribution.
4. Repeat steps 1 to 3 for upstream and downstream sectors to map out a wider portion of the value chain for the product of interest.

Box 8.1 applies this concept to computer storage devices, Malaysia's main export product. The analysis reveals that the product is small and peripheral to the manufacturing production network (based on U.S. I-O tables) and that the product's main buyers are relatively concentrated in more sophisticated sectors, which are all likely to require higher technological and skill content. Matching these findings to trade data, the analysis shows that although Malaysia's position as an exporter of downstream products is relatively marginal, its most important competitor in producing computer storage devices is China, which is also the largest buyer of Malaysian exports of the product, as well as a leading exporter of downstream products—factors that may help shape GVC entry strategies.

Step 3. Identify Which Tasks within a Broad Sector or Value Chain Create the Largest Domestic Value Added or Promise for Growth and Development

In the absence of market failures (monopolistic rent or exclusive or controlled access to resources), tasks tend to depend on the know-how (quantity and quality of workers) and capital stock (including technology) available to perform them. If only a fraction of the workforce is highly skilled, launching into tasks that depend primarily on skilled workers does not make sense for a country. The goal is to choose tasks that create the largest domestic value added, given the labor and capital endowments in the home country.

That is indeed what Morocco did to develop its aerospace industry (box 8.2), based on its predominantly low-skilled workforce. Good performance allowed the country to transition to higher value-added segments.

Information about the value added of tasks cannot be easily obtained using available statistical data. Using I-O tables and gathering firm-level data are two ways to address some of the data constraints

Box 8.1. Network Analysis of a Product Value Chain Using I-O Tables

Figure B8.1.1 shows the inter-sector links for the sectors in manufacturing, using the highest available disaggregation provided by the U.S. input-output (I-O) tables (388 products) for 2007.[a] The node size is proportional to the so-called OUT-degree: bigger/darker nodes are those that supply intermediates to a larger number of industries (the color is correlated to the size of the node—that is, they deliver the same information). Links, from sector *i* to sector *j*, are proportional to the share of *i* in the overall input demand of *j*, excluding *j*'s inputs sourced from *j*. The network is built considering all intermediate flows from *i* to *j*, using all the information available in the network structure. For visual clarity, only flows above the 1 percent threshold of total intermediates requirements in the production of *j* are shown. North American Industry Classification System (NAICS) product 331110, iron and steel mills and ferroalloys, is the most structurally integrated into the manufacturing production network, supplying inputs to a large number of manufacturing industries. The network visualization also puts into perspective the position of product 334112, computer storage devices, which is an important export product of middle-income countries—such as Malaysia—in the electronics global value chain (GVC). The figure shows that the product is relatively small and peripheral to the manufacturing production network (in red).

(Box continues next page)

Box 8.1. *(continued)*

Figure B8.1.1. Manufacturing Inter-Sector Links, NAICS 31–33, 2007

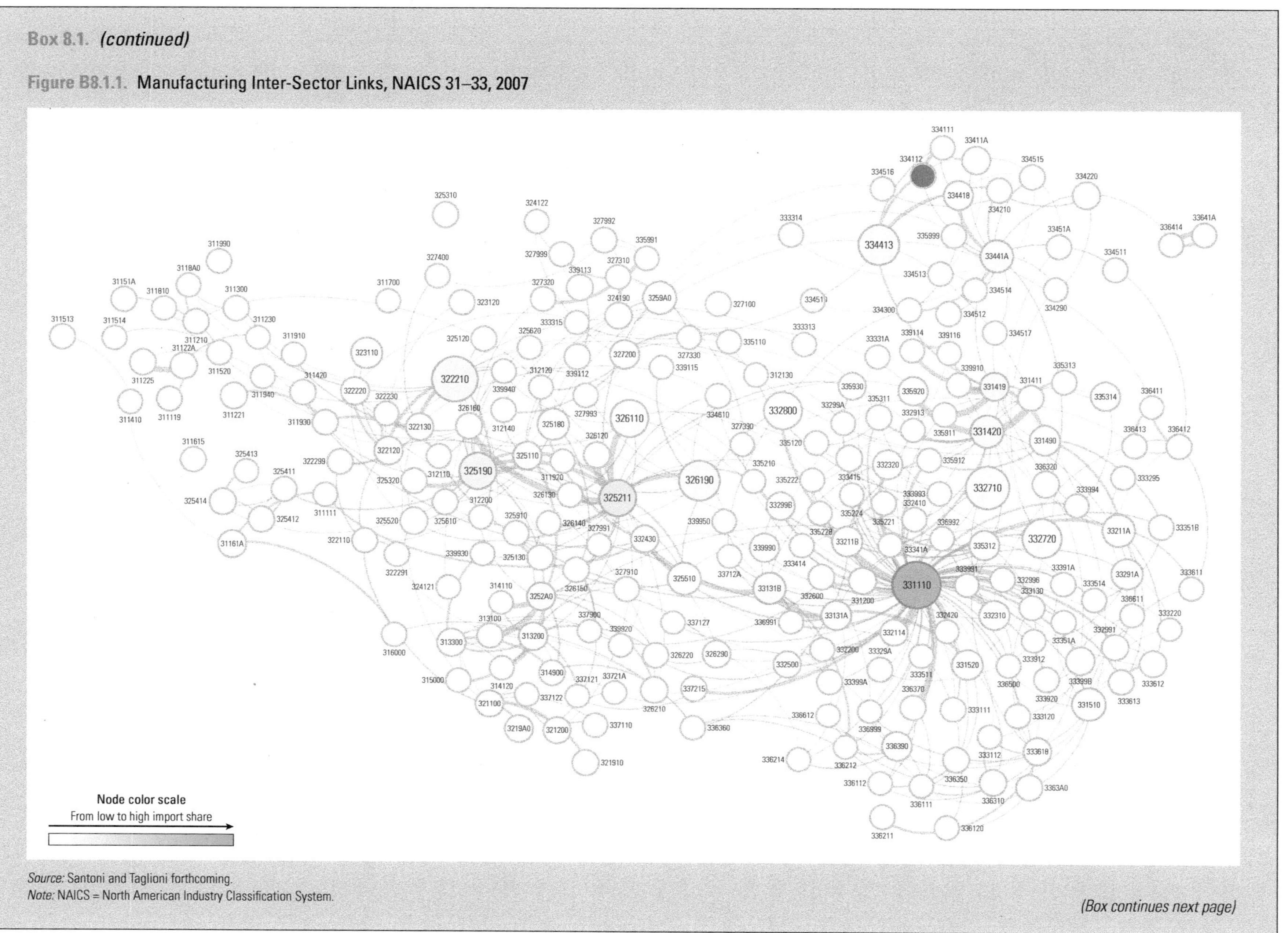

Source: Santoni and Taglioni forthcoming.
Note: NAICS = North American Industry Classification System.

(Box continues next page)

BOX 8.1. *(continued)*

Sector Buyers of This Product

Figure B8.1.2 reports the outflows of sector 334112 (red node). The green nodes represent industries that use 334112 as inputs in production and for which computer storage devices constitute at least 1 percent of the total input requirements for their production (for visual clarity, we highlight only the links associated with sector 334112). These are sector 334510 (electromedical and electrotherapeutic apparatus), sector 334111 (electronic computer manufacturing with the U.S. Small Business Association small business standard, which includes manufacturing and assembling electronic computers, such as mainframes, personal computers, workstations, laptops, and computer servers), sector 33411A (other computer manufacturing), sector 334511 (search, detection, navigation, guidance, aeronautical, and nautical system and instrument manufacturing), and sector 33451A (other measuring and controlling device manufacturing).[b] These sectors are more sophisticated than computer storage devices, which suggests that entering the downstream stages of production may imply for Malaysia a need to upgrade its technology and skills. A detailed analysis of the production structure and relative value added of the downstream products to the item of interest—such as the one suggested in Step 3 of the method—would further make it possible to assess how easy jumping to the next step in the downstream value chain would be.

Figure B8.1.2. Most Relevant Buyers of Computer Storage Devices

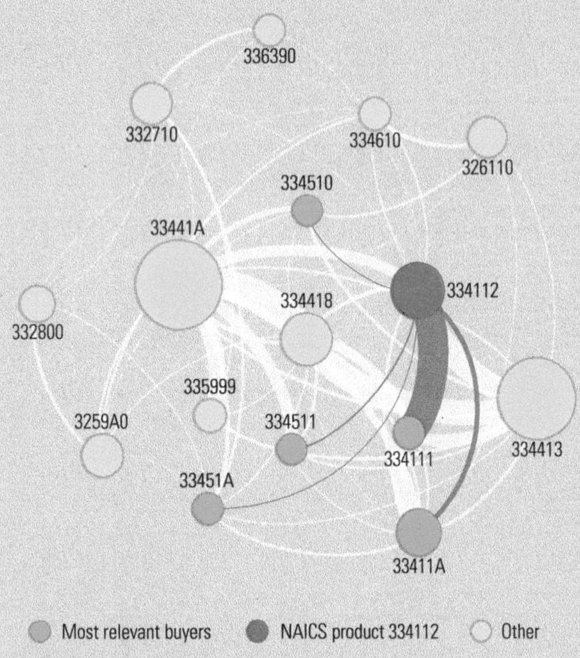

Source: Santoni and Taglioni forthcoming.
Note: The red lines designate flows of computer storage devices (red circle) to main buying sectors (green circles). NAICS = North American Industry Classification System.

Sector Suppliers of This Product

Figure B8.1.3 displays the inflows to 334112 (red node)—that is, the most important suppliers of intermediates for this sector (green nodes): sectors 334610 (software reproduction), 33411A (other computer manufacturing), 334418 (printed circuit assembly), 335999 (all other miscellaneous electrical equipment and component manufacturing), 33441A (other electronic component manufacturing), 332800 (metal treating), 3259A0 (other chemical product and preparation manufacturing), 326110 (plastics packaging materials and unlaminated film and sheet manufacturing), 334413 (semiconductor and related device manufacturing), 332710 (machine shops), and 336390 (other motor vehicle parts manufacturing).[c]

Figure B8.1.3. Most Relevant Suppliers for Computer Storage Devices

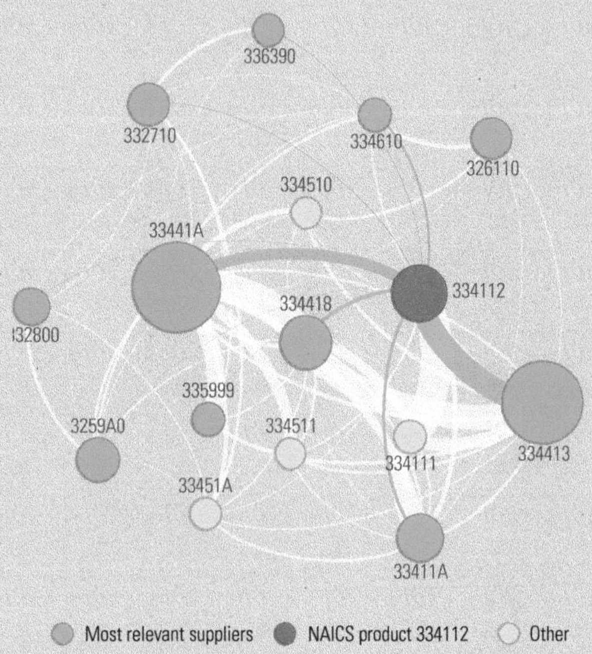

Source: Santoni and Taglioni forthcoming.
Note: The green lines designate main input flows from supplying sectors (green circles) to the computer storage devices sector (red circle). NAICS = North American Industry Classification System.

Relative Positions of Countries as Suppliers of This Product

Figure B8.1.4 depicts the relative position of Malaysia (red node) as a supplier of computer storage devices in 2012 (NAICS 2007 code 334112, computer storage devices). The links between the other nodes show the exports of downstream products—products that use computer storage devices as major inputs—using U.S. I-O tables for 2007.[d] The node size is proportional to a country's market share in world exports. For Malaysia, the market share for computer storage devices exports in 2012 was 5.6 percent. The most important competitor was China.

(Box continues next page)

BOX 8.1. *(continued)*

Figure B8.1.4. Computer Storage Devices Network for Malaysia

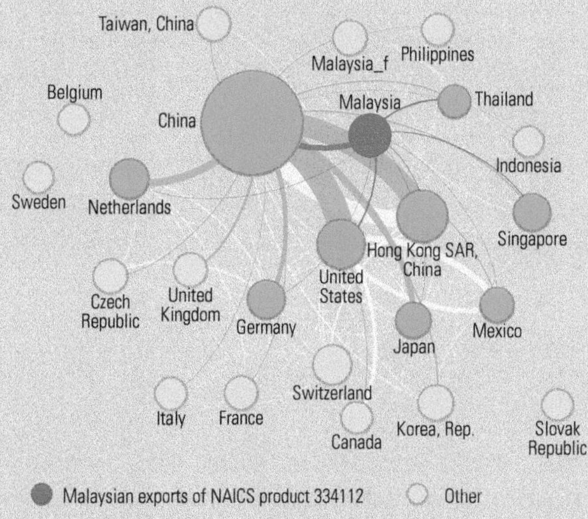

Source: Santoni and Taglioni forthcoming; BACI World Trade Database, CEPII.
Note: The red lines designate export flows of Malaysian computer storage devices (red circle) to most relevant buyers (green circles). The green lines designate export flows of downstream products that use computer storage devices as inputs. NAICS = North American Industry Classification System.

Figure B8.1.5. Malaysia as an Importer of Downstream Products

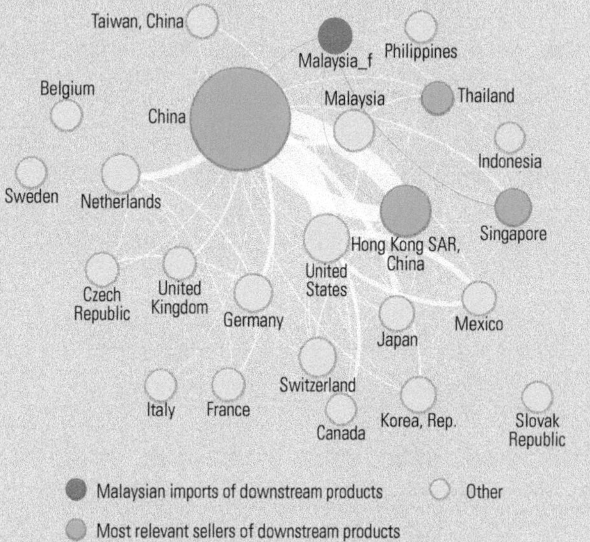

Source: Santoni and Taglioni forthcoming; BACI World Trade Database, CEPII.
Note: The green lines designate import flows of downstream products that use computer storage devices as inputs to Malaysia (red circle) from most relevant sellers (green circles). NAICS = North American Industry Classification System.

The nine largest buyers (green nodes) of Malaysian exports of computer storage devices absorbed 50 percent of the country's exports in this sector. For the other countries, the size of the node reflects the market share in exports of downstream products: China (green links) is the most important exporter of downstream products, with an export market share of 37.3 percent. Exports from China to the United States are 10 percent of world flows, and flows from China to Hong Kong SAR, China, are 8.2 percent of world flows. (In the other direction, exports from Hong Kong SAR, China, to China represent 6.3 percent of overall world flows.)

Figure B8.1.5 visualizes the position of Malaysia as a buyer of downstream products (with respect to computer storage devices) from other countries. The node MYS_f considers the position of the country as an importer of downstream products (the largest exporters are the green nodes). Figure B8.1.6 reports the position of Malaysia as a seller of downstream products (with respect to computer storage devices) to other countries. The node MYS_f considers the position of the country as an exporter of downstream products (the largest importers are the green nodes).

Figure B8.1.6. Malaysia as an Exporter of Downstream Products

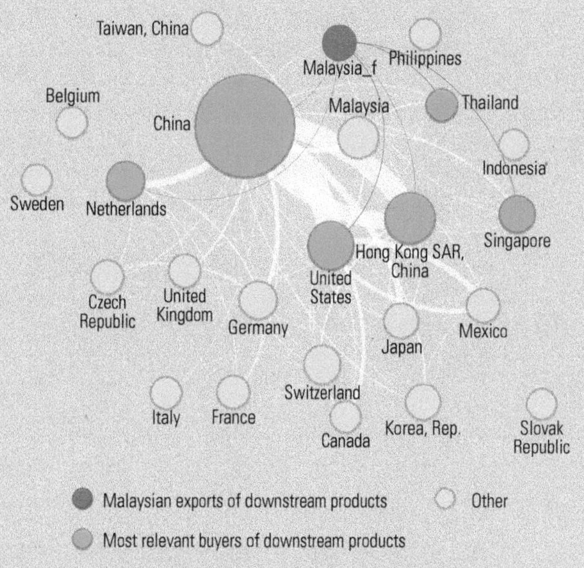

Sources: Santoni and Taglioni forthcoming; BACI World Trade Database, CEPII.
Note: The red lines designate Malaysian export flows of downstream products that use computer storage devices as inputs (red circle) to most relevant buyers (green circles). NAICS = North American Industry Classification System.

(Box continues next page)

BOX 8.1. (continued)

a. The network representation is built on the 2007 Commodity-by-Commodity Direct Requirements table from the U.S. Bureau of Economic Analysis, which provides only the total requirement table (TOT); the direct requirement was derived as $DR = (TOT\text{-}I)xTOT^{-1}$, following Acemoglu and others (2012). The data are in the form of a square matrix, where the (i, j) entry represents the share of commodity i (row) used in the production of commodity j (column). Column sums provide the total share of intermediate inputs in each commodity.

b. Sector 33451A from the I-O tables groups the following NAICS (2007) codes: 334518 (watch, clock, and part manufacturing) and 334519 (other measuring and controlling device manufacturing). Sector 33411A corresponds to 334413 (semiconductor and related device manufacturing) and 334419 (other electronic component manufacturing).

c. Sector 33441A corresponds to the following NAICS (2007) codes: 334411 (electronic computer manufacturing); 334412 (bare printed circuit board manufacturing), 334414 (electronic capacitor manufacturing), 334415 (electronic resistor manufacturing), 334416 (electronic coil, transformer, and other inductor manufacturing), 334417 (electronic connector manufacturing), and 334419 (other electronic component manufacturing). Sector 3529A0 corresponds to 325920 (explosives manufacturing) and 32599 (all other chemical product manufacturing).

d. Downstream industries are those that use 334112 as input in production and for which computer storage devices represent at least 1 percent of the total input requirements for their production. Those industries are depicted as green nodes in figure B8.1.2.

Box 8.2. The Moroccan Aerospace Industry

Over the past decade, leading aviation companies, such as Boeing of the United States and Bombardier of Canada, have invested in increasingly sophisticated factories in Morocco. That investment is part of the government's strategy to expand into more advanced manufacturing, including aerospace and electronics—a move that is expected to attract more basic industries in its wake.

In 2001, Boeing and French electrical wiring company Labinal opened a small operation, Matis, to prepare cables for Boeing 737 jetliners. Workers assembled wire bundles and shipped them to Boeing plants in the United States for installation. Initially, that work did not require any technical background, but workers hit 70 percent efficiency of industry norms within two years. As the company expanded, job openings attracted many highly educated applicants, more than 80 percent of them with few job opportunities in traditional industries. Today, Matis workers prepare wires not just for Boeing, but also for General Electric, Dassault Aviation, and Airbus.

Matis's parent company—now called Safran—then invested in more advanced manufacturing. In 2006, its Aircelle division opened a plant that produces jet engine housings.

Morocco's aviation industry recently employed almost 9,000 people (figure B8.2.1), who are paid approximately 15 percent more than the country's average monthly wage of about US$320.

Sources: Michaels 2012; interviews with people from the private sector in Morocco.

Figure B8.2.1. Upward Mobility: Approximate Employment in the Moroccan Aerospace Industry

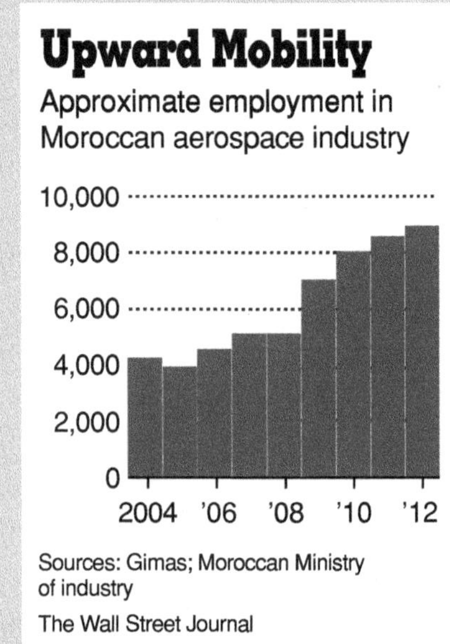

Source: Reprinted with permission from *Wall Street Journal*.
Note: GIMAS = Moroccan Aerospace Industries Association.

and quantify value added and manufacturing links; nevertheless, those data sources have limits. With I-O tables, in most cases, relationships cannot be documented at the fine level of disaggregation necessary. GVC frameworks that use firm-level analysis to determine the different stages of production of a sector and the value of each task are very costly, because they often have to be based on ad hoc surveys. Firm-level official information, such as census and balance sheet data, seldom has the detailed information required, and when it does, access to the data is very frequently restricted. Improving such data sets would enable analysts to apply new theoretical GVC models to firm-level data. One such attempt has been made by Del Prete and Rungi (2015), who apply the property rights model by Antràs and Chor (2013) to Italian firm-level data.[10]

For these reasons, the assessment must be based on different sources and methodologies. Methodologies for identifying tasks within sectors include gathering qualitative information from one or more of the following: industry associations, chambers of commerce and industry, ministries of trade and industry, companies, experienced technical experts in companies and academic centers, and existing value chain case studies. For a detailed assessment of suitable tasks, countries can follow methodologies that combine strategic analysis with cluster change-management tools (Christensen and Kempinsky 2004; Conejos and others 2000; USAID 2006).[11] These tools are not a substitute but a complement to the analyses suggested in this chapter.

The methodology used for the strategic analysis usually is based on the concepts initially developed by Michael E. Porter, a professor at Harvard University.[12] It includes evaluating the sources of a cluster's competitive advantage; detailed and forward-looking industry analysis, with emphasis on future trends; evaluation of the strategic positioning for the producers and firms in a country and recommendations for attainable strategic options; and highlights of the value chain in which firms operate and main areas of improvement.

Strategic analysis as applied to GVCs requires the utmost attention to the international (regional and global) dimension of production and demand. Specifically, it requires a market analysis that includes a benchmarking exercise that (1) assesses key attributes of firms (that is, quality, price, reliability of supply, flexibility, and time from order to delivery) against local, regional, and global competitors; and (2) keeps an eye on how technology and increasing global integration of goods, services, capital, and knowledge flows change the boundaries of the industry and the competitive space. Such an analysis also should segment end-markets as much as possible, because generally multiple actual and potential end-markets exist, each with different demand characteristics and returns, as well as different opportunities and challenges. Finally, identification of the policy area of intervention should be multidimensional, assessing the subnational, national, regional, and multilateral levels. Such an approach allows an assessment of the strategic positioning of firms and recommendations for attainable strategic options in the global context.

Once strategic analysis has identified suitable tasks, methodologies focusing on the process of change can help specify actions to generate short-term results and engage an industry or a cluster in the dynamics of change (USAID 2006). Box 8.3 provides examples of how such methodologies allow

Box 8.3. Examples of Strategic Analysis and the Dynamics of Change Management: The Ventilation Industry and the Truck Cluster in Sweden

Companies of all sizes are globalizing production, often through value chain clustering. Low-cost countries may create satellite clusters of companies to a lead firm, as seen with Bangalore's hi-tech cluster or Timisoara's footwear and auto clusters. High-income countries have responded by moving jobs and business models in an entire industry or cluster to higher-productivity tasks. Strategic analysis methodologies have helped companies redefine their business model and identify tasks of comparative advantage. Greater value added can be created either through incorporating new technologies originating from strong research and development capabilities, usually upstream from the production process, or through inserting (or expanding) value-added services, which originate from a deep and sophisticated knowledge of customers with technology (such as using "Big Data").

Duch (2000) proposed an analysis of two clusters in Sweden—the ventilation and truck industries—based on 10 steps: (1) mapping of the cluster, (2) strategic segmentation, (3) evolution of the segment's attractiveness, (4) advanced demand analysis, (5) generic strategic options for the future, (6) key success factors for the options, (7) ideal value chain and cluster diamond for chosen option/s, (8) benchmarking of the cluster against the reference/ideal cluster, (9) feasible options for firms in the cluster, and (10) areas of improvement.

That approach allowed the country's ventilation industry to understand the need to shift from selling (heating, ventilating, and air conditioning equipment) to selling clean air services—to stay in business. The approach also encouraged the truck industry to refocus from selling trucks to offering full transport solutions. In both cases, the shift entailed moving from selling products to selling concepts and services, such as fleet management systems.

Although this approach seems most useful to the private sector, it is important for public policy, too. The approach can align private initiatives and public interventions.

Sources: Conejos and others 2000; Christensen and Kempinsky 2004.

identifying tasks in high-income countries that are challenged by the loss of jobs and business to lower-cost countries.[13]

Which Risks?

GVC integration entails not only economic benefits, but also risks on the sourcing and selling sides, and countries must be aware of those risks. Yet governments cannot control the risks directly, because GVC participation is the endogenous result of a choice made by firms.

The seller's risk refers to demand shocks, including end-market risks, and to a wide range of other downstream risks along the value chain. Similarly, the buyer's upstream risks refer to supply shocks on the sourcing side that result from unforeseen events or bottlenecks taking place along the value chain of upstream suppliers.

Downstream and upstream risks are larger in GVCs than in non-GVC trade or exports based on purely domestic value chains. The risks also are larger for more complex goods, such as automobiles, for which parts and components are produced in different countries and assembled in one location. The higher is the number of countries involved in key tasks of production and the higher is the customization of the task to the downstream output, the higher is the exposure of participants to potential risks. Conversely, exports of unprocessed consumer goods, goods produced by purely domestic value chains—which are organized in a single country—or final goods produced in shorter and less sophisticated GVCs are likely to be more resilient.

Downstream and upstream risks in GVCs can more generally be related to operational risks because of the supplier's dependence on a monopsony for its product; multiple border crossings, modes of transport, hand-offs, and countries; and disparate technology issues and security concerns.[14] Risks can also be caused by shifts in a firm's strategies, such as GVC consolidation or task bundling.

A final risk is the uncertainty of firms in an economic downturn. Such uncertainty is greater for more peripheral firms and occurs more frequently among upstream firms. When demand for final goods slows, exporters can continue for a while on inventory rather than order new intermediates. Having less information about any fall in demand for final goods, suppliers of inputs may start avoiding risk—by cutting production and trade in intermediate goods—faster than if they had the same information as final goods producers.[15]

The next subsections look more closely at sellers' end-market and downstream risks and at buyers' upstream risks.

Sellers' End-Market and Downstream Risks

A seller's end-market risk has been discussed for quite some time. Sector, firm, or geographic concentration is a potential source of high volatility in value added and a likely determinant of sharp readjustments in a country's gross domestic product (GDP) during a crisis. By contrast, a diversified portfolio generally helps dampen price fluctuations, as having more products, firms, or production facilities in diverse geographic areas is likely to lead to independent price dynamics, with smoothing effects on total earnings. Put differently, a more diversified production portfolio should lead to a more stable stream of export revenues.

The export diversification discussion applies well to a world of final goods exporters (rather than to a world characterized by importing-to-export in which countries export intermediates to the lead firm or final goods producer). Suppliers in GVCs, by contrast, do not have that option because they often produce specialized (customized) inputs for only one or a few buyers (see, for example, figure 1.6 in chapter 1). The suppliers may also depend on the technology and know-how provided by the lead firm. Or, in an effort to become a supplier in GVCs, they might incur specific sunk cost investments, which make finding alternative buyers more difficult. That risk also applies to contract manufacturers that produce final goods for large buyers.

The risks are also greater for suppliers in GVCs than for lead firms. GVCs adjust quickly to demand changes in end markets, as lead firms seek to shift the burden of risks (associated with declines in demand) to supplier firms, especially when supply chains are well coordinated.[16] Such burden shifting came through strongly in the economic crisis of 2008 and importers' ensuing inventory changes, revealing GVC countries' vulnerability.[17] For the apparel GVC, declining demand from leading apparel-importing countries led to a fall in apparel volumes and values for suppliers in LMICs and to higher unemployment and more factory closures.[18]

A "pecking order" of risk exists among suppliers. First-tier and second-tier suppliers tend to face less risk than marginal suppliers. In a financial crisis or another unexpected shock, buyers tend to transfer business from marginal outfits to their core operations. During the 2008–09 global trade collapse, foreign-owned Polish firms were more resilient than average, partly as a result of intra-group lending mechanisms that supported affiliates facing external credit constraints.[19] Many foreign-owned firms in Poland were turnkey suppliers for foreign multinationals.

From a seller's perspective, the major novel risk elements in many value chains are changes in the strategies and management of lead firms. The asymmetric power relations between suppliers (competing with each other) and the lead firm (frequently, a buyer that is far downstream in the GVC with oligopoly power) enable strategic changes.

Thailand's high-technology and small and medium corporate sectors, for example, are highly dependent on the decisions of Japanese companies in Thailand. Some of them, such as Nikon (cameras) and Yazaki (car parts), are shifting production of lower-value manufacturing to lower-income neighbors, such as Cambodia and the Lao People's Democratic Republic.[20] Improvement of regional transport links is therefore increasing the opportunities—and risks—for the region's economies overall, as the lower-income countries continue their moves to attract foreign investment.

Buyers' Upstream Risks

From a buyer's perspective, the novel risk element relates to upstream supply shocks, because importing goods (or services) to export increases a buyer's dependence on upstream inputs. Two such upstream risks are natural disasters and changes in—this time—suppliers' strategies.

The 2011 flooding in Thailand (box 8.4) and the triple Tohoku disaster in Japan—earthquake, tsunami, and nuclear—starkly revealed the vulnerability of GVCs to natural events. Tohoku was especially pernicious in automotive products, computers, and consumer electronics, where downstream producers rely heavily on Japanese suppliers of specialized parts and components.[21] In addition to the severe effects it had on Japan's economy, the Tohoku disaster took a toll especially on other Asian countries, which have higher shares of intermediate goods imports than other parts of the world.[22]

Changes in upstream supplier strategies may also pose a risk for intermediate buyers in GVCs. Suppliers that—because of the underlying GVC governance structure—have more market power or target economic upgrading within the GVC could perform new tasks to supplement and build on existing ones. That type of change poses a threat to existing downstream suppliers of those tasks, particularly

Box 8.4. The Impact of Thailand's 2011 Flooding

Thailand's 2011 flooding—combined with the government's inefficiency in managing the recovery—led to price hikes and production cuts in third countries.

The flooding hit many industrial clusters in central areas. According to a business survey by the Bank of Thailand in 2012, 43 percent of businesses reported that usual operations could be restored within only three months, 46 percent in four to six months, and the remaining 11 percent in more than six months.

Manufacturing was hit hardest. Whereas 56 percent of manufacturing firms reported that the impact on their businesses was "severe" or "very severe," only 41 percent of nonmanufacturing firms made that claim. In contrast, 31 percent of nonmanufacturing firms reported "no or a small impact," but only 14 percent of manufacturing firms reported that level of impact. The stronger impact on manufacturing stemmed largely from disruptions of intermediate input supplies in the automotive and electronics sectors, and in computers and optical instruments.

The flooding had a ripple effect on final production in other countries. Shortages of auto parts from an inundated plant in Ayutthaya forced Honda to cut production around the world.[a] It also caused price hikes for hard disk drives, because of the direct impact of production stoppage and the indirect impacts of defensive purchases by consumers and inventory hoarding by resellers and wholesalers.[b]

The flooding and the government's inefficiency in managing flood recovery have raised investor concerns about rising production costs stemming from higher insurance premiums and firms building their own flood defenses. Those concerns could undermine Thailand's longer-term investment attractiveness. Of 50 multinational firms directly affected by the floods, 38 percent intend to "scale back" activities.

Source: JETRO 2012, reported in Ye and Abe 2012.
a. Chongvilaivan (2012).
b. Ye and Abe (2012).

if the upstream supplier manages to offer the bundled tasks at a competitive cost.

Which Form of Governance?[23]

As GVCs have developed, and suppliers have increased their technological sophistication and scale of operations, the dichotomy between in-house ("make") and arm's-length ("buy") global supply relations has given way to a multiplicity of lead firm–supplier relations. Those relations involve various degrees of investment, technical support, and long-term contracting and monitoring, as reflected in the growing importance of NEMs for internationalization. Largely for that reason, the form of governance matters (box 8.5).

Which form of Governance between Lead Firms and Suppliers?

GVCs can be organized in one of five governance structures: market, modular, relational, captive, and hierarchy (figure 8.2).[24] They can be measured by three variables: complexity of information between actors in the chain, how the information for production can be codified, and supplier competence.[25]

Market Governance

The market governance structure involves fairly simple transactions. Information on product specifications is easily transmitted, and suppliers can make products with minimal input from buyers. Exchanges between the lead firm and its suppliers usually occur at arm's length, requiring little or no formal cooperation, and the costs of switching to new partners is low on both sides. The central governance mechanism is price, rather than a powerful lead firm.

Modular Governance

The modular governance structure exists when complex transactions are fairly easy to codify. Suppliers in modular chains typically make products to a customer's specifications and take full responsibility for process technology, using generic machinery that spreads investments across a wide customer base. Such governance often appears in industries dominated by transactions between a lead firm and turnkey, full-package suppliers—especially in the domains of autos, apparel, footwear, electronics, and business services. This structure keeps the switching costs low and transaction-specific investments few, although buyer-supplier interactions can be very complex. The links (or relationships) are more substantial than in simple market structures, because of the high volume of information flowing across the inter-firm link. Information technology and standards for exchanging information are key to how this structure functions.

Relational Governance

With the relational governance structure, buyers and sellers rely on complex information that is not easily transmitted or learned, which leads to frequent

Box 8.5. Why the Form of Governance Matters

The scope for entering global value chains (GVCs) and determining the value of exports in GVCs is not fully in the hands of countries. Most lead firms decide strategically where to produce (domestically or offshore) and whether to make some levels of the value chain abroad (foreign direct investment) or buy them from an external firm either at arm's length (domestic or offshore outsourcing) or through non-equity modes of investment, such as contract manufacturing.

The firm's governance decisions go beyond mere transactions costs and core competencies. A theoretical model may be considered, in which firms, on the basis of productivity and sector characteristics, decide whether to integrate production of intermediate inputs or outsource it.[a] Firms with different productivity levels choose different ownership structures and supplier locations, and those choices affect the relative prevalence of different organizational forms. But the motives for offshoring and outsourcing for the strategic firm also encompass the pursuit of greater flexibility, diversification of location to reduce risk, and lower production costs.[b] Comparing vertical foreign direct investment versus arm's-length outsourcing in a North-South framework, Grover (2011) postulates that outsourcing is more welfare enhancing in the South if the domestic absorptive capacity, defined as the ratio of skilled relative to unskilled labor, is above a certain threshold level. Bernard and others (2010) show that the choice between these two forms of governance is sector-specific.

Similar to firms, countries should think strategically about the forms of GVC participation that will best advance their development goals. The firms may not be able to choose the governance structure, but they should be aware of how governance characteristics can mediate the impacts of GVC participation—and therefore condition firms' decisions.

a. Antràs and Helpman (2004).
b. Milberg and Winkler (2013).

Figure 8.2. Five GVC Governance Structures

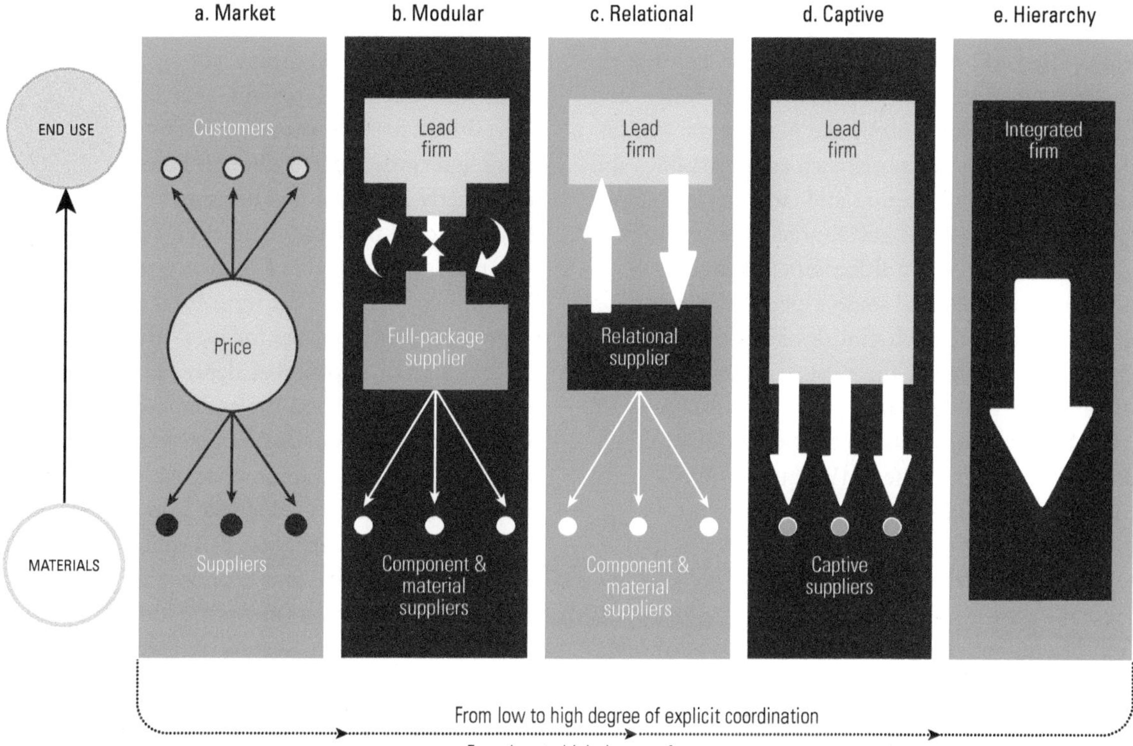

Source: Adapted from Gereffi, Humphrey, and Sturgeon 2005, 89.
Note: GVC = global value chain.

interactions and knowledge sharing between the parties. Such links require trust and generate mutual reliance, which are regulated through reputation, social and spatial proximity, family and ethnic ties, and the like. Despite mutual dependence, however, lead firms still specify what is needed and thus have the ability to exert some level of control over suppliers. Producers in relational chains are more likely to supply differentiated products based on quality, geographic origin, or other unique characteristics. Relational links take time to build, so the costs and difficulties in switching to a new partner usually are high.

Captive Governance

With captive governance structures, small suppliers depend on one or a few buyers that often wield a great deal of power. Such networks feature a high degree of monitoring and control by the lead firm. The power asymmetry forces suppliers to link to their buyer under conditions set by—and often specific to—that buyer, leading to "thick" ties and high switching costs for both parties. The core competence of the lead firms tends to be in areas outside production, so helping the suppliers upgrade their production capabilities does not encroach on this attribute but benefits the lead firm by increasing the efficiency of its value chain. Ethical leadership is important to ensure that suppliers receive fair treatment and an equitable share of the market price.

Hierarchical Governance

With the hierarchical governance type of structure, chains are characterized by vertical integration, and managerial control exists within lead firms that develop and manufacture products in-house (make). This structure usually exists when product specifications cannot be codified, products are complex, or highly competent suppliers cannot be found. Although it is less common than in the past, this sort of vertical integration is still important in the global economy.

Buyer- or Producer-Driven Value Chains?

Over time, any of these forms of governance can change as an industry evolves; similarly, governance patterns within an industry can vary from one link of the chain to the next. Depending on the nature of the lead firm in the chain, the analysis can also distinguish between buyer-driven and producer-driven value chains.[26] The former occur mainly in consumer products, such as apparel, footwear, and toys. The GVC is driven by large retailers that do not manufacture but focus instead on design and marketing and subcontract the production. The latter are typical in industries such as automobiles and aeronautics, which require mid- to high-technology production as well as substantial scale economies. They are driven by multinational producing firms that may subcontract some aspects of production but that keep research and development and final goods production at the firm. However, there are major cases of buyer-driven relationships, in which the buyer focuses solely on the postproduction segment—for example, the BMW (buyer)–Aprilia (producer) relationship in motorcycles.

Which Power Relations in GVCs?[27]

The governance structure of GVCs is particularly important, because it defines the GVC's power relations, which determine how financial, material, and human resources are allocated within the chain.[28] GVCs with different governance structures have different degrees of power asymmetries (box 8.6 and figure 8.2), including GVCs in agrifood, consumer electronics, textiles, and apparel.

Although extremely useful from an analytical perspective, the five governance structures do not consider a firm's location. Firms in GVCs have two basic locational decisions: stay in their home country or open an affiliate or NEM abroad. These options generally apply to lead firms and large, first-tier suppliers with market power in GVCs. Lower-tier suppliers do not have the capacity to carry the sunk costs of foreign investment. Although governments cannot directly influence that decision (it is the firm's), they can adopt policies to attract FDI or NEMs.

A major determinant of country policies to attract FDI is the potential to deliver substantial knowledge or productivity spillovers for local firms and workers. A vast set of empirical evidence has been amassed over the past decade on the existence and direction of FDI-generated horizontal and vertical productivity spillovers. In a comprehensive meta-analysis, Havranek and Irsova (2011) take into account 3,626 estimates from 55 studies on FDI spillovers and find evidence for positive and economically important backward spillovers from multinationals on local suppliers in upstream sectors and smaller positive effects on local customers in downstream sectors. However, the authors reject the existence of horizontal FDI spillovers.

Local firms, including NEMs, can similarly benefit from international trade within GVCs, particularly when exporting inputs to international buyers abroad, but also when importing intermediates from international suppliers. The extent of spillovers to

Box 8.6. Four Strategies to Widen Power Asymmetries in GVCs

Asymmetric power often is endogenous to the formation and governance of some global value chains (GVCs), as oligopolistic lead firms follow a cost-cutting strategy managed through offshore sourcing in GVCs. Such endogenous asymmetry can take a variety of forms, depending on the lead firm's strategic focus. Four strategies stand out:

- *Inducing competition* is the process of diversifying among suppliers to spur competition among them. Playing one supplier off another, working with multiple suppliers, and even creating new supplier firms have become standard strategies of lead firms in GVCs, to keep input prices low. Such diversification also reduces risk after, say, a political, economic, or natural disaster in a country or a unionization effort or work protest at a given plant. Inducing competition is easiest where global capacity is already excessive.
- *Offloading risk to suppliers* has been documented in a variety of industries, including apparel and electronics. The surge of offshoring and outsourcing practices also helps lead firms offload risks that they previously faced when producing those segments in-house. Such risks include end-market and downstream risks.
- *Branding* is a textbook example of constructing an entry barrier. Despite considerable theoretical analysis of entry barriers, study of the economics of pure branding within GVCs has been limited. Branding tilts the bargaining power in production to the firm that holds the brand. In industries with standardized production technology—including apparel, footwear, airlines, computing (at times), consumer electronics, and automobiles—branding is a key part of a lead firm's strategy.
- *Minimizing technology sharing* is a strategy in which lead firms protect their proprietary assets through patents, trademarks, and other forms of intellectual property regulations, especially when investing abroad, to reduce the amount of potential technology leakages. For example, Boeing carefully controls technology in its sourcing with Japanese, U.K., and U.S. parts producers.[a]

Source: Milberg and Winkler 2013.
a. Nolan, Sutherland, and Zhang (2002).

domestic suppliers depends on the type of governance structure between the lead firm and its local suppliers.

In addition to the governance structure in GVCs, international buyer characteristics can mediate potential spillovers from belonging to a GVC. The buyer's motives (whether market, cost, resource, or asset seeking), global production and sourcing strategies (which could also involve co-sourcing and co-location), technology intensity, home country, and the duration of supplier relations can all—through international trade—influence potential spillovers in a way similar to how foreign investor characteristics mediate FDI spillover potential.

Likewise, some host country characteristics and institutions that are important for FDI spillovers can lead to spillovers through domestic firms' involvement in international trade. Host country characteristics and institutions that affect the availability and quality of labor (a country's learning and innovation infrastructure) and the international movement of goods and services (a country's trade policy) are of major importance to spillovers. These mediating factors for spillovers in GVCs will be discussed in more detail in chapter 9.

Policy Options

Lead firms think strategically when making decisions, so governments should too, when reviewing two sets of policies: (1) creating world-class links in GVCs to optimize international flows of inputs and outputs among production facilities and create efficient links with global markets and (2) creating a world-class business climate for foreign tangible and intangible assets (see the example of Bulgaria in figure 2.14 in chapter 2).

Creating World-Class GVC Links

Countries can join GVCs either by facilitating domestic firms' entry or by attracting foreign investors. The foreign investment option includes more direct access to foreign know-how and technology. Countries such as Costa Rica and Thailand have managed to attract FDI and turn it into sustainable GVC participation in very different ways. In all cases, however, providing excellent infrastructure, streamlined export procedures, and a tariff-friendly environment is necessary. One way to jumpstart that process, particularly for countries with poor national infrastructure and high import tariffs, is to create "competitive spaces"—enclave locations where the rules of business are different from those that prevail in the national territory, and the costs of factors are lower. An example is export processing zones (EPZs), which are rapidly built sites equipped with excellent infrastructure, streamlined procedures, and favorable tax conditions (such as tariff drawbacks on imports of intermediates).

Jumpstarting GVC Entry through the Creation of EPZs and Other Competitive Spaces[29]

In many lower-income countries, exports come overwhelmingly from EPZs, which—along with the other types of competitive spaces—can provide a way for the country not only to attract foreign capital, but also to connect the local labor force to established GVCs. The critical second step is then to connect the competitive spaces to the rest of the economy.[30] So, within the framework of GVCs, competitive spaces have a clear rationale, but empirical research also shows that their ability to generate development yields mixed results. The case of EPZs illustrates the complex issues that converge to determine the ability of competitive spaces to deliver development.

EPZs are spaces in a country that are intended to attract export-oriented companies by offering those companies special concessions on taxes, tariffs, and regulations. Some of the typical special incentives for EPZs include the following:

- Exemption from some or all export taxes
- Exemption from some or all duties on imports of raw materials or intermediate goods
- Exemption from direct taxes, such as profit, municipal, and property taxes
- Exemption from indirect taxes, such as value-added tax on domestic purchases
- Exemption from national foreign exchange controls
- Free profit repatriation for foreign companies
- Provision of streamlined administrative services, especially to facilitate import and export
- Free provision of enhanced physical infrastructure for production, transport, and logistics

Other, less transparent features of EPZs sometimes provide further incentives for firm investment and export. One such feature is a relaxed regulatory environment, including labor rights and standards (notably the right to unionize), foreign ownership, and leasing or purchasing of land. Another feature (although clearly not available to all countries simultaneously) is an undervalued currency that renders costs lower (in foreign currency terms) and raises export competitiveness.

EPZs continue to contribute an important share of national gross exports in many LMICs, particularly lower-income economies. During the 1990s, many countries vastly expanded their EPZ exports: Costa Rica's EPZs, for example, shot up from 10 percent of manufactured gross exports in 1990 to 50–52 percent in the early 2000s; Bangladesh saw its gross EPZ exports rise from 3.4 percent in 1990 to 21.3 percent in 2003.[31] In some smaller LMICs, EPZ exports accounted for 80 percent or more of gross exports in 2006.

For EPZs to contribute to sustained economic development, however, they have to be linked to the rest of the economy. The problem is that, by their nature, they resist such links for several reasons. For one, EPZs are generally created to attract foreign firms to promote jobs and exports precisely because domestic firms are uncompetitive internationally and cannot generate foreign exchange. So, from the start, domestic firms are behind in their capacity to provide low-cost, high-quality inputs to production in EPZs.

Another reason for resistance may be that EPZs are dominated by foreign firms that have well-established relations with foreign input producers. Many foreign firms may follow a co-sourcing strategy, relying on imported inputs from established suppliers abroad, or they may follow co-location strategies that require established foreign input suppliers to enter EPZs. Most studies find that the backward links from firms in EPZs are minimal, with domestic orders remaining very low and technology spillovers rare. That finding underpins the terms-of-trade weakness for many LMIC manufacturing exports.

Moreover, most EPZs allow duty-free imports of material inputs. Non-EPZ domestic firms may not import inputs duty-free, putting them at a cost disadvantage in input production. The share of inputs purchased from domestic suppliers commonly ranges from 3 to 9 percent, as reported for El Salvador, Guatemala, the Philippines, and Sri Lanka in the mid- to late 1990s. In the Dominican Republic in 2004, after 30 years of EPZ presence and robust growth in EPZ exports and employment, EPZs purchased 0.0001 percent of material inputs from the domestic market.[32]

Some notable exceptions include the Republic of Korea, where the share of inputs purchased from the domestic economy rose from 13 percent in 1972 to 32 percent in 1978 and remained that high through the 1980s.[33] The country's EPZs were set up to attract foreign investment and promote the electronics sector. The level of integration is particularly impressive, given that about 80 percent of investment in the EPZs was foreign. The state played an important role in fostering the link by providing duty drawbacks to non-EPZ firms in its "equal footing policy."[34]

Technology spillovers also are limited, as the low-skill, assembly-type production so common in EPZs is simply not conducive to technology transfer. And the higher skill-intensive EPZs, such as those involving software or other business services, often are enclaves, de-linked from the rest of the economy except for its high-skills labor force. The technology is embodied in imported capital, and the knowledge is embodied in management. Evidence shows—for example, in the case again of Korea in the mid-1980s—that knowledge transfers increase when the skill intensity of production rises.[35]

At least two other characteristics of EPZs restrain their potential to advance development. First, EPZs may indeed create employment and pay average wages slightly higher than those of similar jobs outside EPZs, but they generally have not been associated with notable improvement in wages and labor standards. Second, EPZs raise an issue of the compatibility of some incentives with World Trade Organization (WTO) agreements—notably, offshore production creates obstacles to aligning domestic onshore rules with best international practices.[36]

Attracting the "Right" Foreign Investors

EPZs and other competitive spaces are a special case. A sustainable longer-term strategy of investment attraction requires that governments target more general, nationwide measures. In designing investment promotion measures, various factors are important for policy makers to consider, particularly factors that explicitly target FDI. Attracting foreign investors is the first of two sets of approaches for countries entering GVCs. The other is facilitating domestic firms' access to GVCs, which is the focus of the next section.

Foreign investors vary in their potential to deliver spillovers.[37] Governments therefore must identify and attract the "right" foreign investors, taking steps that include assessing the nature of the investment and the motivations of potential FDI or NEM (for example, efficiency seeking/export platform, resource seeking, or market seeking), as well as their technology contribution and the technology gap with domestic firms. Investment promotion should not only focus on lead firms in GVCs, but also target turnkey global suppliers and, possibly, important lower-tier suppliers.[38]

A light-handed industrial policy can foster participation in GVCs and links with the domestic economy by overcoming market failures or capturing coordination externalities. Urban policy provides an analogy: if individual initiatives are completely uncoordinated, the result can be over-congested cities that fail in the basic goal of improving citizens' lives. At the other extreme, government control of every investment decision can stifle growth and innovation—and so also fail to improve everyone's lives—in cities, towns, and rural areas.

A key difference between GVC-led and other avenues of development is that GVCs require government coordination at the micro level. Still, governments should not aim to pick a sector as the "winner" (box 8.7). They should instead help firms plan and encourage entry into the appropriate tasks and, consequently, densification of already-begun GVC participation (see, for example USAID (2006), as discussed in Step 3).

The following are recommendations for designing public policy to attract FDI and NEMs with potential for spillovers.[39]

- Keep the most important policies focused on ensuring an attractive general investment climate and a trade-conducive policy environment.
- Ensure that investment policy explicitly considers the nature of investment and the motivations of potential FDI and NEMs, as their degree of spillover is likely to vary.

Box 8.7. Lessons from Failed Industrial Policies

Many countries have designed and run industrial policies to promote production transformation, reconversion, or upgrading. Some policies have achieved their objectives, but many others have failed. Even the success stories include elements of failure over time, as countries learn through trial and error. Focusing on the lessons from success is common, but failure can be just as instructive.

- *Indiscriminate subsidies.* Granting subsidies without conditions increases the risk of adverse selection of beneficiaries and the development of assistance-dependent behavior among firms. Such a policy rarely translates into productivity improvements.
- *Never-ending support.* The absence of sunset clauses (a provision that if a contract is canceled, neither buyer nor seller shall be subject to penalty) in support programs to companies discourages efforts to increase productivity.
- *Cathedrals in the desert.* Building factories or research laboratories in remote locations works only when it is part of a broader plan for creating backward and forward links, or when the policy is matched with programs to foster local infrastructure development.
- *Prevention of competition.* Although the creation of new activities and industries may require support in the early stages (the traditional "infant industry" argument), gradual exposure to internal and external competition can ensure that those activities grow in a productive way.
- *Closed-door, bureaucracy-led priorities.* This type of policy cuts the chances of generating the information flows and trust essential to get the private sector to commit to investing in innovation and production.
- *Capture by incumbents.* Consultations with the private sector often end up being led by incumbents, but innovation and production diversification also depend on the creation and expansion of new firms. Targeted mechanisms to encourage the creation of startups are needed to avoid the risks of policies that will only help to maintain the status quo instead of catalyzing dynamic change.
- *Low critical mass for investments.* If the government's contribution is too small, the government will not be able to mobilize the matching funds from the private sector.
- *Short-term horizon and annual budgeting.* The creation and strengthening of domestic scientific, technological, and production capabilities take time, so industrial policies with short-term horizons and based on annual budgets tend not to be credible. Multiyear plans and budgets are necessary to achieve results, but they require robust monitoring and evaluation (M&E) to correct failures during implementation.
- *Lack of M&E mechanisms.* The limited capacity to generate feedback between policy design and implementation reduces the effectiveness of policies that evolve through trial and error. That lack also narrows the scope for regularly revising the policy to reduce the risks of capture and adverse selection.

Source: OECD-WTO 2013b.

- Assess the appropriate technology contribution explicitly during FDI evaluation. The assessment could include ascertaining how much the technologies that investors may bring are likely to be absorbed in the economy, given the current capacity.
- Target promotion efforts beyond original equipment manufacturers and lead firms to tier-one global suppliers and beyond. This means that the requirements and incentives to promote spillovers should be pushed down below the lead firms to include first-tier—or even second-tier—suppliers and the investors to whom they contract out operations.
- Avoid bidding away the benefits of spillovers by offering excessive firm-specific incentives to attract FDI and NEMs. Incentives tend to be most commonly associated with attracting export platform investment, given its more footloose nature, although realizing spillovers from exactly that type of investment may be the most challenging.
- Recognize that the "right" investment to deliver spillovers requires foreign and domestic investors, so ensure that investment policies are not biased against domestic investors and that they support mutual interaction. EPZs are one example of bias: they often are established primarily for foreign investors and may have explicit or de facto barriers to domestic investors. Countries that are home to large and competitive companies have an advantage in attracting FDI because the domestic firms can act as turnkey suppliers. Countries in which firms are predominantly small and medium enterprises (SMEs) find attracting FDI more difficult and so become inclined to provide overly generous incentives. Devoting some of those resources to helping SMEs become part of a well-established and integrated industrial cluster brings greater "bang for the buck."[40]
- Facilitate joint ventures (JVs) where they can add value, but avoid coercion. JVs seem to be effective for facilitating spillovers, particularly of older technologies and know-how (which, for low-income countries, are likely to be most relevant). However, this admonition should not be misread as encouraging attempts to force investors to engage in JVs with local partners. The correlation depends on the FDI or NEM motive, and demand-led JVs are more likely to share knowledge openly than are forced partnerships.
- Use industrial policy light-handedly. Weaknesses in institutions, private sector capacity and organization, and skills and absorptive capacity are the norm in low-income countries, which raises an array of challenges to fostering links. The trick is to fashion a light-handed industrial policy (in chosen sectors that conform to reasonable projections of comparative advantage) that focuses on overcoming market failures or capturing coordination externalities, including packages of infrastructure expenditures and public-private vocational training.

Helping Domestic Firms Find the "Right" Trade Partners and Technology Abroad

Governments can help potential buyers and suppliers—domestic and international—by making the right connections, say, by setting up an online firm directory that includes the sector, expertise, and firm profile. Such directories should include information on certificates that local suppliers have obtained. Becoming a supplier to lead firms requires meeting specific quality, legal, labor, health, safety, environmental, and other standards. Walmart, for example, provides a manual that includes "responsible sourcing" requirements with which potential suppliers need to comply.[41] And the International Trade Centre (United Nations Conference on Trade and Development/WTO) has launched a tool called Standard Maps, which provides comprehensive, verified, and transparent information on voluntary standards and other initiatives, covering issues such as food quality and safety. This tool also includes self-assessments for producers to rate their business against standard requirements.[42]

Government assistance can also include e-tools to help domestic companies (1) commercialize their intellectual property, (2) identify and take advantage of freely available technologies, or (3) assist them to establish licensing agreements, as Morocco does through the Office Marocain de la Propriété Industrielle in the framework of its Horizon 2015 program.[43] Other practical advice that governments can provide to potential local suppliers includes the requirements they must meet to become exporters of intermediates. Effective forms of matchmaking include holding buyer-supplier fairs or meetings.

The government's role also covers the promotion and marketing of exports and imports. Export promotion ranges from country image building, to export support services (such as trade fairs), to market research and publications. Japan's External Trade Organization (JETRO), for example, has been successful in promoting exports partly because of its emphasis on researching foreign markets and providing information to Japanese firms.[44] Chile's export promotion agency—the Chilean Trade Commission, or ProChile, for short—has helped promote Chilean salmon in the U.S. market, working with Canadian producers.[45] Chile's 2001 Internationalization Plan has helped improve the exporting skills of smaller exporters and encouraged new SME exporters (box 8.8).

In a world of GVCs, however, importing to export also requires public efforts to focus on import promotion, because a country's ability to participate in GVCs depends on its capacity to import world-class inputs. JETRO, for instance, established import promotion facilities as early as the 1990s to adapt to the increasing openness of Japan's trade.[46]

Improving Connectivity to International Markets

How effectively does a country's logistics infrastructure operate and connect to its neighbors and to global markets? Geography plays a role, with countries in remote locations (such as Chile, Kazakhstan, and Mongolia) or with large archipelagos (Greece and Indonesia) at a disadvantage. However, policy also matters for logistics performance, whether for infrastructure investment and operation or regulatory matters (licensing, implementation, enforcement, or trade facilitation at the border). In short, policy is key for creating an overall conducive environment for logistics services (figure 8.3).

Rarely does a single "magic bullet" of policy reform exist, and improving the international connectivity of a country touches on many dimensions: tightening forward and backward links within GVCs; securing the flow of inputs and outputs; creating efficient links with global markets; reducing "the thickness of borders;"[47] lowering traditional barriers to trade; and promoting trade facilitation. Improved connectivity also serves the goals of GVC participation by lowering costs, increasing speed, and reducing uncertainty.

Regarding cost reduction, GVCs have changed the perspective on traditional barriers to trade, such as tariffs. Some recent studies suggest that reducing supply chain barriers to trade (border administration, transport and communications infrastructure, and related services) would have greater impact on the growth of GDP and trade than the complete elimination of tariffs. Cutting supply chain barriers to trade could increase GDP by nearly 5 percent and trade by 5 percent, against less than 1 and 10 percent, respectively, for complete tariff removal.[48] LMICs would be the main benefactors of trade facilitation (figure 8.4). Transport costs, according to LMIC suppliers, remain the main obstacle to entering, establishing, or upgrading in GVCs.[49]

Box 8.8. Chile: ProChile Internationalization Plan

Chile is a middle-income country that relies heavily on mining and metals but has substantial agricultural export capacity. In the past two decades, Chile has become a major export success in agriculture and agroprocessing, including products such as salmon and wine, and horticulture. ProChile is widely acknowledged as having played a critical role in the country's export growth.

To improve the export skills of smaller existing exporters and encourage new small and medium enterprise (SME) exporters, ProChile developed its Internationalization Plan in 2001. One component, Interpac, is for agricultural SMEs; the other, Interpyme, is for industrial SMEs. Those programs provide Chilean companies with systematic training in the exporting issues faced by SMEs. The programs include training parts on production capabilities, market research, logistics, marketing plans, banking, international law, searching for partners, and the export process. Interpac and Interpyme are operated by a team of private sector consultants hired by ProChile, and participants receive individualized, one-on-one counseling. They complete one part at a time, and when they have completed the full program, they become eligible for ProChile co-financing programs if they have promising export plans. The programs take about one year to complete. ProChile covers up to 90 percent of the cost if participants have an exportable product for which international demand exists and if they use labor-intensive production methods.

Since the early 1990s, the number of exporters in Chile has doubled. The diversification of sectors, products, and markets has been dramatic, with the number of new products doubling, the number of markets growing by more than 50 percent, and the relative concentration of the mining sector falling sharply. Between 1996 and 2006, Chile's nontraditional exports (which account for 90 percent of its SME exports) increased from US$6 billion to US$15 billion. Several impact evaluation studies have shown that ProChile has had a positive and significant impact on export participation, new product introduction, and firm-level technological and management improvements.

Source: Partly derived from Nathan Associates 2004.

Figure 8.3. Logistics Services in a Typical Supply Chain

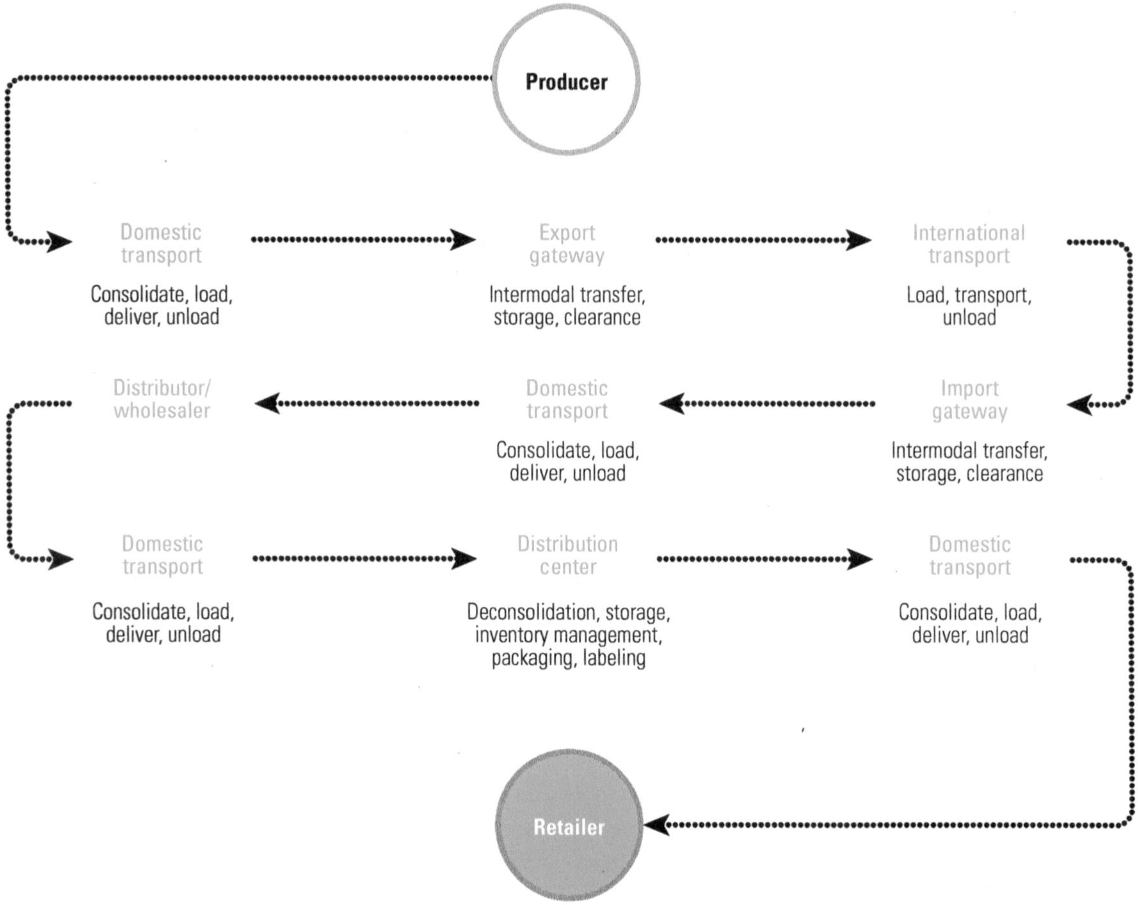

Producer

Domestic transport
Consolidate, load, deliver, unload

Export gateway
Intermodal transfer, storage, clearance

International transport
Load, transport, unload

Import gateway
Intermodal transfer, storage, clearance

Domestic transport
Consolidate, load, deliver, unload

Distributor/ wholesaler

Domestic transport
Consolidate, load, deliver, unload

Distribution center
Deconsolidation, storage, inventory management, packaging, labeling

Domestic transport
Consolidate, load, deliver, unload

Retailer

Although drivers for offshore outsourcing often have been linked to a desire to cut labor costs, other drivers include predictability, reliability, and timeliness—that is, increased speed and reduced uncertainty.[50] Many countries cannot join certain stages of GVCs because of their inability to meet requirements for timely production and delivery; time really is money. A day of delay in exporting has a tariff equivalent of 1 percent or more for time-sensitive products.[51] Slow and unpredictable land transport keeps most of Sub-Saharan Africa out of the electronics value chain.[52] Sellers often are willing to pay more for air freight. Delays in GVCs also create uncertainty, inhibiting countries from participating in GVCs for goods such as electronics or fruits and vegetables.[53]

To guide policy makers in enacting reforms of the logistics sector, the World Bank launched the now widely accepted concept of logistics performance in 2007. The World Bank also introduced a framework—now a standard—to analyze national supply chains. Logistics performance captures the different dimensions of supply chain efficiency, including how supply chains connect globally and regionally and how each is influenced by national endowments and policies. The three pillars of logistics performance are

- Availability and quality of trade-related infrastructure: ports, airports, roads, and railroads
- Friendliness and transparency of trade procedures implemented by customs and other border control agencies
- Development and quality of logistics services, such as trucking, warehousing, freight forwarding, shipping and customs clearing, and value-added logistics services (third- and fourth-party logistics)

Logistics performance and the ability of countries to connect to international markets therefore depend on a range of policy interventions that can be implemented at the national or, increasingly, regional level.

Figure 8.4. Reducing Supply Chain Barriers: Impact on GDP and Trade Growth

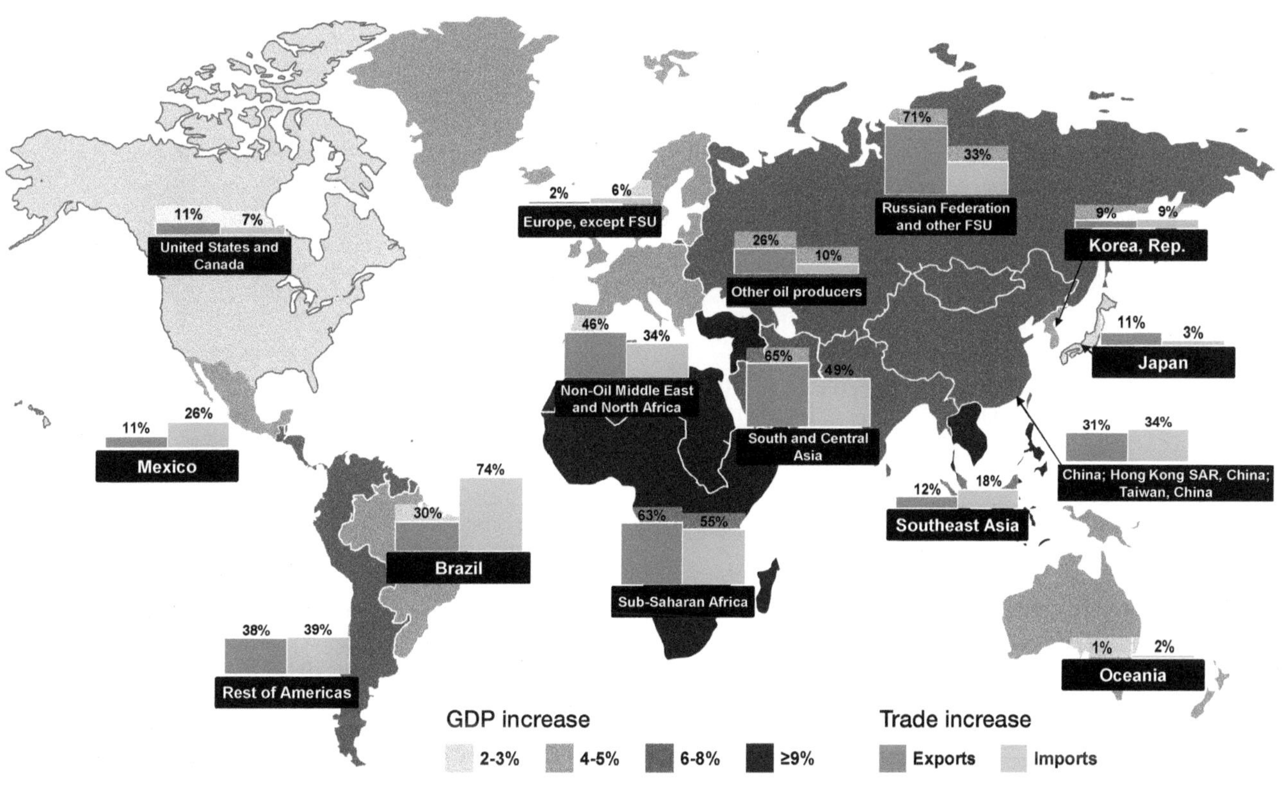

Source: Reprinted with permission from WEF 2013.
Note: GDP = gross domestic product; FSU = former Soviet Union.

Priority areas for logistics performance improvement in most countries include the following:

- Regional integration and development of trade corridors: border crossings and transit regimes
- Customs reform and trade facilitation
- Border management extending beyond customs
- Port reform
- Regulation and development of logistics services (such as trucking, third-party logistics, freight forwarding, and warehousing)
- Development of performance metrics
- Public-private coalitions for reforms

Addressing Obstacles at the Border[54]

Policies on obstacles at the border (table 8.1) should address traditional barriers to trade, as well as customs matters, notably efficiency and procedures, including rules of origin. When production is within GVCs, addressing the traditional barriers to trade is much more critical, for two main reasons.

First, GVCs broaden the scope of traditional export barriers to include barriers to imports: a country's competitiveness and ability to participate in GVCs depends as much on its capacity to import world-class inputs efficiently as on its capacity to export processed or final goods.

Second, trade within GVCs magnifies the costs of tariff protection when intermediate inputs are traded across borders multiple times, and the efficiency of the value chain could be challenged if a country at an intermediate stage of production has high tariffs.[55] Tariff escalation is a further, direct obstacle to the offshore outsourcing of key stages of production; it reduces the length of a GVC and the upgrading prospects of LMICs in the chain.

Customs efficiency can be another obstacle at the border, often in LMICs. One approach to simplify border processing and clearance is a national single-window system, in which buyers and sellers submit all information through a single electronic gateway. But establishing such a system requires a strong government mandate supported by political will and stakeholder engagement, as well as the cooperation of multiple government agencies, many of which have to undergo substantial institutional reform.[56]

Table 8.1. Addressing Obstacles at the Border: Policy Objectives and Performance Indicators

Policy objectives	
• Address obstacles to trade at the border, including trade facilitation • Suppress quotas and other quantitative restrictions on imports and exports • Reduce tariffs, suppress tariff peaks and tariff escalation, or simplify tariff schedules • Modernize (reform) customs, and harmonize procedures and cooperation across borders	• Simplify customs procedures, including sanitary and phytosanitary; technical barriers to trade; and other certifications, rules of origin, valuation, and so forth, to conform with agreements or international best practices • Implement WTO or regional/bilateral commitments (for example, common external tariff)
Performance indicators	
• Trade restrictiveness indexes: OTRI, TTRI (WTI 1.1) • Binding coverage and bound rates (WDI) • Share of tariff lines with peaks/specific rates (WDI, WTI 1.6) • MFN applied tariffs: AV+AVE or AV only (WDI; WTI 1.2, 1.3) • Applied tariffs, including preferences (WDI, WTI 1.4) • Tariff escalation (WTI 1.5) • MFN 0 tariff lines/import value (WTI 1.7) • Tariff bounds/overhang (WTI 1.8) • Non-AV tariffs (WTI 1.9) • Nontariff measures (WTI 1.10) • Customs duties (WTI 1.11)	• Export restrictions (WTI 1.13) • Logistics Performance Index and its indicators—efficiency of customs and other border procedures (LPI, WTI 4.1) • Trading across Borders—Doing Business (IFC, WTI 4.2) • Trade-enabling and global competitiveness indexes—goods market efficiency: burden of customs procedures, prevalence of trade barriers, trade tariffs, efficiency of customs administration, efficiency of import–export procedures, transparency of border administration (WEF GCI 6.10, 6.11, 6.13; ETI 1.01–4.02) • Average time to clear exports through customs/time to export/import (WDI) • Documents to export/import (WDI)

Sources: Cattaneo and others 2013, based on OECD 2012a.
Note: AV = ad valorem; AVE = ad valorem equivalent; ETI = Enabling Trade Index; GCI = Global Competitiveness Index; IFC = International Finance Corporation; LPI = Logistics Performance Index; MFN = Most Favored Nation; OTRI = Overall Trade Restrictiveness Index; TTRI = Trade Tariff Restrictiveness Index; WDI = World Development Indicators; WEF = World Economic Forum; WTI = World Trade Indicators; WTO = World Trade Organization.

Increasing the Connectivity of Domestic Markets

The policy objectives and measures in table 8.2 aim to increase the connectivity of domestic markets through improvements in logistics and transport and telecommunications, with a greater focus on transport for goods and telecommunications for offshoring services.

Importer logistics performance is associated with higher components and parts trade.[57] Its influence is much higher for trade in parts and components than for trade in final goods. The quality of logistics in the importing country is thus an important determinant in a lead firm's location decisions, but the relationship between logistics performance in the exporting country and trade in parts and components is less clear.

In addition to logistics performance, the development of GVCs—particularly offshoring services—to a large extent has been fostered by information and communications technologies (ICTs). ICTs transmit codified design specifications between actors in product-based chains and are the main medium for participation in cross-border services exports. ICTs have enabled information to be uncoupled from physical storage, which renders the transfer of huge amounts of data possible in seconds, eroding the prior dominance of producing and consuming a service onsite.

LMICs have caught up on ICT penetration and interregional Internet bandwidth, which has increased their ability to produce and export services. But the poorest among those countries still have a long way to go. The progress in LMICs has been accompanied by liberalization of services sectors, which has been fostered by constant privatization, competition, and independent regulation over the past two decades. Most LMICs that are now attracting large amounts of FDI in the services sector were characterized by protectionist policies before opening to foreign ownership of companies.

Creating a World-Class Business Climate for Foreign Tangible and Intangible Assets[58]

Ensuring Cost Competitiveness While Avoiding the Trap of Low-Cost Tasks

Low wages may be a way for countries to enter GVCs. According to firm surveys, costs (production, labor, transport, and investment) and tax incentives are major drivers of lead firms' decisions to invest or source production in LMICs. Wage differentials have

Table 8.2. Increasing the Connectivity of Domestic Markets: Policy Objectives and Performance Indicators

Policy objectives	
Increasing the accessibility and connectivity of the domestic market and the security, predictability, reliability, and efficiency of transports/logistics, telecommunications, and ICT: • Reform the telecommunications sector, including infrastructure, regulation, competition, and access for all segments; to include fixed lines and mobiles • Develop the ICT sector and the Internet (infrastructure, regulation, competition, access)	• Reform transport, logistics, and ancillary services, including infrastructure, regulation, competition for land (road and rail), maritime/water, and air • Harmonize regional infrastructure for trade corridors, and ensure other forms of regulatory cooperation • Improve vertical governance in infrastructure, including through fast-tracking and streamlining the regulatory environment, private–public dialogue on regulatory changes needed, and enhancement of budget capital execution
Performance indicators	
• Logistics Performance Index and its indicators—quality of transport and IT infrastructure, international transport costs, logistics competence, traceability and timeliness of shipments, and domestic transport costs (WDI, LPI, WTI 4.1) • Trading across Borders—Doing Business (IFC, WTI 4.2) • Trade enabling and global competitiveness indexes—infrastructure: quality of infrastructure overall, roads, railroads, ports, air transport, available seats, fixed telephone lines/100, mobile phone subscriptions/100, availability and quality of transport infrastructure and services, and availability and use of ICTs (WEF GCI 2.01–2.09, WEF ETI 4.01–7.05, WDI) • Technological readiness (WEF GCI 9.01–9.06) • Africa Infrastructure Country Diagnostic (AICD) • Liner Shipping Connectivity Index (UNCTAD, WTI 4.3) • Baltic Exchange Dry Index (WTI 4.3) • Lead time to export/import (WDI) • Port container traffic (WDI, WTI 4.3) • Total/air freight and costs (WTI, 4.3)	• Number of seats available, airlines, international routes, and airport passenger statistics (IATA, WDI) • World telecommunication/ICT indicators database and ICT development index (ITU) • Foreign participation/ownership in telecoms (ITU, WTI 1.14) • Competition index in telecoms (ITU, WTI 1.14) • Number of international gateways, landing stations, licenses for fixed and mobile phones, and Internet providers (national data, WB and OECD STRI) • Mobile and fixed-line telephone subscribers/population covered by mobile cellular network (WDI, WTI 4.4) • Average cost of 3-minute call to the United States (WTI 4.4) • Personal computers (WTI 4.4) • Internet or broadband users/subscribers (WDI, WTI 4.4) • Internet bandwidth and secured servers (ITU, WDI)

Sources: Cattaneo and others 2013, based on OECD 2012a.
Note: AICD = Africa Infrastructure Country Diagnostic; ETI = Enabling Trade Index; GCI = Global Competitiveness Index; IATA = International Air Transport Association; ICT = information and communications technology; IFC = International Finance Corporation; IT = information technology; ITU = International Telecommunication Union; LPI = Logistics Performance Index; OECD = Organisation for Economic Co-operation and Development; STRI = Services Trade Restrictiveness Index; UNCTAD = United Nations Conference on Trade and Development; WB = World Bank; WDI = World Development Indicators; WEF = World Economic Forum; WTI = World Trade Indicators.

been primary drivers of the globalization of production. But costs encompass a wide range of drivers, and high costs could, for example, stem from a lack of infrastructure or competition in basic services. High costs could also result from excessive administrative burdens (including those at the border), strict labor laws (a weak business environment), or widespread political and social insecurity or corruption.

However, the goal should be higher labor productivity and higher wages, allowing the country to remain cost competitive despite rising living standards. Unit labor costs in themselves are irrelevant. For example, China remains competitive even with rising labor costs. Recent research finds, for example, that minimum wage growth in China allows more productive firms to replace the least productive ones and forces incumbent firms to strengthen their competitiveness.[59] Although job creation and labor productivity growth are sometimes viewed as competing goals, if more value added is created with the same amount of workers (static productivity effects), this book argues that GVC integration not only has a strong potential for productivity gains via several transmission channels (dynamic productivity effects), but also creates jobs because of the increased vertical specialization and value added in GVCs (densification), as discussed in the next chapter.

Productivity and the capacity to meet production requirements must also be considered when assessing costs. If cost savings because of relocation go hand in hand with productivity losses, lead firms might end up facing higher overall costs. Moreover, value chain tasks based exclusively on labor cost advantages tend to be easy to relocate. A strategy based on low wages exclusively is therefore risky and unsustainable over the long term. Investment or tax incentives should

Table 8.3. Improving Cost Competitiveness While Avoiding the Trap of Low-Cost Tasks: Policy Objectives and Performance Indicators

Policy objectives
• Ensure cost competitiveness related to production, labor, transport, and investment. • Foster productivity gains, skills development, and technological empowerment.
Performance indicators
• Unit labor costs and wage data (ILO ILOSTAT and KILM, OECD) • Labor productivity (ILO KILM, OECD) • For skills development and technological empowerment indicators, see table 9.1.

Note: ILO = International Labour Organization; ILOSTAT = ILO database of labor statistics; KILM = Key Indicators of the Labour Market; OECD = Organisation for Economic Co-operation and Development.

be carefully used to foster productivity gains, skills development, and technological empowerment (for a list of performance indicators, see table 8.3).

Improving Drivers of Investment and Protecting Foreign Assets

Drivers of investment, particularly the protection of foreign assets, have a large influence on a country's location attractiveness for foreign investors. Those drivers affect a country's participation in GVCs, regardless of their governance structure.

Protecting assets is mainly about protecting firm-specific technology and know-how, but only some of those elements can be defended through patents, trademarks, and other forms of intellectual property laws. Many other elements cannot be protected this way, including business and organizational models, managerial practices, production processes, and export procedures. As global production networks necessarily involve contracting relationships between agents in countries with differing legal systems and contracting institutions, contracts often are incomplete.[60] The reasons for incomplete contracting in international settings include a limited amount of repeated interactions; lack of collective punishment mechanisms; and natural difficulties in contract disputes, such as determining which country's laws apply—and even when that is known, local courts may be reluctant to enforce a contract involving residents of foreign countries.[61] The way in which different national systems deal with contractual frictions and incomplete contracts is therefore important in driving firms' choices of location and boundaries in global sourcing.[62]

That statement is also proven empirically. The annual Doing Business (World Bank) and Global Competitiveness (World Economic Forum) reports provide lists of key measures for business operations, as well as indications of a country's performance based on selected criteria. The range of measures is very large, from the regulatory environment to the functioning of markets (such as state trading enterprises and government procurement). Protection of intellectual property is a decision tipping point for many lead firms. The cost of administrative burdens also becomes larger in GVCs, as management needs to coordinate a wider cast of actors.

A country's political stability, governance, and degree of corruption are other factors to consider in the decision to join a GVC. Those metrics (with others, summarized in table 8.4) relate to security (including assets and personnel) and predictability, the key drivers of intra-firm GVC trade (FDI) and on-time delivery to consumers. Within GVCs, suppliers often are expected to meet the lead firm's corporate social responsibility codes, which raise challenges for audit and execution in small, LMIC firms.[63]

To prevent a "race to the bottom" on incentives, however, policy makers can seek to promote investment through regional integration. That process includes four steps: (1) identifying regional investment barriers (such as through intensive private sector consultations and interviews), (2) defining the reform agenda, (3) implementing reforms, and (4) benchmarking reform progress against the defined reform agenda. Throughout the process, an important measure is to engage the private sector with the national public sector and regional institutions (such as through private-public dialogues) as a feedback mechanism and reform engine.[64]

GVC entry through foreign investment requires maximum fluidity in the mobility of production factors. Barriers to FDI are likely to exclude a country from major GVCs, or confine the country to certain forms of GVC governance. Stability clauses in contracts and participation in major international (including regional) arbitration and dispute settlement mechanisms are also important (table 8.5).

Organizing Domestic Value Chains and Improving the Quality of Infrastructure and Services

How well the domestic segment of the value chain is organized is as important as that for the international segment (see figure 8.3). The benefits of efficient transport and logistics at the border, for example, can be undermined by inefficient domestic links, including the unreliability or high cost of

Table 8.4. Improving Drivers of Investment: Policy Objectives and Performance Indicators

Policy objectives

Intellectual property protection:

- Improve the intellectual property regime and administration to comply with trade agreements, to include patents, authors' rights, geographic indications, and so forth
- Improve enforcement mechanisms and practices
- Promote the intellectual property regime and related training or technical assistance

Competition, including privatizations and concessions:

- Privatize, offer concessions, and open sectors to competition
- Elaborate and implement a competition framework, including competition law, competition authority (for example, independence, resources), competition law enforcement (for instance, investigations, sanctions), and related training or technical assistance

Government procurement:

- Adjust laws pertaining to public procurement, including transparency, selection criteria, national preference, and so forth

Corruption:

- Reform to fight corruption in the public (for instance, customs) and private sectors
- Promote and adopt international instruments for corruption reform

Administrative burden:

- Adopt administrative reforms to simplify and reduce administrative procedures (as an example, guillotine reform); increase transparency, predictability, timeliness, and security of administrative decisions (for example, suppression of authorizations)

Other constraint resolution:

- Create EPZs, business clusters, technology centers, and the like
- Revise labor regulations for greater labor market efficiency
- Revise regulations regarding the form of business operations and partnerships (for instance, franchises, multi-sector partnerships)
- Increase security for operations and staff against crime and violence

Promote investment through regional integration:

- Eliminate barriers to expansion of cross-border investments within the region
- Converge levels of investment protection within the region and increase transparency to prevent "race to the bottom" on incentives

Performance indicators

- Ease of Doing Business Index (IFC, WTI 3.1, WDI)
- World Governance Indicators—corruption, rule of law, government effectiveness, regulatory quality, political stability (WTI 3.2)
- Enabling Trade and Global Competitiveness Indexes
- Regulatory environment (WEF ETI, 8.01-08)
- Institutions: property rights, ethics and corruption, undue influence, government inefficiency, security (WEF GCI 1.01-1.16)
- Labor market efficiency (WEF GCI 7.01-7.09)
- Goods market efficiency (WEF GCI 6.01-6.16)
- Business sophistication: state of cluster development (WEF GCI 11.03)
- Enterprise ownership (government, private foreign, private domestic) (ADI)
- Cost of business startup procedure/procedures to register a business (WDI)
- Time spent in meetings with tax officials/expected gifts/informal payments to public officials (WDI)
- Firms using banks to finance investment (WDI)
- Strength of legal rights index (WDI)
- Time required to enforce a contract (WDI)
- Time required to obtain an operating license/register property/start a business (WDI)
- Value of seized counterfeited goods (national statistics)
- Number of registered trademarks, patents, and the like (WIPO, WDI)
- Number of competition investigations and sanctions (national statistics)
- Public procurement penetration ratio—public imports/public demand percentage (national statistics)
- Security costs (ADI)

Sources: Cattaneo and others 2013; also based on OECD 2012a and World Bank 2014.
Note: ADI = Africa Development Indicators; EPZ = export processing zone; ETI = Enabling Trade Index; GCI = Global Competitiveness Index; IFC = International Finance Corporation; WDI = World Development Indicators; WEF = World Economic Forum; WIPO = World Intellectual Property Organization; WTI = World Trade Indicators.

domestic transport, the fresh product cool chain, and low-quality storage. Regional markets and stocks are critical for agriculture's inclusion in GVCs.

Locational attractiveness to foreign investors is also determined by the ease of access to efficient services and infrastructure, including access to energy (cheap and reliable), financial and trade support, telecommunications, and transport. Access to finance (for 52 percent of the firms surveyed) and transport infrastructure (for 39 percent) were the two most serious national supply-side constraints identified by LMIC GVC suppliers as affecting their ability to enter, establish, or upgrade in a GVC.[65]

The "servicification" of manufacturing is particularly important as production internationalizes because as many as 40 services may be involved when a manufacturing firm internationalizes (figure 8.5). Recent trade in value-added data suggest that

Table 8.5. Encouraging and Protecting Foreign Investment: Policy Objectives and Performance Indicators

Policy objectives

- Remove barriers to foreign investment
- Allow more foreign equity/ownership/partnership
- Facilitate the free movement and employment of key personnel across borders
- Remove discriminatory policies (including licensing, taxes, subsidies, and so forth)
- Increase the protection of foreign assets
- Strengthen investor protection, including rights to challenge domestic regulations/decisions
- Develop alternative dispute resolution mechanisms for foreign investors (for example, recognition of international arbitration, bolstering of domestic arbitration capacities)
- Adjust the laws on nationalization, expropriation, foreign ownership, stability clauses, and the like

Performance indicators

- GATS commitments (WTO), regional commitments, and domestic laws
- Services trade restrictiveness indexes (WB, OECD)
- Arbitration awards (ICSID and other arbitration bodies' statistics)
- Protecting investors (ADI)

Sources: Cattaneo and others 2013, based on OECD 2012a.
Note: ADI = African Development Indicators; GATS = General Agreement on Trade in Services; ICSID = International Centre for Settlement of Investment Disputes; OECD = Organisation for Economic Co-operation and Development; WB = World Bank; WTO = World Trade Organization.

services represent at least 30 percent of the share of value added in manufacturing trade (see also chapter 6).[66] Thus, a country cannot be competitive and join GVCs—even in manufacturing—unless it has efficient domestic services or is open to importing them. Managing the complexity of the value chain and preserving production standards along it require strong coordination efforts that rely on efficient services (auditors, lawyers, and managers) and the movement of key personnel across borders (table 8.6).

Improving a country's domestic logistics environment—a key services sector in GVCs—requires infrastructural interventions and regulatory changes spanning many different sectors, as seen in the example of Greece (box 8.9).

Figure 8.5. Services Involved in the Internationalization of Production (at Sandvik Tooling)

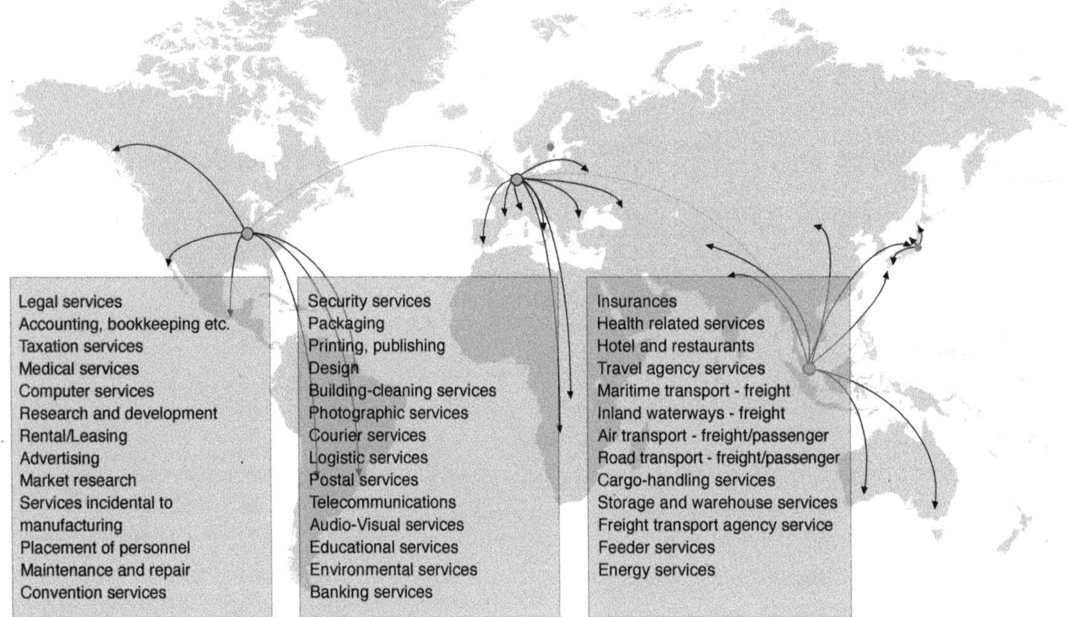

Source: Reprinted with permission from the National Board of Trade 2010.

Table 8.6. Improving Domestic Services Infrastructure and Market Structure: Policy Objectives and Performance Indicators

Policy objectives	Performance indicators
Improving access to finance: • Reform the financial sector, including microfinance, to increase the affordability and availability of financial services • Ensure export credit and trade finance	• Banking GATS commitment index (USITC, WTI 1.14) • Export credit—insured exposures (WTI 4.5) • Indicators of financial structure, development, and soundness (IMF) • Access to finance (WDI) • Enabling trade and global competitiveness indexes—financial market development (WEF GCI 8.01-8.08)
Improving other domestic infrastructure, including storage and energy: • Upgrade storage infrastructure • Reform access, regulation, and competition in energy (production and distribution) and other natural resources essential to certain activities (for instance, water in agriculture)	• Procedures and time to build a warehouse (WDI) • Time required to get electricity (WDI) • Energy statistics/access to electricity (IEA, WDI) • Quality of electricity supply (WEF 2.07) • Power outages in firms/value lost in power outages (WDI) • Electricity cost (WTI 4.6) • Pump price for fuel (WTI 4.6)
Improving business support and the organization, connectivity, and performance of markets, including e-commerce: • Adopt export and investment promotion and incentives • Give analyses and information on markets, opportunities, threats, and so forth • Undertake marketing, branding, international presence, and promotion efforts • Form sector, professional, or other forms of associations (such as chambers of commerce) and consultations • Develop trade corridors and other regional forms of hard and soft networks (for example, regional regulatory agency, regional distribution network) • Develop regional markets and stocks, boards of trade, and price regulation mechanisms • Organize value chains and sectors, including storage and distribution channels • Develop e-commerce (including infrastructure, legal framework, protection of data, security of payments)	• Logistics Performance Index and its indicators—quality of transport and IT infrastructure, international transport costs, logistics competence, trackability and timeliness of shipments, and domestic transport costs (WB, WTI 4.1) • Global Competitiveness Index—business sophistication: extent of marketing, state of cluster development, value chain breadth, control of international distribution production process sophistication, delegation of authority (WEF GCI 11.05-11.09) • Value of e-commerce, number of ICT firms, number of secured servers (WDI, ITU, national statistics) • Postharvest losses (African Postharvest Losses Information System)

Sources: Cattaneo and others 2013, based on OECD 2012b.

Note: GATS = General Agreement on Trade in Services; GCI = Global Competitiveness Index; ICT = information and communications technology; IEA = International Energy Agency; IMF = International Monetary Fund; IT = information technology; ITU = International Telecommunication Union; USITC = United States International Trade Commission; WB = World Bank; WDI = World Development Indicators; WEF = World Economic Forum; WTI = World Trade Indicators.

Box 8.9. Case Study: Regulatory Reform and Infrastructure Building in Greek Logistics

More than 95 percent of goods traded between Europe and Asia are transported over deep seas, through two primary routes. Large container ships leave ports in Asia and go to Rotterdam, the Netherlands. Many go through the Suez Canal, entering the Mediterranean, usually bypassing Greece. However, Greece's economic crisis has helped focus domestic policy makers' attention on the potential benefits of being a regional transport hub in the way the Netherlands is in Northern Europe.

But becoming a regional gateway requires competitive logistics along the whole supply chain—beyond efficient ports and railway connections—requiring extensive reforms and strategic investments. To facilitate that goal, the Greek government, advised by the World Bank, is taking steps to remove regulatory bottlenecks and improve the country's international connectivity. Those steps include reforms in transformational sectors such as trucking, rail, and ports; in the regulatory environment; and in smaller micro initiatives, such as improving the enforcement of regulations, promoting coordination between authorities, enhancing transparency vis-à-vis the private sector, and better monitoring the performance of the sector and evaluating the impact of

(Box continues next page)

BOX 8.9. *(continued)*

reforms using modern methods. Key actions enacted since 2010 include the following:

- *Privatizing port operations at the Port of Piraeus (Greece's main port) of the Piraeus Port Authority and the national railway company, Trainose.* Piraeus is the focal point of a logistics push by the government. Part operated by the China-based Cosco Pacific Ltd., Piraeus is the 11th largest container-shipping port in the European Union, and it is the fastest growing port in the European Union (by number of containers) since Cosco started operations.
- *Investing in infrastructure.* In 2013, the government completed a long-delayed 17-kilometer link from the port to the national rail network following Cosco Pacific's arrival. This is now attracting international investors such as Hewlett Packard to Greece.
- *Improving the regulatory environment.* Reforms should improve the viability of Greek logistics companies, improve logistics efficiency, and encourage competition along all the segments of the logistics value chain. Key actions include drafting a logistics strategy and a logistics master plan, passing a new law on the logistics industry, and establishing a strong institutional framework by which the private sector has the power to hold the public sector accountable.
- *Adopting a trade facilitation strategy.* The strategy has established a single window for trade facilitation and additional initiatives, such as setting up business process analysis to map export procedures, improving customs procedures, and introducing risk management methods.

Source: Taglioni and others 2013.

Notes

1. Farole and Winkler (2014a).
2. Farole and Winkler (2014a). Knowledge spillovers can diffuse from foreign firms to local producers within the same industry (intra-industry, or horizontal spillovers) or to another industry (inter-industry, or vertical spillovers). In the latter case, spillovers can affect local input or services suppliers in upstream sectors (backward spillovers) and local customers in downstream sectors (forward spillovers).
3. Dimelis and Louri (2002); Takii (2005).
4. Crespo and Fontoura (2007); Toth and Semjen (1999).
5. Farole and Winkler (2014a).
6. The value added generated by the lead firm comes from preproduction activities, such as design, and postproduction activities, including marketing and retailing.
7. UNCTAD (2011).
8. The RCA can be computed based on the domestic value added embodied in a country's gross exports (see, for example, the World Bank's Export of Value Added database and the OECD-WTO's TiVA database in Appendixes G and H). For countries for which trade in value-added data are unavailable, or for customized aggregations of products and sectors (for example, a specific cluster of activities spanning different broad sectors, such as the automotive cluster or the textile cluster), RCA indexes can be constructed based on intermediates, parts, and components, which can be identified using the informed classifications discussed in part 1 and appendixes B through E.
9. This step draws on ongoing research at the World Bank by Jean Francois Arvis, Daria Taglioni, and Gianluca Santoni.
10. Gereffi and others (2001). For the goods sectors, the value added of a task can be determined as the difference between the costs of inputs and outputs. If reliable information on the value added of tasks is unavailable, which often is the case in services sectors, then the skill intensity of a performed task—that is, the employee's educational level or work experience—can serve as a good proxy for the task's value added (Gereffi and Fernandez-Stark 2010). An example is offshore services GVCs. Call centers or routine business process outsourcing tasks can be performed by workers with a high school diploma. Market research, however, generally requires workers with a minimum of a bachelor's degree, and the highest value-added tasks often are carried out by workers with master's degrees or PhDs. That classification helps policy makers identify which tasks may be entered based on the skill levels of their workers (Gereffi and Fernandez-Stark 2010).
11. A separate project of the World Bank Group, Trade and Competitiveness Global Practice, is creating a framework for such detailed analysis and identification of tasks.
12. Porter (1980, 1985, 1990, 1998).
13. Based on the preceding concepts, a separate World Bank Group project is producing a framework for systematically applying strategic analysis and cluster change management tools to identify GVC tasks in World Bank client countries.
14. MacDonald (2006).
15. Ferrantino and Taglioni (2014).
16. Milberg and Winkler (2010).
17. Alessandria, Kaboski, and Midrigan (2010, 2013).
18. Gereffi and Frederick (2010).
19. Kolasa, Rubaszek, and Taglioni (2010).
20. Peel (2014).
21. Lohr (2011); Escaith and Gonguet (2011).
22. IMF (2011); Cattaneo and others (2013).
23. This section draws on information from Cattaneo and others (2013, box 2).
24. Gereffi, Humphrey, and Sturgeon (2005).

25. Frederick and Gereffi (2009); Gereffi, Humphrey, and Sturgeon (2005).
26. Gereffi (1994).
27. This section draws on information from Milberg and Winkler (2013).
28. Gereffi (1994, 97).
29. This section draws on information from Milberg and Winkler (2013).
30. Milberg and Winkler (2013).
31. Engman, Onodera, and Pinali (2007); Aggarwal (2005).
32. Engman, Onodera, and Pinali (2007, 34–35).
33. Kusago and Tzannatos (1998).
34. Engman, Onodera, and Pinali (2007, 39).
35. Engman, Onodera, and Pinali (2007).
36. Farole and Akinci (2011).
37. Farole and Winkler (2014c).
38. Farole and Winkler (2014b).
39. Farole and Winkler (2014b).
40. Becattini 1990; Porter (1990).
41. Walmart (2014).
42. www.standardsmap.org.
43. www.directinfo.ma.
44. Beltramello and others (2011).
45. Pietrobelli (2008).
46. Beltramello and others (2011).
47. OECD (2012b).
48. WEF (2013).
49. OECD-WTO (2013a).
50. WEF (2013).
51. Hummels and others (2007).
52. Christ and Ferrantino (2011).
53. Arvis, Raballand, and Marteau (2010); Christ and Ferrantino (2011).
54. This section draws on Cattaneo and others (2013).
55. OECD (2012a).
56. McLinden (2013).
57. Saslavsky and Shepherd (2012).
58. This section draws on Cattaneo and others (2013).
59. Mayneris, Poncet and Zhang (2014).
60. Rodrik (2000).
61. Antràs (2014).
62. Antràs and Yeaple (2014).
63. UNCTAD (2012).
64. World Bank (2014).
65. OECD-WTO (2013a).
66. OECD (2014).

References

Acemoglu, Daron, Vasco M. Carvalho, Asuman Ozdaglar, and Alireza Tahbaz-Saleh. 2012. "The Network Origins of Aggregate Fluctuations." *Econometrica* 80 (5).

Aggarwal, Aradhna. 2005. "Performance of Export Processing Zones: A Comparative Analysis of India, Sri Lanka and Bangladesh." Working paper 155, Indian Council for Research on International Economic Relations, New Delhi.

Alessandria, George, Joseph P. Kaboski, and Virgiliu Midrigan. 2010. "The Great Trade Collapse of 2008–09: An Inventory Adjustment?" NBER Working Paper 16059, National Bureau of Economic Research, Cambridge, MA.

———. 2013. "Trade Wedges, Inventories, and International Business Cycles." *Journal of Monetary Economics* 60 (1): 1–20.

Antràs, Pol. 2014. "Grossman-Hart (1986) Goes Global: Incomplete Contracts, Property Rights, and the International Organization of Production." *Journal of Law Economics and Organization* 30 (suppl 1): i118–i17.

Antràs, Pol, and Davin Chor. 2013. "Organizing the Global Value Chain." *Econometrica* 81 (6): 2127–204.

Antràs, Pol, and Elhanan Helpman. 2004. "Global Sourcing." *Journal of Political Economy* 112 (3): 552–80.

Antràs, P., and Stephen R. Yeaple. 2014. "Multinational Firms and the Structure of International Trade." In *Handbook of International Economics*, vol. 4, edited by Gita Gopinath, Elhanan Helpman, and Kenneth Rogoff, 55–130. Amsterdam: Elsevier.

Arvis, Jean-François, Gaël Raballand, and Jean-François Marteau. 2010. *The Cost of Being Landlocked: Logistics Costs and Supply Chain Reliability.* Washington, DC: World Bank.

Becattini, G. 1990. "The Marshallian Industrial District as a Socio-Economic Notion." In *Industrial Districts and Inter-Firm Cooperation in Italy*, edited by F. Pyke, G. Becattini, and W. Sengenberger. International Institute for Labor Studies, Geneva.

Beltramello, A., K. De Backer, V. Mercader, and L. Moussiegt. 2011. "Opening Japan: Comparisons with Other G20 Countries and Lessons Learned from International Experience." OECD Science, Technology, and Industry Working Papers, 2011/02, Organisation for Economic Co-operation and Development Publishing, Paris. http://dx.doi.org/10.1787/5kg6nk6w3v7c-en.

Bernard, Andrew B., J. Bradford Jensen, Stephen J. Redding, and Peter K. Schott. 2010. "Intra-Firm Trade and Product Contractibility." *American Economic Review*, Papers and Proceedings, 100 (5): 444–48.

Cattaneo, Olivier, Gary Gereffi, Sébastien Miroudot, and Daria Taglioni. 2013. "Joining, Upgrading and Being Competitive in Global Value Chains: A Strategic Framework." Policy Research Working Paper 6406, World Bank, Washington, DC.

Chongvilaivan, Aekapol. 2012. "Thailand's 2011 Flooding: Its Impact on Direct Exports and Global Supply Chains." Asia-Pacific Research and Training Network on Trade (ARTNeT) Working Paper Series 113, ARTNeT, Bangkok.

Christ, Nannette, and Michael J. Ferrantino. 2011. "Land Transport for Exports: The Effects of Cost, Time, and Uncertainty in Sub-Saharan Africa." *World Development* 39 (10): 1749–59.

Christensen, Lars, and Peter Kempinsky. 2004. "Reinforcing the Competitiveness of Clusters." Translated by Emiliano Duch. Originally published as "Att stärka klusters konkurrenskraft," chapter 15 of *Att molilisera for regional tillväxt: Regionala Utvecklingsprocesser, Kluster och Innovationssystem.* Lund, Sweden: Studentlitteratur.

Conejos, J., E. Duch, J. Fontrodona, J. M. Hernández, A. Luzárraga, and E. Terré. 2000. *Cambio Estratégico y Clusters en Cataluña.* Barcelona: Gestion.

Crespo, Nuno, and Maria Paula Fontoura. 2007. "Determinant Factors of FDI Spillovers—What Do We Really Know?" *World Development* 35 (3): 410–25.

Del Prete, Davide, and Armando Rungi. 2015. "Organizing the Global Value Chain: A Firm Level Test." IMT Lucca EIC Working Paper Series 04, Institute for Advanced Studies, Lucca, Italy.

Dimelis, Sophia, and Helen Louri. 2002. "Foreign Ownership and Production Efficiency: A Quantile Regression Analysis." *Oxford Economic Papers* 54 (3): 449–69.

Engman, Michael, Osamu Onodera, and Enrico Pinali. 2007. "Export Processing Zones: Past and Future Role in Trade and Development." OECD Trade Policy Working Paper 53, Organisation for Economic Co-operation and Development, Paris.

Escaith, Hubert, and Fabien Gonguet. 2011. "International Supply Chains as Real Transmission Channels of Financial Shocks," *Journal of Financial Transformation,* Capco Institute 31: 83–97.

Farole, Thomas, and Gokhan Akinci. 2011. *Special Economic Zones: Progress, Emerging Challenges, and Future Directions.* Washington, DC: World Bank.

Farole, Thomas, and Deborah Winkler. 2014a. "Introduction." In *Making Foreign Direct Investment Work for Sub-Saharan Africa: Local Spillovers and Competitiveness in Global Value Chains,* edited by Thomas Farole and Deborah Winkler, 5–22. Washington, DC: World Bank.

———. 2014b. "Policy Implications." In *Making Foreign Direct Investment Work for Sub-Saharan Africa: Local Spillovers and Competitiveness in Global Value Chains,* edited by Thomas Farole and Deborah Winkler, 263–79. Washington, DC: World Bank.

———. 2014c. "The Role of Mediating Factors for FDI Spillovers in Developing Countries: Evidence from a Global Dataset." In *Making Foreign Direct Investment Work for Sub-Saharan Africa: Local Spillovers and Competitiveness in Global Value Chains,* edited by Thomas Farole and Deborah Winkler, 59–86. Washington, DC: World Bank.

Ferrantino, Michael J., and Daria Taglioni. 2014. "Global Value Chains in the Current Trade Slowdown." *Economic Premise* No. 137, Washington, DC, World Bank.

Frederick, Stacey, and Gary Gereffi. 2009. "Value Chain Governance." USAID Briefing Paper. U.S. Agency for International Development, Washington, DC. http://www.cggc.duke.edu/pdfs/Frederick_Gereffi_ValueChainGovernance_USAID_BriefingPaper_Feb2009.pdf.

Gereffi, Gary. 1994. "The Organization of Buyer-Driven Global Commodity Chains: How U.S. Retailers Shape Overseas Production Networks." In *Commodity Chains and Global Capitalism,* edited by Gary Gereffi and Miguel Korzeniewicz, 95–122. Westport, CT: Greenwood Press.

Gereffi, Gary, and Karina Fernandez-Stark. 2010. "The Offshore Services Value Chain: Developing Countries and the Crisis." In *Global Value Chains in a Postcrisis World. A Development Perspective,* edited by Olivier Cattaneo, Gary Gereffi, and Cornelia Staritz, 335–72. Washington, DC: World Bank.

Gereffi, Gary, and Stacey Frederick. 2010. "The Global Apparel Value Chain, Trade, and the Crisis: Challenges and Opportunities for Developing Countries." In *Global Value Chains in a Postcrisis World: A Development Perspective,* edited by Olivier Cattaneo, Gary Gereffi, and Cornelia Staritz, 157–208. Washington, DC: The World Bank.

Gereffi, Gary, John Humphrey, Raphael Kaplinsky, and Timothy J. Sturgeon. 2001. "Introduction: Globalisation, Value Chains and Development." *IDS Bulletin* 32 (3): 1–8.

Gereffi, Gary, John Humphrey, and Timothy J. Sturgeon. 2005. "The Governance of Global Value Chains." *Review of International Political Economy* 12 (1): 78–104.

Grover, Arti. 2011. "Vertical FDI versus Outsourcing: A Welfare Comparison from the Perspective of the Host Country." *Review of Development Economics* 15 (2): 293–306.

Havranek, Tomas, and Zuzana Irsova. 2011. "Estimating Vertical Spillovers from FDI: Why Results Vary and What the True Effect Is." *Journal of International Economics* 85 (2): 234–44.

Hummels, David, Peter Minor, Matthew Reisman, and Erin Endean. 2007. "Calculating Tariff Equivalents for Time in Trade." Technical Report submitted to the U.S. Agency for International Development, Nathan Associates, Arlington, VA.

IMF (International Monetary Fund). 2011. "Tensions from the Two-Speed Recovery: Unemployment, Commodities, and Capital Flows." *World Economic Outlook,* IMF, Washington, DC.

JETRO (Japan External Trade Organization). 2012. "Survey of Business Sentiment on Japanese Corporations in Thailand for the 2nd Half of 2011." JETRO, Tokyo. http://www.jetro.go.jp/thailand/e_survey/pdf/jccaut11eng.pdf.

Kolasa, Marcin, Michal Rubaszek, and Daria Taglioni. 2010. "Firms in the Great Global Recession: The Role of Foreign Ownership and Financial Dependence." *Emerging Markets Review* 11 (4): 341–57.

Kusago, Takayoshi, and Zafiris Tzannatos. 1998. "Export Processing Zones: A Review in Need of an Update." Social Protection Discussion Paper 9802, World Bank, Washington, DC.

Lohr, Steve. 2011. "Stress Test for the Global Supply Chain." *The New York Times,* March 19. http://www.nytimes.com/2011/03/20/business/20supply.html?pagewanted=all&_r=0.

MacDonald, Andrea. 2006. "Managing a Global vs. Domestic Supply Chain." *World Trade Magazine,* July 6. http://fyketrading.homestead.com/World_Trade_Article_reprint.pdf.

Mayneris, Florian, Sandra Poncet, and Tao Zhang. 2014. "The Cleansing Effect of Minimum Wage: Firm-Level and Aggregate Effects of the 2004 Reform of Minimum Wage Rules in China." Working Paper 2014-21, CEPII, Paris.

McLinden, Gerard. 2013. "Single-Window Systems: What We Have Learned." *The Trade Post* (blog), World Bank Group, April 30. http://blogs.worldbank.org/trade/single-window-systems-what-we-have-learned.

Michaels, Daniel. 2012. "Morocco's Aviation Industry Takes Off." *Wall Street Journal* March 20. http://online.wsj.com/news/articles/SB10001424052970204059804577226763868263758.

Milberg, William, and Deborah Winkler. 2010. "Trade, Crisis, and Recovery: Restructuring of Global Value Chains." In *Global Value Chains in a Postcrisis World: A Development Perspective*, edited by Olivier Cattaneo, Gary Gereffi, and Cornelia Staritz, 23–72. Washington, DC: World Bank.

———. 2013. *Outsourcing Economics: Global Value Chains in Capitalist Development.* New York: Cambridge University Press.

Nathan Associates. 2004. "Best Practices in Export Promotion." Technical report submitted to USAID, Nathan Associates, Arlington, VA.

National Board of Trade. 2010. "At Your Service. The Importance of Services for Manufacturing Companies and Possible Trade Policy Implications." *Kommerskollegium* 2010:2.

Nolan, Peter, Dylan Sutherland, and Jin Zhang. 2002. "The Challenge of the Global Business Revolution." *Contributions to Political Economy* 21 (1): 91–110.

OECD (Organisation for Economic Co-operation and Development). 2012a. "Managing Aid to Achieve Trade and Development Results: An Analysis of Trade-related Targets." COM/DCD/TAD (2012) 12/FINAL. OECD, Paris.

———. 2012b. "Reducing the Thickness of Borders to Promote Trade and Participation to Global Value Chains: An Issues Paper." COM/DCD/TAD/RD (2012) 2/RD4. OECD, Paris.

OECD-WTO (Organisation for Economic Co-operation and Development and World Trade Organization). 2013a. "Aid for Trade at a Glance 2013: Linking to Value Chains." OECD, Paris.

———. 2013. *Perspectives on Global Development 2013: Industrial Policies in a Changing World.* Paris: OECD.

———. OECD. 2014. "Global Value Chains and Africa's Industrialisation." *African Economic Outlook 2014.* OECD, Paris.

Peel, Michael. 2014. "Thailand Political Turmoil Imperils Foreign and Domestic Investment." *Financial Times,* March 9. http://www.ft.com/cms/s/0/6a2c75f4-a5e7-11e3-9818-00144feab7de.html#axzz48Z7q1AoR.

Pietrobelli, Carlo. 2008. "Global Value Chains in the Least Developed Countries of the World: Threats and Opportunities for Local Producers." *International Journal of Technological Learning, Innovation, and Development* 1 (4): 459–81.

Porter, Michael E. 1980. *Competitive Strategy: Techniques for Analyzing Industries and Competitors.* New York: Free Press.

———. 1985. *Competitive Advantage: Creating and Sustaining Superior Performance.* New York: Free Press.

———. 1990. "The Competitive Advantage of Nations." *Harvard Business Review* 78 (2): 73–93.

———. 1998. *On Competition.* Boston: Harvard Business School.

Rodrik, Dani. 2000. "How Far Will Economic Integration Go?" *Journal of Economic Perspectives* 14 (1): 177–86.

Santoni, Gianluca, and Daria Taglioni. Forthcoming. "Benchmark Input-Output Data." Bureau of Economic Analysis, U.S. Department of Commerce, Washington, DC.

Saslavsky, Daniel, and Ben Shepherd. 2012. "Facilitating International Production Networks: The Role of Trade Logistics." Policy Research Working Paper 6224, World Bank, Washington, DC.

Taglioni, Daria, Baher El-Hifnawi, Jean-Francois Arvis, and Lauri Ojala. 2013. *Greek Logistics: Unlocking Growth Potential through Regulatory Reform and Complementary Measures.* Washington, DC: World Bank.

Takii, Sadayuki. 2005. "Productivity Spillovers and Characteristics of Foreign Multinational Plants in Indonesian Manufacturing 1990–1995." *Journal of Development Economics* 76: 521–42.

Toth, Istvan Janos, and Andras Semjen. 1999. "Market Links and Growth Capacity of Enterprises in a Transforming Economy: The Case of Hungary." In *Market Links, Tax Environment and Financial Discipline of Hungarian Enterprises*, edited by Istvan Janos Toth and Andras Semjen. Budapest: Institute of Economics, Hungarian Academy of Sciences.

UNCTAD (United Nations Conference on Trade and Development). 2011. WIR11. World Investment Report 2011: Non-Equity Modes of International Production and Development. New York and Geneva: United Nations]

———. 2012. *Corporate Social Responsibility in Global Value Chains: Evaluation and Monitoring Challenges for Small and Medium Sized Suppliers in Developing Countries.* Geneva: UNCTAD.

USAID (United States Agency for International Development). 2006. "Implementation of Best Practices for Value Chain Development Projects." Draft for discussion. USAID, Washington, DC.

Walmart. 2014. Standards for Suppliers Manual, available online at: http://cdn.corporate.walmart.com/d1/7e/ee6f5c8942f69ad4183bc068377 1/standards-for-suppliers-manual.pdf

WEF (World Economic Forum). 2013. *Enabling Trade: Valuing Growth Opportunities.* Geneva, Switzerland: WEF.

World Bank. 2014. "Investment Policy Product." *Investment Climate, Trade and Competitiveness Global Practice.* Washington, DC: World Bank.

Ye, Linghe, and Masato Abe. 2012. "The Impacts of Natural Disasters on Global Supply Chains." Asia-Pacific Research and Training Network on Trade (ARTNeT) Working Paper 115, ARTNeT, Bangkok.

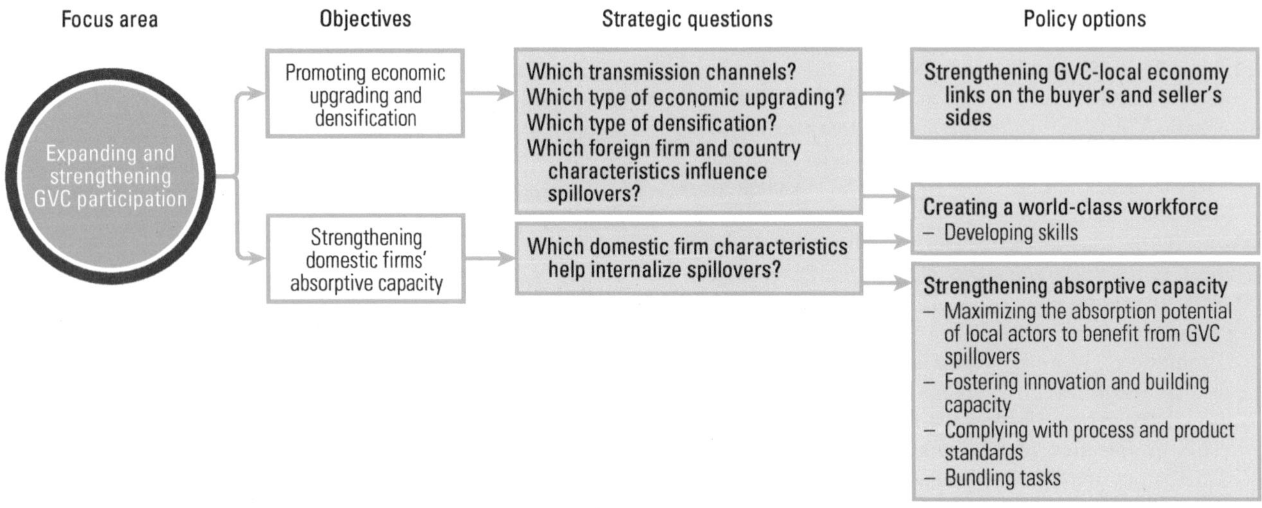
Focus area
Objectives
Strategic questions
Policy options
Expanding and strengthening GVC participation
Promoting economic upgrading and densification
Strengthening domestic firms' absorptive capacity
Which transmission channels?
Which type of economic upgrading?
Which type of densification?
Which foreign firm and country characteristics influence spillovers?
Which domestic firm characteristics help internalize spillovers?
Strengthening GVC-local economy links on the buyer's and seller's sides
Creating a world-class workforce
– Developing skills
Strengthening absorptive capacity
– Maximizing the absorption potential of local actors to benefit from GVC spillovers
– Fostering innovation and building capacity
– Complying with process and product standards
– Bundling tasks

Chapter 9

EXPANDING AND STRENGTHENING GVC PARTICIPATION

Introduction

This chapter focuses on strengthening a country's participation in global value chains (GVCs) and upgrading to higher value-added activities. Policy makers must focus on strengthening existing GVC–local economy links, as well as the absorptive capacity of local actors, to help them maximize the benefits from GVC spillovers. Policy makers need to decide which type of economic upgrading (product, functional, or inter-sector) they want to pursue. By locating various stages of production in countries where production costs are lower, firms decrease the marginal cost of production but raise other costs by increasing the complexity and uncertainty associated with organizing production across several locations. Changes in this "trade-off" affect outsourcing and offshoring decisions and can be heavily influenced by national policy choices. In recent years, some evidence of "back-shored" activities caused by rising costs, intellectual property rights concerns, and digitalization of the economy, and changing perceptions about the stability and reliability of GVCs has started to emerge, pointing to the critical role of domestic policies to retain GVC-related investment and ensure that it leads to positive spillovers for local actors.

Promoting Economic Upgrading and Densification in GVCs: Strategic Questions

How can countries complete the ecosystem of firms beyond the initial GVC enclave and ensure that GVCs are integrated into the domestic economy? The logic of that effort is that strong links with the domestic economy result in greater diffusion of knowledge, technology, and know-how from foreign investors or trade partners abroad. Unfortunately, foreign investors and trade partners do not actively pursue—and sometimes resist—such integration for reasons ranging from economic constraints to technological and quality gaps with domestic suppliers, and to shortages of specialized workers and skills.

For policy makers, economic upgrading and densification are keys to turning GVC participation into sustainable development. The concept of economic upgrading is largely about gaining competitiveness in higher value-added products, tasks, and sectors. GVC densification involves engaging more local actors (firms and workers) in the GVC network. In some cases, this could mean that performing lower value-added activities on a large scale can generate large value addition for the country. Raising domestic labor productivity and skills contributes to the overall goal to increase a country's value added as a result of GVC participation. Although static labor productivity effects are sometimes viewed to be negative for employment creation (if more value added is created with the same amount of workers), GVC integration has strong potential for productivity gains via several transmission channels (dynamic productivity effects), as discussed in this chapter, which go hand-in-hand with the increased labor demand caused by more vertical specialization and higher value added in GVCs.

This chapter concentrates on two options to expand development beyond the initial enclave: (1) promoting economic upgrading and densification in GVCs and (2) strengthening domestic firms' absorptive capacity to benefit from spillovers in GVCs (see figure O.1 in the Overview).

Policy can help move a country's resources into higher value-added activities. Value added is defined as the sum of wage income, profit income, and tax revenue. All factors that influence these three elements can be considered determinants of value added, including the ability to produce goods at a higher level of quality and sophistication, as well as access to skills, knowledge, innovation, and technology. But before discussing such policy options, the chapter focuses on four basic strategic questions facing low- and middle-income countries (LMICs).

Which Transmission Channels?

To target policy efforts efficiently, countries should identify the main transmission channels for economic and social upgrading (see figure 1.11 in chapter 1):

- *Forward links* are sales of GVC-linked intermediates to the local economy, spurring production and/or productivity in downstream sectors.
- *Backward links* are GVC-linked purchases of local inputs, spurring production and/or productivity in various upstream sectors.
- *Technology spillovers* are improved productivity of local firms in the same or related downstream or upstream sectors as a result of GVC production.
- *Skills demand and upgrading* are similar to technology spillovers but transferred through the training of and demand for skilled labor.
- *Minimum scale achievements* occur, for example, when GVC participation stimulates investments in infrastructure that would otherwise not be profitable and that may spur local production in other sectors.

These transmission channels enable GVCs to support development and industrialization in four ways.[1] First, GVCs—through forward and backward links—generate a demand effect (lead firms tend to require more or better inputs from local suppliers) and an assistance effect (lead firms can assist local suppliers through, for example, sharing knowledge and technology, and advance payments) in the host country. The forward and backward links generate technology spillovers, which improve the productivity of local firms through the diffusion effect (the assistance effect diffuses knowledge and technology in the supplier's industry) as well as the availability and quality effects (GVC participation increases the availability and quality of inputs).

Second, GVC participation can translate into pro-competitive market restructuring effects that extend to nonparticipants through the pro-competition effect. GVC participation increases competition for limited resources in the country—between multinational corporations (MNCs) and local firms, and between participants and nonparticipants in GVCs—raising overall average productivity in the medium run.[2] GVC participation also increases competition through the demonstration effect of GVC products, business models, marketing strategies, production processes, or export processes. Knowledge and technology spillovers arise from direct imitation or reverse engineering by local firms, whether or not they are GVC participants.

Third, minimum scale achievements have a twin impact. In the amplification effect, they amplify pro-competition effects, stimulating investment in infrastructure and backbone services, which would not be realized without the scale of activity generated by GVCs. The infrastructure, once in place, is likely to spur local production and/or productivity in other sectors and in the non-GVC economy. With the sustainability effect, minimum scale achievements strengthen the country's ability to sustain GVC participation over time. The GVC literature is rife with examples of the key role of improvements in backbone infrastructure and services, such as logistics, to improve timeliness and reliability in transporting goods, parts, and components, which enables countries to integrate vertically into GVCs.[3]

Fourth, GVCs benefit labor markets through the following:

- *Demand effect.* GVC participation is characterized by higher demand for skilled labor from MNCs or other GVC participants. Multinationals may temporarily bid away human capital by paying higher wages or offering enhanced employment benefits, but that effect tends to dim as soon as the productivity of domestic firms is raised or the market adjusts to the tightening labor supply.
- *Training effect.* Local firms in GVCs are more likely to receive training (for example, from MNCs or their international buyers).
- *Labor turnover effect.* Knowledge embodied in the workforce of participating firms (such as MNCs or their local suppliers) moves to other local firms.

Which Type of Economic Upgrading?

Economic upgrading does not necessarily mean to "move up the value chain"—in other words, to perform or integrate downstream activities—but offers a wider range of possibilities. Depending on the type of economic upgrading that a country pursues, three objectives can be defined:

- *Moving into more sophisticated products in the existing value chain (product upgrading).*[4] Product sophistication can be measured in increased unit values (value added per unit of output).
- *Increasing value-added shares (in output of final product) in existing GVC tasks (functional upgrading).* Functional upgrading is defined as the move into more technologically sophisticated or more integrated tasks of a production process and relates to the overall skill content of activities.[5] It is usually measured as a higher share of value added in the output of the final product.
- *Moving into new value chains with higher value-added shares (inter-sector upgrading).* Firms can pursue inter-sector upgrading, moving horizontally into new value chains that require similar knowledge and skills.[6] To qualify such a move as economic upgrading, it should involve tasks with a higher unit value (value added per unit of output). For example, knowledge acquired in the television GVC may be used in the monitor/computer GVC. Taiwan, China, has been successful in such inter-sector upgrading.[7] Another possible example could be the move from sewing products in Nicaragua's apparel and footwear industries to sewing covers for car seats (figure 9.1).

How can countries upgrade inter-sectorally? Once countries have singled out the tasks in which they have a comparative advantage (as described in chapter 8), they need to identify sectors that require similar tasks but add more value. The following measures can be used:

- Labor's share in value added can be used to get a first indication of a sector's labor intensity.
- The skill intensity of sectors can be calculated if sector data by type of labor input are available (say, by using firm-level data).
- Technology intensity is a more sophisticated measure to identify similar sectors. The classification by Lall (2000) has high-, medium-, and low-tech; resource-based; and primary sectors/products.

Figure 9.1. Example of Possible Inter-Sector Upgrading in Nicaragua

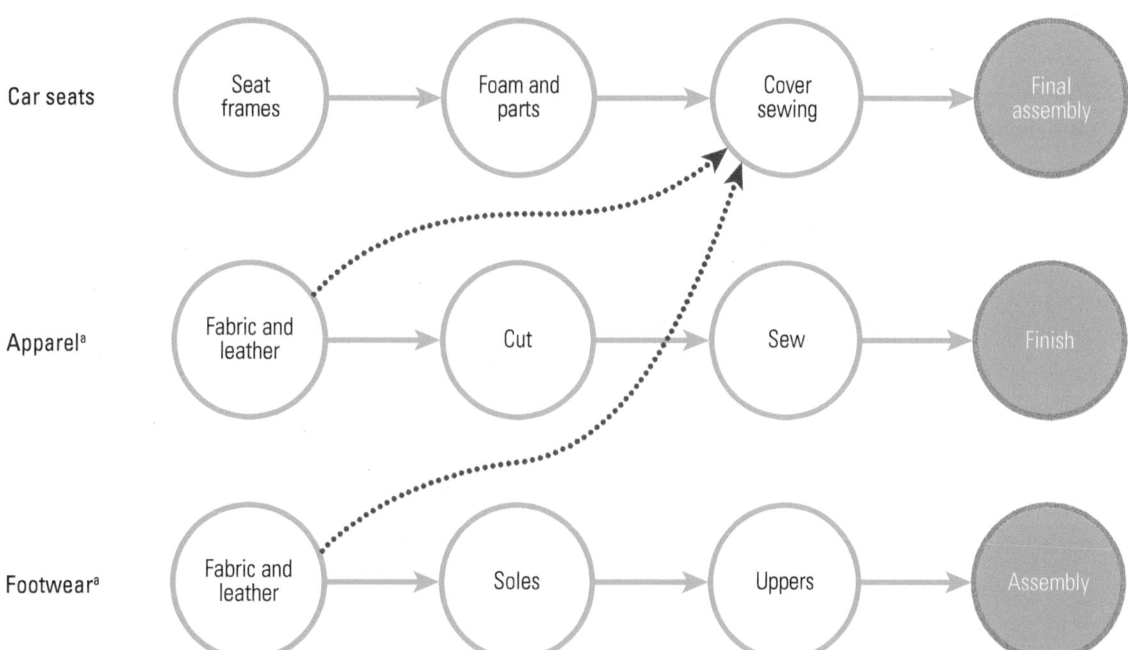

Source: Adapted from Sturgeon and Zylberberg 2012.
a. Industry value chains currently active in Nicaragua.

The measures are most meaningful if they are undertaken at a highly disaggregated sector level. To detect similar tasks with higher value added in other industries, analysts should also use qualitative information from technical sources, companies, and other field experts. That information can help identify which sectors are similar in their processes and required tasks, and which type of inter-sector upgrading has been successful in other countries. Ideally, that information should be backed up by evidence of past success (with firms that have moved into higher value-added products in other sectors).

Other measures of economic upgrading include profit growth, export growth, growth in export market shares (especially if associated with unit value/ quality growth), reduced relative incidence of unit labor costs, and increase in capital intensity.[8]

The three objectives can be achieved by upgrading the production factors of labor and capital, and also by increasing total factor productivity (see figure 1.9 in chapter 1). Policy options and indicators are discussed in more detail in this chapter. The policy options should aim for the following:

- *Improving the skills and know-how of the workforce (skills upgrading).* Developing skills is a key element of competitiveness, and it affects the ability to participate in GVCs and achieve economic and social upgrading within GVCs. This can happen by increasing the skill content of a country's workforce.
- *Improving the absorptive capacity and technology of firms (capital upgrading).* Strengthening the absorptive capacity of local firms requires general and industry-specific investments to upgrade technical capacity and achieve quality standards and innovation capabilities.
- *Increasing productivity in existing GVC tasks (process upgrading).* Domestic firms performing GVC tasks can pursue process upgrading by better organizing their production or introducing new technologies to capture efficiency gains.[9] In other words, process upgrading refers to total factor productivity growth in existing activities in the value chain that cannot be directly attributed to the production factors of labor or capital.

Which Type of Densification?

Densification is about engaging more local actors (firms and workers) in the GVC network. Densification—in addition to economic upgrading—contributes to the overall goal to increase a country's value added that results from GVC participation.

The concept of economic upgrading is based on the premise that existing local GVC participants become more competitive, which enables them to advance into new products, tasks, and sectors with higher value added. Densification, by contrast, aims at facilitating the participation of more local firms and workers in already existing GVC-related products, tasks, and sectors in a country. Value addition in the latter case happens through scale effects, as densification creates higher profit income, wage income, and tax revenue. In some cases, this could mean that performing lower value-added activities on a large scale can generate large value addition for the country.

The key is to enable local firms and workers to participate in GVCs that are already present in the country by strengthening domestic firms' absorptive capacity and developing worker skills. Policy makers should assess which of those is the priority for a country.

Which Foreign Firm and Country Characteristics Influence Spillovers?

A major determinant of country policies to attract foreign direct investment (FDI) and non-equity modes of investment (NEMs) is the potential to deliver substantial spillovers of knowledge—and ultimately productivity—to local firms and workers. A vast set of empirical evidence has been amassed over the past decade on the presence and direction of FDI-generated horizontal and vertical productivity spillovers. Overall, the results are mixed and suggest that the theoretical postulated spillover effects do not automatically materialize with FDI, which indicates the need for still more research.[10]

Three groups of mediating factors determine potential spillovers to domestic firm productivity: (1) the spillover potential of the foreign firm, (2) the absorptive capacity of firms in the host economy, and (3) the national characteristics and institutions of the host country. GVC entry via FDI attraction is mainly determined by the first and third factors, which are discussed following the conceptual framework developed in Farole, Staritz, and Winkler (2014). The second group is discussed in the next section.

Given the increasing importance of GVCs and export platform FDI, understanding how spillover potential differs is likely to become an important policy priority, particularly for small and low-income countries that rely on that type of investment.

Which Foreign Firm Characteristics Influence Spillover Potential?[11]

The degree of foreign ownership affects local firms' potential to absorb FDI spillovers. A higher share of foreign ownership—thus, larger control over management and lower potential for knowledge leakages—correlates positively with the parent firm's incentive to transfer knowledge, such as in the form of technology.[12] A larger domestic ownership share, however, could also be beneficial for local firms, because the foreign investor's interests are less well protected, which makes technology leakages more likely. Larger domestic participation might further increase the likelihood of relying on domestic suppliers.[13] Empirical studies controlling for different structures of foreign ownership tend to support the more positive spillover effects of joint ventures.[14] Explanations include the possibility of more vertical links, as well as stronger technology leakages for partly owned foreign firms.[15]

Various motivations for FDI and NEMs are likely to mediate spillover potential. The conventional wisdom is that resource-seeking investment has less potential for spillovers because of its capital and technology intensity and limited time horizons. By contrast, manufacturing investment often is considered to have higher spillover potential because it is driven largely by efficiency-seeking motives. Indeed, manufacturing investment that is more labor-intensive, has greater requirements for a broad range of goods and services inputs, and has lower barriers to domestic links (relative to resource-seeking investment) is a strong candidate for contributing spillovers. Market-seeking investment, particularly in retail, is also considered to provide higher spillover potential, because retailers tend to source from local producers—in particular, food and other perishables. The evidence remains ambiguous, however, which suggests context specificity.

Analogously, a multinational firm's sourcing strategy may affect spillover potential. If an MNC sources on a global scale, it may follow a co-sourcing strategy, which increases its reliance on imported inputs from established suppliers abroad. An MNC might follow co-location strategies that require an established foreign input supplier to enter the host country. Both circumstances could make the entrance of new local suppliers more difficult, which is a particularly common situation for multinationals in the clothing, footwear, electronics, and automotive sectors.[16] Moreover, the share of intermediates sourced locally by multinationals is likely to increase with the distance between the host and the source economy. The share is also likely to be larger for multinationals originating in countries outside the country's preferential trade agreement, because such a trade agreement makes imports from the home country less attractive.[17]

Spillovers also depend on the technology intensity of the multinational's goods produced in the host country.[18] Products characterized by greater technology—or products that are more intensive in research and development (R&D)—generally contain a greater element of knowledge and a broader set of skills. However, the production of high-tech products might also involve low-tech processes, which could offset that effect.[19]

Related to technology intensity is the foreign investor's home country, which may have an effect on the production strategy and technologies in host countries, but also may have other effects on spillover potential. The home country more generally influences managerial practices and cultures on the use of expatriate workers, attitudes toward training local workers, and skills development. Further, end-market segmentation—closely linked to foreign investors' home countries through historical, cultural, and language ties, as well as trade policies—is common. All these patterns affect spillover potential.[20] The foreign investor's home country also positively influences domestic firms' absorptive capacity, because workers in domestic firms observe and imitate technologies, management practices, and cultural values.[21] And a foreign affiliate's distance to its parent firm affects its spillover potential, particularly for efficiency-seeking investment. Several studies find that foreign investors are more likely to purchase local inputs from domestic suppliers if the home country is further away.[22]

A multinational firm's entry mode may influence the pace or extent of investment-induced benefits for local firms. For example, a greenfield investment is more likely to be accompanied by technology, whereas with mergers and acquisitions (M&As), the multinational firm is more likely to adopt the host country's technology and only gradually improve it.[23] Whereas greenfield investments self-evidently increase investment, capacity, and employment, M&As and other types of brownfield investments may not do so, because the new foreign owners may rationalize and even reduce capacity and employment.

The pace and irregularity of foreign entry can also affect spillovers, by constraining multinationals from building stable relationships with local suppliers, which results in multinationals being less likely to rely on domestic inputs. Further, local firms might not have enough time to observe and imitate good practices and for local workers to acquire skills, which results in negative competition effects.[24]

Finally, the length of foreign presence may affect spillovers. Foreign firms with a longer presence in the country may have a more positive effect on productivity spillovers, largely resulting from longer supplier relationships, although that effect may taper off.[25]

Which Host Country Characteristics and Institutions Influence Spillovers?[26]

Host country and institutional factors can influence foreign and domestic firm characteristics, as well as the transmission channels for knowledge diffusion from multinationals to local firms. Although the focus here is on spillovers from FDI, many host country characteristics can also be expected to lead to spillovers from GVC participation through NEMs of investment.

Labor market regulations may influence the effect of foreign investment on domestic firms through various channels. Higher absolute and relative labor market flexibility than in the foreign investor's home country seems to have a positive effect on the chances of securing initial foreign investment.[27] Labor market regulations in general, and wage constraints in particular, can affect the skills in a firm, and hence their absorptive capacity.[28] Overly rigid labor markets can reduce the likelihood of labor turnover and FDI spillovers.[29] Conversely, overly flexible labor markets may generate frequent labor turnover, which reduces the time for domestic workers to acquire skills and knowledge from foreign firms.

The strength of intellectual property rights in a host country may help attract high-quality foreign investment initially and, therefore, create the potential for FDI spillovers. But some people argue that although strong intellectual property rights may help attract such investment and allow knowledge and technology to be transferred to the affiliate, they may also hinder the transmission of those advances to the local market.[30] Multinational firms use several instruments—in addition to ensuring strong property rights—to protect technology spillovers to local competitors in the same sector, such as paying higher wages to avoid labor turnover, ensuring trade secrecy, and locating in countries with few serious competitors.[31] Policies that mandate technology transfer to local firms may increase the transmission of knowledge and technology between the affiliate and the local market, but such policies may result in the foreign investor limiting the level and nature of knowledge transfers to the affiliate.

Financial markets in LMICs may also be a factor in the absorption of spillovers.[32] Multinationals can have an ambiguous impact on access to finance for local firms: multinationals may ease such access by bringing in scarce capital to LMICs; but if MNCs borrow locally, they may increase local firms' financing constraints.[33] That, in turn, can influence a local firm's absorptive capacity, and well-developed markets may facilitate a domestic firm's absorptive capacity links.[34]

A country's trade policy shapes the amount and type of foreign investment. Spillovers are larger in countries that are more open to trade. A country's trade policy regime is related to its capacity to attract foreign firms, because foreign investors are less constrained by the size and efficiency of the local market.[35] Moreover, foreign investors in an open trade setting are more integrated globally and thus tend to adopt the newest technologies. However, it can also be argued that foreign investors in an outward-oriented trade policy regime tend to focus more on international distribution and marketing and less on new technologies.[36]

Trade policy also affects domestic firms. In an open trade regime, domestic firms are more exposed to international competitive pressures, which will prepare them to absorb spillovers.[37] Moreover, a country's trade policy also affects the likelihood of domestic firms' becoming exporters and learning by exporting. Although the effect of exporting on domestic firms' absorptive capacities is ambiguous, exporting clearly moderates the direction and extent of FDI spillovers. FDI spillovers are larger in countries that are more open to trade.[38] For example, for China, horizontal and vertical spillover effects from FDI are negative when final goods and input tariffs are higher.[39]

Investment policy and promotion mediate spillovers by helping to attract foreign investment in general (the focus of most export promotion efforts) and by encouraging policies to promote spillovers (much less common). Investment promotion contributes to bringing in firms that should have higher spillover potential, given their quality and technology position.[40] For example, positive FDI spillovers in Chinese manufacturing are higher from foreign firms enjoying investment subsidies and exemptions from value-added taxes relative to spillovers from foreign firms that do not reap those benefits.[41]

Special economic zones (SEZs) may affect spillovers. Local Chinese manufacturing firms in SEZs have smaller productivity spillovers from FDI than do non-SEZ domestic firms.[42] That may occur because most SEZs focus on export processing combined with a high percentage of imported inputs, which limits the potential for FDI spillovers because demand for local suppliers is constrained. Moreover, the spatial and legal structures that govern SEZs often inhibit their integration with the local economy.

Industrial policies, particularly programs to support the development of local small and medium enterprises, can mediate FDI spillovers, especially where the technology and productivity gaps between foreign and local firms are large, or where few local firms exist. Collaboration with foreign firms and support to develop local supplier networks through supplier development programs run by foreign affiliates but supported by governments have done much to facilitate spillovers in, for example, the automotive and electronics sectors. Local content provisions that require a certain share of inputs to be sourced locally have also gained prominence, as in China, but the track record of those provisions is mixed, and they depend on domestic absorption capacity and supplier development.

Weak institutions—including corruption, red tape, and intellectual property rights—are linked to protection for local firms, network-driven business practices, and inefficient markets, which possibly constrains foreign investors from fully exploiting their competitive advantages. That drawback may influence the types of FDI and NEM that are initially attracted, as well as domestic firms' absorptive capacity. The empirical evidence is mixed. Firm-level data for 17 emerging countries during 2002–05 reveal no evidence that the extent of FDI spillovers is affected by the degree of corruption or red tape.[43] The evidence also shows that a country's transparency has a U-shaped effect on FDI spillovers: countries with a medium level of transparency benefit the least from FDI, whereas countries with low and high levels show stronger FDI spillovers.[44]

The local innovation and learning infrastructure influences the share of human capital in firms (most studies find that FDI spillovers increase with average education and innovation) and is particularly important for expanding GVC participation.[45]

Strengthening Absorptive Capacity: Which Domestic Firm Characteristics Help Internalize Spillovers?[46]

At the domestic firm level, R&D, human capital, firm size, firm location, export behavior, technology gap, type of ownership, and sector competition are mediating factors that allow countries to adopt complementary policies for leveraging the opportunities of GVC participation. These factors determine the local firm's absorptive capacity. Although the focus here is on spillovers from FDI, many firm characteristics can also be expected to lead to spillovers from GVC participation through international trade and NEMs, especially in modular or relational governance forms in which the degree of knowledge sharing is relatively high (see the section "Which Form of Governance between Lead Firms and Suppliers?" in chapter 8).

The technology gap between foreign and domestic firms has been identified as one the most important mediating factors for FDI spillovers.[47] A large gap can be beneficial for local firms because their catching-up potential increases,[48] but local firms might not be able to absorb positive FDI spillovers if the gap is too big or too small.[49] Some studies reconcile the two views and find a nonlinear relationship between a domestic firm's technology gap and FDI-induced productivity benefits.[50]

The supportive role of R&D in local firms is solid in high-income countries, such as Ireland, Spain,[51] Sweden, and the United States.[52] It is also strong in LMICs or emerging countries, including the Czech Republic, Hungary, India, Indonesia, and the Slovak Republic, and a large cross-section of 78 LMICs.[53]

A domestic firm's ability to absorb foreign technology can be positively related to its share of skilled labor,[54] but that benefit may apply only to smaller firms.[55] In that case, FDI does not affect large domestic firms with a high proportion of human capital, because those firms are probably the most similar to multinationals in technology and market share. No evidence exists for the positive effect of skilled workers.[56] In contrast, the competition effect might enable larger domestic firms to keep skilled workers more readily, compared with smaller firms, which may lead to negative spillovers for the latter. Smaller firms have fewer means to attract skilled workers by paying higher wages or offering additional benefits.[57]

Firm size has been positively related to a domestic firm's capacity to absorb FDI spillovers.[58] Larger firms may (1) be better positioned to compete with multinationals and imitate their tools;[59] (2) pay better wages and therefore find attracting workers employed by multinational firms easier; and (3) be more visible, perhaps organized in associations, and thus more likely to be selected as local suppliers by foreign firms.

Several aspects of domestic firm location are important in FDI productivity spillovers. Foreign firms co-locating (agglomeration) in the same sector and region, for example, can significantly increase the productivity and employment of local firms.[60] However, firm location in SEZs can have a negative impact on FDI spillovers if the zone focuses on export processing and has a high share of imported inputs. More regional development and a domestic firm's geographic proximity to multinational firms seem to have a positive effect.[61]

Exporting has been linked to a domestic firm's absorptive capacity for at least two reasons. First, local exporting firms generally are characterized by higher productivity—whether through learning by exporting or self-selecting into exporting—which makes them more competitive against negative rivalry effects created by multinationals.[62] Second, the more a local firm exports, the less the competitive pressures from multinational firms are felt (assuming that the multinational firm does not enter the same export market); hence, there is an incentive to improve, which lowers the extent of positive FDI spillovers. However, empirical studies show no clear evidence of whether exporting increases or lowers the productivity gains from FDI.[63]

Spillovers can also depend on the sectors in which domestic firms operate.[64] FDI-enhanced productivity spillovers in food processing, for example, seem to be driven by efficiency improvements, whereas technological progress seems to be the main driver in electrical machinery. FDI spillovers may be smaller for domestic firms in services sectors because of the lower absorptive capacity of firms in those sectors. A foreign presence in technology-intensive or high-tech industries tends to lead to larger positive spillovers compared with foreign presence in labor-intensive or low-tech industries.[65]

Type of ownership is another factor. Some studies have focused on the difference between private versus state-owned firms, which can be studied best in the context of China or the transition economies in Central and Eastern Europe. Private firms may be more likely to benefit from FDI spillovers because of their willingness to restructure and imitate (demonstration effect), and because of their larger export orientation, which enables those firms to access knowledge internationally.[66] By contrast, state-owned enterprises typically are larger, are technically competitive, and may have easier access to finance, which increases their absorptive capacity; but they tend to be less market oriented, which may lower their absorptive capacity.[67]

Finally, the level of competition influences the extent of FDI spillovers. Competitive pressures from multinational firms might be lower if the local firm already faces stiff competition at the sector level. As with exports, local firms in competitive sectors may have less incentive to improve, which results in lower benefits from FDI spillovers. Still, local firms may be better equipped to benefit from positive demonstration effects.[68]

Policy Options

Expanding GVC participation requires three sets of policies: (1) to strengthen existing links in GVCs, (2) to strengthen a country's absorptive capacity to benefit from intensified GVC integration, and (3) to create a world-class workforce (see figure O.1 in the Overview). Although some policies in the third set aim to strengthen a country's absorptive capacity—for example, by promoting skills development—a broad range of policies target other aspects of upgrading.

Strengthening GVC–Local Economy Links on the Buyer's and Seller's Sides[69]

Strong links with the domestic economy—through forward and backward links, technology spillovers, skills demand and upgrading, minimum-scale achievements (see figure 1.11 and the subsection "Which Transmission Channels?" in this chapter), and other forms of collaboration and interaction—should offer greater benefits of GVC participation at home. The development of links can focus on the breadth of links (variety of local inputs) and on their depth (degree of local value added), so making a distinction is key.[70] Policies that promote links between GVCs and the local economy primarily target foreign investors, but can also include other international buyers outside the country. The policies include the following:

- Ensure that the incentives used to attract foreign investors do not create a bias against local integration. The most important issue is to ensure that foreign-owned companies do not have privileged access to instruments such as import tax and duty concessions or duty drawbacks. Similarly, reserving EPZs for foreign-owned companies can create barriers to supply by domestic firms.
- Leverage investment and other incentives to promote actions that support spillovers. If generating spillovers is among the principal rationales for offering incentives to foreign investors or other international buyers, if those incentives are not predicated on spillover outcomes (which are difficult to measure), the incentives should be predicated at least on foreign investors or other international buyers engaging in activities to support spillovers.
- Ensure that local content regulations operate under the right conditions and are clearly defined. (For example, what is "local" and what is "content"?) The focus should be on value addition rather than in-country ownership. Regulations can be effective, but only when the domestic supply side is up to the task of being a competitive supplier. Otherwise such regulations are likely to weaken the competitiveness of investors, thereby undermining the overall outcomes. In any case, setting strict local content targets can be counterproductive and difficult to enforce. Instead of establishing rigid local content requirements, the aim should be the collaborative development of flexible localization plans, in which investors come up with their own proposals for delivering spillovers to the local economy. That approach allows for sufficient flexibility across sectors and firms.
- Have a clear and comprehensive framework to support the upgrading of domestic firms. This step is important to facilitate supplier development programs initiated by foreign investors or other international buyers. Traditional linkage programs merely scratch the surface; they are likely to be effective only in the context of a more comprehensive set of policies on links. A comprehensive framework should include bridging information gaps by facilitating exchanges of information on foreign investors' and other international buyers' needs and local supplier capabilities, as well as establishing skill requirements. The framework should also include addressing gaps in domestic contract enforcement and other barriers to formal contracting with local suppliers.
- Establish incentives for foreign investors and other international buyers to work with local universities, research institutes, and training institutes. Such incentives include research funds, matching grant programs, and fiscal incentives for R&D in the host country, as well as internships, outplacements, and joint training and curriculum development.

Although these policy options target international firms—particularly foreign investors—in GVCs, policies for developing links should emphasize (1) the absorptive capacity of domestic firms to benefit from GVC participation and (2) the development or improvement of worker skills. The next two subsections address these areas.

Strengthening Absorptive Capacity

Maximizing the Absorption Potential of Local Actors to Benefit from GVC Spillovers[71]

Attracting foreign investors and other international buyers and linking them to the domestic economy should create the conditions for local firms and workers to benefit from spillovers of knowledge and technology. The degree to which they ultimately benefit, however, depends on the absorptive capacity of the domestic actors. This is the area of spillover policy in which government has the most important role, particularly by building the absorptive capacity of firms and workers and by helping local firms and workers access opportunities. For example, the Czech Republic has policies to help create a competitive local supplier network, as described in box 9.1.

The policies should include the following:

- Support supply-side capacity building, taking into account the heterogeneity of domestic firms. The potential of domestic firms to supply foreign investors and other international buyers and to upgrade in higher value-added activities varies enormously across domestic firms. Supplying foreign investors and other international buyers should be an activity for the most productive, high-potential domestic firms. Government programs focused on upgrading technical capacity should focus primarily on those firms, setting out clear requirements for firm participation.

Box 9.1. The Czech Republic's Supplier Development Program

After the country's emergence from communism and entry into the European Union, CzechInvest (the investment promotion agency—CI) learned from surveying investors that multinationals considered the local supplier network a key determinant in their investment decisions, second only to labor availability. Yet multinational investors imported 90 to 95 percent of their components to meet production requirements.

CI's top management saw an opportunity: to address investors' demand for inputs and willingness to source locally by strengthening the capabilities of Czech suppliers. From CI's perspective, creating a robust, competitive Czech supplier base for key prominent sectors was a way to embed foreign direct investment (FDI) into the economy and channel its benefits, thereby helping to retain and attract investors while supporting domestic suppliers. CI launched the Pilot Supplier Development Program (also called the Twinning Program) in electronics, the country's fastest-growing and second largest FDI sector after automotives.

The program's orientation was demand driven and practical. Its overall objective was to equip suppliers with the information and skills to meet investor requirements and win more (and higher) value-added contracts. The program had three elements:

- Collecting and distributing information on the products and capabilities of potential Czech component suppliers to enable foreign manufacturers to shortlist and contact potential suppliers.
- Matchmaking by identifying the components and services foreign investors were considering subcontracting (Meet the Buyer), arranging seminars and exhibitions with Czech suppliers and foreign affiliates, and taking proposals to potential foreign investors.
- Upgrading selected Czech suppliers. CI managers selected suppliers according to predefined criteria in high-technology industries, and then produced an upgrading plan. In an electronics pilot, CI identified 45 companies as potential candidates, trained them, and after seven months reevaluated them; CI subsequently offered tailored assistance to the 20 most promising firms.

An evaluation of the pilot 18 months after it ended in July 2002 showed that 15 suppliers had landed new, renewable contracts, worth more than US$46 million for 2000–03. Based on those results, CI rolled out Twinning II, which extended the program to aeronautics, automotives, pharmaceuticals, and engineering.

Source: Potter 2001.

- Build the absorptive capacity of local firms. This requires general and industry-specific investments to upgrade technical capacity and, most important, achieve quality standards. Because licensing of technology from foreign investors and other international buyers is a significant source of spillovers, governments should provide incentives for it. The biggest gap in support, however, is likely to be outside the technical arena—in basic business and financial management. Flexible delivery and financing models are necessary to allow for sector-specific approaches and collaboration with foreign investors.
- Narrow the technical and managerial skills gap with foreign investors and other international buyers. This includes actively engaging universities and research institutes to embed spillovers.
- Adopt open policies to promote imports and skilled immigration. This step may be critical to promote localization in the long term. A policy of openness—not only for access to imported goods and services, but, more controversially, for access to (imported) skilled workers—is likely to pay off in the long run by improving the sophistication and competitiveness of local firms.

Fostering Innovation and Building Capacity[72]

GVCs ease capacity constraints because a country does not need to develop a fully integrated industry to participate in GVCs. Still, capacities and productivity (as much as cost) are important drivers for foreign investors and lead firms that search for global offshore locations. Given the significance of flows in the new trade paradigm (as opposed to stocks), a location's responsiveness, capacity to innovate, and adaptability to the lead firm's requests are also key factors.[73]

With the shift in demand to emerging markets, lead firms have to define strategies in which innovation "centers" are in fact decentralized. According to the concept of reverse innovation, lead firms need to innovate in LMICs—often in clusters—and eventually bring the results back home.[74] That requires the host country to develop innovation capabilities, based on education and skills, often involving public-private partnerships for R&D (box 9.2), increasing the supply of qualified researchers at local universities, and aligning higher education curricula and training with the local economy's needs.

Economic upgrading is often about "creating the knowledge behind the product," but a country might not be able to upgrade because of barriers in other stages of production, such as services. The diversification into services tasks and the promotion of services exports offer largely untapped potential for many LMICs, but also require them to be well prepared. For example, moving out of production and into R&D, engineering, or marketing services requires flexibility in trading those services, including the temporary movement of service providers. It may also require establishing and enforcing intellectual property rights.

Table 9.1 summarizes possible policy objectives to foster innovation and capacity building, as well as available performance indicators.

Box 9.2. Case Study: Renault-Dacia Regional Design and Development Activities in Romania

In 2007, Renault-Dacia moved part of its regional design and development activities to Renault Technologie Roumanie (RTR) in Romania, the largest Renault engineering center outside France, with some 2,500 engineers.

RTR mainly accommodates engineering functions, along with purchasing, design, and support. With three locations in Romania, RTR brings together all the activities needed in an automotive project.

The relocation of the design and development activities was driven by Dacia's entry-level car and the idea that designing cars in an emerging market would help the company respond better to new consumer markets in Eastern Europe and Asia. The center now oversees the development of all entry-level vehicles (about 35 percent of all Renault vehicles worldwide).

Source: Based on interviews with private sector stakeholders.

Complying with Process and Product Standards

Although respect for standards might vary depending on the maturity of the GVC's lead firm and the final market, it is a key element for the functioning of GVCs—so much so that "failure to comply with these standards can result in exclusion from the GVC."[75]

According to a recent business survey in the agri-food sector of 250 lead firms and suppliers in LMICs, about 60 percent of the firms named the ability to

Table 9.1. Fostering Innovation and Building Capacity: Policy Objectives and Performance Indicators

Policy objectives
Bolstering productivity, production, and innovation capacities, including human capital and other resources:
• Adopt innovation policies and incentives (for example, R&D, innovation centers) and adapt/diffuse technologies in trade-oriented sectors.
• Provide education and training to match domestic skills with international standards and demand in trade-oriented sectors; upgrade skills.
• Develop production capacities in trade-oriented sectors, both hard (storage, conditioning, cooling chains, and so forth) and soft (value chain management, for instance).
• Create clusters and other task-bundling efforts.
• Change production (methods and equipment) to more efficient and sustainable use of natural resources and energy.
Performance indicators
• Computer, communications, and other services; ICT goods and services imports/exports (WDI)
• Investment in telecoms with private participation (WDI)
• Firms offering formal training (WDI)
• Number of patent applications filed by residents and nonresidents, domestically and abroad (WDI, WIPO)
• Education statistics: secondary and tertiary education, specialties, male/female, and so forth (UNESCO, ILO, WDI)
• Global competitiveness index–business sophistication (WEF GCI 11.01–11.09)
• Innovation (WEF GCI 12.01–12.07)
• Extent of staff training (WEF GCI 5.08)
• Labor statistics—activity rates, unemployment, male/female, and so forth (ILO, WDI)
• Innovation indicators and surveys—public and private R&D expenditure, high and medium-high technology manufacturing, knowledge intensive services (OECD)
• Production capacities—sector output—and productivity statistics (national statistics, WIOD)

Sources: Cattaneo and others 2013, based on OECD 2012.

Note: GCI = Global Competitiveness Index; ICT = information and communications technology; ILO = International Labour Organization; OECD = Organisation for Economic Co-operation and Development; R&D = research and development; UNESCO = United Nations Educational, Scientific, and Cultural Organization; WDI = World Development Indicators; WEF = World Economic Forum; WIOD = World Input-Output Database; WIPO = World Intellectual Property Organization.

meet quality and safety standards as the main factor influencing sourcing and investment decisions in GVCs.[76] Similarly, 40 percent of the firms pointed to noncompliance with mandatory import requirements as a typical trade problem with LMIC suppliers. About 37 percent suggested that improving the standards infrastructure and certification capacity would be the most effective way to integrate new suppliers in LMICs into GVCs; almost 50 percent of the firms providing trade-related technical and capacity building focused on compliance with safety and quality standards.

Standards relate to processes (such as labor, social, and environmental standards, often in corporate social responsibility or code of conduct) and products (such as quality). The standards must be respected along the entire value chain, because every stage of production could affect the quality of the final product or service. In agrifoods, for example, such standards translate into traceability requirements aimed at protecting consumer health and increasing product information for consumers.

Standards in GVCs are public and private, with an increasing prevalence of "voluntary" standards imposed by lead firms (buyers or producers) on all input providers and assemblers along the chain.[77] Despite the role of private standards in GVCs, public standards, public infrastructure for certification and accreditation, and the enforcement by public authorities of health, safety, and environment rules are essential to attract GVC production segments. Inadequate public standards can raise the cost of local production or create unnecessary obstacles to trade—or both (figure 9.2).

Excessively low or badly enforced local standards minimize the backward links and positive spillovers of FDI and offshore production in a country: inputs will have to be imported to meet the lead firm's standards, and the local tasks will be confined to basic transformation and manufacturing. Analysis of the retail sector suggests three phases: a first phase in which no local products meet the retailer's standards and most products are imported; a second in which local producers adjust to the standards of the retailer (often with its help), and local products replace imported ones; and a third in which the best local products that meet international standards are exported and distributed by the retailer abroad.

Conversely, excessively high local standards are equally disturbing and could constitute unnecessary

Figure 9.2. Standards in Agrifood GVCs

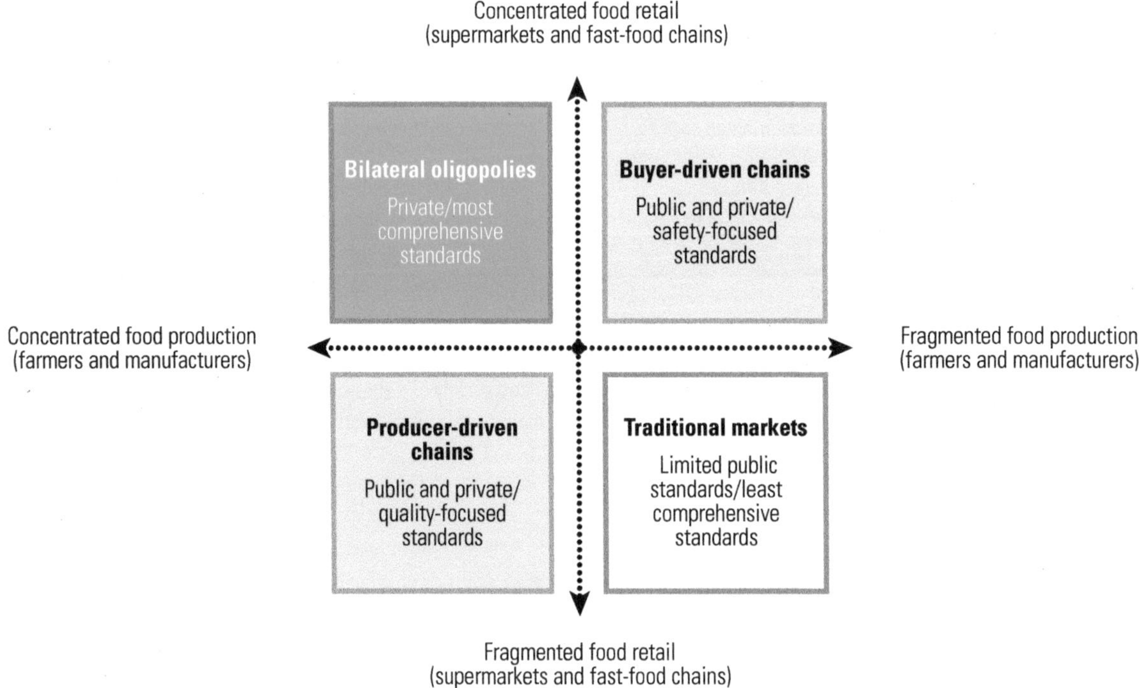

Source: Adapted from Lee, Gereffi, and Beauvais 2012.
Note: GVC = global value chain.

Figure 9.3. Diffusion of Standards and Other Codes of Conduct in GVCs

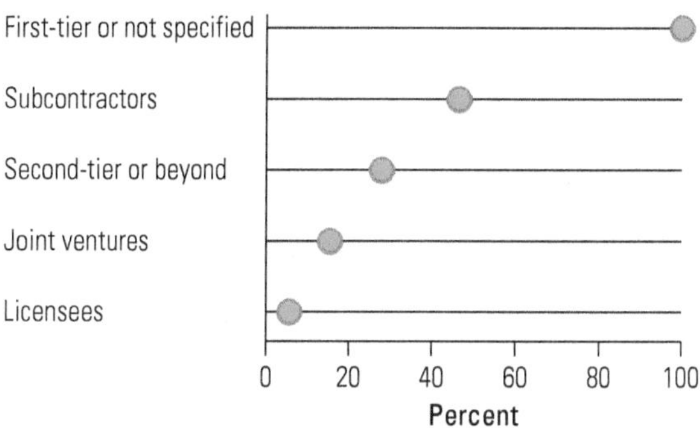

Source: Adapted from UNCTAD 2012.
Note: GVC = global value chain; UNCTAD = United Nations Conference on Trade and Development.

obstacles to trade or disguised protectionism. Several questions have been raised, for example, over eco-labeling and border adjustment taxes (so-called carbon taxes).[78]

Where local standards and certification and accreditation meet international standards and best practice, the costs of value chain management are sharply reduced, which increases a country's attractiveness to FDI. GVCs therefore make a strong case for regulatory convergence, harmonization, mutual recognition, and diffusion of international standards. Imposing respect for standards is very difficult and costly for lead firms on their own, although many do so (figure 9.3): some transparency mechanisms, such as mapping pollution at the micro level in China, help to enforce green supply chains by providing an independent monitoring mechanism to lead firms' subcontracting production in China, as well as to civil society (IPE.org.cn).

Considering the risks associated with the prevalence of private standards in GVCs—particularly for smallholders and producers in LMICs, as well as consumers—the case is strong for multi-stakeholder dialogue and cooperation in defining and enforcing standards (table 9.2).[79]

Bundling Tasks

The trend toward GVC consolidation suggests that a country cannot offer a single task but must offer a bundle of tasks. Economic upgrading trajectories often reflect performing new tasks that build on existing ones (figure 9.4), which this book defines as functional upgrading. Economic upgrading does not always mean to perform or integrate downstream activities, but offers a wider range of

Table 9.2. Improving Standards: Policy Objectives and Performance Indicators

Policy objectives
Technical and sanitary and phytosanitary standards: • Build capacity for certification and accreditation (labs, personnel, resources, and so forth). • Adopt or reform domestic norms and standards to comply with international best practices. • Promote standards—including voluntary standards—and related training. • Ensure private sector support to comply with standards.
Performance indicators
• Diffusion of voluntary standards and ISO certification ownership (WDI, national statistics) • Adoption of international standards • International accreditation of domestic accreditation/certification agencies

Sources: Cattaneo and others 2013, based on OECD 2012.
Note: More specific policy objectives and measures of labor and social standards are presented in table 10.1 in chapter 10. ISO = International Organization for Standardization; WDI = World Development Indicators.

possibilities (see the subsection "Which Type of Economic Upgrading?" in this chapter). Task bundling is necessary for consolidating GVCs, in which lead firms reduce the number of intermediates and expect their suppliers to provide a more comprehensive package with larger services content. Task bundling might also be necessary for potential offshore locations to attract the production of some tasks that cannot be performed independently.[80] For example, some tasks that can be easily offshored may be bundled with tasks that cannot, making it possible to offshore the first set of tasks only to countries that can also perform the second set.

Figure 9.4. Tasks Performed by Apparel Industries in Torreon, Mexico

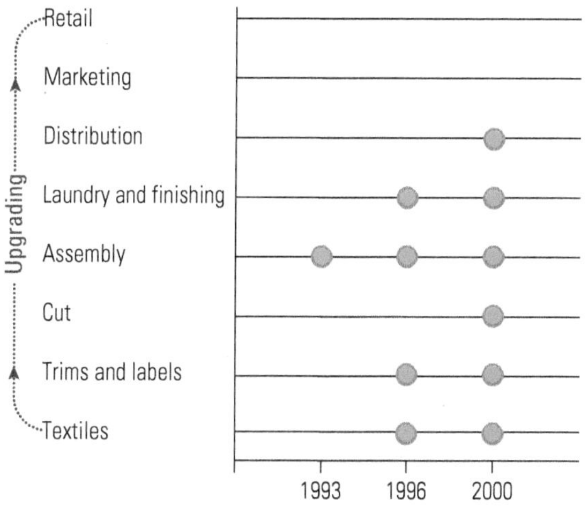

Source: Adapted from Bair and Gereffi 2001.

Creating a World-Class Workforce[81]

Skill development is a key element of competitiveness, participation in GVCs, and economic and social upgrading within GVCs. A positive and statistically significant correlation exists between human capital and services exports, for instance.[82] Economic upgrading requires new skills and knowledge, either by increasing the skill content of a country's activities (and thus workforce) or by developing competencies in niche market segments.[83] In other words, economic upgrading and social upgrading are mutually dependent.

Skill shortages can impede a country's upgrading. In Chile, Costa Rica, Ethiopia, and Rwanda, upgrading strategies in GVCs have been most successful when accompanied by complementary workforce development interventions.[84] In Rwanda, economic upgrading into the high-quality specialty coffee segment required skill development for managing workers, plantations, financial risks, and other areas. For workforce development to be successful, it must be part of a coherent overall upgrading strategy that involves key stakeholders. In addition, workforce development must be customized to the specific job requirements.[85]

GVCs contribute to skill development through lead-firm transfers. Lead firms indeed have strong incentives to train their workforce to comply with their standards. Beyond private initiatives, a strong case exists for public investment in skill development to meet the needs of international trade and participation in GVCs. Table 9.1 lists performance indicators related to skill development.

A look at the link between economic upgrading and skill development in four GVCs (apparel, tourism, offshore services, and fruits and vegetables) in some 20 LMICs reached the following conclusions.[86]

On workforce skills:

- Appropriate worker skills are essential to economic upgrading.
- The focus of skill development must reflect local needs and those of the global economy.
- A new and evolving set of workforce skills is needed to participate in GVCs.
- Required skills and workforce development needs vary substantially by stage within industry-specific upgrading trajectories.
- Workers need soft skills (in addition to hard skills, which are more easily quantifiable and directly linked to the job) in today's world of work.
- In LMICs, managerial skills for GVCs are in short supply.
- Upgrading in GVCs requires more and better professionals and technicians in bottleneck positions.

On stakeholders and institutions:

- Local education systems currently do not provide the range of skills required by GVCs.
- Technical training institutions and universities should coordinate more closely with industry stakeholders.
- New actors—such as individual firms, industry associations, nongovernmental organizations, and special government programs—can provide many of the skills required by GVCs.
- Private sector intermediaries can facilitate upgrading and skills development.
- Public-private partnerships have emerged as an efficient and effective method for skill development.

On global standards:

- Global standards define the upgrading requirements for the local workforce.
- Multi-stakeholder partnerships in LMICs coalesce in response to global standards.
- National certification of skills can be a powerful tool for GVC labor markets in LMICs.

The successful upgrading in GVCs through developing a more skilled workforce is illustrated by the apparel industry in Turkey (box 9.3).

Box 9.3. Own Design and Branding in Turkey

Turkish firms moved into the design segment of the value chain as part of a broader strategy to establish the country as a fashion center. Industry associations and government agencies collaborated to promote Istanbul, targeting it to become a top-five global fashion center by 2023.

Tight relationships of local manufacturers with large global retailers, such as the United Kingdom–based Marks & Spencer, facilitated upgrading into design services. In 2007, Denizli was designing 10 percent of Marks & Spencer's garments made in Turkey. Upgrading into own-design manufacturing required a specialized workforce, which was built with government support. Organizations such as the Istanbul Textile and Apparel Exporter Association (IKTIB) worked with the private sector and government agencies to establish fashion design vocational training schools. Istanbul Fashion Academy, established by the European Union and IKTIB, trains students.

The Turkish government supported upgrading into own branding, the next stage after own design, by granting incentives for firms willing to upgrade into branding. The incentives included reimbursements up to 60 percent of the cost for a maximum of three years of personnel expenses, machinery, equipment, software, consultancy, and research and development material. Leading local firms with their own brands and retail outlets abroad include Sarar, Mithat, and Bilsar. Erak clothing, which was originally a full-package supplier with international brands such as Guess, Esprit, and Calvin Klein, is now selling its own brand, Mavi Jeans, in 4,600 specialty stores in 28 countries. Developing own branding has required additional efforts to foster workforce development, from bodies such as IKTIB and KOSGEB *(Small and Medium Enterprises Development Organization)*, a quasi-governmental organization affiliated with the Ministry of Industry and Trade.

Source: Fernandez-Stark, Frederick, and Gereffi 2011.

Notes

1. The discussion on mechanisms triggered by GVC participation partially evolves from the taxonomy introduced by Farole, Staritz, and Winkler (2014).
2. In the short run, average productivity may decrease and local firms may lose market shares as a result of intensified competition.
3. WEF (2013).
4. Humphrey (2004); Humphrey and Schmitz (2002).
5. Humphrey (2004); Humphrey and Schmitz (2002).
6. Humphrey (2004); Humphrey and Schmitz (2002).
7. Humphrey and Schmitz (2002).
8. Milberg and Winkler (2011, 349).
9. Humphrey (2004); Humphrey and Schmitz (2002).
10. Havranek and Irsova (2011).
11. This section draws on Farole, Staritz, and Winkler (2014).
12. Takii (2005).
13. Crespo and Fontoura (2007).
14. Abraham, Konings, and Slootmaekers (2010).
15. Javorcik and Spatareanu (2008).
16. Paus and Gallagher (2008).
17. Javorcik and Spatareanu (2011).
18. Lin, Liu, and Zhang (2009).
19. Paus and Gallagher (2008).
20. Staritz and Morris (2013).
21. Zhang and others (2010).
22. See, for instance, Javorcik and Spatareanu (2011).
23. Crespo and Fontoura (2007).
24. Wang and others (2012).
25. Gorodnichenko, Svejnar, and Terrell (2007).
26. This section draws on Farole, Staritz, and Winkler (2014).
27. Javorcik and Spatareanu (2005).
28. Hale and Long (2011).
29. Gorodnichenko, Svejnar, and Terrell (2007); Javorcik (2004a).
30. Havranek and Irsova (2011).
31. Javorcik (2004b).
32. Alfaro and others (2010).
33. Harrison, Love, and McMillan (2004).
34. Aggarwal, Milner, and Riaño (2011).
35. Crespo and Fontoura (2007).
36. Meyer and Sinani (2009).
37. Havranek and Irsova (2011).
38. Havranek and Irsova (2011).
39. Du, Harrison, and Jefferson (2011).
40. Harding and Javorcik (2012).
41. Du, Harrison, and Jefferson (2011).
42. Abraham, Konings, and Slootmaekers (2010).
43. Gorodnichenko, Svejnar, and Terrell (2007).
44. Meyer and Sinani (2009).
45. Farole and Winkler (2014a).
46. This section draws on Farole, Staritz, and Winkler (2014).
47. Kokko, Tansini, and Zejan (1996); Grünfeld (2006). The technology gap usually is measured as a domestic firm's productivity level relative to a benchmark productivity level within the same sector, often of the lead firm's or foreign firms.
48. Smeets (2008); Jordaan (2011).
49. Winkler (2014); Blalock and Gertler (2009).
50. Girma and Görg (2007).
51. Barrios and others (2004).
52. Barrios and others (2004); Karpaty and Lundberg (2004); Keller and Yeaple (2009).
53. Kinoshita (2001); Kanthuria (2000, 2001, 2002); Damijan and others (2003); Blalock and Gertler (2009); Farole and Winkler (2014a).

54. Blalock and Gertler (2009).
55. Girma and Wakelin (2007).
56. Farole and Winkler (2014a).
57. Sinani and Meyer (2004); Winkler (2014).
58. See Jordaan (2011) for Mexico and Farole and Winkler (2014) for the 78 LMICs.
59. Crespo and Fontoura (2007).
60. Barrios, Bertinelli, and Strobl (2006); Farole and Winkler (2014a).
61. Girma and Wakelin (2007); Winkler (2014).
62. Crespo and Fontoura (2007).
63. Blomström and Sjöholm (1999) for Indonesia, Ponomareva (2000) for Russia, Sinani and Meyer (2004) for Estonia, and Abraham, Konings, and Slootmaekers (2010) and Du, Harrison, and Jefferson (2011) for China confirm that the potential for positive productivity spillovers is less pronounced for exporters compared with nonexporters or firms exporting little. By contrast, Jordaan (2011) for Mexico, Barrios and Strobl (2002) for Spain, Schoors and van der Tol (2002) for Hungary, Lin, Liu, and Zhang (2009) for China, and Farole and Winkler (2014a) for a large sample of LMICs find positive spillovers from exporting or operating in more open sectors.
64. Temenggung (2007); Suyanto and Salim (2010).
65. Buckley, Wang, and Clegg (2007); Keller and Yeaple (2009).
66. Sinani and Meyer (2004).
67. Du, Harrison, and Jefferson (2011).
68. Barrios and Strobl (2002); Farole and Winkler (2014).
69. This section draws on Farole and Winkler (2014b).
70. Morris, Kaplinsky, and Kaplan (2011).
71. This section draws on Farole and Winkler (2014b).
72. The following three sections draw on Cattaneo and others (2013).
73. World Bank (2010).
74. Govindarajan and Trimble (2012).
75. Kaplinsky, Terheggen, and Tijaja (2010); Gereffi, Fernandez-Stark, and Psilos (2011, 243).
76. OECD-WTO (2013).
77. Lee, Gereffi, and Beauvais (2012).
78. Brenton, Edwards-Jones, and Jensen (2009).
79. Lee, Gereffi, and Beauvais (2012); Cadot, Malouche, and Saez (2012).
80. Gereffi and Frederick (2010); Lanz, Miroudot, and Nordås (2013).
81. This section largely draws on Cattaneo and others (2013).
82. Saez and Goswami (2010).
83. Humphrey and Schmitz (2002).
84. World Bank (2014a).
85. World Bank (2014b).
86. Gereffi, Fernandez-Stark, and Psilos (2011).

References

Abraham, Filip, Jozef Konings, and Veerle Slootmaekers. 2010. "FDI Spillovers in the Chinese Manufacturing Sector Evidence of Firm Heterogeneity." *Economies of Transition* 18: 143–82.

Aggarwal, Natasha, Chris Milner, and Alejandro Riaño. 2011. "Credit Constraints and FDI Spillovers in China." China and the World Economy Research Paper Series No. 2011/21, University of Nottingham, United Kingdom.

Alfaro, Laura, Areendam Chanda, Sebnem Kalemli-Ozcan, and Selin Sayek. 2010. "Does Foreign Direct Investment Promote Growth? Exploring the Role of Financial Markets on Linkages." *Journal of Development Economics* 91 (2): 242–56.

Bair, Jennifer, and Gary Gereffi. 2001. "Local Clusters in Global Value Chains: The Causes and Consequences of Export Dynamism in Torreon's Blue Jeans Industry." *World Development* 29 (11): 1885–903.

Barrios, Salvador, Luisito Bertinelli, and Eric Strobl. 2006. "Coagglomeration and Spillovers." *Regional Science and Urban Economics* 36 (4): 467–81.

Barrios, Salvador, Sophia Dimelis, Helen Louri, and Eric Strobl. 2004. "Efficiency Spillovers from Foreign Direct Investment in the EU Periphery: A Comparative Study of Greece, Ireland, and Spain." *Review of World Economics* (Weltwirtschaftliches Archiv) 140 (4): 688–705.

Barrios, S., and E. Strobl. 2002. "Foreign Direct Investment and Productivity Spillovers: Evidence from the Spanish Experience." *Review of World Economics* 138 (3): 459–81.

Blalock, G., and P. Gertler. 2009. "How Firm Capabilities Affect Who Benefits from Foreign Technology." *Journal of Development Economics* 90 (2): 192–99.

Blomström, M., and F. Sjöholm. 1999. "Technology Transfer and Spillovers: Does Local Participation with Multinationals Matter?" *European Economic Review* 43 (4–6): 915–23.

Brenton, Paul, Gareth Edwards-Jones, and Michael Friis Jensen. 2009. "Carbon Labeling and Low-income Country Exports: A Review of the Development Issues." *Development Policy Review* 27 (3): 243–67.

Buckley, Peter J., Chengqi Wang, and Jeremy Clegg. 2007. "The Impact of Foreign Ownership, Local Ownership and Industry Characteristics on Spillover Benefits from Foreign Direct Investment in China." *International Business Review* 16 (2): 142–58.

Cadot, Olivier, Mariem Malouche, and Sebastian Saez. 2012. *Streamlining Non-Tariff Measures: A Toolkit for Policy Makers.* Washington, DC: World Bank.

Cattaneo, Olivier, Gary Gereffi, Sébastien Miroudot, and Daria Taglioni. 2013. "Joining, Upgrading and Being Competitive in Global Value Chains: A Strategic Framework." Policy Research Working Paper 6406, World Bank, Washington, DC.

Crespo, N., and M. P. Fontoura. 2007. "Determinant Factors of FDI Spillovers—What Do We Really Know?" *World Development* 35 (3): 410–25.

Damijan, J., M. Knell, B. Majcen, and M. Rojec. 2003. "Technology Transfer through FDI in Top-10 Transition Countries: How Important Are Direct Effects, Horizontal and Vertical Spillovers?" Working Paper 549, William Davidson Institute, University of Michigan, Ann Arbor, MI.

Du, L., A. Harrison, and G. Jefferson. 2011. "Do Institutions Matter For FDI Spillovers? The Implications of China's 'Special Characteristics.'" NBER Working Paper 16767, National Bureau of Economic Research, Cambridge, MA.

Farole, Thomas, C. Staritz, and D. Winkler. 2014. "Conceptual Framework." In *Making Foreign Direct Investment Work for Sub-Saharan Africa: Local Spillovers and Competitiveness in Global Value Chains*, edited by T. Farole and D. Winkler, 23–55. Washington, DC: World Bank.

Farole, T., and D. Winkler. 2014a. "The Role of Mediating Factors for FDI Spillovers in Developing Countries: Evidence from a Global Dataset." In *Making Foreign Direct Investment Work for Sub-Saharan Africa: Local Spillovers and Competitiveness in Global Value Chains*, edited by Thomas Farole and Deborah Winkler, 59–86. Washington, DC: World Bank.

———. 2014b. "Policy Implications." In *Making Foreign Direct Investment Work for Sub-Saharan Africa: Local Spillovers and Competitiveness in Global Value Chains*, edited by Thomas Farole and Deborah Winkler, 263–79. Washington, DC: World Bank.

Fernandez-Stark, Karina, Stacey Frederick, and Gary Gereffi. 2011. *The Apparel Global Value Chain: Economic Upgrading and Workforce Development*. Durham, NC: Duke University. http://www.cggc.duke.edu/pdfs/2011-11-11_CGGC_Apparel-Global-Value-Chain.pdf.

Gereffi, Gary, Karina Fernandez-Stark, and Phil Psilos. 2011. "Skills for Upgrading: Workforce Development and Global Value Chains in Developing Countries." Center on Globalization, Governance & Competitiveness, Duke University; and RTI International. http://www.cggc.duke.edu/pdfs/Skills-for-Upgrading-Workforce-Development-and-GVC-in-Developing-Countries_FullBook.pdf.

Gereffi, Gary, and Stacey Frederick. 2010. "The Global Apparel Value Chain, Trade, and the Crisis: Challenges and Opportunities for Developing Countries." In *Global Value Chains in a Postcrisis World: A Development Perspective*, edited by Olivier Cattaneo, Gary Gereffi, and Cornelia Staritz, 157–208. Washington, DC: World Bank.

Girma, Sourafel, and Holger Görg. 2007. "The Role of the Efficiency Gap for Spillovers from FDI: Evidence from the UK Electronics and Engineering Sectors." *Open Economies Review* 18 (2): 215–32.

Girma, Sourafel, and Katharine Wakelin. 2007. "Local Productivity Spillovers from Foreign Direct Investment in the U.K. Electronics Industry." *Regional Science and Urban Economics* 37 (3): 399–412.

Gorodnichenko, Yuriy, Jan Svejnar, and Katherine Terrell. 2007. "When Does FDI Have Positive Spillovers? Evidence from 17 Emerging Market Economies." Discussion Paper 3079, Institute for the Study of Labor, Bonn, Germany.

Govindarajan, Vijay, and Chris Trimble. 2012. *Reverse Innovation: Create Far from Home, Win Everywhere*. Cambridge, MA: Harvard Business Review Press.

Grünfeld, Leo A. 2006. "Multinational Production, Absorptive Capacity, and Endogenous R&D Spillovers." *Review of International Economics* 14 (5): 922–40.

Hale, G., and C. Long. 2011. "Did Foreign Direct Investment Put an Upward Pressure on Wages in China?" *IMF Economic Review* 59: 404–30.

Harding, Torfinn, and Beata S. Javorcik. 2012. "Foreign Direct Investment and Export Upgrading." *Review of Economics and Statistics* 94 (4): 964–80.

Harrison, Ann E., Inessa Love, and Margaret S. McMillan. 2004. "Global Capital Flows and Financing Constraints." *Journal of Development Economics* 75 (1): 269–301.

Havranek, Tomas, and Zuzana Irsova. 2011. "Estimating Vertical Spillovers from FDI: Why Results Vary and What the True Effect Is." *Journal of International Economics* 85 (2): 234–44.

Humphrey, John. 2004. "Upgrading in Global Value Chains." Working Paper 28, Policy Integration Department, World Commission on the Social Dimension of Globalization, International Labour Organization, Geneva.

Humphrey, J., and H. Schmitz. 2002. "How Does Insertion in Global Value Chains Affect Upgrading in Industrial Clusters?" *Regional Studies* 36 (9): 1017–27.

Javorcik, Beata Smarzynska. 2004a. "The Composition of Foreign Direct Investment and Protection of Intellectual Property Rights: Evidence from Transition Economies." *European Economic Review* 48 (1): 39–62.

———. 2004b. "Does Foreign Direct Investment Increase the Productivity of Domestic Firms? In Search of Spillovers through Backward Linkages." *American Economic Review* 94 (3): 605–27.

Javorcik, Beata Smarzynska, and Mariana Spatareanu. 2005. "Do Foreign Investors Care about Labor Market Regulations?" *Review of World Economics* 141 (3): 375–403.

———. 2008. "To Share or Not to Share: Does Local Participation Matter for Spillovers from Foreign Direct Investment?" *Journal of Development Economics* 85: 194–217.

———. 2011. "Does It Matter Where You Come From? Vertical Spillovers from Foreign Direct Investment and the Origin of Investors." *Journal of Development Economics* 96 (1): 126–38.

Jordaan, Jacob A. 2011. "Local Sourcing and Technology Spillovers to Mexican Suppliers: How Important are FDI and Supplier Characteristics?" *Growth and Change* 42 (3): 287–319.

Kanthuria, Vinish. 2000. "Productivity Spillovers from Technology Transfer to Indian Manufacturing Firms." *Journal of International Development* 12 (3): 343–69.

———. 2001. "Foreign Firms, Technology Transfer and Knowledge Spillovers to Indian Manufacturing Firms: A Stochastic Frontier Analysis." *Applied Economics* 33 (5): 625–42.

———. 2002. "Liberalisation, FDI, and Productivity Spillovers—An Analysis of Indian Manufacturing Firms." *Oxford Economic Papers* 54 (4): 688–718.

Kaplinsky, Raphael, Anne Terheggen, and Julia Tijaja. 2010. "What Happens When the Market Shifts to

China? The Gabon Timber and Thai Cassava Value Chains." In *Global Value Chains in a Postcrisis World: A Development Perspective*, edited by Olivier Cattaneo, Gary Gereffi, and Cornelia Staritz, 303–34. Washington, DC: World Bank.

Karpaty, Patrik, and Lars Lundberg. 2004. "Foreign Direct Investment and Productivity Spillovers in Swedish Manufacturing." Working Paper 194, Trade Union Institute for Economic Research, Stockholm.

Keller, Wolfgang, and Stephen R. Yeaple. 2009. "Multinational Enterprises, International Trade, and Productivity Growth: Firm-Level Evidence from the United States." *Review of Economics and Statistics* 91 (4): 821–31.

Kinoshita, Y. 2001. "R&D and Technology Spillovers through FDI: Innovation and Absorptive Capacity." CEPR Discussion Paper 2775, Centre for Economic Policy Research, London.

Kokko, Ari, Rúben Tansini, and Mario Carlos Zejan. 1996. "Local Technological Capability and Productivity Spillovers from FDI in the Uruguayan Manufacturing Sector." *Journal of Development Studies* 32 (4): 602–11.

Lall, Sanjaya. 2000. "The Technological Structure and Performance of Developing Country Manufactured Exports, 1985–1998." Working Paper 44, Queen Elizabeth House, University of Oxford, United Kingdom.

Lanz, Rainer, Sebastien Miroudot, and Hildegunn Nordås. 2013. "Offshoring of Tasks: Taylorism versus Toyotism." *World Economy* 36 (2): 194–212.

Lee, Joonkoo, Gary Gereffi, and Janet Beauvais. 2012. "Global Value Chains and Agrifood Standards: Challenges and Possibilities for Smallholders in Developing Countries." *Proceedings of the National Academy of Sciences of the United States of America* 109 (31): 12326–31.

Lin, Ping, Zhuomin Liu, and Yifan Zhang. 2009. "Do Chinese Domestic Firms Benefit from FDI Inflow? Evidence of Horizontal and Vertical Spillovers." *China Economic Review* 20 (4): 677–91.

Meyer, Klaus E., and Evis Sinani. 2009. "When and Where Does Foreign Direct Investment Generate Positive Spillovers? A Meta-Analysis." *Journal of International Business Studies* 40 (7): 1075–94.

Milberg, William, and Deborah Winkler. 2011. "Economic and Social Upgrading in Global Production Networks: Problems of Theory and Measurement." *International Labour Review* 150 (3–4): 341–65.

Morris, M., R. Kaplinsky, and D. Kaplan. 2011. "Commodities and Linkages: Meeting the Policy Challenge." Discussion Paper 14, Making the Most of Commodities Programme, The Open University, United Kingdom.

OECD (Organisation for Economic Co-operation and Development). 2012. *Managing Aid to Achieve Trade and Development Results: An Analysis of Trade-Related Targets*. COM/DCD/TAD(2012)12/FINAL. Paris: OECD.

OECD-WTO (Organisation for Economic Co-operation and Development and World Trade Organization). 2013. "Aid for Trade at a Glance 2013: Linking to Value Chains." OECD, Paris.

Paus, E. A., and K. P. Gallagher. 2008. "Missing Links: Foreign Investment and Industrial Development in Costa Rica and Mexico." *Studies of Comparative International Development* 43 (1): 53–80.

Ponomareva, N. 2000. "Are There Positive or Negative Spillovers from Foreign-Owned to Commodities and Linkages: Meeting the Policy Challenge." Discussion Paper 14, Making the Most of Commodities Programme, The Open University, United Kingdom Domestic Firms." Working Paper BSP/00/042, New Economics School, Moscow.

Potter, Jonathan. 2001. *Embedding Foreign Direct Investment*. Paris: Organisation for Economic Co-operation and Development. http://www.icpr3.org/en/foreign-direct-investment/czech-republic/.

Saez, Sebastian, and Arti Grover Goswami. 2010. "Uncovering Developing Countries' Performance in Trade." *Economic Premise* 39, World Bank, Washington, DC.

Schoors, K., and B. van der Tol. 2002. "Foreign Direct Investment Spillovers within and between Sectors: Evidence from Hungarian Data." Working Paper 2002/157, University of Gent, Gent, Belgium.

Sinani, Evis, and Klaus E. Meyer. 2004. "Spillovers of Technology Transfer from FDI: The Case of Estonia." *Journal of Comparative Economics* 32 (3): 445–66.

Smeets, Roger. 2008. "Collecting the Pieces of the FDI Knowledge Spillovers Puzzle." *The World Bank Research Observer* 23 (2): 107–38.

Staritz, Cornelia, and Mike Morris. 2013. "Local Embeddedness and Economic and Social Upgrading in Madagascar's Export Apparel Industry." ÖFSE Working Paper 38, Austrian Foundation for Development Research, Vienna.

Sturgeon, Timothy, and E. Zylberberg. 2012. "Global Value Chains, Special Economic Zones and Domestic Links: The Extension of Automotive Global Value Chains into Nicaragua and Macedonia." Presentation to the World Bank's International Trade Department, Poverty Reduction and Economic Management (PREM) Network. World Bank, Washington, DC.

Suyanto, Suyanto, and Ruhul A. Salim. 2010. "Sources of Productivity Gains from FDI in Indonesia: Is It Efficiency Improvement or Technological Progress?" *Developing Economies* 48 (4): 450–72.

Takii, Sadayuki. 2005. "Productivity Spillovers and Characteristics of Foreign Multinational Plants in Indonesian Manufacturing 1990–1995." *Journal of Development Economics* 76: 521–42.

Temenggung, Della. 2007. "Productivity Spillovers from Foreign Direct Investment: Indonesian Manufacturing Industry's Experience 1975–2000." Dynamics, Economic Growth, and International Trade Conference Paper c012_048, Kiel Institute for the World Economy, Kiel, Germany.

UNCTAD (United Nations Conference on Trade and Development). 2012. *Corporate Social Responsibility in Global Value Chains: Evaluation and Monitoring*

Challenges for Small and Medium Sized Suppliers in Developing Countries. Geneva: UNCTAD.

Wang, Chengqi, Ziliang Deng, Mario I. Kafouros, and Yan Chen. 2012. "Reconceptualizing the Spillover Effects of Foreign Direct Investment: A Process-Dependent Approach." *International Business Review* 21 (3): 452–64.

WEF (World Economic Forum). 2013. "Enabling Trade: Valuing Growth Opportunities" WEF, Geneva.

Winkler, D. 2014. "Determining the Nature and Extent of Spillovers: Empirical Assessment." In *Making Foreign Direct Investment Work for Sub-Saharan Africa: Local Spillovers and Competitiveness in Global Value Chains*, edited by Thomas Farole and Deborah Winkler, 87–114. Washington, DC: World Bank.

World Bank. 2010. *Innovation Policy: A Guide for Developing Countries.* Washington, DC: World Bank.

———. 2014a. *Republic of Burundi: Skills Development for Growth—Building Skills for Coffee and Other Priority Sectors.* Washington, DC: World Bank.

———. 2014b. "Turkey: Trading up to High Income: Country Economic Memorandum." Report 82307, World Bank, Washington, DC.

Zhang, Yan, Haiyang Li, Yu Li, and Li-An Zhou. 2010. "FDI Spillovers in an Emerging Market: The Role of Foreign Firms' Country Origin Diversity and Domestic Firms' Absorptive Capacity." *Strategic Management Journal* 31 (9): 969–89.

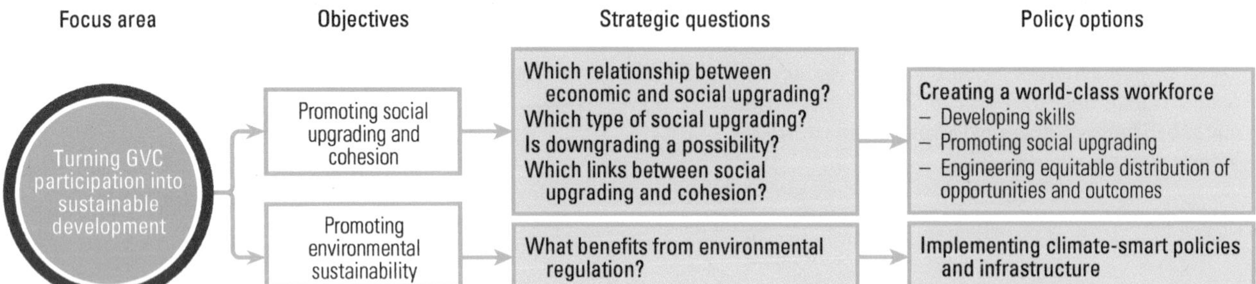
Focus area
Objectives
Strategic questions
Policy options
Turning GVC participation into sustainable development
Promoting social upgrading and cohesion
Promoting environmental sustainability
Which relationship between economic and social upgrading?
Which type of social upgrading?
Is downgrading a possibility?
Which links between social upgrading and cohesion?
What benefits from environmental regulation?
Creating a world-class workforce
– Developing skills
– Promoting social upgrading
– Engineering equitable distribution of opportunities and outcomes
Implementing climate-smart policies and infrastructure

Chapter 10

TURNING GVC PARTICIPATION INTO SUSTAINABLE DEVELOPMENT

Introduction

This chapter tackles the challenge of how to turn global value chain (GVC) participation into sustainable development. Three areas of sustainable development are important: macroeconomic sustainability, social sustainability, and environmental sustainability. Not only are they important development objectives per se, they also ensure the sustainability of a GVC-centric approach to development. This chapter focuses on social and environmental sustainability and leaves the discussion on the macroeconomic implications of GVCs for further work.

Labor market–enhancing outcomes for workers at home and more equitable distribution of opportunities and outcomes create social support for a reform agenda aimed at strengthening a country's GVC participation. Climate-smart policy prescriptions and infrastructure can mitigate the challenges for firms from climatic disruptions, as the firms seek to ensure the long-term predictability, reliability, and time-sensitive delivery of goods necessary to participate in GVCs. Because climatic disruption can impair firms' ability to access inputs and deliver final products, countries' preparedness is an increasingly critical factor in firms' location decisions.

Promoting Social Upgrading and Cohesion: Strategic Questions

The issues of social upgrading are not new and have been discussed in the literature under the role of multinational corporations in development. However, linking economic and social upgrading shows that economic upgrading may lead to social downgrading. That is, economic upgrading may lead to lower-value economic activities and weaken workers' employment, wages, rights, and protection, strongly suggesting a role for policy to counter this possibility.

Which Relationship between Economic and Social Upgrading?

An often implicit assumption is that economic upgrading in GVCs will automatically translate into social upgrading through greater employment opportunities and higher wages. However, the link between those elements is unclear from a theoretical standpoint. If productivity growth is a proxy for economic upgrading and wage growth is a reasonable representation of social upgrading, economic theory can explain the relationship between the two. Neoclassical theory implies that, other things being equal, social upgrading will result from economic upgrading. From an institutional perspective, however, social upgrading is de-linked from technological change and associated with social institutions, including union density, bargaining rights, minimum wages, and active labor market policies.[1]

Empirical research also shows that economic upgrading can translate into social upgrading, but not necessarily. Therefore, it is important to know the circumstances for economic upgrading to lead to its social equivalent. Conversely, it is necessary to understand how to stanch economic and social downgrading. If economic upgrading does not automatically lead to social upgrading, policy has a clear role.[2]

Figure 10.1. Social Cohesion as an End of and a Means for Development

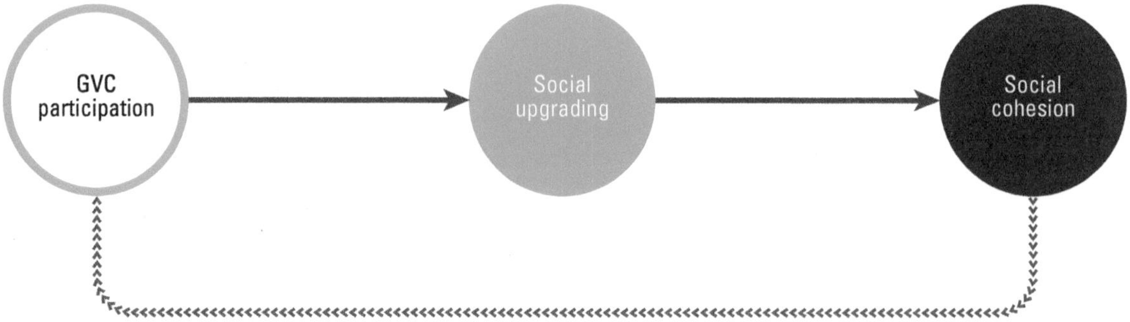

What does economic upgrading through GVCs mean for living standards, including employment, wages, working conditions, economic rights, gender equality, and economic security? Improvements in "the terms, conditions, and remuneration of employment and respect for workers' rights, as embodied in the concept of decent work" can be referred to as social upgrading.[3] But although substantial research has been done on economic upgrading in GVCs, little systematic research exists on what such economic upgrading actually means for employment and living standards, despite growing interest in understanding the social spillovers to the domestic economy of countries already participating in—or thinking about joining—GVCs.

Evidence and intuition suggest that the impact of GVC participation on living standards depends on many factors. One factor is where a country, industry, or firm is positioned in the value chain. The effect for countries performing assembly tasks is likely to be different from that for countries specializing in preproduction stages. The gains may also differ by the type of value chain, because some industries are more labor intensive than others (as are some product lines within the same industry). Different GVCs also may involve different combinations of low-skilled, labor-intensive, and higher-skilled technology-intensive workers. And the spillovers generated by trade flows in GVCs in a specific sector may differ across countries, depending on how integrated the sector is with the rest of the economy of each country.

Multinationals and large global buyers are under increasing pressure to comply with international labor and health, safety, and environmental (HSE) standards, which apply particularly to electronics, apparel, and food GVCs, in which final consumers perceive a more direct link between the consumer good and the working conditions. Although lead firms are largely able to require the implementation of similar codes of conduct from their first-tier suppliers or contract manufacturers through monitoring or audits, monitoring and improving working conditions at lower-tier suppliers becomes increasingly difficult. The lead firm's ability to influence suppliers also depends on the power relations in a GVC. Increased price pressures from the lead firm create negative incentives for first- and lower-tier suppliers to cut labor and other costs by violating international labor standards (failure to pay minimum wages, requiring illegal overtime, or using forced and child labor) and other HSE standards (failure to install ventilation systems or fire safety features, as the 2013 Rana Plaza disaster in Bangladesh demonstrated).[4]

Social upgrading is linked to a country's social cohesion, which can be understood as working toward the well-being of all the members of a society by (1) creating a sense of belonging and active participation, (2) promoting trust, (3) offering the opportunity of upward social mobility, and (4) fighting inequality and exclusion. Living standards—notably the result of jobs—are major elements linking social upgrading and cohesion. Although social cohesion can be an end (or goal) of development outcomes, it is also a means for development, especially as greater social cohesion and political stability make countries more attractive for investment (figure 10.1).[5]

Which Type of Social Upgrading?

The literature divides social upgrading into two mutually complementary parts. Measurable standards refer to aspects of worker well-being that are more easily observed and quantified. The most basic

Figure 10.2. Social "Grading" of Jobs

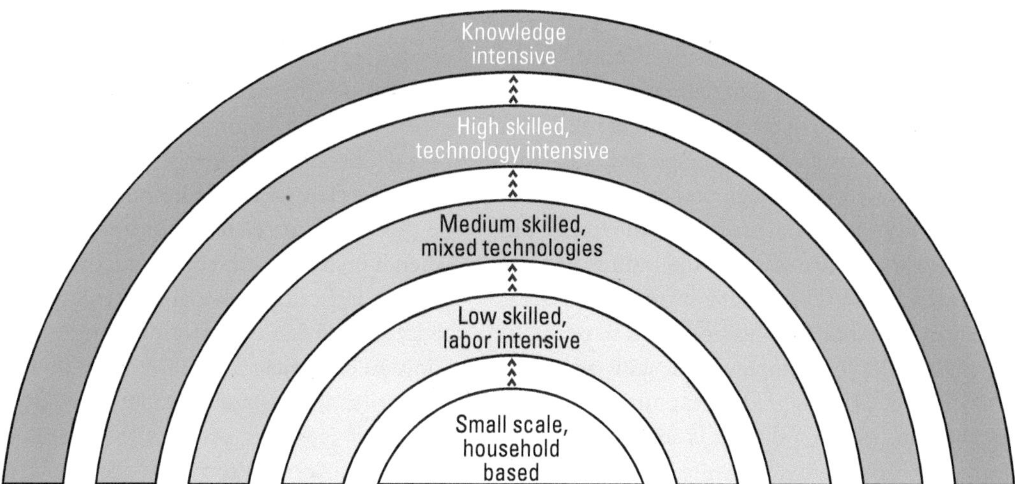

Source: Adapted from Barrientos, Gereffi, and Rossi 2011.

expressions are employment and wages, but others include physical well-being and working conditions, such as health and safety, working hours, and employment security. Enabling rights are less easily quantified; they include empowerment, nondiscrimination, rights to bargaining, and freedom of association.[6]

Different types of work can be given a different "grade" subjectively, with knowledge-intensive activities valued at the top and household-based, small-scale activities at the bottom (figure 10.2).[7]

In this framework, three possible "trajectories" of improved measurable standards are possible:[8]

- *Small-scale worker upgrading.* Workers in home-based production can experience improvements in their working conditions. Establishing producer organizations and providing more secure contracts, better payment, and upgraded personal health and safety equipment can support this goal.
- *Labor-intensive upgrading.* Less-skilled workers can move to other types of labor-intensive work characterized by better working conditions. An example is the move of female workers in Bangladesh or Sri Lanka from subsistence farming to wage employment in apparel firms (if the latter have buyers' codes of labor practice).
- *Higher-skill upgrading.* Workers can move to more skilled and better-paid jobs (for example, in information technology) if they have been trained at their previous workplace and the firm had higher labor standards.

Which Measures of Social Upgrading?

The most basic indicator of social upgrading is employment growth. Employment growth could also be correlated with various measures of GVC integration, but chapter 7 presents instead more direct measurements of the link by drawing on various indicators already developed in the literature. The expansion of global production in labor-intensive industries has been an important source of employment generation and other positive impacts through strengthened formal job opportunities. Similarly, migrant workers and women who previously had difficulty accessing that type of wage work have filled many of those jobs.[9]

GVC-enhanced employment is a necessary but not sufficient condition for social upgrading, because employment gains may be undermined in other areas. Where employment generates better rights and protection for workers, it can enhance social upgrading. Such employment, however, often is insecure and unprotected, which presents multiple challenges in ensuring decent work and wages for more vulnerable workers. The downward pricing pressure in many GVCs has simultaneously led to negative social impacts.

With the increasing complexity of trade in GVCs, the relationship between trade and employment becomes more complicated. Rather than exports generating only domestic employment (as would be the case if countries were selling only intermediate or final goods abroad), they may generate employment in other countries from importing (or buying) intermediate goods. The discussion in chapter 7 is framed on this basis.

Chapter 7 presents five indicators that link employment and GVC participation in countries and industries: (1) the labor content of exports, (2) the labor component of domestic value added in exports, (3) jobs sustained by foreign final demand, (4) jobs generated by foreign trade in GVCs, and (5) jobs in GVC manufacturing. Employment can be a deceptive measure of social upgrading, because jobs created by GVCs can vary in quality in areas such as pay, work hours, conditions, and so on.

Much broader than employment, skills, or wages, the concept of social upgrading captures more generally the gains in living standards and working conditions over time. Other measures include growth in employment; growth in wages; growth in labor share; increased formal employment; decline in youth unemployment; increased gender equality of employment and wages; poverty reduction; higher share of wage employment in nonagricultural employment; improved labor standards; improved job safety; abolition of child labor, forced labor, and employment discrimination; regulation of monitoring; improved political rights; improved human development indicators; improved standards in plant monitoring; and a higher number of workers per job.[10] These indicators are usually measured at different levels of analysis, such as country, sector, GVC, and firm, and are compiled from sector-based case studies.

Measures of social upgrading are likely particular to trade within GVCs. For example, the employment rate of women has been rising in export-oriented manufacturing industries, services, and agriculture. However, the relative dynamism of female employment growth tends to decrease as countries upgrade economically.[11] In addition, if exogenous changes in external demand are perpetuated along value chains, the stability of employment in GVCs may also be lower than non-GVC employment.[12]

Is Downgrading a Possibility?[13]

If economic upgrading is a possibility, is downgrading also a possibility? If international competitiveness depends in part on production costs, there are two routes to improve competitiveness: lowering the payment to factors of production (in particular, labor and capital) and raising productivity. Without considering capital costs, the issue can be simplified as between lowering wages and raising labor productivity—a low road and a high road. Although the high road does not guarantee that wage growth (part of social upgrading) will follow, the low road of lowering wages has limits because of considerations of political stability and human subsistence.

Pressures for upgrading and downgrading compete within GVCs as suppliers balance higher quality with lower costs. Economic and social upgrading can be positively correlated with improved production when it increases workers' productivity. For example, pay (an indicator of social upgrading) and productivity growth (an indicator of economic upgrading) show an extremely high correlation in a 45-country sample for the apparel and footwear sectors in 1995 to 1999.[14] However, pressure to reduce costs might lead employers to combine economic upgrading with social downgrading, although that challenge is not limited to GVCs. In many labor-intensive industries, the pressure to reduce costs puts significant downward pressure on labor costs, including wages and working conditions.

In theory, four combinations of outcomes are possible (figure 10.3). Economic upgrading may be combined with social upgrading or downgrading. If labor productivity growth is driven by employment declines rather than increased value added, economic upgrading in fact leads to social downgrading. Similarly, a decline in relative unit labor costs can be driven by wage declines rather than productivity increases. Social upgrading may also occur in the absence of economic upgrading, and a country may experience simultaneous economic and social downgrading.

Bernhardt and Milberg (2011) find that the translation is quite varied across countries and GVCs. Their study proposes a simple method for combining economic and social upgrading. To get an indicator for economic upgrading, a weight of 50 percent is assigned to the percentage change in export market share and the percentage change in export unit value. The indicator for social upgrading is obtained analogously, assigning a weight of 50 percent to the percentage change in employment and in real wages.

The development of the economic and social realms between the 1990s and the 2000s for several low- and middle-income countries (LMICs) in the apparel sector shows many cases of overall upgrading (figure 10.4). Five of the eight countries with data appear in the first quadrant of clear overall upgraders. Among them, Cambodia has been the

Figure 10.3. Upgrading and Downgrading

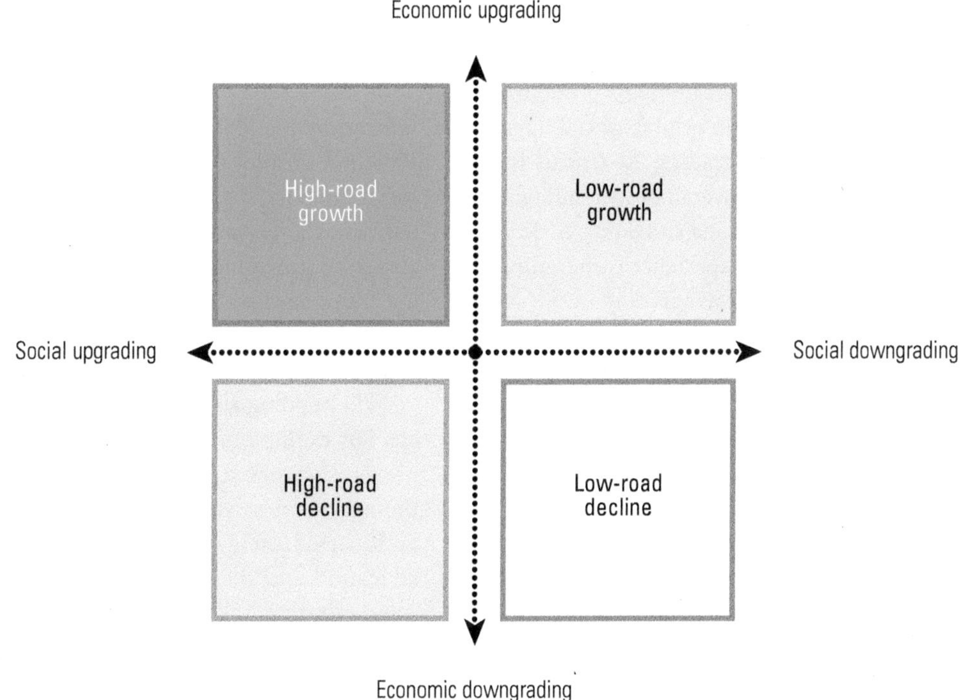

Source: Adapted from Milberg and Winkler 2011, 345.

Figure 10.4. Economic and Social Upgrading and Downgrading in Apparel, 1990s to 2000s

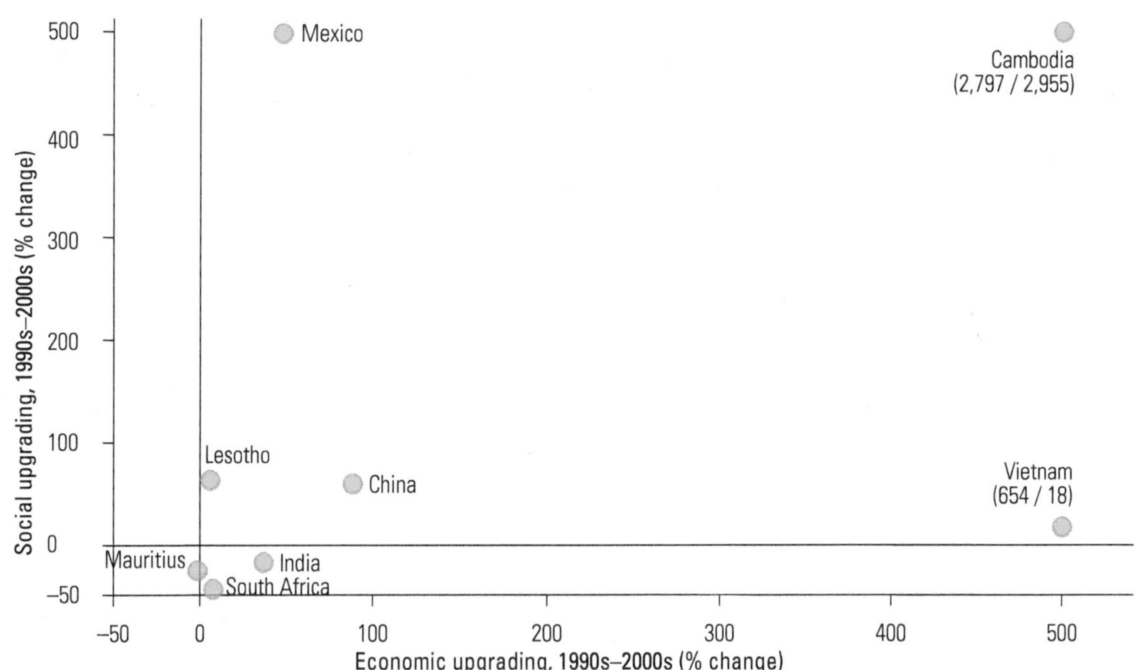

Source: Adapted from Bernhardt and Milberg 2013.

Note: Economic upgrading = average of the percentage change in export market share and the percentage change in export unit value. Social upgrading = average of the percentage change in employment and the percentage change in real wages.

prime performer, with formidable upgrading in economic and social terms. Other outstanding performers include Vietnam (on the economic front) and Mexico (on the social front). The progress of the remaining two upgraders has been less pronounced, particularly China's. Lesotho exhibits social upgrading without economic upgrading. Mauritius is the single case of full-fledged overall downgrading. The remaining two countries, India and South Africa, are intermediate. Both have experienced upgrading in the economic sphere but downgrading in the social sphere. Overall, there seems to be a positive relationship between economic upgrading and social upgrading.

Which Links between Social Upgrading and Cohesion?

Social upgrading can enhance social cohesion in a country. Social upgrading here includes better living standards in the form of more employment, higher wages, better working conditions and education (including skills development), more economic rights, more gender equality, and more economic security (including health insurance and pensions). The following subsections focus on three types of links: jobs and working conditions, education and skill building, and health insurance and pensions.

Jobs and Working Conditions

Jobs are perhaps the most important link between social upgrading and cohesion, because unemployment—especially among the youth—can be related to social unrest, such as during the Arab Spring. Jobs can help alleviate social tensions because they create trust in other people and institutions, as well as contribute to more civic engagement and thus social cohesion. In addition, jobs can shape social interactions by providing social identity to workers, connecting people of different socioeconomic and ethnic backgrounds, raising awareness of different views, and influencing people's aspirations. By contrast, social networks can have a negative impact on social cohesion by excluding people who are not part of the network.[15]

Working conditions in GVCs also contribute to more social cohesion. Better working conditions or corporate social responsibility standards, including economic rights (such as freedom of association) and more security at the workplace (such as increased HSE standards), promote trust and inclusion. Higher labor standards—such as higher minimum wages and more gender equality—can help fight inequality and enhance upward social mobility, thereby fostering social cohesion.

Education and Skill Building

This link enables equal opportunities and upward social mobility. It can result from the lead firm's initiative to train its own or its suppliers' workforce, but also from providing learning on the job. Such training allows workers in GVCs to build their knowledge and perform tasks that require more skills and pay higher wages.

Skill building also can raise aspirations for workers. For example, some workers in Ghana who had previously worked for a multinational company in the agribusiness sector exhibited entrepreneurism and started their own business.[16] When workers' education and skill upgrading lead to better living standards, that link can also create higher education ambitions for their offspring.

In addition, training initiatives at the firm can enhance a sense of active engagement and trust in the company, especially if that training covers a broader set of skills. Supplier assistance, including training, is associated with formal contracting because of the risk that informal suppliers may side-sell products to other clients. A large share of contracts, especially in agriculture, is informal, which limits skill building through training.[17] Because training measures target only parts of the population, they should not be considered a substitute for addressing the deeper challenges of a country's education system.

Health Insurance and Pensions

LMICs have low health insurance and pension coverage rates (less than one-quarter, on average), especially in Africa and Asia. Coverage is particularly low for low-income workers, often less than 10 percent. Social upgrading in GVCs can lead to more economic security for workers in the form of health insurance and pensions. Access to health insurance and pension programs usually is linked to jobs because those programs are largely financed through payroll taxes (from employers, employees, or both).

On the downside, financing social insurance programs through payroll taxes excludes informal workers, which in turn discourages employers from creating more formal jobs (if the taxes are fully or partially paid by the employer) and discourages employees from working in the formal sector (if the taxes are fully or partially paid by the employee). According to recent surveys, workers in LMICs highly value access to health insurance and pensions, and would be willing to contribute a significant share of their income to social insurance.[18]

Unequal coverage can also discourage workers who enjoy social insurance from moving to other firms that do not offer social insurance, which limits positive knowledge spillovers through labor mobility. A recent World Bank survey in Sub-Saharan African countries, for example, confirmed that working for multinationals in the mining sector seems to be attractive to local workers, so they tend to stay there rather than move to other firms or start their own businesses. That finding has a double negative impact: such firms attract and keep the best workers, which leads to skills shortages elsewhere in the local labor market, and the reluctance of those workers to move on inhibits labor turnover and knowledge spillovers.[19]

Equalizing opportunities in access to health insurance and pensions in a country therefore enhances social cohesion by integrating the disadvantaged and helping people build an encompassing social contract. It also helps to reduce inequalities and fosters (generational or intergenerational) social upward mobility, which contributes to a sense of well-being.[20]

Promoting Environmental Sustainability: What Benefits from Environmental Regulation?

Firms today are more vulnerable than ever to shifts in the economy and exogenous disruptions. The changing climate and the resulting changing policy landscape are creating new challenges for firms as they seek to ensure the long-term predictability, reliability, and time-sensitive delivery of goods necessary to participate in GVCs. Climatic disruption can impair firms' ability to access inputs and deliver final products, making countries' preparedness an increasingly critical factor in firms' location decisions.

Climate change is a multi-sector and uncertain phenomenon. Those attributes make evaluating economic impacts and designing robust and appropriately prioritized adaptation strategies difficult for countries. For example, estimates for Vietnam—one of the world's five most vulnerable countries to climate change—suggest that climate change is likely to reduce the country's national income by 1 to 2 percent by 2050, but that number doubles under more extreme projections.[21]

The global trade landscape is trending toward more climate-friendly international standards and mandatory sustainability reporting regimes. Some of the issues affected include wildlife trafficking, illegal logging, sustainable management of ocean and coastal resources, energy efficiency, infrastructure for electric vehicles, responsible mining practices, chemical health and safety cooperation, trade in environmental goods, and aviation emissions.

For countries to comply with such standards long term, strategic policy responses are necessary. That will require the mainstreaming of a triple bottom-line approach to planning that accounts for financial, social, and environmental policy implications. The world's most successful firms are already embracing a culture of "disruptive thinking" when envisioning how best to plan for the future. More participation in GVCs can have a "pro-competition effect," leading to increased competition for limited or vulnerable resources. Increasing the scale of production can further amplify that effect, requiring carefully planned investments in infrastructure. With an effective strategic vision, countries can strengthen the ability of their firms to sustain GVC participation over time.

Policy Options

Policy has a role in promoting social upgrading and cohesion, and environmental sustainability through GVCs. This section presents complementary preconditions and policies for government to maximize the sustainable development impact of GVC activities.[22]

Creating a World-Class Workforce

Developing Skills

Skill development is a key element not only of competitiveness and economic upgrading, but also of social upgrading. In other words, economic and social upgrading are linked and dependent on each other. Skill shortages can impede upward social mobility, and low social mobility can impede economic upgrading. In Chile, Costa Rica, Ethiopia, and Rwanda, upgrading strategies in GVCs have been most successful when accompanied by complementary workforce development interventions. For workforce development to succeed, it must be part of

Box 10.1. Succeeding in New Knowledge-Intensive Niche Sectors

Nordic Europe has produced many global niche players. Its governments recognize the need to encourage more entrepreneurs if they want to provide their people with highly paid jobs. They therefore encourage universities to commercialize their ideas, generate startups, and invest in promoting entrepreneurship—rather than rely on large local companies to generate business ecosystems on their own.

Three main factors explain the ability of firms in those countries to develop successful ventures in knowledge-intensive niche sectors.[a] First is a commitment to relentless innovation and its application to even the most basic industry. Innovation explains the continuing success of the Danish toy company Lego and the ability of a small country such as Denmark to be the world's eighth largest exporter of food products in the world. Second, and related to the first, those countries make a continuing effort to upgrade processes through capital-intensive inputs, adding value. Third, flat governance structures and a culture that promotes trust and cooperation allow for consensus-based decisions and long-term planning, thereby creating a business-friendly environment.

Particularly instructive is the way in which Finland responded to the decline of Nokia, on which it had become overly dependent. Nokia fostered multiple startups that produced goods and services as diverse as online gaming, automatic recycling systems, do-it-yourself family dining services, and devices that improve people's moods by firing bright light into the ear canal. The company created an agency that focused on fostering entrepreneurship, Tekes, and endowed it with a large staff and budget. A venture capital fund, Finnvera, found early-stage companies and helped them get established. Finally, a large network of business accelerators was financed either with fully public money or through public-private partnerships.

Innovation in Finland and other Nordic countries goes well beyond the generation of high-tech. Bridging the gap between engineering and design, innovation in marketing and financing is equally important. The success of Rovio Entertainment's Angry Birds, for example, comes largely from combining skilled mastery of technology with red-hot business acumen. Indeed, innovative business models explain much of the success of recent Nordic startups.

a. *The Economist* 2013.

a coherent overall upgrading strategy.[23] An example is the case study from Nordic Europe in box 10.1. For a more detailed discussion on the importance of skill development, see section "Creating a World-Class Workforce" in chapter 9.

Promoting Social Upgrading

Social upgrading can be supported through labor regulation and monitoring. Host countries must ensure that GVC partners observe the local and national labor regimes, which should meet core international labor standards (for example, the Organisation for Economic Co-operation and Development Guidelines for Multinational Enterprises, the Core Labour Standards of the International Labour Organization (ILO), and the United Nations Guiding Principles on Business and Human Rights). However, adopting such standards does not ensure implementation—let alone enforcement—and governments should also ensure comprehensive and systematic monitoring with assistance from watchdog organizations.

Well-functioning labor markets are also important, because the process of integrating into GVCs necessarily entails a reallocation of resources, including labor, among firms or economic sectors or between both. Even as employment opportunities and average real wages improve, some workers may lose their jobs or see their wages decline when they switch jobs. To facilitate that adjustment, governments can, first, reduce frictions that increase the costs to workers of moving between jobs and, second, put in place social assistance programs designed to accelerate the transition.[24] Introducing minimum wages also can promote social upgrading and cohesion (box 10.2).

Some countries, such as Brazil, improved the living standards of workers and fought income disparities by raising minimum wages in the 2000s. And although those increases target only the formal sector, the outcomes can spill over to the informal sector through labor turnover. Misuse of minimum wages can also lead to negative employment effects, however, especially if wages are raised in economic downturns (such as in Colombia in the late 1990s) or too quickly (for example, in Indonesia in the early 1990s). Moreover, the impact on workers is unequal and depends on enforcement and compliance, as well as the labor market segmentation between formal and informal workers. Minimum wages should therefore not be seen as a substitute for an effective social policy to mitigate inequality in outcomes.[25]

Many other factors beyond labor markets and social policies contribute to social upgrading and can be addressed by three sets of initiatives.[26]

Box 10.2. Bangladesh's Minimum Wage in the Apparel Industry

In 2010, following months of violent protests over labor and safety standards, the Government of Bangladesh raised the monthly minimum wage in the apparel industry from Tk 1,662.50 to Tk 3,000 (about US$38 today). The increase of roughly 80 percent—the first in the industry since 2006—includes an allowance for housing (Tk 800) and medical expenses (Tk 200).

Following the collapse of Rana Plaza in April 2013, the Government of Bangladesh faced even stronger pressure to increase safety and labor standards. As of 2013, Bangladesh had the world's lowest minimum wage, one-half the level of Cambodia (US$75) and US$100 less than China (see figure B10.2.1). The government decided to lift the minimum wage to Tk 5,300 (about US$68)—a 77 percent raise.

Sources: Bajaj 2010; Mahmood 2013; Yardley 2013.

Figure B10.2.1. Minimum Wage per Month for Selected Countries

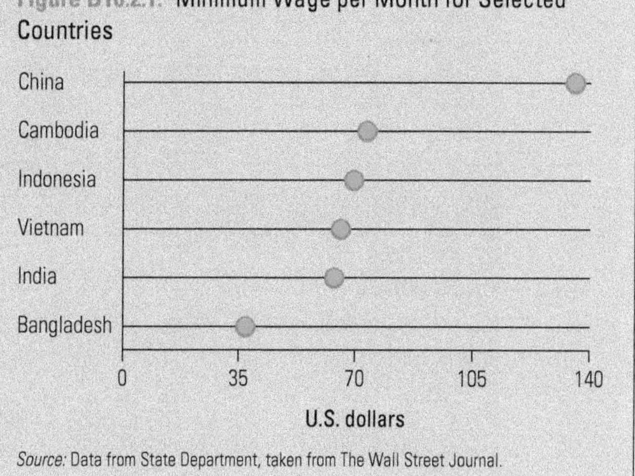

Source: Data from State Department, taken from The Wall Street Journal.

Nonstate Initiatives

Social upgrading can be promoted through private governance in the form of (1) corporate policies that exceed minimum standards, (2) negotiated arrangements between the corporate sector and labor representatives, and (3) civil society and consumer campaigns. Social upgrading can be promoted through voluntary or semi-voluntary agreements by firms to pay living wages and provide other benefits, as well as social institutions that provide services to unemployed workers and the working poor. Such initiatives include standards adopted by industry groups, activities of business associations and chambers of commerce, framework agreements that establish norms of trust and conduct, efforts by development associations to attract certain forms of foreign investment or cooperate with greenfield startups, direct changes in the production process or the structure of buyer-driven value chains and production networks, and corporate social responsibility initiatives by leading brands.

Government Initiatives

Governments in LMICs can address social upgrading by strengthening public institutions for labor regulation (such as labor inspectorates or health and safety inspectorates); developing governance capacities, including social safety nets and other income transfer mechanisms; enforcing labor laws, including working time and child labor laws (as in Brazil, Chile, Costa Rica, and the Dominican Republic); increasing minimum wages (as in Bangladesh's apparel industry in 2010); and regulating overtime and other contract conditions, including insurance and pension requirements.

International Initiatives

These initiatives have been fostered at various levels:

- Multilaterally, the Policy and Performance Standards of the International Finance Corporation (IFC) have included reference to the ILO's core standards and other labor standards.
- Coordinated or collaborative multi-stakeholder approaches include the ILO/IFC Better Work Programme, Ethical Trade Initiative, Social Accountability International, and United Nations Special Representative Ruggie's Guiding Principles on Business and Human Rights.
- As part of its regional trade agreements, the European Union grants bilateral trade concessions to countries that implement the ILO's core labor standards and other basic rights.
- Although regional free trade agreements, such as the North American Free Trade Agreement and the Central American Free Trade Agreement, include side agreements regarding labor, their coverage is more limited and they do not explicitly refer to ILO standards.[27]

Policy Objectives and Performance Indicators

Policies to support social upgrading should be individually tailored to the country's specific situation and consistent with its overall development strategy. To comply with those frameworks, local firms

Table 10.1. Promoting Social Upgrading: Policy Objectives and Performance Indicators

Policy objectives
• Adopt core international labor standards, and ensure implementation and enforcement, as well as comprehensive and systematic monitoring. • Reduce frictions that increase the costs to workers of moving between jobs, and put in place social assistance programs to accelerate the transition. • Introduce and raise minimum wages to improve living standards, and ensure enforcement and compliance. • Strengthen public institutions for labor regulation, and develop governance capacities.
Performance indicators
Labor standards: • ILO NORMLEX *Labor market frictions and social assistance:* • Skills mismatch (ILO KILM) • Employment protection legislation (ILO EPLex; OECD EPL; IFC Doing Business Indicators—Employing Workers) • OECD public expenditure on labor market programs—Public employment services and administration; training; employment incentives; sheltered and supported employment and rehabilitation; direct job creation; startup incentives; and so forth *Minimum wages/working poor:* • ILO Working Conditions Laws Database • OECD Labour Force Statistics (LFS) • Working poor statistics (ILOSTAT) *Implementation and institutional/governance capacity:* • Labor inspection indicators (ILO ILOSTAT) • World Bank CPIA—Quality of public administration rating • World Bank Actionable Governance Indicators (AGI) • Sustainable Governance Indicators (SGI)

Note: CPIA = Country Policy and Institutional Assessment; EPL = employment protection legislation; EPLex = ILO employment protection database; IFC = International Finance Corporation; ILO = International Labour Office; ILOSTAT = ILO database of labor statistics; KILM = Key Indicators of the Labour Market; NORMLEX = Information System on International Labour Standards; OECD = Organisation for Economic Co-operation and Development.

generally require a well-functioning labor market and a strong social governance framework with regulation and capacity building. Table 10.1 lists the policy objectives discussed in this section and the available performance indicators.

Engineering Equitable Distribution of Opportunities and Outcomes

For social upgrading to translate into social cohesion through better living standards, a country must ensure equality of opportunity and outcomes. A society can support the relative poor financially (through income support or progressive taxes) and through provision of services.[28] Of particular relevance to GVCs is the minimum wage.

Promoting equality of opportunities targets excluded groups of the society—such as women, informal workers, rural inhabitants, and minorities—by reducing inequalities and discrimination. Relevant policies for GVCs include granting equal access to jobs, education, health insurance, and pensions. In practice, policies that engineer equality of opportunities and outcomes can be complementary.[29] Income-based scholarships, for example, are cash transfers (promoting equality of outcomes) that are conditional on education for students (promoting equality of opportunity in the future).

Three policy options are recommended: facilitate access to information, remove discriminatory social institutions and establishing rights, and reform social insurance.

Facilitating Access to Information

Equality of opportunity requires including groups of the society that face obstacles to seizing opportunities because they lack information about opportunities or their roles, rights, and entitlements. Equality of access to jobs is the most important opportunity for GVCs. Providing access to widely advertised information about job vacancies and practical advice about how to get those jobs is a precondition of equality of access. A common program is job search assistance, which makes job matching more effective by providing information about job vacancies and job seekers. Assistance can also include job placement and counseling.

Workers must be informed about their rights and entitlements. Farmers, the self-employed, and informal workers often are unaware of their rights in relation to landowners, traders, or employers. Cooperatives, associations of informal workers, and trade unions can be effective channels of information and expression.[30] The need to have a voice extends to formal workers and requires that freedom of association and collective bargaining rights be implemented. Policy makers also have to raise awareness of social assistance and other social entitlement programs, especially pensions and health insurance.

Skill development includes clearly communicating to workers about their specific role in the value chain. Female workers in Chinese factories often were unable to explain exactly what they were doing.[31] Understanding one's role and contribution to the overall good promotes a sense of social identity and belonging, which in turn contributes to social cohesion. In addition, workers and firms need to be given access to information about accredited training programs. Training may be provided by private firms, donor programs (such as the U.S. Agency for International Development), the public sector, and, in some cases, private trainers. For example, in Burundi and Rwanda, private trainers in the informal sector provide fee-based training.[32]

Managing information is particularly important for social insurance, because many LMICs lack instruments for identifying people. Technological advances such as biometric technology can help overcome such challenges and reduce costs, leakages, and corruption. Information management systems must also track people's medical or work history to align benefits with contributions.[33]

Removing Discriminatory Social Institutions and Establishing Rights

Facilitating access to jobs for excluded or disadvantaged groups of society, especially women and minorities, helps economies tap a large productive potential and tightens social cohesion. Antidiscrimination laws and mandatory or voluntary affirmative action programs are a prerequisite for greater equality of opportunities.[34]

Guaranteeing women their property and inheritance rights enhances their security and equality, and can enable them to take advantage of formal job opportunities instead of being confined to lower-paid, informal jobs. Discriminatory barriers include formal social institutions and informal social institutions, such as norms, values, and traditions. Those informal barriers are reflected in gender-related stereotyping that discourages women (and men) from choosing untraditional professions.[35]

Establishing the rights of freedom of association (say, in organizations or trade unions) and collective bargaining enhances social cohesion, thanks to the possibility for social dialogue that can address tensions before they lead to conflict. In an attempt to maintain social cohesion during the labor market transition, China has had collective bargaining mechanisms since the mid-1990s, leading to the Labor Contract Law of 2008, which regulates the governance of collective contracts. The establishment of coordination bodies at the province, city, and prefecture levels accompanied that law.[36]

Although trade unions provide voice to employed workers, they do not cover self-employed or informal workers, who still make up a large share of the workforce in LMICs. The demand for alternative institutions of collective representation resulted in the emergence of associations of self-employed workers, who united to demand better working conditions, including the protection of rights. Anecdotal evidence shows that in some cases, those efforts include filing claims at court, as with street vendors in Lima, Peru, and Durban, South Africa.[37]

Reforming Social Insurance

One right is granting universal access to social insurance. Reforming a country's social insurance systems can facilitate wider coverage of health insurance and pensions. To enable knowledge spillovers through the labor mobility effect, it is important to ensure portable health and pension benefits across jobs. In Indonesia, some provinces extend noncontributory social health protection to uninsured groups. Because funds are pooled at the province level (or even at the district level, as in South Sumatra), the portability of health benefits is limited.[38] In addition, minimum social insurance—notably pensions—can help alleviate economic insecurity. A simulation model of 18 Latin American countries based on household survey data revealed that universal minimum pensions would substantially reduce poverty among the elderly in most of the countries.[39]

The challenge is considerable when social insurance systems differentiate between formal and informal jobs, especially if the financing for formal

Table 10.2. Engineering Equitable Distribution of Opportunities and Outcomes: Policy Objectives and Performance Indicators

Policy objectives

- Facilitate access to information about opportunities, roles, rights, and entitlements.
- Remove discriminatory social institutions by putting in place antidiscrimination laws and mandatory or voluntary affirmative action programs; establish women's rights (for example, property and inheritance rights) and the rights for freedom of association and collective bargaining.
- Reform social insurance systems and combine them with more traditional social assistance programs.

Performance indicators

Access to information:

- IFC Women, business and the law indicators—Accessing institutions
- OECD Public expenditure on labor market programs—Placement and related services

Antidiscrimination laws and rights:

- ILO NATLEX
- IFC Women, business and the law indicators—Using property, getting a job, building credit, going to court, and so forth
- FAO Gender and land rights database—Property and use rights; inheritance rights; and so forth
- World Bank CPIA—Property rights and rule-based governance ratings; gender equality rating
- ILO NORMLEX—Freedom of association cases
- Trade union density and collective bargaining coverage (ILOSTAT)

Social insurance and assistance:

- ILO NATLEX
- Social security indicators (ILOSTAT)—Social protection coverage; public social protection expenditure; and so on
- OECD Social Expenditure Database—Labor market programs; health; old age; and so forth
- World Bank CPIA—Policies for social inclusion/equity; social protection rating
- WDI—Benefits held by first 20 percent of population and program participation (all social insurance; all social protection; all social safety nets; unemployment benefits; and ALMP)

Note: ALMP = active labor market policies; CPIA = Country Policy and Institutional Assessment; FAO = Food and Agriculture Organization; IFC = International Finance Corporation; ILO = International Labour Office; ILOSTAT = ILO database of labor statistics; NATLEX = Database of National Labour, Social Security and Related Human Rights Legislation; NORMLEX = Information System on International Labour Standards; OECD = Organisation for Economic Co-operation and Development; WDI = World Development Indicators.

workers is based on contributions and that for informal workers is based on taxes. Tax-based social assistance programs for informal workers de facto "subsidize" informal work by taxing formal workers twice. The portability of social benefits across firms therefore requires more innovative instruments that target informal workers—who often have the means to contribute to social insurance systems—as well as a country's capacity to manage worker transitions.[40]

One non-tax-based possibility to include informal workers is to offer "unbundled individualized instruments," such as individual retirement savings accounts, which would allow informal workers or workers who switch between formal and informal jobs to contribute. Subsidized contributions by the state could complement the program. Fairly high contribution rates by informal workers in Mexico have related pension reforms along those lines. Similar approaches are plausible in health insurance.[41] Social insurance reforms that target informal workers not only increase overall coverage rates, but also facilitate knowledge spillovers through labor turnover in a country.[42]

Such policies can be combined with more traditional social assistance that targets other uninsured sectors of the population (such as the unemployed and the elderly). Progress has been substantial in offering universal entitlement in health, often by creating a parallel system to cover the uninsured. Thailand's health insurance coverage, for example, reached 98 percent in 2007, although universal coverage was introduced only in 2001. Before the health reform, only employees in the public sector or in firms with more than 20 employees were covered. Social pensions also help narrow the coverage gap, although transfers tend to be small (such as US$2.30 per month in Bangladesh). Nevertheless, social pensions have coverage rates of about 90 percent in Kyrgyz Republic and Lesotho.[43] Table 10.2 shows the policy objectives discussed here and possible performance indicators.

Implementing Climate-Smart Policies and Infrastructure

Climate-smart policy prescriptions can strengthen global competitiveness. Recent research[44, 45, 46, and 47] has shown that the benefits of environmental regulation often vastly outweigh the costs. Proper regulation can induce innovation in green technologies and produce economy-wide benefits.

Policy responses to ensure the sustainability of GVCs and sustained economic growth amid climate change include the following examples:

- Government should continue to invest in information systems to monitor climate change impacts in agribusiness; cooperate with the global community on the development of heat-resistant crop varieties; work to improve water use efficiency; and ensure that standards for infrastructure, such as roads, are designed to endure more extremes (warmer/colder) and a more variable climate.
- Governments in countries with extensive coastal lowlands should consider the gradual channeling of economic activity to safer, higher elevation zones. The location and vulnerability of the capital stock in many LMICs in the coming decades is still a matter of choice. Sea-level rise and the continual threat of cyclones make this consideration critical.
- The development of disaster risk mechanisms will be key to sustainable economic growth. Disaster risk financing markets are a crucial new development that merits closer attention for most countries. Strengthening financial resilience should include enhancing technical and institutional capacities related to crisis management, coordinating various governmental authorities across all levels, and supporting the continuity planning of business.

Notes

1. Milberg and Winkler (2013).
2. Milberg and Winkler (2013).
3. From Barrientos and others (2011, 301).
4. UNCTAD (2013).
5. OECD (2011).
6. Barrientos, Gereffi, and Rossi (2010); Rossi (2013).
7. Barrientos, Gereffi, and Rossi (2011).
8. Barrientos, Gereffi, and Rossi (2011).
9. Barrientos, Gereffi, and Rossi (2010).
10. Milberg and Winkler (2011).
11. UNCTAD (2013).
12. OECD, WTO, and UNCTAD (2013).
13. This section draws on Milberg and Winkler (2013).
14. Flanagan (2005).
15. World Bank (2013b).
16. Kaiser Associates Partners (2014a).
17. Kaiser Associates Partners (2014a).
18. World Bank (2013b).
19. Kaiser Associates Partners (2014b).
20. OECD (2011); World Bank (2013b).
21. Channing, Tarp, and Thurlow. 2015.
22. See figure O.1 in the book's Overview for the strategic questions and policy options for this focus area.
23. World Bank (2014).
24. Hollweg and others (2014).
25. OECD (2011).
26. Barrientos, Gereffi, and Rossi (2011).
27. Barrientos, Gereffi, and Rossi (2011).
28. Shared prosperity refers to expanding a country's income and sharing it such that people in the bottom 40 percent of the income distribution increase their welfare as quickly as possible (World Bank 2013a).
29. OECD (2011).
30. World Bank (2013b).
31. Chang (2012).
32. World Bank (2014).
33. World Bank (2013b).
34. World Bank (2013b).
35. OECD (2011).
36. OECD (2011); World Bank (2013b).
37. World Bank (2013b).
38. ILO (2014).
39. Dethier, Pestieau, and Ali (2010).
40. OECD (2011).
41. OECD (2011).
42. For a collection of studies describing strategies to promote universal health coverage and its effects in 22 countries, see the "Universal Health Coverage Study Series" (World Bank 2013a).
43. OECD (2011).
44. Aguado, Alvarez, and Domingo (2013).
45. Ambec and others (2013).
46. Di Marchi, Di Maria, and Micelli (2013).
47. Eccles, Ioannou, and Serafeim (2014).

References

Ambec, S., M.A. Cohen, S. Elgie, and P. Lanoie. 2013. "The Porter Hypothesis at 20: Can Environmental Regulation Enhance Innovation and Competitiveness?" Review of Environmental Economics and Policy. Oxford Journals: First published online January 4, 2013.

Aguado, S., R. Alvarez, and R. Domingo. 2013. "Model of Efficient and Sustainable Improvements in a Lean Production system through Processes of Environmental Innovation." *Journal of Cleaner Production* 47 (May): 141–148.

Arndt, Channing, Finn Tarp, and James Thurlow. 2015. "The Economic Costs of Climate Change: A Multi-Sector Impact Assessment for Vietnam." *Sustainability* 7: 4131–45.

Bajaj, Vikas. 2010. "Bangladesh Garment Workers Awarded Higher Pay." *The New York Times*, July 28. http://www.nytimes.com/2010/07/29/business/global/29garment.html?_r=0.

Barrientos, Stephanie, Gary Gereffi, and Arianna Rossi. 2010. "Economic and Social Upgrading in Global Production Networks: Developing a Framework for Analysis." Capturing the Gains Working Paper 2010/03, University of Manchester, United Kingdom.

———. 2011. "Economic and Social Upgrading in Global Production Networks: A New Paradigm for a Changing World." *International Labour Review* 150 (3–4): 319–40.

Barrientos, Stephanie, Frederick Mayer, John Pickles, and Anne Posthuma. 2011. "Decent Work in Global Production Networks: Framing the Policy Debate." *International Labour Review* 150 (3–4): 299–317.

Bernhardt, Thomas, and William Milberg. 2011. "Economic and Social Upgrading in Global Value Chains: Analysis of Horticulture, Apparel, Tourism and Mobile Telephones, Capturing the Gains." Working Paper 2011/06, University of Manchester, United Kingdom.

———. 2013. "Does Industrial Upgrading Generate Employment and Wage Gains?" In *The Oxford Handbook of Offshoring and Global Employment*, edited by A. Bardhan, D. Jaffee, and C. Kroll, 490–533. New York: Oxford University Press.

Chang, Leslie T. 2012. "The Voices of China's Workers." TED (Technology, Entertainment and Design) Talk (online video). http://www.ted.com/talks/leslie_t_chang_the_voices_of_china_s_workers.

Dethier, J. J., P. Pestieau, and R. Ali. 2010. "Universal Minimum Old Age Pensions: Impact on Poverty and Fiscal Cost in 18 Latin American Countries." Policy Research Working Paper 5292, World Bank, Washington, DC.

Di Marchi, V., E. Di Maria, and S. Micelli. 2013. "Environmental Strategies, Upgrading and Competitive Advantage in Global Value Chains." *Business Strategy and the Environment* 22: 62–72. Published online May 14, 2012 in Wiley Online Library.

Eccles, R.G., I. Ioannou, and G. Serafeim. 2014. "The Impact of Corporate Sustainability on Organizational Processes and Performance." *Management Science* 60 (11): 2835–57.

The Economist. 2013. "Special Report—The Nordic Countries: Northern Lights." *The Economist*, February 2, 2013 http://www.economist.com/sites/default/files/20130202_nordic_countries.pdf.

Flanagan, Robert J. 2005. *Globalization and Labor Conditions: Working Conditions and Worker Rights in a Global Economy.* New York: Oxford University Press.

Hollweg, Claire H., Daniel Lederman, Diego Rojas, and Elizabeth Ruppert Bulmer. 2014. *Sticky Feet: How Labor Market Frictions Shape the Impact of International Trade on Jobs and Wages*, vol. 1. Directions in Development: Trade, Report 88890, World Bank, Washington, DC.

ILO (International Labour Organization). 2014. "Indonesia—Health." In *Social Protection: Building Social Protection Floors and Comprehensive Social Security Systems.* Geneva: ILO. http://www.social-protection.org/gimi/gess/ShowWiki.action?wiki.wikiId=869.

Kaiser Associates Partners. 2014a. "Sector Case Study: Agribusiness." In *Making Foreign Direct Investment Work for Sub-Saharan Africa: Local Spillovers and Competitiveness in Global Value Chains*, edited by Thomas Farole and Deborah Winkler, 163–207. Washington, DC: World Bank.

———. 2014b. "Sector Case Study: Mining." In *Making Foreign Direct Investment Work for Sub-Saharan Africa: Local Spillovers and Competitiveness in Global Value Chains*, edited by Thomas Farole and Deborah Winkler, 117–62. Washington, DC: World Bank.

Mahmood, Syed Zain Al-. 2013. "Bangladesh to Raise Pay for Garment Workers." *The Wall Street Journal*, May 12. http://online.wsj.com/news/articles/SB10001424127887324715704578479231065424630.

Milberg, William, and Deborah Winkler. 2011. "Economic and Social Upgrading in Global Production Networks: Problems of Theory and Measurement." *International Labour Review* 150 (3–4): 341–65.

———. 2013. *Outsourcing Economics: Global Value Chains in Capitalist Development.* New York: Cambridge University Press.

OECD (Organisation for Economic Co-operation and Development). 2011. *Perspectives on Global Development 2012: Social Cohesion in a Shifting World.* Paris: OECD.

OECD, WTO, and UNCTAD (Organisation for Economic Co-operation and Development, World Trade Organization, and United Nations Conference on Trade and Development). 2013. *Implications of Global Value Chains for Trade, Investment, Development, and Jobs.* Prepared for the G-20 Leaders Summit, Saint Petersburg (Russian Federation). http://www.oecd.org/trade/G20-Global-Value-Chains-2013.pdf.

Rossi, Arianna. 2013. "Does Economic Upgrading Lead to Social Upgrading in Global Production Networks? Evidence from Morocco." *World Development* 46: 223–33.

UNCTAD (United Nations Conference on Trade and Development). 2013. "World Investment Report 2013—Global Value Chains: Investment and Trade for Development." UNCTAD, Geneva.

World Bank. 2013a. *The World Bank Group Goals: End Extreme Poverty and Promote Shared Prosperity.* Washington, DC: World Bank.

———. 2013b. *World Development Report: Jobs.* Washington, DC: World Bank.

———. 2014. *Republic of Burundi: Skills Development for Growth—Building Skills for Coffee and Other Priority Sectors.* Washington, DC: World Bank.

Yardley, Jim. 2013. "Bangladesh Takes Step to Increase Lowest Pay." *The New York Times*, November 4. http://www.nytimes.com/2013/11/05/world/asia/bangladesh-takes-step-toward-raising-38-a-month-minimum-wage.html.

PART IV

COUNTRY ENGAGEMENT

Chapter 11

DESIGNING A COUNTRY ENGAGEMENT STRATEGY BASED ON SOUND ANALYTICS

What Is the Goal of This Guide?

Use of This Book to Help Design a Country Engagement Strategy to Achieve GVC-Led Development

To complement parts I to III of this book, this chapter offers guidelines on engaging with country stakeholders to implement a national strategy to achieve economic and social development through global value chain (GVC) participation. Policy and its implementation in a wide range of influencing areas affect the odds of success in GVCs. Those areas are as different as trade and trade policy, domestic services regulations, investment regulations and incentives, compliance with process and product standards, innovation, industry, entrepreneurship, labor markets, education, and infrastructure and connectivity, as discussed in detail in part III of this book. Thus, creating synergies on the ground requires multiple interventions and long-lasting engagement with a variety of stakeholders within and outside the country. A few important recommendations and lessons learned for interventions at the country level need to be kept in mind:

- The creation of synergies on the ground requires multiple interventions (advisory, analytics, financing, advocacy) and long-lasting engagement.
- Policy advice supporting GVC-based growth models requires sound analytics, evidence, and data. It also requires 360-degree assessment of the competitiveness of a country's economy, in its entirety, and drilling down to specific sectors, GVCs, tasks, and activities, to identify, prepare, and inform all interventions.
- Interventions need to build on analytical foundations and follow well-targeted and action-bound action plans, but they do not need to follow a standard sequence or timeline abstracting from country-specific and context-specific conditions. The coordination, information sharing, and leveraging synergies between different interventions are important. Coordination demands are high within government agencies, GVC stakeholders, and donor partners.
- A participative approach, with alignment on and ownership of the agenda by all stakeholders is critical. Effective stakeholder engagement mechanisms are a central anchor for continued, long-lasting results (but often the least funded). Successful sector-specific, public-private cooperation and dialogue are required to inform national competitiveness strategies, investment climate reforms, and investment attraction with opportunities and challenges at the micro level. Leveraging and reinforcing existing cooperation through systematic consultations and formal mechanisms of bottom-up policy making is fundamental.
- Network effects and positive spillovers from GVC participation across sectors, based on integrated solution packages, are achievable over time. Dynamic learning, replication, and scale-up can be fostered through global/cross-country platforms.
- A shared vision and a common understanding of the project goals and objectives between implementing teams, local and international stakeholders, and other development partners are important for success.

This chapter brings attention to the synergies between these different areas and helps support countries' efforts to identify the necessary reforms to trigger a virtuous cycle of "reform-GVC-entry and upgrading-development." The cycle would encourage the private sector to keep investing retained earnings in the continued improvement of existing and new activities and tasks of comparative advantage in countries' agriculture, manufacturing, and services sectors. The strategic framework for GVC participation developed in this book—mapping focus areas for policy with relevant objectives, strategic questions, and policy options—can guide policy makers in identifying policy options and priorities for fostering GVC-led development (see figure O.1 in the Overview). The framework is to be a first step toward a full GVC participation assessment and strategy. This pre-engagement analytical work and identification of priority policy areas for intervention should be completed with methodologies that drill down within sectors, GVCs, and specific tasks and activities (see box 11.1 for a discussion of complementary work that drills down within GVCs).

Turning back to the pre-engagement, economy-wide analysis, the successful implementation of full GVC diagnostics begins with effective planning and management, and an understanding of how this feeds into the overall country engagement strategy of GVC participation.

A three-step process can be envisaged for the overall country engagement strategy.

Component 1. Pre-Project Assessment: From Macro to Micro (2 to 3 months)

The objective of component 1 of a country's GVC engagement strategy is to provide a comprehensive,

Box 11.1 World Bank Group Approach to Diagnostic Work and Formulation of Action Plans to Strengthen a Country's Position within Specific GVCs

The World Bank Group uses a range of instruments, including advisory services and capacity building, lending, investment support, and guarantees, to help countries, their industrial sectors, and firms in the efforts to enter GVCs, upgrade and densify participation in GVCs, and sustain the engagement over time at the macroeconomic, social, and environmental levels. This is achieved by supporting countries' efforts to improve macroeconomic and horizontal policies as well as their vertical interventions targeting specific sectors, GVCs, products, and firms. Targeted challenges and market failures are grouped into three broad areas:

- Internal to the firm (firm capabilities)
  - Managerial capabilities and workforce skills
  - Technology adoption
  - Innovation capabilities
- Domestic environment
  - Business climate and institutions
  - Financial and labor markets
  - Quality and conditions of output and input factors
    - Education and skills
    - Public policies for innovation
    - Product and process standards
    - Labor and social conditions
- International dimension
  - Infrastructure and policies for connectivity (physical and information and communications technology)
  - International investment
  - Trade costs and openness

The need to cover horizontal policies and vertical interventions in a coherent manner means that the World Bank Group approach complements economy-wide assessment, as presented in this book, with methodologies that drill down to tasks and activities within individual GVCs. The vertical analysis focuses on identifying strategic segments and business models that deliver high-value-added dividends and development prospects in selected industries. These strategic segments of focus are determined through diagnostic work and consultations with the private sector, government agencies and ministries, global buyers, lead firms, and advanced consumers. Where feasible, the approach favors a participative process, so that after its completion, local stakeholders are trained and empowered with the necessary know-how to drive the process of supporting the competitiveness of the country.

The success of value chain competitiveness reinforcement strategies requires continued and lasting effort, as opposed to one-off initiatives. For this reason, the capacity-building and training component and direct involvement in the project of local stakeholders need critically to be built within countries' public sector and/or relevant partner institutions.

Finally, the World Bank Group approach emphasizes results and impact measures. Although this is often not a request of governments, World Bank Group engagements tend to include frameworks to measure results, reforms, and development impacts. This is an important way to assess reforms and correct action in a timely manner if needed. Monitoring and evaluation frameworks developed over the years by the World Bank Group systems are used for establishing monitoring and evaluation protocols and follow-up of results during and after the completion of project and embedded technical assistance.

fact-based, and independent preliminary view of the country's trade competitiveness (particularly measured in value added), performance in GVC integration, economic upgrading, and the role of country characteristics, including the business climate, investment climate, and drivers of competitiveness across economic, regulatory, operational, and infrastructural dimensions. This preliminary view is developed through a desk-based analysis followed by a field-based qualitative assessment and discussion of the identified challenges, opportunities, and policy options with local public and private sector stakeholders. Planning of the pre-project phase should focus on the economy as a whole, but also zoom into key industries, strategic segments therein, and individual value chains (as narrowly defined as the availability of quantitative and qualitative information allows). A limited number of key industries (three or four) and/or value chains (eight or nine)—existing ones that exemplify critical and/or broader opportunities and challenges, or new ones that are considered important by the local stakeholders, as well as subnational specificities—may also be identified at this stage for deeper analysis and discussion of challenges and opportunities. Component 1 provides a first-pass analysis of sector- and GVC-specific issues, which can be the object of more focused and deeper assessments in component 2 of the engagement strategy.

Assessments in component 1 must be based on the widest range of available and applicable methodologies. This process allows for customizing the analysis to country-specific needs and overcoming the limits inherent in specific methodologies. As discussed in parts II and III of this book, none of the available methodologies allows a full and balanced assessment of a country's participation in GVCs. Each tool illustrated in this book was developed for application to comprehensive analyses. Together, the tools form a suite of analytical frameworks and instruments for linking performance (outcomes and potential) to diagnostics of countries' and regions' competitiveness in goods and services GVCs. Table 11.1 provides a summary of the methodologies available to carry out the assessment and their content.

Component 2. Drilling within GVCs and Capacity Building (12 to 24 Months)

Component 2, which can start one month after the start of component 1, includes (1) establishing the model of country engagement and the appropriate institutional setting for identification of strategies in GVCs that offer the promise of the highest value-added growth (see also chapter 4 for further illustrations), as well as further investigation and/or validation of possible binding constraints and solutions, building on those identified in component 1 of the engagement strategy and drilling down within GVCs; and (2) creating a detailed road map for starting to implement reforms. For example, a possible strategy could be to identify a list of four to six major initiatives to maximize shared value added in incorporating global best practices and placing a priority on "quick wins." Various governance models can be used for designing the appropriate institutional setting—for instance, by establishing a working group to work closely with the president's or prime minister's office, or by devising a plan for strengthening the coordinating mandate of one key ministry. Participants can be selected from relevant public institutions, including ministries of economy; ministries in charge of entrepreneurship and domestic economic development; national and subnational agencies for the promotion of trade, investment, and competitiveness; chambers of commerce; associations of employers; regional development agencies; etc. The established governance body will participate in the work of component 2 and may oversee the work of component 3.

Component 3. Execution Phase of Interventions (6 to 18 Months)

Component 3, which needs to start after the completion of component 1, but can start as early as six months after the beginning of component 2 and delivery of early results, covers the execution phase of interventions. It includes revising regulations, re-engineering processes, and investing in infrastructure to achieve measurable improvements across all key dimensions and areas of binding constraint identified at the macro and micro levels.

The material in this book focuses on providing tools to support the assessment in component 1. Component 1 should be treated as a project within the overall GVC engagement strategy, and therefore should be managed accordingly. Preparatory steps must be considered, establishing objectives and roles and determining the main actors and scope.

Who Is This Guide For?

The GVC participation assessment in component 1 is to be led by a small core team, most likely comprising

Table 11.1. Desk-Based Analysis

Component	Content
1. Macroeconomic trends	Value added by broad sector, employment by broad sector, labor productivity by sector, FDI, exports and imports (% of GDP), exports and imports by broad economic category, and other informed classifications
2. Export market share growth, push, and pull factors	Export market share growth; decomposition in push and pull factors using shift-share methodologies
3a. World Bank MC-GVC Dashboard (short or long version)	Trade in main GVCs, exports of GVC products relevant to country, top five exports (see chapter 3)
3b. World Bank MC-GVC Dashboard (long version)	Extension of 3a, including country dimensions and follow-up analysis of interesting patterns (such as product-specific analysis) (see chapter 3)
4a. Network analysis (short version)	Worldwide trade network, country trade network for sector of interest (main buyers), country trade network for sector of interest (main suppliers) (see chapter 6)
4b. Network analysis (long version)	Extension to more sectors (four or five, maximum) (see chapter 6)
5a. Trade in value-added indicators (EORA)	Foreign value added in gross exports, domestic value added in third countries' exports, GVC participation index (see chapters 4–6)
5b. Trade in value-added indicators (OECD-TiVA or WIOD), other GVC indicators, and econometric decomposition of gross exports, for countries covered by these more sophisticated databases	Domestic value added in gross exports (total growth and by sector), decomposition, foreign value added in gross exports, domestic value added in third countries' exports, sourcing and selling patterns, value added by destination, import and export upstreamness and gap, contribution of direct and indirect domestic value added and foreign value added to gross export growth (see chapters 4–7)
6a. Econometric assessment: structural integration into GVCs and economic upgrading	Impact of structural integration in GVCs (network measure) on domestic value added embodied in exports and gross exports (see chapter 7)
6b. Econometric assessment: probability of entry in GVCs	Probabilistic model of entry in GVCs (see chapter 7)
6c. Econometric assessment: economic upgrading	Impact of GVC integration (foreign value added in gross exports, domestic value added in third countries' exports) on value added and the role of national policies (see chapter 7)
7a. Econometric assessment: economic upgrading using Enterprise Surveys	Impact of GVC integration (imported input share, export share, etc.) on labor productivity and the role of absorptive capacity (see chapter 7)
7b. Econometric assessment: economic upgrading using national firm-level data	Impact of GVC integration (imported input share, export share, etc.) on labor productivity and the role of absorptive capacity (depends on whether data need to be cleaned and the extent of analysis, etc.)
8a. Role of services in GVCs (short version)	Zoom into the services dimension of analysis in sections 1 to 7 (see chapter 6)
8b. Role of services in GVCs (long version)	
9. Country- or product-specific case study	Value chain mapping and country positioning, historical/current trends, stakeholder/actor analysis, challenges and opportunities, future implications, policy implications
10a. Policy section (short version)	Policy suggestions based on short GVC analysis (and additional research) (see also part III)
10b. Policy section (long version)	Application of strategic policy framework, policy suggestions based on long GVC analysis, screening of policy performance indicators, additional research (potentially drawing on information from mission trip)

Note: EORA = Environmental Accounting Framework Using Externality Data and Input–Output Tools for Policy Analysis; FDI = foreign direct investment; GDP = gross domestic product; GVC = global value chain; MC-GVCs = Measuring Competitiveness in GVCs Dashboard; OECD = Organisation for Economic Co-operation and Development; TiVA = Trade in Value Added; WIOD = World Input-Output Database.

three to four people. At least one team member should have sound past experience in policy and strategic issues related to trade in general and GVCs in particular, as well as technical skills in analyzing trade and production data at the macro and firm levels. Ideally, the task team leader should have some experience in GVC analysis and, most important, in-depth country knowledge and experience.

If the study participants intend to do in-depth technical analysis as well, technical experts must be involved. If the team considers certain methodologies essential from the outset, then bringing in specialized technical expertise to lead those components may be useful.

The success of component 1 of the GVC participation strategy will depend on combining desk-based assessments with inputs and qualitative information from a wide variety of stakeholders in the country, including government officials and the private sector, by conducting individual consultations and focus group interviews and directly involving counterparts in government in the design of the analysis. In some countries, with sufficiently sophisticated human resources in the public sector, it is also possible to establish a partnership with the local government for conducting the analysis jointly. In some cases, assembling a steering group of key stakeholders (government, business, and labor) to provide inputs and feedback at some well-identified stages of the assessment may also be useful.

Core staff and/or consultants should include the following:

1. One task-team leader, preferably based in the country
2. One project coordinator and/or senior analyst
3. One or two junior analysts.

Steps in Component 1

A full GVC participation study for component 1 of a country engagement strategy is conducted in four key steps:

1. Prepare a preliminary GVC participation assessment based on available data.
2. Conduct initial desk research and prepare a preliminary GVC participation strategy for fieldwork.
3. Perform in-country field research and document findings.
4. Refine the policy recommendations.

The study is to be completed in two to three months, including four to six weeks of fieldwork (although a small country could complete the fieldwork in as few as two weeks). Some steps can overlap chronologically.

Main Activities before Fieldwork

The following are the main activities that should be done before beginning the fieldwork:

1. *Assessment and research of the country's participation in GVCs, through desk research.* The topics to be covered and methodologies are listed in table 11.1 and discussed in part II of this book. An example, applied to Bulgaria, of pre-mission desk research is provided in chapter 2. The following are some of the main tasks to consider for the assessment:
   a. Preliminary assessment of the country's growth in value added over time, sources of value added, location of final demand, and actors that drive the country's participation in GVCs (see chapters 4 to 6).
   b. Identification and first-cut analysis of key sectors, GVCs, and firms that demand closer investigation (see chapter 3).
   c. Identification of peer countries—for benchmarking purposes (see chapter 4).
   d. Preliminary identification of challenges and needs at the micro (firm) and macro (country) levels to support entry and strengthening of GVC participation and long-term sustainability of the country's GVC strategy (see chapter 7).
   e. Preliminary identification of policy areas for intervention and collection of evidence from international best practices (see the strategic policy framework in figure O.1 in the Overview, as well as chapter 7 and part III).

2. *Preparation for in-country fieldwork.* In-country fieldwork is an exercise that has three key objectives. It helps in vetting preliminary findings from the desk analysis. It allows interacting directly with key stakeholders, with a view to understand their objectives, concerns, and operating environment, as well as for further reference. Finally, it represents a means to identify and analyze qualitative information that complements the quantitative, desk-based research. Table 11.2 provides a full list of key private and public sector stakeholders that should be consulted, including exporters, local suppliers, lead firms and global buyers, representatives of advanced consumers, intermediaries, key equipment and service providers, distributors, retailers, standard-setting bodies, key agencies and ministries, leading consulting companies, and international law firms. Meanwhile, the following are examples of information (and relevant target stakeholders) that desk research is unlikely to document and that require field interviews:

Table 11.2. Stakeholders to Target during Fieldwork

Organization	Persons to meet
Government agencies and industry associations	► Representatives of key agencies in charge of regulations that affect the key GVCs identified: – Line ministries – Economic development agencies – Administrations in charge of industrial and business development – Administrations in charge of trade and trade policy – Finance ministry (or agency in charge of tax and incentive policies) – FDI and investment promotion agencies – Chambers of commerce – Standard-setting bodies – Others, when relevant: agencies in charge of domestic services regulations, science, technology, innovation, entrepreneurship, labor markets, education, and infrastructure and connectivity
Firms involved in GVCs in selected industries—for example: – Automotive – Electrical and electronics – ICT – Food and agriculture – Light manufacturing (textiles, apparel, leather and footwear) – Chemicals and pharmaceuticals – Business processing and back office	► Senior management of a representative sample of firms: – Domestically owned exporters – Domestically owned suppliers located in the country – Domestically owned final producers or assemblers that rely predominantly on imported inputs – Local subsidiaries of MNCs in the country that rely predominantly on imported intermediates – Local subsidiaries of MNCs in the country that rely predominantly on domestically produced inputs – A few marginal local firms with high growth potential (for example, innovative SMEs or firms with key capabilities for development and upgrading) – A few examples of firms exemplifying failed GVC participation strategies – International HQ of global lead firms; global buyers; intermediaries; global suppliers; representatives of advanced users that can drive outcomes through their decisions on demand, investment, technology, business models, operational processes, standard setting, and so forth – Very few, carefully selected factory visits may be of interest, but the key priority is to speak with top managers rather than observing production processes; some types of factories (such as assembly plants) can be avoided, as they do not provide major insights about a country's strategic positioning in GVCs or scope for upgrading
Key equipment and services providers (including design, R&D, transport and logistics, BPO, and software providers)	► Senior management
Venture capital and private equity or other finance providers (especially those that offer finance to SMEs)	► Senior management
Distribution sector: wholesalers and large retail chains	► Senior management
Management firms of SEZs and competitive spaces	► Senior management
Business incubators and accelerators	► Manager or business development person
Technological and industrial parks	► Manager or business development person
Management consulting firms, consulting firms specialized in IT and software, and international law firms	► Senior management

Note: BPO = business process outsourcing; FDI = foreign direct investment; GVC = global value chain; HQ = headquarters; ICT = information and communications technology; IT = information technology; MNCs = multinational corporations; R&D = research and development; SEZs = special economic zones; SMEs = small and medium enterprises.

a. Qualitative characterization of the country's participation in GVC manufacturing and services functions, challenges and opportunities in specific business models, power relations within GVCs (including governance structures), business climate, and recent government initiatives likely to influence developments in GVC participation.
   i. Key policy makers and influential decision makers from the private sector. The priority is to speak with the top managers in the country, who are able to provide a clear understanding of the strategic positioning of the country in GVCs. Carefully selected factory visits may be of interest, but some types of factories (such as assembly plants) can be avoided, as they do not provide major insights about the country's strategic positioning in GVCs or on scope for upgrading.
   ii. Large consulting firms or international law firms in the country. These can provide a good assessment of the key factors for attracting GVC lead firms to the country and areas for improvement.
   iii. Decision makers and investors outside the country. The crucial question of "where does the country fit in the GVC?" is often best answered by those outside the country—in the regional or global headquarters of the key global firms, private equity firms, and large consulting firms and law firms.
   iv. Representatives of advanced users. There may be some key in-country consumers demanding above-average goods and services. Interviews with representatives of advanced users outside the country also help in understanding demand trends and likely patterns of future GVC development. Advanced users could be in the public or private sector.
b. The most important global and local players that form a GVC in which the country has a presence, and which of these are present in the country, as well as some of the marginal actors that have high potential for growth (for example, innovative small and medium enterprises):
   i. Global lead firms (or original equipment manufacturers [OEMs]), global buyers, and global suppliers are a good starting point. They can drive development by placing large orders, making direct investments, and introducing requirements that demand technologies, processes, and business models that are more advanced compared with what goes on locally.
   ii. A few innovative local private firms in the activity of interest or in activities that can easily upgrade to the activity of interest.
c. Involvement of domestic firms in key strategic value chain segments and the nature of production, including inputs, intermediate goods, final goods, and services (for example, design, logistics, finance, and business process outsourcing), again being sure to include representatives from the key categories:
   i. Most important global lead firms or OEMs
   ii. Contract manufacturers and service providers, since they work for a variety of customers and can provide a broader view of the country's participation in GVCs than global lead firms or OEMs
   iii. Services and logistics providers, as these sectors represent the areas where the most sophisticated and higher-value-added segments of a value chain usually lie.

Fact-checking prior to the fieldwork on the firms and key public sector stakeholders targeted for the interviews can increase the odds of a successful interview process. Activities carried out locally are not the only important ones. The sector-, firm-, and cluster-level analysis illustrated in part II of this book may help to reveal the upstream and downstream activities in specific value chains. With this information at hand, it is suggested to undertake the following steps before conducting fieldwork:

a. Collect key facts about key firms present in the country and immediately upstream and downstream activities, which are relevant to understand upgrading patterns and potential. For large firms, the key facts available from public sources, including the Internet and sector registries, include
   - Firm age and ownership, key milestones, mergers and acquisitions, problems encountered, main products, main downstream markets and customers, and financial history
   - Role played by the firm in GVCs, if any
   - Upstream supply base: domestic, regional, and global

b. If possible, prepare synthesis tables of the standard firm-level information illustrated in part II of this book (box 6.2 in chapter 6), which is available from the World Bank Enterprise Surveys, or other relevant firm-level information, including data on outsourcing and offshoring by business function, if available. The tables will be useful in assessing whether the interviewed firms are outperformers, low performers, or average performers against relevant benchmarks.

Main Activities during Fieldwork

The aim of the fieldwork is to refine the identification of the key challenges to GVC participation and the operating context, using qualitative information that statistics are not able to capture. The analysis will help in the design of the necessary policy and regulatory interventions that will target the challenges in entering GVCs and upgrading and densifying participation, while also identifying macroeconomic, social, and environmental conditions to ensure the sustainability of a GVC-based model of development.

Activities during the fieldwork include

1. Sharing desk analysis with local policy makers. Present the findings from desk analysis and discuss with policy makers (including government officials) the strategic objectives of the country's GVC participation and pre-fieldwork hypotheses emerging from the desk analysis.
2. Interviews with key stakeholders. A team will conduct field interviews with representative key players in GVCs, including global lead firms and suppliers, leading domestic suppliers, contract manufacturers and services providers, policy makers, professional associations, and services firms (see table 11.2 for a tentative list). The most important topics to raise for discussion during firm interviews are included in the list of relevant questions for each of these topics, as proposed in annex 11A.
3. Preparation of an aide-memoire and wrap-up meeting at the end of the mission to share with key government counterparts, laying out the key findings, gaps in knowledge, lessons learned from stakeholders regarding a strategic vision for the country's GVC-led development, and priority policy interventions identified.

Activities after Fieldwork

The following are the main activities to conduct after the fieldwork:

1. Finalize the report.
2. Plan and prepare an action plan for implementing the reform (for component 2 of the process).
3. Prepare an execution plan (for component 3 of the process).

After validating with interviews, pre-fieldwork desk analysis, and sector selection, the last step consists of providing a detailed understanding of global, regional, and local features of the GVCs of interest, main products, processes, key technology trends, actors, regulations, typical transactions, and all other factors that shape the country's ability to join the GVCs, expand and strengthen its GVC participation, and turn GVC participation into sustainable development. Annex 11B provides a checklist of topics that should be covered in detail by a combination of deskwork and fieldwork, offering a quantitative foundation for starting an effective country engagement strategy.

Annex 11A Interview Guide for Fieldwork

Firm Interviews

1. Firm profile
   a. Description of the firm profile and its role in global value chains (GVCs)
   b. Perspective on structure of the sector, GVC, segment within the GVC, and where the firm fits in
   c. Review of general economic trends experienced by the firm, with a focus on economic upgrading (growth of domestic value added in the past)
   d. Perspective on competitors (countries and firms): comparative/competitive advantage/ disadvantage within the sector, GVC, and segment within the GVC
   e. Description of required and prospective human capital and technology to carry out current tasks and upgrade.

2. Domestic sales and trade
   a. Focus on the most recent two years, indication of export mix (top five products), destination markets (top five destinations), and proportion of exports versus domestic sales and share of domestic sales going to other local exporters
   b. Nature of exports: final products; semi-finished products, parts, and components; packaging materials; raw materials; services; other
   c. Hypothetical question for top export products of the firm: if your firm would increase prices by 10 percent today, what would be the percentage variation in revenues in the domestic market as well as the foreign market, provided that competitors did not adjust their pricing and all other things being equal?
   d. Expenditure, relative to total, in raw materials and intermediate inputs
   e. Reliance on imported raw materials and intermediate inputs for the production of goods to be exported versus the production of goods to be sold domestically
   f. Nature of imports: final products; semi-finished products, parts, and components; packaging materials; raw materials; services; other
   g. Top five origin countries of intermediate inputs used by the firm
   h. What does the firm do with imported intermediate inputs? Transform them for manufacturing of products that are also semi-finished products, parts, and components? Transform them into manufacturing of final products? Use them for assembly of semi-finished products, parts, and components? Use them for assembly of final products? Package them as finished products, parts, and components?
   i. If the firm exports or sells semi-finished products to local exporters, are those semi-finished products incorporated by the buyers into the production or assembly of final products or into the production or assembly of further intermediates?
   j. For firms that sell to local consumers and export directly and/or sell to local exporters, are products/services similar regardless of the customers, or are those sold to local consumers different in variety/quality/ nature?

3. Contractual relationships and issues of contract enforcement
   a. Is the firm engaged in long-term relationships with the main buyers? Through what type of contractual arrangement (arm's length trade, non-equity relationships, or equity stake)?
   b. Local versus global procurement and supply challenges, strategies, strengths
   c. Processes, authorities, regulatory environment for contract enforcement
   d. Are the exports/sales made to fit exclusively to suit unique specifications required by buyers?
   e. Do buyers provide precise information on product design and/or quality standards?
   f. When the contract includes specific quality standards, are there penalties if the quality standards are not met?
   g. Are the prices in the contract negotiated or imposed by the buyers?
   h. What is the firm's degree of participation in the design of the products it manufactures?
   i. What type of assistance is provided by and which type of collaboration is established

with the buyer? (The possibilities include assisting the firm to achieve a particular design of quality standards; assisting the firm with manufacturing technologies; lending, renting, or leasing machinery and equipment to the firm; providing the firm with raw materials or intermediate inputs; engaging the firm in process or product research and development activities; organizing exchanges of personnel with the firm as a way to disseminate and diffuse new technologies to the firm's production facilities; assisting financially with payments in advance or other types of financial assistance; assisting with firm management practices, such as financial planning, inventory management, or personnel practices; assisting the firm to achieve international quality certifications and meet regulatory standards; assisting the firm to meet international labor standards; and assisting the firm in meeting international environmental standards.

j. Who is responsible for the logistics (certifications, customs, and transport)—the firm interviewed or its buyers?
k. Does the firm have long-lasting and substantive collaborative relationships with foreign firms (other than those with its buyers, parent firm, or affiliates of the same group)?
l. If the firm exports, how was the first foreign order obtained? Possible options are through active search for a foreign buyer, a contact at a trade fair, an unsolicited order, a foreign supplier of intermediate inputs, a government export assistance program, or other.
m. If the firm exports, what obstacles are faced mostly? Possible options include the reliability of foreign customers; language and cultural barriers; access to credit/financing; exchange rate risk; political risk; intellectual property risk; contracting problems; transportation costs; customs taxes, fees, and procedures; rules of origin; different standards and regulations; or other.
n. If the firm imports intermediate inputs, what obstacles are faced mostly? Possible options include custom tariffs, nontariff measures (quotas, technical regulations, etc.), or customs and border agency procedures on imports.
o. For firms that do not engage extensively in international trade (export or import side), what is the main reason? Possible options include lack of information on foreign buyers or foreign suppliers, prices offered on international markets are too low, insufficient access to technologies, insufficient quality of the firm's own products, lack of scale to meet a buyer's contract, lack of capacity to meet shipping schedules, lack of finance, or other.

4. Control over decisions/power structure within the GVC
   a. Is the headquarters at the same location as the production units?
   b. Is the headquarters located in the country or abroad? If abroad, what is the time to travel to the headquarters door-to-door?
   c. Where are the following decisions made (within the firm, at the headquarters, in the production establishment, or by the global buyer/supplier)?
      i. Hiring full-time employees
      ii. Providing an employee a pay increase of 10 percent
      iii. Introducing new products
      iv. Advertising products
      v. Sourcing decisions for machinery, key parts and components, standard parts and components, packaging materials, and raw materials
   d. Thinking of all the intermediates that are used to produce a final good, what share of the purchase value can the firm decide from what firm to buy, that is, which suppliers, with the understanding that the remaining fraction is decided by headquarters or the global buyer/supplier?
   e. Does the firm have exclusivity clauses in the contracts with its buyers/suppliers?
   f. Does the firm use data to support decision-making? What type of data?

5. Determinants of upgrading
   a. What features of the firm have been important for connecting with the global lead firm/global buyer?
      i. Product design

ii. Brand recognition
iii. Low price
iv. Product quality
v. Advanced production processes and technology
vi. Advanced material handling
vii. Supply chain and logistics technologies
viii. Advanced use of information and communications technologies
ix. Management practices, including explicit and systematic performance tracking, reviews, and/or bonuses at the managerial level
x. Agile and flexible organization
xi. Total quality management, lean management
xii. Access to skilled workers
xiii. Access to cheap intermediate inputs
xiv. Access to high-quality intermediate inputs and/or raw materials
xv. Product quality certifications
xvi. Environmental certifications
xvii. Managerial certifications
xviii. Labor standards compliance

b. Did you take measures to improve your performance against any of the above parameters in the past two years?
c. What are the obstacles at your firm to obtain the capabilities that would allow you to upgrade?
    i. Human resource issues, including lack of employee training; employee resistance to change; organizational rigidity of the enterprise; difficulty in recruiting blue collar plant technicians, white collar workers/managers in finance, managers in marketing, managers in research and development (R&D), product design, production, or information technology; difficulty in recruiting a chief executive officer
    ii. Product/price issues, including low-quality products, high prices/costs, inadequate product design, packaging, labeling
    iii. Finance, including difficulty in accessing private funds or public funds, or obtaining guarantees
    iv. Technology, including low return on investment; difficulty in integrating new advanced technologies with existing systems, standards, and processes; low information and communications technology (ICT) capabilities; insufficient scale of production; lack of technical support from consultants, customers, or suppliers
    v. Captive relation in GVC, exclusivity contracts
    vi. Information, including limited information on export markets and difficulty in identifying business opportunities
    vii. Procedural, including excessive and complicated paperwork, difficulty communicating with foreign customers/partners, slow collection of payments, and difficulty in enforcing contracts
    viii. Government barriers, including lack of support from government and unfavorable domestic regulations
    ix. Business environment, including unfamiliar business practices of lead firms/global buyers and inadequate infrastructure and regulatory environment for e-commerce
    x. Tariffs and nontariff barriers, inadequate property rights protection
    xi. Customer and foreign competitor barriers, including too fierce competition or different habits/attitudes/tastes

6. Productivity and worker skills
    a. What share of the production costs go into electricity; fuel, energy, and gasoline; wages and workers' compensation; other?
    b. What is the approximate value of the firm's investment in machinery, vehicles, and equipment? What is the value of the investment in land and buildings?
    c. Hypothetically, if the firm had to purchase the assets it uses now, in their current condition and regardless of whether the establishment uses them or not, how much would they cost, independently of whether they are owned, rented, or leased?

d. What is the composition of workers in the firm? What share of production workers, professional/technical workers, managers, and other types of workers does the firm have? What share of white-collar, blue-collar nonqualified, and blue-collar qualified employees? How many employees are at the supervisory level?
e. For white-collar employees:
   i. How much of their working day goes into routine tasks?
   ii. How much into creative thinking (understood as developing, designing, or creating new applications, ideas, relationships, systems, or products)?
   iii. How much into making decisions and solving problems (understood as analyzing information and evaluating results to choose the best solutions and solving problems)?
   iv. How much into unanticipated situations?
   v. How much into communicating inside the organization versus outside the organization versus working with computers?
f. For supervisors and top management, how much of their working day goes into creative thinking, making decisions and solving problems, and unanticipated situations? How much into communicating inside the organization versus outside the organization? How much into working with computers?
g. For blue-collar workers, white-collar workers, supervisors, and managers, how much on-the-job training is required after hiring (none, short demonstration, 1 month, 3 months, 6 months, 1 year, 2 years, 7 years, 10 years, or more)?
h. Do you face a shortage of skills? For which tasks in particular?
i. To what extent is it possible for workers at your firm to do the work on their job without being physically present (all the work, most of the work, some of the work, or none at all)? What tasks, if any, can be carried out from a remote location (via computer or telephone)? What tasks require face-to-face physical presence with the other co-workers, machinery, or locally installed software?
j. Do you monitor key performance indicators? What types? (Possible options: metrics on production, cost, waste, quality, inventory, energy, absenteeism, deliveries on time, or other). How many? (Possible options: 1-2; 3-9; or 10 or more, on key performance indicators.) How often are they reviewed? (Possible options: yearly, quarterly, monthly, weekly, daily, or never).
k. When production targets are met, what percent of workers receives performance bonuses?
l. Does the firm use data to support decision making? What type of data?

7. Innovation capacity
   a. What are the past and future investments in R&D?
   b. What are the areas of innovation/economic upgrading in which the firm is engaged/plans to engage? (Possible options: business processes, functions, products, or new sectors.)
   c. What is the skill upgrading potential within the firm?
   d. What is the current and projected use of ICT (and results)?
   e. What are the requirements of new or external (within and outside the country) expertise to support innovation?
   f. What are the firm's strategies to import technology and know-how and learn new ways of doing business?
   g. What are the strategic partnerships for innovation?
   h. What are the links between innovation and workers/wages? What institutional support is required to accelerate the gains from these links?
   i. What are the risks in innovation?
   j. What is the firm doing/planning to do to facilitate the transfer of knowledge or other tangible or intangible assets from the lead firm/global buyer? Options include no role; joint research projects; joint training programs for blue collar workers/white collar workers/managers; technical assistance from the buyer/lead firm to the suppliers; assistance in product design and development for suppliers; equipment and specialized machinery; assistance in the design

of equipment and specialized machinery; finance for investment in technology and/or innovation from global buyers/lead firms to suppliers.

Firm and Public Sector Entity Interviews

8. Role of exports, imports, foreign direct investment (FDI), and other non-equity types of real (non-financial) investment in the country
   a. Overall and sector trends (temporal, spatial) as they are perceived by the interviewed stakeholders
   b. Drivers of trade, FDI, or other non-equity real investment, today and projected (political, economic, or social)
   c. Impact of regional and global competition on local firms' productivity/performance (within sector and substitute sectors)
   d. Recommendations for improvement (within firms, sector, and government)
   e. Strategy to maximize benefits from open trade environment, FDI, or other non-equity forms of investment
   f. What are the national strategies to support firms' ability to import technology and know-how and learn new ways of doing business?
   g. What are the strategic partnerships for innovation in which the country engages/should engage?
   h. What are the links between innovation and workers/wages? What institutional support is required to accelerate the gains from these links?

9. Quality and competence of the domestic country's infrastructure and services
   a. Role of the domestic country's infrastructure and services (not just logistics/transportation, but also business and technical services) supporting firm entry and deeper integration in GVCs, and growth in the sector (barrier, enabler, or accelerator)
   b. Sufficiency of services in performance, access/availability, and resilience, and suggested improvements
   c. Local, regional, and global connectivity of the domestic country's infrastructure and services
   d. Inter-sector use of the domestic country's infrastructure and services (and implications)

10. Skills and innovation capacity in the country
    a. Are shortages of skilled workers perceived?
    b. Does the education system produce skills matching the demand for labor?
    c. How is vocational training organized?
    d. What are the past and future investments in R&D in the country/region?
    e. What are the areas of innovation/economic upgrading in which the firm is engaged/plans to engage? (Possible options: business processes, functions, products, and new sectors.)
    f. What is the skill upgrading potential within the firm?
    g. What is the current and projected use of ICT (and results)?
    h. What are the requirements of new or external (within and outside of country) expertise to support innovation?
    i. What are the public strategies to import technology and know-how and firms in their efforts to learn new ways of doing business?
    j. What are the strategic partnerships for innovation?
    k. What are the links between innovation and workers/wages? What institutional support is required to accelerate the gains from these links?
    l. What are the risks in innovation?

Annex 11B Checklist of Topics from Combined Desk Research and Fieldwork

The aim of the field interviews is to confirm and deepen knowledge on the points below (which will have already been partly addressed via the desk analysis). These include the following.

1. General overview
   a. What is [INSERT COUNTRY NAME]'s position in global value chains (GVCs)?
   b. What can [INSERT COUNTRY NAME] do now to ensure that it increases its share of domestic value added in these GVCs?
   c. How can [INSERT COUNTRY NAME] leverage its participation in GVCs to increase productivity and innovation?
   d. What are best-practice examples, but also negative lessons that [INSERT COUNTRY NAME] can draw from?
   e. Chain upgrading: what is the transferability of skills across sectors? What key skills (such as skills related to information and communications technology) are transferable to other sectors, including soft skills related to functional upgrading (logistics coordination, services, design, branding, and product development)?

2. Drilling down into specific sectors, GVCs, and market segments within GVCs
   a. Value chain mapping
      - What are the main sectors, product sets, clusters, and markets that comprise the industry in which the country participates?
   b. Identify growth sectors, GVCs, and segments within GVCs
      - Which sectors, GVCs, and segments within GVCs have high growth rates and high growth potential?
   c. Identify the potential for technological learning
      - What sectors, GVCs, and segments within GVCs have high potential for technological learning?
   d. Identify potential for specialization within GVCs
      - What sectors, GVCs, and segments within GVCs have the potential for countries and regions to play specialized roles?
   e. Identify the potential for employment
      - Which sectors, GVCs, and segments within GVCs have high levels of employment or potential employment? Are these low-skilled or high-skilled? Is the average wage above or below that in other countries, in comparable tasks?
   f. Identify sectors, GVCs, and segments within GVCs where the target country has a plausible chance of success
      - Which sectors, GVCs, and segments within GVCs have a current, nascent, or potential presence in the target country, including foreign direct investment (FDI), local firms, exports, and employment?

3. Analysis of global trends
   a. Product mapping
      - What are the main final and intermediate goods that comprise the sectors, GVCs, and segments within the GVCs?
      - What are the main activities in the sectors, GVCs, and segments within the GVCs?
      - What comprises the chain of value-adding activities in the main product areas, and in the case study products in particular?
   b. Key technology trends
      - What is the impact of technology on the sectors, GVCs, and segments within the GVCs, in effects on produced goods and services, processes, logistics, and automation of business functions?
      - How is technology flowing to domestic actors in the sectors, GVCs, and segments within the GVCs? If it does not, what are the key bottlenecks?
      - How is technology impacting the organization of work within sectors, GVCs, and segments within the GVCs? Are these impacts aligned to global trends, or do they reflect local challenges and specificities?
   c. Identification of GVC actors
      - Which firms and organizations "drive" the sector as big buyers, market share leaders, foreign investors, owners of key technologies and other intellectual property, and initiate or "lead" the process of global engagement (sourcing,

FDI, contracting out, licensing, franchising, etc.)?
   - Have specific processes in the sectors, GVCs, and segments within the GVCs been outsourced and offshored (for example, final assembly or call centers)?
   - Has a set of large supplier firms grown on the basis of large-scale outsourcing and/or offshoring? How have business models in the sector changed over the past 20 years?
   - Are there key service providers (such as logistics), equipment vendors, or component suppliers that strongly influence the development of the sector as "platform leaders"?
   - Are there "intermediaries" in the GVC, such as commodity exchanges, powerful trading companies, or large processors that influence international prices and standards?
   - Are there institutional actors that have influenced the structure, location, and growth of the global sector, including governments, multilateral agencies, nongovernmental organizations, certification and compliance bodies, and sector standard-setting bodies?

d. Transaction mapping
   - How is information exchanged across key activities (arms-length, codified, or tacit)?
   - Do certain activities need to be co-located?
   - Can other activities be accomplished at a distance?
   - What role does technology play in the coordination of value chain activities?
   - How has the global sector changed over the past 20 years?
   - Outsourcing and offshoring
   - Role of information technology
   - New markets
   - New product areas
   - New standards, including labor and environmental standards
   - Changes in sector structure (vertical/horizontal integration/disintegration)
   - Market share changes (consolidation or fragmentation)
   - Regulations
   - Resource constraints

4. Identification of key global actors (retailers, lead firms and global buyers, intermediaries, key equipment and service providers, distributors, central exchanges, standard-setting bodies, etc.)
   a. Discover how the target country, sector, and cases are perceived by key sector actors
   b. Discover how the target country, sector, and cases fit (or do not fit) into the past, present, and future sourcing strategies of powerful buyers and lead firms in the sector

5. Evaluation of the domestic sector and its links to GVCs
   a. Which of the actors identified above are present in the country?
   b. Does the domestic sector play a specific role within GVCs?
   c. Quantify the domestic sector in terms of:
      - Number and size of firms
      - GVC roles played by local firms and foreign affiliates
      - Employment and wages
      - Trade (imports and exports)
      - Productivity, value added, etc.
   d. Identify and evaluate the effects of government programs and regulations on the sector.

APPENDIXES

APPENDIX A

DIMENSIONS OF GVC PARTICIPATION: A TENTATIVE CHECKLIST

Global value chains (GVCs) are a multidimensional phenomenon that involves flows of goods and services (discussed at length in part II of this book). Flows of factors of production (workers, ideas, and investment) are also important, as shown in chapter 1. Table A.1 reports a wide set of examples and measures that can be analyzed to complement the task-based and value-added data assessments discussed in part II of the book.

A few examples demonstrate how to use the table. In the "workers" column, the second block of rows (specialization/value addition) in the table indicates that high wages in a country that shows strong performance as a seller in GVCs may be associated with sellers that are also owners of GVC assets, technology, and know-how. High wages are likely to indicate that the buyer is also a producer, close to final demand, and able to generate high value added. Meanwhile, low wages are likely to be predominant in buyers that are mainly assemblers or involved in activities with little transformation. Indicators on flows of international patents, foreign technology licenses, royalties, and fee services are also important indicators of countries' specialization in higher or lower value-added activities, likely position in the GVC network, and other aspects of GVC participation.

Table A.1. A Multidimensional Checklist of a Country's Participation in GVCs

	Tasks		Factors of production		
GVC component	**Goods**	**Services**	**Workers**	**Ideas and know-how**	**Investment**
Role of domestic firms and FDI hosted in the domestic territory in GVCs					
Buyer					
Any buyer	High share of imported intermediates from countries that have a comparative advantage in the same intermediates or immediate upstream or downstream sectors. High foreign value-added content in own exports.	High share of wholesale service imports, and transport and logistics service production and/or imports.	Depends on the type of buyer. Low-skilled, manufacturing jobs and shortage of management skills for buyers specializing in low-value-added activities. High-skilled and service jobs for buyers specializing in high-value-added tasks.	Buyer of licenses and other NEM agreements for nonstrategic assets. Direct capital control (equity stakes) for strategic assets. Technical cooperation and arm's length trade may signal either looser forms of collaboration or less hierarchical power structure in GVCs.	Dominance of inward FDI and NEMs. FDI/NEMs in sectors of specialization and with partners relevant to GVC trade. FDI versus NEMs measures may indicate strategic importance of assets, degree of collaboration, or hierarchical power structure in GVCs (see ideas column).
Buyer of high-value-added tasks (for example, final producer, brand owner, or high-end retailer)	High share of imported intermediates or unbranded finished products from countries with lower costs and/or other comparative advantages. Exports final product to consumers abroad. Specializes in postproduction services.	Imports IT and BPO services from countries with lower costs and/or other comparative advantages. Exports final services to consumers abroad.	High wages (relative to supplier, and often absolutely) because of higher value-added activities.	Domestic companies tend to maintain high-value-added activities (such as R&D or design) in-house. Potential purchasing of international patents or licensing for parts of the product or technology. Sizable revenues through trademarks, royalties, license fees, and so forth.	Investment in knowledge creation. Outbound FDI/NEMs (often cost or resource based) in countries with costs or other comparative advantages for the production of intermediate inputs. FDI versus NEMs measures may indicate strategic importance of assets.
Seller	Produces and exports a high share of intermediates to countries that buy imported intermediates.	Exports IT and BPO services that often have a lower value added.	Wages (relative to final producer, and often absolutely) are a priori indeterminate: low/high depending on position in GVC. Dependence on expatriates (managers, technicians) if supplier is foreign affiliate of final producer firm.	Purchasing international patents or licensing (for example, of technology), also from within the multinational group (lead firm or other entities) if supplier is a foreign affiliate.	Larger share of outward investment than in buyer countries. Investment in scale production. Inbound FDI/NEMs (often cost or resource based) mainly in sectors of high GVC participation.

(Table continues next page)

Table A.1. *(continued)*

	Tasks		Factors of production		
GVC component	**Goods**	**Services**	**Workers**	**Ideas and know-how**	**Investment**
Specialization/value addition					
Mass or primary production/ assembly activities	Low value added from assembly activities and mass or primary production destined to export markets. Buyer-side integration higher than seller-side integration.	Importance of logistics performance. High imports of logistics services. Possible exports of wholesale services; transportation high.	High dependence on low-skill workers (including immigrants from other low-wage countries).	Licensing (for example, of technology); low patent applications. Low rates of private R&D activity.	Investment in scale production. Inbound FDI/NEMs (often cost or resource based) from countries that specialize in preproduction.
Specialization in high-value-added support and knowledge activities (R&D, technological development, or specialized services)	Strong structural integration in GVCs, particularly on the seller side.	High value added from production and exports of R&D, design, commercialization services, and so forth. High exports of royalties.	High wages for researchers, designers, and specialized personnel (domestic and from abroad).	High R&D intensity and innovation. High returns from royalties and fees. High services content in manufacturing. High domestic content of value added in exports.	Investment in knowledge creation. Outbound market-oriented FDI/NEMs in countries that specialize in postproduction.
Specialization in medium-value-added support activities and sales		High value added from production and exports of branding, logistics, after-sales services, and so on.	High wages for specialized workers (domestic and from abroad), particularly mid-skill workers.		Investment in distribution channels. Inward market-oriented FDI/NEMs from countries that specialize in preproduction. Outward market-based FDI/NEMs to support sales abroad.
Type of GVC node					
Headquarter node	High share of imported value added used in production of output.	High share of imported services value added used in production of output.	High share of skilled workers.	High private R&D intensity; high rates of patents and patent applications by private sector.	Investment in knowledge creation. Outbound FDI/NEMs (often cost or resource based) in factory nodes.
Factory node	High share of intermediate goods exported to headquarter node.	High share of intermediate services exported to headquarter node.	Low share of skilled workers.	Lower private R&D intensity than headquarters. Lower than headquarter rates of private patent applications.	Investment in scale production. Inbound FDI/NEMs (often cost or resource based) from headquarter node.

(Table continues next page)

Table A.1. *(continued)*

GVC component	Tasks		Factors of production		
	Goods	Services	Workers	Ideas and know-how	Investment
Position in the GVC network					
Incoming spoke	High share of intermediate goods exported to hubs or central nodes, as identified by network metrics.	High share of two-way trade in business, transport, and distribution services with hubs or central nodes, as identified by network metrics.	Lower wages (relative to hub, and often absolutely). Dependence on expatriates (managers, technicians) if incoming spoke is foreign affiliate of hub or central node.	Purchasing international patents or licensing (for example, of technology), also from hub or central node. High imports of royalties and fees.	Investment in scale production. Inbound FDI/NEMs (often cost or resource based), mainly in sectors of high GVC participation.
Hub	High share of imported value added used in production of output for consumption abroad.	High share of services value added in exports of manufacturing. Good logistics performance.	High wages (relative to spokes, and often absolutely) because of higher value-added activities. Expatriates (managers, technicians) if hub has outward FDI.	Maintains high-value-added activities (such as R&D or design) in-house. Potential purchasing of international patents or licensing. Licensing of technology to incoming spoke.	Investment in knowledge creation. Outbound FDI/NEMs (often cost or resource based) from hubs to incoming spokes in upstream sectors.
Outgoing spoke	High share of final goods imports from hubs or central nodes for domestic consumption or distribution to more peripheral locations. May act as a regional hub.	High share of wholesale services production or trade. May act as a regional hub for distribution services.		Distribution agreements and licenses. High imports of royalties and fees.	Market-based inbound FDI/NEMs from hub or central node to support sales.

Note: BPO = business process outsourcing; FDI = foreign direct investment; GVC = global value chain; IT = information technology; NEMs = non-equity modes of investment; R&D = research and development.

APPENDIX B

BROAD ECONOMIC CATEGORIES CLASSIFICATION

The Broad Economic Categories (BEC) classification, as defined by the United Nations (UN), comprises 19 basic categories that are assigned to the final use of the good—capital, consumption, and intermediate. Three categories—motor spirit, passenger motor cars, and goods not elsewhere specified—are not assigned to any of those 19 categories. The authors suggest classifying motor spirit as intermediate goods and passenger motorcars as consumption goods. The assignment of goods not specified elsewhere cannot be done. In sum, all the items indicated in bold are classified as intermediate (see table B.1). Concordance tables to match the BEC categories to trade data are widely available. One common source in the UN website, which reports concordance tables between BEC and the Harmonized System classifications and Standard International Trade Classification classifications, is http://unstats.un.org/unsd/cr/registry/regot.asp?Lg=1.

Table B.1. BEC Classification

Broad economic category	Final use
1 Food and beverages	
11 Primary	
111 Mainly for industry	**Intermediate goods**
112 Mainly for household consumption	Consumption goods
12 Processed	
121 Mainly for industry	**Intermediate goods**
122 Mainly for household consumption	Consumption goods
2 Industrial supplies not elsewhere specified	
21 Primary	**Intermediate goods**
22 Processed	**Intermediate goods**
3 Fuels and lubricants	
31 Primary	**Intermediate goods**
32 Processed	
321 Motor spirit	**Intermediate and consumption goods**
322 Other	**Intermediate goods**
4 Capital goods (excluding transport equipment)	
41 Capital goods	Capital goods
42 Parts and accessories	**Intermediate goods**
5 Transport equipment	
51 Passenger motor cars	Intermediate and consumption goods
52 Other	
521 Industrial	Capital goods
522 Nonindustrial	Consumption goods
53 Parts and accessories	**Intermediate goods**
6 Consumer goods not elsewhere specified	
61 Durable	Consumption goods
62 Semi-durable	Consumption goods
63 Nondurable	Consumption goods
7 Goods not elsewhere specified	Intermediate, consumption, and capital goods

Source: Based on UN 2002.
Note: BEC = Broad Economic Category.

APPENDIX C

CUSTOMIZED VERSUS GENERIC INTERMEDIATES

Sturgeon and Memedovic (2011) differentiate between customized and generic intermediates in three sectors: apparel and footwear, electronics, and passenger vehicles.

- Customized intermediates are products that are likely to be used in specific final products or at least relatively narrow classes of products.
- Generic intermediates are products that are likely to be used in a wide range of final products, as well as in products made in large, standardized batches and in continuous-process production methods.

Table C.1 exemplifies the range of customized intermediates in the apparel and footwear sector (excerpt from original table).

Table C.1. Customized Intermediates in the Apparel and Footwear Sector (Excerpt)

BEC	SITC	SITC description
22	65225	Other woven fabrics of cotton, unbleached, weight < 200 g/m^2
22	6536	Fabrics, woven, containing 85% or more by weight of artificial staple fibers
22	65112	Yarn of carded wool, containing 85% or more by weight of wool, not put up for retail sale
22	65113	Yarn of combed wool, containing 85% or more by weight of wool, not put up for retail sale
22	65114	Yarn of fine animal hair (carded or combed), not put up for retail sale
22	65115	Yarn of coarse animal hair or of horsehair (including gimped horsehair yarn), whether or not put up for retail sale
22	65117	Yarn of carded wool, containing less than 85% by weight of wool, not put up for retail sale
22	65118	Yarn of combed wool, containing less than 85% by weight of wool, not put up for retail sale
22	65121	Cotton sewing thread, not put up for retail sale
22	65133	Cotton yarn (other than sewing thread), containing 85% or more by weight of cotton, not put up for retail sale
22	65134	Cotton yarn (other than sewing thread), containing less than 85% by weight of cotton, not put up for retail sale
22	65141	Sewing thread of synthetic filaments, whether or not put up for retail sale
22	65142	Sewing thread of artificial filaments, whether or not put up for retail sale
22	65143	Sewing thread of synthetic staple fibers, whether or not put up for retail sale
22	65144	Sewing thread of artificial staple fibers, whether or not put up for retail sale
22	65151	Filament yarn (other than sewing thread), of nylon or other polyamides, not put up for retail sale

Source: Sturgeon and Memedovic 2011, 30.
Note: BEC = Broad Economic Classification; g = gram; m = meter; SITC = Standard International Trade Classification.

APPENDIX D

PARTS AND COMPONENTS

Athukorala (2010) mapped parts and components for manufacturing sectors in the United Nations (UN) Broad Economic Categories (BEC) registry in the product list of the World Trade Organization Information Technology Agreement with the Harmonized System (HS) of trade classification at the 6-digit level. Existing gaps in the list were filled with estimates from firm-level surveys conducted in Malaysia and Thailand. Data compiled at the HS 6-digit level were converted to the Standard International Trade Classification (SITC) for the final analysis, using the UN HS-SITC concordance. For an illustration of 20 (of a list of 525) manufacturing parts and components at the HS 6-digit level, see table D.1.

Table D.1. List of Manufacturing Parts and Components (Excerpt)

Nomenclature
Plates, sheets, etc. nesoi, cellular polyurethanes
Plates, sheets, etc. nesoi, cellular plastic nesoi
Chemical elements doped, used in electronics, discs, wafers, etc.
Articles of leather used in machinery/mechanical appliance
Pipe, reinforced/combine w/metal only, w/o fitting
Pipe, reinforced/combine w/ textiles, w/o fitting
Pipe, reinforced/combine w/ material, w/o fitting
Tubes, pipe, etc., vulcanized soft rubber, with fitting
Endless transmission belt, trapezoidal, circumference > 60 cm, < 180 cm
Endless transmission belt, circumference > 180 cm, < 240 cm
Conveyor belts or belting reinforced with metal
Conveyor belts reinforced with textile materials
Conveyor belts reinforced only with plastics
Conveyor belts/belting of vulcanized rubber nesoi
Endless synchronous belt, circumference > 60 cm, < 150 cm
Endless synchronous belt, circumference > 150 cm, < 198 cm
Transmission belt/belting, of vulcanized rubber, nesoi
Articles of soft vulcanized rubber nesoi
Gasket, washers, & other seals, of vulcanized rubber
Textile labels, badges, etc., not embroidered, woven

Source: Athukorala 2010, 19.
Note: cm = centimeter; nesoi = not elsewhere specified or included.

APPENDIX E

VALUE CHAIN CATEGORIES

The classification by Taymaz, Voylvoda, and Yilmaz (2011) carefully assigns exports (categorized at the 4-digit International Standard Industrial Classification code) to one of five value chain categories—final products, main input/part, standard input/track, raw material, and machinery/equipment—based on engineering considerations. The classification is available for five key Turkish industries (motor vehicles, TV, food, machinery, and textiles and apparel). The product assignment by value chain category for the five GVC sectors is reported in table E.1. This system has at least two downsides. First, being a classification that covers only goods exports, it does not identify the services segments of value chains, such as research and development, design, commercialization, distribution, marketing/branding, logistics, and after-sales services, precisely the segments that allow for functional upgrading. Second, it does not account for the domestic dimension of value chains, thus providing only a partial overview of the situation.

Table E.1. Assignment of Products to Five Value Chain Categories in Five Main GVC Sectors

Final products		Main input/part		Standard input/track		Raw material		Machinery/equipment	
Motor vehicles									
111	Auto	120	Motor	131	Auto parts	140	Flat steel	151	Already designed or engineered parts
112	Camion			132	Other components			152	Other
113	Autobus								
114	Tractors								
TV									
211	Radio	221	CRT	231	Electronic components	240	Plastic	250	Injection machines
212	TV								
Food									
411	Meat/fish products	422	Sugar			441	Meat/fish	450	Food machines
412	Confectionery	423	Cocoa			442	Sugar beet		
413	Chocolate	424	Milk powder, flour, etc.			443	Cocoa powder		
414	Flour products	425	Frozen products			444	Milk, wheat, etc.		
415	Canned food	426	Tea, etc.			445	Vegetables, fruit		
416	Other food	427	Alcohol, vinegar			446	Coffee, soya		
417	Drinks	428	Pulp, waste			447	Mineral water		
418	Waste products								

(Table continues next page)

Table E.1. *(continued)*

Machinery									
511	Consumer machinery	521	Motors, turbines	531	Metal plates, pipes, etc.	541	Iron, copper, etc.	151	Already designed or engineered parts
512	Industrial machinery							152	Other
Textiles and apparel									
Cotton									
311.1	Apparel	321	Fabric	331	Yarn	341	Cotton	350	Textile machinery
311.2	Pajama, t-shirts								
311.3	Sheets, etc.								
Wool									
312.1	Apparel	322	Fabric	332	Yarn	342	Wool	350	Textile machinery
312.2	Pajama, t-shirts								
312.3	Sheets, etc.								
312.4	Carpets								
Synthetic									
313.1	Apparel	323	Fabric	333	Yarn	343	Polyester	350	Textile machinery
313.2	Pajama, t-shirts								
313.3	Sheets, etc.								
313.4	Carpets								
Other									
314.1	Apparel	324	Fabric	334	Yarn	344	Other	350	Textile machinery
314.2	Pajama, t-shirts								
314.3	Sheets, etc.								
314.4	Carpets								

Note: CRT = cathode ray tube.

APPENDIX F

SECTOR AND PRODUCT CLUSTERS

Sectors are a statistics artifact. The same task can be deployed in different sectors (for example, threading and sewing expertise can be deployed in the textiles and apparel sector and in the auto sector), and success in a given sector may depend on comparative advantages in tasks that do not belong to that sector according to official statistics. Services inputs, such as transport and finance, are important for the competitiveness of many manufacturing products. Table F.1 presents an attempt, by the ARD Vest Development Agency in Romania, to identify clusters of activities needed in agrifood, construction, energy, health, information and communications technology, textiles and apparel, and tourism. To some degree, the detailed activities included in each cluster may be influenced by locational factors, so that application to other countries may require small modifications to the compositions of the clusters.

Table F.1. GVC Clusters

AGRIFOOD	
NACE rev. 2 code	**NACE Rev. 2 description**
111	Growing of cereals (except rice), leguminous crops, and oil seeds [01.11]
112	Growing of rice [01.12]
113	Growing of vegetables and melons, roots and tubers [01.13]
114	Growing of sugar cane [01.14]
115	Growing of tobacco [01.15]
116	Growing of fiber crops [01.16]
119	Growing of other non-perennial crops [01.19]
121	Growing of grapes [01.21]
122	Growing of tropical and subtropical fruits [01.22]
123	Growing of citrus fruits [01.23]
124	Growing of pome fruits and stone fruits [01.24]
125	Growing of other tree and bush fruits and nuts [01.25]
126	Growing of oleaginous fruits [01.26]
127	Growing of beverage crops [01.27]
128	Growing of spices, aromatic, drug and pharmaceutical crops [01.28]
129	Growing of other perennial crops [01.29]
130	Plant propagation [01.30]
141	Raising of dairy cattle [01.41]
142	Raising of other cattle and buffaloes [01.42]
143	Raising of horses and other equines [01.43]
144	Raising of camels and camelids [01.44]
145	Raising of sheep and goats [01.45]

(Table continues next page)

Table F.1. *(continued)*

AGRIFOOD	
NACE rev. 2 code	**NACE Rev. 2 description**
146	Raising of swine/pigs [01.46]
147	Raising of poultry [01.47]
149	Raising of other animals [01.49]
150	Mixed farming [01.50]
161	Support activities for crop production [01.61]
162	Support activities for animal production [01.62]
163	Post-harvest crop activities [01.63]
164	Seed processing for propagation [01.64]
311	Marine fishing [03.11]
312	Freshwater fishing [03.12]
321	Marine aquaculture [03.21]
322	Freshwater aquaculture [03.22]
1011	Processing and preserving of meat [10.11]
1012	Processing and preserving of poultry meat [10.12]
1013	Production of meat and poultry meat products [10.13]
1020	Processing and preserving of fish, crustaceans, and mollusks [10.20]
1031	Processing and preserving of potatoes [10.31]
1032	Manufacture of fruit and vegetable juice [10.32]
1039	Other processing and preserving of fruit and vegetables [10.39]
1041	Manufacture of oils and fats [10.41]
1042	Manufacture of margarine and similar edible fats [10.42]
1051	Operation of dairies and cheese making [10.51]
1052	Manufacture of ice cream [10.52]
1061	Manufacture of grain mill products [10.61]
1062	Manufacture of starches and starch products [10.62]
1071	Manufacture of bread; manufacture of fresh pastry goods and cakes [10.71]
1072	Manufacture of rusks and biscuits; manufacture of preserved pastry goods and cakes [10.72]
1073	Manufacture of macaroni, noodles, couscous, and similar farinaceous products [10.73]
1081	Manufacture of sugar [10.81]
1082	Manufacture of cocoa, chocolate, and sugar confectionery [10.82]
1083	Processing of tea and coffee [10.83]
1084	Manufacture of condiments and seasonings [10.84]
1085	Manufacture of prepared meals and dishes [10.85]
1086	Manufacture of homogenized food preparations and dietetic food [10.86]
1089	Manufacture of other food products nec [10.89]
1091	Manufacture of prepared feeds for farm animals [10.91]
1092	Manufacture of prepared pet foods [10.92]
1101	Distilling, rectifying, and blending of spirits [11.01]
1102	Manufacture of wine from grape [11.02]
1103	Manufacture of cider and other fruit wines [11.03]
1104	Manufacture of other non-distilled fermented beverages [11.04]
1105	Manufacture of beer [11.05]
1106	Manufacture of malt [11.06]
1107	Manufacture of soft drinks; production of mineral waters and other bottled waters [11.07]
CONSTRUCTION	
NACE 2	**NACE 2 description**
4110	Development of building projects
4120	Construction of residential and non-residential buildings
4200	Civil engineering

(Table continues next page)

Table F.1. *(continued)*

NACE 2	NACE 2 description
CONSTRUCTION	
NACE 2	**NACE 2 description**
4211	Construction of roads and motorways
4212	Construction of railways and underground railways
4213	Construction of bridges and tunnels
4221	Construction of utility projects for fluids
4222	Construction of utility projects for electricity and telecommunications
4291	Construction of water projects
4299	Construction of other civil engineering projects nec
4311	Demolition
4312	Site preparation
4313	Test drilling and boring
4321	Electrical installation
4322	Plumbing, heat, and air conditioning installation
4329	Other construction installation
4331	Plastering
4332	Joinery installation
4333	Floor and wall covering
4334	Painting and glazing
4339	Other building completion and finishing
4391	Roofing activities
4399	Other specialized construction activities nec
ENERGY	
NACE 2	**NACE 2 description**
3511	Production of electricity
3512	Transmission of electricity
3513	Distribution of electricity
3514	Trade of electricity
3521	Manufacture of gas
3522	Distribution of gaseous fuels through mains
3523	Trade of gas through mains
3530	Steam and air conditioning supply
HEALTH	
NACE 2	**NACE 2 description**
8610	Hospital activities
8621	General medical practice activities
8622	Specialist medical practice activities
8623	Dental practice activities
8690	Other human health activities
8710	Residential nursing care activities
8730	Residential care activities for the elderly and disabled
8790	Other residential care activities
8810	Social work activities without accommodation for the elderly and disabled
8891	Child day-care activities
8899	Other social work activities without accommodation nec
INFORMATION AND COMMUNICATIONS TECHNOLOGY (ICT)	
NACE 2	**NACE Rev. 2 description**
2611	Manufacture of electronic components [26.11]
2612	Manufacture of loaded electronic boards [26.12]
2620	Manufacture of computers and peripheral equipment [26.20]

(Table continues next page)

Table F.1. *(continued)*

NACE 2	NACE Rev. 2 description
INFORMATION AND COMMUNICATIONS TECHNOLOGY (ICT)	
NACE 2	**NACE Rev. 2 description**
2630	Manufacture of communication equipment [26.30]
2640	Manufacture of consumer electronics [26.40]
2680	Manufacture of magnetic and optical media [26.80]
4742	Retail sale of telecommunications equipment in specialized stores [47.42]
4743	Retail sale of audio and video equipment in specialized stores [47.43]
5821	Publishing of computer games [58.21]
5829	Other software publishing [58.29]
6110	Wired telecommunications activities [61.10]
6120	Wireless telecommunications activities [61.20]
6201	Computer programming activities [62.01]
6202	Computer consultancy activities [62.02]
6203	Computer facilities management activities [62.03]
6209	Other information technology and computer service activities [62.09]
6311	Data processing, hosting, and related activities [63.11]
6312	Web portals [63.12]
6391	News agency activities [63.91]
6399	Other information service activities nec [63.99]
9511	Repair of computers and peripheral equipment [95.11]
9512	Repair of communication equipment [95.12]
TEXTILES AND APPAREL	
NACE 2	**NACE Rev. 2 description**
1310	Preparation and spinning of textile fibers [13.10]
1320	Weaving of textiles [13.20]
1330	Finishing of textiles [13.30]
1391	Manufacture of knitted and crocheted fabrics [13.91]
1393	Manufacture of carpets and rugs [13.93]
1394	Manufacture of cordage, rope, twine, and netting [13.94]
1395	Manufacture of non-wovens and articles made from non-wovens, except apparel [13.95]
1396	Manufacture of other technical and industrial textiles [13.96]
1399	Manufacture of other textiles nec [13.99]
1411	Manufacture of leather clothes [14.11]
1412	Manufacture of workwear [14.12]
1413	Manufacture of other outerwear [14.13]
1414	Manufacture of underwear [14.14]
1419	Manufacture of other wearing apparel and accessories [14.19]
1420	Manufacture of articles of fur [14.20]
1431	Manufacture of knitted and crocheted hosiery [14.31]
1439	Manufacture of other knitted and crocheted apparel [14.39]
1511	Tanning and dressing of leather; dressing and dyeing of fur [15.11]
1512	Manufacture of luggage, handbags and the like, saddler, and harness [15.12]
1520	Manufacture of footwear [15.20]
TOURISM	
NACE 2	**NACE 2 description**
5510	Hotels and similar accommodation
5520	Holiday and other short-stay accommodation
5530	Camping grounds, recreational vehicle parks and trailer parks
5590	Other accommodation
5610	Restaurants and mobile food service activities

(Table continues next page)

Table F.1. *(continued)*

TOURISM	
NACE 2	**NACE 2 description**
5621	Event catering activities
5629	Other food service activities
5630	Beverage serving activities
7911	Travel agency activities
7912	Tour operator activities
7990	Other reservation service and related activities
9321	Activities of amusement parks and theme parks
9329	Other amusement and recreation activities

Source: Strategic cluster definition by ARD Vest, Romania.
Note: GVC = global value chain; NACE = General Industrial Classification of Economic Activities within the European Communities; nec = not elsewhere classified.

APPENDIX G

MAIN TYPES OF DATA USED TO MEASURE GVC PARTICIPATION

This appendix describes the five main types of data used to measure global value chain (GVC) participation, as well as their capabilities and limitations. These data help in assessing a country's participation in GVCs along various dimensions.

1. Production Data and Gross Trade Data

Production data and gross trade data measure the amount of goods and services produced and traded, respectively. The data do not indicate the domestic or foreign source of the inputs or the value addition generated in a country. Production data from international sources provide a limited breakdown in industries. Firm-level sources (for example, customs-level trade data) tend to provide a finer disaggregation, as do sector trade data. These data, categorized using informed classifications (Broad Economic Classification, parts and components, or technical classifications) or classified into product and sector clusters allow investigation of specific aspects of GVC participation. A discussion of the main classifications that can be used is provided in appendixes B through F.

2. Value-Added Data

In the GVC context, a country's exports cannot be competitive if the country does not import parts and components from the most competitive suppliers. Put simply, imports are functionally linked to exports. In this new GVC world, exports are not all equal from a national perspective. A million dollars of exports may create few jobs or many, and it may have few links with the rest of the economy or many. To help governments and scholars think more carefully about this topic, several organizations recently released new international input-output (I-O) tables. Box G.1 gives an overview of the available international I-O data.

International I-O data allow the assessment of how primary inputs (workers and capital) in a country are used and how much income they generate through GVC participation. The key concept is "value-added" versus "gross" exports. Gross exports are the traditional measure that has been used for decades—the value of goods when they leave the country. Value-added exports strip out the value that was added in some other country. Therefore, they enable the identification of the ultimate source or destination of the value added that is generated by eliminating double counting in gross export data.[1] Gross and value-added exports are important indicators. For instance, most trade policy is applied to gross trade, but the number of jobs linked to exports depends on value-added exports.

Although value-added trade data provide essential information about GVCs, the data are subject to restrictive assumptions that may significantly bias the quantification of technology coefficients for different types of production.[2] Being based on nonharmonized I-O tables from national sources, any errors in an I-O national table will produce errors in all the value-added trade flows.

Several organizations have started to produce international I-O tables and measures derived from them, such as the World Input-Output Database, the Organisation for Economic Co-operation and Development–World Trade Organization Trade in Value Added database, the United Nations Conference on Trade and Development (UNCTAD)–EORA

Box G.1. Major Input-Output Databases

Table BG.1.1. International Input-Output Databases

Database	Data source	Countries/ regions	Sectors/ products	Years
WIOD	http://www.wiod.org/	40	35	1995–2011
OECD-WTO TiVA database	http://www.oecd.org/ http://www.wto.org/	61	34	1995, 2000, 2005, 2008–2011
EORA MRIO database	http://www.worldmrio.com/	187	26	1990–2012
Asian Development Bank MRIO database	Available through WIOD database	18	35	2000, 2005–2008, 2011
IDE JETRO, Asian International Input-Output Tables	http://www.ide.go.jp	10	78	1985, 1990, 1995, 2000, 2005
EXIOPOL Multi-regional Database	http://www.exiobase.eu/	43	200	2007
World Bank Export of Value Added database	http://data.worldbank.org/data-catalog/export-value-added and http://wits.worldbank.org/datadownload.aspx	120	27	1997, 2001, 2004, 2007, 2011
World Bank LACEX Database	http://wits.worldbank.org/datadownload.aspx	120	24 or 57	1995, 1997, 2001, 2004, 2007, 2011
Daudin, Rifflart, and Schweisguth (2011)	From authors	66 or 113	55	1997, 2001, 2004
Johnson and Noguera (2012)	From authors	94	57	2004
Koopman, Wang, and Wei (2014)	From authors	26	41	2004

Note: EXIOPOL = Environmental Accounting Framework Using Externality Data and Input–Output Tools for Policy Analysis; IDE = Institute of Developing Economies; JETRO = Japan External Trade Organization; LACEX = Labor Content of Exports; MRIO: multi-regional input-output tables; OECD = Organisation for Economic Co-operation and Development; TiVA = Trade in Value Added; WIOD = World Input-Output Database; WTO = World Trade Organization.

WIOD

The World Input-Output Database (WIOD), compiled by a consortium of 11 institutions, was funded by the European Commission from 2009 to 2012. Based on supply-use tables from official national statistics, WIOD identifies the I-O links between 27 European Union members and 13 other major economies (plus "the rest of the world"). The database covers 35 industries and all years from 1995 to 2011.[a] WIOD was the first freely available I-O database and one of the highest quality sources; it is available to download at www.wiod.org.

ADB-MRIO and IDE JETRO Database

The Asian Development Bank multi-regional input-output tables (ADB-MRIO) complements the WIOD, since it has included additional Asian countries to WIOD to facilitate analysis related to the Asia and Pacific Region. Five Asian countries (Bangladesh, Malaysia, the Philippines, Thailand, and Vietnam) have been added for the years 2000, 2005–08, and 2011.

The Institute of Developing Economies, Japan External Trade Organization (IDE JETRO) database is the ancestor of all international input-output tables. Since 1975, IDE-JETRO has been producing international input-output tables with a focus on Asia-Pacific countries.

OECD-WTO TiVA Database

The Organisation for Economic Co-operation and Development (OECD) Inter-Country I-O tables represent a similar effort to WIOD, providing data based on a bilateral trade database and end-use categories as well as several derived statistical measures. The 2015 edition includes 61 economies,[b] plus a "the rest of the world" region, with a breakdown into 37 industries. The I-O tables cover the years 1995, 2000, 2005, and 2008–11, but the goal is to produce a complete time series and extend the country coverage.[c]

EORA MRIO Database

The EORA global multi-region I-O (MRIO) tables, produced by the University of Sydney and funded by the Australian Research Council, bring together a variety of primary data sources that are combined in a single data set that uses interpolation and estimation techniques to provide a contiguous, continuous data set for 1990–2012 for 187 countries. Because the project focuses on environmental issues, it displays important deviations from observed trade flows and gross domestic product, and the tables are balanced to match, principally, data from large economies.

The EORA MRIO was used by UNCTAD to produce trade in value-added indicators. Because standard I-O calculations require a balanced table, the EORA database contains only 26 harmonized sectors. Although it has the most extensive country coverage of the databases discussed, I-O tables for many countries in EORA are not available and have been estimated from the United Nations System of National Accounts and other, more aggregated data.[d]

(Box continues next page)

Box G.1. *(continued)*

World Bank Export of Value Added Database and GTAP Input-Output Tables

The World Bank Export of Value Added database is based on the input-output data from the Global Trade Analysis Project (GTAP), which uses alternative sources and estimates missing data. The GTAP I-O data include social accounting matrices that cover additional countries where no official I-O tables are available. The 2001, 2004, 2007, and 2011 GTAP data cover 57 sectors. The 2007 and 2011 GTAP data cover 129 countries or regions, whereas the 2001 and 2004 data cover fewer countries. Developed by Francois, Manchin, and Tomberger (2013), the World Bank Export of Value Added data set allows for exploiting social accounting matrices spanning intermittent years from 1992 to 2011, to construct country-specific measures of the direct and indirect contribution of goods and services to the value added contained in a given country's domestic production and exports. The Export of Value Added database covers 27 sectors, 120 countries, and the years 1997, 2001, 2004, 2007, and 2011. (See appendix H for further discussion.)[e]

World Bank LACEX Database

The World Bank Labor Content of Export (LACEX) Database was developed based on input-output data from GTAP (Calì and others forthcoming). The database is similar to the World Bank Export of Value Added database, except it looks at the value added remunerated to labor (instead of total value added). As such, it allows the user to compare the direct and indirect contributions of labor in different sectors (goods and services) of an economy with the value added contained in the economy's domestic production and exports. The labor value added is further decomposed between skilled and unskilled labor. The database covers the years 1995, 1997, 2001, 2004, 2007, and 2011 for 24 or 57 sectors.

Other Databases

Other GTAP-based global value chain studies include Daudin and others (2006), Johnson and Noguera (2012), and Koopman and others (2011, 2014). In general, those studies have not included the full dimensionality of the GTAP data set.

Finally, the Environmental Accounting Framework Using Externality Data and Input–Output Tools for Policy Analysis (EXIOPOL) provides international input-output tables (EXIOBASE) that can be used for analysis of the environmental impacts associated with the final consumption of product groups. EXIOBASE covers 43 countries, five world regions, and 200 products in 163 industries. It also provides information on 15 land use types, employment per three skill levels, 48 types of raw materials, and 172 types of water uses.

a. For more detailed information, see Timmer (2012).
b. For better estimation of the value added in Chinese production and trade, the database includes additional I-O tables for three types of economic activity: processing trade, ordinary trade, and domestic-only enterprises.
c. For more information on the international I-O tables and TiVA measures, see OECD and WTO (2012).
d. Lenzen and others (2013) describe the construction of the underlying EORA database, and UNCTAD (2013a, 2013b) describes the related UNCTAD-EORA database.
e. Tsigas, Wang, and Gehlhar (2012) provide a detailed example of how to construct an international I-O table from GTAP.

database, and the World Bank.[3] Table BG.1.1 summarizes and describes in more detail the major international I-O databases.

3. Imports of Intermediates

Data on imports of intermediates indicate the reliance of domestic production on imported intermediates. Combined with export data through the use of international I-O data, intermediate imports data allow the measurement of the import content of exports. The data are subject to the same caveats highlighted in the section on value-added data. A different type of data exists for some countries: data from special customs regimes for processing trade. Those data are collected in cases in which a country suspends tariffs on imported intermediates if all the intermediates are used to make goods that are subsequently exported. Finally, changes in I-O patterns in I-O tables can reveal if the country is entering a new production or technology. However, the level of sector disaggregation is limited.

4. Re-import and Re-export Data

In GVC analysis, re-import data concern countries' exports of intermediate goods that are then re-imported after some processing in the partner country. Re-export data track the inverse flow; they are a mirror concept of re-import data. These data are available at the same (fine) level of disaggregation as are gross exports data. The concepts of re-importing and re-exporting in the compilation of official trade data are different. Re-exports in official trade statistics are goods that have not been transformed since they were imported, whereas re-imports are goods that are returned without being sold.[4]

5. Firm-Level Data

Firm-level data capture the main actors in a value chain: final producers and suppliers. Using firm-level survey data about direct links in GVCs allows the detection of additional aspects of GVC participation—beyond what the aggregate data reveal. Those aspects include the potential for gains (and also risks) from increased GVC integration. The Enterprise Surveys, which are available from the World Bank—and have wide country coverage—allow for cross-country comparisons. Stratified at sector, firm size, and sub-national geographic levels, the surveys provide information on multinational sourcing strategies (domestic versus foreign suppliers), domestic producers' reliance on imported intermediates, and domestic suppliers' share of exports. In combination with data on firm-level output, value added, capital stock, productivity, and employment, which are available from the World Bank Enterprise Analysis Unit or from national sources, the surveys allow for relating GVC participation with firm-level characteristics

Appendix H

THE WORLD BANK EXPORT OF VALUE ADDED DATABASE

The World Bank Export of Value Added database provides information on the domestic value–added content of domestic output and exports for 120 countries across 27 sectors of the economy, including 10 commercial services sectors, 14 manufacturing sectors, and 3 primary sectors, spanning intermittent years between 1997 and 2011. Trade data usually are measured at transaction value, which is the price actually paid or payable for goods and services. Thus, the transaction value of goods and services is a gross value (or value added plus intermediate inputs), which may overestimate or underestimate the real contribution of goods and services to trade. To overcome this shortcoming, a calculation of trade measured in value added, using data based on input-output tables, has been developed. The measure includes the direct value-added contribution of sectors to total output and exports as well as their indirect contribution through links.

This includes both forward links—the value-added contribution of a particular sector as an input to other sectors' output or exports—and backward links—the value-added contribution of all other sectors to a particular sector's output or exports. Specifically, the forward links in the database show the importance of services as inputs to other sectors' output and exports. Services are an input for many other economic activities, which implies the importance of their efficient delivery to increase competitiveness, although some services are also for final consumption. In sum, this type of data set provides information on what the direct and indirect value-added contribution of goods and services to output and exports looks like over time. As such, the database follows up on the pioneering work of Christen, Francois, and Hoekman (2012) and Francois, Manchin, and Tomberger (2013).

Data Source

The underlying data for the World Bank Export of Value Added database come from the Global Trade Analysis Project data set (GTAP, https://www.gtap.agecon.purdue.edu). The GTAP database is a global database that measures and describes bilateral trade patterns, production, consumption, and intermediate input use of goods and services. Because the data are bilateral and developed for various years, they can be used to obtain data for cross-border links in recent years as well as the way those links have changed over time. The data set thus represents an advanced input-output panel—also known as social accounting—of incomes and expenditures linked to trade from 1992 to 2011, covering not only key Organisation for Economic Co-operation and Development (OECD) economies, but also a wide range of developing countries divided by sectors.

The basic structure of GTAP is explained by McDougall (2001) and McDougall and Hagemejer (2005). The database provides explanations of how it was built, its underlying data structure, and its data sources with each new release. The GTAP database is produced by a consortium of institutions, including the World Bank, U.S. International Trade Commission, World Trade Organization, OECD, United Nations Conference on Trade and Development, United Nations Food and Agriculture Organization, and universities and independent research institutes. The project is based at Purdue University. A public good, GTAP is an open-source input that is often used for policy modeling on issues such as climate change, regional trade agreements, and even food security.

Although the GTAP database has been updated continuously with each new release, the authors of the database have maintained a consistent set of regions, countries, and sectors to ensure strong compatibility of the data over time.

Why This Database?

The World Bank Export of Value Added database provides a comprehensive picture of economic relationships between sectors within countries that are accounted for in national income or gross domestic product. The underlying theory stems from economics and is based on a "general equilibrium principle," meaning that every income of an economy has a counterpart in expenditure, so that all receipts and outlays correspond with each other.

The strength of this database, therefore, is in its comprehensiveness in setting out the interrelationships within an economy between links that record intermediate input use and final demand. Importantly, consumption and trade patterns are also recorded in this database, so the value added produced in one sector can be linked in intermediate or final demand to the domestic consumption and external trade demand patterns of other sectors. Those links provide a fuller analysis than national input-output tables.

The undertaking of this database eventually enables analysis of the complex structure of the value-added content of final output and demand, as well as exports. The structure of value-added can be further broken down into direct and indirect value added. Direct value added captures the true sector-specific value added that is generated within an economy and nets out domestic and foreign inputs, whereas indirect value added adds to the direct measure the portion of value added of the inputs produced domestically. Both types of value added can then be expressed as part of the domestic output per sector, as well as a sector's share of exports.

An economy's value added is measured as the "net" output after adding all sectoral outputs and subtracting all intermediate inputs. The direct contribution of each sector to value added, of the domestic economy as a whole or only of exports, is the value added sold directly to final consumers. For example, in Bangladesh, trade and transport services represent 10 percent of the direct value added of the domestic economy and 1 percent of the direct value added of exports. However, the contribution of that sector to the overall value added or export value added of the economy is much higher, because those services enter as inputs into the production function of downstream sectors, continuing to add value to the latter. To account for this, the database also measures the indirect contribution of services to value added through forward and backward links.

Forward links represent the contribution of a specific sector as an input to other sectors' value added. More specifically, they are the supply response of a particular sector to all other (downstream) sectors' demand for more inputs. Typically, when all other sectors are expanding, they demand more financial services. The forward link will indicate how much those sectors are using inputs from the financial sector—in other words, how much the financial sector output will expand. Looking again at Bangladesh, trade and transport services represent 28.9 percent of the value added of the domestic economy, and 24.2 percent of the value added of exports, after considering this sector's contribution as inputs in other sectors' value added.

Likewise, backward links represent the contribution of all other sectors to a specific sector's value added (upstream)—in other words, they represent how much the demand of a particular sector will pull the supply of all other sectors. For example, the construction sector demands from other sectors cement, glass, bricks, and steel, which in turn contribute to the value added of the construction sector. In Bangladesh, trade and transport services demanded only 11.5 percent of the value added of the domestic economy, and 4.9 percent of the value added of exports across all sectors.

Links represent the interdependence of sectors of the economy. Industries with strong backward and forward links play an important role in a country's development strategy. A sector with strong backward links means that an increase in the final demand of those industries' output will have a large effect on industries that supply inputs in the production of those industries' output. And a sector with strong forward links means that an increase in the final demand of other industries' output will have a large effect on the industry. Naturally, strong links to export value added suggest an important role in a country's export strategy.

From a policy point of view, when looking at services, what is of most interest is their services links. But the backward links of dominant manufacturing sectors to upstream services sectors can also reveal the effect of manufacturing demand on the supply of services.

Methodology of the Database

To obtain all the links of value added requires first calculating how much input is contained in one unit of final output. That is the intermediate multiplier matrix, also commonly known as the Leontief matrix (M). The M-matrix holds information on direct and indirect input use in a sector. Second, information about the shares of value added in total output, which is then consumed domestically or otherwise exported, is organized in what we call the B-matrix. The intermediate input use shares of the M-matrix are multiplied by the final output and exports figures (B-matrix) to obtain the corresponding value-added shares.

Writing this more formally, a domestic economy's gross output can be represented in terms of final demand plus intermediate input demand. Let FD denote final demand, INT denote intermediate input demand, and GO denote gross output:

$$GO = FD + INT \qquad (H.1)$$

$$INT = \alpha\, GO \qquad (H.2)$$

where α is a coefficient that indicates the shares of each intermediate input used in a unit of gross output, which can be thought of as being used across different sectors and hence can be expressed in the form of a matrix. Equation (H.1) defines final output by intermediate input use requirements, which is in effect nothing other than the M-matrix. Because we know which sector's value added goes into another sector, we can thus also identify the direct and indirect inputs between sectors expressed in a certain currency. That implies that we can analyze real production activities and measure it by the value of output.

Each industry uses a different amount of intermediate inputs; thus, each link between industries will vary. In addition, final demand (FD) as such is measured in gross terms, whereas the goal of this database is to obtain a cleaner "net" measure of value added. Focusing on value added, we have to disentangle the flow of gross activities and the value-added activities from intermediate to final use. Some share of the gross output measure also involves the value added that is created within each sector. Once we have a clean measure of value-added shares of final demand, we can call that measure β, which then must be integrated with the M-matrix to obtain flows of value added broken down across sector activities. That leads to a new value-added matrix, VA:

$$VA = \beta M \qquad (H.3)$$

In effect, β is a coefficient that indicates the shares of each intermediate input used in a unit of value added, which can be thought of as being used across different sectors. Because the Export of Value Added database also contains figures for total final demand and exports taken from GTAP, we can further split the value-added matrix into value-added flows that result from domestic activities, which is the primary component of gross national product and value-added flows that are recovered from exports. More technically, we can call the former type of value added the G-matrix, whereas the latter is the H-matrix. For both matrices, the figures can be further divided into direct value added and indirect value added.

Example

To apply the methodology, we can provide an example by examining Turkey for 2007. Table H.1 provides five measures based on the Export of Value Added database, for the domestic economy as well as for exports.

The first column shows how much value added (as share of a sector's gross output) is produced in each sector. The second column shows the share of a sector's exports in gross terms as part of the economy's total exports. Similarly, the third column shows the share of exports in value-added terms as part of the economy's total value-added exports. We can see that transport services accounts for an important sector, because it generates 19 percent of export value added in Turkey's economy, although it occupies only 15 percent of gross exports. If we look at clothing, for instance, those figures are reversed.

With this database, as previously explained, we can estimate the value added embodied in exports for Turkey's commercial services sector. Because we can account for all links across sectors, we can estimate in two directions—forward and backward. As for domestic production, forward links tell us how much value added each sector contains, which is exported directly and indirectly in the production of other goods and services. Hence, forward links represent the contribution of a specific sector as an input to other sectors' value added. Backward links represent the contribution of all other sectors to a specific sector's value added (upstream). The shares of forward links and direct exports are shown in the fourth column in table H.1, while the shares of backward links and direct exports are shown in the fifth column.

Turkey's business services, for instance, account for 8 percent of total value added exported directly and 14 percent when including forward links; that number is the value of services used as inputs to other sectors. Backward links represent only 6 percent of total exports (box H.1).

Table H.1 Turkey's Exports, Gross and Value-Added Measures, by Sector, 2007 (%)

Sector	Share of domestic value-added in gross output by sector	Gross value: direct exports	Value added: direct exports	Value added: direct exports and forward links	Value-added: direct exports and backward links
		(1)	(2)	(3)	(4)
1 Primary agricultural goods	65	3	5	5	4
2 Other primary goods	76	2	3	3	2
3 Energy	27	2	1	4	1
4 Processed foods	43	3	3	3	4
5 Beverages and tobacco	54	0	0	0	0
6 Textiles	38	10	9	8	10
7 Clothing	32	7	5	3	7
8 Leather	26	0	0	0	0
9 Lumber	27	1	1	1	1
10 Paper	43	1	1	1	1
11 Chemicals	29	6	4	4	5
12 Non-metal minerals	51	3	3	2	3
13 Metals	22	9	5	5	6
14 Fabricated metals	35	3	3	4	3
15 Transport equipment	39	14	13	8	14
16 Machinery	40	12	11	8	12
17 Other manufacturing	35	2	1	1	1
18 Water	84	0	0	0	0
19 Construction	47	1	1	0	1
20 Distribution	74	1	3	10	2
21 Transport	56	15	19	16	16
22 Communication	86	0	1	2	1
23 Finance	66	1	1	5	1
24 Insurance	66	1	1	1	1
25 Other business services and ICT	61	1	1	3	1
26 Other consumer services	58	1	2	1	1
27 Other services	89	1	3	2	2
Total		100	100	100	100
Total business services (22–27)		5	8	14	6

Source: Based on the World Bank Export of Value Added database.
Note: ICT = information and communications technology.

Box H.1 Value Added in Exports

We measure the value added contained in exports as follows. First, we calculate direct cost shares linked to demand for intermediate inputs:

$$\theta_{z,j} = \frac{e_{z,j}}{\sum_{j} e_{j,j}} \times 100.$$

Direct value added in exports:

$$\alpha_z = v_z x_z.$$

Total (direct and indirect) value added in exports, based on forward links:

$$F_z = \alpha_z + \sum_{i \neq z} .01 \times \theta_{z,j} v_z x_i,$$

Total (direct and indirect) value added in exports, based on backward links:

$$B_z = \alpha_z + \sum_{i \neq z} .01 \times \theta_{i,z} v_i x_z,$$

where $e_{i,j}$ represents expenditure in sector j on inputs indexed by i, including value added, or primary inputs (capital, labor, and land), and intermediate inputs; v_j represents expenditure on primary inputs as a share of total costs of production in sector j; and x_j represents the gross value of exports from sector j.

Appendix I

SURVEY YEAR AND NUMBER OF DOMESTIC AND FOREIGN MANUFACTURING FIRMS, BY COUNTRY

Farole and Winkler (2014) have developed an econometric analysis to assess how foreign investor characteristics, domestic firms' absorptive capacity, and a country's institutional variables influence intra-industry productivity spillovers to domestic firms from foreign direct investment (chapter 7). The econometric estimation uses a cross-section of more than 25,000 domestic manufacturing firms in 76 low- and middle-income economies from the World Bank's Enterprise Surveys, as listed in table I.1.

Table I.1 Survey Year and Number of Domestic and Foreign Manufacturing Firms, by Country

Country	Survey year	Domestic manufacturing firms	Foreign manufacturing firms
Albania	2007	87	23
Algeria	2007	374	10
Argentina	2010	681	111
Armenia	2009	102	12
Azerbaijan	2009	95	23
Belarus	2008	86	13
Bolivia	2010	118	22
Bosnia and Herzegovina	2009	113	10
Brazil	2009	851	59
Burkina Faso	2009	81	16
Burundi	2006	110	28
Cameroon	2009	87	29
Chile	2010	673	102
Colombia	2010	641	65
Costa Rica	2010	272	53
Côte d'Ivoire	2009	144	49
Croatia	2007	364	47
Ecuador	2010	97	22
Egypt, Arab Rep.	2008	1,103	36
El Salvador	2010	104	20
Ethiopia	2006	337	22
Georgia	2008	109	14
Ghana	2007	271	19
Guatemala	2010	315	40
Guinea	2006	122	15
Guinea-Bissau	2006	72	9

(Table continues next page)

Table I.1 *(continued)*

Country	Survey year	Domestic manufacturing firms	Foreign manufacturing firms
Honduras	2010	130	18
India	2006	2,134	37
Indonesia	2009	1,067	89
Jamaica	2010	103	16
Jordan	2006	305	48
Kazakhstan	2009	169	14
Kenya	2007	331	65
Kyrgyz Republic	2009	80	16
Latvia	2009	65	24
Lithuania	2009	85	19
Macedonia, FYR	2009	98	23
Madagascar	2009	125	79
Malaysia	2007	773	321
Mauritania	2006	112	16
Mauritius	2009	157	18
Mexico	2010	1,046	110
Moldova	2009	86	22
Mongolia	2009	115	15
Morocco	2007	354	103
Mozambique	2007	284	56
Namibia	2006	114	37
Nepal	2009	124	4
Nicaragua	2010	115	10
Nigeria	2007	938	10
Pakistan	2007	763	20
Panama	2010	101	14
Paraguay	2010	108	17
Peru	2010	673	87
Philippines	2009	692	262
Poland	2009	137	14
Romania	2009	143	36
Russian Federation	2009	660	39
Rwanda	2006	54	14
Senegal	2007	243	16
Serbia	2009	117	19
South Africa	2007	579	101
St. Vincent and the Grenadines	2010	124	24
Swaziland	2006	68	38
Tajikistan	2008	98	15
Tanzania	2006	247	39
Thailand	2006	800	230
Turkey	2008	866	29
Uganda	2006	276	58
Ukraine	2008	523	46
Uruguay	2010	327	32
Uzbekistan	2008	87	34
Venezuela, RB	2010	71	14
Vietnam	2009	649	130
Yemen, Rep.	2010	238	5
Zambia	2007	236	68
Total		25,199	3,440

Source: Farole and Winkler 2014, 80.

Because the effect of GVC participation is the topic of interest in chapter 2, we merged the data set with two sector measures of structural integration in GVCs: BONwin (buyer's perspective) and BONwout (seller's perspective), as described in chapter 6 and computed by Santoni and Taglioni (2015). Because the measures of structural integration are based on the OECD-WTO TiVA database, fewer observations are available; there are a total of more than 14,000 manufacturing firms in 22 low- and middle-income countries, as listed in Table I.2.

Table I.2 Survey Year and Number of Domestic and Foreign Manufacturing Firms, by Country, Select Countries

Country	Survey year	Domestic manufacturing firms	Foreign manufacturing firms	Total
Argentina	2010	681	111	792
Brazil	2009	851	59	910
Bulgaria	2007	788	114	902
Chile	2010	673	102	775
Czech Republic	2009	79	22	101
Estonia	2009	65	25	90
Hungary	2009	87	29	116
India	2006	2,134	37	2,171
Indonesia	2009	1,067	89	1,156
Latvia	2009	60	23	83
Lithuania	2009	77	19	96
Malaysia	2007	773	321	1,094
Mexico	2010	1,046	110	1,156
Philippines	2009	692	262	954
Poland	2009	137	14	151
Romania	2009	143	36	179
Russia	2009	660	39	699
Slovak Republic	2009	74	15	89
South Africa	2007	579	101	680
Thailand	2006	586	187	773
Turkey	2008	866	29	895
Vietnam	2009	649	130	779
Total		12,767	1,874	14,641

Notes

1. For example, in gross trade data, if a disk drive from Thailand is exported to China, where it is used to make a laptop, which is exported to the United States, the value of the disk drive is included in Thailand's and China's export data. Value-added trade data assign the wages and profits in Thai activities and Chinese activities separately, so it can be seen how each stage of the production process contributes to total incomes.

2. For example, Baldwin and Lopez-Gonzalez (2013) find that the proportionality in the use of intermediates and by different industries in one of the most important sources of these data (the WIOD database) leads to substantially different measures of import content of exports, depending on the aggregate chosen (with or without the data for the rest of the world). Similarly, Feenstra and Jensen (2012), using confidential U.S. firm data, report that estimates of intermediate imports based on the proportionality assumption introduce nontrivial errors in some cases.

3. The Asian I-O database by IDE-JETRO covers 76 industries in intermittent years between 1975 and 2005, but it focuses on Asian economies (China; Indonesia; Japan; Malaysia; the Philippines; the Republic of Korea; Singapore; Thailand; and Taiwan, China) and the United States only.

4. See, for example, UN (United Nations). 2004. International Merchandise Trade Statistics: Compilers Manual. New York: UN, 28. http://unstats.un.org/unsd/publication/SeriesF/seriesf_87e.pdf, 28.

References

Athukorala, Prema-chandra. 2010. "Production Networks and Trade Patterns in East Asia: Regionalization or Globalization?" Asian Development Bank (ADB) Working Paper Series on Regional Economic Integration 56, ADB, Manila.

Baldwin, Richard, and Javier Lopez-Gonzalez. 2013. "Supply-Chain Trade: A Portrait of Global Patterns and Several Testable Hypotheses." NBER Working Paper 18957, National Bureau of Economic Research, Cambridge, MA.

Calì, M., J. Francois, C. Hollweg, M. Manchin, D. A. Oberdabernig, H. Rojas-Romagosa, S. Rubinova, and P. Tomberger. Forthcoming. *Jobs and Wage Content of Trade.* Washington, DC: World Bank.

Christen, Elisabeth, Joseph Francois, and Bernard Hoekman. 2012. "Computable General Equilibrium Modeling of Market Access in Services." In *Handbook of Computable General Equilibrium Modeling*, edited by Peter B. Dixon and Dale W. Jorgenson, 1601–43. Amsterdam: Elsevier.

Daudin, Guillaume, Christine Rifflart, and Danielle Schweisguth. 2011. "Who Produces for Whom in the World Economy?" *Canadian Journal of Economics/Revue canadienne d'économique* 44 (4): 1403–37.

Daudin, Guillaume, Christine Rifflart, Danielle Schweisguth, and Paola Monperrus-Veroni. 2006. "Le Commerce Extérieur en Valeur Ajoutée." *Revue de l'OFCE: Observations et Diagnostics Économiques* 98: 129–65.

Farole, Thomas, and Deborah Winkler. 2014. "The Role of Mediating Factors for FDI Spillovers in Developing Countries: Evidence from a Global Dataset." In *Making Foreign Direct Investment Work for Sub-Saharan Africa: Local Spillovers and Competitiveness in Global Value Chains*, edited by Thomas Farole and Deborah Winkler, 59–86. Washington, DC: World Bank.

Feenstra, Robert C., and J. Jensen. 2012. "Evaluating Estimates of Materials Offshoring from U.S. Manufacturing." NBER Working Paper 17916, National Bureau of Economic Research, Cambridge, MA.

Francois, J., M. Manchin, and P. Tomberger. 2013. "Services Links and the Value Added Content of Trade." Policy Research Working Paper 6432, World Bank, Washington, DC.

Johnson, Robert C., and Guillermo Noguera. 2012. "Accounting for Intermediates: Production Sharing and Trade in Value Added." *Journal of International Economics* 86 (2): 224–36.

Koopman, Robert, William Powers, Zhi Wang, and Shang-Jin Wei. 2011. "Giving Credit Where Credit Is Due: Tracing Value Added in Global Production Chains." NBER Working Paper 16426, National Bureau of Economic Research, Cambridge, MA.

Koopman, Robert, Zhi Wang, and Shang-Jin Wei. 2014. "Tracing Value-Added and Double Counting in Gross Exports." *American Economic Review* 104 (2): 459–94.

Lenzen, Manfred, Daniel Moran, Keiichiro Kanemoto, and Arne Geschke. 2013. "Building Eora: A Global Multi-regional Input-Output Database at High Country and Sector Resolution." *Economic Systems Research* 25 (1): 20–49.

McDougall, Robert. 2001. "The GTAP Database, Version 5." Center for Global Trade Analysis, Purdue University, West Lafayette, IN.

McDougall, Robert, and Jan Hagemejer. 2005. "Services Trade Data." In *Global Trade, Assistance, and Production: The GTAP 6 Data Base*, edited by Betina V. Dimaranan. Center for Global Trade Analysis, Purdue University, West Lafayette, IN.

OECD (Organisation for Economic Co-operation and Development) and WTO (World Trade Organization). 2012. "Trade in Value-Added: Concept, Methodologies, and Challenges." Joint OCED-WTO note. http://www.oecd.org/sti/ind/49894138.pdf.

Sturgeon, Timothy J., and Olga Memedovic. 2011. "Mapping Global Value Chains: Intermediate Goods Trade and Structural Change in the World Economy." Working Paper 10/2010, United Nations Industrial Development Organization, Vienna.

Taymaz, Erol, Ebru Voylvoda, and Kamil Yilmaz. 2011. "Uluslararasi Uretim Zincirlerinde Donusum ve Turkiye'nin Konumu." TUSIAD-Koc Universitesi Ekonomik Arastirma Forumu Calisma Raporlari Serisi. Turkish Industry and Business Association, Istanbul.

Timmer, Marcel P., ed. 2012. "The World Input-Output Database (WIOD): Contents, Sources and Methods." World Input-Output Database Working Paper 10. http://www.wiod.org/publications/source_docs/WIOD_sources.pdf.

Tsigas, Marinos, Zhi Wang, and Mark Gehlhar. 2012. "How a Global Inter-Country Input-Output Table with Processing Trade Account Can Be Constructed from GTAP Database." Paper presented at the 15th Annual Conference on Global Economic Analysis, Geneva, June 27–29. https://www.gtap.agecon.purdue.edu/resources/download/5998.pdf.

UN (United Nations). 2002. "Classification by Broad Economic Categories." United Nations, Department of Economic and Social Affairs, Statistics Division, Statistical Papers, Series M No. 53, Rev. 4. United Nations, New York.

UNCTAD (United Nations Conference on Trade and Development). 2013a. *Global Value Chains and Development: Investment and Value Added Trade in the Global Economy: A Preliminary Analysis.* New York and Geneva: United Nations. http://unctad.org/en/PublicationsLibrary/diae2013d1_en.pdf.

———. 2013b. "World Investment Report 2013—Global Value Chains: Investment and Trade for Development." UNCTAD, Geneva.

ECO-AUDIT

Environmental Benefits Statement

The World Bank Group is committed to reducing its environmental footprint. In support of this commitment, the Publishing and Knowledge Division leverages electronic publishing options and print-on-demand technology, which is located in regional hubs worldwide. Together, these initiatives enable print runs to be lowered and shipping distances decreased, resulting in reduced paper consumption, chemical use, greenhouse gas emissions, and waste.

The Publishing and Knowledge Division follows the recommended standards for paper use set by the Green Press Initiative. The majority of our books are printed on Forest Stewardship Council (FSC)–certified paper, with nearly all containing 50–100 percent recycled content. The recycled fiber in our book paper is either unbleached or bleached using totally chlorine-free (TCF), processed chlorine-free (PCF), or enhanced elemental chlorine-free (EECF) processes.

More information about the Bank's environmental philosophy can be found at http://www.worldbank.org/corporateresponsibility.